Walter Nash

Walter Nash

Keith Sinclair

Auckland University Press
Oxford University Press

© Keith Sinclair 1976

First published 1976

Printed in New Zealand
by John McIndoe Ltd
Dunedin

ISBN 0 19 647949 5

Preface

When Sir Walter Nash died in 1968 he left both a study and a very large garage full of the biggest collection of private papers yet known to scholars in New Zealand. The 3,000 or so bundles and boxes of documents, after being purged of newspapers and journals, still weigh several tons and occupy 700 feet of shelves in the National Archives.

I had, three years earlier, asked Sir Walter if I could write his biography. He declined, wishing to sort the papers himself, and hoping to write his own memoirs. After his death, however, his trustees asked me to write his life—not 'the' life, not an 'official' life, but a life.

I began studying the Nash papers in 1970. In 1971 a generous grant from the Nuffield Foundation, to which I am very greatly indebted, enabled me to employ a research assistant, Mrs Alison Allen, who catalogued the contents of the bundles of papers, and helped my investigations in other ways. Her knowledge of New Zealand Labour history and her good humour made her an ideal assistant and co-worker.

Many people have asked how I could stand reading all these documents, but historians will understand their fascination. No other collection of papers affords a comparable view of New Zealand political history in this century. It includes a very large number of letters from other Labour leaders, including Harry Holland and Micky Savage and Peter Fraser. An extraordinary number of politicians, economists, public servants, academics, parsons, and public figures make their appearances on Nash's stage.

Most of the important episodes in Nash's life are richly and extensively documented in his papers. While he was a cabinet minister he kept his own copies of correspondence relating to any topic he thought significant. Consequently, except in relation to a few topics inadequately covered in his papers, it was not necessary for a biographer to try to follow Sir Walter through the labyrinths of files of the departments which he once headed. However, extensive research was necessary in British archives, chiefly in the Public Record Office, London, to discover the British point of view during Nash's various negotiations with the British government. Some records in the United States, notably the minutes of the Pacific War

Council (in the Roosevelt Papers), revealed something of American attitudes towards Nash and New Zealand. In a few cases where it was necessary to seek official New Zealand records, the author was permitted to read them but not to cite his sources. A certain cloudy reticence was in such places necessary.

Nash's papers document, to an extraordinary degree, his personal participation in the life of New Zealand since 1909. The problem which has so often worried the biographer, of how far his book should be a 'life and times', scarcely arises with the life of someone as continuously active in public events as Nash was. His life was inextricably involved in many of the important events of his time.

If one were writing about a major politician in Great Britain or the USA there would be many published works on the political parties, and on other leaders, as well as the memoirs of the great, for background reading. In New Zealand there are very few such books on modern politics —there is, for example, no thorough study of any government of this century, nor has any politician of the first rank published his recollections. I have had the good fortune to have some very able research students— indeed, fellow students—to carry out parts of the necessary background work. Each year since 1970 several students have spent endless hours 'Nashing' in the National Archives. Mr Bob Hill was, in effect, a collaborator as he worked away at the theology of the guaranteed price. Miss Elizabeth Hanson wrote an excellent account of the political origins of social security. To them, to other students, and to several colleagues who are mentioned in footnotes, I am greatly indebted.

I owe a great deal to Mrs Jane Thomson, who worked as a research assistant, especially in searching the pages of the *Maoriland Worker* and other newspapers. Mrs Judy Brooker assisted with enquiries into Nash's Anglican connections and Mrs Margaret Thompson by checking references for me. Dr R. M. Dalziel helped with checking references and the bibliography. The Chief Archivists, Miss Judy Hornabrook, and her predecessor, the late John Pascoe, and their staff, were invariably helpful. Many other people assisted in various ways. The sharp editorial eye of Dennis McEldowney saved me from many solecisms and errors. Miss Olive Johnson made the index. Mr Richard Northey was an unfailing source of Labour lore. The late Dr R. M. Campbell and his friend, the late Professor A. G. B. Fisher, took a keen and helpful interest in my work. Mr J. A. D. Nash and Mr L. Nash and other members of Sir Walter's family were frank and helpful in answering my queries. The Rt Hon. Harold Macmillan and Sir George Mallaby kindly gave me permission to quote from their published memoirs. Acknowledgements are made to the British Library of Political and Economic Science for permission to quote the Dalton diaries, and to Miss Judy Elphick, who searched them for references to Nash. The University of Auckland gave me leave to visit Great

Britain to follow in the footsteps of my subject. I am very grateful to the Advisory Trustees of the Nash estate for making this biography possible.

Professor Roger Louis of Austin, Texas, generously provided a copy of the minutes of the Pacific War Council and other documents from the Roosevelt Papers. Mr John A. Lee kindly gave me access to sections of his papers not open to public. Professor P. J. O'Farrell generously gave me a copy of his summary of Labour Party Head Office papers destroyed since he read them.

In the course of studying Nash's life I interviewed the surviving cabinet ministers from the first three Labour ministries and some ministers from the last two, several senior public servants, and former assistants and friends of Nash. Much information and many insights into his personality are derived from their remarks, though these are not always what any one person said. Conflicting opinions might be thought of as triangulating or fixing a position in his personality.

Keith Sinclair
University of Auckland

Contents

Illustrations

I

The Old Country

1882-1909

Walter Nash was born in England on 12 February 1882, in a small two-storied brick cottage at 93 Mill Street, Kidderminster. Of his ancestors nothing much is known. One of his grandfather's aunts, Sarah Nash, married Francis Lycett, who made a fortune in gloves and was knighted for it. His grandfather died of sickness after returning from the Crimean War, leaving his widow, Margaret, with one baby son, Alfred Arthur.[1] In 1879 she ran a small shop at 114 Mill Street. She was a 'general dealer in lamps, oil, hardware, toys, confectionery, &c and agent for Assam tea company'.[2] Her son married Amelia Randle who came from the nearby town of Bridgnorth. The young couple lived elsewhere in the town, where three or four of their five sons were born, Ernest, Will, Albert and perhaps Arch, moving to Mill Street in 1880 or 1881.

One of the town's most famous sons, Josiah Mason, who had died in 1881, had been born in the same street, probably on the other side of the road and further up the hill, though Nash always believed that they had been born in the same house. Mason's biographer began his book by saying that he was 'in all respects, a self-made man. He had no advantages of birth, or connexions, or education, or means. So far as regarded the probability of wealth or of personal eminence, no life could have begun in a manner less promising.'[3] He made a considerable fortune in Birmingham from split key-rings, steel nibs, and then electroplating, and founded orphanages, almshouses, and a Science College in Birmingham. Its admission policy was to be as liberal as possible, to help poor students. In time Mason College became the building for the University of Birmingham.

There was similarly little in Nash's background to suggest that he would ever do anything, or be anyone of importance. Whether their lives illustrate the triumph of nature over nurture, of I.Q. over environment, or the power of Christian industry (for they were both religious men) may be debated fruitlessly. Nash was one of the innumerable people, from families of crofters or criminals, farm labourers or factory hands, who have prospered in the new worlds to which millions of English-speaking folk have migrated in recent centuries.

Walter Nash's mother was a weaver in the mills. Alfred Arthur was a clerk in 1879; in 1882 a rug weaver, like Josiah Mason's father. In 1906 he was a clerk again.[4] A few doors away from their house and the grandmother's shop was the local inn, 'The Reindeer' (which still stood in 1973, full of Mill Street drinkers, rather after closing time). Mr Nash repaired there, or to other local hostelries, somewhat frequently. Many years later his son Will wrote to Walter, 'He could turn a hand to anything and make a success of it. Providing other hand hadn't been holding or holding out for Glass of Beer or Whisky. Well yes he drank near enough to fill a well. God Rest his Soul I forgive him. Dear old Dad. He married Dear old Mom. That old fashioned Mother of Ours. God Bless Her.'[5]

Alfred Arthur Nash spent many of his adult years in a circle of poverty and alcohol, each proceeding from and leading to the other. In his harsh, industrial world, for many people alcohol and religion were alternatives, some would say alternative soothing draughts.

Mill Street descends steeply to a gentle slope that was periodically flooded by the little River Stour, which marked the boundary of the Nashes' back yard. Photographs still exist of the street under the water of the flood of 1886.[6]

At the bottom of the street the town flattens out. Kidderminster had been a place of weavers and woollen cloths since medieval times. Carpets had been made there since the eighteenth century. In the mid-nineteenth the power loom, driven by steam from coal fires, had been introduced.[7] Long, low, brick mills came to occupy much of the town, including a substantial part of Mill Street. Within was the labyrinth of the looms with their human attendants; above was the forest of tall chimneys, breathing soot. Not satanically polluted, perhaps, for when Walter was born the town had only 24,000 people; but smoky enough.

Looking down on the brick and chimneys, from high land to the north of Mill Street, was the impressive parish church of St Mary and All Saints, partly fourteenth and fifteenth century gothic, described as both decorated and perpendicular.

Walter Nash's earliest memory was of getting lost in the narrow streets. A man took him out of town to Habberley. Someone else took him home.[8] But, because the town was small, for young people in particular it was not the whole world. It was only a short walk to the fields. He remembered walking through the woods to Habberley valley to pick primroses and bluebells. One winter he walked to Bewdley, a lovely little neighbouring town, to watch an ox being roasted whole on the Severn River, which was frozen.[9] He rambled in the countryside on great days, the sky a pale, mineral blue, crisp late autumn air with the sun unexpectedly bright, thinning trees trailing wisps of leaves on traceries of twigs. But more likely he remembered that English haze, the Severn or Stour, almost hidden in mist, seeming great rivers. Though much inclined to factual recital, he never trusted himself to lyrical description, so we cannot quote him. What always remained was a feeling for England, for what he came to call 'the Old Country'—etched on his memory very early by sights, and sounds, smells of soot, and cold air blown over from the Clee Hills. Few people ever lose a nostalgia for those earliest scenes, the landscapes of the mind.

Walter was sent unhappily to school at what now seems the very early age of three. The 'governess', as the infant teacher was called there, Emily Bradburn, took him from his mother and, he said nearly eighty years later, 'won me within half an hour or so'. He always thought very affectionately of her. She had a considerable influence on him particularly, if we may fairly judge from her much later letters, in reinforcing his mother's Christian teaching. In a letter in 1932, for instance, she prayed that he would be given grace, wisdom and understanding, so that he could achieve righteousness. Twelve years later she was pleased that he had kept God always before him. She hoped God would give him the strength and knowledge 'to carry out His great work he has given you to do on Earth. I am very proud of you!'[10]

The school was an Anglican church school, the St John's School in Chapel Street, which had been built in 1835 for 300 infants. Miss Bradburn taught him for three years. Then he went to the more advanced branch of the school which had been built in 1850 in St John's Street. It was a very small brick building, with about four tiny classrooms for its 310 boys, and a little playground. There was a brick arch over the front door within which the bell hung. It was a few yards up Mill Lane from Mill Street.

Walter sang in the school choir. He went to church with the school every Wednesday. He proved to have a considerable facility at arithmetic and an unusually retentive memory. He could give the average scores of the famous cricketers for a couple of years back.[11] At the age of eleven he won a scholarship to the King Charles I school, the local grammar school, but could not go because his mother could not afford the three suits of clothes which were required. Indeed it was very difficult for her to find the 'school pence', ninepence per child per week, to keep several children at school at once. The school had given her a concession of 2/6 a week for the family.[12]

He had already had odd jobs, for instance as a paper boy. Now he left school and got a job as office boy, in fact a messenger at five shillings a week, for a local solicitor, Spencer Thursfield. Thursfield acted as agent for conservative candidates in local council and parliamentary elections. He employed Walter's father as a part-time agent, canvassing, checking the registers and the like. Since many voters still expected to be 'treated', conviviality was an almost indispensable qualification for the job. Stanley Baldwin, who stood for Kidderminster in 1906, later said that he was 'expected to spend three evenings a week during the time of his probation in one or another of the public houses which jostled each other through the constituency, listening to and vociferously applauding what, for want of a better name, was called, on the *lucus a non lucendo* principle, comic or humorous song'. He called these sessions 'orgies'.[13]

Walter used to help his father on election days by standing outside a polling place and checking on the register the names of people voting: at that time, he later confessed, in his eyes as well as in his father's, blue was right and red was wrong. He gained a good training, however, in election work. Like many other boys, he vaguely conceived the ambition of standing for parliament.[14]

Of this period of his life Walter Nash always recalled how worried he was when the change from the purchase of stamps was incorrect.[15] All his life he was anxious to account for every penny. In a testimonial Thursfield said he had found Walter 'truthful, honest and attentive to your duties'. Walter's own account was different: he wrote that

he there developed an abnormal strain of laziness such as for instance the usual boys method of standing to gaze on all hoardings and he remembered one instance of his master telling him that he could have walked to Birmingham in the time it had taken him to walk to his house from the office a distance of 1 mile. Time $2\frac{1}{2}$ hours.

Well he eventually succeeded in getting himself dismissed, and then went into one of the carpet factories in the borough, and was renowned for his daring feat of crawling underneath the back gates after the doors were closed.[16]

Whether caused by poverty or not, excessive drinking probably brought more misery to poor families than poverty. The man's wages went into the till. He was likely to be confused, morose, or violent at home, creating terrible family tensions. This was as true in England as in the settlement colonies like those in Australia or New Zealand, where the quantity of alcohol consumed last century was incredible by modern standards. In such circumstances the mother had to bring up the children single-handed, if she could. So it was in the Nash family. The mother, Amelia, slaved to keep the family together. A photograph shows her as careworn, anxious. The father looks a pleasant enough man, if a little worn too. In this first surviving photograph Walter, aged about ten, had a gumboil.

When Alfred Arthur died in 1913, his wife said he had been very good to her when she was ill in Kidderminster. 'His only fault was that he couldn't see his fault,' the youngest member of the family, Emily, reported to Walter.[17] The family came to think of him as clever, shrewd, but weak and easily led. Certainly he often treated his wife badly. On one occasion when he said that he 'had the best little wife in the world', Walter answered back, 'Why don't you treat her as such?'[18]

Walter Nash said once that his mother overcame greater difficulties in life than he did: she 'believed in a power beyond the universe'.[19] Her religion helped her to bear her lot. They were Anglicans, but not 'churchy' people—it does not seem that Walter was christened, at least as a baby.[20] But she inculcated a strong sense of religious duty in her children. When there was a dispute about religious teaching in the schools in 1885, she composed some lines (with overtones of a famous hymn by George Herbert), 'on takeing Religious Education out of the Day Schools', opposing the removal of 'true wisdom' out of schools:

> 'Our children need it every day,
> Not one day out of seven.
> If we live six days without help
> Why not live the seven?'

Her son, Will, used to quote some other lines which he called his mother's verse about sin:

> 'when first I commenced my warfare against sin
> many said he'll run away!
> But they all have been decieved:
> in the fight I am today.'[21]

When any of her children's conduct fell short of what she thought right she was not angry, but hurt. On one occasion, probably in about 1900, Walter went out with some men from work and won some money at cards. He told her and she said, 'Oh Walter! you shouldn't do that.' He returned the money, and would never again gamble, though he liked cards.

Kidderminster had been experiencing economic difficulties since the mid-eighteen-eighties. In 1893 the carpet market collapsed after massive dumping of cut-price American goods.[22] Ernest presently moved to Birmingham. The rest of the family followed in 1896 or 1897. At about this time, or not long after, once they earned enough to support their mother, the boys, it is believed, encouraged the father to get out, to protect her from further hurt.[23] For some years the family continued a unit close-knit by poverty, domestic misery, mother-love and mother's love.

Selly Oak, and the nearby villages and suburbs just to the south-west of Birmingham, were enjoying a boom fed by chocolate and riding on rear-chain-driven safety bicycles.

The 'Black Country', where coal and iron ore were found close together, was a very old centre of the metal trades. Now nails and guns were giving way to newer products. The 'safety' bicycle was first made in 1885; the pneumatic tyre was added three years later. In 1897 came the 'free wheel' and in 1903 three-speed gears. Coventry and Birmingham took the lead in this new and profitable manufacture, which acquired an important export market. Some of the factories were set up to the south of Birmingham.

Another development which had altered the character of the area was that the enlightened Quakers, the Cadburys, moved their works from the city to a site in Bournville, in open fields, from 1879 onwards. In the 1890s they created one of the first 'garden suburbs'—originally a 'village', but the city was expanding towards and engulfing that district. The houses, of simple design, were built in pleasant groups. Bournville was world-famous, as a notable attempt to improve the labouring and living conditions of urban workers. There were no pubs, but there was a village institute, Ruskin Hall, playing fields, and a factory dining room.

The old village of Selly Oak, nearby, also benefited from these very rich and enlightened employers. George Cadbury founded a social club there, and built the Selly Oak Institute. It provided reading and billiard rooms. The social club and the Society of Friends met there. The Adult School (and later the Workers' Educational Association) held their classes there, where reading and writing were taught to the illiterate and barely literate, while lectures and discussions laid a basis for a liberal education.[24] The Cadburys sought to introduce an element of civilization into a world technologically progressive but socially barbarous. To some extent they succeeded.

For twelve years Walter's life centred on Selly Oak and the new suburb of Bournbrook, which grew up alongside. Selly Oak was expanding and becoming an industrial area. A bicycle firm, Components Limited, and its associated Ariel Cycle works were the principal employers. It was not a particularly attractive area, though more so than later, when it was quite surrounded by the city. It spread along the Bristol Road, a red brick sea of two-storied cottages, joined on in endless lines fronting the streets, such as Heeley Road, and others nearby, where the Nashes lived.

Walter now had several other jobs, first of all in a metal works, where, having been a solicitor's messenger, he was known as 'lawyer'. In an amusing essay written in about 1904, already quoted on his career, and entitled 'From Mill-boy to Office Manager "How to Succeed"', he described his progress from metal worker to head of the cost analysis department at the Ariel works. He was a sort of unqualified accountant, possibly what might now be called a 'costing clerk':

This work was evidently too hard for him as he began to look ill, but one morning he was locked out, and not being able to get underneath the gates as at Kidderminster he was forced to go back home. Having heard that some Office Boys were required at a new Factory close by he donned his best garment and went and applied for a situation, he was successful and commenced in the Order Dept. after a time the firm decided to have two boys in Livery as Messenger Boy and they selected the writer as one, and as the provision of clothing was a lot to be greatly considered at that time and the Sales Manager taking the two boys down to one of the large restaurants in the city, and gave them such a tuck in, blow out or whatever you like to call it he decided to don the uniform and become a Messenger boy. He was at that time 15 years of age, and his salary 5/- per week, after a time in uniform he got tired and objected to being called 'Buttons' he asked to be releived [*sic*] of the uniform and he was transferred to Adv Dept; after 12 months he was again transferred to the Order Dept, and caused a diversion between the respective heads of these Depts over leaving. [His] salary was increased to 7/- per week. about this time the Company were very busy and there was plenty of money about; and to appreciate the cheek, pluck, audacity or whatever you may call of the writer he once worked 3 hours overtime and was sent 1/6 for doing so which he refused to accept, he was arraigned before the Secretary and the 1/6 was again tendered and again refused, and was asked his reason for doing and bluntly stated it was not enough. Fancy 17 years of age and 6d an hour not enough. The Sec told him to either have that or nothing, and he said he would not have anything and walked away The wonder of it was that he was not dismissed as the Sec was supposed to be a very strict disciplinarian. after 12 months order work and at the age of 18 years he was promoted to the accountancy Dept at a Salary of 8/6 per week as Invoice Clerk from that to agency Stock Clerk and afterwards to Purchase with increases of 1/6 and 2/6 respectively for the next three years this salary was increased half yearly . . . . this time he asked the Sales Manager to appoint him as Assistant Manager at one of the Depots and was successful in his application and his salary was increased to 27/6 per week. after a time through Depression in Trade the Depot at which he was assisting in the management was closed, and he was offered employment at the same salary at the Head Office he accepted same, and was allowed to help whom he liked for a period of six months after that he had trouble with the Accountant as he objected to being allowed to do just as he liked at that time as he was likely to rust, he was then told that he would be required for some special Analysing work by the Managing Director which would commence at an early date.

He had begun to like work just now and after commencing on the Analysis Work and continuing same for about twelve months working on an average 14 hours per day he finished it up and then found that with the assistance that he had he could do the work in about three days per week. he then went to the M.D. & bluntly told him that he had not enough to do & said he did not like it & this seemed to please the M.D. a little & he told him that he had other special work for him to and gave him some important & confidential figures to work out. & gave him an increase to 35/- per week. He is now in receipt of £100 per year with the charge of the Analysis Dept of the Firm.

He concluded his composition, probably intended for some local club journal, or works magazine,[25] with the words: 'Now how has he done it? First and foremost he has always asked himself the question before he did anything whatever "Is it right".' That he learnt from his mother. Though, like everyone else, he could be wrong, or delude himself, it was characteristic all his life that, in a quite simple way, he asked that question.

He was employed by Components Limited for nearly ten years. Later the 'analysing work' referred to struck him as a milestone in his life. He began 'to like work', and laboured excessively hard. He was asked to find out where losses were occurring in the factory, where the employees worked three shifts. He decided to work at least part of each shift himself, and found that he could do with only four or five hours sleep. Apparently he succeeded at his task and pleased the managing director, but he became ill and had to take a holiday in Aberystwyth. When he was an old man he claimed that he 'cracked up' because he stopped this hard work and had 'never stopped since'.[26] Although he was probably not aware of it, the changes in Nash's work were an example of a major change in industrial administration. Managerial functions in factories were shifting from the 'overhand' to the office staff.[27] He was gaining experience, to be of great importance to him, of centralized office methods.

Life was not all work. Walter made many friends in Selly Oak. Two of them, he said, he completely trusted with all his thoughts. One Jim Boylin, later went off to Beaver Falls, Pennsylvania, where he became a photographer. With the other, Ernest Hitchinson, he corresponded occasionally throughout his life. 'Hitch' worked for Components Limited too. They both played for the Selly Oak Cricket Club, 'Hitch' being one of the best players they had. The young men used to go on cycling tours in the country. On one never-to-be-forgotten occasion the two of them walked over thirty miles in a day. They began from Acock's Green, to the south of Birmingham, to Stonebridge, Solihull, and to the beautiful manor town of Henley-in-Arden, with its Tudor and Georgian houses and its Norman church, and back to Selly Oak.[28] Walter and his friends also played billiards a good deal in the Institute. He became very skilled at it.

It seems characteristic of urban people that they do not inhabit a city but some part of it which often, to the locals, retains much of the character of a village community. Certainly that was true of Nash. The houses he and his family lived in in Selly Oak were bounded by a few streets. Most of his friends lived in the close vicinity. He met his future wife, Lotty May Eaton, in the Selly Oak Post Office, where she was head assistant. He offered to get her a bicycle. Her father (who drank every night) was a plumber who lived in Heeley Road, where the Nashes had lived for a time. She was a friend of Walter's friend Jim Boylin. 'Hitch' arranged for his brother to sell Walter the sapphire engagement ring that he gave to Lotty. Their best man was Charles Daniel, who worked for his family's house-decorating business in the High Street. Lot and Wal were married in the parish church of St Mary, in 1906.[29]

At about the time of their marriage, Walter also changed his occupation. On the marriage certificate his occupation was given as 'clerk', but he had already moved into a little shop at 195 High Street opposite the Post Office, and was setting up a small business. He acquired, no doubt rented, two shops, the other at 127 High Street, down the hill towards Bournbrook.[30] It may be, though this is conjecture, that Lotty helped him to make a start. She received a small annual income from a family trust which owned some properties on the Bristol Road.[31] Certainly Walter did not have much capital. His Post Office Savings deposit had grown from 1s. in 1897 to £31 1s. 6d. in 1904.[32] They went by train to Wales for their honeymoon.

Lot and Walter lived in the rooms above No. 195, above a large sign, 'THIS IS NASH'S'. That shop was called 'Wholesale Tobacco Stores' and the other 'Wholesale Confectionery Stores'. He ran a retail business, employing assistants in the shops, as well as a small wholesale one, supplying other nearby shops. He used to cycle round the district selling his goods—York cachous, nougat, caramels, Cadbury's chocolates, French beans, pear drops, mint rock, toffees, marzipans, or Bonbon delice. His assistants received detailed instructions, carefully written out in a notebook: never keep a customer waiting; never deceive a customer in any way; only he could allow credit.[33]

Lot was a lively girl. Their passports presently recorded that she had auburn hair (his was brown), blue eyes (his were bronze), and plump good looks. She was two years older than he was and an inch or two shorter than his five foot six. She was less serious-minded, and had a natural gaiety which made her very good company.

Walter Nash already showed some characteristics which became permanent. People often commented on his immense industry and thoroughness. Though he had few intimates, he was a gregarious man. He had, what he must have learnt from maternal sermonizing, a social conscience. He entered very fully into the life of the Selly Oak community —and he was the sort of person who is almost automatically chosen as secretary. For several years he was secretary of the Selly Oak Social Club, started by George Cadbury, whose son, Edward, was the president. Its finances were in a mess, and they worked hard to put them right. Edward Cadbury wrote of Nash that he 'threw himself with energy into the work that he had to do. . . .' Later Nash was a vice-president of the club. He also acted as organizer of the local Debating Society, arranging, for instance, a debate on women's suffrage. After he started in business he became secretary of the Selly Oak and Bournbrook Traders' and Rate-payers' Association, arranging dances, whist drives, and other gatherings.[34] Such activities may seem trivial, but they gave him experience in committee work and lessons in leadership. Anyone who has served on committees knows how often the secretary is the power beside the chair. For the first time in his life a born activist began to find out what he liked doing, and could do.

He was very conscious of his inadequate education. He attended night classes, from time to time, after leaving school. Now he began to meet a small number of people who could influence his further education, inspire intellectual interests related to his life, and suggest relevant reading; who could set satisfying goals before him; people who became, for him, examples. One such person was Edward Cadbury, a director of the family firm. He and his family stood for honesty in business, for the social responsibilities of business leaders, and in generous measure practised what they preached. It is unlikely that Nash got to know him at all well.

Another, the most important early influence on Nash's ideas, was George Shann, a Yorkshireman who had had an elementary schooling and worked as a part-time spinner and then wool-comber, while attending evening classes. He won a scholarship to the Bradford Technical College, and eventually gained a first class honours degree in economics at Glasgow University, where he lived in a university settlement in the slums. In about 1903 he came to Birmingham University, where he lectured on economic and industrial subjects. Like Edward Cadbury, he taught at the Adult School. Cadbury and he wrote two books, *Women's Work and Wages* (1906) and *Sweating* (1907).

Shann was a very active socialist—he joined the Fabian Society, the Birmingham Socialist Centre and the Independent Labour Party. He was elected to the King's Norton and Northfield Urban District Council, and when this district became part of greater Birmingham, he became a Labour councillor there in 1911. Edward Cadbury, who stood as an 'independent' but was in fact Liberal, gained more votes.[35]

Shann was probably the first educated socialist Nash had known and as an old man he recalled his influence.[36] Ernest and Will Nash were Labour. They both worked on the trams. Will, in particular, was an active trade unionist and socialist. But theirs was an instinctive radicalism, deriving from class feelings and their trade union background. They knew little of the great theories which were shaping international labour movements. While their attitudes were politically extremely influential in the world, they held little attraction to a young brother who was not a unionist and not Labour. Later Will wrote to Wal that he had been what Philip Snowden called an 'unconscious socialist'.[37] In fact, however, Nash's thoughts had been moving in more radical directions than his brother knew.

Shann introduced him to the great world of political ideals; he encouraged him to read, to think, to aim high in life. The first signs of a transformation in the little clerk are to be found in his first lecture.[38] It is not quite clear where this was delivered. Late in life he said it was to a 'church club' or to a 'progressive meeting' on a 'Pleasant Sunday Afternoon'—a church institution intended to popularize religion among the workers, by making church a more informal and social occasion. Possibly it was an adult bible class, which was established in Birmingham, or a class at the Adult School. What is certain is that he was speaking to Mr Shann's 'class' in January 1904.

He began by saying that when asking Mr Shann a question he felt quite confident, but now he had to state his own opinion he was very nervous—if anyone thought of laughing he asked them 'to have a think again before doing so that there is nothing whatever equal to laughter or ridicule for closing a person's mouth or hurting his feelings'.

His talk was about the views on social reform of Charles Bradlaugh, who had been excluded from parliament because he refused to take the oath. A free-thinking republican would not in later years have been his first choice for a subject.

Walter admired Bradlaugh's persistence. After leaving school at eleven, and in the face of persecution for his beliefs, he had become a figure in the land. He advocated, Walter said, teaching political economy to the workers. He cited the economist J. R. McCulloch and Bradlaugh on the subject of economics: 'By this you will see that the actual object in the teaching of political economy is to do away altogether with poverty. Poverty in itself is the impassable barrier between bondage and liberty.' There was one point on which he could not agree with Bradlaugh, who wanted the people to save their money. 'I think the tying up of money in savings bank is the cause of a lot of trade depression today.' In this remark he showed that he was aware of the view of classical economists like John Stuart Mill of the social utility of unlimited saving. He had obviously read John Ruskin's criticism of this, and possibly J. A. Hobson's view, expressed in 1889, that excessive saving led to unemployment and depression.[39]

The speaker noted other points, such as Bradlaugh's support for female suffrage. He also criticized Kipling's view that the 'Eastern races' were unprogressive and unchangeable, noting their great improvement in the last twenty years. He discussed at some length Bradlaugh's views on land tenure reform. Bradlaugh thought land nationalization too difficult to achieve, but wanted to break up the land monopoly. 'Property in land he held is only valid in so far as the proprietor of the land is its improver'. Owners must cultivate their land. Ruskin agreed with this, Nash noted, and went on to talk about the use of a graduated land tax on excessively large holdings, to force subdivision. This programme, deriving from Mill, was becoming very influential in England because of the proselytization of the American, Henry George, with his doctrine of the 'single tax'. It was to be even more popular in Australia and New Zealand.

The idea of a land tax on the 'unearned increment' which landlords received as a result of rising land values, paid for in an expanding society by the taxpayers, in the form of roads, bridges, and other amenities, had an immense appeal of great importance in the political theories of the time. It is hard now to believe its extraordinary influence, but it was adopted, for instance, by the Fabian socialists and Christian Socialists alike. The doctrine was, in its essence, non-socialist. The millenium could be brought about, not by land nationalization, not by confiscating property, but by confiscating rent. Land taxes provided a path to radicalism which enabled the intellectual traveller to avoid the dangers of Marxist or other dangerous —and secularist—doctrines.[40]

Nash's lecture was written in a very inadequate prose, marred by childish expressions, but the opinions he discussed are of great interest. They foreshadow in some degree views he was to hold all his life.

There are references in Walter Nash's early correspondence to his reading *England's Ideal* by the utopian socialist, Edward Carpenter, and another popular socialist writer, Blatchford—'Hitch' called him 'Your old friend Robert Blatchford'. He had begun reading John Ruskin, for instance *The Crown of Wild Olive*, with its elegant criticisms of war, capitalism, the class system, and 'the Goddess of Getting-on'. As an old man he listed many other authors among his youthful reading: Tolstoy, Carlyle, Emerson, Thoreau, William Morris; and somewhat later, the Webbs and Tawney. There is no doubt that one of the main influences on his thinking was the late nineteenth century Christian Socialist revival. He would have come into contact with its teachings not only through Shann, but also in the church. Although not notably active there, he did take part in discussion groups. Charles Gore, one of the founders of the Christian Social Union in 1889, was Bishop of Birmingham, 1905-11, and sometimes preached in Selly Oak. His ideas and those of his associates, like Stewart Headlam and Scott Holland (whose work, as an old man, Nash listed among his early readings) must have been widely discussed in Birmingham radical and church circles.

The extent and nature of these influences on Nash's thinking is clearer a little later in his life. What was important is that he had laid down lines connecting him with many of the chief intellectual forces in the English-speaking world. One line took him from the Christian Socialists to the main body of European and British socialist theory. Marx is not numbered among the authors he read at this time, and it is doubtful whether he ever studied him closely, though some of the British socialists he did read had done so. Another line led to the revision of Liberalism made by J. S. Mill, T. H. Green and others. Quite possibly he had not heard of Green, but almost all men imbibe their philosophy in a watered form, and are none the worse for that. To Green the negative Liberalism of laissez-faire was a class doctrine, ignoring the welfare of the majority, who needed help to participate fully in society. Free enterprise and poverty were alike immoral. Positive legislation was needed before the full human life inherent in the ideal of Freedom could be available to all.[41] Under all of Nash's ideas, then and later, lay such a view of a moral society. The theories which most impressed themselves upon him thus reinforced his mother's teachings; a social conscience was given intellectual as well as cultural roots. Those theories may be summed up and labelled, radical humanitarianism.

He was not yet clear in what grand shape he wished the world remade. But he and his friends had lively discussions. Fred Daniel or Jim Boylin, for instance, would drop in—the latter wrote—for 'a debate in the room behind the shop about 11.30. terminated with, Wal give me a couple of macaroons & I'm off'. When Jim migrated to the USA and 'Hitch' became a commercial traveller he corresponded with them discussing the universe, Christian morality, atheism and other grand subjects. They were very serious-minded young men.

Walter was much concerned about commercial morality. He had strong views on misleading labels and advertising. He asked whether the public should not be told what a retailer *paid* for an article, and why a retailer should make a higher percentage profit on some lines than others. He wrote to Jim Boylin that, in his view, all trade should be confined to 'cooperatives and combinations'. The belief in 'co-ops' was to be found in Christian Socialist and in Bradlaugh's writings. Nash was opposed to excessive competition. But, living in the USA, Boylin had learnt suspicion of monopolies and wrote back defending free competition against trusts.[42]

Walter believed in practising his preachings. He gave his employees an eight hour day and 'top rates' (his brother Will wrote), 'and the only one you nearly killed [i.e. with over-work] was yourself'. After debates with Jim, he also closed his shops on Sundays,[43] which seemed an extraordinary thing to do—but, as it happened, gained him some church trade.

The surviving letters about this period are those written to Nash and not his own. But his own writings of the time, and a few years later, are all markedly youthful and naive. It seems safe to conclude, as might be expected, that his reading and his enquiring mind had not yet made up for his deficient schooling. He was ranging widely, in unfamiliar country, without a map. Yet some of the permanent foundations of his thinking were clearly being formed.

Apart from his friendship with his mentor, George Shann, he had little to do with the Labour movement in Birmingham. His friends wrote of his admiration for Lloyd George—who favoured land taxes. Among a vast crowd, he heard one of Joseph Chamberlain's famous speeches in Birmingham in 1903 or 1904 advocating tariff reform and preference for Empire products. Tariff reform became one of Walter's favourite themes. All his life he belonged to the 'Birmingham School'[44] not that of the Manchester freetraders. He was strongly interested in politics—his friends later wrote of missing their political arguments—but, through the Ratepayers' Association, he was more immediately concerned with local body politics, rating, and land taxes on the unearned increment. Thus his awareness of the world was expanding. But Selly Oak did not offer much room.

It might be supposed, because of his unconventional opinions, he would not do well in business, but in fact he did quite well. The shops lost money in 1906 and 1907, but he 'came out on the right side' and made £225 in 1908. His capital was about £260. By early 1909 it was £864 13s. 1d., of which £50 11s. 8d. was borrowed from Lot. Another £300 was owed to him by customers. Thus he had, roughly, £500 in cash.[45] By this time Lot and he had decided to migrate—they hesitated between Canada and New Zealand.

It is very often difficult to discover why migrants decide to move. Often they do not themselves know very clearly which of various circumstances most influenced them. In the case of migration from Great Britain to New

Zealand it was—and is—clear that more people wish to move when economic conditions are bad. When the Nashes left Britain was experiencing a brief recession, which had hit Selly Oak severely. The firm of Components Limited was closed during 1909. Workers in many other jobs were more or less on short time and business people were making little profit.[46] Prospects were not good.

But it seems that their motives were not mainly economic. When they were sailing Will wrote to Walter, 'Do alter your decision about building a wall to separate yourselves from England'. It would be 'less heartbreaking for Mother' if he promised to come over in a few years[47]—and he did say he would visit her in four years. Precisely what led to so firm a 'decision' to migrate is not known, but it may have been Lot's health. Walter wrote at the time that they were leaving 'for family reasons'. Their first child, Clement Walter, had been born in June 1907. A year later they were thinking of migrating. Lot was pregnant again and they decided that Walter would go out to New Zealand to 'see what New Zealand was like' while she lived in a cottage in the Lickey Hills, a few miles from Birmingham. But the second child, a girl, died. Such an experience, Walter later wrote, caused 'a great sadness in a mother'. Lot, and also the baby boy, were both sick in late 1908, and the mother was very often ill in the next few years. It seems likely that her health was a main reason for leaving. Walter sometimes said, too, that she had a strong desire to travel. Some of the Nash family also believe (nearly seventy years later) that Lot may have urged Walter to leave because, in the absence of his father, he was being cast in the role of head of the family, with a special responsibility to care for his mother and young sister, Emily. Certainly Lot always felt a little guilty about her share in the decision. In 1936 Albert Nash wrote to her, 'I never heard Mother complain about you helping Walter to decide to go to New Zealand; & I do not feel there was anything to forgive.'[48]

Once decided, the move was made speedily. Walter wrote to various tobacco and confectionery firms, and to Bryant & May, seeking their New Zealand agencies. The replies were discouraging.[49] They booked passages in the Second Saloon class on R.M.S. *Tainui*, sailing from Tilbury to Wellington, and calling at Plymouth, Teneriffe, Cape Town, and Hobart. They left Tilbury on 3 April 1909. If, as seem likely, Lot was suffering from depression earlier, she did not show it at the parting. Will wrote that she 'did great work with her cheery Tra la la from the Boat. She kept our Spirits up tho I expect she had her work cut out to keep her own up.'

Everyone was seasick at first, but after that the Nashes really enjoyed themselves. They played whist, cricket, 'bullboard'. The food was very good and they were 'waited on hand and foot'. A photograph taken on board shows a plump young Walter, Lot looking a picture of health and Wal a little wistful, dreamy, like a soulful character from an early H. G. Wells novel, waiting for something to turn up.[50]

II

The New Chum

1909-12

Wellington presents itself to the visitor as a natural fortress. It is difficult of access by land. Those arriving by sea are faced with cliffs, bare hills, surf bursting over rocks and reefs guarding the entrance. Then, quite suddenly, inside the heads there is a spacious harbour, shielded almost right round by hills. In the distance to the north are higher ranges, snow-capped in winter.

The town nestles cosily along the narrow shore and creeps up the valleys and hills of Brooklyn, Kelburn, Karori and other suburbs. Even in 1909, when there were only 73,000 people living there, many of the slopes were built on by people in search of land not actually vertical or the superb views of sea and ranges. It was the capital of the new British 'Dominion' —'the Fortunate Isles', William Pember Reeves had called it—and well endowed by nature for a leading role.

When the travellers landed in mid-May they had an agreeable surprise: they were met by some friends of Lot and taken out to tea. Next day they were invited to another house, and stayed with further friends for two more days. People were extremely friendly. Several others offered to put them up. But they decided to live in a hotel until Wal had found a job. After a 'splendid' passage out, he wrote to his mother, they were all in 'real good trim'; indeed he had 'never seen Lot look better'.[1]

Friends and business acquaintances had written references for him. One said, 'he is one of the right sort, he has a good round sum of money past him and leaves Birmingham not owing anyone a penny. He would like to invest his money in some business. . . .' Another testified that, 'he is one of the steadiest and hardest workers I know, and a thoroughly good businessman'.[2]

Like many immigrants, the Nashes took the advice of and settled near friends from Home. They rented a house in Washington Avenue, Brooklyn, near the grocery shop at the corner of the avenue and Cleveland Street, run by some 'Kiddy' people, the Westwoods, whom they knew, and who became close friends.[3] It cost 20s. a week and had views both of the sea and hills. There was plenty of room so they bought a billiard table among the furniture, which cost, altogether, £156 2s. 11d. A few months later they moved to another house in Brooklyn, in Bruce Avenue, which had a magnificent harbour view and stood on the edge of a precipitous gully full of bush—an excitingly risky adventure ground for small boys.[4] Two more sons, Les and Jim, were born in Brooklyn, Les while they lived in Washington Avenue and Jim in Bruce Avenue.

Wal probably made his first business contacts through the Westwoods. W. J. Westwood was People's Warden and Synodsman of the local Anglican church, St Matthews, which the Nashes started to attend. One of the Vestrymen was Howard Jones, who was a tailor. Another tailor, Edgar Jones, who was possibly his brother, wanted a secretary for a company being formed to purchase the old-fashioned, private tailoring business of Jones & Ashdown, of which Edgar was sole proprietor. Edgar Jones, if not Howard, came from Selly Oak and was known to the Nashes' families.

Wal was willing to invest some of his capital in shares, and was offered the secretary's job on that condition. He took over on 1 July. The speed of this proceeding might suggest some imprudence. Howard had warned him that the firm was insolvent and had a debenture hanging over its head. Edgar, however, denied the existence of a debenture or of any debts other than the rent. Nash formed the impression, as he wrote in 1909, that the concern was 'grossly mismanaged' and 'drafted out systems where I was of opinion that money could be saved and losses checked'.[5]

By bringing in some new shareholders, Edgar Jones was trying to keep his badly water-logged company afloat. The new shareholders, under provisions introduced by the Companies Act 1903, for the incorporation of private companies, were protected by the principle of limited liability, but were of course liable to the extent of the uncalled portion of their shares. The fact that Jones was taking advantage of the principles of limited liability might in itself have given Nash cause for thought.

That Nash did have or soon acquired some misgivings is hinted at by his secretiveness in letters home. A year later Arch was complaining that he had told neither 'Hitch' nor his family what his occupation was. Nor had he told Jim Boylin. When they did learn they were, Lot's sister Nell wrote, 'very surprised to hear of Walter working for Edgar, hope the trade will pick up out there shortly. . . .' Possibly his doubts were about whether tailoring would suitably impress. When Nash left Jones & Ashdown 'Hitch' was glad, for he felt that Wal was 'not cut out' to be a tailor and was more suited to the life of 'a travelling man'.[6] He wrote that he had never known such a chap for knocking his clothes about.

What surprised some of his family even more was that Wal became an ardent churchman. He formed a close friendship with the Reverend Richard H. Hobday, who was newly appointed as the first Vicar of St Matthews. Like most of Nash's early friends in New Zealand, and a high proportion throughout his life, Hobday was an Englishman, educated at

St Paul's School, London, and Sidney Sussex College, Cambridge. He was a handsome young man, with resolute jaw and anxious eyes.

Nash was soon teaching Sunday school, and in December was elected a Vestryman. He helped raise funds to build the vicarage. On 24 April he was, as he wrote many years later to Mrs Hobday, 'confirmed in proper entry as an adult into the church'.[7] Since he had been brought up in church schools and by a religious mother it is perhaps surprising that he had not already been confirmed. (Possibly he was christened just before.) Two days later, at the annual meeting, speaking 'very forcibly', he secured unanimous support for circularizing parishioners to raise contributions for the vicar's stipend fund.[8] Then and later the quarterly payments to Hobday were often in arrears. He was very poor and Nash sometimes helped him with gifts of cloth for suits.

His brother Arch wrote in 1910 saying that he must have changed, 'as you were so much against Church work so socialistic when in the home country'. Lot's sister Nell was equally intrigued: 'If Walter still goes on he will be the Rev. W. N. by the time you pay us a visit.'[9]

Although inaccurate, Nell's was not a misguided prophecy. Indeed Nash may have had such a goal in mind. In late 1909 and early 1910 he began studying for 'matric' (the University Entrance examination) with a coach, but he was too busy to keep it up.[10] Many people who knew Nash later believed that he was a lay reader, licensed by the bishop to take part in divine service. No evidence of this can be found.[11] But he was often asked to preach. And all his life there was something a little parsonical about his personality and voice, which contributed to the strong impression of sincerity which he gave.

Much of Nash's time outside business hours was now taken up with church affairs. Many of his papers concern the stipend fund, church bazaars, or prayer week. He attended a missionary meeting in the Wellington Town Hall. He wrote to the Church Socialist League, founded in Christchurch in 1913. Above all, he became involved in the work of the Church of England Men's Society, which he joined in 1909 and of which he remained a member all his life. He usually wore its medallion on his watch chain, outside his waistcoat.

The aims of the CEMS were to promote the glory to God, true religion, Christian brotherly love and practical helpfulness. Its Rule of Life was daily to pray and to help forward the work of the church. In 1910 Nash represented Brooklyn at the first CEMS conference and spoke twice. He helped to draft its constitution. At the Nelson conference in 1913 he was appointed to collect funds for the appointment of an Organizing Secretary, a task he took up with his never-failing enthusiasm, circularizing on special notepaper brother members and churches throughout the country. Not all Anglicans supported the Society. He lamented that Bishop Averill did not do so and wrote to his friend, the Reverend J. D. Russell (who became the first secretary), that he wanted 'to make our society the Fighting Battalions for the Establishment of the Kingdom of Heaven on Earth'.[12] He had a humourless seriousness about him and a religious enthusiasm which earnest Anglicans in those years found a little disconcerting.

The activist element of the CEMS was very much to Nash's taste. His interest in the complexities of theology was slight; his views on religion and its role were direct and fairly simple. He believed in the existence of a divine power, though he had doubts about the divinity of Christ, and certainly did not believe that Christianity was the only true religion or path to God. He believed in prayer, and prayed throughout his life. He was a sedulous attender at divine service. Above all, be believed in practising Christianity here and now. He accepted literally that it was the duty of every Christian to work to bring about God's Kingdom on earth. Nor, though he would not in later life have used the same phrases, did he waver in this attitude. In 1916 he wrote, 'I believe that Christ's methods and orders if obeyed literally, when understood, are infallible.' In 1932 to a correspondent interested in Christian Socialism, he wrote, 'Personally I am of opinion that the Christian methods are the most profitable ones to employ in solving our economic problems. I find, however, that the greatest difficulty arises from the Christians themselves, in that they feel that Christianity is something exclusively to do with Churches and Services whereas in my opinion these are the means only of getting the necessary help and instruction for the application of Christian principles to normal life.'[13] An ardent Christian, he did not believe in 'churchianity'.

Although he was not bothered by Christian theological niceties, literature of an inspirational sort was always the most attractive to him. From about 1913-17 the greatest influence on him and some of his friends was the religious writings of Tolstoy, who died in 1910. Numerous notes written for his own edification and enlightenment refer to the great novelist's life and words. Some of these are headings for or notes of talks to Sunday schools, sermons and the like: 'First Sunday was Tolstoi & Peace. The main thought was the abolition of Fear. Second Sunday, Mazzini—Duty. . . .' Some of them are mere headings on narrow slips of paper cut from *The Gentlemen's Tailor*. It was always characteristic of his speech notes that a heading, especially including some very emotive word—'Love'—or—'Peace'—with plentiful capitals, seemed to him to constitute in itself a thought or an argument. Others are notes meant for himself: 'when we have reached self-control we can overcome all things'; 'Happiness lies in self sacrifice'.

It is not always clear whether some of these writings, usually close to Tolstoy's thought, are paraphrases or quotations from him or not. Many of them evidently had struck near to Nash's own aspirations and longings: 'There is something in me which compels me to believe that I was not born to be like everybody else.'[14]

Tolstoy believed that one should try to follow the teachings of Christ, which were perverted or misinterpreted by the Orthodox Church. While denying Christ's divinity, he wanted to live by Christian morality. Particularly meaningful to Nash was his stress on a practical Christianity and his advocacy of non-violence. Nash also tried to practise a Christian and Tolstoyan avoidance of evil-speaking.[15]

A draft of a letter to a close friend, Harold Ahearn, in 1917, shows how closely he followed Tolstoyan doctrines. Unselfishness, living for others, he wrote, was the key to a good life. With God's guidance, there was hope of bringing 'into being here on Earth that Kingdom, which is the only Kingdom worth fighting for.' (Tolstoy had written that the Kingdom of God could be achieved by effort 'in our own epoch'.)[16]

'I do not think there are many flaws in Tolstoi's interpretation of Christ's Christianity, but if his interpretation is impracticable, then it is of no real help, and it is not a true interpretation.'

With much Church doctrine he could not agree. 'With regard to Christ's divinity I do not think this weighs much at all. To me it is not the Person so much that is Divine, but the Wisdom.' He had noticed, he wrote, that in his excited moments he had been led to 'make statements that are far from conforming to the ordinary accepted beliefs of the Church, yet I have never once been called to order. . . .'

In another draft of this letter[17] he said that his belief in Christ was 'not founded on the Virgin Birth—the Resurrection—the Miracles—the Ascension or any supernatural Powers. I believe in Him because he appeals to my reason as the wisest and sanest, therefore most divine Explanation of why we are here, and how to make the best of our life.' Christianity appealed to his reason, but to his feelings too.

About this time Hobday, admirer of Tolstoy as he was, felt moved to warn his friend of Tolstoy's egotism: he, Tolstoy, would show the world what Christ's Christianity was. 'I do think you must beware of taking Tolstoy in the place of Christ.' Nevertheless, although, as Nash wrote to Ahearn, 'my thoughts are not orthodox', they were never so far from the generous scope of the Anglican Church as to prevent him from feeling comfortably at home in its ranks, within its walls, at its services, with their consolations and promise.

There was one very important respect in which Nash did not agree with Tolstoy. The latter thought socialism impractical.[18] In 1911, after reading *The Problems and Perils of Socialism* (1908), by the conservative John St Loe Strachey (whom he certainly did not know—he misspelt 'Loe'), he wrote to the author that he would have accepted his book as sound had he not 'been a follower of Jesus Christ'. Strachey had omitted to take into account that Christian Socialists 'have one objective only in their endeavours to alter the existing state of Commercial Morality; I feel tempted to say Commercial Immorality. Their object is so to educate the world in the ways of Christ, that His task will not be so heavy on His return to this small planet.'[19]

The Christian Socialists were another of the great formative influences on Nash's views. Their aims, which included the application of Christian principles to economic and social problems, were entirely attractive to him. They had a generous wish to improve the lives of the poor and the handicapped; one not restricted by any rigidities of economic or political dogma. An intellectual woolliness, an *emotional* theory, as it were, suited him. So did their safeness; for though many people rightly thought their aims threatened established society, their upraised hands brandished the Cross and an olive branch. Their aims and views could settle down comfortably with Ruskin's and not too scratchily with Tolstoy's. They, too, asserted that 'the Kingdom of God had to be realised on Earth'.[20]

Nash was much impressed with the papers presented to the Pan-Anglican Congress in 1907-8.[21] These included several papers on economic and such issues. The Bishop of Birmingham, Charles Gore, presented one on 'Christianity and Socialism', which asserted that nothing in the latter was antagonistic to the former. Socialism was ethical: a cry for justice. Echoes from these papers resounded in Nash's remarks then and later.

To Nash, socialism quite literally was applied Christianity. 'All Christians who are striving to enter the Kingdom of Heaven on Earth are Socialists', he wrote to the Reverend J. D. Russell, whom he called the finest socialist he had met.[22]

The emphasis of the Christian Socialists on morality also strongly appealed to Nash. Radicalism was seen as compatible with his Anglican beliefs and personal feelings. He was always very puritanical, opposing gambling, for instance, as an attempt to get wealth without effort. This was an important issue in church discussions at the time—one of *The Pan-Anglican Papers* said it was an evil reducing men to their passions and destroying the foundations of character in society. Nash thought the government should prohibit the import of contraceptives. Like many conservatives and Christians, he feared that certain sorts of socialism might involve immorality and wrote, in some notes, that there was great danger to the family in the view of 'Materialist Socialists' that 'children belong to the State'[23] and should be brought up in common. Similarly, he was opposed to divorce, which some socialists thought should be made easy. Socialism was thus, in several senses, a moral question.

Although he had begun to read the Christian Socialists and other writers in England, the cumulative effect on his thinking is more noticeable after his migration. This may be partly because fewer of his papers survive from before 1909, but it is clear that he was now expressing his ideas with greater fluency. The flavour of his thought, which persisted throughout his life, may also be gained from reading John Ruskin. In 1913 Nash contemplated writing an essay on him.[24]

Ruskin attacked Ricardo, J. S. Mill, and orthodox economists in general for leaving ordinary humanity out of their calculations. He advocated a *moral* political economy, within which there was room for 'social affection'. The 'real science of political economy' would lead to a fuller life. Ruskin wrote, perhaps his most famous words, 'THERE IS NO WEALTH BUT LIFE,' and went on, 'That country is the richest which nourishes the greatest number of noble and happy human beings.' The Christian Socialists had similarly criticized the stress on self-interest, however enlightened, in free trade, *laissez-faire*, contemporary capitalist thought. The key to social reform was to reform social motives or, rather, to liberate man's better, suppressed inner man. Competition and greed should not be the dynamos of progress; the worker was not a 'covetous machine'; men were capable of self-sacrifice, of cooperation. In Ruskin, Nash also found the idea that distribution and consumption, rather than production, were keys to a new way of economic understanding.[25] These notions, which he added to Tolstoy, were to loom large in his thoughts in years to come. So, too, was the idea he found in Ruskin (he wrote to his brother Will, recommending him to read *Unto This Last* and *Sesame and the Lilies*), that in a true Christian country no one would enjoy luxuries until all had necessaries. This might well be identified as the central sentiment of the New Zealand Labour Party twenty years or more later. Will, another Christian Socialist, wrote back about 'what you liked to be thinking about. The uplifting of Mankind.'[26]

These influences on Nash's thinking may seem oddly assorted today, but they were not. There were many links between the Christian Socialists, Tolstoy and Ruskin. Both writers and some of the Christian Socialists, for instance, encouraged the idea of cooperative communities—we should now say 'communes'. And the people Nash read were immensely influential in encouraging—not socialist revolution—but nevertheless a revolutionary reform of capitalism.

It was at this time and with these thoughts that Nash first became interested in Labour. When he arrived in New Zealand that movement was even more divided than it was in England, where the various groups had at least formally coalesced into a loose party in 1906, although their feuding continued for years. In the Dominion Labour political organizations had been late in appearing in comparison with the Australian colonies, where Labor parties had been formed by 1891. Partly no doubt this was a result of the weakness of unions in a predominantly rural society. The great success of the Liberal government (1891-1912) in introducing measures which the unionists wanted was also an important brake on Labour. Moreover, except during the intense depression of the late 1880s and the strikes of 1890, class feeling was relatively weak—by British standards—until the strikes of 1912-13.

A Political Labour League was formed by the Trades and Labour
Councils in 1904. It put up a few parliamentary candidates, but faded away
by 1909. At the same time there also existed groups of more moderate
'Lib-Labs', supporters of the Liberal-Labour Federation established by the
Liberal Prime Minister, R. J. Seddon, in 1899 in an effort to contain an
incipient Labour party within the Liberal ranks.

The first New Zealand Labour Party was formed, again by the unions
and their Trades and Labour Councils, in 1909. A motion to include in its
platform the words 'socialisation of the means of production, distribution,
and exchange' was rejected. It was a moderate workers' party. Its leaders
were mostly 'old colonists', who had been in the country for a long time,
or New Zealanders.

Since the late nineteenth century there had also been groups of socialists,
followers of the Fabians, of Robert Blatchford or other overseas prophets.
In 1908 these groups formed a Socialist Party, but it, too, declined as a
new brand of trade union radicalism arrived in the country. The doctrines
of syndicalism came with several persons and thousands of pamphlets. Tom
Mann, the militant English union leader, in the years 1902-09 worked in
Australia and New Zealand. A New Zealander, Pat Hickey, returned from
the USA, where he had joined the Western Federation of Miners, a
syndicalist union. Several Australians with similar ideas, including Harry
Holland, secretary of the Socialist Federation of Australasia, who had been
influenced by Mann, 'Joe' Savage, Bob Semple, Paddy Webb, and Bill Parry
came over at about the same time as Nash.

The aim of the syndicalists was to gain control of the economy and
country by taking over the industries. The American Industrial Workers
of the World, the 'Wobblies', like their later New Zealand disciples, wanted
'One Big Union'. Parliament and political action the syndicalists regarded
with contempt. They helped to start Socialist Party branches, and then in
1908 formed a Federation of Miners on the 'West Coast' (of the South
Island) which was in 1909 transformed into the Federation of Labour. Its
members came to be called 'Red Feds'. Its constitution was almost identical
with that of the Western Federation of Miners, although it did include
provision for securing the election of MPs. It repeated traditional socialist
clichés about class warfare and the mission of the workers to abolish
capitalism. Other unions, including the watersiders, joined, though it never
became a federation of more than a minority.

The 'Red' Federation suffered from some severe disabilities, to which its
leaders seemed blind. They were, Pat Hickey wrote, 'all in deadly earnest.
We were often accused of being fanatical. . . . We were so convinced that
our tactic was right that it was inconceivable to us that any intelligent
worker could possibly do otherwise than rally to our cause.'[27] They were
indeed fanatics. To take over by industrial action a country with a rural
economy, where urban industries other than rope yards, brick factories, or

cobbling shops were almost non-existent, where scarcely any large agglomerations of workers were to be found except in mines, on the wharves, and in the Railway Workshops (the biggest factories in the country) would take some doing or, in this case, imagination. Most of the unions were created by W. P. Reeves's Industrial Conciliation and Arbitration Act of 1894, whereby any group of workers could gain an award wage if they formed a union. The most rapidly growing industry was small (capitalist) dairy farming. Class feeling was generally weak in a land where so many hoped to become owners of a farm or business. It would be difficult to think of a doctrine more out of place than syndicalism.

The moderate radicals imported leaders too. In 1911 'Professor' W. T. Mills arrived from the USA via England. He had started as a Quaker, temperance evangelist, and become a well-known orator in both countries. In New Zealand he organized a union of the Labour Party, prohibitionists, 'single taxers' and others, in the United Labour Party of 1912. It had a typically trade union and reformist policy. It stressed increased taxation of land values, one of Nash's old enthusiasms. It did advocate a state bank with sole right of note issue, but did not mention nationalizing the others. It called for a national minimum wage, more pensions, state medical and hospital care, and workers' homes.

Nash took a keen interest in the United Labour Party and kept many copies of its constitution and its recruiting leaflet. He knew some of its leaders, including 'Professor' W. T. Mills, the four-foot-six American organizer, whom Hobday called 'the great little man'. Once in 1914 Nash enjoyed a long discussion with him. He also knew David McLaren, a leading Wellington Labour man who was organizer for the United Labour Party in 1913.[28] He was acquainted with James Thorn, a very active radical born in Christchurch, who had worked for socialist parties in England and Scotland. During the 1911 election Nash helped him with 'the drudgery work' in the Wellington South electorate, where the New Zealand Labour Party candidate, A. H. Hindmarsh, a lawyer, beat the Reform and Liberal candidates. Nash was very pleased with the four Labour men who won.[29]

The election led to the fall of the Liberal Government, after twenty years of power, and the formation of an anti-socialist Reform Party government led by W. F. Massey and dominated by small farmers.

Nash certainly considered joining the United Labour Party. In 1912 Hobday wrote to him: 'Please let me know what you do about the U.L.P. If you do join, I expect you will find yourself acting as a continual brake upon the red hot chariot wheels of some, & I don't suppose will be effective! This sounds very rude, but experience and history seem to show that the steady cool moderates soon have their heads cut off, or are similarly extinguished.' He wished Nash would stand for Parliament and agreed with one of the newspapers that it was 'a shame that the younger educated N.Z. men don't take a keener interest in the welfare of their country.'[30] As

William Pember Reeves had found in the early years of Liberal rule, educated people tended to oppose the radicals and to stand for middle class respectability. And very few locally born people took a leading role in left-wing movements. A majority of middle-aged or older adults were immigrants, so a fair proportion among the leaders was to be expected. But almost all the Labour Party chiefs of the 1920s and 1930s were Australians or British. In addition, it might be said that there were conspicuously few Anglicans among the left and righteous.[31]

There are some slight indications that Nash did join the party. In a pamphlet published in England during World War II, it is asserted in a note in his handwriting that he joined 'shortly after' the 1908 election—in fact it could not have been earlier than 1912. Elsewhere, however, he permitted it to be said that he was 'associated' with the party, or made 'his first contact with the Labour Movement' through it.[32] This is probably correct, but he may have thought it impolitic to stress any associations with the pre-1916 Labour factions, just as Peter Fraser, for example, was later happy to ignore his 'Red Fed' and prison days, in the interests of party unity. Another aspect also affected Nash's attitude. 'Professor' Mills was involved in a scandal and hastily left the country. Nash strongly disapproved of him. Many years later he asked Bruce Brown, the author of *The Rise of New Zealand Labour*, to strike Mills's name out of the introduction: 'Mills was a great orator but there is another side which would not warrant me saying that he was a great man'.[33]

Some of Nash's attitudes and doubts about politics, including considerable caution, are expressed in a letter to a friend, Frederick W. Frankland, of 1913, which partly refers to unfortunate business experiences not yet recounted:

Twelve months ago I set out in search of success in the following four ideals: Christianity—Health—Business—Politics.

A little thought opened up the truth that *real* success in either of my ambitions was entirely dependent on Number 1. Constant reading thinking and meditation convinced me that this alone was the only solution if I desired good Health Christianity taught me that the Body was the Temple of the Holy Ghost, and whatever I did in any way that affected my body [to] an ill degree was sinful.

Success in Business is impossible under the present system to anyone endeavouring to live up to Christ's Ideal.

You cannot be a Christian under the present Business System and make your business a success.

The present game of business I love but it is unchristian. The fourth ideal Politics is dangerous with a large D. . . .

Willing as I am to give the other side credit for desiring to bring about a better state for all, I cannot rid me of the idea that the Church—the powers that be—and the aristocracy of intellect—are not doing what they should to bring the Kingdom of Heaven on Earth into being.

In political questions, it is *not politic* for individuals to set themselves up *in opposition* to those who are *in power*.

Machiavel laid down this for a master rule in his political scheme, that *the show of religion* was helpful to the politician. . . .

What an ambition to endeavour to so alter the *political* system that I may be a *Christian* and yet enjoy the work of *business* which I love without injuring my *health* through mental worries.

I know how to do it but shall have to wait years before getting enough people to believe in it to bring it into being.

Everyone agrees that Socialism is right if it can be worked. If it is right it can be worked. If it is right it is Christian. If it is Christian it will be worked because Christianity—Love must win.'[34]

Socialism, Christianity, and goodness in daily life, then, were indistinguishable. His notions of such living were quite remarkably strenuous. In some of his notes on Tolstoy he referred to his hero's 'Rules of Life', such as were common in Tolstoy's diary. His own prescription for virtue was modelled on them. In about 1911 he wrote:

6.30 - 7	toilet
7.0 - 7.30	prayer
7.30 - 8.0	Home
8.0 - 8.30	meals
9.0 - 1.0	business
1.0 - 1.15	exercise
1.15 - 1.45	meals
1.45 - 2.0	exercise
2.0 - 6.0	business
6.0 - 6.15	exercise
6.15 - 6.45	meals
6.45 - 7.15	Home
7.15 - 7.30	exercise
7.30 - 8.0	Church
8.0 - 8.15	Reserve
8.15 - 8.30	exercise
8.30 - 9.15	Home
9.15 - 9.30	Prayer
9.30 - 10.30	study
10.30 - 6.30	sleep[35]

If he in practice exercised that much it may help to account for the good health he almost always enjoyed. He was an athletic Christian. His Sunday programme included church 10.30-12.30, 3-4.15, and 6.45-8.45. His timetable accounted for 8,736 hours out of the total possible in a year of 8,760. Only eight hours daily were allocated to work, an activity which was to expand, and very little to 'Home', which was to contract.

The business side of Nash's life was the least satisfactory. It had long been a tradition in the colonies that 'new chums' were fair game: stories of their being taken down by shrewd, sharp colonials were endless. So it was with Nash and what Hobday called 'the noble firm of Jones & Ashdown'. He was gullible and gulled.

The original 'Memorandum of Association' of the firm of Jones & Ashdown which was registered as a limited liability company in 1909, announced the intention of the shareholders to purchase Edgar Jones's business in Wellington and Wanganui, including his goodwill, stock-in-trade, fittings, plant, and debts. The capital of £7,000 was to be in seventy shares. When Nash joined he purchased three of these, which he began to pay off at 10s. a week.

Although Edgar Jones had denied the existence of a debenture, Nash rapidly became anxious. When he asked to see the firm's papers its lawyers continually put him off by saying they could not get them until a lease on the firm's premises in Willis Street had been transferred. And reasons for concern rapidly multiplied. Although fourteen shares (other than Edgar Jones's fully paid up vendor's shares) had been allotted, only four deposits had materialized. The company was extremely short of working capital. Moreover, during a short, sharp recession which hit New Zealand (like England) from 1908 to mid-1910, it had suffered and continued to lose money steadily even after things improved. In July 1910 alone it lost £700. Nash also became alarmed at an enigmatic reference by Edgar Jones to a debenture. He managed, after some delays, to call a directors' meeting and only then, in early August 1909, learnt the extent of the company's debt. There was a deficiency of about £3,000, including Edgar Jones's debenture or debentures. Originally, the chairman, E. L. Chatwin, told him, they had proposed to issue a debenture of £3,200 secured on the company's property, to satisfy its most pressing creditors. They had refused and threatened to bankrupt the firm and to stop the flotation of the new limited liability company.

Nash's account of these events, written at the time, is confused, and suggests no great insight into the intricacies of company law or management, but many of the details are confirmed by surviving records.[36]

Despite the fresh revelations, Howard Jones and Nash still decided to try to keep the company going. They offered £400 cash (£200 each) plus a debenture for £600, secured on the firm's assets and their personal guarantees, to the chief creditors. Edgar claimed to have friends who would invest £600 in the company. His shares, for what they were worth, were transferred to the company.

The firm's lawyer advised them (Nash wrote) 'to drop this most confounded and complicated transaction as he saw no hope of us pulling through unless we obtained the Capital promised by Mr E. J. also that I might as well have chucked my money over the wharf into the sea'. Their offer was accepted, however, and Howard Jones and Nash went ahead as joint managing directors. They 'trimmed sail' by reducing four salaries by

10s. each per week and sacked two assistants—thus saving £7 10s. per week!

The loss in the trading account continued, as the company limped along. One of the shareholders, an old man called McKeown, wished to enforce liquidation, but the others resisted, for they would be liable for the firm's debts to the extent of their uncalled capital.

Nash shared in this legal liability, and felt morally obliged for more. His friend Jim Boylin wrote from Pennsylvania that Nash had made the mistake of thinking everyone as honest as himself. 'I know you will pay all the debts', he added.[37] Nash was always proud that he managed in the end to pay all he owed.

At the same time Nash's solicitor in Birmingham, F. B. Darling, was writing that the county court had failed to collect the £300 owing to him there. His debtors knew that he had left the country.[38] He advised Nash not to go to court and because of the fees throw good money after bad (which was what he was doing in New Zealand).

Walter had to tell Lot that he had lost all his money.[39] In March 1913 he left and took a job as a commercial traveller for the firm of Miller & Ahearn, and in about June he and his family moved to Palmerston North. He was already negotiating with Howard Jones to sell his shares.

His 'wish to get J & A off my mind', as he put it in a letter to Howard Jones in 1913, was not easy to achieve. He made various offers. In August 1912 Jones offered to buy him out with £50 a year for seven years but this would have meant a continuing liability for the firm's bad debts and he did not want to be 'perpetually bound to liquidate the debts of the Company', as he wrote to Lot.[40] Eventually, a year later, he transferred his shares to Jones for £159, but was paid only £50 down, the rest to be paid in stages.

Nash had offered to reimburse McKeown for the £70 he had paid on his share if Jones did not do so. In 1914 McKeown called at Miller & Ahearn's warehouse and called Nash a 'bloody rogue'. He threatened to sue Nash until his lawyer advised him that he had no claim.[41]

In 1914 Hobday wrote, 'As to J & A . . . I do not think it right that you should stand to lose all that the firm owes you. You must [not] force by your kindness & generosity H.J.J. into being more mean & slim than ever.'[42] But several years later Howard had not paid anything off his debt.[43] It is doubtful whether Nash ever recovered the remaining £109. He had lost virtually all the money that remained after they had furnished their home.

In 1912 a Wellington firm of men's outfitters and some merchants filed a petition in bankruptcy against Edgar Jones, but it was withdrawn after the bailiff swore that Jones had no goods to seize. Possibly this incident—and the whole episode—was the origin of a malicious rumour which persisted throughout Nash's life that he had been a bankrupt. Howard kept the firm going until 1919, but even in 1915 he had no money, not even £35 to pay McKeown.[44]

These unhappy events naturally caused Nash intense strain. He had been
naive and must have felt a fool, as well as anxious about his family's
welfare. This is one of the few periods in his life when there are references
to his being ill. In 1913 he had an operation, though it is not clear of what
sort.

III

The Travelling Man

1912-16

From 1912 to 1916 the Nashes lived in Palmerston North, a small provincial town with 11,000 people, eighty miles north of Wellington, first at 67 Waldegrave Street and from 1914 at 37 Hereford Street, on the corner of College Street, in a small wooden house, with a small front entrance porch. It still stood sixty years later.

He was a commercial traveller for Miller & Ahearn, woollen merchants, importers and wholesalers of cloths, who were one of Jones & Ashdown's chief creditors. Nash had known the proprietors since 1910. He now travelled about selling cloths to tailors and retailers. This was a most successful venture. He was an outstanding salesman. His employers trusted him completely. It did a great deal to boost his confidence.

Harold Ahearn and his family became life-long friends. He was a very serious Christian like Nash. They exchanged long letters giving their ideas on Life. Ahearn's thinking had been influenced by Tom Paine. One of Nash's letters to him on Tolstoy and Christianity has already been quoted.

Although Nash was an employee, in a sense Ahearn looked up to him, as someone out of the ordinary. His son Robert Ahearn later wrote that his father had never met such a person. Nash talked much of love for mankind, and could quote cricket scores for years back.

In 1916 the firm offered to pay for his mother and sister Emily to come out for a visit.[1] They thought he worked too hard. Hobday asked him to represent Brooklyn at the 1914 CEMS conference and Ahearn urged him to do so: 'Go to this by all means and do not rush it too much, a spell among congenial companions will do you good, if you do not rush it too much.'[2] Nash wrote high-toned letters to him on salesmanship: 'It seems illogical to say that a man can do "better than his best" ' but 'No man is *all* out *all* the time, and yet he is doing his best.' He thought salesmen could be spurred on to do better by having figures showing what sales had been made previously in each town.[3] His moralizing inclinations must have been tedious or irritating to less sympathetic, less Christian companions.

Sometimes his work gave ample scope for his hypersensitive conscience. For instance in 1915 he found that the firm had increased the price of serge

already in stock, taking advantage of a war-time shortage. He wrote to
Lotty that 'the awkward part' was, he had sold a piece at the higher price
by accident. 'Now what am I to do?' He had written to Miller 'hoping he'll
do what is right'.[4] He was, as always, a great worrier over details. In 1916
he wrote to Lot from Rotorua, 'awfully worried over 7/3 which I could
not and cannot account for. Do you remember anything on which I
disbursed this amount?' Of course 7/3 then would be worth several dollars
sixty years later.

What, as a commercial traveller, he called his 'territory' or 'ground' was
extensive. It stretched from Nelson and Blenheim in the South Island, up
the Wairarapa, the East Coast and across to New Plymouth. Trips often
took five or six weeks. Sometimes he travelled by coastal vessel. But in
1914 the firm bought him a car. Characteristically, Nash preferred an
English car, a Humber, but Ahearn insisted that an American Buick would
be better. Not long after he ran down two lambs and had to pay for them.
Probably he was an indifferent driver, and in later life he did not keep a
car, nor was he known to drive.

He was incredibly meticulous in the details of his work and his accounts.
Everything was noted, tabulated, added, analysed. We could (if we wished)
from appointment books and hotel bills and letters, follow him from one
provincial hotel to the next, as he set up showrooms and contacted tailors
and drapers to see his samples of Chintz, Buckram, Haircloth, Holland,
Silesia, Verona, Golden Fleece suitings, Black Anglesea, Optima, Worsteds,
'Saltaire' serges, braids, Lion Coloured Button Hole Twist and buttons. We
could discover, from his letters to Lot and his thousands of copies of
orders, when he got 'a nice order' or only 'a nice little order'.

In 1912-13 alone he sold £12,639 worth of goods in a year. At his peak
he sold over £20,000 worth in a year. His salary was at first £20 and later
£26 a month, plus bonuses and a commission which was, in 1916, 3¾ per cent
on sales over £7,000, plus expenses. By 1916 he was earning several hundred
pounds a year, a considerable income then.[5] In testimonials a few years
later Harold Ahearn wrote that Nash was 'eminently successful' as a
salesman and 'a competent accountant' and had 'exceptional business
capacity'.[6]

A glimpse of him from the customer's point of view has survived. One
firm he called on was Reardon & Wright in Napier, where Mr G. Chetwin
was in charge of purchasing. His boss, Robert Wright, loved an argument.
One morning when Nash was expected he said to Chetwin, 'This man Nash
is a Christian Socialist, isn't he? Send him in after you've finished and I'll
have a piece of him.' Chetwin heard them arguing for a half hour. After the
'traveller' had gone Wright walked down the shop to Chetwin and said,
'He knows his onions. I couldn't knock him back once.' Few people could
talk or put Nash down. He was always courteously combative. Over sixty
years later Chetwin recalled that Nash's 'line of thought' was not popular

with businessmen, yet 'everyone in the trade thought the world of him': for 'his principles shone through everything'. That judgement was not, we may be sure, all afterthought.

One consequence of his new job was that he was rarely home, a situation which in time became habitual. One of his sisters-in-law, Albert Nash's wife Becky, wrote to Lot, 'having Walter away so much it must be all little Honeymoons him staying away so long'.

He was beyond almost any expectations fortunate in his wife—which reflects, perhaps, as much on him as on her. Certainly he was affectionate, thoughtful, kind, and faithful. She was amusing and delightful, warmer, more generally and immediately thought loveable. It was rare for anyone to say an unkind word about her. She had an instant rapport with many people. She was more passionate. That is not to imply that he was cold. But he was rather puritanical, physically fastidious. For instance he did not like people outside his family touching him. Whereas she could be a little bawdy with close friends, was more earthy, he never used coarse and rarely blunt language. He always used euphemisms for the facts of life and death, which was characteristic of his generation.

After ten years of marriage they were as devoted and loving as ever. When she was away on holiday in November 1916 Lot wrote, 'Well darling if you want me as much as I want you I ought to come straight home I think.' He replied, 'darling . . . come home soon. I want you, not physically, not carnally, but just your presence. I want to feel you near.' Their love continued as strong over the years. In 1922 he wrote that he hoped her 'acute longing' for him would return when he came home. Two days later he wrote that he had reread the marriage service—'Nothing was promised there other than I would promise again tomorrow.'

They wrote constantly, so that we know that he had a glass of wine one day in 1916. He was abstemious, but not a total abstainer. In 1911 he tried, unsuccessfully, to stop smoking altogether. Once in 1912 he did not smoke all day to mark the sailing to New Zealand of Lot's sister Nell and her husband Ted Hinton. And he did soon succeed in stopping this habit. In Havelock North one day in 1914 he played billiards, at which he was very proficient. On a train he was studying 'Christ's words on brotherhood' when two travellers asked him to play 'Five Hundred'—the first game of cards he had had 'on the road'.

He gave advice on bringing up the boys—a task which Lot, in fact, performed. She wrote of giving one of them 'a good smacking'. Wal did not believe in this. They should aim 'to control him with love' but not expect him to be 'exactly as we wish'. All they could do was to hope that he would become 'a strong, sound, reliable, loving, man. Our actions will I believe later on be reproduced in him.'

On another occasion when he had spoken unkindly to her he wrote that at times he was so anxious that the Will of God should come into operation that he forgot to practise it himself: 'It is only the old devil of selfishness and egoism that rise at times and extinguishes my sense of equity and justice'.

One letter from Walter in about 1914 refers with remarkable brevity to many of his interests—business, books, politics, religion, and love—in a strange emulsion:

My dear Sweetheart,
When you get the credit note from Utting for a/c on Silk amounting to £4-1-4, will you please attach to the Invoice herewith and send to Wellington.
Please take 'The Soul of the War' to Gifford.

Love

Walter[7]

Lot's letters were more insecure than his in matters of spelling or punctuation, which sometimes produced lively effects: 'Mrs Evans has had all her wound & over (cant spell it) removed they cannot have any more children'.

The Nashes were the centre of a large, complex web of relationships and friendships. First there was family. Those in Birmingham were often very poor. When his wife was ill in 1910 Will had to pawn his watch. Walter often sent 'help', a few pounds, to him and to their mother, who constantly hoped he would return, as promised, in four years. In 1912 Arch died, which saddened the rest of her life. Hobday visited them in Birmingham just before his death. Walter wrote such comfort as he could—'Arch has gone to another sphere and will wait for us, and you Mother dear, will see him once again and I hope that God will guide us all to that home, where we part no more.' Or again—'I am looking forward to once again feel the touch of your dear lips, and as soon as ever I can possibly come to see you I will.' But that was in 1912, when it was not possible.

The Selly Oak shop which they had kept did not bring in enough to support Emily and their mother. Ernest bought another shop in nearby Smethwick for them. At first his mother did not like working in the shop. He wrote to Emily: 'Tell Mother not to worry about working. If she had all the wealth she had earned she would never have to walk she would ride. She would never need to cook her food—it would be cooked—served and a chair placed for her to sit down and eat it and somebody to wash and clean up afterwards whilst she sat eating fruit.' It is not clear how comforting these sentiments were, but Walter often sent advice: 'My dear Emily "*Rotten*" is not ladylike.'

Many people in Selly Oak wrote to Walter in his first few years away. Then there were close friends and relatives who migrated to New Zealand, like his sister-in-law Nell and Ted Hinton, who had had a nervous breakdown in England and was to be similarly ill in New Zealand. They worked at first at a Boys' Training Farm at Weraroa, where Ted taught carpentry.

There were also Eva and Frank Beard, who kept a grocery shop in Wanganui. She always called Lotty 'Lotetia'. Another affectionate friend called her 'Lotchen'.

The Westwoods, Hobdays, Nashes and the rest were a very close group of expatriates. Only a few of them were technically very literate. But they were almost all fluent, like Walter and Eva. There was a constant flow of loving words, whether misspelt, in grammatical order, or not.

Nash kept on making new friends too, a process which continued throughout his life. He lost few friends and forgot none.

Members of the CEMS addressed one another as 'Brother'—'Dear Brother Nash'. But now he came to know people who called one another 'Comrade', not always quite seriously. One such person, who was very close to him, was a very strange man indeed, Frederick W. Frankland. Hobday, to whom Nash introduced him, called him 'the sage of Foxton'.

Frankland and Hobday played a large part in Nash's education. In England the people he knew were almost all much less schooled and not well read. Frankland had been educated at the University of London before becoming the New Zealand government actuary and statistician. He was the son of a knight and brother of a professor at Birmingham University. He had known Seddon and is said to have helped Edward Tregear, the Secretary of Labour (whom Nash knew too), to draft some of the Liberal legislation. He was thought a crank, though to be a socialist at all seemed odd to most people, and was indeed a much less orthodox person than, say, George Shann. An anti-socialist correspondent wrote to Nash in 1913 that Frankland was 'as mad as they make 'em. Only uneducated folk pretend to understand his "philosophy" '.[8]

Frankland was a socialist, a member of the Fabian Society, who had lived and worked as an actuary in New York and had spent a good deal of money publicizing what Nash called 'the splendid work done by Mr Noyes in the Oneida Community'. This was a socialist religious community which believed in communal industry and 'complex marriage' and 'scientific propagation'. They called themselves 'Perfectionists' and preached bodily joy. Like its founder and later leaders from the Noyes family, Frankland believed that man had fallen from an earlier state of tribal communism, to which Christ would restore him. His own chief claim to fame, Frankland believed, was his formulation of 'the system of Objective and Evolutionary Idealism or Panpsychist Realism' in about 1870.[9] He believed that the sexual problem was more important than the economic and wrote to Nash, quoting Kipling, you 'cannot lighten the curse on Adam Till you lighten the curse on Eve'. He advocated birth control, 'sane eugenics', the emancipation of women, and held 'advanced' views on marriage. He propagated his views in pamphlets like *Reverence for and Loyalty to Womanhood*, *Altruistic Eudaemonism The Only Tenable Ethic*, and *Bible-Religion the Most Important Thing in the World*, which he sent to 'Comrade Walter

Nash' in 1909.

Nash's reactions to all this must have been mixed, but he was fascinated. Frankland lent him many books, for instance on American and other socialism. Nash reciprocated with Christian Socialist writings, including an essay by Gore, Frankland's favourite bishop. These two and Hobday had endless discussions, in which Nash was not merely a consumer. Their letters show that they held him in high esteem.

Nash continued to read very widely. In about 1917 (or earlier) he began to study law, but gave it up because the tutor wanted him to cram. 'I said that I would not cram, I would rather study and know all about that I wanted to know, or drop the course.'[10] He sometimes attended the lectures of J. B. Condliffe, later a very well-known academic and author, on economic history at the Workers' Educational Association in Wellington in 1915. The revolutionary socialists, Harry Holland, 'Pat' (later known as Peter) Fraser and some trade union leaders also attended. After each lecture Holland and Fraser would expound the Marxist view and Nash the Christian Socialist. Sometimes Hobday asked them to give talks after his sermons in St Matthews.[11]

Hobday had introduced Nash to Holland, then the editor of the *Maoriland Worker*, a radical socialist periodical, in September 1913 and (he told Frankland) 'in about 5 seconds the two of them were at it hammer and tongs! You can imagine it!'[12]

Holland had been an active socialist in Australia. He had suffered great hardship working for his cause and had been in prison twice, once for libel and once for seditious utterances, threatening violence against the government. As a youth he had been a convert to the Salvation Army and retained what his biographer called a 'sect mentality', a sense of personal mission, scorn of moderation, impatience with piecemeal reform—above all, a sense of undeviating righteousness.[13] Nash said of him, 'I never met a man, very difficult at times, but so earnest in his outlook and determination, never mind the consequences. Harry was the salt of the earth, very difficult to get on with.'[14]

Holland's Marxist-Syndicalist views had been influenced by Tom Mann. Hobday disapproved of the *Maoriland Worker*, which expressed anti-Christian sentiments.[15] Nevertheless, Nash came to know Holland and the other syndicalist leaders, including Semple, Pat Hickey, and Fraser, very well. Holland, Semple, Nash, and Hobday all lived in Brooklyn in about 1912. Although Nash must have seemed rather an odd man out at first, the syndicalists' letters to him were very friendly. It was at this time and in Wellington, where Nash spent much time even after he lived in Palmerston, that the personal alliance was formed which was to dominate the Labour Party.

In 1912 there was a strike in the gold-mining town of Waihi, where the union had joined the 'Red' Federation of Labour. 'Pat' Fraser was sent down from Auckland to represent the Federation executive on the strike committee. In a situation in which there was fear on both sides, the strikers were savagely beaten by decidedly lawless strike-breakers brought in by the employers. One striker was killed. The ULP opposed the strike. The vituperative sectarianism of the Labour cliques at that time is expressed in *The Tragic Story of the Waihi Strike* of which Holland was joint author, with another Australian agitator, R. S. Ross, and another man, in 1913.

The syndicalists continued to believe in the superiority of the strike as a weapon against capitalism. It took an overwhelming demonstration of the power of political action to convince all but the most obtuse of the irrelevance of their views in New Zealand society. Before that occurred, however, a further effort was made to achieve Labour solidarity. Another Labour 'Unity' conference met in Wellington. The 'Red Feds', the Socialist Party, and most of the ULP joined forces to form an industrial organiza-tion, the United Federation of Labour, and a socialist party, the Social Democratic Party, led by Edward Tregear, once head of the Labour Department and an enthusiastic Polynesian scholar. Although the constitu-tion of the industrial organization was more moderate than that of the former Federation, it was dominated by 'Red Feds'.[16]

Nash continued to support the rump of the ULP,[17] while maintaining closer personal links with the Social Democrats. In 1913 his growing enthusiasm for socialism found a new outlet. He sponsored an essay competition on 'What Socialism is' in the *Maoriland Worker*, and provided prizes of £2 10s., £1 10s., and £1. He recommended that competitors should read Robert Blatchford's *Merry England*, Philip Snowden's *Socialism and Syndicalism*, Edward Bellamy's *Looking Backward*, Edward Carpenter's *England's Ideal*, Ruskin's *Unto This Last*, and John Spargo's *Commonsense of Socialism*. The judges were Holland, Frankland, and Hobday. Nash wrote to them about how the marking should be done, approaching the whole thing with elaborate thoroughness. The winning entries were published in the *Worker*.[18]

This literary contest was interrupted by the strike of 1913, the worst example of class warfare in the country's history, relatively peaceful in this respect. Measured by violence of feeling, 1913 was rivalled, but not excelled by the strikes of 1890 and 1951 and the depression riots of 1932.

The extremism of the syndicalists was matched by the anti-socialist prejudices of the new Reform government and its small farmer supporters, who feared and hated the 'Red Feds'.

The strike was confined to the few radical unions, watersiders, seamen, and miners. This time the Farmers' Union organized mounted farmers, who came into town to work on the wharves or to be sworn in as 'special police'. Some of these undisciplined forces got out of hand. There was some fighting in Wellington between stone-throwing crowds and Massey's

'Cossacks', swinging batons. The *Maoriland Worker* had a field-day, with rhapsodies of violence, stories of drunken 'Specials' (with criminal records), tanked up at the 'Royal Tiger Hotel', of cavalry charges, of 'Specials' batoning innocent people, pursuing boys, making indecent proposals to girls, invading homes and firing revolvers.[19] But the extreme left wing were not the only ones appalled by the violence of the 'Specials'. As late as 1936 Hobday wrote to Nash asking after their friend, 'Fighting Bob' Semple: 'I haven't forgotten the raids round his house in Washington Avenue during the 1913 strike by the invading "Uhlans" from the country.'[20]

What shocked Hobday was this brute demonstration that wealth was backed by law, police, judges, army and navy. He thought that the forces of law and order are 'arrayed to bolster up "things as they *are*" against "things as they *ought* to & might be"—*against* men who see visions & dream dreams who *must* in the very nature of things finally triumph.'[21] He saw in syndicalism great possibilities because it was 'spiritual & not purely material'. But he could not support the strikers completely. He thought that Pat Hickey's conduct was alienating potential supporters. 'They will not be bluffed into striking just by insolence & bad language', he wrote to Nash and added, 'Oh, for some better leaders! Your time will come old man one of these days'.[22] Nevertheless, he did support the strikers, and made himself unpopular in the church for doing so. He wished he had 'Comrade Nash' to support him and told him later that the Canterbury clergy's idea of a model clergyman was not Christ but the Vicar of Bray.[23] Most Anglicans thought Hobday and Nash too partisan. One minister wrote to Nash in 1916, about the strike, 'we must not drag Christ in the dust of political controversy'.[24]

Nash found everyone he met—employers, church friends, customers— hostile to the strikers, and his life had become 'one perpetual battle'. 'I was so lonely on the road fighting the battles of the Strikers day after day and not a *visible* word of sympathy that I decided to visit Brooklyn to get inspiration for further battles or get into an atmosphere of agreement', he wrote to Frankland. 'You would have leapt for joy had you been present on Sunday evening at St. Matthews, Brooklyn. Comrade Hobday preached a glorious Sermon on the Strike. . . . Your work has quickly borne fruit. He . . . now has declared himself in favour of Socialism i.e. Co-operation —as against competition.—His remarks shook the congregation to such an extent that they nearly all left the Church in a rage.'[25]

In early November Holland, Fraser, Semple, and other strike leaders were arrested, Holland for using seditious language which came close to advocating violence against the government.[26]

Hobday and Nash visited Holland in prison. Many years later Nash described what happened:

They made me stay outside the door, they would not let me inside his cell.

Right Young Walter Nash

Below Alfred and Amelia Nash with their five sons: from left, Archibald, Ernest, William, Albert, and Walter; and Emily on her mother's knee

Above Walter Nash's sweet shop in Selly Oak

Left Walter and Lotty Nash with young Walter on board the *Tainui* bound for New Zealand, 1909

They would not let him have a razor so he was all bristly with ugly growth out of his face. . . . I had a talk with him, with somebody standing by me to listen to what I said. He said, 'I didn't say what they say I said, but if I said it I would justify it.' And you would see the gleam of fervour at what he thought to be right coming out of his face.[27]

Nash thought of paying his legal expenses, but Hobday advised that Holland would probably make his lawyer's defence useless by his own remarks.[28] And so it proved: he made a fiery speech from the dock and was sentenced to a year in prison. At that time he had a zeal for martyrdom.

In most respects Nash supported the strikers. A correspondent called Holland a 'jailbird' and Nash replied, 'I have met him four times and have found him a gentleman on every occasion. He cares for his home—loves his wife and children—and desires, in my opinion, to so alter the present system that the labourer whether with brain or hand shall have the results of his toil.'[29]

He told Frankland that 'There is more Christianity in the Strike leaders than in many of our church leaders.' 'Pat' Fraser was a most abstemious man. Nash wrote, 'what sound advice the leaders are giving "Don't drink, you want your brains as cool as ice". Good on you Fraser.' But he could not approve of the waterside workers stopping work at 8 a.m. in breach of their agreement. Nor could he accept the view of the 'Red Feds' that strikes were the best method of gaining their ends. It would 'be a year or two before the working class realise that the best way to strike is through the ballot box'.[30]

In the view of conservatives it was the 'Red Feds', not the 'Specials', who were using intimidation to cause and keep the strike going. The *Dominion* was demanding that a secret ballot should be obligatory before men went on strike.[31] A few days earlier Nash had suggested a way to end the strike to Hobday and Frankland. The strikers were to vote by secret ballot on whether they preferred to work under an Arbitration Court award or under their previous agreement but with a penalty clause. The government was to conduct the ballot. He thought of putting his proposal to the Prime Minister, Massey, but was, he said, 'too shy'. However, he did present it to Hickey. He feared that the Federation would be smashed if it lost the strike.[32] It was not to be his last unsuccessful attempt to stop a strike. No one took any notice and the strikers were indeed smashed.

The events of 1913 forced the 'Red Feds' towards political action. They had a very powerful effect on Nash. His opinions moved somewhat to the left; thereafter they were remarkably stable throughout his life. More important, he moved towards the unions and working men. He was clearly not going to get much support among his church friends for achieving his brand of heaven on earth. Though never remotely like a trade unionist, he had come to identify with them, as well as with the poor. At least he came from the working class and the poor. The unionists came to trust him as he came to rely on them.

He became progressively much more active politically. In 1914 he had a lively discussion in a pub in Wanganui with a Reform candidate and some farmers, trying to convince them 'that Socialism was right and that even some of the "Red Feds" were better than the average type of citizen'.[33] That conversation must have required all his courtesy to off-set his scarlet volubility! In early 1916 he was 'befriending wharfies' and heckling a speaker on the wharf. Hobday told him he was 'going the right way to be a labour M.P. one of these days'. He thought it would be no bad thing if Nash should join another CEMS member, James McCombs of Christchurch, who had been elected to parliament in December 1913. He had long had the impression that Nash's future lay in politics. In 1912, when Nash became a salesman, he had written to him, 'You should get a very good idea of the people & country in your travels, which should be of great use to you when you are Prime Minister.'[34]

A variety of people who met Nash during his early years in New Zealand thought he was a remarkable person. Some of them were, or were to be, in their own way worthy of notice too: Holland or Fraser for instance. Even Frankland and Hobday, minor figures as they now seem, appear respectively in the *Dictionary of New Zealand Biography* and *Who's Who in New Zealand*. But how *could* a little salesman become Prime Minister? It was known in the USA: *From Log Cabin to White House; From Tanyard to White House*. It was known in H. G. Wells's novels. And there, too, the hero had this belief in success, shared by his friends, who talked about their futures in the world. But no Labour people had been successful anywhere. By 1912 Australia had had two Labor Prime Ministers, who had achieved very little in comparison with, say, the Liberals Alfred Deakin or W. P. Reeves. Perhaps Hobday was not very serious.

For the 1914 election miscellaneous, more-or-less *ad hoc* organizations, Labour Representation Committees, as well as the SDP, put up candidates.[35] The ULP had virtually disappeared, but Nash continued to support its rump. He asked Holland why the SDP opposed the ULP leader, D. McLaren. Holland said that there was no ULP, and that McLaren was 'an enemy of Labor'[36]—as he was later to prove when he became a spokesman for the anti-socialist Welfare League.

One curious episode in Nash's life in Palmerston North deserves to be recalled. He continued as active as ever in the church—fighting, for instance, for the abolition of pew rents in the town, a significant issue in England when he left. Some of his attitudes struck his friends as punctilious to absurdity. For instance he thought it disrespectful to women in the choir that it had to rise when the priest entered. Hobday told him that the choir was part of the congregation and that rising was simply a mark of respect for the priest. He gave him some advice he was not always to follow: 'Don't get worried about these things. Keep your mind on the big issues & not on the pinpricks.'[37]

His finest effort arose from his duties as national fund raiser for the proposed CEMS organizing secretary. He worked hard, aiming at £1,000 to start with—the salary was to be £300 a year, with £100 expenses. Unknown to his fellows, Brother Nash held the old-fashioned opinion that usury was a sin—an opinion shared it seems, by others in his family.[38] He wrote to Hobday quite definitely: 'interest is robbery'.[39] Consequently, instead of depositing funds collected, amounting to £123 in mid-1914, in a Post Office Savings Bank account as expected, he placed it with the Palmerston North churchwardens, enabling them to reduce the church's overdraft. When asked by a member of the CEMS committee, Cyril Burdekin, and by the bishop, where the funds were, he seemed at first to suppose that they suspected him of dishonesty and took a high and mighty line. He told the bishop that he had saved the church money, in interest, since the Post Office rate was $3\frac{3}{4}$ per cent whereas the overdraft rate paid by the churchwardens was 6 per cent, so that the funds were 'undoubtedly doing Our Lord's work'.[40]

Nash offered to pay the interest himself. A friend, the Reverend J. D. Russell, who later became the first CEMS secretary, took over the fund-raising on the tactful grounds that Nash was worried about his wife's health. Russell wrote quoting biblical texts justifying usury. When Burdekin checked the accounts he found, as expected, that they were absolutely correct.

Hobday was stern. He wrote that Nash should have known both the bishop and Burdekin well enough to realize that they did not intend the construction Nash placed on the enquiry. Moreover they had as much right to their point of view as Nash did. 'But really, old man, I do not want you in any way to be running yourself into a position in which what you say, however right & sound, will be heavily discounted because the words come from you. . . . There is nothing to be gained by making folks so vexed with you . . . that they won't be bothered by listening to you at all.' Nash, how-ever, was always sore that he had been pushed out of his job as fund raiser.

Hobday's remarks to Nash do seem to indicate what his best friends feared might be his weakness at this time. In 1908, after Jim Boylin had left Kidderminster for Beaver Falls, Nash wrote telling him that he had lost a contract to supply the workhouse with tobacco twist. His tone led his friend to write back that there was no point in making a fuss: 'I imagine one can do more in any line . . . minus the reputation of a crank or faddist'.[41]

Nash and his socialist and some close Christian friends were opposed to the war. In this they were not alone. In an official poll of men of military age in 1915, although a majority indicated their willingness to serve

in an expeditionary force, 44,800 (23 per cent) were willing to serve only
in a civil capacity, while 35,700 (19 per cent) were unwilling to serve in
any capacity at all.[42] But mostly they were a silent minority: conscientious
objectors were persecuted.

At first Hobday spoke out. In a speech to the Student Christian Union
at the university in Wellington he took an advanced Tolstoyan view which
'fell like a Zeppelin bomb upon the astounded audience'. But soon he was
despondent at the lack of support, and declared on occasions that the war
was justified.[43]

Nash was frankly a pacifist. In 1915 he told a CEMS meeting that
'militarism is an infectious disease' and that the Germans 'are now
undoubtedly fighting for their freedom'. At a retreat he spoke of how hard
it was 'to realise our fellowship with German and Austrian believers'.[44]
Germans were hated but Nash courageously allowed one to stay with him
in Palmerston North.

In 1915 the *Dominion* newspaper in Wellington urged that the clergy
should fight. Nash wrote a letter, signed 'Socratus', questioning whether
Christians should go to war. He said, 'God is love' and asked how much
Christian love there was in a bayonet charge. He could not 'imagine a God
of Love leading anyone to war'. This produced several letters attacking him
and an editorial reprimand.[45]

Not much needs be said of Nash's pacifist views, which derived from
Tolstoy and from his own interpretation of Christ's message. Tolstoy had
himself been influenced by the Quakers,[46] of whom the Cadburys were
distinguished examples. Nash's pacifism preceded his reading of Tolstoy
and was shared, for instance, by his mother, who wrote in 1915, 'why dont
the Kaizer and all the other kings fight it out there selfs not let thousands
be slain for them for after all wee shall not gain what theay fighting for
now dont you think it his enugh to make some think there his no loveing
God but it his not Gods fault at all it his man there greed for Gold and
pleasure and wee all have to work for it dont you think so if thay would
pull some of the Slums down and every working man and woman have
comfortable homes to lie and rest in when their work his done there would
not be half the drunkess there his nor so many doctors bills to pay.' And
his brother Will wrote that the war was planned by 'Bloodthirsty Capitalist
—the militarists have been making bombs for years'.[47] These views were
also exactly shared by the former 'Red Feds'. Tim Armstrong wrote from
prison in 1917, 'Let the Kings and Kaisers go and murder one another if
they like. . . .'[48]

Many New Zealand socialists had held the view of the Second Socialist
International that a war could be prevented by simultaneous national
general strikes. But when World War I began the socialists did not expect
it and failed to act. They surrendered in general to patriotic war fervour.
In Germany the Social Democrats voted in August 1914 for war credits.[49]

In Australia the government held two unsuccessful referenda seeking support for conscription. The New Zealand government introduced conscription in 1916 without benefit of referenda. 'Pat' Fraser, F. R. Cooke, Semple, James Thorn, H. T. Armstrong, Tom Brindle, and other socialist leaders were imprisoned for using seditious language in opposing it. There was a police raid on the *Maoriland Worker* office.[50] The newspapers were delighted. One editor, especially pleased at Semple's arrest, thought that some striking miners were worse; if they would not work 'a shipload or two of Japanese miners' should be brought in.[51]

The war contributed to the belated achievement of Labour unity. The defeat of the strikes of 1912-13 had disheartened the syndicalists. Some of them, notably Holland, held the Leninist belief that the war represented a crisis for capitalism. It was caused by imperialism, the dying phase of capitalism, and heralded its collapse. The workers must be united and ready to take over. The SDP, the UFL and the Labour Representation Committees combined to form the (present) New Zealand Labour Party.[52] Nash now definitely joined it.[53]

But these were distressing years for everyone, not least for those not buoyed up by patriotic exhilaration. Charlie Herzog, the son of a close friend, was killed. A friend volunteered and Nash wrote to him, 'They tell me you are going for a soldier. It is good to fight for Freedom altho' better still not to have to fight.' James Thorn wrote in 1916, 'I suppose you are still scattering the seeds of Socialism and Peace. Rather stony soil at present—'.[54]

Although Nash enjoyed his travelling he was very restless by 1915. He wrote to his wife, 'In lots of things I am "all over the shop" just at present. Hardly know where I am, but hope to land fair and square on the side of truth, equity—justice and mercy'.[55] He wondered whether to continue with Miller & Ahearn or start on his own or 'go farming'. He and Ahearn thought of buying 'a decent patch of land' for apple orchards. He investigated this and Ahearn took an option on some land at Upper Moutere. Nash was thinking of spending some £800, though he did not have that much in cash.[56] In 1916 his firm offered him the job as traveller in the Auckland province, assuring that he would earn more there than 'on your old ground'—up to £1,000 a year,[57] a very high income in those days. He accepted and wrote to Lot, 'We are now about to enter on a new sphere of life. Shall we pray that we may draw closer to one another, and that we both may be instruments in helping toward the establishment of the Kingdom of Heaven on earth.'[58] Not many travellers can have hoped for such a consummation from moving. For a few months he was to be found in Ohaeawai, Rawene, Rotorua, Whangarei, extending his extensive knowledge of the country. But later in the year he decided to go into a business in New Plymouth, a small coastal town with only 7,600 people, in

Taranaki. He wrote to his employers that he had been very happy with them. 'During the past four and half years life has slipped by very fast.' If he had been 'in any way successful' it was due to them. They had given him 'inside knowledge as to how you conduct your business' as well as personal friendship.[59] But he did not *feel* successful. He was now thirty-four. He felt that he was still serving an apprenticeship, prolonged—but for what? Several years more were to pass before he found out.

IV

Profit-Sharing
and Politics in New Plymouth

1916-20

In the course of his travels for Miller & Ahearn Nash had become very
friendly with a Stratford tailor, Bill (or Will) Besley. He often helped him
with his purchases of cloth, with his balance sheets and his income tax
returns. Once he found that Besley had paid too much rent and saved him
£25 tax.

In 1915 Nash suggested to him that he should start a cooperative
tailoring company, which would provide the public with cheaper suits,
employees with higher income and the proprietors with higher profits—a
combination of benefits not often realized. He believed that the clothes
would retain 'the individuality and special genius of each cutter', that the
cloth would be of the best quality, and that suits could be made for £1 or
£1 5s.[1] This novel idea was much discussed among the Taranaki master
tailors.

The idea of cooperative tailors, and of profit-sharing among them and
their employees, had great appeal to Nash. The Christian Socialists in
England had themselves sponsored a tailors' cooperative association, with
a dozen tailors working in a rented house. Charles Kingsley wrote his
pamphlet *Cheap Clothes and Nasty* at that time (1850) attacking production by sweated contract labour and also referred to a co-op in his novel,
Alton Locke, which Nash had read.[2]

Within a short time Besley was pressing Nash to join two other tailors
and himself in the project: 'the more I think of the scheme the more you
seem inseparable from it . . . its the special ability you have for finance,
buying, business management etc. which we are lacking in, that you can
supply.'[3] This was indubitably true. Where else in the country could he
have recruited a businessman who believed in profit-sharing and co-ops?
Miller & Ahearn were willing to release him, while warning that there were
'risks' as well as 'possibilities'. Hobday, who had been reading a book on
profit-sharing, wrote strongly recommending the change. He thought Nash
might be able 'to show us a more Xtian spirit in business'. Moreover, he

doubted whether 'in the long run speechmaking, pamphleteering etc etc give any such real opportunity for permanent work' as did devoting one's life to one's family.[4] He wrote of the need for close companionship between fathers and sons, and of the importance of a father's example. This impressed Nash, whose long trips had disrupted his family life, and he wrote to Lot of the advantage that he could be with her and the boys all the time. He also hoped to have a chance to introduce profit-sharing. The only danger, he told her, was that Besley and George Pearce (one of the partners) might think him more capable than he would prove.[5]

Because of his own high current and potential earnings, quite reasonably Nash was only willing to join the firm on equal terms. Eventually it was agreed that the three chief partners should have 850 shares each. Nash paid no cash, though he was liable to pay the full value of the shares if the company failed. In addition it was decided that the firm would pay for Nash to visit his mother in 1919, as Miller & Ahearn had apparently offered to do. On the other hand Nash was to receive only £6 a week salary, so he accepted a considerable drop in income.[6]

It was necessary to get an efficient foreman to do the cutting, fitting up and to run the workroom, so an additional partner, H. Townsley, was brought in. Besley was to exercise a general supervision and instruct the hands; Pearce to do the pressing; Nash to order the cloth and manage the business side. He acted as chairman and kept the minutes.

Trouble in Modern Tailors Ltd began from the start. Even with a division of labour it proved impossible to make suits of average quality, as Besley had asserted, for £1 5s. Pearce resented being confined to pressing. He was called up in the army and sold his shares to Besley and to Nash, who borrowed £425 from Besley to pay for them. George Pearce remained a life-long friend of Nash.

When he arrived in New Plymouth Nash had only £140, so he had not recovered from the Jones & Ashdown affair, despite good earnings for a couple of years. They found it impossible to get a house or to live on their income, so that they lived partly on their small capital.

They lived briefly at 123 Devon Street and then for a long time at 'Marsland View', a two-storied boarding house which still stands in Weymouth Street. It was run by a Mrs Golding, who also became a lasting friend.

In its first year the company made only £144 net profit. Nash had to borrow £400 from Lot and to mortgage his insurance policy to obtain funds. He found the year so 'harassing' and 'worrying' that his health was 'completely undermined'. In 1917 he had another (unspecified) operation in Dunedin.

Other problems followed. The Taranaki tailoring employers and employees were both split over the fairness of the practices of Modern Tailors Ltd. Its opponents claimed that it ran a factory system and did not make 'tailor-made' suits as it claimed. Some tailors felt that it contravened 'real tailors' principles' of giving a personal service.[7] The firm successfully applied to the Arbitration Court to get its award amended to permit a subdivision of labour.

Eventually business improved. In 1919 the firm was advertising suits at £7, claiming that it gave better value because it had bought stock when prices were low, and that its employees gave good service because they were paid wages well above the award.[8] A local paper reported that the firm had the largest local stocks of high quality tweeds, worsteds, and serges. The foresight was Nash's. His connection with Miller & Ahearn helped in getting supplies. As the war ended there was a great demand for good quality clothing.[9] In 1918 profits were £469 and in 1919 £1,337. Nash's own income was £329 in 1917-18 and £312 in 1918-19. (His tax was £5 7s. 3d. in 1918 and 9s. in 1919.)

In late 1918 Nash made his first small attempt to reform the world, but he failed to convince even the Taranaki master tailors that this was their duty. He did, however, succeed for a time in inducing the other two directors, Besley and Townsley, to try out his profit-sharing scheme. This was worked out in great detail and must be one of the most unusual items recorded in the minutes of a New Zealand company. He sent it to Harry Holland for his criticisms but he had just been elected to Parliament and its length deterred him from reading it.[10]

'A first charge' (a phrase which Nash was to use throughout his life in a rather different context) on net profit was to pay 6 per cent a year on the paid-up shares, which all belonged to Besley. Of the remaining profit, various sums were distributed to reserves and shareholders' dividends, and for division among employees. The criteria for this division were specified in typical Nashian detail, so many points being allocated for long service and efficiency, the directors severally awarding marks for the latter. These points were recorded in the minutes too. At the first distribution, the best hand received £36 18s. 4d.; last was the 'Stratford boy' who got only 11s. for the first four months of the scheme.

The minutes concluded:

The Principle in mind of the Secretary when working out this System was that the soundest title to anything is Creation. (Remembering the part that organisation and study plays in the average Manufacturing or Trading Establishment).

This Title is not recognised (altho often emphasized in the Churches in connection with the Divine Creator).

It should be noted that the transfer of commodities from the Creator to other persons, will not affect the Title of the Transferee provided the commodity was held for use.

Owing to the present Capitalistic System it is not expedient to give Employees the whole of the value they create, but when returning to them a portion, they should be urged to use every legitimate opportunity for altering the System to

one that would enable them to exercise full control over all that they create or
its equivalent in value.

Mr W. H. Besley said that while not agreeing altogether with the last
paragraph of the Report he would move

'That the Profit be distributed among Employees on the System suggested.'

Mr Townsley seconded and it was carried.[11]

Not much is known of Nash's social life in New Plymouth and indeed
he was so busy there must have been little time for it. A relative of George
Pearce recalls that when they went off in Pearce's car for picnics, though
Lot would swim, Walter would not, but would always have a book in his
hands.[12] His relations with his wife were as usual most considerate and
loving, but naturally they had their little differences. On one occasion she
wrote to him, 'no thanks I am not looking for work at present, altho you
may think I do not do enough, I do, so that settles it don't you think'. He
replied, 'Someone has said "you must be very careful when writing as the
written word often sounds harsher than the spoken and sometimes conveys
a totally different meaning." Your remarks re yourself and work hurt very
much.'[13]

His son Walter did very well at school, and won a Junior National
Scholarship of £5 a year to attend the local Boys High School. For a time
Nash served on the Committee of the West End Primary School, which his
son attended.[14] As always, Nash was an outstanding example of an activist
in the local community. In 1918 he called a meeting of householders to
discuss extending the education system. His circular letter pointed out that
in 1916 the USA spent 32s. 1d. per head on education and New Zealand
only 25s. 8d.[15]

He continued to be very active in the CEMS. As always, he took a keen
interest in practical reform. The Sunday School at St Mary's Church was
run on old-fashioned pedagogical lines, with the sixty or so children sitting
on raised tiers. He announced that he would reform it according to the
Montessori method. Probably no one else in New Plymouth had heard of
Montessori, nor were her methods taught at the Wellington Teachers'
College. Local gossips said, 'he's a tailor!' But he proceeded to put the
older children in small rooms, to remove the tiers and turn the hall into an
open space. The younger children, in small groups, had their bible lessons
and reconstructed them with models in sand trays. They could walk about
and see what their friends had done, enjoying the freedom of movement
advocated by Montessori. He recruited teachers from the adolescent bible
class and gave them weekly instruction for a month in the principles of
learning by doing. He believed that to say 'listen to this' or 'learn that' was
fatal to good teaching. For at least one of his new teachers he was an
inspiration.[16]

His outstanding example of public service at New Plymouth occurred
during the terrible influenza pandemic of 1918, which killed millions of

people all over the world. The new virus of 'Spanish influenza' was apparently brought to New Zealand in October 1918 by the vessel *Niagara*, which also brought the Prime Minister, W. F. Massey, and his war-time associate, Sir Joseph Ward, back from the imperial war cabinet. It spread rapidly, coinciding with the armistice celebrations and crowds of mid-November. By that time the situation in New Plymouth was so bad that the town (like others) was closed. Volunteers were called for to combat the disease. One of the first to volunteer was Nash who ran a central bureau, with a telephone, 'a beacon of immediate succour to so many sick and helpless people', as a man later wrote to him.

The town was divided into blocks. Volunteers went from door to door locating cases of sickness and advising on ventilation. Everyone was told to stay home and to keep the windows open. A ladies' committee prepared soup and other food. Lemons were distributed. Inhaling chambers, where zinc sulphate and other vapours were available, were set up. Emergency convalescent homes were established. The risks were great—every nurse but one in the hospital contracted the disease. By 19 November $11\frac{1}{2}$ per cent of the population had 'flu and 16 per cent by the 23rd. But it passed away quickly. By early December the crisis was over.[17]

It was long remembered that in Wellington Pat Fraser had taken a lead in this risky service. Nash's role, and M. J. Savage's in Auckland, were less well known.

In England Nash had been interested in land tenure reform by means of taxing unimproved (in the colonies 'prairie') values. In New Zealand he had read Henry George's book, *Poverty and Progress* (at the same time as Kropotkin's *Fields—Factories—and Workshops*) in about 1913.[18] In New Plymouth he took the lead in a campaign to introduce rating on unimproved values instead of the current practice of rating on the annual value (5 per cent of the capital value—that is, of improvements plus the unimproved land value).

There had since about 1890 been a strong movement towards taxing unimproved values, which was a policy of the Liberal Government elected in that year. The Rating on Unimproved Values Act of 1896 had allowed local polls to be taken on the issue. By 1914, of 151 such local polls, 116 had favoured the new rating method.[19]

Advocates of this system argued that increased land values were due to roads, bridges and other improvements paid for by the community. Nash wrote, 'The Community value of the land does not in equity belong to the individual.' If one man worked hard on his land, his neighbour's land values rose effortlessly. If an owner knew that it would not pay to hold undeveloped land for speculation he would sell it. Under the proposed new method rates would not rise in proportion to capital expended by a man developing his land, which was especially attractive to urban land owners. Opponents, including the two newspapers, urged that the change would reduce the size of building sections, since it would encourage owners to subdivide unused land. It would force town settlers to move into the country.[20]

Nash was by no means alone in advocating this reform.[21] He, however, got up a petition to the Borough Council, which 376 ratepayers signed, calling for a poll on rating. They invited P. J. O'Regan, a Wellington lawyer and former parliamentarian, to speak in New Plymouth. Nash addressed meetings himself and wrote to the newspapers. He wrote to ratepayers telling them what their rates would be if they voted for rating reform. The *Daily News* conceded that he and his friends had organized their campaign well.[22] The Council decided to hold a poll at the same time as the municipal election.

While Nash lived in New Plymouth, probably unknown to him (though such practices did come to his notice a few years later), his mail was set aside by the Post Office for police scrutiny.[23] This was certainly because of his pacifism and association with Fraser and Holland and their friends. In the public (that is, the conservative, patriotic, and newspaper) mind at that time there was no difference between socialism, pacifism, disloyalty, sedition, and perhaps treason.

Holland and Fraser were both elected to parliament as the war ended. The former wrote to Nash that in his first speech to the House he

gave them something to think about by telling them that, if this war failed to end Capitalism, wars would still be inevitable and all the sacrifice of life would have been in vain. I . . . predicted revolution in every country unless a mighty change were peaceably allowed. . . . One could see that the matter was new to the members. I really don't think they quite gripped the meaning of it all for the time being. . . . When I concluded the silence was like the chill of the South Pole. . . . [After] they had carried the motion to adjourn they sang God Save the King—and it was well. It may be that this is the twilight of the Kings.[24]

Holland's support for the German socialist revolution and denunciation of secret treaties, and the Labour Conference's sympathy for the Bolsheviks, were making Labour even less popular than usual with the newspapers. The *Taranaki Daily News* said Labour was dragging New Zealand's 'loyalty and patriotism' through the mud.[25] Holland and Fraser were labelled Bolshevik candidates and supporters of the Kaiser.[26] Because Labour was critical of the secret diplomacy and later of the Treaty of Versailles, it was damned as both pro-German and pro-Bolshevik—an improbable but daunting charge to answer.

It was in this unpromising atmosphere, heated by the more-or-less Marxist speeches of leaders like Holland and Semple, that Nash began his serious life's work. In 1918 he was corresponding with Holland, John Glover, and other leaders in Wellington. A man called S. G. Smith was being talked of in New Plymouth as a possible 'Lib-Lab' candidate for parliament, but the Labour men would not support him because he was not a party member and opposed their policy in some respects. He kept talking of 'sane Labour'. Moreover, there was no local party branch to support a candidate. Holland wrote that he wished Nash would stand and that the Taranaki Labour people would form branches and Labour Representation Committees. LRCs were organizations of branches and local unions. The national secretary, Glover, sent membership cards and Nash formed the New Plymouth branch of the Labour Party, with twenty-five members. Peter Fraser wrote that this was 'a splendid start', but that he must now get the unions to form an LRC.[27]

The branch first met on 25 October 1918.[28] From this moment until his death, fifty years later, Nash was increasingly and soon incessantly active on behalf of his party. Very few politicians can have been more continuously energetic in their cause.

The next step was, for the first time, to put up Labour candidates for the New Plymouth local body elections in mid-1919. The *Taranaki Herald* disapproved of bringing 'political considerations', factions and class war into local politics.[29] But Labour put up candidates for the Hospital and Harbour Boards and for the Borough Council, for which Nash stood. As secretary of the local branch, he also played a big part in organizing the campaign. Twenty-six thousand leaflets were distributed.

Labour's policies looked many years into the future. They included a municipal milk supply, with the council running the milk business 'from the grass to the baby's bottle',[30] and municipal housing. Nash wanted the council to borrow £30,000 to finance housing. The occupiers were to have a right to purchase. The profits of the electric light department were to be distributed.[31] Some of these policies came directly from the platform of the United Labour Party of 1912.[32]

Nash campaigned for rating reform, which had been part of the ULP policy but was not a party policy in the New Plymouth elections, at the same time as he fought for Labour.

One practice they adopted was for several Labour candidates to address a meeting, each tackling a different subject. On one occasion Nash's topic was septic tanks. He also expressed his views and his party's in letters to the local papers. The main principle of private enterprise, he told Taranaki readers, was 'profit, not service. Labour contends that service should come first'; 'Private enterprise is out to make money. The Labour Party is out to make citizens.'[33] In another letter, after the election, he discussed the division of the profits of industry, juggling millions of pounds, as he always loved to do in speeches: 'The creators should control, and will control, their creation.'[34] One of his brothers, Will, devoted much of his time to sending ill-composed letters on every conceivable topic to the newspapers. Had he not harnessed his epistolary proclivities to a single cause, Nash might have become something of a crank too.

In opposing the profit motive and stressing cooperation, Nash sounded vaguely like Ruskin, but it would be wrong to think that he was moderate. The nationalization of land, transport, and banks (the means of production, distribution, and exchange) he said, would bring socialism about.[35]

Some of Nash's main political opinions and aims were formed by 1919. He was an unusually stable person, and over many years rarely deviated from them. In particular it is worth glancing at the origins of his ideas on social security. In some notes on 'The Labour Party and Health' written about this time, presumably for a speech, some of them in connection with a visit by Pat Fraser in 1919, he wrote, 'The wealth of the community is entirely dependent on the health of its citizens. The highest national economy would ensure that the health of all the people was well cared for—'. 'The care of the aged and infirm should be a first charge on the wealth created.'[36]

The phrase, 'a first charge', came in Nash's mind to be a shorthand verbal symbol for his ideas on social security, and he believed that it marked the beginning of his thought on that subject. It was throughout the rest of his life his favourite expression when he referred to the welfare state, though he would later add to his list of beneficiaries, 'the young'. He came to believe and often said that he first heard the above formula at the Second Socialist International in Geneva in 1921,[37] but this was a mistake. He almost certainly derived it from Anglican sources. The expression, 'a' or 'the first charge' appeared several times in the papers of the 1908 Pan-Anglican Congress, in which it was stated that 'a first charge upon industry' should be adequate payment for the workman. It appeared in other Anglican publications in 1919 and 1920.[38]

Nash had other intellectual contacts with the idea of the welfare state. State medical and hospital care had been in the 1912 policy of the United Labour Party. In 1913 Frankland had lent him an issue of the *Fabian News* with a review by B. Moore of a book on *First Steps Towards a State Medical Service*.[39] In 1914 an article by Hobday on a state medical service had appeared in the *Maoriland Worker*.[40] Thus, from Christian Socialist and other sources, he had derived some of his basic ideas about the welfare state and certainly had thought about that subject over some years. This humane or humanitarian interest became the centre of his political attitudes, linking the others in a generous web of thought and feeling.

With 728 votes Nash was the top Labour candidate, but they were all beaten. The *Taranaki Daily News* commented that the Labour Party 'must put forward common-sense and practical—not visionary—proposals to get support,' and ridiculed Labour's policy of 'speedy national control of pictures [i.e. movies or the cinema] from the camera to the screen'.[41] But Nash had in fact promoted one 'practical issue'. Rating on unimproved values was approved by the ratepayers by 780 to 593.[42] Lot wrote, 'I was sorry for your sake as you are so keen on labour that you did not succeed, but for your health's sake I was not for I am quite sure you have enough to do. I think you should be quite happy to think the unimproved value had won through. I was pleased to see you topped the others.'[43] It was to be some years before she could share his enthusiasm for Labour; she never did share his love of politics.

Labour learned a few lessons from the results. Hundreds of votes were lost because of supporters not being on the rolls.[44] Clearly more Labour publicity was needed. The branch wrote asking Pat Fraser and later Bob Semple and Bill Parry to speak. Despite the party's shortage of good platform speakers they obliged. Some 900 came to one of Fraser's ten meetings, in the Everybody's Theatre, which Nash claimed was the biggest public meeting ever held in the town. Since Nash organized the tour, the size of the audience must have impressed his abilities on the speaker.[45]

Nash began to realize more clearly the importance of the unions, from which the party had sprung. When the secretary of two important freezing works and wharf unions wrote in late 1919 asking the party president on whose authority he was contesting a parliamentary seat, since they had not been consulted, Nash wrote back a most conciliatory letter, urging that only his party represented the worker, but conceding that the union view should have been heard. He drew up a constitution for an LRC. He also dashed about, helping to start branches in Eltham, Patea, and Hawera. He wrote to his selected activist helper in Hawera, P. O'Dea, that what the world needed was for people who had 'a good notion as to the road we ought to travel to come out, and tell the people the way'.[46]

Now he began, in a small but not insignificant way, to play his first role in Labour affairs on the national stage. In 1919 he was the New Plymouth delegate to the annual conference of the party, and was elected to the Press Committee and to a special Land Committee, which included Joe Savage, Harry Holland, and Bob Semple. The latter committee came out with a new 'plank' for the party platform, 'usehold' tenure, which supposedly meant that occupancy and use were to be the conditions of holding land.[47] This expression, vaguely hinting at public ownership, was to bedevil the party's work for years. In the debate on defence, after which Conference voted in favour of a voluntary citizen army, Nash uttered some words he would later doubt: 'an unarmed nation would be an impregnable nation.'[48]

Nash was also elected to the National Executive and declined a nomination to be secretary. But his work continued restlessly. He wrote to the new national secretary, Joe Savage, about a new fund-raising effort. Fifty thousand half crown certificates were hopefully to be issued, stating, 'WE PROMISE to give to bearer ———— full Industrial and Political Rights.' He thought the money should go to Head Office and not the LRCs which raised it.[49] The New Plymouth branch needed a headquarters. He helped to purchase the Good Templar Hall, which became the Workers' Social Hall, and he drew up the deed of trust. It became a very popular dance hall, and raised £15 or so each weekend.

By mid-1919 Holland had written asking him to become the party organizer in Wellington. At first he was interested to accept the job, though only for say a year, for he wished to 'go home' in 1920. But he doubted whether the party could afford the £7 a week he estimated would be needed to keep his family.[50]

His mother had continued to look forward to seeing him. In 1909 he had promised a return visit in a few years which poverty and war had prevented.[51] But she had died in April 1919, and was buried with her husband, who had preceded her in 1913, and Arch. Apart from rather perfunctory references to his death, their father was scarcely mentioned in family correspondence. If a biographer were looking for some psychological wound in Walter Nash, he would certainly examine his feelings about his father. But any conclusions would be highly speculative, for there is very little evidence. As we have seen, he strongly disapproved of the way in which his father treated his mother. Walter did not keep in touch with him after he migrated. In January 1914 (a month after his father had died, though he did not know that), he wrote to his mother, 'Give Father my love when next you see him. I may write to him later, but cannot be sure.' Alfred Arthur Nash had died in the Union Infirmary—the Workhouse hospital.[52] Whether he had lived there is unknown, but the family, other than Walter by 1909, were far too poor to keep him. The Workhouse or its Infirmary were shameful things, not thereafter to be mentioned. Just before he died the old man told Emily's boy-friend that it was his own fault he was there. Apart from saying once or twice that his father had been a political agent, Nash seems never to have referred to him in correspondence or speeches.

In 1952 a man called Hinton, no doubt a relative of Lot's sister's husband, wrote to Nash about his father and sent him a photograph. Nash replied that it was the only one he had, and said that his father had died before he migrated to New Zealand.[53] A man might forget when his father died, but it is more difficult to believe that he would forget whether he was near him or 12,000 miles away. Such forgetfulness suggests a powerful repression. Alternatively, it might be thought that the statement was a lie. If so it is the only one—other than a politic evasiveness—which his biographer has detected, and it would seem to have little motive, unless to throw the enquirer off the scent.

Nash never forgot his debt to his mother who he said, years later, had faced and overcome greater difficulties than he. He was to attribute his success in life chiefly to her.[54] The remark was not merely conventional filial piety.

Now he still intended to visit the UK to see his family and to secure book publishers' and other agencies in order to start a new business.

In the firm of Modern Tailors, Nash's profit-sharing system had been continued in 1919 and wages were also increased. But by August the directors decided that merit alone should be the deciding factor, and that

Above The family about the beginning of
World War I. The boys from left are
Walter, Jim, and Leslie
Right Labour member for Hutt,
early 1930s

The first Labour cabinet, December 1935. From left, back row: W. Lee Martin, P.C. Webb, F. Langstone, H.G.R. Mason, F. Jones, D.G. Sullivan, H.T. Armstrong. Front row: W.E. Parry, P. Fraser, M.J. Savage, W. Nash, M. Fagan, R. Semple

Besley should apportion the distribution. 'Merit' was to include quality of work, punctuality, attention to the job, and cooperation with the directors. By October it was decided to raise wages and drop the profit-sharing scheme. The union was demanding that female coatmakers should be paid 'on the same basis as the men'. Besley did not accept this, however.

Nash had fallen out with Besley because the latter exerted continual pressure to increase prices, which 'jarred' with Nash's 'method of doing business'. Despite his great concentration on detail, and the success of the company, it is clear that a man who believed in profit-sharing and opposed taking interest was not cut out for success in the business world. When things had been going badly, Ahearn had written to him in 1917, 'You are not out to make money'[55] and, beyond the reasonable needs of his family this was generally true.

His disillusionment with business was by now great and produced another squabble with a bishop, A. W. Averill of Auckland. Nash lectured him on Christian obligations to Caesar; such service must be a godly service. 'You mention business. May it not be that the present day business system is such that God will not sanction. I believe that it is impossible to apply the whole of Christ's principles in present day business AND LIVE. The whole system is based on making it pay.' And again, 'Our Church authorities are so keen on running the Church in a business manner that they forget their mission which is to run business in a Christian manner.'[56]

It was agreed that Nash should leave the firm and go to England. Both he and Townsley transferred their shares to Besley. Nash was to receive £1,500 for his shares and £500 for his trip, the firm thus making good its earlier promise. He lent the £1,500 to the firm and took Besley round purchasing stocks of cloth. Besley was to pay him on nine bills due in 1920-1 and payable to Miller & Ahearn (presumably because Nash might still be abroad).

In March 1920 the Nashes sailed from Wellington. Hobday, Ahearn, Westwood, and Tom Brindle, a 'wharfie' friend, saw them off. The two younger boys, Les and Jim, became boarders at a church school, Croydon, in Day's Bay, on the east side of Wellington harbour. Hobday was the headmaster. Walter junior was boarding at the New Plymouth Boys' High School. Nell and Ted Hinton were to take them to Russell, at the Bay of Islands, for the summer holidays at the end of the year.

V

The Second Socialist International: Travels and Troubles

1920-2

Although Walter was very seasick at first, Lot and he enjoyed their shipboard life of whist drives and deck chairs, of visits to tropical Panama and Colon. They left the ship in New York and rented a hotel room for $20 a week. They went to a play and a show. He spoke about New Zealand at an 'Open Forum' at the Church of the Ascension in Fifth Avenue and was thanked for his 'kindly humour'. He attended a banquet of the American Booksellers' Association in Philadelphia. He heard Siegfried Sassoon reading his poems in a synagogue. They visited Washington and inspected George Washington's house at Mount Vernon. In Washington he called on the Plumb Plan League, which favoured nationalizing the railways. In Chicago he visited two left-wing bookshops, 'Clarion' and the 'Radical'. They saw Niagara Falls, visited Canada and attended a Federation of Labor meeting, chaired by the great Samuel Gompers. It passed a motion, against his wishes, favouring the Plumb Plan.

For a time they stayed with their friends, Jim and Kitty Boylin, at Beaver Falls, Pennsylvania. As usual, he was busy. On one day, and this was not unusual, he wrote twenty-four letters. Then they crossed the Atlantic from Montreal in the liner *Scandinavia*. By the end of June they were back in England.[1]

Their families were delighted to see them. Walter visited his old teacher, Emily Taylor (now married), and spent 'a very pleasant hour on Education'. He enjoyed revisiting 'Kiddy' and Birmingham. Bournville was 'good enough for a Christ to live in. Why cannot all the workers have nice homes?' he asked himself.[2] In London he went to a revue, 'Hello America', a concert and plays, sitting in 'the pit'.

Most of his time in England was taken up by correspondence with and calls on publishers and other manufacturers. He acquired agencies for various goods including Dean's Rag Dolls and their Rag Books (which were to prove profitable lines). He became the New Zealand representative for The Sports Co., Manchester, which sold tennis racquets and similar goods, and for Hitchinson & Co. of Birmingham, which made electroplated goods. This was his old friend 'Hitch's' firm.[3]

His main effort went into securing publishers' agencies. He wanted to start a bookshop and agency business. In his eyes a bookshop was not a store but a cause, a view not uncommon up to the nineteen-thirties or nineteen-forties. It would, he wrote to Harold Ahearn in 1919, be a benefit to the country and the world if someone specialized in 'first class reading matter' on social, political, and religious questions. M. J. Savage called it Nash's idea of 'a Reformer Book Shop'.[4] Some years later Nash said that booksellers should be 'another formative agency in society', 'in the front lines of the battle for enlightenment, for social security, for spiritual well-being', by ensuring that the public had access to books 'breaking new ground' on such subjects. 'We can judge a society by its book shops'.[5]

He wrote in similar terms to publishers such as Stanley Unwin.[6] During his visit to England, and later, he secured a considerable number of agencies, including those for Allen & Unwin, the Student Christian Movement publications, the Rationalist Press Association, J. M. Dent, and others.

Equally to the front of his mind was politics. On 28 June, the day after they reached London, he visited the Labour Party offices to discuss the possibility of going to Geneva for the forthcoming meeting of the Second Socialist International.

The Second International, formed in 1889, had collapsed in 1914 when most European socialists—'social patriots', Lenin called them—rallied to the war and their national flags. The Russian revolution had then completely split the international socialist movement. In 1919 the Russians and their friends moved to establish the Third International, which called for world revolution.

At the end of the war the British and other more moderate socialists tried to revive the Second International, but at a meeting in Berne in 1919 there were many defections, including the Bolsheviks, Italian socialists, and the British Independent Labour Party. The social democrats or reformist socialists were split among themselves. In some countries, notably Germany, there were also numerous but unsuccessful revolutionary socialists. Thus the meeting which Nash wished to attend in Geneva was one of the rump of the old Second International.

Before Nash left New Zealand Savage had written to the chairman of the Independent Labour Party, saying that Nash was 'a true friend of the toilers' who had 'rendered fine service to the Working-class Movement—both as an Executive Officer and from the platform'. Now Arthur Henderson, secretary of the British Labour Party, cabled Peter Fraser suggesting that Nash have a watching brief for the New Zealand Labour Party at Geneva, and Savage authorized him to be their representative.[7]

Nash met many of the Labour leaders, including Philip Snowden. He

went to the Albert Hall to hear the report of a British delegation back from
Russia. It was chaired by another Christian Socialist, George Lansbury.
Some of the speakers, from the ILP and the TUC, gave idealistic accounts
of the revolution, admitting its brutal side, but likening the deaths to social
birth pangs.[8]

The great issue of the time for radicals was how to regard the revolution.
In most countries some, like Harry Holland, proudly identified with the
Bolsheviks, but others were much more doubtful. In Britain and New
Zealand there was, at least, unity over opposing the intervention after the
war ended of British and other forces against the revolutionaries. Three
'independent' New Zealand MPs issued a statement in London professing
to express a labour view on the opposition of British workers to this
intervention. Nash wrote to the *Daily Herald* denouncing their pretensions
to speak for his party.[9]

He wanted Lot to come to Geneva with him, but she refused,[10] possibly
because (as always) she found politics and (at that time) radical politics
distasteful. In late July he left for Paris, where he met some French
socialists, including Pierre Renaudel, before going on to Switzerland.[11]

Although the conference was important in the history of socialism,
perhaps rather for what it ended than began, the attendance was very poor.
Before the war there would have been eight or nine hundred delegates.
Now the largest group was twenty-five from Britain, and the Communal
Hall seemed empty. F. W. Jowett wrote that 'the fire of enthusiasm could
not be kindled from the spent, battered and visionless delegates. . . .'[12]

The British and some of the German Majority socialists were supported
by Belgians, Swedes, Danes, and Dutch. Several socialist parties sent
observers only, so uncertain were they about the course to follow. (The
Third International held a rival conference a few days before.) There were
small groups from Georgia, Azerbaidjan, Lithuania, and Poland. E. G.
Theodore represented Queensland. Britain was given thirty votes, Australia
fifteen, and New Zealand five.

For the first time in his life Nash was becoming acquainted with
important and famous men. He met Ramsay MacDonald, Noel Buxton,
Sidney Webb, Fred Jowett, Camille Huysmans, Emile Vandervelde from
Belgium, the Germans, Philipp Scheidemann and Ebert, and others whose
names and personalities remained in his memory for the rest of his life. His
new country was affording him a step on to a larger stage than was likely
to have been possible for a small shopkeeper in Selly Oak.

Several Commissions reported to the Congress. That on War Responsibilities (Jowett wrote) 'graciously consented to accept from the German
delegation their humble admission of sins committed by the German
Government (which the said delegates had supported)' and their admission
of German and Austrian war guilt.[13]

The Report on Socialisation and the Political System of Socialism caused the main contention. This document (Nash wrote) contained many anti-Bolshevik clauses. It stressed democratic political processes and repudiated violence and dictatorship. As a sop to syndicalists and British Guild Socialists there was some talk of worker participation in management and of a possible National Industrial Council, representing trades and professions, to exist alongside parliament. It stressed reformist, step-by-step socialism. There was to be no expropriation of property without compensation, nor were all industries necessarily to be nationalized.

It was mainly the work of Sidney Webb and based on Beatrice's and his views. Fabian constitutional legerdemain made some delegates, like Jowett and Nash, very impatient. To the former it seemed to concentrate on technicalities of administration instead of the essential thing, getting wealth for the workers. Neil Maclean and Jowett moved an amendment, that 'It is the function of the community as a whole to establish a priority of claim on all commodities for children, for aged and ailing persons, and for all those engaged in the production and distribution of essential utilities'.[14]

Ever afterwards Nash supposed that they had used the expression 'a first charge', not 'a priority of claim', and regarded this amendment as the basis of his own views on social security.

The main debate, in which Nash spoke for the only time, was on this Report. He supported the amendment. He wrote in an account of the congress that the Report gave to many the impression 'that a form of State and Municipal Ownership was being recommended which would take a century or more to introduce' and that then it would 'leave the world with a form of State Capitalism almost, if not more evil, than that which we were trying to escape from. It was a characteristic Webb contribution but even Sidney Webb said [to Nash] that he had found it necessary to compromise with some of the Continental delegates. The Swedish delegate who happened to be the Swedish Minister for Finance was opposed to the Nationalisation of Banks. . . .' Nash said to the Congress that 'The Worker's control of the wealth which he creates seemed to me to be the fundamental of rational Socialism. If the recommendations of the Commission were adopted industries would be socialised step by step, but would end in the Non-Worker getting a State guaranteed share of wealth under the title of Interest and the Capitalists would not mind how they got their share or what it was called provided that they got it.'

He went on to tell them of 'the State and Municipal owned utilities of New Zealand and said that if State Ownership was Socialism then there was much Socialism in New Zealand', but 'unless State Ownership led to Democratic Control—with the fundamental that Service was the only title to a share of the wealth created—then it is not Socialism but a bigger menace to the workers than the private Capitalism of today'.

The basis of the Bolshevik success, he said, was 'the principle of wealth to the worker and NO WORK, NO VOTE'. A 'lazy class' always meant trouble. Socialism was 'not essentially a System for producing more commodities but . . . also, and more important, a system to ensure an equitable system of distribution. CREATION IS THE PUREST TITLE TO ANYTHING. THE WORKERS, WITH BRAIN AND HAND, CREATE. THEY SHOULD CONTROL.'

In conclusion he suggested that 'the Second International was dying' if it denied 'to those who create the right to control their creation'. 'This brought forth a bitter attack from the [Dutch] presenter of the Report, and the discussion livened up'.[15]

In this speech Nash brought up two of the central problems of late nineteenth and twentieth century radicalism and socialism: whether to divide the economic cake more equally or to bake a bigger one; whether state control equalled socialism. To the second question most people would now say 'no'. For what he was describing and criticizing, in radical sentiments for 1921, sounds very like the economy of German or Italian Fascism of the early nineteen-thirties, or the slightly later 'mixed economies' of the 'welfare states'. Only the politically very conservative would since then equate state control with socialism as most Fabians did in about 1900.

To the first question most radicals since—say—the mid-twentieth century would reply 'both'.

Most of the rest of Nash's life was to be concerned with these issues: the care of the old and the young; the distribution of wealth; economic growth—and bank nationalization. Perhaps he obscurely guessed or wished for this future. Certainly he was attracted to Geneva as a young artist at that time would have been drawn almost instinctively to Paris.

Ramsay MacDonald had just returned from a tour of Germany. He reported to the Congress on the shortage of food there and 'the sacrifice of child life'. Nash thought this the most inspiring speech at the meeting, and that MacDonald 'stood out from all the other delegates'. It was decided to organize relief through the 'Save the Children Fund', and Nash tried to assist this cause in England. He also wrote to the Wellington *Evening Post* about conditions in Europe.[16]

The secretariat of the Second International was transferred to London, but it faded out. It became the Labour and Socialist International in 1923, but the New Zealand party did not join.

The Nashes' return to New Zealand was immediately followed by the most difficult period of their life. Walter's outspoken socialism did not make for easy sociability in the closed world of a month's sea voyage in a liner. On 28 December 1920 he wrote in his diary, 'Passengers rather agitated against me but do not express feeling openly—Lot much upset'. Next day he wrote, 'Atmosphere on boat rather bad'.[17] At that time the ship was berthed near Melbourne, where he called at the Socialist Hall. The stewards went on strike and the passengers helped out. He wondered whether to do so. He felt that he could not let the other passengers wait on him, yet he did not want to 'scab' on the stewards. In the end he did do some work. Eventually they left the ship, the *Argyllshire*, and crossed the Tasman in the *Moeraki*.

While in Melbourne he visited a publisher and importer, Will Andrade, who gave him a parcel of pamphlets for his bookshop. They were samples, not meant to be sold, and he did not open the package. He must have been under surveillance. At the Wellington wharf a detective was waiting for him. He asked if Nash had any literature and opened the parcel. Nash was prosecuted under war regulations for bringing into the country documents encouraging and inciting violence and lawlessness. These were two communist pamphlets, one of them Bukharin's *Programme of the World Revolution*. Nash's plea that his aim 'was to bring home to the Labour Party the principles underlying Christianity and to interest Christian people in New Zealand', did no good. The magistrate said that the publications were 'as dangerous to the body politic as typhoid germs deliberately placed in a city reservoir'. Had Nash distributed them he would have imposed the maximum penalty of a £100 fine and a gaol sentence. In the circumstances, however, he fined him £5 and £7 costs.

The case was very widely reported, with the incorrect detail that Nash had pleaded guilty. The *Taranaki News* carried the headlines: 'FORBIDDEN LITERATURE. BOLSHEVIK AGENT FINED'! The Wellington *Evening Post* published an editorial article saying that though free speech was a cherished possession which distinguished British communities, order had been its essential condition. Free speech was subject to legal limits. 'To punish crime while allowing incitements to crime a free run' would be absurd.[18]

Harry Holland wrote sympathetically that he was 'disgusted to learn that Prussianism is on your track already'. He had the *Communist Programme* himself and did not know it was banned.[19] The New Plymouth Labour Party sent a message of sympathy and asked him to stand for Secretary-Treasurer of the Party. He declined because launching his new book business was so urgent.[20] He was asked to speak in Petone, and Lot wrote that she had been told that his name and actions were 'the talk of the city'.[21]

An even greater blow than the prosecution fell at the same time. When he left Modern Tailors Nash had received £300 towards his trip Home, and £200 from the profits earned between the time he transferred his shares and when he actually left the firm. Instead of receiving the money for his shares, valued at £1,500 on the basis of the company's profit over three-and-a-half years, however, he had accepted promissory notes (sometimes called 'bills' in the correspondence) payable at various dates over fifteen months. Miller & Ahearn discounted some of these to help pay for his trip.[22] It was decided that it would be good for the business to purchase stock ahead, and Nash took Besley round the sellers—thereby spending money which otherwise might have paid for his shares.

When Nash returned he had been paid only £650, and the remaining £850 was still owing. Already he had received warning of trouble. As early as mid-1920 Ahearn had written that Besley was unable to meet a bill and that he had advanced him the money to pay Nash.[23] So part of the money Nash had received was owed to Ahearn.

As soon as he arrived in Wellington on 2 January, Ahearn told him that Besley would not meet the outstanding bills. Nash went up to New Plymouth (while Lot travelled to the Bay of Islands where the boys were staying with Ted and Nell Hinton). Besley told him he felt he had paid too much for Nash's shares. He felt that Nash had got £2,000 more-or-less for nothing, since none of the shares were paid up. Nash felt that he had given up an immediate income of over £100 a month (at that time) for £1,500.[24]

Nash shortly learned from lawyers that Besley was suing to recover the £500 (for fares and extra profit) and to cancel the remaining bills on the ground of Nash's 'fraud and undue influence'.[25]

Nash was now in debt, for books ordered abroad, and almost penniless, for he had counted on the remaining money to start his new business and a new home. Negotiations went on for months until even his lawyer admitted that the delays were unconscionable.

He wrote to his brother Albert, who lent him £200 to pay for purchases in England. Tom Brindle, a waterside worker and left-wing Labour man, lent them £250 and helped devotedly with the new business. Ahearn offered to stand by them. The Hobdays let them have a room for a time. Then they rented a 'tiny home', a cottage attached to Hobday's school, in Ferry Road, Day's Bay, near Wellington, for £4 6s. 8d. a month. Mrs Hobday sold Lot a bed for £5 and curtains at half price. Walter wrote to Lot, 'of course you have done the best you could with the money dear. If you can scrape a Home together on £40 you are a marvel'. They transferred young Walter (whom Nell, and sometimes his parents, called 'McNab') from the High School in New Plymouth to Wellington College—where he won a Senior National Scholarship to go to University.

Their friends and relatives knew (as Nell wrote) that they were having 'a rotten wretched time'. And it was, as Lot wrote to him, 'hard to have worked so hard at home then to return to all this worry'. Sometimes they were both depressed, as their letters show (written as he travelled the country again, about his new business). In August he admitted that he sometimes felt he would 'bend under the load', but that her spirits helped him to keep going. Lot replied that Les (her second son) said that she was 'always laughing' and that it was getting so monotonous that she must stop. At other times he wrote to her 'Everything will be all right darling—in the long run—the road will be very hard—but we can get through all right—keep smiling'. Lot's friend Eva Beard wrote to her, 'His unbounded energy & lightheartedness should be an inspiration to other folks'. 'I think your husband is one of the *Great* men & goodness knows they are all too few & far between'. It was certainly true that his resilience was remarkable.

Nell, who was very emotional, wrote that Walter seemed to have caught on 'to rotters all the time in this country' as he had earlier found a rotter ('names need not be mentioned') in the Church in England. But Walter declined to adopt her attitude. He wrote to Lot, 'If I let myself go and said exactly what I thought of Besley . . . I am afraid the air would get blue— but I want to look at it as much as possible in the best light'. By early 1922 (when it was all over) he wrote to Lot saying how good people had been to them and added, 'Besley loved his Mother. . . . There's a little bit of good in the worst of us'. (Besley had tried to justify his conduct by saying he was worried to the point of breakdown about his sick mother.[26]) This kind of attitude, very natural to Nash, could seem to others either inspiring or insincere.

Like many disputes among former friends, it was nasty. Besley said to Pearce, of the prosecution, that Nash had been 'fairly caught'. To a suggestion that his row with Besley arose from political differences, Nash replied that the latter was one of the first members of the New Plymouth Labour Party and had contributed to party funds. There was some difference of opinion between Nash and Ahearn about whether Miller & Ahearn had in fact promised to pay for his trip home, or merely to give him six months' leave on full pay (as Ahearn recalled). However, there was no doubt that Besley had agreed to the former. Besley asked Pearce if he had kept the early correspondence on the matter. He had destroyed his papers, but said that Nash would not have done so. Besley said, as Pearce reported, 'No, that's the worst of it.' But Nash did not have the Company's minute book, nor (with one exception), its balance sheets, nor the Articles of Association, and was uncertain whether they were registered.

By December Besley was willing to abandon his claim to the money for the shares and willing to make a cash offer, but Nash would not agree while there remained the suggestion of fraud.

Eventually Nash won the case. The dispute was placed before the arbitration of a Wellington accountant, Duncan Menzies, who in January 1922 found in favour of Nash (with costs) on all the points in dispute.[27] Even then it was some time before Nash got his money. Of Besley's first payment of £600, in March, £478 was owing to Miller & Ahearn. At that time he had only 1s. 7d. in the bank.

It is difficult to know what conclusions may be drawn about Nash from this episode. Certainly he was naive or very trusting. Probably an unwillingness to rely on the work of others, very noticeable later in his life, may be traced to his experiences with Jones & Ashdown and with Besley. His written submissions to the arbitrator are rather muddled and lack the cogent presentation which might be expected from (say) a trained accountant. However, the firm was successful, so he did not lack business ability.

Another of Nash's most striking characteristics may be related to the Besley affair. He was already careful in keeping papers, but henceforth the preservation of every document, indeed of almost any scrap of paper which concerned him in any way, became an obsession.

Throughout 1921 Nash worked very hard to establish his new businesses, a bookshop and his agencies. The latter required him to be away from Wellington for six months out of twelve. Over the next few years he had a sample room, showing cutlery, rag dolls, model aeroplanes and other goods, in Wellington.[28] To start with he combined this with the Clarté Subscription Agency and the Clarté Book Room (presently a shop), in Dixon Street and then in Willis Street.

He named his shop after the Clarté movement, which he probably heard of when he visited France. Clarté had been started there in 1919. It was a movement to organize writers, scientists, and other intellectuals of both the allied and 'central' powers in an international league, with the aim of bringing about a moral revolution in the world. The sole purpose of the Clarté Agency, he wrote to Moses Ayrton, secretary of the Labour Party from 1920 to 1922, was to spread the knowledge which would enable the workers of New Zealand to understand the forces which surrounded them.[29]

The agency took subscriptions for a wide range of journals dealing with economics, international affairs, and socialism. Harry Holland, for instance, subscribed to the *New Statesman*, the *Economic Review*, and various socialist papers. Although he was an MP (since 1918), he could not afford to pay by the year, and did so monthly.[30]

While Walter was travelling, Lot helped to run the book room and agency office. He sent her detailed instructions on how to take orders and send out magazines. At first there was little to do. In July 1921 she wrote to him, 'There is not much buiz doing here shall have to go & work if things don't buck up a bit soon'.[31] A month later he wrote to her, 'If you cannot sell people books—lend them to them. They will probably do the same as Mr Wolke—buy them after reading'.[32]

Nash's mail was obviously still watched by the police. One night at 10 p.m. Tom Brindle, who helped Lot a great deal, saw a postcard and a letter in their box at the post office. When Nash went to get it at 9 a.m. it was not there. When he enquired at the post office he was told 'that maybe they had blown out of the box'. By 11.15 a.m. they were back, both showing signs of having been examined. He wrote to Harry Holland, 'The Letter Card was from my wife and read peculiarly strange. They will think there is a huge plot afoot. I wonder why they are harassing me so much?'[33] He wrote to Lot later, 'I hope they are not opening my letters again—but they will do just what they are disposed to. They are a law unto themselves—yet they expect people to obey the law'.[34] He also had difficulty with the

Customs Department, which controlled the censorship of literature. It would not tell him which books were banned unless he asked about a specific title. Eighteen copies of *Christianism and Communism* were seized.[35]

From March 1921 to March 1922 he managed to earn only £429 (which probably included the £122 from Besley). His commission on book sales between January 1922 and July 1922 was only £65.[36] In January 1923 he found that though his commissions amounted to £732, office and travelling expenses took £481 (the Dixon Street premises alone cost £200 a year). By this time he also received £130 salary as Secretary of the Labour Party. But another year's work had left his bank account overdrawn by £61. They had lived on £441 'personal drawings'.[37] Things were 'on the mend', but they had had a very hard time. They continued to live in the Day's Bay cottage until May 1922, when they moved nearby, into the headmaster's house at the Croydon School. Then, in 1925, they went back to Brooklyn, renting the Westwood's house in Karepa Street. In that year he was also able to repay the £200 to his brother Albert.

VI

Secretary of the Labour Party

1922-32

The first secretary of the Labour Party had been 'Joe' Savage. A former Australian miner, cellar-man in an Auckland brewery, and agitator, he was appointed in 1919, after Tom Brindle and Nash declined nomination at the conference. In 1920 Brindle was beaten by Moses Ayrton, a Methodist minister. Under him the party's affairs were a muddle. He did not answer letters, write up minutes, nor keep clear accounts. In 1922 Nash was nominated for the job by the Taranaki branches and the Auckland LRC. The Taranaki LRC also nominated him for the New Plymouth electorate in the forthcoming general election. He accepted the former but declined the latter nomination, as incompatible with the secretaryship if he were elected.[1]

Before accepting he spent a couple of afternoons discussing it with Jack McCullough, a workers' representative on the Arbitration Court. McCullough offered to travel round the country trying to induce unions to affiliate with the Party. He also talked to 'Pat' Fraser.[2] A national plebiscite of party members was held, as was then the procedure, and he was elected. Lot hoped he would not find life too strenuous, since he was to do the job part-time.

He found that the party was £150 in debt, but since £70 of capitation fees paid in advance had been included in the balance sheet, it was in fact £220 in debt. The manager of the *Maoriland Worker*, John Glover, lent £100 interest free and Nash managed to lend some too, so that the debts were paid.[3]

Nash set himself three related initial tasks, to raise funds and membership and to open a head office, which the party had not been able to afford. His first effort was to renew Savage's 50,000 half-crowns fund-raising campaign, but reduced to shillings, and to launch a National Office fund. His notion of the sort of appeal likely to attract money sounded more like that of a church than of a Labour group. He announced in the *Maoriland Worker* that the goal was 'FIFTY THOUSAND SHILLINGS AND FIFTY THOUSAND MEMBERS IN THREE MONTHS', and he quoted John Addington Symonds's hymn:

> When they tell you we are dreamers tell them
> 'These things shall be ; a loftier race
> Than ere the world has known shall rise
> With flame of freedom in their souls,
> And light of knowledge in their eyes.'

He proclaimed that 'The fundamental of the Movement is that a first charge on all wealth created shall be the care of the aged, the ailing, the young. . . . The Labor Party goes to the country on the basis of SERVICE. Service is the only title to wealth. . . . It will bring about a state where Truth and Equity, Justice and Mercy will govern the mutual dealings of men and of nations. . . . It appeals to all those Christians who believe in the Social Principles of Christ'. In the *National Record* Nash announced that 'the Labour Party is for the Higher Ideal'.[4]

At this task, with his previous experience as fund-raiser for the CEMS, Nash was about as successful as anyone could be in an organization whose supporters were poor. Often LRCs were late with, or could not pay their capitation fees. Few of the targets set were achieved. But the party survived.

After nine months, and despite fighting an election, the deficit was only £5 14s. 9½d. (Nash always counted his half-pennies). By 1924 over £1,100, which exceeded the target, had been raised for a head office. A Political Fighting (i.e. campaign) Fund was then started, and £10,174 was raised by 1927. Thereafter, during the depression, finances became very difficult again. In 1931, for instance, £1,100 was raised for the election, but the party's £200 credit came from two legacies.

Nash received £130 in 1922 but then he was not paid for two years. At the 1924 conference Bob Semple said that the party 'did not stand for sweating'. It should pay Mr Nash a salary, 'for he had the capacity to impress classes whom we had not yet won by our propaganda'. Fraser moved that he should be paid at the same rate as an MP for the proportion of his time that he worked for the party. This was a recommendation from the National Executive and was approved. It is estimated that Nash received £6 or £7 a week thereafter.[5]

At the 1923 conference the executive reported that the party had made its most astonishing advance since its inception, both in the 1922 election and by opening its head office in Hood's Building in Lambton Quay, Wellington. Later it was moved to Willis Street and, in 1929, to the Wellington Trades Hall, just built in Vivian Street.

Nash acquired a typist, Miss Minnis, who worked for the party (indexing all the correspondence for him, for instance) and also acted as his secretary for his agency business. This was a big help in Wellington, but not when he was travelling. One day in Oamaru in 1923 he spent seven hours writing and typing.[6]

During the 1922 election the office sent out nearly 500,000 pamphlets,[7] as well as running correspondence with all the branches and fund-raising.

Even with the help of devoted party members like Brindle and Semple, Nash had to work extraordinarily hard. By 1926 the National Executive decided that he needed an assistant. David Wilson, a Scottish immigrant, was appointed. When Nash was working for Miller & Ahearn he had met Wilson in Nelson where he was a tailor. Then he had become a paid Secretary of the Auckland LRC.[8]

The task closest to Nash's heart was partly of his choosing. Fraser and he were keen to start an Information (or Research) Bureau within Head Office. Articles in the *Maoriland Worker*, some of them written by Nash, constantly stressed the need for *facts* as 'munitions of war for the intellectual political struggle which will free the working people of New Zealand from the various forms of exploitation. . . .'[9]

£1,000 was needed for this information service. Eventually it was financed jointly by the Alliance of Labour, the successor to the Federation, and the Party.[10] By early 1924 the first bulletin was issued. It was followed by a series of papers on all sorts of topics such as wages, day labour, armaments, local bodies, the standard of living and family allowances.

Holland, Fraser, Nash, Thorn, and others kept up a constant stream of propaganda in the *Maoriland Worker* (renamed the *New Zealand Worker* in 1924). The party did not control the paper, which had begun as a shearers' and then a 'Red Fed' journal, but it bought a large block of shares in 1927. Nash became a director, and wrote numerous articles, on such topics as workers' compensation, the Government Statistician's rent and wages index, and 'CHRIST—THE AGITATOR', in which he proclaimed that 'to practise the principles of Christ in our present commercial system is impossible, if what is called success is desired. . . .'[11]

What effect such educational (or propaganda) work had is difficult to say. The *Maoriland Worker* was probably not much read outside self-conscious Labour and trade union circles. Certainly its views made little headway beyond trade union suburbs and city centres. Membership did, however, increase, partly at least because of the persistent drive Nash gave to branch organization. He helped set up branches, and spurred others on. Over matters like sending out membership cards, collecting capitation fees, answering correspondence, or urging all branches and affiliated unions to send representatives to the annual conference, he was meticulous. When there were disputes in branches he was conciliatory. If anyone was half-hearted he spurred them on. In 1923 the Napier Secretary doubted whether anyone would come to meetings in outlying districts. Nash reminded him that the party did not merely seek office, but wanted to bring about 'as soon as possible a new type of system'; they needed the 'understanding' of people everywhere to 'create an atmosphere that will ensure that when our legislation goes on the Statute Book, it will be fruitful'.[12]

Membership had doubled in 1918-19, to 21,000. Thereafter it fluctuated. The Hutt LRC Secretary wrote, 'it seems peculiar to N.Z. that interest in

Political matters only awakes at election times and then fades away'.[13] But by 1924 there were branches in all but nine electorates; a year later there were over 45,000 members. During the depression membership declined, but active supporters were more active. In 1932 twenty-three new branches were formed.

Because it could expect few large donations, a political scientist has written, the Labour Party was obliged to rely on union contributions supplemented by the enthusiastic support of many 'more-or-less permanently active branches'. The branch workers 'were keen to attend the annual conferences of the Party and to debate policy. . . . Moreover, branch workers and affiliated unionists chose the candidates. In consequence, the twenties saw the spread, improvement and consolidation of New Zealand's first modern political organisation with a mass basis in a membership of thousands'. The Reform and Liberal parties remained 'loose aggregations of individuals'.[14] It should be added, however, that Labour membership figures can be misleading, since they included affiliated union members. The number of party activists was very much smaller. But this is true of all large political parties. Moreover, each affiliated union paid fees, which were as important as supporters 'on the ground'.

Obviously large sections of the unionists thought, and voted, in class terms. Yet Labour's numerous membership obscured its weakness, for unionists were in a minority in a predominantly rural society. Moreover, although it sprang from the unions, the party was far from enjoying their universal or unqualified support. It had more-or-less absorbed the old 'Red Feds', whose leaders had become Labour Party leaders. But after the war there was a revival of syndicalism, when the Alliance of Labour was formed. It scoffed at parliamentary and advocated industrial action. It did not, however, achieve the 'One Big Union' it aimed at. Two strikes by unions belonging to the Alliance, of seamen in 1923 and railwaymen in 1924, were disastrous failures and—in the opinion of Peter Fraser—fatal blunders. The Labour Party had nothing to do with calling the strikes, but it did try to bring about settlements. In 1923, for instance, Nash went with the President of the Alliance and the Secretary of the Seamen's Union to call on Massey to discuss a settlement. But there was little the party could do and the strikes split the Alliance.[15] By the mid-nineteen-twenties the Alliance had drawn somewhat closer to the party. But, whereas there was only one labour political party, the union side of the movement remained weak and divided. The Trades and Labour Councils Federation, based on craft unionist principles, continued to exist alongside the Alliance.

Although Nash lacked the union experience of most of the other Labour leaders, union affairs, especially involving the LRCs, occupied a good deal of time and he came to know most of the union leaders.

Much of Nash's work involved organizing meetings, like the No-More-War demonstrations of 1922 and again an International Anti-War Day in

1924, and arranging for speaking tours by Harry Holland and the other MPs. But he was a remarkably peripatetic secretary himself. He was constantly reported addressing branch or public meetings all over the country, work which at first he combined with travelling for his agencies.

By 1924, Nash found he could not cover the whole country and do his party work. So he engaged a traveller. A year later he entered a partnership with J. R. Kissling, who had importing experience. Kissling did all the travelling and administration for the agencies. Five years later, when Nash was elected to parliament, he sold out to Kissling, who continued trading under the name of Nash & Kissling. In 1938 he became ill and went to Australia. The firm was taken over by a rival. Although it was made public that Nash had had nothing to do with the firm for years, this episode probably gave further currency to a rumour that Nash had gone bankrupt.[16] One of Nash's amusing stories in later life concerned his book agencies. He said, in a radio interview, 'I was keen to propagate Christianity. I wanted to make Christians Socialists and I wanted to make Rationalists Christians. And I was agent for Watts and Co., which is what is known as the R.P.A., the Rationalist Press Association. They found out I was propagating Christianity as well as trying to get Christians rational, and they cancelled the agency, but none of the Christian firms did, they kept me going. Someone reported to one of the houses that they ought not to have a Bolshevik represent them, and the publishing manager of the Student Christian Movement wrote back again and said, "Well, if you can find anyone else who will sell more of our books than Walter Nash is selling, let us know".'[17]

He also gave up his bookshop. By 1924 he found that, with all his work for the party, the losses were too great for his pocket. The Labour Party took it over and his stock was moved to the party office. The stock—of books and pamphlets on sociology, economics, religion, and so on—was valued at £294.[18] It was kept going as the Clarté Bookroom until it was decided in 1934 to call it the Labour Book Room. At that time the assets were valued at £667. They included one Rag Book and some ostrich feather fans.[19]

This was the end of Nash's business career. It might be said that, though not a failure, he had not been a great success, despite his industry and thoroughness. But he did well as a salesman for Miller & Ahearn, and Modern Tailors Ltd flourished while he was, in effect, secretary-manager. Nash was not poor—he frequently donated money to the party and other causes, and lent money to friends. He was thrifty personally but generous to friends and charities.

J. C. Beaglehole, the historian, who used to drop in at the Clarté bookshop as a young man, said that Nash was not very interested in making money.[20] And this was true. As a bookseller he used to 'push' League of Nations publications, on which he lost money, and tried to create a market for Student Christian Movement books for which there was a negligible demand.[21] When asked (in a CEMS questionnaire), 'What effect does the making of money have upon the soul?' he replied, 'detrimental'.[22]

To a peculiar degree, Nash combined in perfect inner harmony the qualities of a visionary and a bureaucrat. When he retired from the secretaryship he was appropriately presented with a filing cabinet, but he might equally well have been given the works of Mazzini—or Tolstoy.

Years later James Thorn, who had been a big man in the Party, and lived in Palmerston North when Nash did, wrote to him,

What wealth of service you have given to our Movement since I first heard of you—and at that time took so very little notice of you! Until you came among us we were little more than a band of agitators, with humane feelings and some brotherly ideals, but speechifying generalities and carrying no responsibility. You brought to us what we had never known before—a knowledge of the business world, the inside on banking, the filing system, orderly office procedures, and the practical conception of socialist progress in the face of capitalist institutions and long-standing prejudices.

And your patience, your loving-kindness, your true religious feeling—all these have been an inspiration to some of us, and helped to keep us sweet and comradely.[23]

The value of Nash's work was widely recognized in the party and often praised—for instance the *New Zealand Worker* said in 1927 that the party's progress was largely due to the efficiency he had brought to its administration. Harry Holland said the same in 1930. Nash was rarely reported attending the socials, parties, and bazaars which were the chores of MPs. His 'sense of duty, his comradeship is an inspiration. With a love of work he amazes his friends by the multitude of the tasks he accomplishes', the *New Zealand Worker* commented in 1930. It was not only his assiduity which impressed. The article said that 'To him effort to realise Socialism is a passion'.[24] Business-like secretaries are always treasures, but, even so, his popularity is shown by the absence of rivals. In 1924 three people were nominated for president, thirteen for vice-president, but only Nash (nominated by twenty-five branches and unions!) for secretary.[25]

The basis of Nash's later power was laid in the twenties. No one had comparable knowledge of the details of branch affairs, personal antipathies, and the whole party organization. But his influence did not stop there. He was a member of most of the important policy committees and election platform committees, and usually wrote their reports.

Nash helped draft the 1922 election programme, which contained some of his characteristic phrases—there was the 'first charge on all wealth'; 'Service shall be the foundation. . . . Truth and Equity the governing factors in the mutual dealings of men and nations'. He wrote the 1928 and the 1935 manifestos. He was a member of the important land policy committees of 1919, 1924 (for which he collated the submissions and wrote the report), and 1926-7; of the 1929 land settlement committee, the important 1933 Policy Committee, and a good many others.

Naturally leading party members helped on these committees and made submissions—men like Frank Langstone and W. E. Barnard, Ben Roberts and Tom Brindle, Jim Thorn, Savage, and Fraser. But some leaders were not very fluent on paper, however remarkable their oratorical flow, so that little evidence survives of their role. It is impossible to say how many people contributed to the formulation of policy at caucus and conference. But there is no doubt that the chief influences were Fraser and Nash. The latter, as secretary, summed up discussions in his own way. His persistent influence on the drafting of statements meant that he controlled the tone, the temper of the party's public utterances. Sometimes his contribution to specific policies may also be identified. Fraser also played a major role in party organization and tactics, and acted for Nash when he was out of town.

Quite apart from ability and industry, their influence rested on the fact that they lived in Wellington. Not only were parliament and Head Office there, but in 1921 a smaller Resident Executive permanently in Wellington had been added to the National Executive, which met only quarterly.[26] The secretary was a member. He and Fraser were sedulous in their attendance. Others, like Holland, who lived on the West Coast, were rarely there when parliament was in recess. Some such members used to complain about the difficulty of getting to executive or committee meetings. In 1926 Frank Langstone wrote that he attached little importance to being on the land committee, 'as on a previous occasion I was never given intimation in time to permit my being present at any meetings. . . .'[27]

Langstone bore on his shoulder a permanent chip, the size of a kauri log, but it is fair to say that the life of an MP was very arduous. For months each year they lived in Wellington (the Labour MPs in cheap boarding houses), travelling overnight to Auckland, Christchurch or elsewhere, by train or boat, on Friday nights and back again on Monday night. It was more tedious, but perhaps less nerve-racking, than the same routine by air in more recent times.

Other leaders, like Savage, Thorn, Langstone, and Semple were important, but the party was increasingly run by Holland, who devoted his efforts to parliamentary attendance and leadership, Fraser, and Nash. The Nashes and Frasers were personal as well as political friends. They lived almost next door and saw a good deal of one another, as they had for some years. On Christmas Day 1922, for instance, when Lot was away, Walter went for a four-hour walk with the Frasers. (On Boxing Day he walked from Day's Bay over to the Orongorongo and back, starting out before breakfast.)[28]

Nash continued to be friendly with Holland too, but of course saw his family less often. Of the three men, Fraser was probably the cleverest. Nash said Fraser could read a book twice as quickly as he. He also had a capacity Nash lacked, to be extremely clear and concise. He went to the heart of the matter faster; Nash had an excessive respect for masses of detail. All three read very widely in political and general economic literature. Nash read plays, short stories, novels, and religious literature too. Fraser was well acquainted with New Zealand books. Holland rivalled them in the breadth of his reading: in 1921 he subscribed to nine of the journals Nash distributed. There were few people in New Zealand as well read as these unschooled men. Many of those who were as widely read, and better educated, were their friends. Hardly any of the Liberal or Reform leaders, with the notable exception of Downie Stewart (also very friendly with Nash), were in the same class. Indeed in the whole of New Zealand political history they had few peers in this respect: some of the early immigrant politicians like C. W. Richmond, William Rolleston, or Robert Stout, or the first New Zealand-born intellectual, William Pember Reeves—the list would be short.

Though there were striking differences of temperament, Fraser and Nash had much in common. Fraser was as devoted to his Janet as Walter to Lot. They were both unusually industrious and both abstemious. Fraser often appeared to live on cups of tea and toast. Nash, on rare occasions, would have a stronger drink.[29]

Like Holland, they were very serious men. Fraser was a dour, humourless, schoolmasterly Scot, with a quick temper. He could be scathingly sarcastic in debate, a quality in which his brevity was a main element and for which Nash's prolixity was usually a disqualification. He came from Fearn in Rosshire, and had joined the Independent Labour Party in London before coming to New Zealand in 1910. He was a modest man, of very great political acumen, far shrewder and tougher, more ruthless, than Nash. He detested cant and show—and showed it. When be became leader, he led by ability and toughness, not through love. He was the most dominant Labour leader of his generation. Before he was leader he was a very loyal lieutenant to Holland and then to Savage.

During his first years in New Zealand Fraser, like Holland and Savage and Semple, was much more left-wing than Nash. Later he was to become, in some respects, notably his anti-Communism, to Nash's right, but in the 1920s and early 1930s they were politically close to one another.

Holland had a decreasing influence on policy. Nash consulted him in writing election manifestos. He admired him, but found him difficult to work with. While kind and gentle in his private life, Holland was humourless, at times bitter in his speeches. Though his party's programme was far from so, he seemed to breathe a revolutionary air. In 1921 he wrote that a Labour government would seek 'economic transformation. A conscious working class cannot tolerate the idea of merely administering the class state'.[30] This was a not unfair comment on policy at the time. But though he did modify his views a decade later, he never changed his resolutely socialist public image. Whether his apocalyptic visions faded is uncertain. Holland had suffered very greatly from poverty and hunger in Australia, keeping a socialist paper going.[31] Poverty continued in New Zealand, even though he was Leader of the Opposition 1925-8 and 1931-3. He had secretarial assistance only when the House was in session, and expended his energies on the many articles he wrote to help earn money, and as propaganda, and on his correspondence—he received 679 letters in January to March 1930 alone. Eventually Head Office paid one third and he paid two thirds of a secretary's salary. But he was (in 1929) in debt. He had no life or fire insurance. He did not drink or smoke and rarely went to a play or to 'the pictures'.[32]

Holland far out-did Fraser and Nash in the quantity of his writings, including his journalism and political pamphlets. He wrote verse of a sentimental and rhetorical sort then fashionable on the left and published a book, *Red Roses on the Highway* (1924). He printed some of his verse on his Christmas cards. His daughter Agnes quoted one of his couplets on her Christmas card in 1926:

> 'The duty ours in waning age as in life's shining youth
> To hold aloft upon the way the flaming torch of truth'.[33]

Nash later adopted this practice of distributing inspiring verse messages at Christmas.

The post-war depression favoured Labour in the election of 1922. The election manifesto stressed motherhood endowment, and free medical treatment. There was to be a state bank and a state shipping line. As a minority party with a large vote (almost as numerous as the Reform Party in 1919) but only eight MPs, Labour favoured proportional representation. There were to be free school books. And 'the twin scourges of war and capitalism' were to be 'driven from the earth'. The land policy, clearly influenced by Nash, stressed 'occupancy and use' and a tax on 'community created values'. There was enough socialism to lead newspapers to warn voters of 'the Russian terror conspiracy'.[34]

The results of the election led to premature jubilation. Labour won a quarter of the votes (a slight increase on 1919). In city seats its vote rose from 29 per cent to 38 per cent and its city seats increased from seven to thirteen. But its voters were densely concentrated in a few electorates. A political scientist has written that Labour 'had reached an invisible barrier of prejudgments about their Party'.[35]

Labour's history for the next thirteen years was a search for support outside the cities. The central issue was its land policy, which alienated rural voters. It was radical, even socialist, but what the Labour leaders did not realize was that their land policies belonged to the past, not the future. In New Zealand questions of land tenure excited less interest than forty years before. When Labour's policies attracted attention it was as a threat. Taxing the unearned increment (so dear to Nash), leasehold tenure, and even land nationalization had had a popular following when the Liberals came to power in 1890. But Labour ignored the cry of 'freehold'—and the victory of Bill Massey—in 1912. This could not be reversed.

The 1919 land policy was drawn up by a committee of which Savage, Semple, Holland, and Nash were members. It was almost certainly inspired by Nash—his first influence on party policy. It said that land tenure was to be one of 'occupancy and use'. This phrase, and the idea it embodied about rights to ownership, reflected what John Ruskin had written in *Fors Clavigera*: 'each man shall possess the ground he can use—and no more'; '*possession* is, and must be, limited by use'.[36]

Land could only be sold 'to or from the state'. Fraser thought this meant gradual land nationalization, an idea strengthened when the clause was altered to read that private land could not be sold or transferred *except* to the state.[37]

As Nash explained the land policy in the years 1922-4,[38] Labour's views on land tenure were very vague, but the clause on transfer to the state appeared to mean that all land would gradually become Crown land and be leased out. Labour's policy involved hostility to land speculation, mortgages, and the profits made by land agents and lawyers from land transfers. The state was to become the land agent (and eventual owner). Labour also favoured taxing the unearned increment.

In 1924-5 another land committee, of which Nash acted as convener and wrote the report,[39] collected data on the exorbitant profits made by land agents, lawyers, and speculators. The actual occupier and user of land was to have 'absolute security of tenure' and full rights to inherit and to bequeath land. These points, which marked some adjustment to rural opinion, were spelt out in the very detailed (far too detailed) land policy in the 1925 manifesto, but it still said that 'all transfers would be made to the state', which seemed to imply slow land nationalization.

The term 'usehold' (referred to by Labour's opponents as 'loosehold') was a liability to the party. What it meant was expressed by Savage, who said in 1925 that a 'usehold' title was better than a mortgage.[40] 'Usehold' was a perpetual lease, as was clear in the party's 1925 manifesto, as well as in that of 1928. But Savage was ignoring the opinion of most New Zealand farmers, for whom a mortgage at least implied the possibility of an eventual unencumbered freehold title and the possibility of sale at increased values.

Some of these problems were recognized by party members whose thinking was not clogged by accepted socialist dogmas, or who were attracted to credit policies. John A. Lee, an Auckland MP, wrote to the land committee that the policy clauses on state valuation of all land and state land transfers were unworkable while land values were governed by prices paid for exports in overseas markets. It would be necessary 'to control prices of produce and make the return from the land fixed and definite' first. 'To endeavour to socialise Land with Production in its present

Anarchic State is to start at the wrong end'. He suggested cooperative marketing by farmers' boards and that advances up to 80 or 90 per cent of the value of farm and stock should be granted to approved farmers.[41] Frank Langstone wrote that 'The question of fixed prices for farm products' for local consumption should be considered.[42] These points of view were not taken up, but pointed the way to future party conflict.

The land policy was in 1925 'the show-piece of the Party's platform . . . the most distinctive, detailed and comprehensive item of policy possessed by any political party in New Zealand'.[43] It was also, as Lee wrote to Nash during a rural by-election in 1925, 'a hell of a grill to toast a candidate on when the audience is hostile'.[44] The Labour man was heavily defeated.

The policy was offered again in the general election of 1925, when Nash stood for the first time, as candidate for the Hutt. His opponent was Thomas Wilford, a former mayor of Wellington and Minister of Justice, who had been the MP for the Hutt since 1903 and was now Leader of the Opposition and of the Liberal Party (called National in 1925). He was virtually unbeatable, but it was usual for a new candidate to be tried out in an unwinnable electorate.

Though Nash had much assistance from his party he was not helped by his family. A Labour supporter, Bertha Whyte, was asked why Mrs Nash and the boys did not help. She replied, unfortunately in Mrs Nash's hearing, that Mrs Nash was not Labour and that she had more influence on the boys' opinions that their father. She wrote a long letter of apology.[45]

Nash was to stand in fifteen elections from 1925 to 1966. Only the most ardent psephologist would wish to have them all recounted at length. Labour election practices changed little over the period. The house-to-house canvass, getting voters on the roll, street corner meetings, the distribution of 'dodgers' to announce meetings, slide advertisements at the movies, speaking in factories, meeting as many voters as possible, shaking hands, posters on hoardings—these have scarcely altered. The 'hall' meeting was more important before the 1950s, and more numerously attended before the advent of television. Like most candidates in 1925, Nash concentrated on canvassing and public meetings, at which Holland or Fraser sometimes spoke in his support.

He was known in one part of the electorate, Day's Bay, which was an advantage. The Hutt included quite wealthy as well as poor areas. Naturally he concentrated on the latter. He tried to woo some of the Liberal voters. Indeed the *Evening Post* said that he was a man out of his class, who would have made an excellent Liberal-Labour candidate.[46] In the Labour movement at the time that public 'image' was an asset. He sounded much less frightening than men like Semple, whose political views later moved very far to his right.

His speeches were predictable to those who knew him; his theme—that the title to wealth should be service. The 'first charge' was given a good airing. He advocated free hospitals, 'the nationalisation of the medical service', and an allowance of 10s. a week for each child in a family after the first. (That figure was to remain in his mind for twenty years and, unlike most political promisers, he was to carry it out—and to include the first child too.) In general he spoke up for a system of 'social welfare', including cheap houses. He had seen that the Railway Department had built homes for its workers and thought that surely the community 'with scientific organisation' could do likewise.[47]

Although the local LRC had told him that in his electorate there was little interest in land policy[48] he could not resist expatiating on his favourite themes, land tenure and land transfers. He explained the iniquities of insurance companies and the power wielded by banks. He covered in detail the history of the Bank of New Zealand, which Seddon had saved from liquidation in the 1890s. In 1925 Nash wrote a pamphlet on this subject, *Financial Power in New Zealand. The Case for a State Bank.*[49] He thought that a State Bank, with an agricultural credits department, was a first priority, so that the Associated Banks should not continue to exercise their politically irresponsible control of credit for the benefit of shareholders.

As always, Nash was very polite to his opponents, and regretted that Wilford was ill and unable to join in the fight. The *Worker* boosted Nash as 'an idealist who knows capitalist business inside out',[50] (Haldane once said that politicians should be both idealists and 'men of business'). But the voters preferred the man they knew. Wilford won by 6,080 to 4,286 votes.

Though Labour's urban support was fairly stable, its number of victories depended on the vagaries of the confused, three-party battles. In 1925 the Labour vote increased, but it lost five seats, including two in cities. This election confirmed the lesson of 1922, that the loyalty of trade unionists and blue collar workers could establish only a minority party. Without support from tradesmen, shopkeepers, professional people and white collar workers the party could not even dominate the cities, certainly not New Zealand as a whole.[51] Continued defeat forced the party once more to move away from its pre-1914 doctrinal basis and towards the voters, especially the farmers.

Dan Sullivan, an MP from Christchurch, a former journalist and trade union leader, who was touring in northern rural districts in 1927, wrote to Nash that to the dairy farmers 'Labour means, not the political party & its ideals so much, as every worker in the Freezing Works who strikes for higher wages: the watersider who wont load his produce. every worker with whom they have ever had a difference, the shearer who hasnt done his job. . . .'[52] Clearly some very substantial shift was needed in Labour's 'image'. He also said that the farmers wanted to be represented only by farmers, and he suggested subsidizing the price of fertilizers.

The party leaders set about modifying land policy again. Another committee including Nash, was set up and a new clause was added to Labour policy giving 'Full recognition to the owners' interests in all land including tenure, right of sale, transfer and bequest'. Increased loans to farmers were also provided. The freehold had now been accepted, but the committee still thought that the transfer of land upon which state loans had been made should be subject to approval of the State Advances Department. At the 1927 conference even this feeble relic of state control was deleted after it was attacked by the Auckland MPs, H. G. R. Mason and John A. Lee.[53] 'Usehold' was retained only for lands acquired by the Crown for closer settlement.

In the discussions on land policy, though he offered to help the sub-committee, Holland played little part. His view of the farmers as capitalist exploiters was becoming an anachronism in party thinking. His biographer describes him as confused and drifting into a state almost of 'psychic paralysis'.[54] At most he could slow down the retreat from socialism. But the retreat was obvious. During the discussions on land policy Semple, Barnard, Savage, Armstrong, Mason, Lee, and others attacked the old policy. Nash, too, was losing his obsession with leasehold. In 1923 he and Bill Parry had hoped they could move nearer to the dairy farmers and create a workers' and peasants' party. Now he was coming to think about controlled markets and pricing for farm products. In 1927, in a sentence which casually summed up central features of future policy, he wrote to Parry that 'the man who desires to work the land for profit can only do so safely with an assured market at guaranteed prices'.[55] Langstone, Lee, and others were, by contrast, talking not of markets but of credit reform as the key to Labour's future.

By 1926 the situation of many New Zealand workers was deteriorating. Unemployment was as bad as in 1922, and was to increase annually for several years. But the economic decline initially favoured not Labour but the old Liberals, now called the United Party, and led by the ageing and sick Sir Joseph Ward, supposedly a 'financial wizard' (though some would have said 'evil spirit'), since about 1894. He announced early in the 1928 election campaign that his party would borrow £70 million abroad, and rescue the people without recourse to increased taxes. It was hastily explained by his colleagues that this was to be done not in one year, as he had said, but over eight to ten years (which was about what the Reform government had been borrowing).[56] While Forbes and others were explaining the £70 million loan away, the Press continued to ridicule and publicize it. And the voters loved it. New Zealand's old-fashioned remedy for poverty —more debt—had a wider appeal than Labour's state prescription.

Nash again stood for the Hutt. He explained to voters that borrowing, even at the rate of £8 million a year, on top of existing loans, meant a debt which no country of New Zealand's size had ever dreamt of contracting.[57] According to the *New Zealand Worker*, at one meeting his sincerity made a 'deep impression' and his peroration was 'divine'. Several voters confessed to the reporter 'to a "huskiness" in the throat'.[58] But at another meeting a motion of confidence in the candidate received little support.[59] This time, though he reduced Wilford's majority, he was beaten by 6,858 to 5,793. The local paper said it was the biggest fight Labour had put up in the Hutt.[60]

The most cheering aspect of the campaign for Nash was that for the first time his family helped him. Lot wrote to his sister Emily that she should be proud of him. Wilford, she said, was 'what one may call a rotter and twister'. She added 'I think I have quite changed as regards politics this election. This election has quite converted me. I feel like fighting for the worker for all I am worth, Wal reckons this election has been worthwhile as he has us all with him instead of against him, Walter junior reckons he will come in from the start next time he helped election day [this time]'.[61]

The Reform government was badly defeated. United did handsomely, but did not gain a majority over the other two parties. Many city voters turned to United—in Auckland, John A. Lee lost his seat. In the country the new land policy produced no significant results.[62] Overall, Labour won seven more seats, but the results were very discouraging. In parliament the nineteen Labour men voted to put United in power and Reform out.

Like many New Zealand politicians, Nash was active in local body politics. In 1927 he stood unsuccessfully for the Wellington City Council. Two years later he stood for the mayoralty and was beaten by the 'non-party' (that is, in New Zealand terms, non-Labour) Civic League candidate. In 1933 he was elected to the Wellington Harbour Board and continued to be a member until 1938. This duty does not seem to have taken up much of his time.[63] By now he was a Member of Parliament.

Ward appointed Wilford as High Commissioner in London. In December 1929 Nash stood as candidate in the ensuing by-election. Peter Fraser acted as his very energetic campaign manager and Mark Fagan, a former Australian miner who was friendly with Nash, as election secretary.[64]

The campaign was much more heated than the earlier ones, in which he was given little chance of success. For the first time, he had two opponents. The Reform candidate, who caused Nash the most trouble and the least damage, was Harold Johnston. Hobday wrote from Auckland, 'What a weird looking creature Johnston is! He looks exactly like one of the *vultures* in our Zoo here!'[65] Nash replied more charitably. The *New Zealand Worker* said Johnston had been educated at Wanganui College and Oxford which had 'left him with the attractive personality of a graduate of these institutions'—the writer thought him a Reformer by association rather than conviction.[66] The United man was James Kerr, editor of a local newspaper and former chairman of Wilford's campaign committee.[67]

Nash's friends worked very hard. Eight hundred names were added to the electoral rolls. A businessman called Nash had recently been divorced and the rumour spread that he was *Walter* Nash. Nash's advertisements were intended to squash this canard. They featured him with his family. His pamphlet revealed a bespectacled and possibly severe man, looking more like a schoolmaster than a Labour agitator. He informed electors that from his business experience and after a close study of political economy and finance, he was satisfied that 'proposals which are ethically sound can be practically carried out'.

At Nash's first meeting, in Petone, the power failed and he spoke for an hour and forty minutes by candlelight. The hall was full and enthusiastic.[68] But at other meetings he had trouble from Junior Reform League interjectors. Allegedly 'a fleet of motor cars' was used to take them from Wellington to a meeting at Day's Bay. His loyalty to the Crown was questioned by an interjector, and a vote of confidence was lost by a large majority.[69] The *Hutt News* said he wanted to introduce a Soviet-like form of government.[70] Johnston said that Nash wanted to confiscate private land and repudiate interest payments on Post Office Savings Bank accounts. Privately-owned shops in Moera 'would be taken over by the State'. The country would be dominated by unions—indeed Labour men had to hand to the 'Trades Unions Council' a sealed letter containing their resignation which would be made effective if they ignored trade union control. All this Nash had to deny: Labour would probably raise interest rates in 'the People's Bank'.[71] The other line of attack on Labour was to ask how its promises would be paid for,[72] a tactic as old as New Zealand radical parties.

Johnston, however, had his own troubles. At one meeting interjectors denounced his party because 'They put us in a swamp'—a reference to local unemployed who were given relief work. The 'nine bob a day' they received was the subject of another interjection. The meeting concluded with cheers for Nash and Holland.[73]

Nash received 5,048 votes, Kerr 4,883 and Johnston 2,570. When the results were announced, the winner spoke at the Upper Hutt mayor's office, saying that harsh words should be forgotten and all should work together for good. A 'rough, tough-looking man from the crowd shouted: "You are a true Christian Gentleman, Walter", and he had tears in his eyes'.[74]

The *Evening Post* thought that Nash would be a moderating influence on Labour policy, while at the same time warning that the 'short steps of moderate Socialists', led to more trouble than the 'long strides' that extremists talked of.[75] William Downie Stewart, a former Reform minister and a friend, wrote that though United had tried to get their man in, 'the next best thing was that you should have it on grounds personal to yourself & not political. . . .'[76] Ahearn wrote that Walter would probably be Minister of Finance within twelve months.[77] His old friend 'Hitch' went further: 'I have named you as the future Prime Minister of New Zealand, so look to it'.[78] Such remarks were not the merely conventional flattery of friends. He inspired many people with a genuine faith.

VII

International Relations, Electoral Affairs, and Private Life

1922-32

Walter Nash was a political being; he lived and thrived in the atmosphere of politics. As for most successful politicians, perhaps most successful people, his interests were his work; his work was his daily bread and nightly dreams. He was very single-minded; his actions were integrated in pursuit of his goals. Most of his non-political activities were related to and assisted the central one. Even so it would be wrong to imply, what was said of Richard John Seddon, that he had no other interests but politics. Nash led a very full life all his life.

Even in his middle age (he was forty-seven when elected to parliament) he had a real gift for getting on with people. In the nineteen-twenties and thirties there was a wide range of individuals with whom he corresponded or whom he saw frequently. He knew all the leading men of the left wing, most of the Anglican leaders, most of the activists of radical or Christian persuasion who were working in whatever way to improve society, most of the small groups whose intellectual interests included economics or politics. Indeed he knew most of the Dominion's intellectuals, few as they may have been, in universities, churches, journalism or the professions. It is hard to think of any notable people in such spheres who do not appear in his correspondence.

J. B. Condliffe, the economic historian, had known him since WEA days. He knew G. H. Scholefield and W. T. G. Airey, another historian and active Christian, and sold his book, *Onward*.[1] Donald Grant, a friend of Airey, and secretary of the Student Christian Movement, was another acquaintance. John Malton Murray, secretary of the New Zealand Alliance (for the prohibition of alcohol), was a close friend. Anything like a complete list might read like a *Who's Who*. He did not, however, seem to know scientists, who were few, or poets, who were fewer and perhaps raffish.

Some of the people he knew in the nineteen-twenties and early thirties became trusted advisers. These included A. G. B. (Allan) Fisher, Professor of Economics at Otago. In 1929 Nash was his best man. Nash later wrote

that he was one of 'the quietest, and most clear-headed thinkers' he had
known.[2] Another friend was the young economist, R. M. (Dick) Campbell,
who went off to the London School of Economics to get his doctorate in
1927. He wrote thanking Nash 'for your manifold kindness, your helpful
advice, and inspiration'.[3] From London he wrote long chatty letters. He told
Nash that the High Commissioner, Sir James Parr, was 'a menace to the
peace of the world. . . .' When Wilford succeeded Parr he asked, 'could
you imagine any greater farce than linking that bounder with the League
of Nations?'[4] In 1930 Nash tried to get Campbell back to replace him as
secretary of the Labour Party, but instead he joined J. G. Coates's staff.
He became a close friend and Nash often called on him in Coates's office.
Coates never complained. Back in London in the later thirties, he sent Nash
lists of all the latest books on politics, housing, or world food problems and
selected £50 worth of books a year for him.[5] Such people helped to keep
Nash in touch with the intellectual world of economics and history. Within
New Zealand he was himself an active member of the intellectual
community.

His church work continued without flagging. In 1923 he was elected to
the executive of the CEMS.[6] He often spoke to student groups—for instance
at the Auckland University College on 'The S.C.M.—Its Value and
Methods', in 1924. On another occasion, in 1928, he spoke to the SCM
conference at Waitaki on 'The Pacific, the Gospel and the Future'. Something of the atmosphere of these conferences may be gathered from a letter
Hobday wrote to Nash about a conference in 1925. He said that the students
'were all as keen as mustard on doing something the very next minute for
the Kingdom of God . . .' but that they did not realize 'what they were up
against'. Nash replied, 'They are certainly tackling heavy subjects, but there
is a tremendous lifting power on the spiritual side of the average human.'[7]
The SCM was a centre of left wing, especially Christian Socialist, thinking,[8]
and hence an organization Nash liked. Many of the people he knew, like
Condliffe and Airey, were active in the movement at one time.

Nash enjoyed the company of Christian students who wished to practise
on earth what was preached of heaven. In the early twenties, when in
Dunedin on business, he used to stay at a cheap unlicensed hotel, the
'Leviathan', and often spent an evening with a group of undergraduates at
Knox College, talking about what were called 'social questions'. There he
met Arnold Nordmeyer, J. D. Salmond, and Alan Watson, all of whom
became Presbyterian ministers and influential citizens. He was the first
person whom Dr Watson heard speak of the right of every citizen to free
medical care. They discussed pensions for all who needed them. Nash grew
'very heated about the "wickedness" of people profiting by the wealth
created by the community'—the 'unearned increment'. Dr Salmond wrote
that, without using 'propagandist methods', he greatly influenced their
thinking. Dr Watson wrote, 'Our normal practice was to talk for hours over

such subjects, then have supper, and one or two of us would walk down the hill and along George Street late at night, to Knox Church corner. Then usually Nash would walk back with us to the Gardens corner, and not infrequently we would walk back with him again to George Street'. He thought that Nash 'had a quick mind, and expressed himself in a splendidly uninhibited manner'; 'Nash was so intensely interested in ideas, and in plans for social reform, that he sometimes gave me the feeling that these concerned him more than people. In my recollection I would say that his passion was more evident than his compassion'.

Throughout his life, Dr Salmond wrote, Nash believed that to care for the world's hungry peoples, at home or abroad, was the mark, not of a Christian but of a civilized society.[9] This life-long concern, and Nash's pacifism, involved him in a keen study of international relations. This was an interest which he shared with Fraser and with Holland, who wrote pamphlets on the government's treatment of the Samoans. (When his colleagues tried to dissuade Holland from putting an item on Samoa in an election manifesto because it would not be politically helpful, Holland protested, 'But it's right!' John A. Lee thought that Holland offended British patriots by saying that Samoa was not British, and told him that 'he had a Samoan complex'.[10]) An interest in world affairs—foreign policy —would not be worthy of remark of politicians in many countries, but it was very unusual indeed in the small New Zealand community, complacent in its Britishness and ignorance of the outside world.

When the Institute of Pacific Relations (an offshoot of the American institute) was founded in Wellington in 1926, largely on the initiative of J. B. Condliffe and J. B. Gow, a Member of the Legislative Council, Nash became an original member of its council. He served for a time as Wellington chairman and as a national vice-president, and he helped to start a branch in Otago.[11] It was an organization devoted to studying the problems of the Pacific basin and, hopefully and indirectly, to contributing to their solution. Scholefield, Condliffe, and Nash were among the handful of New Zealanders interested in Pacific affairs, other than in the construction of a large British naval base in Singapore. Even New Zealand's unhappy record as the mandatory power in Western Samoa, where there was a revolt in 1929, aroused little public concern. Nash collected statistics on the populations and areas of Pacific countries; he wrote to the Mexican Director of Education for books on his country.[12]

William Downie Stewart, who had been a minister in Massey's government and in the Coalition, 1931-3, helped to start a branch of the (British) Institute of International Affairs in Wellington in 1934. He became the first president and Mr A. D. McIntosh, then a parliamentary librarian, became the secretary (as also of the IPR). Nash wrote the letter inviting people to the first meeting, at which he was one of the speakers.[13] In such a small community these bodies were almost indistinguishable. Nash was also an active member of the Council of the League of Nations Union, started in Christchurch by Condliffe and Airey, and often addressed its meetings.[14]

These interests brought Nash two of his most memorable experiences of that time. In 1927 he led the New Zealand delegation to the second Institute of Pacific Relations Conference, which met in Honolulu. The other leading delegates were an Auckland lawyer, Hollis Cocker, and Dr Peter Buck (Te Rangihiroa). The latter, one of the most distinguished Maoris of modern times, already lived in Hawaii, where he was an anthropologist in the Bishop Museum. So did J. B. Condliffe, now research secretary of the IPR. The New Zealand delegation was thus a strong one.

On board the RMS *Aorangi* the New Zealand and some of the Australian delegates met to study the data papers for the conference. At Hawaii they were greeted by Condliffe. There was plenty of time for sightseeing. Nash was taken to sea in an outrigger which was swamped a mile out. It took half an hour to bail it out. The Hawaiians seemed to think this was fun but Nash's feelings were less positive.[15]

At the first session Peter Buck brought the house down with his oratory and Maori chants. After Nash's opening statement, he wrote to Lot, dozens came up and said 'how interesting' or 'instructive'. He only wished he had been able to express his own thoughts and not to interpret New Zealand's —a wish which was greatly to increase on his return home.

He became friendly with a large number of delegates, many of them academics, including Japanese and Chinese. Much of the discussion centred on China's problems, which greatly impressed Nash. He said in his main speech that, with the rise of Asian industries, British exports would decline, and therefore the buying power of the British would decline, so New Zealand would suffer too. For New Zealand to achieve 'a readjustment of exports' might take a long time—a sentiment valid nearly fifty years later.[16]

Meeting educated Asians, and people like Buck, made a permanent impression on Nash, whose previous experience of non-Europeans was very limited. On his return he wrote that we should all 'look behind the mask of race and colour and nation. Our natural reaction to persons of another colour, another language, other physical features is one of aversion, but if we look beyond the barrier of colour we shall find as many beautiful souls underneath coloured skins as under white'.[17] After his return he opposed racial discrimination in immigration policy.[18]

Nash's main statement, reported and then published in a book edited by Condliffe, got him into hot water at home. He rehearsed the arguments for and against constructing a great naval base at Singapore, towards which the government had offered to contribute £1 million. He tried to do this fairly —the security of the Pacific, and the defence of Australia and New Zealand, required the presence of a British fleet; on the other hand, the base would seem a potential source of aggression.[19] He said twice that the majority of New Zealanders supported the government's policy.

The objectivity aimed at by the IPR was not altogether compatible with the duties of the Labour Party secretary. The Minister of Justice, F. J. Rolleston, brought Nash's statement up in the House and taunted Holland into saying that the Labour movement utterly repudiated Nash's statement. Holland's own speech strongly opposed the base, seeing it as a 'war gesture', and affirming that 'human nature' was not warlike: 'Warfare is not the reflection of what is human in nature'. He quoted the London *Spectator* on the difficulties of getting a fleet to Singapore and supplying it once there.[20] Nash had to make a public explanation, that he had said (which was quite correct) that a majority supported the base because they believed it would be defensive. He added that in fact it would be 'the greatest menace to peace' and a waste of money.[21]

In this argument both sides were to be proven wrong. The left-wing idealists persisted in believing that Japan would not become aggressive;[22] the right-wing realists supposed that a British fleet could or would defend New Zealand although, even during World War I, the British could not maintain naval superiority in the Atlantic and Pacific at once, and Japanese ships had protected New Zealand convoys.

The next IPR conference in Kyoto in 1929 led Nash into a similar difficulty. There was some talk of his going, but instead he wrote a paper, 'New Zealand Labour and the Pacific', which the Institute published. Like his previous paper, it stressed how fundamentally 'British' New Zealand was. It expressed his idealistic hope that the world's goods should be better distributed for the benefit of the poorer peoples of the earth. Like other New Zealand Labour men, he saw the difference between standards of living in advanced and underdeveloped countries as an important, if indeed not the main cause of war. The level of the lowest standard of living in New Zealand, he twice asserted, was comparatively high.[23] Tom Bloodworth, a personal friend and a leading trade unionist, remonstrated with him: what Nash said was probably true, but a politician should not tell the whole truth, and certainly not the secretary, who might thus smash his Party.[24]

Nash was proud of leading the New Zealand delegation to Honolulu, and often listed the episode among his qualifications in his political pamphlets and in *Who's Who*. The experience not only broadened his knowledge. It helped to make him more conscious of the Pacific, indeed that New Zealand *was* in the Pacific, than most native-born New Zealanders many, if not most, of whom still called Great Britain 'Home'. In those days the New Zealanders were often said to be 'more British than the British'. More British than the native New Zealanders in one sense, Nash was also less impressed with the mythology of the local British tradition, which all too often ignored British poverty and class distinctions. His was not that idealized England. He was also much more international in his attitudes than most of the locally born.

Nash had another trip abroad, this time as an MP, in 1933. The fifth

IPR conference was held in Banff and a British Commonwealth Relations Conference followed in Toronto. He discussed with Savage whether he could go and he replied that he would personally approve, but on the whole thought he should stay in case parliament met during his absence. If he decided otherwise, Savage wrote, 'you may count on, at least, one friend at this end'.[25] Holland was apparently ill, and there were also by this time disputes in caucus and dissatisfaction with his leadership.[26]

There was a little rivalry as to who should lead the delegation. Professor A. G. B. Fisher wrote to Nash that he should lead it, as W. D. Stewart's outlook was 'too incurably that of the politician (in the bad sense of the term)', since he related everything to his career and would not be an independent member of the conference. This was rather harsh, for Stewart had just resigned from cabinet after a dispute with Coates over the exchange rate. This was the last occasion when a New Zealand minister resigned over a principle.

In the event Nash led the delegation to Banff and Downie Stewart to Toronto.[27] Once again, Nash met many well-known people—Professor Ernest Scott from Australia, Professor Zimmern, Lord Samuel, Arnold Toynbee, G. M. Gathorne-Hardy, Secretary at Chatham House, the parent body of the NZIIA. The theme of the conference was 'Conflict and Control in the Pacific Area'. As at Honolulu, the conference divided into 'Round Tables' (committees), one of which, on trade adjustment in the Pacific, Nash chaired. He also submitted a paper.

With his usual energy Nash lectured, visited Niagara, which Lotty and he had seen in 1920, visited Jim and Kitty Boylin again at Beaver Falls, met socialists, travelled to Washington and New York.

At the Commonwealth Relations Conference in Toronto, sponsored by the Canadian Institute of International Affairs, the theme was Commonwealth constitutional evolution. A typical New Zealand ultra-old-fashioned imperialist view was expressed in a paper by the Wellington lawyer, H. F. Von Haast. A draft called the Balfour Report 'a poisonous subterfuge'. After Nash objected this was toned down to 'the Balfour Formula shirked real issues and was largely responsible for the rapid disintegration of the British Empire'.[28] It is not clear who wrote this amendment, but it was still very much a New Zealand point of view. In Canada or South Africa or Great Britain it was more commonly thought that the attempt of the Balfour Report to define constitutional relations was aimed at preserving the British Commonwealth.

At Banff a Japanese delegate, Sobei Mogi, author of *Eastern Trial of Socialism*, asked that a Pacific organization of Labour and Socialist parties should be created to exchange information and help one another. Nash worked with him to draw up some draft proposals. The 1934 Labour conference resolved to proceed with this proposal, and the National Executive referred it to Nash and 'Big Jim' Roberts, one of the trade union leaders, to open up negotiations. On 31 December 1935, after the 1935 election, Nash minuted, 'No action Not possible to attend to now'.[29]

Though Nash had numerous friends, his increasing public activities probably left even less time for a private life than when he was a commercial traveller. When, in old age, he was asked about his home life, he wrote, 'Rarely at Home Except to sleep'.[30] That had been true for very many years. Consequently the boys continued to be brought up by his wife. And when he *was* home, their delight was not always unqualified.

His sons' letters to him are very affectionate, but at home he was a slightly remote, not quite a stern, parent. He made the rules; the boys obeyed. They regarded him almost with awe. Yet Lot had a bigger influence. Both parents guided their children by example and precept. Nash almost never lost his temper with his sons, and never hit them.

The boys dreaded gardening. Their father took no interest in it except that he liked the flowers to be in neat, perfectly weeded rows. When the garden was becoming overgrown Nash would say, 'Tomorrow we'll clear up.' That meant that he would work, and make the boys work, from dawn to dusk. He would make them pull out every single weed. Lot would be on edge all day on these occasions. When his oldest son, Walter, married, he refused at first to garden at all because his father had made him clean up all the hedge clippings after him. Nash would drive them, and never permit a job to be left unfinished. Once Les and a friend cycled to Auckland and, having reached Stratford on the way back, took the train. His father never let him forget this—failure, he thought it, or dereliction.

He was a fond father. He was very good at any ball game, and when he was home often took his sons out to play. He was, one of his boys said, a 'great kidder'. He could always say the right word to make them feel good. If one of them brought him a morning cup of tea he would say, 'This is the best cup of tea I've ever had in my life'. But they did not always understand how affectionate he was. Perhaps the fairest thing to say is that he loved his sons and dominated them. He expected too much of them, it may be, and to some extent tended to crush initiatives. He dominated because, while strongly believing in being fair, he also believed, almost invariably, that he was right. The family, by and large, had to fit into his way of things, his ways, his *rightness*.

Nash found it difficult to show his feelings, except to his wife. He loved children yet, one of the family said, if he tried to coax a baby it would bellow. He was both prim and proper. His oldest son would shock him, but generally his family avoided earthy language or stories. At the movies the Bloodworths and Lot would laugh out loud at risque jokes, but never Walter. Sometimes Lot would tell a mild story and say, 'Don't tell Walter I told you that!'

Only once could the Bloodworths recall Nash using any strong language at all. In January 1926 the Nash family stayed with them at their cottage at Manly, a few miles north of Auckland. (His Labour and business correspondence was forwarded by Miss Minnis.) A girl spilt tea on him twice and he said 'damn!'

At the beach he would go for walks, dressed in a suit and wearing a tie, but never fishing or swimming.

The Nash finances slowly improved. In October 1927 his 'liquid assets' were £656.[31] He bought a section for £700 in Aitken Street, near parliament, on which three flats were erected, which bore the initials 'W.N.' above the entrance. During the depression he had trouble letting them, and afterwards kept the rents far lower than the market rate. In 1933 he had a bank overdraft of £1,894, secured by his insurance policy, a second mortgage on the flats, and a guarantee of £300 from the two sections in Brooklyn owned by his wife.[32]

In 1930 Nash built a house at 14 St Albans Grove, Lower Hutt, within his electorate, where he lived for the rest of his life. It is a pleasant, modest bungalow with an oak-panelled hall. Emily wrote, 'Don't feel guilty about having a new home'.[33] (He must have made some comment about the contrast between his relative comfort and the poverty with which he was surrounded.) The people who were to be his closest friends, Mary and Craig Mackenzie, soon came to live almost opposite.

Though not wealthy, Nash was again from time to time able to help his family in England with small gifts of money. He also lent more to his sons —and expected it back in full in due course. Although in many respects he was very self-centred, Nash was far from mean or selfish. Indeed, throughout his life he was unusually helpful to his friends and active in charitable works. When he was very busy himself, in 1925 to 1927, he spent much time assisting with the business problems of Edward Golding, son of the boarding-house keeper in New Plymouth. Though he had difficulty raising the money he lent him £100 to buy a chemist's shop.[34] His brother-in-law, Ted Hinton, suffered from mental depression and had to retire from teaching woodwork in 1935. Once, when the Hintons were having severe problems, Nash rushed up to Auckland in the train, efficiently coped with everything, and returned the next night.[35] In quiet practical ways he helped very many people throughout his life.

When Nash was elected to parliament the country was already suffering severely from what is usually, but in the case of New Zealand, erroneously, called 'the depression of the thirties'. By 1926 export earnings were falling; unemployment was as bad as in 1922—and was increasing.[36] Since the Hutt housed thousands of trade unionists, there was a high proportion of unemployed, a problem which confronted him in his electorate before it did in the House of Representatives. In New Zealand, MPs have always been regarded first and foremost as local representatives, social workers, and 'fix-it' men. Nash took his constituency work very seriously.

Every Sunday morning for years after his election, Nash held what his friend, John Stanhope Reid—later an ambassador—called his séances at his house.[37] Large numbers of unemployed people would call. Nash tried to see that they were offered more than sympathy with the endless cups of tea provided by Lot. Often a great deal of running about was necessary in order to assist people over their rates, their rent, their pensions. He had to call on the State Advances Corporation, local councils or landlords, for instance. The kind of problem that arose may be illustrated by Mr J. Perry, a man with a wife and two children, who in 1931 earned £1 8s. 1½d. a week on relief works, but was given work only three weeks out of four. He was £12 in arrears on his monthly payments of £5 1s. 5d. on his mortgage. It was arranged that he should pay 13s. 4d. each week that he worked. Nash became chairman of the local Rent and Mortgage Adjustments Committee, set up to help such cases.[38] He wrote to the State Advances Corporation about his scheme to arrange a sliding scale of such payments, according to circumstances, and wanted the state to guarantee mortgagors until the economy improved, so that they would not be turned out in the street.[39]

One very practical step Nash took was to assist in organizing a free issue of milk daily to the children of the Randwick School, who a medical officer said were the most undernourished in the country. A former mayor of Lower Hutt, Sir Alexander Roberts, agreed to pay for the milk and Nash arranged for a local farmer to supply it. Dan Sullivan organized a similar system in Christchurch. In the House, Nash quoted Department of Health statistics that over 600 children in 10,000 were suffering from malnutrition and urged that milk should be freely available to the whole population. In 1935 and 1936 the government began to subsidize free milk issues to school children generally.[40]

Nash was a very effective practical man. In November 1930 he convened a conference of local mayors and the County Council chairman in the Hutt Valley to discuss unemployment. They set up a Relief Committee which sought, in cooperation with Hospital Boards, Social Welfare Committees, and the district nurses, to relieve the worst cases of distress. It sold cheap food to the needy. In 1934 it paid £6,545 for food which was sold for £4,842. Grants from the lottery (the Art Union) and the government Unemployment Board subsidized this effort.[41]

In early 1930 Nash was spending about two hours a day trying to find jobs for the unemployed.[42] Work of all sorts was found, road work, gardening, and scrub cutting. At Christmas 1930 and 1931 he arranged with Sir Francis Bell to employ some men cutting gorse on his property at Lowry Bay. The Relief Committee paid half their wages. Fourteen married men wrote him a heartfelt letter of thanks for making their Christmas—much the most important holiday in New Zealand—possible.[43]

So many letters from distressed people were sent to the Wellington paper, the *Evening Post*, that it decided 'to exclude individual statements of hardship'.[44] But a busy MP could not ignore individuals. Nash's papers give details of many hundreds of cases. A few examples are not irrelevant detail, for those were the stuff of which the centre-piece of politics was woven. Cases like these made Labour what it became, a party not of socialist dogma but of 'social justice'. These are individual cases, but the depression was in sum a national trauma. Like World War I, it left scars almost permanent on the thoughts and feelings of large numbers of people, on society itself.

On 16 February 1933 Eva Scotson wrote to Nash that her fourteen year old girl earned £1 a week in a tobacco factory. There were several children, and their father paid no maintenance. That was all the family's income: 'We have no table, a chair, two boxes, and have our meal off a bench'. Nash was trying to get some clothes for her daughter.[45]

An elderly man, John Robertson, was deserted by his wife. He received £1 4s. a week in government sustenance, from which he paid her 7s. 6d. His wife had taken all the furniture and he could not pay the rent. Nash arranged for him to stay with a family.

W. W. Carter, a man with eight children who wanted a job, wrote that now the Hospital Board had cut rations in half he had 'been wondering all day how I was going to keep my wife and family all week. . . . In November I got £6.0.8 to keep the family on. I paid £4.4.0 of that for rent so you can see what we had over to buy food and coal, light etc. Of course clothes are out of the question just now. The amount of our rations this week were 6 loaves, 6 lbs of meat, and 6 shillings of groceries. Now where in H—— are we going to get more after about Monday when that is all gone. I am not writing this with the hope that you can do any more than you are already doing . . . but to give you something more to work on. . . .'

Nash gave away some of the family blankets. Lot got friends to donate baby's clothes. They went to great trouble to get medical treatment and a holiday for a sick child. When a widow's son was sent into the sanitorium (with tuberculosis), Nash offered his own coat. Whether or not this was accepted, he did take off his shoes and give them to a man whose own were worn out.[46]

Of the innumerable sad experiences of those years one stuck in Nash's mind all his life with symbolic force. At one of his Sundays at-home (Nash said over thirty years later), 'It was half past two. I had had nothing to eat. I had a cup of tea that my wife brought in, the same as the others. And he came in in his turn and he cracked up and said, "Mr. Nash, it isn't fair. Nobody wants me. I can fashion wood with my hands as well as any man in this valley, I have some knowledge of fashioning metal too, but nobody wants me". His clothes had been donated by a doctor and his relatives, his boots from the relief depot. "There is nothing on me that is mine. Nobody wants me" '.[47]

By about 1930 Walter Nash had become a fifty-year-old 'smiling public man' whose inner life became increasingly masked, inaccessible, in comparison with that of the young man who read Tolstoy and Ruskin. The public man never missed a chance of attending a prize-giving or any function at which he could identify himself with his district, and at which identification would be seen to occur. By 1932 he was patron, president, or vice-president of sixty-six tennis, boating, cricket, cycling, boxing, basketball and other clubs and chairman of the Boy Scouts' committee, not to mention the Red Cross and Anglican Boys' Home Society and the amateur actors.[48] Often his family felt a mere backdrop to his staged appearances.[49] Over many years Mrs Mary Mackenzie would drive him on a single Saturday to eight or so official openings or closings of club seasons. He would serve, kick or bowl the first ball.[50] Such assiduity, in conjunction with the real help he gave to people, earned him the highest electoral praise a New Zealand MP can enjoy—he was 'a good local member'.

Is there a contradiction or paradox in his somewhat inhibited personal relations with those close to him, except Lot, and his helping, and reaching out to, the masses of people? There was nothing false, no ulterior political motive in his helping of strangers. He not only helped, he could instantly recall the names of very large numbers of people. His interest in individuals was genuine. Perhaps we may see nothing more than a deep wish to be loved and to love—which he could express better with acquaintances than with intimates. If so, this was a changing aspect of his nature. For with his early close friends, like Hobday, the mutual love was clear and open.

VIII

'The Way Out of the Labyrinth'

1930-1

From 1930 onwards several months of each year were devoted to the life and work of parliament. Its affairs were not, of course, new to Nash. He had necessarily followed them closely and had frequently listened to debates, an experience only the most devoutly committed could voluntarily endure.

His maiden speech, during the Imprest Supply Bill debate, on 27 June 1930, brought up some of the issues which were to occupy and perplex his party and himself for years. He spoke on poverty and unemployment. Like his party, he did not consider that unemployment in New Zealand was a consequence of unfavourable export prices. He accepted the dogma that it resulted from increasing mechanization (and, a point he stressed in other speeches, immigration). The unemployed would always be there, because there would always 'be a stage of transition from one form of production to another'. The government and the community must create new jobs and care for the jobless. A mere 400,000 people, he claimed, received half the value of the national production of £121 million; 1,100,000 got the rest. There was a 'maldistribution of production', which had to be cured in order to get rid of underconsumption. He quoted the unorthodox—but non-socialist—English economist, J. A. Hobson, a favourite with the Labour Party, on the need for a better distribution of income. Following him, Nash saw no point in increasing production without increasing the people's purchasing power. How to do so soon became the main divisive issue within the party. In Nash's opinion it should be done through taxation and social services such as family allowances which benefited the less, at the expense of the more, well-to-do.[1]

The speech was well received in the House. The *New Zealand Worker* praised his clear and concise delivery and well-marshalled facts.[2] The conservative *New Zealand Herald* reported that he was forceful and thoughtful, fluent, and considered that it would not be surprising if one day he were leader of his party, for his ability was well known before his election.[3]

Although not a principal speaker for his party, as one of a small band he spoke very often. As draughtsman of various policy statements he had as good a grasp of Labour policy as any of the leaders, and could be called upon to speak on many topics. He was not then a dynamic speaker, certainly not in the same class as Bob Semple or John A. Lee as a mob orator. But he was very effective in the House, where demagoguery was at a discount. He became, in time, a formidable debater. Unlike the fiery Bob, he never lost his temper and rarely sounded irritable. Bob's spontaneous outbursts of picturesque language had great appeal to the mass of Labour voters, but less in the House, though even there his natural showmanship made him a centre of attention. Nash was always courteous and generous to his opponents. There were, he said, 'just as clean, straightforward, and good-living men believing in the road they are following' on the Reform and Liberal as on the Labour benches.[4]

Something of Nash's qualities and shortcomings as a public speaker are suggested by a letter from a Labour friend, a farmer, Ben Roberts, in 1932. Nash had spoken at a small town and made, Roberts told him, a 'magnificent' impression, better even than Peter Fraser. 'I gathered (which I anticipated) that your address had appealed to the highest intelligence of the audience, which was probably unique for political meetings in Martin-borough.'[5] Appealing to the 'highest intelligence' was not necessarily the quickest route to the hearts of voters. By contrast, Joe Savage, who was not nearly as clever as Nash or Fraser, exuded sympathy and warmth in cloudy phrases.

Another characteristic of Nash's speeches was that he loved verbally juggling with arithmetic, tossing millions of £s about. He loved details, especially facts and figures.[6] Bank deposits, land speculation profits, sterling funds, interested him exceedingly, and he had a remarkable memory for them. In speeches it impressed, but it did not exhilarate.

This is not to say that he could not on occasion be moving and move his audience. When he spoke, as in his first year in the House, of the 'first charge' on wealth being the care of the aged, the ailing, the young, the producers, he spoke with passion.[7] In 1935 John A. Lee (back in the House since 1932) wrote to his wife: 'Unemployment. Walter Nash delivered a very fine and moving speech which had in it a fine tragic period which however came near for a moment to bathos. But it managed to pause perilously on the brink and then move away. He had a large house and crowded galleries verging on tears.'[8] Lee was one of the best writers—and public speakers—in the country.

Nash's feeling for the oppressed was scarcely separable from his religious sense. At times a note of piety could be heard in his more arousing speeches which could sound variously, to followers or critics, sincere, parsonical, or sanctimonious. On one occasion John A. Lee wrote that Nash and Bill Jordan, a former London policeman and Methodist preacher who was a Labour MP, had made speeches about 'The Master', clever but more suitable, he said, for synod than parliament.[9] Nash's references to 'the

Apostle of Service' were somewhat frequent and on one occasion his
familiarity with holy names brought editorial reprimand.[10] He did sometimes irritate his religious political opponents by sounding as though he had
a corner on Christ. Still, his strong attraction to the idea of putting
Christianity into practice had ample scope, for his election to parliament
coincided with the worst poverty that most voters had known.

As we have seen, New Zealand suffered very severely from the
depression. Almost all its exports were sold in one market, that in Great
Britain, which was itself equally depressed. International terms of trade
turned strongly against countries exporting primary produce. Prices fell
dramatically and New Zealand's export earnings dropped some 40 per cent
in three years.[11] New Zealand governments had been borrowing recklessly
—the public debt was by 1931 22 per cent higher than in 1919 and double
that in 1914. It was said to be the highest per capita debt of any country in
the world. The fixed interest charges on this debt in the early thirties ate up
about a quarter of the returns from exports and constituted some 40 per
cent of total government expenditure.[12]

This situation caused enormous financial and budgetary difficulties. But
government policy added both to the problems and to the national suffering.
By July 1933 it is estimated that there were 81,000 unemployed, including
women, Maoris, and minors (aged fifteen to twenty), in all 12 per cent of
the work force.[13] There was also much 'concealed unemployment', large
numbers of people moving to or staying on farms, often living in poverty
and working for not much more than their keep. There was a drop in real
income of some 20 per cent over four years.[14] Possibly this was to some
extent ameliorated by people turning to non-monetary sources of income.
It was often feasible to supplement diet with shell-fish, fish, fruit, mush-
rooms, vegetables from home gardens, farm butter and other produce from
near-by farms. There was a good deal of bartering, for instance of old
clothes for food. Large sections of the population became in effect tribes
of hunter-gatherers. Even so, life was scarcely endurable. The effect of
unemployment on morale, for school leavers or job losers, was devastating.

The United (formerly Liberal) Government soon made it clear that it
had no intention of borrowing its golden £70 million. In a situation of great
hardship, especially for the unemployed, trade unionists, small farmers and
the elderly, the government's chief preoccupation, in line with current
economic orthodoxies, was to balance the budget. One economist has
written that their aim was 'closer to conventional morality than to economic
analysis', while another has referred to 'a sort of primitive morality,
requiring that adverse conditions be conquered by sacrifice and hardship.'[15]

Following the recommendations of bankers, of committees of economists
and businessmen, the government's response was to cut salaries and wages
and introduce new taxes, including increased duties, for instance on tea,

sugar, tobacco, and beer,[16] which fell hard on the poorer people.

The result of a deflationary policy in an already contracted economy was a further contraction of employment and income. Government revenues were falling, for instance because of a decrease in customs duties. The government's measures reduced demand, so that its policies encouraged a downward spiral. The budget was balanced, while export sterling earnings piled up in London for the lack of a demand for imports.

This depression was the greatest crisis in New Zealand since the Anglo-Maori wars of the eighteen-sixties, the slump of 1879-95, and the world war. The public political results were fears of unemployment and poverty almost incomprehensible to the next generation. The immediate political result was a dramatic transformation of party political alignments and policies. The Liberals combined with the Reform Party. The Labour Party abandoned almost all pretence of being socialist: indeed 'socialist' came to be the adjective applied to it by its foes, not the proud boast of would-be revolutionaries or social and economic reconstructors.

At first, after the 1928 election, the Labour MPs had continued to vote with Ward to keep United in office. It was, Holland said, a preference of bad to worse.[17] But as the government's policy tightened this alliance caused great stress in the Labour movement. Tom Bloodworth wrote to Nash that feeling in the Carpenters' Union was very bitter.[18] Bloodworth frankly sympathized with the Alliance of Labour. As we have seen, it had somewhat modified its attitude towards the Labour Party by about 1924, but its leaders, 'Big Jim' Roberts and Arthur Cook, still uttered a good deal of anti-parliamentary bluster. At the 1930 party Conference, Cook assailed the party for supporting the government and urged that the industrial wing of the Labour movement should dictate policy. There was much bitterness over this dispute,[19] but as the Alliance lost most of its following during the depression, it became more conciliatory. Tension continued, however, up to 1935.

Much of the party's effort was, of course, directed to trying to help the unemployed. When the government set up a fund for the relief of unemployment financed on a flat rate of tax (paid by adult European males), Labour's view, Nash said, was that the tax should be graduated.[20] He thought that the government should guarantee food, fuel, and clothing to 'all persons registering themselves as ready to work'.[21] He made many speeches on the problem, and joined a deputation of the Alliance of Labour to discuss it with George Forbes, Ward's lieutenant and acting Prime Minister.[22] Increasingly, Labour's efforts were also directed to defending the Arbitration Court, whose powers the government was dismantling. It provided at least a partial protection for the workers' wages.

Some Labour men were growing restive at these piecemeal efforts. W. E. Barnard, a lawyer who was the Member for Napier, wrote to Nash that the party should announce its policy. Nash replied that there was so much urgency in coping with actual distress that it was difficult to get down to the work of drawing up a constructive programme.[23]

Labour cannot be blamed, perhaps, for having no convincing positive proposals for dealing with an unforeseen and unprecedented calamity. But the question went much further: what should replace the confident socialist religion of the nineteen-tens? Labour had become a working-class party without a message.

It did soon begin to move in a new direction arising from the fact that the depression and the unemployment could scarcely, any longer, be blamed on inventions and immigration, but must somehow be seen (a point which could scarcely have escaped a Marxist) as related to the capitalist system. Marxism was not, however, to be the instrument of enlightenment.

In 1931 the parliamentary party abandoned the government, now led by Forbes after Ward's death in 1930. It fought a long 'stone-wall' from 16 to 28 March against a Finance Bill which cut civil service salaries by 10 per cent, increased taxes, and enabled the Arbitration Court to 'review awards' (that is, as it was to do, make a general reduction of 10 per cent in wages). Eventually the government had to apply the closure.[24] Labour's view was that it was necessary to meet the depression by expanding consumer demand through a redistribution of national income, not by deflation.[25]

In August J. G. Coates, the Leader of the Opposition, moved for an inter-party conference to draw up an economic plan. The government and Labour agreed. Holland, Savage, and James McCombs sat on the committee, which took evidence for several weeks. Forbes then demanded that the elections be postponed and an all-party (national) government be formed. He admitted to the committee that if the government introduced the drastic economies he thought necessary, it would be committing electoral suicide.[26] The outcome was that United and Reform formed a Coalition government (and eventually their parties coalesced into the modern National Party). Holland became Leader of the Opposition. The way was open to a Labour government.

On the day the Coalition was announced, Holland made a pronouncement on policy which marked a clear shift of emphasis.[27] The revised policy was not socialism but the revival of the capitalist economy under state direction. The drop in world prices was attributed to 'monetary causes', and a monetary solution was proffered. The state should completely control credit and currency through a Reserve Bank. It was necessary to increase wages and hence effective demand. Credit must be used to create employment and get the economy moving forwards again. There must be a bold policy of developing primary and secondary industries, if necessary, in the case of the latter, by giving state financial assistance.

Other points were that overseas marketing should be regulated through bilateral bulk purchase trade agreements. Labour also hoped to pay farmers a guaranteed price based on average prices for primary produce over a five-yearly period.

The policy was explained in Holland's Address-in-Reply speech in September 1932,[28] which was published by the Clarté Book Shop as a pamphlet, *The Way out of the Labyrinth*. He said that currency reform alone could not end unemployment, but must play a part in a scheme of social and industrial reconstruction. He quoted Keynes and other economists to argue that increased purchasing power, not deflation, was what was needed. Though he thought the issue of bank notes, based on the volume of goods and services, could be increased, he was not advocating inflation, but state control of credit.

It is in the nature of committee or party policies that it is often very difficult to say exactly who is responsible for a particular point or emphasis. What is certain is that the new policy was that of the MPs: it was not endorsed by the party until the 1933 conference.[29] It was hammered out— and there would have been a good deal of hammering—in caucus, in 1930 and 1931. The policy was adumbrated in the parliamentary Labour Party's report to conference in 1930.[30] This statement was produced after a special caucus meeting in February 1930, which was probably the first Nash attended. It must have been discussed at further caucuses, before Holland announced it in the House, but no minutes have survived.

It seems likely that Holland's contribution was slight. He persisted in believing that capitalism was near to collapse. In his address to the 1930 conference the president, James Thorn, had repudiated this view and urged that party policy should not follow theories but respond to immediate problems. Moderation and practical policies were being called for by others, like Savage and Bill Jordan. The party was turning its back on old socialist dogma and dogmatists. But even Holland was showing signs of a revisionist spirit.[31]

The main change in Labour policy was the emphasis on credit and banking. This was not altogether new. The party had since 1916 advocated setting up a state bank to reduce the cost of credit and—still an aim in 1931—to control the issue of bank notes. The historian of the Reserve Bank has pointed out the irrelevance of the latter aim in New Zealand, where bank notes were only a small part of credit. Nash had, however, come closer to the idea of a central bank in his pamphlet, *Financial Power in New Zealand*, in 1925, when he argued that it should control the level of credit in the community.[32]

But Labour's new policy went much further in stressing public control of credit. Credit reform had now moved alongside a humanitarian welfare programme to form the twin centres of Labour policy. The socialists of 1913 had become an anti-bank party. Instead of attacking capitalism they were attacking, and intended to reform, its financial structure. And the aim was to cheapen and extend credit within the capitalist system. The 'foreign doctrines' of the 'Red Feds' had been discarded for a more domesticated product. Only a minority of New Zealanders had—or have —ever voted for socialism. But cheap and plentiful money had always had immense appeal. Indeed overseas loans and credit had been among the main threads from which New Zealand politics were woven. In the 1880s a State Bank League and in the 1910s a State Currency Association had sought easier money. Usually what was demanded was easier loans for capitalist farmers. Now Labour wanted cheap money for capitalist indus- trialists—socialist, state industries were not part of policy—and for the poor.

The new policy was undoubtedly due directly to two influences. One was such under-consumptionist theories as those of J. A. Hobson. The other was the views of Major C. H. Douglas, which had been spreading in New Zealand since the early nineteen-twenties.[33] Douglas noticed, during World War I, what New Zealanders could scarcely fail to notice during the depression, that money could easily be found for any wartime purpose, and asked why this was not so in peacetime. He concluded—and New Zealand Labour came to agree wholeheartedly—that production was not the problem, but distribution. There was a shortage of purchasing power inherent in the economic system. He invented his famous and absurd A + B theorem to demonstrate this. The Treasury would make up the deficiency. Inflation would be turned into a system.[34]

It would not have been surprising if Nash had been attracted to Social Credit, for some of Douglas's ideas, for instance his equation of wealth with well-being, with the general quality of life, had something in common with Ruskin. But he was not. Probably his leading thoughts were already too fixed to be altered easily. Several of the Labour Members were, however, converts in some degree, notably Langstone and H. G. R. Mason. There can be no doubt that it was this group which was responsible for the new credit face of Labour policy.

Some policies may be more directly attributed to their authors. Undoubtedly Savage was the source of a recommendation that internal loans should be raised for investment in approved primary and secondary industries. At that time he opposed both overseas loans and inflationary credit issues.[35] Later he could sound as inflated as the best of them.

Holland's biographer thinks that the 'form and approach' of the statement seemed the work of Nash. This is debatable—for instance he would certainly, had he had the chief say, have used the word 'socialism' from time to time.[36] However, as secretary, he had been more continuously involved in policy discussions than anyone else. He was one of the authors of at least two of the new policies which were to assume importance.

The idea of 'fixed' or 'guaranteed' prices for exported primary produce had a long history, going back to a resolution of conference in 1921 that farmers should receive 'guaranteed fixed, fair prices for their products'.[37]

Douglasites and their sympathizers, like Frank Langstone, referred to 'fair' or 'fixed' prices in the early nineteen-twenties.[38] There is little doubt that Nash found the idea in the proposal of the British Labour Party to purchase food in bulk at 'enforced standard prices', to prevent price fluctuations. This was publicized in the *New Zealand Worker* in 1924. In the same journal, in 1926, Nash wrote of the need for bulk marketing to ensure 'stabilised prices'. He was one of the first, if not the first, to refer to 'guaranteed prices' in anything like the form they were to take. In a letter to Parry in 1927 he wrote that the best way to help farmers was to support the Dairy Control Board while it sought a cooperative marketing policy: what they needed was 'an assured market at guaranteed prices'.[39]

This remark was made in reference to unsuccessful efforts by the Dairy Board to fix London prices in 1926-7. It showed that Nash, like others, was moving away from an obsession with land tenure to see that the farmers' real problem was produce prices. *How* to stabilize prices was the crucial problem, then as since.

In linking an assured market with guaranteed prices, Nash was already making the essential connection which the currency reformers missed: they wished to make up any shortcoming in overseas prices by issuing credit in New Zealand.[40]

It followed that Nash's other emphasis should be on bulk sales agreements with Great Britain. Guaranteed prices and bilateral agreements became favourite themes in his speeches for several years.

The idea of bulk sales was not new. There had been a war-time 'commandeer' of New Zealand produce for Britain. Holland and Savage and Langstone had favoured the general idea of organized marketing, which the former saw as a step to socialism, in the nineteen-twenties, when Labour supported the Dairy-produce Export Control bill.[41] The fact that the British Labour Party proposed bulk purchasing gave new stimulus to the idea. Nash discussed it in 1927. The party did not follow up the idea, but he kept thinking about it. In an article which appeared in 1929 in the first book published by the New Zealand branch of the Institute of Pacific Relations he advocated reciprocal trade arrangements between China and Japan as well as between New Zealand and other countries. In 1930 he wrote to Ted Hinton's brother, Professor W. J. Hinton, in England, that he had great hopes for reciprocal bulk trade agreements between Britain and New Zealand. He told him that Empire Free Trade was not practicable, otherwise he thought he would have been a keen supporter.[42] In the House in the same year he attributed the idea to Savage, and again linked such contracts with price stabilization in New Zealand. His arguments in favour of bilateralism will be considered later.[43]

Some of the phrases in the party's 1931 election manifesto echo the note of Nash's—or Savage's—sentimental optimism, sounded even in the worst conditions: 'We have wonderful natural resources'. But the emphatic stress on credit, again, obviously derived from the credit reformers, such as the president of the party, H. G. R. Mason.[44] It asserted, 'The flow of credit . . . has been blocked'; the Labour Party 'proposes to use the nation's credit for reconstruction purposes'; 'Credit is the first essential'. A central bank would be established to control credit resources. However, there was a credit antidote in the same bottle. The manifesto twice asserted that the necessary extra credit could be raised under existing banking laws. This enabled Labour speakers not enamoured of daring finance to proclaim, as Fraser did, that there would be no departure from sound finance, 'no rash inflation, no repudiation'.[45] However, equally, it permitted candidates to stress credit to their liking. In Wellington, on 4 November, Holland made an attempt to rival Ward's successful £70 million loan proposal of 1928.[46] He was not announcing party policy, and it seems that his political grip was weakening. The state would intervene to provide funds for development. Pending the setting up of a Reserve Bank, and under existing banking laws, Labour would raise £25 million in three years, partly by relaxing the laws regulating bank note issue, partly by 'employing methods somewhat similar to those adopted during the war'. He did not make it clear whether there was to be an internal loan or whether the government would borrow direct from the banks, but in either case credit would be increased.[47]

Holland had made a mistake about evidence given by bankers to the inter-party economic conference, and believed that they had said that eight or nine million pounds a year could be raised. Forbes and Coates—and Savage—promptly corrected him.[48] A much lower figure had been mentioned. The loan proposal seems to have been dropped during the election.

Nash's view of credit certainly inclined towards Fraser's caution but, typically, he tried to keep out of the internal discord. He did not stress credit in his campaign speeches. Again and again he referred to unemployment, government policies aggravating it, and Labour's remedial proposals, such as productive employment at standard rates of pay. He also spoke of land taxation and government cuts in education expenditure.[49]

Nor did he emphasize socialism. When accused of writing an outspoken article in the New Zealand Worker and asked to define his socialism, he denied authorship and said his definition came from a school Reader approved by the Education Department. He was learning a political cunning.[50]

An advertisement in the Hutt Elector got him into trouble. Immediately above a copy of Labour's manifesto, bearing his signature, was a Labour advertisement showing a picture of men pulling a harrow. It quoted Coates as saying that relief workers were cheaper than horses, while Seddon declaimed, 'This! In God's Own Country?' Nash denied having anything to do with placing the advertisement but had to admit, when challenged in the House, that he was present when these slogans were chosen. Coates said he was a past master at misrepresentation.[51]

For Nash the election was a triumph. He beat his opponent, James Kerr, by 9,187 votes to 6,364. He was surprised and pleased. The *Worker* gave him a headline, 'Walter Nash Gets Greatest Vote in New Zealand's History', the highest, it said, since single-member constituencies were reintroduced, in 1905.[52] For the party the results were not encouraging. Labour won more votes than either Reform or United and increased its seats, but it did not beat the Coalition.

During the campaign Lot was very ill. Her health had been indifferent for years and she would occasionally, as in the summer of 1924, go to Rotorua to bathe in the hot pools. Perhaps she had the beginnings of the rheumatic complaint which was later to become a crippling arthritis. Her doctor said she must stay away from the Hutt for she was on the verge of collapse. She stayed with Nell Hinton in Auckland, suffering from a racing heart, crying fits, and a 'bad state of nerves'. In Queen Street she felt that the buildings would fall down on her. She wrote to Walter, signing herself 'Your no help wife'. He urged her to keep away. If people lied and intrigued, he wrote to her, 'you would want to knock them out—and the chances are that they would knock you out'.

Their son Les had written firmly to his father (much more so than the boys usually did) after the first session of 1931 that he hoped he would now be home more often: 'Mother is entitled to see you more often than she did when I was home last.' And now, Les wrote to Lotty that at last Dad had decided to have a holiday. They went up to the Bay of Islands for Christmas and part of January. Lotty said Walter was 'as brown as a nigger'.[53] The election of 1931 marked a turning point in Nash's life. He decided not to stand for National Secretary again. A trade union friend, later the Mayor of Lower Hutt, Percy Dowse, wrote that his name was 'so interwoven with the party' that every year there was unanimity on who should fill one office, the secretaryship.[54] In 1932 he became a front-bencher, with Holland, Fraser, Savage, and the two whips, Dan Sullivan and Ted Howard. John A. Lee, Parry, Armstrong, Langstone, McCombs—and probably Semple—sat immediately behind them.[55] Nash became the main spokesman on finance. J. G. Coates, a former Prime Minister and, in 1933-5, Minister of Finance, now often thought him worth his shot. Sometimes they had running exchanges.[56] One of the ministers, Sir Alfred Ransom, said of Nash that there was 'no finer debater in the Labour Party'.[57] Instead of being a servant of the party—he would have said 'as well as'—he had become one of the leaders. That was a role he was not to relinquish for a generation.

IX

The Politics of Depression

1932-4

Probably no New Zealand Government has faced such grave and simultaneous difficulties as the Coalition did in 1932 and 1933. The ministers had some very able public servants to advise them, including B. C. Ashwin of Treasury and three young economists, R. M. Campbell, Horace Belshaw, and W. B. Sutch. But the leaders, other than J. G. Coates and W. Downie Stewart, were among the least impressive the Dominion had elected. Coates showed great strength of character, an ability to learn and to rise to the occasion. But he was not supported by his colleagues and became, quite unjustifiably, hated by Labour voters and some of his own former supporters. Property and poverty were at war, fear and faith-healing at large, in all parties and parts of the community. Government, parties, and society itself were torn apart in the economic whirlwind.

Early in 1932 the desperation of the unemployed and 'relief' workers found an outlet in ugly scenes. There was street rioting in Dunedin, Auckland, and Wellington. 'Special police' were enrolled and took part in incidents reminiscent of 1913.

John A. Lee and Nash blamed the government and 'special police' for the trouble. Lee claimed that he had seen the explosion coming, and he had marched in the front rank of the procession which led to the rioting in Auckland.[1] He, and no doubt others, half-expected worse to follow. He wrote to his wife of the dangers of a rebellion or even of guerilla warfare. 'Joe' Savage told him that 'he would like to see a spontaneous industrial upheaval. Not one provoked by mere verbiage but occasioned by revolt against existing injustice. "I believe it will come" he said.'[2] Such opinions reflect how emotional the situation was, how nearly out of control as in many countries. But the unemployed settled down to a sullen resentment against the government and the system.

Early in 1932 a committee of economists recommended further reductions in costs and also a devaluation of the New Zealand pound. Severe economies and a new sales tax were accompanied by measures to help the farmers. Mortgages were, for instance, compulsorily written down.

After a prolonged public debate the £NZ, which had already depreciated against sterling, was devalued to NZ£125 = sterling £100. This, too, was calculated to benefit farmers and exporters, since every sterling £100 earned brought NZ£125 into their bank accounts. Imports became correspondingly dearer. Treasury and most of the banks opposed the change. The Minister of Finance, W. D. Stewart, resigned over the issue and was replaced by Coates.[3]

Coates was the force behind this decision. He was not content to sit back and follow the negative, deflationary policies followed, for instance by the British government, and by the Coalition until 1933. As the first New Zealander who had been Prime Minister for any length of time, he was also sympathetic to measures of economic nationalism. An independent currency was a small symbolic step.[4]

In 1930 B. C. Ashwin, of Treasury, had observed that New Zealand sterling funds, earned by exports, were being used for Australia's benefit— and 'unfairly to the people of this Dominion'. Most of the banks were 'foreign', both owned and directed, and there was much hostility to them. A Bank of England official, Sir Otto Niemeyer, who was invited to New Zealand to discuss its exchange problems, suggested that a central bank should be set up to regulate the monetary system. The need for such a bank had been discussed in the nineteen-twenties and its creation had been advocated by the Labour Party. The Coalition government did not, however, implement this recommendation until Coates became Minister of Finance in 1933. He then set up the Reserve Bank, extending its objective to a more general one, 'that the economic welfare of the Dominion may be promoted and maintained'.[5]

Labour's response to these measures was mixed. It thought that the Reserve Bank should be state-owned and directed, not partly owned by private shareholders. It opposed the 1933 devaluation. Economic historians believe that that action was belated, but did aid New Zealand's recovery.[6] Nash argued that it was, in effect, a premium paid by the consumer to the exporter, and amounted to a duty on imports. Moreover its beneficial effects would be transitory, an opinion probably correct.[7] But the government's expectation was that the improvement in the position of the farmers (called 'the backbone of the country') would seep through the body social and economic.

The active intervention of Coates in the economy, while falling far short of Labour's wishes, caused him to be regarded by many conservatives as dangerously socialistic. Various right-wing groups were formed including the Legion, and the Democrat Party which contested the 1935 election. It opposed state activities and regarded the Coalition government and the Labour Party as almost equally dangerous. Much of the force behind these movements came from urban groups hostile to government measures, such as devaluation, favouring the farmers.

Dr D. G. McMillan, secretary of the Waitaki Labour Representation Committee (and later one of the leading currency reformers among the MPs) wrote a pamphlet attacking the Legion. Nash thought the Legion had fascist undertones, but warned McMillan against alienating its supporters, some of whom he thought worthy men—McMillan told him that 'Down this way it is being run by Reform Party Racketeers'. A Labour Party sub-committee had a meeting with its leader, Dr Campbell Begg, and others but could find little common ground because the Legion opposed 'party' government.[8]

Almost equally strong tensions were created within the Labour Party, which threatened its progress throughout the decade and in 1940 led to a split.

As in most parties, there had always been criticism of the leadership. In his first year as secretary Nash corresponded with some Labour supporters who were early converts to the doctrines of Major Douglas, and wanted to get rid of Holland. Nash tried to soothe them.[9] The deputy leader, Savage, was increasingly critical too, and thought that Sir Joseph Ward's illness (in 1929) was no good reason why the party should not attack him. He did not see why 'the illness of one stupid old jackass' should be an excuse for holding up everything (a view he did not take when he himself was a sick premier). H. G. R. Mason was also impatient with Holland, while John A. Lee, for his part, was contemptuous of Savage.[10] As early as 1927 Tom Bloodworth wrote to Nash, 'at heart I am not sure that we have even a Labour Party. We have a Savage party, a Parry party —a Lee party. . . .'[11]

Like most parties, again, Labour contained people of very different persuasions, originally more, or less, left wing, but increasingly divided on quite different lines. More and more, they differed over credit policy, which did not escape the notice of their opponents. R. A. ('Monkey') Wright, a Wellington MP, taunted the Labour Opposition with having a back-bench, Lee and Langstone, policy not supported by the front bench.[12]

Personal differences complicated the issue. Savage was keen on the idea, promulgated by Holland in 1931, of solving the unemployment problem by a compulsory loan, graduated according to income, to be devoted to fostering industries and employment. (Lee wrote to his wife that the idea gave him a pain.)[13]

Savage, McCombs, and Nash worked out a loan proposal which led to heated caucus meetings in March 1933.[14] Savage grew annoyed at Lee's interjections. Lee 'lobbied furiously' and ensured a majority against the scheme. Only the three authors and Fraser, Frederick Jones, and D. W. Coleman, voted in favour. Holland, as well as Mason, Barnard, Semple, Langstone, and Lee, voted against. By this time Holland was beginning to sound on occasions like a credit reformer—he said in the House that one day the country's transactions might be based 'on internal levels instead of the unscientific method of an export price-level', but probably his vote was more a result of friction with his deputy.[15] At least thereafter, Savage could sound as strong a credit reform note as any of them.

'The popes are in retreat', Lee wrote to his wife; it was 'a complete victory for the free money advocates'; there would be 'some sore sad hearts for a few days'.[16] As far as Savage was concerned, the soreness lasted to his death.

In a debate next day, though caucus had agreed that members could mention the loan proposal, Nash did not speak 'out of consideration for the views of the other members'. Holland moved that bank credit should be used for industrial development, while Savage spoke of the need for peace credits, like those in war,[17] a formulation sufficiently vague to support the caucus majority, while sticking to his guns.

There was a widespread acceptance, except among the politically and economically most conservative, that what was needed to alleviate the depression were some inflationary measures to stimulate the economy. But in what form should the stimulus be administered? Coates had tried devaluation. Within the Labour Party there was a widening difference of opinion. Fraser and Nash agreed that there was need for expansion. The latter spoke of a shortage of 'spending power'.[18] But they believed that inflationary measures should be carefully controlled. They could not swallow the Social Credit doctrine that there was a permanent shortage because of a congenital defect in the monetary system.

Nash was strongly opposed to extensive 'credit creation', fresh currency issues, and unrestrained inflation. He thought bank advances could be much extended—the banks' lending policies were very conservative. He inclined to think that much of the necessary credit could be obtained from local institutions such as the Post Office Savings Bank, State Advances, and the state insurance office. Basically he believed that economic development should be paid for mainly from taxation and loans, which should be raised locally and not overseas. He believed in balancing the budget, with which Holland agreed (although they favoured inflationary measures in other areas, such as guaranteed prices). On such points his views could be, and were, called conservative by the currency reformers, or by anyone who thought Social Credit was left wing. But he sometimes spoke in terms very like theirs. In 1934, for instance, he advocated the nationalization of all banks and said that credit must be controlled in the interests of the community as a whole.[19]

Nash had a much clearer and more realistic conception of how the economy in practice worked than did his critics. 'Our income is conditioned by the return we get for the produce we send overseas', he said flatly to the 1934 Monetary Committee.[20] It was not the only factor, as he realized. Nevertheless, New Zealand was exceptionally dependent on exports of meat, dairy produce, and wool, almost all to the British market. This was a fact which no New Zealand government could overlook.

The leading currency reformers in the party sometimes denied that they agreed completely with Douglas, but their assumptions were close to his.[21] They did not believe that the local standard of living should be at the mercy of overseas price movements—here they agreed with Nash. But they pushed that attitude much further. They did not understand, or would not accept, the extent to which the economy was regulated by its sterling funds. The 'sterling exchange standard' had been clearly explained by an economist a decade earlier,[22] when the New Zealand £ equalled the £ sterling, which was worth its face value in gold. For each £1 of exports, £1 was deposited in the banks' London holdings and simultaneously in the farmers' accounts in New Zealand. Overseas sterling paid for imports, and determined whether there was a credit squeeze or expansion in New Zealand. Thus, until the creation of the Reserve Bank, the London funds regulated the banking system.[23] And ever since they have been a major determinant of New Zealand's economy.

The credit reformers would have none of this. From 1932 to 1935 they pressed their own views strongly in parliament, in caucus, at conference and in public. H. G. R. Mason brought in several private member's Currency Bills to stabilize internal prices at pre-war levels, and wrote a pamphlet to spread his views. He was one of the few university graduates among the Labour MPs—he was an MA in physics and mathematics and an LlB. He believed that the depression resulted from bankers deliberately restricting the amount of money in circulation. It was necessary to stabilize internal purchasing power and price levels, which were more important than the overseas reserves. A central bank should issue interest-free credit so that the amount of money in circulation was the same as in more prosperous years. He accepted a version of the Social Credit doctrine of a shortage of purchasing power. He wanted to finance superannuation, pensions, and public works, plus the payment of a bonus to all producers to raise their income to the average before the depression, all out of interest-free credit. To support his proposals he quoted Nash's favourite author, Ruskin.[24]

Nash's reply was that there was 'no more dangerous philosophy than the idea that the issue of credit' would overcome their problems. The 'absolute control of credit' was 'the main factor in introducing a Socialist State, but lightly undertaken it may destroy the possibility of Socialism for a century. Lenin used the method to destroy the value of old currency and succeeded, but I do not think our policy is to destroy all equities. . . .' He did not think they should destroy the value of people's savings by inflation until the state could guarantee everything needed for 'a full life'.[25]

The proposals of the currency reformers would have grossly inflated prices and incomes within New Zealand, while overseas sterling funds were severely rationed. This latter point they realized.

Frank Langstone, who learnt his economics running the railway station refreshment room at Taumarunui, was at first the best-known Labour currency crank. In a pamphlet in 1934 he explained how New Zealand could fix its own internal price level irrespective of overseas earnings. By way of example he proposed that if butter earned 6d. per lb. overseas, while the average price over a period had been 1s. 3d., the farmer would be paid 1s. 3d. The farmer would then be charged 1s. 3d. for any import costing 6d. abroad. He had—he claimed—solved the problem of inflation: 'Naturally, prices cannot rise, under our New Economic Policy, above the stipulated level.' Fixed prices would be introduced, and interest-free credit would be created to sustain that level above overseas prices.

An 'era of free money' would be issued in. There would be no borrowing, no national debt, no payment of interest. Colonialism would be ended too. New Zealand would emancipate itself from Great Britain by establishing its own internal price level.[26]

Nash wrote a reply addressed to the Labour MPs (but apparently decided not to send it) simply pointing out that, while ridiculing exchange manipulations, Langstone was suggesting an exchange tax of 150 per cent. Moreover, Nash wondered whether it was practicable to fix the price of all commodities and services.[27]

Since Langstone was president of the party, his New Economic Policy attracted much ridicule and adverse publicity from the government side. The inflationary consequences of his proposals were easily predictable. Inevitably, he quoted William Jennings Bryan: New Zealand man must not be crucified on a Cross of Gold.[28] Had he been turned loose with his NEP the populace would have been looking for a golden Ark in a rising Flood of paper money.

Mason and Langstone in 1933 put proposals to Conference whereby bank credit would 'stabilise the value of export produce in accordance with the stabilised internal price level'.[29] The external economic facts were to conform to the internal situation. The party did not join them. But they had many supporters, notably John A. Lee, who was as good as them at ridiculing the 'inflation bogey', and arguing that the use of Reserve Bank credit would free the country from 'capitalist debt'.[30] But to attack banks had now become the favourite pastime of all the Labour men. Banks 'created credit': this mere truism became an accusation. It was like charging hens with laying eggs.

The new policy was extremely attractive to large numbers of people who had not been Labour and would not have been attracted to socialism. Not only the unemployed, but farmers weighed down by mortgages and many other people agreed with Mason's simplistic summary: 'the trouble is that money is lacking'. Previously Douglas's views had been of interest mainly to small discussion groups, but now politicians, doctors, ministers, teachers, even poets like A. R. D. Fairburn, received 'Douglasism' as a new religion. In 1932 the Social Credit Movement held its first national meeting and set up a national organization to spread the gospel.[31] Despite rebuff and ridicule, its persistence ever since is significant in the context of New Zealand politics. It has offered plenty for nothing. It has been the country's Aladdin's Lamp, golden-egged goose, state lottery, and 'cargo cult'.

The Labour leaders were of course perfectly conscious of Social Credit's growing appeal. Mason wrote to the assistant secretary, Dave Wilson, in 1933 that the movement was going through Auckland like a plague. They would have to convince its adherents that Labour would give Shylock short shrift.[32] Lee, too, stressed the need to placate or attract them.[33] One Labour Party member said that 'Douglasism' was an 'avalanche'. He thought Labour should add the word 'Social' to its credit policy statement.[34] Social Creditors, with no political party of their own, pressed the Labour party from within and without. One of the Labour credit reformers, W. E. Barnard, wrote to James Thorn in 1932 that five of the branches near Napier wanted Labour to adopt a Social Credit policy. When Douglas visited New Zealand in 1934 Barnard thought the party should welcome him, but the Executive rejected the idea.[35] However, the leaders were as conciliatory as possible. Nash wrote to one devotee that Douglas had made 'a splendid contribution towards the reconstruction of our Monetary system', but he could not quite accept his proposed method of 'putting the matter in order'.[36] In 1933 a Social Creditor was allowed to address the Labour conference.[37] In 1932 Nash, Savage, and Jordan held a meeting with the members of the (Social Credit) Auckland branch of the Farmers' Union. The chairman was Colonel S. J. E. Closey, leader of the Social Credit Movement. They passed resolutions on the need for public control of the financial system, and increased payments to farmers and workers and unemployed.[38] A loose, unofficial alliance was formed, which lasted until about 1936. This gave Labour an extra organization, with touring lecturers spreading a gospel rather like Labour's.[39]

Being in opposition, amidst the terrible scenes of the depression, created powerful motives for unity. The conflict of opinions had somehow to be contained. This was what Nash, always conciliatory, was good at. At the 1933 conference, a month after the caucus dispute over internal loans, a Policy Committee produced a report which was adopted. In effect it superseded the old 'Platform' with its socialist 'Objective',[40] and became the basis of the 1935 election manifesto. Nash convened the committee, which included Holland, Savage, Semple, Jim Roberts of the Alliance of Labour, Mason, and Langstone.

The Report was drafted by Nash, but a good deal of what he wrote was deleted in the version approved by the committee and, as amended, by conference. He wrote of the 'transition from the present economic order to one of cooperation and socialism'. His references to socialism vanished.

The final version contained much that was pure Nash: 'The basis of all credit and currency must be production (goods and services).'[41] But altogether it was a victory for the credit reformers. The first point and that most emphasized was 'Banking Credit and Currency'. The Report asserted flatly that 'New Zealand can establish her own living standard'. No longer should overseas prices be permitted to depress it. The result of committee drafting was a kind of political mermaid, platypus, or minotaur, parts of various animals being tacked together in an improbable fashion.

The ambiguities in the Report adequately shrouded the discord in party opinions from the public. But there were in fact two policies. Nash's draft had the main points 'linked together'. For instance, guaranteed prices to primary producers rested on negotiated agreements for bulk sales to Great Britain and other countries. Exchange and import controls necessarily followed so that the required goods could be purchased under bilateral agreements. In the Report guaranteed prices were coupled with overseas marketing agreements in this way, as Nash always saw them. But the general picture looked different to the credit reformers. In their eyes, generous inflation at home would require import selection or exchange rationing to prevent the dissipation of overseas exchange because of over-importing. Both sides agreed that as an additional aim more local industries could be encouraged by import selection. In this simple ambiguity lay much of the party's troubles over the next seven years. But import or exchange controls, twice mentioned in Nash's draft, were not explicitly mentioned in the Report, either by accident of drafting, or because the idea would alarm farmers and importers.

The assistant secretary, Dave Wilson, wrote to Nash that he and Jim Thorn thought the document 'a splendid statement of our case. Neither of us feels competent to alter it in any degree. . . .' Fraser wrote that it was very thorough and concise. With his usual instinct for practical and popular politics he made the suggestion, which Nash added, that there be a definite assurance that immediately on assuming office Labour would raise the payments to relief workers.[42]

Dissent had been contained, but only just below the surface. There was dispute between Nash and Mason a year later over the Labour-Social Credit report of the minority members of a government Monetary Committee, of which Langstone and Captain Rushworth were members. Nash and Mason had been given the job of scrutinizing the report, which was very largely Social Credit. They disagreed and the matter went to caucus.[43]

Disputes over credit were influential in the line-up in caucus over much more important matters. Holland's partial conversion to credit was his last contribution to his party's policy. By 1933 the executive thought him an electoral liability. In October he dramatically died, attending the funeral of the Maori King, and insisting on climbing with the cortege the steep hill,

Taupiri, where the Kings are buried.[44] At Holland's funeral there was an enormous crowd of mourners. Nash had in July gone off to the IPR conference in Canada, and Lot wrote that it was the biggest funeral ever seen in Wellington, with three lorry loads of flowers.[45] In the absence of an election or of public opinion polls it was the first clear intimation of a swing of public opinion towards Labour.

At caucus shortly afterwards, Savage was elected Leader after Fraser refused to stand. Lot wrote to her husband: 'Things were not too rosy at the Caucus meeting. Barnard Lee crowd including Langstone were getting together to oppose Savage & elect Fraser & one of themselves as deputy, they did not put anyone up for leader after Fraser nominated Savage but they did for deputy. Cant remember what the votes were but Barnard did not get *one* Armstrong told Mrs Fraser all this. . . .' In fact, as Wilson informed Nash, there were seven nominations for deputy leader, but Fraser won on the first ballot.[46]

Lee was a very clever man and a powerful writer, but his bad judgement could scarcely have been revealed more clearly than in a letter he wrote to his wife at this time. He conceded that Savage could be very generous and likeable. He was justified in stressing his lack of 'concern or understanding of culture' and in describing him as a 'good old fashioned trade union leader'—to which he might have added that, as concomitants, he was shrewd and, at that time, tough. Lee was probably right in saying that 'He leads by following. Being unimaginative he has no sense of contemporaneity and advances with the common mean.' But Lee also wrote that Savage had 'not much contact with the mass of human beings'; 'I think he can be inspired but can never inspire'[47]—these things of a man soon revealed as the only charismatic leader New Zealand has ever had, except for Richard John Seddon, who had died in 1906. 'Micky' Savage, as the public called him, identified himself with the poor; was indeed one of them. Ordinary people came almost to worship him. In him, ordinariness became sublime.

X

'This is the Year'

1935-6

By 1935 Walter Nash was a very different man from the commercial traveller who had gone to New Plymouth as secretary of a small company twenty years before. People often find such changes, in acquaintances who continue, as it were, to grow, difficult to credit. And for many years he was talked of by some people associated with Bill Besley, in New Plymouth, in a hostile or belittling way, as the man they thought they had known, or the one they had heard about. But by 1935 he had acquired a public image.

He had been of importance in his party for ten years and was about the most experienced political organizer in the country. He had joined a group of ambitious men and more than held his own. Behind the scenes, and now increasingly out front, he had come, with Savage and Fraser, to hold the reins of party power. In part this was by accident. Others like Holland or James Thorn had died or somehow faded. Some, like Langstone and Barnard, lived away from the capital city, the centre of power—though this proved no handicap to Savage, perhaps because as a bachelor he was less tied to Auckland than married men like Lee. But character was undoubtedly the main force. Above all, Fraser and Nash had the seriousness, the devotion, the energy, the devastating, single-minded concentration on politics, which mark the successful politician. Others shared their idealism, but lacked the capacity to pursue it and to put it into practice.

It was becoming clear to the public that Nash was a figure at the centre of the political stage. Within the party and without, he was known personally and amiably to a very large number of people, not an insignificant fact in a small democracy. In 1935, after being nominated for the position by numerous branches and Labour Representation Committees (LRCs), he was elected president of the Labour Party, easily beating Tim Armstrong, the previous president, and other less notable opponents. Despite intrigue and wrangling, he was to keep an impregnable position within the party for nearly another thirty years, with massive support from both branches and unions, a fact important when recalling his vicissitudes.

In 1935 the party was in several ways in a very bad state. There was endless trouble in the branches. The Palmerston North branch had threatened to break away and form an independent socialist party. In December 1934 the central executive had dissolved it and suspended the LRC. This dispute was still smouldering. In Auckland there was a complicated row between the Labour MPs and the LRC, which was dominated by Fred Young, the secretary of the Hotel and Restaurant Workers' Federation. The LRC selected a weak candidate to contest the mayoral election against 'Ernie' Davis, a wealthy Jewish brewer, and it appeared to be working in the 'liquor' interests. It was very generally believed that he contributed both to union and Labour Party funds. At the same time Bill Jordan decided to stand for the Electric Power Board despite an LRC decision not to contest the election. At an LRC meeting trade unionists denounced politicians. Young said they were 'slimy', 'greasy'. John A. Lee wrote to Young denouncing his conduct and saying that he was 'collecting material for a Labour Novel which I shall one day publish . . .'—an unusual threat from a Labour MP to a leading unionist. Savage wrote to Nash that one LRC meeting was 'the greatest exhibition of hate against Parliamentarians' he had ever witnessed. Lee wanted the executive to suspend the LRC and select a new mayoral candidate, H. G. R. Mason, who wished to stand. But despite Savage's urging in favour of Mason the National Executive, including Fraser and Nash, unanimously voted not to intervene. They did not want an open breach with a powerful unionist like Young with a general election coming.

At the Labour Party conference there was a bitter dispute, with Semple abusing Young and even Fraser accusing the LRC of helping the brewers. There were accusations of bribery and a special committee was set up to investigate accusations made by Lee. Much of this was reported in a weekly paper, *Truth*. Such were the problems with which a party president had to deal.[1] And there were many others—for instance resisting the frequent offers of cooperation from the Communists and their 'front' organizations.[2] Labour had no wish to be associated with the Friends of the Soviet Union. Their overtures were likely to lead politically to the kiss of death.

Labour might not have seemed, at least from the inside, a party likely to win an election. Its finances were as precarious as ever. During the depression affiliated unions fell into arrears with party fees—in 1933 the Hotel and Restaurant Workers' Federation rescued Head Office by paying £100 fees for its 2,666 members. In 1934 the president, Langstone, reported that the Office was continually on the verge of bankruptcy: it needed £30 a week to keep going.[3] Even so, with its mass union and branch base, it was easily the most effective political organization. The Democrat Party and the Coalition of Reform and United, which formed the National Political Federation (then called 'Nationalists') in 1935, had only the most vestigial of grass-roots or central organizations. The Democrats, in August, were still trying to find a leader.[4]

Amidst all the pre-election pressures, Nash still found time to answer all his mail. A man who wanted to be an MP wrote in September, asking for advice. Nash replied with characteristic points, among them: '1. Cultivate Self-Control and determine to follow the urge for right purposes without giving too much thought to the consequences for yourself. 2. Cultivate the habit of thinking. Do not be satisfied with ready made opinions either from books or newspapers. 3. Study so that you have some reasonable knowledge of the purpose of Life. . . . 5. Remember that whilst you have thought out the subject you are speaking about, the other person's thoughts are worth examining and they may be right.' He was urged to study world trade, New Zealand's resources, banking practice and currency theory, and war and peace.[5] In later years this democratic urge to deal with every letter—and detail—was to become a pronounced weakness, but such attentiveness to voters was a strength in a vote-seeker. Nash knew this perfectly well, but it was in any case something he could not resist.

The 1935 election, which was one of the most exciting in the country's history, rivalled by those of 1890 and 1949, and one of the most momentous in its results, was held on 27 November. Excitement is difficult to recapture. The feeling arose from the depression: the depression was the issue. Such an election is the civil war of a democracy, no less decisive in its results for leaving the losers their heads.

The Coalition was in a desperate position, and knew it. In 1932 it had prolonged the life of parliament for a year. Members of the government admitted its unpopularity.[6] But it is difficult to imagine any New Zealand government surviving such a depression. Economic conditions were improving in 1935, and the best that Coates could claim was that the government had successfully piloted the country through the storm.[7] (The voters remembered the storm perfectly well but hated the pilot—might he not have charted another course?)

The Coalition began to look into health and national insurance schemes. Nash ridiculed this: the government had begun to investigate universal contributory pensions in 1914 and had been twenty-one years about it. Vague promises of welfare measures when conditions warranted them contrasted poorly with Labour's definite promises.[8] The Democrat Party came out with a policy of checking state socialism and introducing extensive welfare measures very like Labour's, while at the same time lowering taxes.[9]

Nash wrote two of the principal pieces of Labour propaganda. The main one was the election 'manifesto'. He sent the first draft to Joe Savage on 3 November: 'It's been a devil of a job writing it and you should watch out with Fraser and the others [on the Publicity Committee] that every word will help.' (The party had no paid ad-men, PR men, or other synthetic image-builders in those days: it had to roll its own publicity.) Although

Nash was the author, he thought it too long for a leaflet,[10] and certainly the four large pages of dense prose were not easy reading, while contrasting favourably in this respect with more modern specimens of Labour electoral prose. Interested voters presumably contented themselves with the summaries in newspaper headings and in speeches.

The main points were guaranteed prices, a statutory minimum wage, a national health and superannuation scheme, and greater educational opportunities. State control of credit was stressed 'to control the flow of credit, the general price level, and the regulation of foreign exchange operations'. The Reserve Bank would be nationalized. Reciprocal trade agreements were to form the basis of guaranteed prices. Foreign policy would aim at promoting international cooperation and the League.

In Nash's mind the main points in the 'manifesto' were joined together in a coherent policy arising from the Christian and humanitarian doctrines he had believed in since he was a young man. The 'first charge'—still his favourite phrase—on the community was to be the care of the worker, the old, the young, the sick. A statutory minimum wage, increased child allowances, pensions for the needy, and a national health scheme would redistribute wealth so that everyone would be cared for. People who served would receive an equitable share of what was produced. He agreed with the credit reformers that the ills of society lay in maldistribution, not in production.

The guaranteed price to farmers would serve the same end. Labour would give every farmer a guaranteed standard of living, he said; like the urban workers, they would have (a favourite adjective) a 'decent' standard of living. The economy would serve and meet human needs.[11]

The socialist 'Objective' (in the sense of public ownership) had almost vanished. The Red Flag had been furled, replaced by Nash's cornucopia of pink candy floss: 'The Objective of the Labour Party is to utilise to the maximum degree the wonderful resources of the Dominion'. Every person was to get 'a decent living standard', with an income 'to provide him and his dependents with everything necessary to make a "home" and "home life" in the best sense of the meaning of those terms'.

Nash's attitude towards socialism had changed with the Labour Party's. His 'socialism' had been tamed, though he still used the word. He said in Canada in 1936 that Labour's aim was 'to create a decent Socialist state' in New Zealand. In 1937 Nash said that 'co-operation' was the most beautiful word in the English language, as it was practised by Robert Owen: 'There is only a very fine line between the two terms—co-operation and Socialism.'[12] When he tried to define his socialism in 1943, it was almost identical with his humanitarianism: 'I am a socialist in the sense that I believe that a major responsibility of Government is to provide collectively for the economic welfare and security of the individual. But I am conservative in the sense that I look upon the family as the foundation of the nation.'[13] It could be said that Nash had never been a Marxist and that his Christian socialism had not greatly changed in content. Yet it had changed in tone. Nash's was now a sentimental socialism. So was his party's.

What New Zealand experience had principally added to his earlier attitudes was that he foresaw a massive role for the centralizing state. It was to have complete control of export marketing, as well as over the distribution of income. Before he left England Nash had believed in the benefit to be derived from monopolies and cooperation. By 1925 he was arguing that the whole trend of modern production was towards monopolies. He instanced the Meat Pool, the Tobacco Trust, the Shipping Combine. These agencies, controlled by one or two men, were inevitable—but it was essential that they 'should come completely under the control of the whole of the people'.[14] He was able to write blandly to a newspaper editor, Oliver Duff, in 1935, 'My personal outlook is conservative'. However, he believed that current economic trends were towards ordered production, regulated marketing, and more even incomes. These trends should be encouraged in the interests of the greatest liberty of the maximum number.[15]

Such beliefs and attitudes, expressed by one of so mild a manner, explain why he was regarded by some of his party as an arch-conservative, but as a dangerous and possibly lunatic 'red' by many more opponents. Allan Fisher wrote to Nash that some people regarded him 'as a representative of "sane" labour. . . . For the most part it means that while you say on the whole the same things as your colleagues, you say it with a friendly smile and without ranting or theatricalism'. He believed that these people misunderstood Nash's 'sweet reasonableness'.[16]

Nash believed that state-managed trade offered the best prospects for the world, as well as for New Zealand (an aspect of his views to be taken up later). It was from an inter-government trade treaty that guaranteed prices would be fixed. He refused to believe, what Coates reported, that Baldwin would have nothing to do with it.[17] The question arose, however, supposing Coates were right, where *was* the money coming from? This problem accounted in part for the embarrassing delays in the production of Nash's second publicity effort, a pamphlet on guaranteed prices. He was working on it in July. He sent drafts to two of the leading economists in the country, Horace Belshaw and A. G. B. Fisher, as well as to W. B. Sutch, one of Coates's economic advisers, to Savage, Ormond Wilson, and others. Some of their comments were hard-hitting. Fisher wrote to him that he would be justified in forgetting guaranteed prices and reserve bank credit and getting on with laying the real foundations of socialist policy.[18] The hardest problem, however, was not to please economists but somehow to reconcile the conflicting opinions within the party in a statement palatable to voters.

In August Nash attended a meeting of party candidates in Palmerston North at which he explained policy. He and Langstone differed over a section of his pamphlet in which Nash had asked what would happen if, over a period of years, price fluctuations had not balanced out good with bad years and there was a deficit: farmers had received more than exports earned. Langstone argued that the buoyancy of the economy under Labour would prevent this (as though that would affect overseas prices, instead of vice versa). Ormond Wilson, a local candidate, wrote to Nash, 'Mr Nash speaks only of orderly marketing, and the prices that must follow from that: Mr Langstone doesn't mention marketing, but proposes to inflate currency. (Thus the enemy).'[19]

The problem was not merely to find a verbal formula to satisfy the currency reformers. A wide variety of statements had been made by Labour spokesmen, within recent years, on how the scheme would be financed. The 'why' of guaranteed prices was easy; the 'how' was difficult to answer. No satisfactory answer, indeed, was known.

The financially more orthodox, like Semple or Fraser, were bluntly realistic. Semple said that the price was simply a repayable advance to producers. Fraser said it was a self-balancing scheme of price stabilization, the surplus in good years cancelling out the bad years' deficit. Confusion abounded. Morgan Williams, the candidate in Kaiapoi, was telling people that Reserve Bank advances to the dairy industry would be a loan 'ultimately to be repaid either by the industry or the community'. The credit reformers, of course, would have none of this—internal prices could be fixed irrespective of overseas ones. Nash inclined to agree with Fraser, but added a typical idealistic, humanitarian gloss to Fraser's realism, by insisting that the price would also be related to the farmer's costs and to his social needs: it was to be socially a just as well as an equalized price.[20]

While Nash revised his text and brooded on these mysteries, candidates wrote to him through September and October saying that since the guaranteed price was 'the bone of contention' they wanted to know what to say. He replied that only the extraordinary pressure of work prevented him from completing the pamphlet.[21]

In the end two sections of his pamphlet, referring to a loss in some years balancing a gain in others, and to the repayment of a deficit to the Reserve Bank, were deleted in the published version, which left an unanswered question, for in the draft it had been implied that the community would somehow have to repay any overdraft at the Reserve Bank, if accounts failed to balance over a period.[22] Now that question was ignored. This was not the only occasion when the 'woolly-mindedness' for which Nash was sometimes criticized was a result of political shrewdness, in this case to placate the credit reformers within the party and without. But there was more to it than that. The party leaders like Nash and Fraser were not sure how to finance the scheme. If prices received abroad did not balance internal payments over a period there would be a deficit. If (social) credit provided the money for the farmers there would be inflation. If the British would not agree to bulk purchases it was hard to think of an alternative basis. If the costs of inefficient farmers were covered, efficient farmers would reap a bonus and land prices would be inflated. But such problems can be left by political oppositions until after elections.

Guaranteed Prices Why and How and the manifesto were not out until early November. They were regarded by the executive as Labour's chief weapons—51,000 of the guaranteed prices pamphlet and 30,000 of Savage's *The Case for Labour* were distributed.[23]

As president, front bench spokesman, chief policy writer and candidate, Nash was extremely busy. Candidates had to be selected. The party contested seventy out of the seventy-six European seats—and had an unofficial alliance with the Ratana movement in the four Maori seats. There were seven clergymen among the Labour candidates. There was a high proportion of credit reformers. A certain amount of horse-trading had to be done. Nash and others had discussions with the Country Party, a minor, more-or-less Social Credit group. Labour did not oppose several of its candidates. (Two of them, once elected, generally supported Labour in the House.) The Country Party did not oppose some Labour candidates. Several active Social Creditors stood as Labour candidates. One of them, pushed in by Langstone against Nash's wishes, was president of the Social Credit Movement in Hamilton.[24]

Nash made an extraordinary number of speeches in 1935. For instance, in August, before the campaign began, within a week he spoke to six public meetings near Auckland, besides talking to branch meetings and a candidates' meeting in Wellington. In November, during the election, he spoke all over the country, on all aspects of policy. He was courteous to the enemy. He praised Coates's 'delightful personality'. He always had a couple of jokes. He always carefully handed out notes or a typed summary of his speech to reporters.[25] He seemed not merely tireless, but refreshed by new burdens and the anticipation of others. In those days a two-hour speech was common. Indeed, in some hints for candidates, Lee advised that two hours was long enough.[26] 'Hall' meetings were very numerous and well-attended—those of the leading men by very large audiences. Ormond Wilson, a young candidate, had about forty-two meetings![27]

Public meetings and canvassing were the main activities of candidates. There was little money for anything else. Head Office plans to make 'talkies' were abandoned and slides were used instead for advertisements in the 'picture theatres'. They could afford few large newspaper advertisements—only £576 was spent by Head Office on these. However, the branches in the electorates also put out pamphlets and advertisements. Some of the national and local publicity was very effective—an attack on the Coalition, for instance: 'Remember the Cuts'. Or a leaflet showing a child leaning on a school door reminded voters that the Coalition had raised the school entry age to six: ' "Locked Out!" For the Children's Sake . . .

Vote Labour!' Control of credit was frequently stressed. Mackenzie King was quoted on the merits of social credit and New Zealand voters were exhorted to 'Follow Canada's Lead'.[28]

Head Office succeeded in raising only £820 for publicity. Its total expenditure for this purpose was only £1,030. The national campaign was run by the assistant secretary, David Wilson (James Thorn meanwhile campaigning in Thames) and three women assistants. The total cost of Nash's campaign in the Hutt was a mere £94 2s.[29]

The Nationalists (as the Coalitionists now called themselves) ran many more large advertisements. Some of these showed a picture of Baldwin and urged the nation to 'Follow Britain's Lead'. Some publicized a run on the Savings Bank in New South Wales as a warning: 'Don't Let It Happen Here'. The Associated Banks weighed in on the Nationalist side, publishing many advertisements stressing the dangers of inflation.[30] But the Press was so hostile to Labour that the Nationalists scarcely needed to pay for their advertisements. 'Labour's Real Policy Exposed', the *Dominion* shouted, and an editorial was headed, 'TO GO OUT AND SMASH THINGS'. J. W. Munro, a Dunedin MP, foolishly said—though he denied it—that if Labour could not get a mandate to carry out its policy, 'then the only thing to do will be to go out and smash things'. It made him very unpopular with his colleagues.[31]

Labour had its own unofficial publicists. In Auckland an extremely popular broadcaster, the Reverend C. G. Scrimgeour (Uncle 'Scrim'), ran a weekly 'Man in the Street' session which attracted a mass audience for its progressive evangelism. A few days before the election his programme was 'jammed' and it was discovered that some Post Office equipment had been used, with the knowledge of the Postmaster General, Adam Hamilton.[32]

The Labour candidates spent little time denouncing the government. Their campaign speeches concentrated on Labour's 'Plan'. Most candidates seem to have placed their main emphasis on credit reform, as Savage did in speech after speech.[33] The reason seems obvious. The trade unionists and unemployed were clearly going to vote Labour. So Labour candidates tried to direct their appeal to sections of the community whose vote could not be counted on—farmers, voters in small towns, 'white collar' workers, shopkeepers. And Labour men obviously believed that credit reform attracted them. Lee wrote later that the activities of the Douglas Social Credit Movement were 'the corridor' through which tens of thousands of voters—such as had previously thought Labour 'too vulgar'—entered the party.[34] Guaranteed prices were also given much stress, especially in speech after speech by Nash, even in his own electorate.[35]

Labour promised. Sir Alfred Ransom, the acting Prime Minister, estimated that these promises would cost the country £30 million—a figure alarming to conservative or nervous voters, and a great underestimate. This was taken up by the Press. He also said that Labour would have to start a paper pulp mill to manufacture the money to pay for guaranteed prices.[36] Conservatives were frightened, especially by rumours of bank failures if Labour were elected. Though Nash had written in July to Fraser, who was in England, that there was no popular 'vindictiveness' towards the government,[37] he was mistaken. The unemployed and the poor were filled with hatred.

Perhaps no one fully realized the extent of the swing of opinion to Labour. Nash told Fraser that his friends were talking of a 3,000 majority, but he would be pleased with 1,500. Savage thought Labour would win forty-three or forty-four seats.[38] In fact Labour won fifty-three seats, a gain of twenty-eight, Ratana won two, the Nationalists only seventeen. Three ministers lost their seats. Nash won by 7,757. His vote of 11,873 was said by a newspaper editor to be the biggest in New Zealand history. Lee had the largest majority, 8,012. It was a famous victory. A political scientist has written that it was the first time in any British country that a Labour party had won office with a majority that enabled it to do as it chose.[39]

Previously Labour held only two rural or small town seats. Now it won eight rural and eleven country-town electorates, especially in dairy farming districts.[40] How far this change was a result of Labour's credit policies or of guaranteed prices—which Nash and other candidates constantly stressed —or of other causes it is difficult to say.

The leader of the Douglas Social Credit Movement, Colonel Closey, wrote to Nash in December enclosing a map showing the coincidence 'between the areas worked by Social Credit and the electorates won for Labour'. Labour had not done well, for instance, in Taranaki, where Social Credit had not been very active. He claimed that 'the Social Credit Movement was the cavalry attack prior to the Labour advance'. Nash was unimpressed and replied in a pretty cool note.[41]

Various writers have argued either that the guaranteed price or that credit reform was the decisive factor, but it is scarcely possible to distinguish between their appeals, or to know whether a large proportion of rural voters were simply voting against the government. Recently a scholar has argued that, whether or not Social Credit had been active, the vote for Labour increased according to the poverty of the farmers. The appeal of Labour and of credit reform was greater where farmers were poorer.[42] Whatever the reason, at last Labour had powerful support in the country. The Nationalists had been pushed back into their strongholds in the wealthier city and town, sheep farming, and some dairying electorates.

On 3 December, fifty-five very excited Labour MPs (including the two Ratana members, H. T. Ratana and Eruera Tirikatene) met at the first Labour government caucus. Seven members of the National Executive, including Jim Roberts, Dave Wilson, Percy Dowse, and Tom Brindle, as

well as two Members of the Legislative Council, Mark Fagan and T. F.
O'Byrne, and Rangi Mawhete, who had translated Labour's policy into
Maori and was soon to be appointed to that Council, met with them.

John A. Lee wrote to his wife as he sat in the room:[43]

                                                    3rd *December* 35
Dear Mollie

Savage kicks off and is cheered. Jas Munro on his feet protesting against the
manner in which a lot of those present today objected to his utterance. Not that
they objected to that but that old time colleagues blamed him for being influenced by the enemy to say what he did. A resolution of congratulations is now
being moved and seconded Sullivan, and Semple. Bob after a good opening
spoils it a little by referring to Harry Holland. This is not the moment. But
Bob is allready away from danger and is striking the correct note. But heres
hoping he doesnt strike it for too long. Alas Bob is getting back to Harry
Holland. Harry is our martyr. But we are up and singing. 'For he's a jolly good
fellow' As we sit down Tirikatene and his co Ratana-ite call a Moari greeting.
Old Joe hands out a few kind words to the Moari. Old fellow deeply stirred.
Cables from Britain, Australia, Forgan Smith, Collier, JT Lang [Australian
Labour leaders] and from Major Douglas. Rex Mason who had insisted on a
ballot in private conversation ups and recommends that Joe be made the
Ministererual sole selector. That intreprets the will of the meeting however and
it would be absolutely useless to even breathe anything against that resolution.
Joe will be sole selector and his judgment will prevail: No one will object until
we get to policy

                                            Love
                                            John

Over half of those present were new members who would scarcely have
known for whom to vote unless the Prime Minister told them, so it was
reasonable to ignore the Australian precedent whereby caucus elected
cabinet. In that emotional scene it was also obviously intended as a
compliment to the leader—one which would plague them all for years.

Savage went off to consider his choices; Fraser to talk to his wife Janet
about his own list; Nash to consider his own proposals, partly, at least,
while talking with Ormond Wilson. The leaders then met to discuss the
difficult task of 'building up a cabinet'.[44] Some of Nash's notes on this
process survive; parallel columns of the various portfolios, with the
Coalition minister and his Labour replacement. He also listed the ministers
according to the location of their electorate—there had to be a good
geographical spread. In the final list there were three from Auckland,
Savage, Mason, and Parry, and three from Wellington, Fraser, Semple, and
Nash. Lee, another Aucklander, was listed as Under-Secretary to the Prime
Minister, with a seat in cabinet. The other ministers were from widely
scattered electorates including the Waikato (Lee Martin), the King Country
(Langstone), the West Coast (Paddy Webb), two from Canterbury (Dan
Sullivan and Tim Armstrong), and Fred Jones from Otago.[45]

The Press expressed surprise at the omission of the Christchurch Labour leader, 'Ted' Howard, but the person most bitterly disappointed was John A. Lee. He had sat, in the House, directly behind the front bench, and he had hoped for a portfolio. He was not, however, generally expected to become a minister: of the newspapers in the four cities only those in Wellington included his name in their lists of likely ministers. He was, in the judgement of that time, very young. He was only forty-four. The average age of Savage's cabinet was about fifty-seven and none of the ministers were under fifty. Lee's appointment as Under-Secretary was welcomed by the Press: it would give him a chance to gain administrative experience and it was thought that he would get early promotion.

Undoubtedly, one reason for Lee's exclusion was that Savage disliked him. He had opposed Savage's loan proposals and his selection as leader in 1933. It seems that Savage did not want Lee at all. Both Fraser and Nash, however, thought he should have a place, and apparently they prevailed upon Savage to include him as an Under-Secretary[46]—a post not previously known in New Zealand politics.

When Savage offered Lee this position he thought it 'a joke' and refused. Later that day, 3 December, however, when Savage announced his cabinet to caucus, it was clear that caucus felt that Lee had been unjustly treated. On the motion of Sullivan and Barnard he was elected Under-Secretary,[47] which he accepted.

Fraser seems to have disliked the whole selection procedure. Earlier that year he had written to Thorn disapproving of the fact that in New South Wales J. T. Lang had been given the power to choose cabinet. He wrote, 'That means that able men who opposed the leader to any extent would be cast aside'.[48] He and Armstrong and others expressed their regrets to Lee. Lee wrote to his wife on 13 December, 'Only Nash has so far expressed no condolences but has been exceptionally friendly'.[49] If Nash had any reservations about Lee he did not show them.

The treatment Lee received turned out to be a great mistake. Some very ordinary men had been included, for geographical considerations, like Jones, or from old loyalties, like Webb. An able and aggressive man like Lee might more justly and more wisely have been given a very demanding job. To make him Under-Secretary to a man with whom he did not get on was worse than casting him aside. By January Lee was writing to his wife, 'Can see myself emerging from it all as the leader of the revolutionary faction'.[50]

Nash became Minister of Finance, Minister of Customs, and Minister-in-Charge of various important offices such as Government Life Insurance, State Advances, and of Land and Income Tax. He ranked third after the Prime Minister and Fraser, who took Education and Health, and was also Minister-in-Charge of the Police Department. Nash had suggested this—he thought the police needed firm control.[51] Dan Sullivan took Industries and

Commerce. Mason was Attorney-General. Semple was Minister of Public Works and Langstone Minister of Lands and Commissioner of State Forests.

There were six New Zealanders, five Australians—one of them, Mark Fagan, Leader of the Legislative Council, a member of the Executive Council without portfolio. The ministry was dominated by a Scot, an Englishman, and five ex-Australian miners—who included the Prime Minister. This mixture was not as surprising as it might seem. Up to that time very few leading politicians had been New Zealand-born. A high proportion of mature adults, say over fifty-five, were immigrants.[52] Moreover, the radical unionist movement of about 1912-13, which furnished many of the Labour Party leaders, had been almost entirely immigrant-led.

For Nash it was a marvellous time. His mother had once prophesied that he would be Chancellor one day; his friend 'Hitch' that he would be Prime Minister. Nor was he alone in that expectation, for Nash gave people a very striking impression of great ability. All sorts of congratulatory messages poured in, from many parsons, for instance. One man wrote, 'I know something of your passion for social righteousness. To me it is assuring to know that the one who is now handling the finances of our country is a man of prayer. . . .' And James Thorn wrote, 'The spirit of Goodness has in you a powerful instrument. . . .' Joe Heenan, the Under-Secretary of Internal Affairs, one of New Zealand's most influential civil servants and a close friend of Nash, was delighted; he'd known nothing like election week's 'fervour' since World War I. 'The great satisfaction to me personally lies in your rare amalgam of moral worth and intellectual ability and capacity for work'.[53] Nash was human enough to be gratified by all the adulation, though less susceptible to flattery than he was in later life. Savage was carried away by it all. By contrast, Fraser instantly detected and loathed any sign of insincerity or cant.

Not all the letters were fulsome. Lee disapproved of Nash getting the finance portfolio and had apparently warned Savage against him. Nash wrote him a Christmas letter—from Bulls, where he was staying with Ormond Wilson and his family. Lee replied: 'Yourself I pick to work harder and more serviceably than anyone. I don't think you are a Field Marshal but you have no superior as a Quarter-master General. . . . Yours will be the severest test. Apart from the feeling I have that you reverence a little too much outworn orthodoxy I know you will do the work of a dozen, certainly you will be 10 times as painstaking as I should be in similar circumstances'. Nash replied that he would look up the peculiar qualifications of the officer concerned.[54]

Lee also wrote to him over Christmas about his anomalous position, neither in the government nor quite out of it. Lee was treated like a minister in being given an allowance for a house in Wellington which, he said, betrayed 'a keenness to be kind', but Lee did not want to take it until he found that he had a job to do. If, he wrote prophetically, 'I cant play a major part in the game I shall at least tell the story'.[55]

While the Under-Secretary waited not too hopefully in the background for a role to emerge for him, the ministers were very busy getting to know their departments, learning the ropes, for of course none of them had been in a cabinet before. The main job was preparing to turn Labour's great promises into small print and action—discussing, drafting bills, revising, discussing.

Then there were party matters to attend to. Caucus had decided that if Labour were elected groups of backbenchers would be co-opted to assist each minister, and all salaries would be pooled, a democratic procedure meant to create the team spirit necessary for men about to bring about 'a transformation to a new order'. This was discussed at the first caucus in 1936 and Nash and others formed a committee to draw up details. This was a task much to his taste. An elaborate scheme was prepared and adopted whereby ministerial salaries were lowered and ordinary Members' salaries raised to £520—since the Coalition's salary cuts these had been reduced from £450 to £405. All other earnings of MPs had to be paid into a pool to be divided up annually. The Prime Minister received only £600 plus a special allowance of £350. Other ministers got £600; one Under-Secretary £550. Nash must have recalled his profit-sharing tailors.

The MPs were not in fact 'co-opted' but volunteered to cooperate with particular ministers, as Ormond Wilson, W. J. Lyon, and some others, including Nordmeyer, did with Nash.[56]

The salary pool continued until 1944 but the system of cooperation seems not to have been put into practice, though much discussed in caucus. Lee wrote to Nash in 1936 that some members thought they should sit in a minister's office to decide whether he should sign a letter or not. H. G. R. Mason wrote that 'there may have been an idea that there would be no difference at all between the minister and the helper except that the minister held the formal appointment'. However, he wrote, though the ministers gave up their extra salary there was no attempt to give the expected assistance.[57] In Nash's papers the only signs of this 'assistance' are a letter from Fraser listing those who had chosen to cooperate with him and a letter in mid-June 1936 which they wrote saying that they had no official status to give them authority to get the information they needed to discuss anything—in this case, new industries. They asked to be appointed as a properly constituted committee with specific duties, but it does not seem that they were given them. Nash was happy to reduce his salary in the interests of others, but it was soon clear that he was very reluctant to share responsibilities.[58]

The twentieth party conference in April 1936 was a triumph for Nash and the party. Its members and supporters were wildly excited. They were in power at last. The government had given a Christmas bonus of £270,000 to the unemployed and other needy people. Santa Claus had arrived—and indeed, Micky Savage sounded very like him. The Reserve Bank had already been nationalized—the people's credit was their's. Nash spoke, as president, of the years of trial, the death of Holland, the years ahead. Many of his powerfully obsessive phrases, or ideas, were paraded: life is 'maintained on goods and services'; these are the product of work: 'Work must be the title to wealth'. Capitalism had revealed the possibilities of production but the old order had failed. 'Its spirit—the spirit of acquisitiveness—has perished in its effort'. 'We believe in the full individual life'. 'Individuality —creative activity—home in the best sense of the word—These are the joys of life. We can make them possible by banishing fear. Fear of want— fear of old age—fear of ill-health—fear for the youngsters'. It would be up-hill, but the issues could not be shirked.

It must have been a moving occasion and an inspiring performance. This Nash could usually do well, rise to the mood of his audience. And in this case his mood, his jubilation, were theirs. The members of the party felt that they were crusaders. He ended with some sentimental, hymnal verses by the American poetess, Charlotte Perkins Gilman—which were threatening to rival the 'Red Flag', usually sung at Labour conferences, as the party's theme song. Nash had quoted them in the *Maoriland Worker* in 1923; they had appeared in some of his reports to conference in the 'twenties; Langstone, a great reciter, had used them to conclude his own speech to the 1934 conference:

> Forget all the buried and welcome the born,
>   Those that are coming are real,
> Plough for the beautiful dream of the corn,
>   Build the ideal.
>
> Changeless the past, but the future is ours,
>   Open for us to endow.
> Fruit of our purpose, proof of our powers,
>   Work for it now.
>
> All we desire is for us to create
>   Here in our hands, here.
> This is the hour that is never too late,
>   This is the year.

XI

Minister of Finance

1936

The depression had beaten the Coalition. Now it was passing away and, although there were still thousands of unemployed, rising export prices helped the new government to implement its policy. It did not introduce all its measures in the first year, but it went at such a pace that this could have seemed its intention. Later on a few disgruntled Labour men accused the ministers of dragging their feet, or even of not fulfilling their promises, but a more justified criticism might have been that they used up their ideas too quickly. Caucus was impatient for action, however, and spurred over-worked ministers on. At the beginning of the year John A. Lee got the impression in cabinet that Fraser and Nash hoped to postpone guaranteed prices for a year. Impatient and resentful, Lee thought Nash was acting as a brake on financial progress. His own views on monetary policy were simple: 'We shall make Walter print and print and print to the limit of commonsense'. He thought there was 'no drive, no energy, just drift', but this was an illusion born of frustration, for he was given very little to do. In fact, the ministers and their public service advisers were acting with immense drive. To have a man so disaffected at cabinet meetings was not wise. Nash decided that he should be put in charge of state housing,[1] and later in the year Lee became Nash's Under-Secretary.

Nash's position, as Minister of Finance, was not easy—trapped between the election rhetoric of Savage, Lee, or Langstone and the judgement of moderate men, like himself, that the British, the voters, and the economy would only stand so much printing. Government by printing press was a relatively novel idea and such examples as came to mind were not encour-aging. Savage had no firm grasp of economics beyond the need for higher wages and pensions. In any case, he was always willing to let his rhetorical heart rule his economic head to the benefit of his political position. More than once Nash had to make his actions conform, as comfortably as might be, to his leader's ill-considered pronouncements.

Just after the election Savage announced that the government would restore wage cuts, expand pensions, guarantee farmers' prices, and revalue the currency. The English *Economist* commented that deflationary exchange manipulation rested uneasily with the former inflationary measures.[2] Various well-informed people wrote to Nash about the consequences of revaluation. The Labour Party had an emotional commitment to revaluation. It had opposed Coates's devaluation, which was meant initially to benefit farmers, and revaluation had become a rigid dogma. Nash shared this attitude to some extent. Devaluation had been a traumatic act. It was difficult to believe that a £ was no longer a pound. But Nash had, at least initially, an open mind,[3] and it was not now closed, a valuable asset for a new minister. He received and was receptive to frank advice.

Bernard Ashwin wrote from Treasury pointing out that the current exchange rate against sterling afforded some protection for industry, by penalizing imports. He mentioned how transfers of capital in search of speculative profit had increased before devaluation in 1933. Dick Campbell wrote from England, listing the advantages and disadvantages of revaluation to parity with sterling. It 'would again set in motion a downward spiral of deflation, reducing internal purchasing power, reducing the profitableness of enterprises, increasing unemployment, and generally checking the tendency towards recovery'. He ridiculed the view widely held in New Zealand that it was 'artificial and "unnatural"' for the NZ £1 not to equal the sterling £1, and enclosed a letter from W. F. Crick, 'an able, leftish person', who was the Midland Bank's economist. Campbell and he argued that revaluation would be 'disastrous'. Crick argued for regarding the NZ £1 as a free unit and for a 'continuously expansive policy', on the lines of current, progressive thought, accepting the possibility of a rise in prices, stimulating recovery by capital works, and removing any impression of a deflationary trend. Nash took all this in, and replied to his trusted friend Campbell, that his letter was 'particularly valuable, although very, very *difficult* to use'. He obviously took some notice. When a well-known ex-New Zealand economist, Douglas Copland, made the same point in public Nash wrote to Campbell that it 'would have been better if he had left the question alone. However, I hope to have a talk with him, when he is in Wellington, before he returns to Melbourne'. Labour had heralded guaranteed prices as an alternative to Coates's exchange devaluation. Now it was pointed out to Nash that revaluation might make guaranteed prices more difficult to finance; it would lower the price received in NZ £s for exports while the government was raising payments to farmers.[4] In the event the *Economist's* forecast was accurate, that the deflationary part of Savage's policy would 'fade decorously into the background'. The change did not cause much soul-searching in the party which had enough to satisfy it. The first caucus met in an 'expectant atmosphere' on 20 and 21 February, 'chirruping merrily', as Lee put it.[5] Nash reported on his plan to nationalize the Reserve Bank, which was closer to Members' hearts than the subtleties of exchange rates.

The government's first legislation was the Reserve Bank Amendment Act. In moving the second reading of the bill on 3 April, Nash spoke of the controversy about whether a central bank should be free of political control. An Associated Banks' bulletin had spoken of the political bias unavoidable in nationalized banking. Nash argued that this impugned the integrity of every MP, and asked why 'so delicate a set of machinery' as the credit and currency machine could be run by private bankers, but not by the elected men who ran, for instance, the health and education systems of the community.

The state bought out the private shareholding of the bank. The sanctity of contracts, which Nash acknowledged, ensured that they received a good price. His aim was 'absolute control of our monetary system'. The Governor of the bank, Leslie Lefeaux, a stiff Englishman, who had been a senior officer of the Bank of England, and had been appointed on the recommendation of its Governor, Montagu Norman, believed that he had some degree of independence from government control. Nash now sought to define the bank's relationship to government: its function was 'to give effect as far as may be to the monetary policy of the Government as communicated to it from time to time by the Minister of Finance'.[6] For this purpose, and to promote 'the economic and social welfare of New Zealand', the bank was to 'control credit and currency' and also all the overseas funds earned by exports. Nash did not, however, intend to introduce exchange controls at once: 'we have in general such confidence in the men who are worth while in the Dominion that we do not think they will take any money away. . . .' He had been warned by a banker that 'Capital is a very "shy bird" and takes fright and flight very quickly', and had looked into the possibility of blocking transfers of funds through the purchase of Australian shares, but for the moment he was optimistic about business confidence in the government.[7] The government would use credit to enliven the economy, but neither too much nor too little.

Coates asked who was to decide on the dosage, cabinet, or the minister, or whether the views of the bank would be considered. Nash defended the principle of a coordination of state and private interests. But he was not heated. Lee thought that Nash's speech was too moderate, that he had a 'slight desire to play to the orthodox whom he can't win rather than to the revolutionary who would cheer'.[8] But of course Nash was trying not to alarm business and banks more than necessary.

The government wanted to keep interest rates low. In September Nash told Lefeaux that he wanted to convert an internal loan and raise money for State Advances at $3\frac{1}{4}$ per cent. Lefeaux informed the Board that in his view the amounts needed could not be raised at that rate. Nash had appointed an old friend, a Dunedin cabinetmaker and city councillor, Mark Silverstone, to the Board. He wrote to Nash that, far from accepting the minister's direction, the Board was hostile and obstructionist and passed resolutions endorsing Lefeaux's views. Nash was about to go to London and Lefeaux argued that a failure to raise the money would weaken his negotiating position there. Nash gave in to some extent. The State Advances Loan was made at $3\frac{1}{4}$ per cent but the conversion at $3\frac{1}{2}$ per cent. This caused strife in caucus, which did not like dictation by bankers. In the event Lefeaux's judgement proved sound. Treasury reported to Nash that the $3\frac{1}{4}$ per cent loan was a fiasco. But the episode was one which led Nash to determine to strengthen the government's control over the bank. Lefeaux believed that while government decided policy, the bank should decide how to implement it. As early as August, however, in instructing the bank to create credit of £5 million, Nash also specified how this was to be done.[9]

The second leg of Nash's 1936 financial policy was guaranteed prices. The Reserve Bank was to provide the funds to pay the farmers for their produce, once it had been purchased by the government and before it was sold. How guaranteed prices were to be implemented was a much more complicated matter than the banking legislation.

Although Labour candidates' statements on guaranteed prices during the election had been contradictory and confusing, Nash, at least, had been fairly clear about how they were meant to work. He had explained to audiences that for the first year the prices paid would be based on average prices over the past eight to ten years. Thereafter the level of production and the price would be based on reciprocal trading agreements.[10] But, as we have seen, he often added quite a different aim to this summary. After the trading agreements had been made, he explained in the *Standard* on 6 November 1935, a detailed investigation would be made of the farmers' costs of production, so as to ensure that he received a fair return for his labour and one covering his working expenses. This objective, which was one closer to his heart than orderly marketing (which he always stressed too), had nothing to do with the market place. It arose from his ideal, of many years standing, that rewards should be measured by service rendered to the community, not by harsh economic laws. It seems to have come, in fact, from John Ruskin, who believed that value should not be measured in monetary terms; the true cost of production involved investigating the human cost, the conditions of life and work of the producers; every industrial process must be reduced to terms of human satisfaction: 'THERE IS NO WEALTH BUT LIFE'.[11]

In terms of actually fixing the price to be guaranteed, this ideal involved endless difficulties, which friends, including economists, pointed out to him.[12] Would the price cover costs of production on inefficient, average (if any), or efficient farms? If the former, labour and investment would be encouraged in inefficient industry, and discouraged from moving to new opportunities. If the guaranteed price were well above market price, production would rise, causing market prices to fall further. And, a candidate wrote to him during the election, at one of his meetings he was asked how Labour would measure the value of a farmers' services: would he be classed as a labourer or a doctor? Nash's reply was oracular: it would be 'a standard of comfort in accord, as far as it can be measured, with the productive resources of the Dominion'.[13] He was becoming a master of saying nothing in phrases heavy with meaning.

Unlike the credit reformers, Nash knew perfectly well what his economic advisers told him bluntly, that fluctuations in overseas prices must always affect New Zealand. But he did not accept the advice of his economist friend, Allan Fisher, who feared that there was no chance of getting the price abroad that was needed to provide the income level in New Zealand that Nash aimed at.[14] In other words, with obstinate optimism, Nash counted on getting a bilateral agreement with Britain which would enable him to even out prices at a high level for a period of years.

There were other, immediate practical problems, such as how the government would purchase produce in New Zealand and administer its sale in Britain, and—the point that came up endlessly—how a deficit would be paid for if price realizations abroad fell far short of payments to farmers at home. Towards these, too, he maintained his usual cheerfully energetic attitude.

Five months were spent in arduous negotiations and discussions, of a sort familiar to weary ministers and civil servants, but of which voters, supporters, and backbenchers seem so often oblivious. Lee was aggrieved that Savage, Nash, and Lee Martin, then Minister for Agriculture, met to discuss the guaranteed price without him. In a cabinet committee he expressed his dissent 'pretty forcibly. . . . The PM got annoyed and suddenly cleared out from the table and sat away like a sulky kid for about half an hour'. This early instance of Savage's petulance, emotional responses hardly or not controlled, was ominous for the government's future. Almost certainly his health was deteriorating—he had been very ill as long ago as 1932.

Unaware of all the background negotiations, Lee saw himself as fighting for a higher price for farmers. Nash seemed to be aiming at twelve pence a pound; Lee thought (in mid-February) that he had 'jumped them' to thirteen pence—'a great win for me'. In fact a significantly higher price was paid, but not because of his advocacy.[15] Cabinet debates were the least of Nash's difficulties.

The dairy industry, through the Dairy Produce Control Board and later the Dairy Board set up by Coates in 1934, had since the world war been striving to rationalize production and marketing, though its efforts had met strong opposition in London and at home. The existence of the Board, with its experienced administrators, and the significant degree of centralization already achieved, meant that the dairying business was already organized to a degree which made state control easy.[16] By comparison the meat and wool producers, who sold to private companies or by auction, had achieved no administrative unity.

The government had some tough discussions with the Dairy Board, which sought to maintain self-government for the industry, including control of overseas sales, but it failed to get its way, for this would have meant that the Board sold produce already bought by the state. An advisory committee was set up, chaired nominally by Nash but in practice by an experienced dairy administrator, George Duncan. Its secretary was Dr W. B. Sutch. The dairy administrators and public servants worked out the details of how guaranteed prices would function, within guidelines laid down by Nash. Much, but not all, of what they recommended was accepted. The committee doubted, however, whether the price guaranteed could achieve Nash's aim of social justice for farmers. Their costs and efficiency varied too greatly to be easily assessed. This Nash ignored, as well as the committee's view that the best way to improve the farmers' lot was to control land values and land speculation[17]—aims with which he had once been almost obsessed.

The Primary Products Marketing Bill dealt only with butter and cheese —the government never did guarantee meat and wool prices, although up until 1947 Nash still hoped to do so. Nash became Minister of Marketing. The Dairy Board was to act as national executive for the producers and control dairy affairs within New Zealand. The government was to purchase the butter and cheese. The Primary Produce Marketing Department was set up to sell the produce, mostly in London.

Nash introduced the Bill on 29 April.[18] The long-term aim of the government, he said, was 'a balanced economy for every section of the community'. He reviewed the wild swings in overseas prices for dairy produce; showed how from 1911 to 1921 prices rose faster than production, while from 1921 to 1935 production had trebled but the gross return had declined. It was from this uncertainty that guaranteed prices were to rescue the farmers. He listed many countries which already organized their marketing of exports. He contrasted the needs of Britain's poor for food with New Zealand's untapped resources. His Bill aimed to match Britain's need with New Zealand's, to provide food for Britain in peace as in war. He deprecated talk that money alone could solve New Zealand's problems. A friend (Allan Fisher), had written to him, 'Human needs will be ineffective to create a demand if they are not backed by an income which must depend upon some one's production, either that of the income receiver or of someone else'. Nash went on to say, however, as did his Bill, that the aim was to 'ensure for Producers an Adequate Remuneration for the Services rendered by them to the Community', and he said that the state's duty was to see that this was paid 'irrespective of the price that his commodity receives overseas'. In such remarks his humanitarian zeal took his rhetoric close to the social creditors'.

It was the ethical aim that he stressed, and it was written into the Bill, in the title and in the section which specified the criteria by which the price would be fixed. They included the costs of efficient producers and the 'general standard of living' of dairy farmers as compared with those of the community. If the mechanism of the measure, to which he referred, was to be a reciprocal trade agreement, its spirit was to be the goal of reward for service. The Bill stated that the price was to give an efficient producer a return 'to enable him to maintain himself and his family in a reasonable state of comfort'. How that price was to relate to prices received abroad to which the Bill also referred, it did not say. This section of the Bill, that closest to his heart, was to be used to beat him about the head in the near future.

The payments to farmers were to come from a Dairy Industry Account at the Reserve Bank, and there was to be no limit on government borrowing from that account. A Member interjected, 'what about balancing the budget' and Nash replied, 'We will also balance the budget. The point I am making is that this account will be left entirely on its own'. So his professed belief in a balanced budget was not incompatible with some inflationary credit.

Coates bluntly called the measure the 'Primary Products Pirating Bill'. He and Adam Hamilton saw it as a step towards socialism: the government had taken over exchange, and now distribution; socialization of production would follow. Coates regarded the Bill as an attack on the incentives and initiative of the farmers. 'The national destiny of this country was ordained', he said, 'by those early pioneers who arrived from the Mother-country nearly a century ago'. That destiny was the 'sturdy independence' of the farmer. He denounced the government's emphasis on developing local manufacturing. The climate and soil and 'the bent of our people' meant that the country's destiny lay in farming and farmers—now threatened by 'red socialism'.[19]

During the third reading Coates complained that Savage had used his majority to 'bludgeon' the Bill through, as he had. Coates's comments were much to the point, those of a man experienced in farming and in dairy politics. He said that Nash would not get his bulk trade agreement—the British Prime Minister had already refused such an agreement with New Zealand; moreover the British did 'not take kindly to State-organized marketing systems'. As for the vaunted guaranteed price, it was merely an 'equalised' price, a levelling device; in the long run the farmer would have to equalize the overdraft at the Reserve Bank; it was 'a repayable advance' (which Nash denied in an interjection). Moreover, it would not work; it was impractical and would break down. 'New Zealand cannot insulate the price against the impact of external conditions'.

Nash replied that if there were an ultimate loss it would be a national loss, not borne by the farmers. Not unnaturally he was a little pleased with himself, as well as determined, and closed the debate with one of his favourite verses, by Edgar Guest:

> Somebody said that it couldn't be done
> But he with a chuckle replied
> That maybe it couldn't,
> But he would be one

Who wouldn't say so till he tried.
So he bucked right in
With a trace of a grin
On his face.
If he worried he hid it.
He started to sing
As he tackled the thing
That couldn't be done,
And he did it.[20]

Opposition MPs and farmers had all along been anxious to know how a deficit in the dairy account would be met, and what would happen to a surplus. Nash had often been vague or evasive, probably because he did not know what his chances were of getting a bilateral agreement. The Dairy Industry Advisory Committee had worked out average prices over the previous eight, nine, and ten years. For 1936-7 the Government took the highest of these and added an amount to cover rising wages.[21] The pay-out, higher than that promised, soothed the troubled farming world for a time.

At one stroke Nash had given purpose and direction to what became the biggest dairy business in the world. It is scarcely possible to improve on the verdicts of the historian of these events, Mr R. J. M. Hill. In the long run, 'guaranteed prices' meant price-levelling. A product almost entirely exported could not be shielded altogether from the ups and downs of world prices and tastes. But while this repudiates Nash's opinion, it recognizes his achievement. The dairy farmers gained a degree of security they had never known. His Act brought other great changes to one of the country's main industries. Sectional controversy was brushed aside by a determined government, but efficient management by the industry's own administrators, not some remote bureaucratic control, was the end result. Cooperation, dear to the minister's heart, was fostered. He was the driving force, the 'principal architect and builder', even though the ultimate shape of the dairy industry was not quite what he hoped.[22]

The third leg of Nash's financial policy was the State Advances Corporation Bill. State advances to settlers—in other words cheap loans to farmers —had been introduced by the Liberals in 1894. Savage had announced that he was taking over where Seddon left off in 1906. In this case Labour returned to somewhere near that position. The Coalition had replaced the old State Advances Office with a Mortgage Corporation with private shareholders. The state now bought these out. The directors were to administer the Corporation under the minister's direction. One of Nash's aims was to keep interest rates down. And he hoped that the Corporation would stimulate the building of houses, up to 5,000 a year. He hoped to stop the land-agents and land-grabbers from reaping the profits—and managed to get in a reference to 'usehold' as a desirable tenure for householders. The Corporation would also administer government loans to promote industries.

Nash said that the guiding principles of the Corporation would be 'generous', its operation 'conservative'. This sentiment pleased Adam Hamilton, who praised Nash's moderation and fairness.[23]

Then there was Nash's first budget, which surveyed the government's measures past and future in their financial aspects. Revenues were buoyant and left a surplus. Nash was buoyant too. It was not too alarming to opponents, but it was a Labour budget. Pensions were up. Salary cuts had been restored. The education vote was raised considerably. The provision for free milk in schools was being investigated—and was soon implemented. And taxes were to be raised too. He increased income tax by about £1 million and land tax by £.8 million. This gave him a chance to trot out one of his hobby-horses—the purpose of land tax was to secure for the community the values it created, and the maximum rewards to those who actually used the land. The 'first charge' was also given an airing when he spoke of pensions.

Coates, quite fairly, said that Labour leaders were constantly reassuring: 'We are going onwards and upwards' (one of Savage's favourites); 'We are builders not wreckers'. Nash's message was the same, that there was nothing to fear. But Coates feared that behind these doses of soothing syrup lay inflation, ruined industry and enterprise and possible economic collapse. Little that he said carried much conviction. The country was too evidently improving, whether due to Labour or not. He did, however, make one remark worth recording. He said that Nash was so burdened that much important work was held up, perhaps the first time that criticism was made.[24]

The *Financial News* later said that Nash's first budget was exemplary in its orthodoxy, though there was danger from inflation in other areas, such as guaranteed prices.[25] Certainly it seemed orthodox—it balanced!—to credit reformers in the party. Coming down to Wellington on the train, the night before the financial statement, John A. Lee and other northern MPs had improvised a version of the 'Red Flag', then usually sung at Labour conferences:

> The people's flag is palest pink
> It's not as red as you might think
> We've heard the Budget, now we know
> That Nash has changed its colour so
> Then raise the scarlet standard high
> Beneath its fold we'll live and die
> Though cowards flinch and traitors sneer
> We'll tone it down while Nash is here.[26]

In its first year Labour's achievements had been remarkable. The Arbitration Court, set up by the Liberals, had been restored and required to fix a basic wage for unskilled workers, providing a fair standard of comfort. The government also introduced compulsory unionism by a pro-vision that anyone subject to an Arbitration Court award or an industrial agreement must belong to a trade union. This was to be much criticized by radicals who wanted strong, active—and voluntary—unions and conser-vatives who disliked compulsion and unions alike. The forty-hour, five-day week had been introduced for most workers, a pioneering measure. Reserve Bank credit had been set aside to pay for state houses to be let at a low rent. Parliamentary debates were broadcast to the nation—not an unmixed blessing, perhaps.

The government felt so pleased that it brought out two pamphlets on its first year, David Wilson's *History in the Making* and Nash's *Labour Rule in New Zealand*, published in London by the New Fabian Research Bureau.

Greater things were planned. In February W. E. Parry, the Minister in Charge of Pensions, began looking into a proposal to raise old age pensions to £1 10s. a week, and other interim improvements. The Treasury reported that his proposals would cost over £10 million, two-and-a-half times the existing pensions bill, at a time when income tax was expected to bring in only £6 million and the total estimated ordinary expenditure revenue was only £31 million. Treasury wanted to know where the money was coming from and so did the ministers. Their hesitation led to friction in caucus. In the end the government decided on two increases of 2s. 6d., raising the pension to 22s. 6d. by December. Meanwhile a parliamentary committee under Dr D. G. McMillan and a cabinet committee under Nash were set up to study the over-all health and pensions legislation. An inter-depart-mental committee, of some of the leading public servants, including B. C. Ashwin, reported to Nash on this topic on 1 October. It estimated that the universal superannuation, at 30s. a week, various other pensions and a complete health service (all without a means test) would cost nearly £30 million, a sum almost equal to the ordinary government revenue. An increase of 150 per cent in income tax and a special tax of 2s. 6d. in the £ would be needed to pay for it.[27] Needless to say, this report gave the ministers reason for sober reflection.

A good deal of ill-feeling was coming into the open in caucus, because the ministers seemed to be dragging their heels over pension increases and were not sufficiently strong in controlling the Reserve Bank. The credit reformers wanted more rapid progress still, and more credit. But these were minor irritants at that stage. On 10 October there was a dispute because Nash wished to convert the internal loan at $3\frac{1}{2}$ per cent and not $3\frac{1}{4}$ per cent —as he had hoped and the credit-men wished. A motion to defer a decision until he returned to New Zealand was defeated by one vote. According to Lee, Savage had miscounted.[28] Probably Savage was not too bothered either by $\frac{1}{4}$ per cent or a miscount. Nash was presented with a wallet and 'accorded musical honours'. He was off, in a few days, to London, in search of his long-dreamed-of bilateral trading agreement.

XII

London and Other Capitals

1936-7

The Nashes sailed in the *Aorangi* on 13 October for Vancouver, en route for Southampton. On the Auckland wharves was a sight notorious among New Zealanders, whether trade unionists or not, and ominous for the future of Nash's party. The waterside workers were having a 'go slow'.

The 'wharfies' were one of the few groups of workers congregated in sufficient numbers to form a strong union. In September Nash had told a wharf delegation led by 'Big Jim' Roberts that if there were disorganization in the industry the standard of living must go down. He was not cheered by what he now saw. He wrote to Fraser that the men were working at a studied pace. The handling rates, he said, were far below those in Sydney and elsewhere and this would do the country much harm.[1]

On the long voyage 'Home' Nash and his colleagues, who included Dr W. B. Sutch, had ample time to brood on their purpose. Bulk trading agreements were meant to form the basis of guaranteed prices, as we have seen. And Nash had long believed that they might make a contribution to international cooperation. At the Institute of Pacific Relations Conference in Banff in 1933 he had chaired a round table discussion at which he had advanced his views. Though, in theory, free trade would give the best results, he argued, it was not practicable. 'Economic nationalism expressed in the quota or agreement system' might produce better results. There, and elsewhere, he urged that (as the free traders believed) each country should specialize in producing what it could best produce. But after that, not market forces, but international agreements should dispose of the exportable surpluses. The credits earned by exports should be allocated to various purposes, including of course, the (reciprocal) imports. Orderly marketing should aim at planned economic expansion, until human needs were met.

This doctrine must have fallen on startled ears for bilateral agreements were anathema to economic orthodoxy and had contributed to the decline in the volume of world trade during the depression. To see them as a means to international order was decidedly unusual. Various critics urged the inefficiency of state as opposed to private enterprise and made other objections. Certainly Nash was naive if he expected to find much support.

On his return to New Zealand in 1933 he had summed up his own brand of international idealism in a series of fifteen 'affirmations' which he read to the House. 'Economic self sufficiency and isolation' were antagonistic to the country's economic and social progress, and dangerous to world peace. 'National economic and production planning' was inevitable but it did not imply a selfish and inward-looking autarchy. National economic plans must be coordinated. The success of a New Zealand planned economy would 'be greater if world trade is regulated through negotiation and cooperation'. 'The world is the ultimate unit, and our national economic plan should be so built as to realize as soon as practicable the spiritual and economic unity of all peoples'. The world economic order must ensure justice, for 'No nation of equal virility, mental efficiency, and vision can be permanently kept on a lower living standard' than its equals. (He was thinking of the Chinese and Japanese.) The economic system must ensure 'full development' for every individual as well as for every nation.[2]

The great goal was to meet 'human needs' (a favourite expression) then sadly unsatisfied in New Zealand as in the world. Fortunately for New Zealand, this was especially true in 'the Old Country'. If the British consumed as much butter as New Zealanders, he argued in 1935, they would need another 240,000 tons. If they ate a pound of butter per home per week, as advocated by a dietary expert, they would need another 480,000 tons.[3]

Had Nash's world economic order come about it would have involved not only state trading but state-regulated production. This latter point was one he did not often stress in New Zealand[4] for quantitative restrictions on production were quite unacceptable to the farmers. It was, however, implicit in his scheme: the state could not pay guaranteed prices for limitless unsaleable produce, so production must be restricted to equal local and overseas demand. Nash elaborated these points in a talk to the Institute of International Affairs held in William Downie Stewart's house in Dunedin in 1934. Under the British Agricultural Marketing Act, he said, the British were regulating the marketing of agricultural products. The British policy of regulating supply would compel countries exporting to Great Britain to control their exports. 'The regulation of exports from a country with undeveloped and partly-developed land resources will ultimately compel its Government to control the commodities to be produced.' And he went on, 'The ultimate saturation of the British Market with products now exported to it from New Zealand will compel the reorganisation of our primary production system.'[5]

It is evident that Nash had given a great deal of thought to this whole subject. His vision of New Zealand, British Commonwealth, and world trade was, however, one very distasteful to the British government which was committed, though more notably in theory than in practice, to a return to freer trade, regulated by market forces. The United States government, in the person of Cordell Hull, was at that time seeking to revive world trade by negotiating tariff reductions. In American or British leaders' eyes, Nash's dream of cooperation appeared liked a Nazi or Communist nightmare.

Not only was what Nash wanted incompatible with the political and economic ideals of British leaders, but a special deal for New Zealand would breach the imperial economic policy which Britain and the Dominions had adopted in the face of world economic collapse.

When the depression began most governments heard the cry, *sauve qui peut,* and adopted various restrictive measures intended to protect their domestic economy, whatever happened to any other country. High tariffs, quotas, competitive devaluations, exchange controls, became the order of the day. There was a great drop in the volume of world trade.[6] New Zealand, which had one of the lowest tariffs in the world, the highest volume of trade per person, and a minute local market, was singularly vulnerable and paralysingly dependent on Britain, which took almost all of its exports —almost all of which were products of the cow and the sheep.[7]

Britain's response was to hope that the Empire trade might prove its salvation. In 1931 it introduced a protective tariff and, at the Ottawa conference, accepted the idea of imperial preference which the Dominions had been advocating for forty-five years and practising for thirty or so. At Ottawa—by a series of bilateral agreements—the Dominions gained exemption from the new British 10 per cent duty, while Britain retained and extended her preferential position in Dominion markets. Tariff protection against British manufactures was to be given only to Dominion industries 'reasonably assured of sound opportunities for success'. Even then, British producers were to be given 'full opportunities of reasonable competition'. This agreement, which was the basis of New Zealand's privileged access to the British market, was generally ignored by New Zealand advocates of currency reform and rapid industrialization. In regarding the Commonwealth as an economic unit, the agreement assumed some specialization in production in the different countries.

The next four years were stormy, for the Empire unit functioned imperfectly. The Dominions could not absorb all Britain's exports, so the British had to consider foreign points of view, such as those of Argentina, a chief rival of the Dominions. Moreover, the British government moved in various and sometimes mysterious ways to protect British farmers. First there was a threat that the British would impose quotas on Dominion and foreign supplies of meat. Then, in 1935, the British proposed to impose a levy on meat imports to subsidize home industry. As the chief supplier of sheep meat New Zealand would have had to pay the largest share of the subsidy. In 1935 the British government dropped this proposal temporarily—the levy would not be introduced for at least three years. The Dominions had to continue to regulate supplies to the British market instead. At the same time, the British government introduced subsidies on local milk and cheese.

What New Zealand wanted was an expanding market, even if the expansion were regulated by quotas or some other means. But this was under threat. Gordon Coates had to warn farmers that the British market was not bottomless. On behalf of the dairy farmers, the government asked whether Britain would give unrestricted entry to New Zealand produce if tariffs on British goods were drastically reduced or even removed. Baldwin could not consider a suggestion put forward by particular trade interests. Coates then asked whether the British would consider a bilateral reciprocal trade agreement with New Zealand. Baldwin replied, in July 1935, that at Ottawa each Dominion had been given (in separate agreements) much the same concessions. Any modification of this equal treatment would need to be discussed at an imperial conference.[8]

Nash was very well-informed about all this and widely read in the relevant literature. His Secretary-Economist, W. B. Sutch, had just written a book on the subject, for which Nash wrote the preface. But, in any case, these were problems he had lived with for many years. He can have had little doubt that his prospects of success were dim. Indeed, in retrospect they appear to have been non-existent. W. K. Hancock commented, in 1940, that since, counting invisible items, Britain had a favourable balance of payments with most Empire countries, it was naive to suppose that she would accept Nash's principle of balancing agreements, which would have slashed her export trade.[9] A less optimistic man would have concluded that his journey was not really necessary. But there were some reasons why he could think that there was at least a chance of securing an agreement.

The British were infinitely flexible in practice. At Ottawa, while professing the ideal of lower tariff barriers, they had negotiated schedules which raised them against foreigners;[10] while preaching equal treatment for the Dominions, they had given Canada preferential bilateral treatment for bacon and ham.[11] Though they made speeches about the liberalization of trade, the British leaders had been as affected as anyone by what Hancock called 'the economics of siege'. While regretting the trend, in the early nineteen-thirties they had made a series of bilateral trade agreements with foreign states. Nearly half Britain's non-Empire trade was conducted by this method. Very often such agreements, sometimes backed by credits to foreign importers, were the only ways of arranging for trade exchanges. For instance, by an Anglo-German Payments Agreement of 1934, 55 per cent of the value of German exports to the United Kingdom was ear-marked by the Reichsbank to pay for British exports to Germany. By 1939 even the USA had descended to a direct barter with Britain of rubber for cotton.[12] The collapse of the World Economic Conference in 1933 had led writers like Arthur Salter, a leading British public servant and intellectual, to write that trade negotiations had more chance of success if they were bilateral and not universal.[13]

Generations of British politicians and civil servants have left minutes and memoranda, now stored in the Public Record Office in London, about the visits of colonial politicians. Their frame of mind was usually that of weary, impatient schoolmasters; their tone tart and superior. It did not alter much if they were dealing with a rough ignoramus or someone much better read and articulate than most of themselves, a man like Alfred Deakin of Australia, for instance. Nash suffered from a treble disability: he represented a Dominion, a small one, and he was easily 'placed' in a hierarchical society —as a Midland shopkeeper. If he suffered from moving in higher and sniffier circles he did not show it; on the other hand, without being a sycophant, he enjoyed meeting and was impressed by the great.

The fact that he had come at all was irritating to start with. The British government had informed the New Zealand, before he left, that it was not its policy to enter into balancing agreements, except in 'special circumstances' (that is, ones from which the practical gain to Britain outweighed the loss in principles), nor to give New Zealand different treatment from the rest of the Empire. The New Zealand reply had ignored British views. The Board of Trade thought the first task would be to persuade Mr Nash 'that we cannot re-cast our general trade policy to suit New Zealand's convenience'.[14]

The British 'establishment's' attitude to the New Zealand government was hostile. It was also, in some very unsympathetic ways well, or at least directly, informed. Lefeaux apparently regarded himself as an agent of the imperial government and the Bank of England.[15] Lord Balfour of Burleigh, a banker, visited the Dominion and after a conversation with Savage wrote that he was an 'honest idealist', willing to try anything to achieve his aims: 'His attitude suggests to me that of a small boy in a power station happily pulling one switch after another to see what happens. One day he may pull a switch which will fuse the whole of the works'.[16] Only Fraser and Nash, of the ministers, at all impressed British visitors and officials.

The British Trade Commissioner, Robert Boulter, wrote from Wellington that official contacts in London should correct the views Nash had 'formed in a small, isolated and self satisfied territory', but doubted whether he would be able to convert his colleagues to his 'adjusted views'. He added that Nash would be terribly disappointed if he did not get his agreement.[17] London officials took up this note. A colonial politician had earlier complained that some of his colleagues were 'duchessed' at consecutive colonial and imperial conferences. Perhaps Nash could be converted by less aristocratic means.

S. D. Waley wrote to another Treasury official, Sir Frederick Phillips, on 12 November 1936, that Nash had arrived but that the Board of Trade officials wanted to put off discussions with him until he had met a few people and discovered 'that his ideas are regarded here as retrograde and barbarous'. Meanwhile, he could safely be kept talking about beef. They thought that the Chancellor of the Exchequer, Neville Chamberlain (who became Prime Minister when Baldwin retired in June 1937), would prefer to postpone meeting him until his ideas had become 'somewhat tamed'. Another official minuted, 'I don't see, therefore, why he sh'd be shut out from the civilising influence of a talk with the Ch of the Ex'.[18] Treasury suggested that a 'purgative lunch or dinner' should be arranged with Montagu Norman, Governor of the Bank of England.[19]

Nash had met the Secretary of State for Dominion Affairs, Malcolm MacDonald, in the Clarté bookshop when he came out to New Zealand with the Oxford Union debating team in 1925. Their personal and official relations were always cordial.[20] They talked on 10 November. Nash told MacDonald that he was very keen on his proposals which were the product of many years of thought. When MacDonald said they could not give New Zealand advantages over other Dominions, Nash asked if this was quite impossible, since New Zealand had the lowest tariff on British goods.[21] On the 13th he had a meeting with MacDonald, Walter Runciman, President of the Board of Trade, and W. S. Morrison, Minister of Agriculture, to discuss beef. At the next meeting, on the 19th, MacDonald wanted to discuss it again, but Nash 'had not brought all his beef advisers with him', and launched into an outline of New Zealand's case for a bilateral agreement. He wanted the maximum proportion of New Zealand's exports to go to Britain, even to the extent of diverting trade with Australia to Britain. All credits earned would be at the disposal of the New Zealand government, to be spent on shipping and insurance charges, interest and redemption of the London debt, and the purchase of British manufactures. British manufacturers would be notified, for instance through the Federation of British Industries, what funds were available to pay for their products. He agreed that this would be easier for New Zealand, most of whose exports were controlled by Export Boards, than for Britain, but he saw no great problem in this.

Runciman said that Nash seemed to be proposing 'the institution of a Clearing House based upon a monopoly'; British industries 'had been built up on an individualistic basis'. MacDonald again objected to Nash's request for 'preferential treatment'. If New Zealand gained a five per cent advantage over Australia, Australia might demand the same preference over South Africa, and so on.

But the complications of Nash's proposals were worse. He mentioned that, since Britain could not, for instance, supply tea, some of New Zealand's London funds would be diverted to Ceylon, 'subject no doubt to Ceylon concluding a similar agreement with the United Kingdom' to purchase goods equivalent in value to the tea exports to New Zealand. Oil would require a similar arrangement. This was getting into fantasy. For, should Britain conclude balancing agreements with the Dominions, it would be involved in consequential agreements with endless other countries. The result would have been an international network like Britain's nineteenth century most-favoured-nation treaties. The prospects of a small Dominion bringing about such a change were nil.

Nash regarded his scheme as self-evidently sensible. New Zealand needed an expanding market and Britain needed New Zealand goods. In his judgement the British people 'could not be allowed to go hungry for ever, when the produce of countries such as New Zealand was available for their consumption'.

Morrison brought up the threat of a quota or levy on British food imports. Nash replied that a levy would inevitably lead to a demand for more protection for New Zealand manufactures—for instance a levy on imported boots. He said that 'if New Zealand followed the practice of other Dominions and built up large industrial establishments, she could make a better country in a decade. He enquired whether the United Kingdom really wanted New Zealand to follow Australian practice in regard to tariffs'.[22]

Another inescapable problem was exposed by this discussion. W. K. Hancock wrote, 'History had determined that the basic problem which the New Zealanders had to face was the problem of markets'.[23] Both as an Englishman and a New Zealander, Nash saw this clearly. He thought in Empire terms. He was even willing to contemplate that certain industries should be prohibited in New Zealand in the interests of British manufacturers. But to reconcile his ideas on marketing with another of Labour's policies, industrial development, would not be easy. He frankly accepted the principle adopted at Ottawa, easy to express but difficult to reduce to examples, that only 'economic' industries should be developed in New Zealand. Many in his party, however, including Savage and Dan Sullivan as well as John A. Lee, were less interested in whether new industries were 'economic' and more in their potential for providing jobs, import substitutes, ultimately a less dependent economy, and (in Lee's case, at least), national cultural progress.[24]

The negotiations were interrupted by the abdication crisis in late November and December.

Edward VIII was very popular in New Zealand, as indeed in other Dominions, as a supposedly egalitarian monarch. At first the New Zealand government, while opposing Mrs Simpson becoming Queen, favoured a morganatic marriage without the King abdicating, a suggestion made by the King himself. However, only De Valera inclined to agree with New Zealand, and he thought Irish public opinion would not stand it. The other Dominions refused to accept a morganatic marriage, and New Zealand conceded that there were insuperable difficulties.[25] Nash cabled Savage that he and Jordan had been kept fully informed by the Secretary of State. He said that they thought abdication was inevitable if the King married Mrs Simpson and that their main concern was that parliament must govern and the King accept the advice of ministers, or the ministers should resign. Even now, when he heard of the King's intention to abdicate, Savage cabled his government's 'dismay and deepest regret', and asked him to reconsider.[26]

It seems obvious from the cables that the government did not know how to respond, and knew next to nothing about the situation. Apparently Savage asked the Governor-General who Mrs Simpson was. It was said that Nash held 'more decisive' views. If so, it was because he was in closer touch with British 'establishment' opinion.

Nash was invited to the Accession Council, on 12 December, with the Privy Council and other 'Gentlemen of Quality', when the King subscribed the oath relating to the Church of Scotland and arrangements were made to proclaim the new sovereign. Nash refused to wear court dress and the Privy Council gave him permission to wear morning dress. In Wellington the cabinet had sat up all night to hear the final news. Early in January Nash was called to St James's Palace to sign the proclamation of the new sovereign on New Zealand's behalf. The *Dominion* remarked that he had met two English Kings in two weeks.[27]

Nash had two further meetings with MacDonald and other ministers and officials in the second half of December. The discussions were courteous but discouraging. There were arguments the British could not press. For instance a Board of Trade brief read, 'In explaining the difficulties of the proposal to Mr Nash, it is important to avoid as far as possible using arguments which Mr Nash could use in his turn against the accord of preferences to United Kingdom products entering New Zealand over similar products from . . . other Dominions'.[28] However, there were plenty of arguments left. Britain opposed balancing agreements in principle. The government would not regiment British industries, nor could it prohibit certain manufactures—nor would Canada nor Australia—as New Zealand was willing to do. Unrestricted imports from New Zealand might cause a price fall damaging to British agriculture. The 'unbalanced' Empire which Nash envisaged would leave Britain with an economy so dependent on Dominion food that it could not long survive a European war.

Nash assumed that there was an approximate equality of debts and credits between the two countries, once 'invisibles' were taken into account, despite the substantial favourable balance of trade that New Zealand enjoyed. British officials disputed this and argued that the balance of payments heavily favoured New Zealand, a fact which the latest New Zealand *Year Book* had been cooked to conceal. Hence, in the British view, any concessions must be made by New Zealand.

Nash was stubborn, but there was little he could oppose to the British barrage. What New Zealand *wanted* was not, in itself, a powerful argument. Nor was the view which he advanced, that it was 'immoral' to deny New Zealand the right to sell to Britain what its people needed; that New Zealanders ate 93 lbs of mutton a year and the British only 28 lbs.[29]

After the first of these meetings E. G. Machtig, Assistant-Under-Secretary at the Dominions Office, wrote to MacDonald 'it was to be hoped if not expected' that Nash would now realize that no progress could be made in the direction he wished, and would 'come down to earth'—to discussing a detailed revision of the Ottawa agreement. MacDonald had been friendly and had suggested that perhaps some other kind of agreement could be reached.

But Nash did not yet surrender. In a letter to MacDonald on 8 January 1937 he reiterated his policy and his arguments. The public servants, not otherwise known to historians or to fame, continued their amusing little exchange of minutes. On 1 February S. D. Waley of Treasury wrote that the Chancellor might want to talk to Nash before an ultimatum was delivered, but that 'Mr Nash is magnificently impervious to argument'. Another added that the Chancellor had decided that 'Mr N. is as impervious to food as to argument' so that it might be better for him 'to guide Mr N. to sensible courses *after* he has taken his knock'. On 19 February MacDonald replied to Nash's letter that the difficulties involved ruled out any possibility of such an arrangement as Nash wanted.[30]

These negotiations were only the beginning of Nash's problems. So far he had been struggling to achieve a vision of imperial trade which might have provided a high standard of living, but which would have confirmed New Zealand's colonial economic status. Now, negotiating in detail over specific products, he found that Britain's needs and British attitudes at once blocked any guarantee of the expanding markets New Zealand needed, while being inimical to the industrial development which might make the Dominion less dependent. By mid-April he had had twenty-two meetings with British ministers. There had been many others between officials. These showed that New Zealand's economic future was very questionable—as doubtful, indeed, as its physical security was soon to prove. If there seems to have been a restrained desperation in Nash's persistence, it must be remembered that these were years of fear for Britain too, fear of European war and fear of renewed depression. In 1937-8 world economic conditions did deteriorate to the extent that economists wrote of another slump.[31]

To follow Nash through the mass of official documents generated for and by all these meetings would be tedious and is unnecessary. The stubborn issues arose right away. The British wanted Nash to proceed by revising the Ottawa agreement. He said that it could not be modified to suit New Zealand's needs. He told MacDonald that powerful interests were pressing for industrial development, at present prevented by low tariffs, and hitherto 'kept in check by the argument that it was necessary to come to a trade agreement with the United Kingdom'. This constraint would now vanish. But he was, the British leaders thought, pleasingly conciliatory, and he produced an outline of an agreement revising Ottawa. The British counter-proposals included a reduction of New Zealand tariffs in Britain's favour which, since they were already lower than those of any Dominion, and among the lowest in the world, Nash said could not be 'meant seriously'.

The British ministers disliked the idea of New Zealand licensing imports and rationing foreign exchange. Lefeaux had opposed these measures. He had said that he hoped that pressure in London would induce Nash to drop the idea. However, Nash told Montagu Norman and the British ministers that they would be introduced whether he got his agreement or not. The Board of Trade saw a threat to a British market in his wish to stimulate industrial development in New Zealand. He had the idea of encouraging British manufacturers to start industries in New Zealand by offering them a virtual monopoly of the market. If New Zealand prohibited certain imports then the imperial tariff preference on British manufactures would be nugatory. Nash argued that without a monopoly of the small local market new industries could not survive. He was negotiating with several British tyre manufacturers to start a New Zealand industry. Oliver Stanley, the new President of the Board of Trade, told him that 'monopolies and quotas were clearly against the spirit, if not against the letter, of the Ottawa Agreement'—forgetting for the moment, Britain's own threatened meat or dairy produce quotas.[33] The Ottawa formula had envisaged Dominion industries reasonably assured of success, but Nash now wished to add the words, 'or essential in the public interest'. The British response was to endeavour to include all goods in which their manufactures had 'a substantial interest' in schedules of goods on which New Zealand would agree not to impose an embargo.[34]

It should be added that, while the British were defending their markets and Nash his country's industrial growth, they did see his point of view. On one occasion Euan Wallace, Parliamentary Secretary to the Department of Overseas Trade, said that New Zealand must develop a balanced economy; it was not supposed that she would be contented with primary production forever.[35] But any compromise suiting both interests was difficult to envisage.

The same appeared true of New Zealand exports to Britain. Nash's draft agreement of 8 March provided for a five per cent annual increase in sheep meat exports in 1937-40. And in general, the main thrust of his argument was for an expanding market. But the British could not agree to any percentage increase. Indeed the Minister of Agriculture told him that it might be necessary to put a stop to the expansion of imports from New Zealand. Nash said he was being offered an agreement worse than Ottawa.[36]

What alarmed him most was the British insistence that it might be necessary either to impose a levy or to regulate imports of dairy produce without warning. He fought hard for the exemption of New Zealand from any levy, and for a year's warning of any quota, so that production in New Zealand could be planned. Both requests were refused. All he could get was a promise of as much notice as possible. The British ministers would not surrender their right to control imports in the interests of the British farmer. They were not unsympathetic. At a meeting of the British ministers alone, MacDonald told his colleagues that Nash had been very conciliatory and 'would undoubtedly have real political trouble' when he went home. He emphasized 'the difficulty of reaching an agreement with New Zealand so long as a Sword of Damocles was suspended over her head'. They must decide whether to use a levy or quantitative restriction.[37]

The difficulty was that the British government did not know what its milk policy, to help British farmers, would be, and did not expect to decide until July. New Zealand's welfare and that of home producers were not the only issues. For instance, because of imperial preferences, a levy on Dominion produce would require an increase in tariff duties on Scandinavian and Baltic produce, and at a time when there was a movement to reduce trade barriers. It might be that 'considerations of high policy, affecting our political as well as our economic relations with other countries', would preclude such an increase. The British could not surrender one of their options, quantitative regulation, to New Zealand, when they might lose the other.[38]

Over mutton and lamb the problem seemed almost as difficult. The British were insisting that, if home prices fell unduly, Australia and New Zealand must accept a $3\frac{1}{2}$ per cent reduction in their allocation for 1937. Antipodean fears were not relieved by the fact that if the market were firm there could be a similar increase. The British were, once again, trying to protect the home producer. However, in early April, the ministers made a concession over this item, and dropped the threatened reduction. In the event there was a small increase. Nash did not, however, get the guarantee of an annual expansion.[39]

The British realized that Nash was 'desperately anxious' to get an agreement to take home, but they disagreed among themselves to some extent, and had little room to manoeuvre. In mid-April agreement had been reached over beef and sheep meats, but otherwise there seemed little hope of success. Nash went off with some of his assistants to Europe to discover whether there was scope for trade agreements there. There is no doubt that he was very disappointed, but he did not show it, and impressed some of the British ministers with his fair-mindedness, even if they had mixed feelings about his persistence.

Nash and his advisers were in Berlin for Hitler's birthday and Moscow on May Day. Nash spent some time with Dr Schacht, Minister of Economic Affairs and President of the Reichsbank, to whom Norman had written 'a private warning':

He is at once charming and dangerous—an extreme Socialist and a complete Christian. He is a Minister not because he likes politics but because through politics he wishes to benefit first his own country and then the whole world. Sooner or later the schemes he is arranging . . . will bring trouble to [his country]. But in the meantime he is perfectly honest and is doing what he believes to be right from all points of view. Thus, you will find him serious even if misguided and I myself have enjoyed many conversations with him this year though I have found it difficult to agree with him in any particular.[40]

After negotiations with various departments they made an agreement whereby Germany bought some New Zealand butter in quantities related to New Zealand imports from Germany. The Germans might also buy some fruit. So Nash had his first bilateral trade agreement, even if it covered only a few hundred tons of butter a month.

There was a minor contretemps at the Polish-Russian border. Dr Sutch, whose tactlessness sometimes amounted to genius, had a Nazi flag and some Nazi literature in his bag. Their bags were searched, despite Nash's protest that it was an infringement of his diplomatic status. However, Nash induced the Russians not to search the 'diplomatic' bags, and he succeeded in placing Sutch's bag with these. The episode remained vividly in his mind all his life.

They went to the opera. They visited Tolstoy's house. He met Krupskaya, Lenin's widow, who was now a minister. Nash and Dick Campbell called on Litvinov, the Commisar for Foreign Affairs. Nash had met him in Geneva, in January, when Jordan and he attended a meeting of the Council of the League of Nations, where Nash gave an account of government policy in Western Samoa. Litvinov was friendly. At that time New Zealand was voting with the USSR at the League of Nations. When they entered his room he had on his desk a newspaper reporting the bombing of Guernica by the Fascists. He said that he hoped the western democracies would now learn something. They had long discussions with A. P. Rosengoltz, the Commissar for Foreign Trade, and other officials. The Russians were interested in New Zealand wool and hides, but they told him that the USSR produced the foods which New Zealand had to sell.

At the Foreign Office he said to Neyman that people on low incomes could not afford to pay for opera tickets and expressed scepticism about equality in Russia. He thought it still had classes. Neyman lectured him: classes arose not from differences in income but in the source of income. On May Day, they watched the procession. Nash broadcast a cautious message to New Zealand about his visit to the USSR, saying it was not necessary to agree with all the methods adopted to admire the country's efforts to solve its problems in its own way. Two of the commissars they met were soon to be executed in the great purges.[41]

They also went to Copenhagen, where they studied the Danish system of exchange controls, and to Paris for further fruitless trade talks. The French were willing to grant New Zealand their lowest tariff, in exchange for most-favoured-nation treatment, on certain items, but Nash said that the tariffs did not matter much while France had quotas. In July Nash visited the Netherlands briefly for similar talks.

Nash's European mission led to much criticism by his political enemies.

The mere fact that he had visited Moscow enabled them repeatedly to hint in later years that he was a Communist. O. C. Mazengarb, a lawyer, and unsuccessful Nationalist candidate in 1935, said in April 1937 that the failure of Nash's negotiations in London had prompted him to 'make contacts with Berlin and Moscow in order to arrange foreign trade agreements which may operate to the detriment of Great Britain just when she is embarrassed by the necessity of rearmament'.[42]

Pressed by Nash and persuaded by C. A. Berendsen,[43] the Head of the Prime Minister's Department, Savage came to London for the coronation and the Imperial Conference which followed. Nash wrote to him several times about what he should wear. The King agreed to relax the rules about dress for gentlemen from abroad, while still expressing his wish that uniform, court dress, or evening clothes with knee breeches should be worn. Nash proposed to wear 'ordinary dress'.

He enjoyed some of the perquisites of power, getting an invitation to the coronation for his old infant teacher and her husband and for the Hobdays. Hobday was now a minister in Fulham. He wrote to Mrs Nash about how delightful it would be for them to be all together in the Abbey, 'recollecting all the old battles in the old days, 1913 for instance'—an unlikely thought perhaps.[44]

Mrs Nash dictated a diary over the coronation period to send to friends and family:

Wednesday, May 12, 1937. Rose at 4.30 a.m. The hairdresser slept on couch to make sure she was here to get six feathers and veils into position. . . . We left here about 7 a.m., and the going was quite good. Was rather disappointed in our seats as we understood they would be excellent. We could see plenty of people but not the main actors in the play. We certainly did see the King crowned, and I saw much more than [that] because several seats by me were not occupied so I ran up and down the row. A pillar was in the way, otherwise the seats would have been good. I liked the part where they took off all the King's clothes except silk shirt and pants—He looked like a boy. You will see the film of it all, so no need to go into detail. After the ceremony we went to the House of Commons to lunch. Mrs. Armstrong and Sir James Parr were taken ill. Sir James went home in the ambulance, but Mrs. Armstrong wouldn't so she had to wait as no cars were allowed to leave until Their Majesties were back at the Palace. Rain started as we were going across to lunch. Then the fun started—The traffic 'phones became out of order, causing a traffic jam and some of the people did not get away from the Abbey until 10 p.m. . . .
Thursday, May 13. This was the day of the Banquet, which to my idea was the best of all. We arrived in grand state with footmen, etc. We were given the name of the person who would take us *from* dinner, not take us *to* dinner. Mine was Mr. Clynes, the Labour M.P., but when I arrived at my table this had been changed, and to my surprise Lord Nuffield was the man. (No, he didn't offer me a car)!! Said he would like to start his tour all over again, New Zealand to be the beginning. We discussed each and everyone and the man on my right was the Hungarian Minister. He asked how much one would require to have to

be able to retire in New Zealand. I said for myself £500 would fill the bill; Lord Nuffield thought £1500, but that the Hungarian Minister would want £12,000 or more. The decorations were wonderful, and the walls were adorned with gold plate. We also ate from gold plates—in fact everything was gold except the knives. I asked Lord Nuffield if he thought they would miss a salt spoon!! The flowers were all in the most delicate shades to tone with the gold. [Wal] and I were in the King's room, quite close to the main table, and saw everyone. After dinner the King and Queen again sent for [Wal] but not for me. This was the third time of asking. I shook hands with them both before dinner, also with Queen Mary. After dinner we went into the drawing room for coffee and liqueurs. Lord Nuffield said he would introduce me to the woman with the most wonderful diamonds in the world—the Marchioness of London-derry. I said afterwards—'just fancy, not really, and I possess none'. He was amused and told all I had said at dinner and afterwards. He is a very nervy man, and I wouldn't change places with him for all his money. His wife is rather ordinary.

Friday, May 14. This was the night of the Ball at Buckingham Palace. Everyone seemed to have a new dress but myself. I didn't mind as some of the new ones didn't outshine mine, and it would have been too much to try and get one that day, so I went to the four functions in the same dress. . . .[45]

In February Janet Fraser had written that 'according to an English journal & blazoned in all the N.Z. papers,' Lot was, 'the most perfectly dressed woman'. 'What a triumph & a smack in the eye for some N.Z. people'. Mrs Fraser, a Scot, did not have a high opinion of all New Zealanders. 'Had a note from Mrs Jordan [the High Commissioner's wife] she is enjoying life, she is loving every minute of it. Why are some of us born sensitive? Silly of us, we should have been born in the Colonies.' In another letter she wondered how Savage would react to London life and society. 'I think just as Mrs Jordan reacts to the situation. I think people born in the Colonies react differently. They take it all for granted'.[46] So perhaps Mrs Nash's one dress was good enough.

She had a lot more fun in her than her husband and enjoyed it all very much. She did admit in her journal that having to walk the length of the room by themselves, on arriving late for the ball, was an ordeal. But she seems not to have been unduly overawed. In his undemonstrative way, Walter also found much satisfaction in great occasions.

The 1937 Imperial Conference lasted from mid-May to mid-June. The New Zealand representatives, Savage, Nash, Jordan, and their twelve secretaries and advisers, were kept very busy, usually serving on several committees and sub-committees. Even then the delegation was too small to be represented on every committee. The main burden fell on Nash.[47] He chaired the imperial shipping committee and was a member of several others, including those on economic questions and food supplies.

Ormond Wilson wrote to Nash of Savage, 'Don't let Savage succumb to the duchesses' embrace (I don't think he is likely to as he has no wife), and see that he makes a good stand for democracy and international cooperation at the conference. He'll say anything radical that you tell him to. . . .' Savage's main speech on foreign policy was certainly written by Carl Berendsen, but was revised a little by Nash.[48] It was very critical of Britain's policy of appeasing the dictatorships and her failure to consult with the Dominions, particularly over the Hoare-Laval pact, which involved a reversal of the policy of applying 'sanctions', under the covenant of the League of Nations, against Italy, which had attacked Abyssinia. The Dominions had not, he said, received 'one word of warning'. He denounced this attempt 'to buy off the aggressor at half-price'—half of Abyssinia—and urged genuine support for the League of Nations. The way to peace must also involve considerations of 'economic justice' for all peoples. Statesmen 'ignored the fact that war was almost entirely the result of economic causes, the chief of which was the inability of the people to purchase to the same extent as they had produced, an omission which inevitably brought them into conflict with other nations over foreign markets. . . .' This doctrine, one close to Nash's heart too, may not have greatly impressed Neville Chamberlain, J. B. M. Hertzog, the Maharaja Gaekwar of Baroda, or Sir Muhammad Zafrullah Khan. Neither Britain nor any of the other Dominions joined New Zealand in defending collective security.

At the economic committee Nash took the opportunity to press his own views, equally novel to most of his audience. He described the guaranteed price and the importance of the 'nutrition movement'. Improved standards of nutrition might mean bulk purchases of food at agreed prices, but this was 'going beyond what the present Government of the United Kingdom will undertake'. The second-best was 'regulated expansion' in food supplies —and in came his bilateral agreement, at some length.[49]

After the conference the Labour Party entertained the New Zealanders at dinner. Nash dined elsewhere, but Mrs Nash went, sitting beside Hugh Dalton, chairman of the national executive. Jordan sat on the other side. He asked why the menu was in French, as Hugh Dalton wrote in his diary, and went on, 'When I asked them this in a West End restaurant a few weeks ago, they said, "The chef's a Frenchman". I said, "It would be a cow, wouldn't it, if he were a Maori?" '

Dalton's diary went on:

Savage made a most admirable speech. He spoke in clear, simple, forcible English. Some passages might have been by Abraham Lincoln. He read extracts from their election pamphlets. These were written, I think, by Nash, who also has this same gift of language. He was clearly most impatient at the attitude of British, and some other Dominion, Ministers at the Imperial Conference. He thinks the Conference has achieved nothing. He spoke of the very slow advance of the New Zealand Labour Party; how they had been 'going very slowly up the hill'; how many of their supporters had been 'losing themselves in blind alleyways'; how many had become disheartened; and then, how 'it all came with a rush' and they found themselves with a large clear majority over the Opposition. Since then, they had been doing what they promised. To-day he was sure that if there was a general election in New Zealand, they would come back with an even greater majority. Of political opponents, he said 'the closer you get to him, the smaller he appears.' He showed great self-confidence. He thought that the broadcasting of the principal speeches in Parliament had been a great success. It had roused and held public interest in Parliamentary proceedings. He had told 'people in high places', in reply to the question whether he thought New Zealand could defend itself, that of course they could not (he used a picturesque phrase, which I cannot recapture, about a herring on a grill) and that the British Commonwealth must stand together and they must all be loyal to Collective Security through the League. He was now threatened with 'quotas and levies' on New Zealand exports to this country. And yet millions of people here did not get enough to eat. He had tried to make 'people in high places' understand that you could not have one-way trade, but that if New Zealand sent more food to Britain she would buy more British manufactures and so create wages for British workmen to enable them to buy more food. If the British population was to be properly fed, that would mean much greater prosperity both for the British farmer and for the farmer in New Zealand.[50]

Savage took his own unimpressed view of all the pomp and imperial platitudes. When he returned to New Zealand he said that Nash and he left the conference 'without having had any sort of screw put on them in connection with foreign policy, defence or anything else.'[51]

While Savage was in London he and Nash attended meetings of the Committee of Imperial Defence, as the latter had earlier. There, as at the imperial conference, they discussed the security of the Pacific, threatened by Japanese militarism. Someone leaked some material from the Committee of Imperial Defence to a Communist newspaper and after an enquiry Sir Maurice Hankey, Secretary of that committee and also Secretary-General of the imperial conference, said that grave suspicion fell on Sutch. What evidence there was for this conclusion is not known. Sutch had walked across Russia in 1932. While in England on Nash's staff he had taken part in a march in favour of the Spanish republicans. He came to be regarded with much suspicion in New Zealand, too, by conservatives and anti-Communists like Peter Fraser—though he seems never to have been a Communist himself.[52]

Savage went with Nash to meetings with MacDonald and other British ministers over the trade negotiations. Savage made a blunt, simple summing up of the situation. The New Zealand population 'must be able to earn its living, either in primary industries or in secondary industries. If New Zealand's production of primary goods were to be restricted by levies or quotas, New Zealand must either embark upon secondary industries or find other markets for her primary goods'.[53] It was now obvious to the Labour ministers, as it had been to Coates, that the British market was limited. New Zealand was being thrust into economic development and independence. A world war was soon to intervene, preventing market diversification though encouraging industrialization, but in the long run New Zealand had to pursue both the options that Savage mentioned.

The trade discussions concluded without any general agreement, whether bilateral or revising Ottawa. The fact that the British government did not know what its dairy policy would be gave Nash an excuse which he could use, as he indicated, for going home without an agreement. For their part, the New Zealanders were as helpful as possible over Britain's current trade negotiations with the USA,[54] which involved some modification of imperial preference.

The British ministers had never privately been convinced that they could impose quotas or levies on New Zealand dairy produce. As early as April Walter Runciman had asked other ministers whether they should imperil trade relations with New Zealand by 'keeping in reserve a weapon which we are, in fact, unlikely to use'.[55] In September, after Nash had gone, Oliver Stanley wrote that either duties or regulated imports would be very unpopular with British voters and that Nash should be given no excuse for saying that he was kept on tenterhooks longer than necessary. He urged that they 'make a virtue of necessity' and give up the right to use these weapons. In November the New Zealand government was told that the British government did not propose to impose a levy—instead a subsidy was used to stimulate milk production. The British government was willing to give up the right, claimed at Ottawa, to use duties or levies, and asked the New Zealanders to examine the suggested tariff revisions which had been presented to Nash.[56] There the negotiations rested.

An account of Nash's trade negotiations gives no impression of the range of activities of his staff and himself on one of the most prolonged of New Zealand ministerial missions, certainly in this century. Dr Sutch helped to investigate the sugar beet industry, tyre manufacturing, council housing, dairy produce marketing, and so on.[57] A research officer, Mr Harold Innes, went to England separately, on a half-secret mission, at Nash's request. One of his tasks was to spend long hours checking records for evidence of linked directorates between British companies trading in New Zealand, and between these and American or New Zealand companies. This was one of Nash's old interests. He wanted to find out how far companies spoke with the voice of monopoly or cartel. He had a splendid memory and the information Innes gleaned was very useful. When Nash spent several days personally investigating marketing procedures for meat and dairy produce, representatives would call and find him unexpectedly well informed on who owned and controlled what proportion of their companies. In this respect Nash was very deceptive; he was much shrewder than people gave him credit for.

Mr Innes recalled one of his minister's striking characteristics, an astonishing ability to turn from the important to the trivial without any sign of noticing. He was shocked at the price charged by Moss Bros. for the 'glad rags' that Savage and he had to hire for formal occasions, and told Innes to check that company's records. Innes told him of their great profits in recent years and Nash said, 'Mr Innes, it confirms my worst fears'.[58]

Nash visited the meat and fruit markets. He travelled to Glasgow, Bristol and other cities, urging people to buy New Zealand goods so that New Zealand could buy more British. He delivered forty-three speeches, for instance to the Royal Empire Society, at the Empire Parliamentary Conference, and over the BBC. He addressed radical clubs at Cambridge University, where he received an honorary doctorate of law. Lord Rutherford lent him his cap and gown. He spoke at Oxford and lunched at New College with G. D. H. Cole. He preached at St Lawrence Jewry. He spoke at a League of Nations Union meeting, urging the powers to stop the war in Spain. One such speech greatly impressed Lord Davies, founder of the New Commonwealth movement, which sought to promote international law and order by establishing international armed forces. He wrote saying that a leader was needed. Nash was urged to return to Britain and stand for parliament 'with the possibility—I would say the probability—of becoming some day the P.M.' Nash declined politely, saying that New Zealand was his country.[59]

Altogether, in ten months abroad, about two of which were spent in ships, he visited sixty-six factories. At one of these, in Birmingham, the party was shown old account books dating back to the eighteenth century. While others studied the lists of tools, Nash ran a finger down a column of figures and said, 'That column's a farthing out'.[60] To those who knew Nash well this story was always thought 'typical'. He had meetings with 300 individuals and groups, including over 100 meetings with ministers and officials. Lot and he went to endless private lunches and dinners—with George Bernard Shaw, with the Baldwins, the Chamberlains, the Bledisloes. In addition, he ate 143 official luncheons and 98 dinners.[61] His digestion was excellent.

One of the things he enjoyed most was meeting all the famous Labour leaders, whom he had admired for years. He addressed a Labour meeting. Over 100 attended including Tom Mann, Ben Tillett, and Sidney and Beatrice Webb.[62] Probably he admired the latter couple more than anyone else. Lot and he stayed with them over two weekends.

If the books of world records included the names of the most active politicians, Nash's would be near the top. Much later in his life, Nash gave the impression that activity was an end in itself, one perhaps giving him an illusion of achievement, but in 1936-7 most of the activity was highly purposeful. For one thing, it generated a great deal of publicity about New Zealand, New Zealand exports, and himself, in the metropolitan and provincial Press. 'The Incredible Nash' was a headline in the London *Star*. The *Daily Express* described how an 'OFFICE BOY Returns to London as Finance Minister'. Even *Tobacco* talked about him, 'always neat, always courteous, always affable'.[63]

On 1 March he was given the Freedom of the Borough of Kidderminster.

He wrote that this was one of the happiest days of his life, meeting people he had not seen for so many years. He visited his old teacher and spoke at the St John's School Old Boy's Association. One old boy was 'deeply impressed . . . chiefly by his open and fearless witness of what he owed to Jesus Christ'.[64]

In early July he sailed in the *Empress of Britain* for the USA. In Washington he met President Roosevelt and Cordell Hull. He had trade discussions in Ottawa and visited Kitty Boylin in Beaver Falls, Pennsylvania. His old friend, Jim, was dead. Even in Panama he could not stop, so he interviewed the President, the British diplomats, and many other people.[65] He was back in New Zealand on 14 August.

His trip cost the taxpayer £2,374—the expenses of the whole delegation were £12,123.[66] Was it worth it? In May David Wilson had written that there was a feeling in the party that his mission was not likely to succeed, but 'everyone agrees that if you couldn't do it then nobody else could'. Now that Savage had joined him, 'we all trust that you will eventually "bring the bacon home" '.[67] His sons had written to tell him that his enemies were saying that he was gallivanting about the world at New Zealand's expense and had achieved nothing.[68] Some of the newspapers were sceptical about the results of his trip, though the Labour *Standard* had a headline, 'MR NASH'S TRIUMPH'.[69] It was generally felt that the mutton agreement was a real success. Nash claimed that because the British had dropped the threatened possible $3\frac{1}{2}$ per cent reduction, the way was open to 'regulated expansion'. This was grasping at straws—yet he did receive some public credit for saving New Zealand from a threatened levy and for securing a high quota for New Zealand mutton and lamb exports.[70] He was able to do a certain amount of boasting: he said that his mission would 'probably be the most profitable work ever done' in discussing future expansion of trade with Britain.[71] But he had not secured the bulk purchase agreement he wanted. He did not tell the House that the British had flatly rejected his offer, but that negotiations were 'not yet complete'.[72]

Dr Sutch wrote later:

Nash's negotiations and discussions abroad in 1936 and 1937 were necessary not only because of the specific proposals he had to make but because New Zealand, outside London, was comparatively unknown as an independent country and Nash had to make good, to the extent that one man can, the lack of diplomatic and government contact between New Zealand and foreign countries. In addition to the work of Jordan at Geneva, Nash did a great deal to increase the status of New Zealand in economic discussions in World War II and thereafter.[73]

Certainly Nash himself benefited from the trip. He was no longer politically unknown outside New Zealand. Indeed, in Great Britain he was now much the best-known New Zealand politician. He had an exceptionally wide acquaintance with British politicians—greater, probably, than any other New Zealand leader has had. Over the next few years this was to prove useful to him and to New Zealand.

XIII

Triumphs and Troubles

1937-8

Considering the magnitude of the government's legislative achievements in 1936, there was a remarkable amount of discontent and disaffection within the union and party ranks in 1937, mainly at the slowness of the pace towards the millenium. Since New Zealand was one of the least populous independent states, the most dependent on world trade, and hence least in control of its economic fate, its people must have been one of the most optimistic, naive, and demanding in the world. Its leaders needed to be not politicians but magicians. Early in 1938 Savage wrote to a lady who was secretary of a branch of the Unemployed Association, and a Social Creditite, that Labour had, indeed, promised a reasonable standard of living for all, but added 'I did not say, nor did I infer, that we could do this over-night'.[1]

During his travels Nash heard a good deal about the situation at home. Apart from cables from Savage and Fraser, he received many letters from John A. Lee (mainly about state housing), John S. Reid (about pensions), Ormond Wilson and others. At the 1937 conference Savage's speech, read in his absence abroad, was a demand for loyalty and unity. He urged the party not to provide ammunition for their enemies. The ministers who attended also sounded defensive against the 'implied charge' that they had not done enough, Ormond Wilson wrote. This apologetic attitude irritated him—as did Bob Semple's habit of calling anyone who urged radical measures a Communist. Still, Wilson admitted, there was overwhelming opposition to the admission of members of the Friends of the Soviet Union or Communists to the Party—the issue which created the greatest excitement.[2]

Janet Fraser wrote to Lotty Nash that Peter was, as usual, trying to keep the party 'on the right track' and getting 'disliked for his pains', amidst 'all kinds of stupid remits' (that is, recommendations on policy from branches or unions). He was, as usual, rising at 6 a.m. and working from 8 a.m. to 1 a.m. seven days a week. Moreover, he had almost lost the sight of one eye (he always wore thick glasses and peered a few inches from the page). She thought he was 'under a great nervous strain, he seems sometimes on the verge of tears . . .'.[3] He had unending problems to deal with. The government's entry into new activities like housing and marketing had produced all sorts of accusations of 'scandals' or worse. There was an outcry in the Press when the Reverend C. G. Scrimgeour, who had broadcast in favour of Labour in 1935, was appointed Controller of Commercial Broadcasting, without the post being advertised, with a salary and a commission on business turnover. This would have brought him an income of thousands. Even Mrs Fraser thought he would get £3,000 and Opposition men thought £8,000. There was much public denunciation. Mrs Fraser wrote to Mrs Nash that her husband was blamed because Savage was abroad—'*You* know who was responsible'. In fact it was Savage, who was a friend of Scrimgeour. Eventually his income was fixed at £1,500, but there was still criticism that he should get more than top public servants. The Opposition called him the 'Minister of Propaganda'.[4]

Caucus was growing increasingly uneasy. Wilson wrote that a left and a right wing was appearing over the proposed health insurance legislation. Fraser seemed inclined to bow to the British Medical Association policy that the scheme should not be universal, but merely be free for the poor.[5]

The reasons for the restiveness were no doubt numerous. One was the persistence of some unemployment; another the disappointment of the Social Creditites. But the main cause was undoubtedly that the government's programme, relatively vast for New Zealand, involved very careful and detailed planning. The public servants (like the ministers) were not, in general, very well educated nor experienced in sophisticated administration. Men like Ashwin or Campbell or Duncan or Sutch were scarce. Setting up state marketing, planning social security, organizing state housing, took many months.

During Nash's absence, and on his return, there were signs which time was shortly to prove ominous. It was, of course, widely believed by people, credit-worthy or rich, that ignorant radicals were likely to undermine, not merely them, but 'the economy'. Such people did not vote for the Labour government, but they could damage it. There was evidence of investors moving funds out of New Zealand. Nash was warned of this while in England by Wilson and by reports in the Press. New Zealand stocks were falling in England. The Beaverbrook Press was reporting that the guaranteed price had been set too high, so that inflation threatened the New Zealand economy. Savage did not help matters by saying that the government would approach holders of New Zealand securities to arrange a conversion of their stock at a lower interest rate. Nash, and when he reached England, Savage, tried to reassure investors with soothing noises to the effect that the New Zealand Labour government was not like J. T. Lang's in New South Wales —it would keep its contracts; that monetary manipulation was not the New Zealand government's method; nor was it going to nationalize the banks.[6]

Nash was very sensitive about this. When W. A. Bodkin, the MP for

Central Otago, raised the question of a flight of capital, Nash grew unusually agitated and accused him of damaging the country's credit. He did
concede that some funds might have moved to Australia, since interest on
gilt-edged securities was higher there.[7] But perhaps his faith that 'men who
are worth while' would not remove their money was a little shaken. Still,
conditions were not too bad when he presented his 1937 budget.

B. C. Ashwin of Treasury had sent him a survey of the finances in April.
There had been a surplus in the public accounts because the pensions vote
was under-expended, possibly a result of people not applying for the
increases available. Vote expenditure had gone up 70 per cent in two years.
In view of the forthcoming health and superannuation scheme, he did not
recommend increasing taxation in 1937-8. But he was a little alarmed that
£20 million had to be found from borrowing (including £3 million for state
housing to be provided by the Reserve Bank). A 'huge army' was employed,
largely paid from borrowed money, on relatively unproductive public works.
Like Sutch, Ashwin wanted to see the Bureau of Industries moving much
faster to stimulate industrial growth. The trouble was that instant industries,
to provide jobs and import substitutes, were hard to think of. Like many
countries New Zealand was employing its depression unemployed on public
works—and, soon, in the armed forces. He was sufficiently anxious to urge
Nash—and Savage—to return as soon as possible.[8]

Nash's second budget was relatively quiet. Export prices had been rising
for two years, for which he claimed no credit, and revenues were buoyant.
He did not increase the rates of income or other tax, an omission relatively
rare since then. His financial statement was mostly a report on the progress
made. Health expenditure, pensions, education and defence expenditure
were up and were to increase further. Most of the increasing government
expenditure went on social services. The House did not fail to note that the
Minister of Lands, Frank Langstone, followed up with a Social Credit
lecture on banks creating credit which implicitly repudiated Nash's soothing
message.[9]

In many ways the government was making real progress, for instance in
state housing. Nash was the Minister in Charge until the end of 1938.
Although he does not deserve the chief credit, his role was still important.
He had seen the value of municipal housing in Birmingham. In the nineteen-
twenties he had thought about how state housing could be managed in New
Zealand. He had visited a factory at Frankton where the Railway Department made cottages for its workmen and been impressed with the possible
extension of its operations.[10]

James Fletcher, an Auckland builder, a Scot, though a supporter of the
Reform Party, had reached the conclusion in 1935 that Labour would win
and wrote to Nash about the need for a housing scheme. Nash had a
number of friendly acquaintances who were successful businessmen, and

these connections proved very valuable to the government. The day after
the election Fletcher wrote offering to assist the government with housing.
He was invited to Wellington to talk with the three leading ministers and
he drew up some plans for building houses in numbers and quickly. The
government—particularly Nash—wanted to buy Fletcher's organization, as
the basis for a government department of housing construction, and to
appoint Fletcher as its director. (In the same way, the government did
purchase the plant, premises, and stock-in-trade of Picot Brothers, the
largest wholesale dealers in primary produce for the local market, as a
beginning for an internal marketing organization for dairy produce, bacon,
eggs, and honey.)[11] At first Fletcher would not agree, and various other
suggestions were considered, including his own proposal to build *all* the
houses at a fixed net profit per house.[12] But in 1937 and up until the end
of 1938 Fletcher gave serious consideration to the proposal. He informed
Nash that he had valued the total assets and stocks of his firm (at £130,000)
and put forward proposals that he should become Director in Charge of a
State Building Construction Department.[13] The negotiations again came to
nothing. Fletcher did, however, build a very high proportion of the state
houses, though not without difficulties, for at the same time he was advising
the government and public servants on the whole programme, which led to
suspicion among the latter that his advice was in his interests as contractor.[14]

Fletcher discovered that, with rising wages and import prices, costs were
increasing rapidly. He found he was going to lose money on every house,
for no escalation clause had been included in his first contract. In order to
keep the project moving the government guaranteed at the Bank of New
Zealand a £200,000 overdraft for one of his firms. Fletcher was widely
criticized for making a fortune out of state housing, but he said then and
later that it was his least profitable undertaking.[15]

It was recognized by the government that, without Fletcher's experienced
advice, and the new skills of his organization, state housing would have
taken much longer to organize. Nash and the Under-Secretary in charge of
housing, John A. Lee, both acknowledged this debt.[16] Fletcher became a
very big businessman by New Zealand standards, but his restless energies
were not all self-seeking. He had large ideas, and a genuine interest in state
housing. During World War II he became Commissioner of Defence
Construction.

Fletcher's cooperation was very important to the government. The
ministers knew little about building and less about organizing and administering a large scale enterprise like state housing. Indeed, none of their large
projects, guaranteed prices, welfare, or housing, had been planned in detail
or costed. In opposition they had no research staff. This makes their
achievements the more remarkable: the distance between dream and action
was so great.

The other two people most responsible for state housing were Lee and

Arthur Tyndall, an engineer, who was Under-Secretary for Mines, whose appointment was recommended by Fletcher.[17] Lee tackled his task with energy equal to Fletcher's. By February 1936 he had written a very long report on overseas public housing and New Zealand's housing problems. He also wrote a report on defence. Sir Alister McIntosh, who assisted him, has remarked how few New Zealand ministers have been capable of writing their own reports.[18]

Like Fletcher, Lee was not pleased with the escalating costs and shortage of skilled workers, about which he reported to caucus.[19] Like Langstone, while advocating more credit in general, he administered his own department with considerable financial caution. He even sounded mildly complaining in letters to Nash about wage increases—he would have preferred a lower wage and a larger family allowance for every child. (Nash agreed and wrote that he would welcome a family allowance of 10s. per child, though it might take 'some time to reach that position in the future'—in fact, ten years.)[20] One important influence Lee had was to insist that Reserve Bank credit—£5 million was initially approved—should finance the scheme.[21] Nash sent him details of Manchester housing. Fletcher, in England in 1937, looked into brick-making plant. Everyone worked with enthusiasm. By September 1937 Savage and Semple and Lee and Nash helped a tram conductor, Mr David McGregor, and his wife to move into the first state house, in Miramar, in Wellington.[22]

The houses were solid looking single units, more substantial in construction than much public housing; no two were supposed to be of the same design in any street. The rents were higher than people had expected, and not much lower than those prevailing, so that the very poorest people probably could not afford them. (Lee did not advocate free houses.)[23] In any case, it was intended that the houses should go to a cross-section of the community and not merely to the most needy.[24] At first they were allocated by ballot and then by a committee Nash set up to select the most urgent cases, such as applicants with large families.[25]

Undoubtedly political influence helped. In Nash's Papers there is a long list of applicants for houses in the Hutt, headed, 'Hutt Urgents on Ministerial List'.[26] There was nothing dishonest about this. Someone would approach Nash—or some other MP—with a genuine hard-luck story. Whether Nash intervened to influence the decision or not, if the applicant were lucky enough to get a house, Nash would write to him that he should be hearing good news in the future. He undoubtedly would attribute his good fortune to the minister's help. One of the first housing developments was in Nash's electorate, and he can rarely have failed to ensure that the occupant, probably a Labour voter in any case, had his loyalty reinforced.

There were other ways in which the state housing programme might have been attempted. Some groups of carpenters wanted to select their own foremen and build houses themselves, and this was attempted.[27] The possibility of a state building department was also considered. Nash apparently suggested and certainly favoured taking over Fletcher's firm. The idea of a state monopoly, or a government-dominated monopoly, attracted him. But the outcome was that the state stimulated private enterprise and sought to regulate profits.[28] This sort of cooperation between private and public enterprise was characteristic of what came to be called the 'welfare state', or the 'mixed economy', in New Zealand. Of course in those days Marxists regarded state capitalism as Fascism, which explains how it was that a builder of a welfare state could so consistently be regarded as left and right wing at the same instant by different observers.

If Lee had been more cooperative, more of a team man, he would certainly have become a minister, despite Savage. But he could not contain his resentments at the leadership—at authority. Only the Minister of Finance could authorize housing loans. While Nash was away (and Fraser was acting minister) State Advances asked for the minister's signature on one of Lee's recommendations. In September he wrote a letter, characteristically truculent, to Nash: 'if I have no authority to make commonsense recommendations of this nature, the age of stupidity and circumlocution is at hand. Obviously, my signature having become, as it were, debased currency, the next move is with yourself.'[29] It was not a letter likely to impress a superior. Tyndall later referred to Lee, in a letter to Lee himself, as 'a certain pugnacious personality'.[30] He could not work under anyone. Indeed it is doubtful how long he could have worked *with* anyone who was a rival. He acted as though every man's hand was against him, like a man on the run, as he had been on the run from oppressive authority as a boy. 'I never ask for quarter and I never give any', he told the Speaker. He loved a scrap. One day during World War I, he told the House, 'I was bored and it was mid-day. The sector was quiet. I did not know what to do so I thought I would pitch a bomb into No-Man's Land. I did not want to hit anybody. I did not wish to kill anybody. I merely wanted to pull the safety-catch out of my bomb and break the monotony with an explosion.'[31]

Lee was the most colourful figure in politics, one of the few with any depth or resonance of intellect and character; one of the most exciting public speakers, rivalled by Semple and Langstone in that respect. He was very well-read, very clever, one of the best writers of fiction (thinly disguised autobiography) in the country. Politically he had a suicidal urge. He said in the House that he would 'bend the knee' to overseas financiers only 'when they run me out of politics';[32] not the only occasion when he spoke in this way. As early as May 1936 he wrote to his wife, 'I have reached the stage wherein nothing will keep me quiet, not even a portfolio.'[33] He resented 'the almighty power of the triumvirate'; but, above all, there was his 'shallow but longtime hatred' of Savage. He wrote to his wife: 'What a complex thing a simple cold fishlike antipathy persisting over time is.' Savage's injustice to him returned at times 'like a neurosis'. And again, 'I am sure the antagonism between Joe and myself will never be resolved this side of the grave as far as Joe is concerned.'[34] It was to be true of them both.

Lee was by no means the sole source of the friction which intensified in caucus from 1936 to 1940 but he was, in personality, its focus; he pressed his opinions and rivalry furthest. In him the conflict was given dramatic form and literary expression in a series of pamphlets and books written over the years from 1938 to 1975.

Essentially the struggle was one by the credit reformers in the party to force their policies on the leaders. Two of them were in cabinet, Langstone and Mason. Outside were able men, like Lee and D. G. McMillan, a general practitioner just elected to parliament. There were a number of other credit reformers among the new MPs. In 1937 they came to form a fairly stable group of dissidents in caucus. Since one of their leaders was Lee, and their principal interest was credit, the government's financial policy and the Minister of Finance himself were usually in or near the centre of the battle.

In 1937 one new MP, Jack Lyon, twice moved that the Bank of New Zealand should be nationalized. This was a step dear to the heart of the credit reformers, who were repeatedly to return to the attack, but this time Lyon was fobbed off by Savage.[35] Lee gave notice of motion that funds for local body loans and conversions, State Advances loans to settlers and workers 'wherever the security warrants', for new industries and for all capital (public) works should be provided by the Reserve Bank. This was at a time when, as Under-Secretary in charge of housing, he was complaining of rising costs and a shortage of skilled workers. He called cheap loans to local authorities 'Socialist funds for Socialist Local Bodies'. He also wished to lower or hold existing interest rates.[36] Instead of borrowing money locally, as Nash was doing, he wished, in short, to find it at the Reserve Bank. This was in line with his view, expressed in a pamphlet in 1934, that 'Each penny of bank created credit is stolen from the community.'[37] In his eyes Labour policy was to be based on credit creation. But in the eyes of Nash and Fraser, Reserve Bank loans were to be used as little as possible. Moreover, it was difficult to hold down interest rates while borrowing on the local market. This question had been fought in 1936, and a State Advances issue at $3\frac{1}{4}$ per cent had been a fiasco. B. C. Ashwin of the Treasury estimated, in April 1937, that some £20 million would have to be raised in loans—'In fact low interest rates and heavy borrowing are a contradiction in policy.'[38]

Lee, too, was pushed off by Savage. The only point in his financial proposal to be voted on by caucus was the nationalization of the Bank of New Zealand. The voting was 14 to 14 and the motion was lost on the Prime Minister's casting vote.[39] There were other elements in this running dispute. For instance A. H. Nordmeyer, Lee, and McMillan were pressing for more encouragement to local industries. But so was Ashwin and so, for instance in his negotiations with rubber manufacturers in Britain, was Nash. It is true, however, that he was more concerned with reconciling industrial growth with the dictates of the Ottawa agreement and imperial trade than were Lee and his allies.

1938 saw two of Labour's greatest triumphs, the Social Security Act and the election of that year. It was a year of tremendous tension within the party. It was a year of mounting economic problems, which led to one of the greatest economic crises in the country's history, though a brief one, which was terminated by the beginning of World War II, for it was also the year of Munich.

In 1936 Nash had set up an inter-departmental committee of civil servants, including B. C. Ashwin and J. S. Reid. It was to investigate the government's superannuation and pension proposals. Nash's instructions had been that the government wanted everyone to receive an old age pension regardless of means. He suggested a 30s. pension for men at sixty and women at fifty-five. He envisaged a special tax to finance the benefits, on the lines of the unemployment tax, at a flat rate. This was the result of the Treasury's estimate in March, that the proposed pensions would cost over £10 million. On 1 October, as we have seen, the inter-departmental committee reported that the health and superannuation proposals would cost £30 million, almost the total government revenues.[40] With this un-welcome blow still ringing in his ears Nash left for England in search of his bilateral agreement a few days later.

While Nash was abroad the inter-departmental committee worked away. His friend and assistant, John S. Reid, kept him in touch with their thinking. In September 1937 they brought out their third report which outlined pension proposals very like those eventually adopted. It included a wide range of health, unemployment, and other benefits and pensions, but suggested that the proposed 30s. superannuation should be means-tested. Everyone should be assured of a minimum of 30s. a week at sixty-five (or sixty for women). The committee recommended that, as a step towards fulfilling Labour's election promise of superannuation for all at sixty, a universal pension of 10s. a week should be paid to all persons at sixty-five.[41]

Meanwhile, Dr McMillan's committee was drawing plans for a health scheme acceptable both to the government and to the doctors. This proved impossible to achieve. Tension developed very quickly between McMillan and the leaders of the local branch of the British Medical Association. McMillan did not enjoy great prestige among his professional colleagues. He was an active Labour man, which was very unusual for a doctor.[42] However, he was one of the very few doctors who devoted their attention to questions of public health. Indeed, with the exception of a surgeon, Douglas Robb, it is difficult to think of anyone else who did so.[43] The BMA's notion of public health reform was to oppose any alteration in the existing system except to provide free medical service to the very poor. They published their own scheme, dividing the population into four classes according to income.[44] Anything more out of touch with public opinion than a scheme of charity, when the public wanted social security, is hard to imagine. When Dr McMillan's committee reported it said, 'Unlike overseas people, self-respecting, freedom-loving New Zealanders will never respect or tolerate a service which gives one type of service to the poor and another type to the well-to-do.'[45]

McMillan's committee reported to cabinet in September 1937, shortly after Nash returned. It advocated a national health service providing medical, hospital, maternity, pharmaceutical, and dental services including free general practitioner service for all. It thought the general practitioner should receive a capitation payment per patient.

It seemed that the health and superannuation legislation was near at hand, but there was a long delay. The *National News*, by April 1938, was bombarding the ministers with quotations from their own speeches promising imminent action. On seeing this article, Savage wrote a pathetic note to Nash. It reveals, not only how little he had to do with this major legislation, but how little he could have contributed.

I suppose I have done my share in having these matters shelved from time to time—

If we find the scheme in its present form is unworkable to get the greatest benefit to the greatest number (though the scheme is to benefit all) then I think (for what it is worth) that if we told the taxpayers [& others (deleted)] why it is being held up—as we strive we learn we all find—then nothing but good *can* accrue.[46]

There were two reasons for the delay. One was the total opposition of the doctors to the health proposals, which increasingly involved Fraser in arduous negotiations. The other was that Nash had been meditating upon the apparently prohibitive cost of the superannuation proposals. He was beginning to consider how to fulfil Labour promises at an acceptable price.

The doctors fought resolutely for the principle that it was good for a patient to pay his doctor.[47] They were led by a pertinacious Shetland Islander, their president, Dr J. P. S. Jamieson.

They argued that a doctor's service to his patient is a very personal thing which does not lend itself to contractual restrictions of time or duties. A contract service would lead to a deterioration of services. Dr Jamieson argued that ordinarily a doctor did the best he could do in order to advance his reputation; but that under a panel system (whereby he received so much per patient per year for instance), his advancement would be in quantity of patients rather than quality of treatment. It was feared that doctors would give patients very brief consultations, or perhaps would send patients to hospitals to be treated for minor complaints. This argument, often advanced at the time, did not reflect favourably on the profession. Nor was the assumption correct that the government had in fact decided on the British panel system, with a payment per (poor) patient. Another argument advanced by Dr Jamieson against the capitation system of payments was that it meant an 'unknown sickness risk to the profession for a known sum': the price would be fixed but not the services.[48] Later the doctors were also to fight against a fee for service—that is for each visit to a doctor—but what was intolerable at five bob became quickly acceptable at seven and six.

The doctors smugly and repetitively asserted that there was no call to improve medical services (except for the very poor) since the standard of medicine was higher than in Britain, Germany, or elsewhere. In fact, as Dr Douglas Robb wrote, it was mediocre, lacking a high quality super-structure.[49]

Above all, they opposed a scheme for every citizen. This would mean that the state paid every doctor. The advancement of doctors would depend on the state. They would be government officials. In short, it would mean socialism. Soon the state would be dictating treatments![50]

It is true that money was not their chief objection to social security. They objected to what Jamieson called 'so revolutionary an innovation' as a universal scheme. Without benefit of Edmund Burke he wrote that, had they accepted that it was desirable, they would still have urged 'that these changes should be brought about gradually'.[51] Evolution, not revolution, was what was required.

In the absence of an hereditary aristocracy, the doctors joined the bankers and a few other small groups in forming an extremely conservative right wing. Both doctors and bankers—as in Australia—conducted newspaper and other protest campaigns against the government. The Legislative Council had long been moribund. The physicians, however, constituted themselves as an upper house of review, opposing the government, and trying to force it to revise its plans; opposing most of the people; opposing —not socialism—but the welfare state.

The lords of the BMA conceived a growing respect for Fraser, who they found to be able and generally conciliatory. Nash they thought much less so. After Nash returned he joined Fraser and sometimes Savage in negotia-tions. At a meeting with Nash and Fraser in December 1937 they found Nash resolutely opposed both to providing a free service for the poor alone and to interposing any fee between the patient and his doctor.

Both Fraser and Nash found some of the doctor's arguments hard to stomach. For instance, Jamieson said that there was nothing he could think of so personal 'as the personal relationship between the patient and the doctor, and in that relationship the patient is the doctor's first consideration before everything, and it was the patient's payment to the doctor that ensured that.' Fraser commented acidly that in that case the government must assume that everyone treated under the health scheme (and the doctors themselves agreed to a scheme for the poor) would be inefficiently treated.

At this meeting Fraser, in general, adopted the reasonable, almost benign manner appropriate to the leader, while Nash was more aggressive, at times leaning on the doctors none too lightly. He made Jamieson angry. Fraser intervened in their argument to suggest that a reasoned statement of their views should be drawn up.

Jamieson's impression of Nash was later summed up in a book by another doctor:

It was now obvious to the profession that they had a new and formidable figure to deal with in the shape of the Minister of Finance. Mr Nash, as the acknowledged party dialectitian, was obviously most interested in and intimately concerned with the setting up of a universal health service, and his intervention in the negotiations was, for the officers of the B.M.A., a new and disturbing development. Nash's approach was essentially dogmatic and rigid. He appeared to be obsessed with the idea that the B.M.A.'s opposition to the Government's ideas was political in origin, and his intense and unremitting suspicion of the profession's motives was to colour the atmosphere in which subsequent negotiations took place. Jamieson in particular found Mr Nash very difficult to deal with, and the two men found it virtually impossible to discover any common ground intellectually. Jamieson confessed to an instinctive antipathy for Mr Nash, and there seems little doubt that this feeling was heartily reciprocated. The B.M.A. discovered that Mr Nash had none of Fraser's genial and pragmatic approach, nor were they able to establish during the negotiations the feelings of mutual respect that lay between them and Fraser. When dealing with Mr Nash, any proposals they offered were placed upon the procrustean bed of his particular brand of Socialism, and many of their ideas were faced with suspicion almost paranoid in intensity.[52]

At a further meeting in February the negotiations with the BMA broke down completely. Once again Nash angered the doctors.[53] In the same month, while playing the socialist bogey before the doctors, Nash figured as a financially orthodox renegade in front of a majority of caucus. He came forward with a scheme of 'social insurance' whereby everyone contributed throughout their working lives to a fund from which they drew an income-related pension on retirement. This was insurance not charity, but was quite different from the scheme supported by caucus, of paying superannuation from current taxation. Such schemes as Nash's new one were of course common—in New Zealand it resembled government superannuation or the universal superannuation introduced by another Labour government in the nineteen-seventies. To credit reformers like McMillan and Lee, however—and to a majority of caucus—in 1938 it seemed conservative because it would be financed out of savings. Lee wrote that, though creating an 'enormous interest-bearing fund', it would create £300 million more debt.[54]

The new scheme involved all workers contributing $2\frac{1}{2}$ per cent (6d. in the £) of their income into a fund. This would be supplemented by the state. The superannuation paid (at sixty for women, sixty-five for men) would be income-related, but the differences were small. For instance, a single man earning £5 a week would retire on £2 3s. 3d. a week, but the single man earning £10 would receive £3 7s. 9d. No one would get less than 30s.[55]

Previously Nash had instructed the public servants to work out a scheme paid for from current taxes. Precisely when he changed his mind is uncertain. Possibly, while overseas, he grew out of touch with New Zealand opinion and in touch with English actuaries.

In late 1936, after Nash had left, Sir Walter Kinnear, Controller of Health and Unemployment Insurance at the Ministry of Health, and Godfrey Ince, Chief Insurance Officer at the Ministry of Labour, visited New Zealand to discuss the government's plans. Nash later talked with Kinnear in England and he suggested the secondment of a British government actuary to New Zealand.[56] The man selected, George Maddex, travelled back to New Zealand with Nash. Perhaps he influenced Nash's thinking.[57] In any case, he was not the only person involved who was likely to think on actuarial lines. It had been clear for some time that the country could not afford a 30s. pension for everyone without a means test. The extra taxes required were politically unacceptable. What *could* be afforded? B. C. Ashwin had earlier suggested that actuarial principles should be adopted for part of the scheme.[58] John S. Reid had proposed in 1937 that an insurance scheme should be introduced for people under twenty.[59]

These three men became Nash's 'team' to work out the details of social security. He took them to Lake Waikaremoana, 'to think', during the summer of 1937-8. There was a consensus among them that a system of 'social insurance' might solve the financial problem. It would fulfil Labour promises of a universal scheme, while postponing most payments, except for the pensioners, into the future. A 'social insurance' scheme had a further, powerful and probably irresistible appeal to Nash. It would have involved building up a huge fund from people's contributions. It could be used, he noted, and explained to caucus, to pay off the national debt.[60] Nash disliked the national debt and came to like it even less within a year or two.

Nash's new scheme was presented to caucus in February 1938. At the same time Peter Fraser sought to compromise with the BMA, apparently by introducing a means test for medical and health benefits.[61] Caucus was in no mood to compromise, and in no mood for Nash's complex tables—his 'beautiful material', Lee called it.[62] Fraser (who chaired the meeting) agreed, after a long discussion, that the health scheme should be universal in its scope. No vote was taken but Nash had to agree to bring down 'an alternative scheme' of superannuation and pensions.[63]

Both Nash and Fraser fought a brief rearguard action,[64] but they were forced by caucus opinion to return to and reconsider the kind of health and superannuation schemes that they had wanted in 1936, before they ran into costs and the doctors. A caucus committee and then a parliamentary select committee drew up the—almost final—plans for social security. Nash was a member of both, but for the moment eclipsed by Nordmeyer who chaired the select committee and presented the report of the other committee to the full caucus.

The caucus committee worked on the basis that the scheme should be comprehensive: that contributions should be according to means and benefits according to needs. They recommended a social security tax of 1s. in the £ to pay for the scheme. There would be free hospital and general practitioner treatment. Superannuation would be 30s. a week for men and women at sixty, but subject to a means test. The government's promise of superannuation for everyone had been put aside: caucus had had to bend to the financial wind too. The other important qualification was that the doctors refused to cooperate, so that the general practitioner service had to be postponed.

When the doctors presented their evidence to the National Health and Superannuation Committee they once again crossed swords with Nash. He pressed Jamieson very hard to get him to admit that everyone should have the same quality of service, irrespective of who paid for it. He also tried to get him to admit that, provided that the patient could choose his doctor, and that the doctor was paid, the source of the income did not matter. On this point the doctors stuck. Dr W. P. P. Gordon twice asked whether the government would let the patient pay *part* of a fee-for-service, and Nash said 'No'. Gordon said that this was the crux of the matter.[65] Nash could not see why this was important, if the fee was agreed upon and paid. The doctors themselves accepted that poor men's fees could be paid by the state, so why should the more affluent have to pay in part? The doctors would not accept the suggestion that they intended to overcharge the patient for his portion. What was left was the old-fashioned notion that self-help was good for people; that partial free enterprise was better than none. So Nash was right: their opposition *was* political.

When Savage, at long last, announced the government's proposals at a meeting in Wellington in April 1938 he received a tumultuous, an ecstatic welcome. Later criticism, however, led the government to adopt, in principle, a suggestion made originally by John S. Reid, one of Nash's assistants, that it would be fair if every contributor, whatever his means, received 'some return, by way of pension'. He suggested a means-tested pension of 30s. at sixty and a universal pension of 10s. a week at sixty-five.[66] The universal pension was, however, fixed initially at £10 a year, on the suggestion of the government actuary, Stanley Beckingsale. This, as it now seems, token benefit was the first of its kind in the world.[67]

Nash became Minister in Charge of Social Security. Bill Parry, the Minister in Charge of Pensions, was a simple soul who would have found mastering so large and complicated a brief rather difficult. On the other hand Nordmeyer or McMillan, who could have mastered it, were at once new MPs, and leading caucus dissidents. Nash, on the positive side, was an old hand, acceptable to the old hands; moreover, social security was a money matter as much as a health or social security matter. So he introduced the Social Security Bill, 1938, possibly the most important single piece of legislation in New Zealand history. To ensure that every single person in the community would enjoy a minimum acceptable standard of living, in sickness or in health, in employment or not, married or widowed, and including 'free' medical treatment was a great deed. No other country had done it. Nash had dreamed of it for many years. Though, for once, he did not mention it, the 'first charge' must have rung in his ears, a triumphant peal, as he spoke in the House on 16 August 1938.

He praised Dr McMillan's work and that of the committees. He recalled that when 'King Dick' Seddon had introduced the old age pensions bill in 1897 the conservatives had cried 'financial ruin', as they did now; and on each occasion the critics cried 'socialism'. Nash said that the benefits proposed would lead to increased production and to a more just distribution of income and prosperity. (This was a central Labour reply to the criticism of expense. Social Security would not reduce the resources available in the community, but would redistribute them in favour of the old, the sick, the poor, the young. . . .)

The universal superannuation proposal, he said, was 'the best step forward ever taken in this or any other country—small in itself but magnificent in its conception to give everyone by right what they ought to have received years ago. That is the first and major principle embodied in the Bill'. He concluded by saying that the Act would be

the first Social Security Act, on any proper definition of that term, ever written in any statute-book in the world. All those people in this country who to-day are suffering from circumstances over which they have no control will be within seven months' time, as far as it is humanly possible to do it by a Government, freed from the circumstances that they are facing to-day—namely, the circumstances of dreading where to get the money from to make provision for their old age ; where to find the money to pay the doctor ; where to provide the ordinary things associated with health ; how to provide for the youngsters if the father and mother are dead. There is more security in the proposals contained in this Bill than in any proposals that have been set out by any Government in any other country up to the present. We have the responsibility of writing the Bill into the law, and of administering the legislation when it is written into the law. If it brings the benefits I believe it will bring, then once more this country will be 'God's Own Country'.[68]

It was a justifiable boast: from each according to his means; to each according to his needs. It was the most comprehensive system of public health, pensions, and superannuation in the world. Years later Sir William Beveridge, author of the post-war British scheme, wrote to Nash that he never ceased to cite New Zealand as the only country ahead of his own.[69]

When Nash was an old man, one of his proudest recollections was of the time when Maddex, the British actuary, said privately and publicly that the government would ruin the country with its frighteningly expensive scheme. 'You cannot do it', he said. Nash replied, 'We are going to pass a bill.'[70]

The details of the bill finally presented were not primarily the result of his own thinking and work, but rather the product of several committees. Some civil servants, as well as McMillan and Nordmeyer, had contributed. Caucus, notably the credit-reforming dissenters, had had the final say on the broad principles. They believed that the country could afford it because they believed that the money could be created. Cost was of no account. And they were, in a sense, proven right by increasing future production and inflation, which made the cost less onerous.

Yet the old Labour leaders deserve some credit. Savage, Holland, Fraser, Nash, Sullivan—they had held to their ideal for twenty or more years. They had helped to create a climate of opinion within which social security was acceptable. Moreover, Fraser and Nash had had the more-or-less continuous responsibility for deciding on action, action to make the ideal 'practicable'. When Savage spoke in the social security debate he began by acknowledging Nash's 'monumental work' on the bill. (He managed to out-Nash Nash by describing the scheme as 'applied Christianity'.)[71]

Nash's name did not (like Abou ben Adhem's) lead all the rest, yet it stood high on the list (in a democratic book of gold) of those who loved their fellow men.

The Social Security Act was to come into force after 1 April 1939, a provision which held the implied threat that if Labour were defeated, a National government would not introduce it. Nash considered that the Act, with this provision, which was Savage's doing, won them the election.[72] Although he was by this time very sick, with the cancer which was to kill him, Savage had not lost his trade union shrewdness.

The election was fought with some bitterness by the National Party, which was in better shape than in 1935, having got rid of splinter parties, but it was weakly led by Adam Hamilton, of whom a political scientist has written that, if asked a question at a meeting, he 'was usually able to think of a good answer next morning'.[73] Conservatives felt that they were losing, and among them there was a great deal of fear. 'Junious & Coy.' distributed a pamphlet in Nash's electorate one night which described his 'Communistic proclivities', his prosecution for bringing in seditious literature, and his address in Moscow 'on May (Red) Day . . . to hundreds of thousands of Russian and foreign cut-throats'. (The National Party assured him that they had not put this out.)[74]

Hamilton said that private enterprise and individualism were now threatened by socialism and supreme state authority: this, in his view was the chief issue. In the House and on the hustings, Hamilton reiterated that the objective of the government was to socialize all property and wealth. It was bringing about the state control of industry—namely, two joinery factories, so far—state houses, state control of production and marketing and prices. Nash's opponent, J. W. Andrews, the Mayor of Lower Hutt, took the same line. Socialism was 'a poisonous foreign product' aimed at destroying the system of government. 'This may be your last opportunity to exercise a free vote at the Ballot Box', he said, 'the Government has already taken Dictatorial powers.' He added that 'The man below the average is out for socialism; the average man and the man above average are out for private enterprise.'[75] (It turned out that a majority were below the mean.) Andrews, a builder, repeatedly denounced state housing. Like Hamilton, he also denounced the Social Security Act, on the grounds of its cost.

Labour's policy was drawn up by a committee, which included Semple, Webb, and Lee. Mainly it stressed Labour's achievements—the five-day, forty-hour week, unemployment down to a very low level, guaranteed prices —above all, the promise of social security. There was still talk of credit for industries, low interest rates, and the continuance of negotiations for bilateral trade agreements.[76]

This time Head Office had £17,000 to spend on the election.[77] The party published a pamphlet by Nash, *Guaranteed Prices—A Successful Reality*, in an attempt to quell the mounting criticism among farmers of the guaranteed price system. In 1936-7 there had been a small deficit in the Dairy Industry Account—in other words, the guaranteed price had been higher than overseas prices. But in 1937-8 there was a surplus. Farmers who had been happy to receive the subsidy the year before, now loudly demanded that the surplus be paid to them. Nash announced in mid-1938 that an extra payment would be made. He claimed that this was not sacrificing the principle of the guaranteed price, but was retrospective compensation for increased costs, such as wages. While his supporters saw this as 'not submitting to political expediency' but as playing their cards well, others, like Ormond Wilson, thought it a betrayal.[78] A well-known economist, Colin Clark, had said in February that New Zealand farmers had the highest standard of living in the world. He wrote to Nash, 'I doubt if any where in the world will be found such an insatiable lust for money as in the bosom of the New Zealand farmer.'[79]

The Farmers Union executive and the Dairy Board wanted the price to be fixed by a joint government-industry tribunal, but a National Dairy Association conference did not support its leaders and deferred to Nash's view that the government should decide.[80] The government set up a committee to advise on the price and it unanimously recommended a large increase. Nash believed then and thereafter, as he hinted darkly in announcing the price for 1938-9, that enemies of his system sought to wreck it by suggesting a price which would result in a large deficit. In this case the recommended price would have caused a deficit of £2.8 million.[81] The government would not accept it. Nash announced a price significantly lower, though still causing a deficit. Although, in his view, and quite correctly, the government had the final decision, the farmers felt they had been betrayed. They brooded about this for years and never forgave him. Nash attributed the loss of several 'butter-seats' in the 1938 election to this decision.[82] But it does not seem that the adverse effects were so immediate.

Though Nash's majority dropped to 6,814, the government had a crushing victory. It won 56 per cent of the votes, the first majority victory of any party for thirty years. (It won only 46 per cent in 1935.) Though it lost three rural seats, possibly because the non-Labour vote was not split by splinter parties as in 1935, it won many more rural votes than in the previous election, and nearly as many as National. The three Ratana Maori MPs supported the government, so it had fifty-three seats to National's twenty-five. (There were two independents.)[83] This election was to prove to be the peak of Labour's popular support.

In denouncing the increase of state controls, which was very marked under the Labour government, National had not struck a note which the public heard loudly. It has, indeed, rarely shown signs of fearing the state. Nor, in a period of rising prosperity, was there much response to Opposition denunciations of rising taxes. During the budget debate, Hamilton had pressed this line of attack, but, in fact, Nash had not increased income taxes in 1937 or 1938. Hamilton had come nearer to finding the government's Achilles heel when, in the same debate, he referred to the declining overseas funds, and referred darkly to the fate of Newfoundland, which had borrowed and spent too freely, and finished up in 1933 in the hands of a receiver, in the form of a British Commission, losing its independence.[84] But this had not been his main weapon during the election.

XIV

The Exchange Crisis

1938-9

During the depression New Zealand built up in London a large reserve of sterling funds, not spent on imports because of a lack of effective demand among the poor and the hungry. These overseas assets totalled sterling £38 million in December 1935. They drained away, especially in 1936. Then, between 30 April and 30 November 1938, they declined from £28.6 million to less than £8 million.[1] Since these funds, which paid for imports, had been regarded as a key indicator of the state of the economy, and had long been its unacknowledged regulator,[2] this was a dangerous situation.

For most of 1938 the government turned a blind eye towards the London balances. Savage and Nash denied that there was a flight of capital or that the sale of foreign exchange was restricted, and attributed contrary assertions to a lack of patriotism and a desire to damage the country's credit.[3] But that was being damaged by figures, not words.

Even before the election there was great public unease about money. The country was swept by rumours that the deposits in the Post Office Savings Bank were not safe. An officer of a trading bank wrote to Nash in November that they were trying to reassure their clients and telling them to leave their money in the Savings Bank.[4] There were heavy withdrawals. Similar fears encouraged a flight of capital abroad.

The transfer of these funds abroad, for instance by purchasing Australian shares, had attracted Nash's attention in 1936. Probably this movement was a result of people having left funds in New Zealand to benefit from Savage's promised revaluation, and transferring them when it did not eventuate.

An economist of the time estimated that the 'panic' export of private funds accounted for more than half the loss of reserves in 1938. Whether he was correct it is not possible to say,[5] but there certainly was a large-scale transfer of funds. Bankers and others wrote to Nash about the requests for capital transfers and the unpatriotic actions of some of the meat companies, for instance, who were selling their funds to the highest bidders.[6]

The 'flight of frightened capital' did not alone explain the economic crisis. There had been considerable over-importing—import costs exceeded export receipts by over £3 million in 1938. But, as Nash explained, New

Zealand needed about a £12 million surplus to service public debts and make other payments. The increase in imports had been largely generated by the government's expansionist policies: for instance the public works programme created a demand for machinery. It was not possible (as the credit reformers supposed) to divorce internal from external expenditure.

To conservatives, like Lefeaux of the Reserve Bank, the situation was quite clear: the country was not living within its income, a situation which could not continue indefinitely. The government must refrain from inflationary measures, reduce expenditure to match income.[7] The traditional response to a drop in reserves was for banks to call up overdrafts, the government to introduce 'cuts', reducing demand and producing unemployment. This, Nash explained to an importers' conference in January 1939, the government had declined to do or to accept. Instead, it decided to 'meet our commitments; maintain our living standards' and reduce imports by introducing exchange controls and import selection.[8]

There can be no doubt that this measure, not taken until December 1938, was belated.[9] In 1937 Nash had been collecting information on the Danish system of controls. He had told caucus in November 1937 that exchange controls would be introduced.[10] He had told the British in 1936-7 that this would be done. He was well aware that funds were being transferred abroad through 1938.[11] Later he claimed that the situation did not become serious until November, but one reason for the crisis was the lack of earlier restraints.

Why had the government not acted? There were several reasons, of which one was probably decisive. Nash had seen exchange controls primarily as a consequence of a bilateral trade agreement with Britain. He lost interest when his mission to London failed. The British strongly opposed the introduction of such controls. They would probably result in a breach of the Ottawa agreement, which had promised British exporters the opportunity for reasonable competition with domestic producers on the New Zealand market.[12] Import regulation or selection might involve an effective prohibition of certain British exports. Lefeaux was extremely hostile to exchange controls, and argued against them on many grounds, faithfully acting as the mouthpiece of British authority.[13] It cannot be said that Nash yielded to imperial views but he could not ignore them; he had to give them due weight. For one thing, a large London loan conversion had to be arranged in 1939.

Probably the main reason why nothing was done for so long was that it was election year. To admit that there was a crisis, to introduce exchange or import restrictions, would have been an admission of failure and a powerful stimulus to the Opposition. Mark Silverstone, Nash's agent on the Reserve Bank directorate, had written to him on 1 June, 'I can see serious trouble coming', but he did not think Nash should act before the election.[14] That he postponed action for this reason cannot be proven, but is very convincing. Certainly that was what John A. Lee thought.[15] The introduction of Social Security had been postponed to win votes; exchange controls so as not to lose them.

Nash was frank in explaining the controls as due to the need to conserve funds. Savage pretended that they were introduced to 'insulate' the Dominion from unfair overseas competition and to encourage industrial development. This explanation was pressed by W. B. Sutch. Allan Fisher wrote to Nash, 'Sutch tells me that it is a mistake to suppose that pressure on London funds is the complete explanation and that control is intended to be a weapon of genuine socialist reconstruction with "selective importing" as the key-note. (A ribald enquirer might ask, selective by whom? by Sutch? which would no doubt be unfair).'[16]

Some Labour MPs, like D. G. McMillan and Lee, as well as Sutch, had for some time seen import controls as the key to industrial growth. However, they were not introduced as part of a large economic strategy, but in an atmosphere of emergency. Ashwin of Treasury and Wood of Customs advised that it was impossible to reduce imports to the extent required to balance receipts and payments—some £10 million to £12 million—without cutting industrial raw materials and other essential items, endangering employment and living standards. Other measures such as taxation, local borrowing, and a reduction of public works would be needed; a large rise in local costs and prices must somehow be avoided.[17]

The months from November 1938 to late 1939 were politically among the most anxious and tense in Nash's political life. He had met the fate of all but the luckiest of New Zealand Ministers of Finance. In a small democracy with a dependent economy, in which the voters expect glittering promises, the Treasury was the most vulnerable position where able men and wizards of finance, like Julius Vogel, Harry Atkinson, J. G. Ward, and Gordon Coates, trying to make the ends of promises and economics meet, had fallen. To some extent Nash was lucky. He was saved, not by the whistle, but the war.

While he was trying to cope with the internal crisis, and soon with its consequences in London, he was also at the centre of the biggest storm the Labour Party has ever experienced. His financial policies were under fire from almost every direction at once, but undoubtedly the party criticism was the most wearing.

The first caucus after the election, on 3 and 4 November, was the occasion of a very unpleasant dispute. Nash outlined the financial problem. McMillan and Anderton moved that a caucus committee, including four credit reformers and three of the leading ministers, be set up to investigate the financial crisis and report back. It was scarcely the time for committees. McMillan withdrew his motion, apparently after a heated debate, when Fraser and Nash moved that cabinet should consider exchange controls, embargoes, or tariffs, in that order of preference. If the former were feasible, cabinet would impose them without reference to caucus; if not, there would be another meeting.

The government had not adopted the dissidents' policies. They were now trying to seize the power to implement them. Already two credit reformers were in cabinet. They wanted a stronger representation. In May 1936 Dr McMillan, a new MP, had moved that in future all cabinet ministers should be elected. Savage had ruled the motion out of order on the grounds that it was the present system, which was quite untrue.[18] The issue had smouldered for two and a half years; now they were trying again. Lee now moved, at the meeting in November 1938, that cabinet should be elected by a preferential vote of all caucus members. According to him, Savage threatened to resign. There was an emotional debate, and the motion was carried by 26 to 22. Savage said that he would not feel bound by the resolution, and would refer the issue to the annual conference,[19] which was not unreasonable, since the method by which cabinet was chosen was as much a matter for the party as for caucus. In the event, however, six members of the central executive attended the next caucus, in early February, to submit the executive's own proposals for selecting cabinet. A joint caucus-executive committee then drew up rules which were accepted. The leader was to be elected by caucus in the year of each general election, and could nominate his own cabinet, but its members had to be approved by a caucus vote. If any names were not approved, members could recommend others to the leader. He would then select those he wanted from among the nominations. These names, too, had to be approved by caucus.[20] Altogether it was an unwieldy attempt to combine leadership with democracy.

After the November meeting Ben Roberts, a farmer MP and an old Labour man, wrote Nash a letter which ought to have been consoling. Certainly it revealed the piety with which some of the party regarded their works:

I feel I should write you a few lines, this Sabbath evening, & let you know that I am sending a few sympathetic 'Thoughts' to yourself & Joe.
You are both carrying a terrific burden. (Altho I was not in Caucus to hear your Statement) I have gathered sufficient information to know that the burden is heavy.—However, it is the 'Inner' trouble which is the burden, & I feel like saying 'Father forgive them, they know not what they do'.
Our comrades are worshipping at the shrine of 'Democratic' Form & letter—but they know not the Spirit.
The Work that we have been able to accomplish during the past 20 years has been wonderful & our political success is the wonder of the Age ; & what took place the other day, while regrettable & undesirable is almost inevitable. Do you & I expect to evade the trials of the Carpenter of N.—It cannot be done. . . .[21]

He went on to say that Nash's role—and to a lesser extent his own—were not confined to New Zealand budgets. They must contribute to a ' "New Deal" in World Affairs'.

In December Lee, Nash's Under-Secretary, launched a powerful attack on Nash himself. He wrote a long letter to members of the Labour caucus. Apparently W. J. Lyon, an Auckland MP and one of the leading Labour credit reformers, intentionally or not, began to circulate it. It was soon published, possibly by National supporters, as a pamphlet, *A Letter which every New Zealander should read.*[22]

The 'Lee Letter' denounced Nash as a conservative blocking the intro-duction of radical Labour reforms. It publicized caucus disputes over pensions and said that Nash's was 'the greatest opposition to the present Social Security Scheme'. But principally it attacked his financial policy. Nash had adopted a 'god-like attitude' and was persisting with financial orthodoxy against party policy. He was denounced for not introducing exchange controls earlier, and for not being more daring in his recourse to Reserve Bank credit. Lee wrote, 'We took over the Reserve Bank to free Labour development from capitalist debt', and asserted that they should have used its credit to wipe out most of the public debt. How London investors could be induced to accept a New Zealand credit issue was not perhaps clear. Lee suggested that loans should have been refunded at a much lower interest rate. He always objected to paying interest to private investors to provide for national development. He ridiculed 'the inflation bogey'. He advocated further credit expansion—at a time when New Zealand was suffering acutely from over-importing because of internal inflation. Thus the cure for New Zealand's post-election hangover was to be more of the stimulus that caused it. Someone wrote to Nash that Lee had seen a man walk steadily after three whiskies and refused to believe that a whole bottle might have a different effect. The 1939 conference condemned Lee's action in issuing the letter as a breach of party loyalty and discipline and passed a vote of confidence in Nash and in his financial policy. But Lee continued as Under-Secretary—sharpening up his pen.

Caucus pressure was one factor which led the government to introduce exchange and import controls, but not the principal factor. Given the delay in acting before the election, even if the government had been willing to adopt deflationary measures, some kind of exchange controls or quotas had become essential.

One of the government's main difficulties was that, to deal with its extensive policies, it had very limited resources of administrative skills and other expertise, whether among the ministers or in the public service. It had promised much, and could not deal with everything at once, as caucus seemed to ask. For instance industrial development had long been a plank in policy, one now especially desirable, to get men off public works into more productive enterprises. This had come up in caucus, raised by

McMillan and Nordmeyer. The government had taken prompt action to protect industries against Australian competition.[23] But new industries had not assumed a focal role in strategy, because of the hope of getting a new trade agreement with Britain, because industrialization was a slow process, and because other things seemed to have a higher priority. Semple's public works provided immediate jobs; the Bureau of Industry seemed sluggish. But now industrialization assumed urgent importance in policy. Import substitutes were vital to economic survival.

On 16 April 1939 Nash wrote for cabinet a paper on import selection, doubtless notes for a talk, which surveyed the economic crisis. It began, 'To ensure the promised facilities for the expansion of secondary industry —the amount of sterling required in excess of the sum estimated to be available is £14,750,000'. Moreover, a loan of £17 million was to reach maturity in early 1940. 'If Primary and Secondary Industry is to expand in accord with the Government's policy' it would be necessary to borrow the money to refund it.[24] The emphasis was on industrialization; the instrument was the one New Zealand had used whenever it wanted to speed up economic development—overseas loans.

Labour had let things go before the election. It had ignored a slight drop in export receipts from the previous record years, ignored import levels and capital transfers. Nash was to concede, talking to British ministers in June, that they had acted 'perhaps rather imprudently'.[25] Certainly he could not be given high marks for economic management, though he might receive them instead for political shrewdness leading to electoral victory. Now he had to find the right economic medicine which was—again—a loan. Without overseas borrowing New Zealand could neither industrialize nor meet its overseas obligations.

In normal times the short-term remedy for over-importing would have been borrowing; the long-term prescription, to live within the means afforded by export earnings. But in mid-1939 the situation could scarcely have been less propitious. Europe was on the verge of war; New Zealand's credit, among conservatives and investors, was nearly nil.

W. J. Jordan, the High Commissioner, had inquired at the Bank of England about a £10 million loan and was told it would be next to impossible; nor could the £17 million maturing loan be renewed unless some £10 million of it were repaid in cash. Nash had approached the British government for a £5 million loan to improve defences. The British had said that New Zealand must pay for its defence out of its own resources.[26]

In England the manufacturers were protesting loudly at losing their New Zealand market because of the import controls. They were getting big headlines. In business and financial circles there was a 'whispering campaign' against the New Zealand government.[27] New Zealand stocks fell in Britain after the election.[28]

Official British views of the Labour government varied from impatience to scorn to outright hostility. In February Sir Eric Machtig of the Dominions Office wrote in a minute that, 'The Treasury, as you know, are incensed over the policy of the New Zealand Government which has brought about this situation. . . .' A Treasury officer, S. D. Waley, wrote to the Dominion Office, 'I profoundly hope that this [loan] proposal will be turned down.' A cable drafted in Treasury to Sir Harry Batterbee, the British High Commissioner in Wellington, said that 'it appears little short of childish that the New Zealanders should waste their substance over a period of years and then complain because H.M.G. is unwilling to come to their assistance financially at the first hint of difficulty'.[29]

The initial response of the British to news of the import controls and queries about loans was very unsympathetic. Malcolm MacDonald sent informal comments to Jordan on the need for New Zealand to live within its income and of the difficulty of resisting pressure from British industry to denounce the Ottawa agreement. The Secretary of State hinted at the same possibility in a despatch to the Governor-General.[30] A series of 'friendly warnings' was sent to the errant Dominion, forwarding the complaints of the Federation of British Industries (a powerful lobby influencing economic foreign policy) about, for instance, the complete prohibition on the import of some British goods such as woollen goods and hardware.[31] The British violently objected to New Zealand developing 'unnecessary' or 'uneconomic' industries, contrary to Ottawa.[32] A memorandum written in the British Department of Overseas Trade said that Nash's proposals to revise Ottawa in 1936 had been 'revolutionary'. Now he wanted to control all primary produce marketing and make trade agreements so as to determine what would be imported and in what quantities. This was 'economic totalitarianism'. The British Trade Commissioner in Wellington, Robert Boulter, wrote to the author of the memorandum that it was interesting that he had 'spotted what Nash is after'. A Bank of England official, R. N. Kershaw, an Australian, wrote that New Zealand was following Germany in trying to use exchange controls to develop industries, but he doubted whether New Zealand had equal skill in planning.[33]

What irritated the British most was that the New Zealand government appeared to be using a temporary economic crisis to establish permanent industries, contrary to Ottawa, and asking for British money to finance the venture. This was the view of Oliver Stanley, President of the Board of Trade, who expressed it clearly to Nash himself in June.[34] Other aspects of Labour policies were subjects of frequent comment in the Bank of England and at government meetings. One was the scale of New Zealand public works, proportionately vast in comparison with Britain's or Australia's. And there was a strong feeling that New Zealand was asking for a British subsidy for its standard of living and its social security system.

There was some understanding of New Zealand's problems, notably in the Dominions Office. One of its staff wrote that the British might have to recognize, as with Australia, 'that industrial development for reasons of defence, migration, employment and even of amour propre has got to come in the case of countries at the other side of the world, and that the case of a small country such as New Zealand we must accept the position that for many years no industry can be economic in the United Kingdom sense of the term without a virtual monopoly of the market.'[35] But the predominant feeling was that New Zealand should be pressed hard. The question was, how hard? For Britain to terminate the Ottawa agreement or for New Zealand to default or devalue would, ministers and officials felt, have a bad psychological effect on some of Britain's allies. If New Zealand received no financial help, the result would be an intensification of the policy of import restriction, damaging British exports further. Britain could not—the Secretary of State for Dominion Affairs, Sir Thomas Inskip, said at a meeting of ministers—'take over' New Zealand like Newfoundland. (G. E. Boyd Shannon had reported from the British High Commissioner's office in Wellington that the Opposition saw in the recent appointment of the first British High Commissioner in New Zealand 'the forerunner of a financial commission from England'.[36]) Consequently, Inskip said, they had to consider whether they could afford to let New Zealand go bankrupt. But the consensus was definite: there would be no assistance from the British government with a loan. New Zealand must put her own house in order and live out of her own garden.[37]

It was decided that Nash should go to London again. On instructions from London, Batterbee sped him on his way with a personal and secret (and holier-than-thou) letter on 30 April, saying that Britain was restricting progress in social legislation and even cutting her standard of living to prepare her defences. New Zealand should look to her national safety too.[38]

Nash was leaving a tattered utopia. The import licensing scheme, in its first six months, was a mess. Obviously there had not been adequate detailed planning. In the first half of 1939 imports were much greater than in the same period in 1938. Licences had been issued for all goods on order in December 1938, and those orders had proven to have been inflated, possibly by importers fearing controls. Moreover, the government had had to authorize increased orders for plant, machinery, and raw materials for new industries.[39]

While Nash was travelling to England, the situation deteriorated further. An Auckland importer challenged the validity of the import control regulations and a judge ruled that they were not authorized by legislation and invalid.[40] Savage cabled that a 'critical situation' was rapidly developing. Overseas funds did not accumulate during March to May, in the usual way. The trading banks were 'heavily over sold in sterling' and the Reserve Bank could not reimburse them. Import licences had been issued well in excess of available overseas funds. Soon the newspapers were full of alarming stories of trading banks refusing to provide funds to pay for imports which had been licensed. Eventually the banks agreed to make a confidential sterling £2 million loan to the government so as not to wreck Nash's London negotiations. He cabled Savage in early June that news of New Zealand banks refusing to provide funds 'made discussion very difficult.'[41] So did an announcement by Savage that the import licensing would be permanent, in the interests of industrialization, which British officials quoted to Nash,[42] who was well aware that Savage meant it.

Nash was a man who disliked unpleasantness and believed in being pleasant. Some of the meetings in London in 1939 were among the most distasteful in his life. On arrival, Nash had a preliminary chat with Sir Thomas Inskip. Nash was very conciliatory. For instance he said that in his view, though not perhaps Savage's, the need for import restrictions would gradually tail off. He was even willing to contemplate that New Zealand would be prepared to accept advice from British industrialists about what industries might be 'economic'! Nash wanted £17 million to convert the loan—less, say, £6 million to be paid off—plus £10 million for 'ordinary government purposes', plus £6 million for defence. Inskip told him 'there was no political prejudice here towards New Zealand, and that his requests would be considered purely on their merits.'[43]

Nash also talked with Montagu Norman and Allan Fisher, who was now in England, and others. He cabled Savage that the general view was that it would be next to impossible to raise new loans in London in present circumstances. Inskip, however, was 'very helpful' and thought the government might assist.[44]

On 7 June Nash met some of the ministers. His explanation of New Zealand's predicament did not produce sympathy. He explained that, partly because of miscalculation, imports would be as high as in 1938. Oliver Stanley 'interposed' to point out that this was no consolation to British manufacturers threatened with a permanent curtailment of their trade. Nash claimed that a major reason for New Zealand's difficulty was that, whereas it had borrowed £89 million in London, in the years 1920-32, it had not borrowed since. Hence it was short of sterling. The argument did not carry conviction. Sir John Simon, the Chancellor of the Exchequer, told him to see Montagu Norman about the conversion loan. Nash said the Bank had directed him to the government, now the government were sending him to the Bank.[45] This was a game, it turned out, which could be played for two months, even with relish.

Next day Nash talked with Sir Frederick Phillips of Treasury. Nash would not admit that government policy was a cause of New Zealand's difficulties though, Phillips reported, 'He did say that he was considering some reduction of the number of men employed on public works . . . but his plan seemed to be to employ them instead in secondary industries with large Government subsidies to their wages while so employed.'

Phillips pointed out that the British government was itself borrowing nearly £400 million a year for defence and could not continue with old style lending. Apart from rare loans to Dominions, lending abroad had almost ceased—80 per cent of a new Australian issue was left to the underwriters. He told Nash it was impossible for the British government to lend money for New Zealand's defence. Neither a government loan nor a public issue was possible for the £10 million loan Nash wanted. He should concentrate on dealing with the £17 million conversion. But he seemed to Phillips to have no programme but wait and see.[46] From Phillips, Inskip, and Norman, Nash got the impression that some funds might be offered for defence, but nothing more until the New Zealand government provided for the redemption of the maturing loan. Norman suggested that a proportion of New Zealand's export receipts should be set aside for this purpose.[47]

Nash began to receive conflicting or contrary advice from different authorities, which was confusing, but at least showed that the 'establishment' was not single-minded, which must have been encouraging. Kershaw of the Bank told him that it might be possible to get a loan for defence, but the conversion loan could not be considered until late that year. Inskip told him he should deal with the conversion first.[48]

It must have been a disconcerting experience to find himself regarded in England much as he regarded John A. Lee in New Zealand. Kershaw lectured him on the iniquities of Reserve Bank credit and excessive public works. While giving him little comfort, more responsible people realized that something would have to be done. New Zealand was discussed in cabinet on 21 June.[49] Inskip said that New Zealanders were beginning to contrast Britain's willingness to give loans and credits to the Roumanians, and recently to the Poles, Turks, and Greeks, with her attitude to the Dominion, a contrast which was not escaping notice in the Press.[50] He said that Nash should not leave without some help. Another point was that Nash was in touch with the Labour Opposition. Lord Halifax, the Foreign Secretary, said that they were 'living in what was virtually a state of concealed war' so that financial aid to the Roumanians or Turks was really military, not commercial. There was an Export Credits Guarantee Department, which assisted British exports by underwriting private commercial credits to foreign importers, and could guarantee New Zealand's payments. Oliver Stanley said, in this connection, that he doubted whether New Zealand would welcome a grant of an export credit 'under a scheme which implied that she was not credit-worthy'. The Prime Minister, Chamberlain, said that this point would be met if Stanley consulted with Inskip, Simon, and Halifax in deciding on the exact amount of the increased figure for non-commercial guarantees which parliament should be invited to sanction. Stanley had presented a memorandum suggesting non-commercial guarantees of up to £10 million should be raised. The Prime Minister had now directed that New Zealand should be helped. Cabinet agreed.

After a chilly beginning, in which most of the British with whom Nash talked offered (in the words of the Treasury brief for ministers), 'little or nothing',[51] the negotiations now entered a second phase in which the British set the most arduous terms for assistance.

The Board of Trade was under strong pressure from businessmen. The New Zealand High Commissioner's office had been suggesting that manufacturers should take advantage of the import regulations by setting up branch factories in New Zealand. This idea, that British industry should export itself instead of its products, was Nash's main idea about how New Zealand could industrialize. He was at the time negotiating with tobacco and tyre firms. It was a way of getting the capital and know-how at once. The Federation of British Industries protested strongly about this and even more at an offer that New Zealand would lift embargoes on imports from firms willing to leave the payment in New Zealand. The Federation said this was 'vicious' and called on the government to revise Ottawa.[52] New Zealand was not merely to pay a stiff price, but to be taught a lesson.

On 22 June Montagu Norman suggested to Nash that he accept a short-term loan of £16 million repayable at £4 million per year, and made a specific charge on New Zealand's export receipts.[53] Nash strongly objected to accepting what was called 'a bond with a charge', for it would be a public indication of distrust of New Zealand's credit. He said he could not recommend his government to accept unless some arrangement could be made to pay for imports and defence. Next day Inskip committed the British government to cover New Zealand's defence needs through the Export Credits Guarantee Department.[54]

New Zealand had almost always converted its London loans when they fell due. Norman's demand was unprecedented and onerous. It was doubtful if New Zealand could pay £4 million annually. Nash protested vigorously against the 'specific charge' at a meeting with the British ministers on 29 June, but Simon said the terms were necessary in Norman's opinion, if the loan were to attract investors. The ministers were also adamant that they would not lend direct to the New Zealand government for import payments and that the Export Credits Guarantee Department must endorse bills covering individual contracts and provide the money only when a payment fell due: 'This was the procedure applied in the case of Russia, Roumania and other countries'.[55]

Later in the afternoon R. S. Hudson, the Parliamentary Under-Secretary of State for Overseas Trade, was even tougher. He presented Nash with a set of demands:

1. The New Zealand Government to declare
    (1) that present import control scheme is temporary and will be abandoned as soon as financially possible ;
    (2) that uneconomic industries will not be set up, nor will existing industries be extended to manufacture goods which cannot be made economically in New Zealand ;

HEAVY GOING

BUSY DAY AT THE TREASURY NURSERY

Top Nash goes to London in 1939, as seen by Minhinnick. *Above* Sir John Simon feeds Turkey, Rumania, and Poland while Montagu Norman lectures New Zealand on the benefits of slimming; a Low cartoon

Top Left On the way to meet Roosevelt at Hyde Park in 1939. *Top Right* Nash in the 1940s. *Above* With Attlee, 1942

(3) that protection, whether by quota or duty, will not be afforded to New Zealand industry in conflict with Ottawa commitments ;

(4) that some undertaking should be given with regard to the granting of monopoly of manufacture to individual concerns or to existing manufacturers to the detriment of other interests in export, import and manufacturing.

2. The New Zealand Government to agree to take into consultation representatives of the appropriate United Kingdom trade association whenever a proposal is under consideration for establishment or extension of New Zealand manufacturing.

Nash protested against point 1 (4) that it was astonishing: 'You are taking charge of our country. Surely we have rights.' Hudson replied, 'yes, and we have too.' Hudson said 'You have broken your promise given at Ottawa'. Nash also protested at the idea of consulting British businessmen on New Zealand industrialization. He said it was futile—no manufacturer would advise the exclusion of his own trade.

Hudson threatened to apply a 'Clearing and Payments Agreement', a procedure whereby a proportion of New Zealand's export receipts defined by the British Government would be paid into a special account and earmarked for the payment of British exports to New Zealand specified by the British government. Despite its dislike of bilateralism, Hudson said, Britain had been forced to negotiate such agreements with Germany and Italy, specifying what goods they would take. Nash said Britain already set a limit to New Zealand's exports to her markets. He did not see what right she had to control New Zealand's imports.

This must have been one of the strongest threats used by a British minister against New Zealand. Nash cabled to Savage that they might agree to give assurances about 'non-economic' industries (and he and the British had discussed what they might be) and to consultation with the British on new industries, but that they should not agree to the annual 'specific charge'[56]—surely a new form of the 'first charge' to him.

Nash's and New Zealand's cup of humiliation was not yet full. On 5 July Norman laid down his terms. The only consolation he offered was that in two years it might be possible to borrow long term to replace the commitments he now suggested. There would be a five-year £16 million loan. Every month £266,666 13s. 4d. from New Zealand's export receipts (£3.2 million per year) was to be placed in a special account. The Bank of England would publicly announce monthly the receipt of these payments —the 'specific charge'! The Reserve Bank was to give 'irrevocable instructions' to the Bank of England authorizing it to draw any deficit in monthly instalments from the Reserve Bank's account in London.[57] Norman then departed to Basle for a week to a meeting of gnomes and bankers.

Savage replied that Hudson's suggestion of a Clearing House procedure was 'intolerable'. Norman's demand that the Bank of England would announce monthly that New Zealand had paid up was 'unnecessary and humiliating'.

Savage underlined the harshness of the terms by reporting that if any-thing like £4 million had to be repaid in 1940, after repaying the £2.5 million lent by the trading banks, interest on government and local body loans and other remittances, only £35.8 million would be left for imports, assuming that export receipts were about £55 million, as in 1939. This would mean a huge reduction of £19 million in imports, in comparison with the cut of about £8 million to £10 million which the government intended. It would disorganize the economy and cause much unemploy-ment.[58]

On the 7th Nash saw the Deputy Governor of the Bank, B. G. Catterns, and objected to the monthly announcements of repayments. At one stage Nash said to him, 'You are our agent: It seems a funny position—I am fighting our agents all the time.' Catterns told him that New Zealand would not get any help from the government if it was 'going to default on the loan in January'. Another bank officer, Kershaw, referred to Australian experi-ence in developing industries to replace imports. Nash said, 'The United Kingdom Government won't let us do that'. Nash offered to repay the £16 million loan over eight years, but Catterns refused. Catterns annoyed Nash exceedingly with his dogmatic manner.[59]

Nash had planned to leave but now. with Norman away. he had to cancel his passage. His staff, including his secretary, Reg Aickin, sailed to New York in the *Aquitania*. Mrs Nash went with them. Their trip had been less joyful than the previous one. Nash had done a certain amount of travelling about Britain, mainly talking to disgruntled crockery and other manufac-turers. They had seen John Steinbeck's 'Of Mice and Men' at the Appollo, Sybil Thorndike in Emlyn Williams's 'The Corn is Green' at the Duchess, a musical comedy, 'Me and My Girl', which they enjoyed very much, and a few other plays and shows. But, as for the world in general, these were not expansive times. On 18 July he wrote to his wife from the Savoy Hotel,

18.7.1939

My dear Sweetheart,

The past ten days have been very lonely. All engagements were off, but they are gradually filling up. I have kept on the rooms at the Savoy as we needed the office. Miss Wylie is working in the sitting room. Taps as annoying as ever, but not too annoying to be irritating—although the valet asked this morning (after I had looked after everyone else) did I require my shoes cleaned. I answered 'Yes! At least once a week'—Very rude. I will have to put it right somehow.

All business arrangements that I came for are completed except the Bank— and it seems that they are making it as awkward as possible. . . .

On Sunday I endeavoured to clear things up—and went to [R.M.] Campbell's for the night.

The week has been trying owing to delays—particularly Wednesday when the Bank could not decide in time to enable me to catch the 'Queen Mary'. Nearly a week has passed since then and still no positive decision—although tentative agreement was reached on terms etc. However I hope the subject will be finalised long before you receive this letter.

On Saturday I spent the day on the East Coast on Secret Official business. . . .

Sunday lunched with the Jordans and Langstone. Afterwards a drive to the Devils Punch Bowl—and a call on the Webbs—both of whom wished to be remembered to you. . . .

It is still not possible to determine when I will leave. U.K. Government arrangements were finished this morning, subject to agreements on procedure which I hope to complete this week—and then Home—if the Bank has answered. . . .

> Heaps of love darling, God Bless you.
> Your loving
> Walter[60]

By 'engagements', he meant lunches, dinners, speeches. The ten days had been very wearing by most people's standards. The British took the view that the three loans were linked, as well as being dependent on certain assurances. Consequently negotiations were very involved. The £5 million for defence orders placed in Great Britain was now secure, but the British ministers would not fix a total for commercial credits for New Zealand importers, wishing to leave this to the Export Credits Advisory Council. Nash asked for £10 million and on 7 July the Chairman of the Council agreed to £2 million. Nash said that this was 'no use to him at all'. He then cancelled his passage home. There were more meetings at which he demanded £8 million (Savage cabled that at least £5 million was needed).[61] At a meeting on 11 July Inskip said that £2 million 'was the limit tonight; it will be the same tomorrow morning or tomorrow afternoon or next week.'[62] Nash indicated that he would compromise at £5 million. Next day the Chairman of the Council, Inskip, Simon, and Stanley decided to offer £4 million, which Nash promptly accepted.[63]

At the same time Nash was engaged in long discussions, involving many cables and telephone calls to Wellington, on the assurances which New Zealand might give to the British government and manufacturers about import controls and New Zealand industries. There was much discussion about what an 'uneconomic' industry was. The British ministers defended their manufacturers vigorously. Oliver Stanley opposed 'monopolies' in New Zealand, protected by import prohibitions, but he added 'that if the license is to be confined to one "we want our people to have the chance to be that one".' In reference to pressure from manufacturers, he said to Nash, 'we're both politicians and have our difficulties'.[64]

The main difficulty arose over the paragraph which referred to obligations already incurred by the New Zealand government in encouraging new industries which, in the opinion of the government (the British draft read) required a 'monopoly' of the local market in order to operate efficiently. Nash objected to the use of this term. Savage was suspicious—were the British trying to discredit New Zealand? There was no justification for

referring to a 'monopoly'. Eventually London agreed to Wellington's suggestion that the paragraph should refer to industries which 'required some
measure of restriction of import in order to operate efficiently'. In the eyes
of the British negotiators, this gave a 'wider assurance' than they had asked
for.[65] On 12 July, Oliver Stanley and Nash signed a memorandum. Though
much watered-down, it was still a humiliating document, which was
presently published. In part it read:

2. United Kingdom Ministers recognise that in the circumstances that existed
in New Zealand last December, and still exist, some effective measure for
reducing total imports into New Zealand below their recent abnormally high
levels was, and is, inevitable, and they do not raise objection in principle to
the method which the New Zealand Government have adopted though they are
conscious of the difficulties it has caused in individual cases. Mr. Nash has
undertaken that the New Zealand Government will examine and do their best
to meet the representations by United Kingdom industries with regard to such
cases. United Kingdom Ministers welcome this assurance. They appreciate also
the fact, which was confirmed by Mr. Nash, that the New Zealand Government's
intention is to administer the policy as favourably as possible in relation to
United Kingdom interests. They informed Mr. Nash, however, that they were
apprehensive as to the permanent effects on the United Kingdom export trade
of a policy designed to meet a temporary difficulty in New Zealand.

Nash acknowledged that the scale of import restrictions was abnormal.
New Zealand would aim at a relaxation to encourage expanding trade with
Britain.

4. Mr. Nash assured United Kingdom Ministers that it was not the intention of
the New Zealand Government to employ the import licensing policy in order to
give protection to New Zealand industry against imports of United Kingdom
goods on a scale which prevented full opportunity of reasonable competition.
He explained that difficulties arose in cases where the New Zealand Government
had already incurred obligations by taking action to encourage the establishment
of industries which, in the opinion of his Government, required some measure
of restriction of import in order to operate efficiently. He undertook to investigate the matter fully on his return to New Zealand, and gave an assurance that,
pending this investigation of the position, such protection would not be extended
to other industries.
5. He also agreed on behalf of the New Zealand Government that their policy
of licensing imports would not be used to foster uneconomic industries, and that,
in order to assist them in determining what goods could be economically
produced in New Zealand, they would invite the views of the United Kingdom
industries concerned and would take such views into account in reaching a
decision.
6. In cases where it is proposed to grant a limited number of licences to manufacture particular kinds of goods, the New Zealand Government would give
United Kingdom interests the opportunity to put forward, should they so desire,
proposals for undertaking such manufacture.[66]

Nash's troubles were not yet over. On 11 July Norman returned from

Basle and met Nash, who had now booked a passage on the *Queen Mary* on the 13th. Norman spoke to him as though to an erring schoolboy. Nash's transcript of the opening of this conversation went as follows:

MR. NORMAN at the outset said that two things were perfectly clear:
(1) We cannot finish this if Mr. Nash is leaving tomorrow
(2) Unless you have agreement with your friends in Whitehall—the Board of Trade and Sir Thomas Inskip—there will be no arrangement. 'We must all stand together'. He enquired whether Mr. Nash was going away?
MR. NASH: Those are my present plans.
MR. NORMAN: From the beginning I have felt you did not want to improve your credit position.
MR. NASH queried this.
MR. NORMAN: 'You have been up and down talking figures that damage your credit. If you had set out to destroy your position you could not have done it better.' He referred further to the difficulties of making arrangements. 'Nobody can know what they can do a week hence: you have only to look at the map of Europe'.
MR. NASH said they were agreed that the money to repay the 16 millions should be met half-yearly ; that arrangements should be made for the Bank of England to draw from Reserve Bank of New Zealand's funds if necessary. There should be no special charge on exports.
MR. NORMAN: What if the money were not there or if the Reserve Bank account were withdrawn from the Bank of England?
MR. NASH: We would give an undertaking that the funds would be there. He was prepared to recommend legislation to set up an Overseas Debt Redemption Fund.
MR. NASH repeated that the proposed announcements that moneys were being paid on due date by New Zealand were objectionable. 'It is like the declaration of a bankrupt's dividend'.
MR. NORMAN: I won't say you're bankrupt but you have no credit. Further discussion whether the giving of priority on a new redemption loan would infringe the security of existing loans.
MR. NORMAN: We still want some charge on the 'funds arising from the sale of primary products outside the Dominion'.
MR. NASH: We are prepared to pay from our own Government funds.
MR. NORMAN could not say this evening whether a phrase on those lines would meet requirements. He mentioned that Mr. Nash was seeing the Dominions Secretary at 9p.m. (9.30p.m. was the hour), and repeated 'We all stand together'. 'You settle with all before you settle with any.'

Instead of a 'first charge' on New Zealand exports, Nash offered to give an undertaking to repay from government funds. Norman replied that 'an irrevocable undertaking to supply from a fund that may or may not exist cannot be very reassuring.' He insisted that a New Zealand government promise to repay must be backed by an order-in-council or an act of parliament.[67] An order-in-council was objectionable enough, and the New Zealand Solicitor-General advised that it would amount to no more than a solemn declaration. Nash protested that the prospectus of a loan was in itself a binding contract. But the government had to comply. On these terms the bank dropped its demand for montlily repayments and for a 'specific charge'. Even so, the loan of £16 million had to be repaid in five annual instalments. Some British newspapers thought the terms impossibly onerous; indeed blackmailing.[68]

There followed what Nash called an 'annoying delay' by the bank.[69] So far the 'establishment' had twisted Nash's arm, meaning to impel him towards wiser, in other words more orthodox courses, more in Britain's interests. Now Norman intervened decisively to help him, just as, almost certainly unknown to Nash, Chamberlain had done. It would not do to go too far in publicly punishing an erring Dominion, or quasi-colony.

It was difficult to induce brokers and financial houses to assist with the loan. Machtig wrote to Batterbee, 'It is a testimony to the depth to which New Zealand's credit had fallen in the City that it took the Governor of the Bank nearly a week before he could secure the necessary support for floating the proposed loan, and even then, we are told, he had to "ram it down the bankers' throats".' What Norman did was to force the six banks operating in New Zealand to take up some £6 million. The Bank of England underwrote the rest. His biographer, Sir Henry Clay, wrote:

One territory incensed the issuing bankers, which had always met its needs, by talking about re-funding sinking funds and by pursuing a policy of domestic inflation which made it very unlikely that it would be able to meet its external debt service. When its Finance Minister arrived in London with very large maturities to re-fund, he found his former friends all disinclined to lend him anything. Norman sympathised with the issuing bankers; but he could not let an Empire Government face default. For a week he kept bankers and Ministers in conference, putting the case of each to the other and extracting concessions from both, until agreement to float the re-funding issue was—with a large undisclosed subscription from the Bank—agreed. The Adviser who had assisted him remarked as they left the last meeting, 'I do not know how even you stand a strain like this last week's'. 'I could not have done, ten years ago', the Governor replied.[70]

Norman also assisted by arranging that the underwriting commission and other expenses would be below normal. The loan was floated at the very low rate of $3\frac{1}{2}$ per cent[71] and only some £3.5 million was applied for in cash or conversions. £12.5 million was left with the banks.[72] The *Times* was 'helpful' in encouraging a good atmosphere for the loan.[73]

Nash at last got away on the *Queen Mary's* next crossing on 2 August. In exceedingly difficult circumstances he had done fairly well. He had got most of the money he wanted. Beneath his courtesy he was exceedingly stubborn. Not as aggressive as Fraser, he was very hard to throw off balance; he kept cool. He was a good negotiator. Although there was a press campaign against New Zealand's finances, personally he had a good Press. He was very attentive in listening to the complaints of manufacturers. His praise of his government's achievements impressed Labour listeners.

He wrote to Inskip that he was grateful to him for his help. Other ministers pleased him less. Oliver Stanley, in particular, he recalled many years later, had been rude.[74]

In 1945 he wrote to Lord Norman in terms similar to those he used to Inskip. Norman had been very ill and had little recollection of the episode.[75] Nearly thirty years after the event Nash looked back with much gratitude to Norman's help and wrote a newspaper article about it. He said that when he was about to sail in the *Aquitania*, Norman called at his rooms in the Savoy and said that if Nash would postpone his passage he would arrange the loan. Norman did call on him on 1 August on the day before he left.[76] If Norman called during the crisis, it must have been on the 12th or 13th of July, at the time of the interview just quoted. Nash was then booked on the *Queen Mary* and uncertain whether to leave, as he told Mrs Nash and Savage, while Norman was urging him to stay on. It was after this that Norman pressed the banks to assist New Zealand.[77] Though these events were, not surprisingly, a little scrambled in his memory when Nash was an old man, there is no reason to doubt that something of the sort happened. Norman did help Nash very considerably—had he gone home without a loan his political prestige would have suffered severely. What impressed Nash most, however, was that Norman had called on him, a borrower.

Just after he left England, Mr H. V. Hodson, the editor of *Round Table*, a journal which tried to be objective about British Commonwealth affairs, wrote to him:

I find it difficult to comment on the arrangements that you succeeded in making here. I imagine they will be regarded by many people in New Zealand as more onerous than might have been expected, and that ill-will towards a Labour Government on the part of the City of London may be blamed a good deal, as it has been in the past. There must inevitably be suspicion on the part of investors of money towards a reformist régime, but it is my view that this motive has been, in the last resort, much less important in placing obstacles in the path of your obtaining the finance you want than the sheer lack of investing power of Great Britain today. We have neither the necessary margin on our balance of payments nor the necessary margin between savings and investment at home. Indeed, I think we may be in for a substantial measure of inflation on the latter score within a short space of time—a development likely to be not unfavourable to the economy of New Zealand. When there is really little or no money to lend, the political excuses for not lending it always seem to be decisive.

While crossing the Pacific in the *Mariposa*, after crossing the USA, Nash replied:

The London negotiations were conducted in very mixed atmospheres.

Some splendid friends whom it is good to remember, others whom it is well to forget.

Once fears in the financial and investing world have been created it is difficult to remove them. Stressing of advisability or necessity only extends the fear of the Trustee or ordinary investor—and the more publicity that was given to the question—the more difficult to obtain rational thought and reasoned procedure.

Whilst recognizing the extent of the accommodation provided and without commenting on terms or other conditions I regret personally that the opportunity was not seized to be completely generous in every way—with party politics—and class prejudices completely set aside.

Such an opportunity to tie up the goodwill of New Zealand whatever its form of Government may not occur again.

We can manage but with many difficulties—difficulties that could have been avoided and replaced by memories of generous thought and treatment that would never have been forgotten.

However the United Kingdom has its difficulties and whatever New Zealand can do in its small way to help the Old Country will be done—even though the cost may be heavy.[78]

One of Nash's reactions to the events in England was that his dislike of overseas borrowing was greatly reinforced. In a cable to Savage from London he referred to 'the menace of overseas debt and redemptions'.[79] This had been an attitude very common in the Labour Party during the depression, as among the earlier Liberals during the depression of the eighteen-eighties. When export receipts fell, or import expenditure rose too high, the interest on and redemption of overseas loans was a heavy burden which left the government exposed to the kind of pressures Nash had experienced.

What other thoughts he may have had are speculative. Though he would not have approved the form, a clever parody of a speech by Savage, he would have understood one passage in 'The Sky is a Limpet' (the sky is the limit), which A. R. D. Fairburn, a New Zealand poet and credit reformer, wrote at this time: 'We owe in continual constultification with Histrajesty's Garblement in Got Bitten.'[80]

Undoubtedly the events of mid-1939—and much more, those of 1941-5 —pushed the New Zealand government towards independence, towards a lesser reliance on 'the Old Country'. The British ministers had not proposed to *tax* the Dominion, but they had certainly wanted to control its economic development—in their own interests: an attitude not much different from those of eighteenth-century mercantilists.

Some people must have thought that Nash was getting his deserts, for profligate radical government, when he was being pushed around in London, in the hard, real world. But was this fair? In the light of later events one might see Chamberlain and Montagu Norman—the 'appeasers'—as living in an unreal world, trying to hold fast to economic and political views which most governments repudiated. (During World War II, the Americans suspected Norman of still being in touch with Schacht. One of Norman's biographers called him a 'sleep-walker', for he persisted in trusting the German authorities even into 1939.)[81]

On his way back to New Zealand Nash paid another official call of much greater long-term and symbolic significance than his time in London. He visited Washington, where he discussed trade with Sumner Welles. He requested an interview with President Roosevelt and was taken to Hyde Park on 11 August. He had a cup of tea with Eleanor Roosevelt and the President in his study at 5 p.m. Nash wanted to discuss seeing Jessie Jones of the Export Bank—which Roosevelt did arrange for him to do in San Francisco—and other important matters such as Pacific air landing rights, but Roosevelt chatted on and on about a recent visit of King George and Queen Elizabeth. He asked Nash how he got on with his wife. At last when Nash's hour appointment was nearly up he managed to raise business matters. When they were talking about the world situation, including the defence of New Zealand, Roosevelt said that the Americans would certainly help to protect Australia and New Zealand if they were threatened. Roosevelt said that he had an Adams precedent. Nash's notes of the interview went:

'1790 Precedent re warning nations not to approach within certain limits of U.S.A. Territory. President suggested that this precedent might be used if necessary to confine war to certain areas—Suggested line in Pacific from Alaska to Pearl Harbour and then to Phillipines [*sic*]—This would keep main sections of war out of Southern Pacific.'

Nash left at 6.10 p.m. On the train he made notes of the interview in a copy of the *Best Stories of 1938*, which is still filed in his papers, and later wrote some fuller notes. In their way these are major New Zealand historical documents. Nash clearly thought so, and filed a photograph of the dust-jacket notes with the longer version written later.[82] It must have been very reassuring to Fraser and Nash, in the darkest days of 1941, to recall Roosevelt's spontaneous assurance, even if it was not exactly a promise.

Nash enjoyed a little revenge on the British, which must have given him some quiet, ironical satisfaction. On 4 September the New Zealand government declared itself at war with Germany. On 5 September Nash came ashore from the *Mariposa*. On the same day the British government cabled that (according to arrangements finalized early in 1939) it was prepared to buy New Zealand's entire exportable surplus of meat. Next day they requested the entire exports of dairy produce.[83] His 1936-7 search for a bulk sales agreement had been rewarded. And over the next few months sterling reserves built up with gratifying speed.

XV

Party Strife

1939-40

Labour could scarcely have been in worse shape to lead the nation in war. Savage, who had been ill and in pain, from time to time, for years, had an operation, for cancer of the bowel, in August.[1] Fraser became acting leader of the House and effectively the country's leader thereafter, except for a period in late 1939 when he went to a ministerial conference in London while Savage, very sick, was briefly back at work.

Over these months of the 'phony war' and up to the time of the smashing Nazi victories in western Europe in mid-1940, the Labour caucus dissidents made their final drive to dominate the party. A new element was added to the party conflict by the war itself. The cabinet contained an ex-pacifist, Nash, and four men who had been gaoled for sedition, but not one person who had served in the armed forces. Some of the ex-servicemen in caucus, like Barnard and Lee, found the idea of the existing ministers running a war effort hard to stomach. ('I defy an ex-C. O. [conscientious objector] to recruit', Lee later wrote.)[2] At the 1939 conference these two and another ex-serviceman and credit reformer, W. J. Lyon, had tabled a minority report calling for a greater recruiting effort. They did not 'subscribe to the viewpoint that New Zealand cannot defend herself'. When war was declared some of the dissidents began to press for the appointment of a serviceman or ex-serviceman to cabinet. There was also much talk among them—and elsewhere—about war aims. Was it an imperialist war? What were they fighting for? In London in November Fraser failed to induce the British to say.[3] Perhaps they did not know or had not thought.

By now the dissidents disapproved of most things the government was doing, or not doing. In the House in August Lee came close to advocating repudiation of the overseas debts, and was accused of having done so. In London, he said, 'financial gangsterdom' was bringing New Zealand to its knees. When an agreement (like that which Nash had been forced to sign) was 'unconscionable' it might be necessary to denounce it.[4] Soon McMillan and others were going about talking of a 'debt-free war'—a remarkable innovation for modern times. He claimed that if the war was financed by Reserve Bank credit there would be no need to repay the capital or to pay interest, because 'the debt will be owed to the Reserve Bank which is the Government'. Barnard and Lee had expressed similar views.[5] The government, in contrast was acting on orthodox lines—for instance in raising a local loan in 1939 at 'market rates'—four per cent. The budget, presented by Savage in 1939, in Nash's absence, had increased income and beer and petrol taxes. He said that Reserve Bank credit had obvious limitations; that the country was suffering from a shortage not of money but of goods.

The disillusioned, disaffected credit-men launched another offensive. In early September caucus met for three days, with Fraser in the chair. He immediately accused 'certain members'—Lee was one of them—of writing articles for the left-wing journal *Tomorrow*. Nordmeyer and Carr countered by moving a vote of no confidence in Fraser as deputy leader. This was defeated by 39 to 3. Nash moved a vote of confidence in Fraser which was unanimously carried. Fraser and Semple moved that the ex-servicemen in caucus form a committee to advise on military matters. This was agreed. McMillan and Lyon then moved that the Bank of New Zealand should be nationalized immediately. Fraser and Nash moved an amendment to adopt the suggestion made by Savage, that cabinet should be authorized 'to take over the whole or part of the banking system as and when determined'—by cabinet. If this were not done within six months or if a number of members of caucus requested it, caucus would discuss the subject again. This amendment, though obviously a delaying one, was carried unanimously. Caucus also resolved to take complete control of the Reserve Bank. Finally Fraser reported that he had discussed with Savage the need to enlarge cabinet to cope with its growing responsibilities. Savage wanted only to appoint some under-secretaries. Barnard and McCombs moved that additional ministers should be appointed, which was agreed. Fraser and Nash seem to have wanted at this time to conciliate their critics. Twenty members then voted to appoint two extra ministers, and nineteen wanted four. A few days later the new ex-servicemen's committee recommended that one or more returned soldiers 'or any other member of caucus' should be selected for cabinet.[6]

Nash was at this time continuing his running fight with Leslie Lefeaux, Governor of the Reserve Bank. As Nash had learnt in 1936, in Lefeaux's view the government did not completely control the bank, which retained some independence in carrying out government policies. Nash decided to put the government's authority beyond doubt, and introduced amending legislation to do so. Lefeaux threatened to resign. He complained that the amendment was unnecessary, unfair and unwise. He complained that it removed all restrictions on the government's power to demand more credit from the bank. The way was open for 'unlimited inflation'. Thereafter he continued to write Nash complaining letters. He was a stiff Englishman, too inflexible to adapt to a new or changing environment. The historian of the Reserve Bank has written that he was 'never an effective adviser to Nash'.[7] B. C. Ashwin was a far more influential voice. Lefeaux opposed Nash over

low interest rates, Reserve Bank credit beyond the most limited and
temporary, and exchange controls. But beyond and more important than
the specific issues, were their quite incompatible outlooks. Like the authorities in Britain, Lefeaux regarded Nash as recklessly inflationary. In fact he
was financially, not orthodox in a depression and deflationary sense, but
distinctly cautious.

The proposed nationalization of the Reserve Bank aroused strong party
political feeling. Fraser and Nash—and Savage—did not want to divide
public opinion any further in war-time by pressing an issue as emotionally
charged as the nationalization of trading banks. It could be thought that,
in seeing an overriding need for national unity, they were as patriotic as
the professed or super patriots like Lee and Barnard, who wrote pamphlets
such as *I Fight for New Zealand* and *The Speech of a New Zealander*.

When the question of nationalizing all the banks first came up in caucus,
at the September meeting, Fraser and Nash raised it. The credit reformers,
except on one occasion, pressed to nationalize the Bank of New Zealand
alone. This would not have been difficult, for it was a New Zealand bank.
Indeed, the government already controlled its policies in a broad sense,
both through the Reserve Bank and because it appointed a majority of its
directors. To nationalize the other banks would be more difficult. Several
had their main business in Australia. All were directed from Australia or
Britain. Most of their shareholders did not live in New Zealand. A caucus
committee reported that it would be difficult to legislate banks out of
existence, but recommended that the Bank of New Zealand, once nationalized, 'might' be given power to purchase the New Zealand assets of its
rivals.[8]

Lee and the dissidents regarded themselves as a left wing fighting
orthodox, conservative ministers, but it is difficult to see the dispute in this
light. A socialist would have regarded bank nationalization as part of a
programme of state ownership of the means of production and distribution
—as well as of exchange. But neither the government nor its critics had
such a programme. The dissidents' aim was not socialism but cheap credit.
Lee believed that a trading bank should be taken over to make credit
available for industry.[9] In the eighteen-eighties the State Bank League had
similarly wished to get cheap credit for farmers. But why Lee thought that
to nationalize the Bank of New Zealand was the best way of providing
cheaper credit was and is not obvious. The nationalization of one bank,
though the largest, would not have threatened capitalism, but to the credit
reformers it was an emotional symbol—one moreover, with which ex-
socialists could identify. Nash himself had written his pamphlet attacking
the bank in 1925.

In October McMillan returned to the attack. He and W. T. Anderton
moved in caucus that the shareholders of the trading banks should be
compelled to sell their shares or New Zealand assets to the Reserve Bank.

How Englishmen or Australians could be compelled to sell their shares he had apparently not thought, but the motion was carried. Two days later Nash reported that he was having difficulty in drafting a clause to this effect, as well he might have done. It was decided to nationalize the Bank of New Zealand instead, within six months[10]—a decision which cabinet ignored.

On 4 November, while Fraser was abroad, Savage returned for his last caucus, at which Nash welcomed him. Lee has written that 'he had been doped to deaden pain. He was fuzzy, hysterical. . . .' Savage opened with some confused remarks about the war. He said that the army might turn Fascist and throw out the government, but in the next breath added that they must not be surprised to hear him delivering patriotic speeches. It is clear from John A. Lee's accounts[11] of the meeting that the Prime Minister was far too ill to be at work. He wanted to add David Wilson to cabinet. Wilson was a Scot who was now secretary of the party and leader of the Legislative Council. When Barnard tried to move that caucus reaffirm its previous resolution about enlarging cabinet, Savage threatened to hit him. The meeting became so emotional that it was adjourned. When they met again, Nordmeyer moved that McMillan should replace Wilson. Savage insisted that they should vote only for or against Wilson, who was now elected by nineteen to eighteen. When new under-secretaries were discussed, Savage refused to accept any but his own nominees. He threatened to assault various other members including Lee, who cruelly said to his leader's face that he had been 'made mentally sick by physical illness'. The sight of this drugged, dying, little man, more or less raving, must have been very distressing. Caucus resolved to adjourn until Fraser returned.

Early in December Lee struck one more merciless blow. He wrote an article, 'Psycho-Pathology in Politics' in *Tomorrow*.[12] It discussed examples of leaders who were pathological as a result of physical illness. Unless a political party with such a leader 'managed to cut off the diseased limb, it went down to crashing defeat'. This time Lee had gone too far even for his supporters in caucus. However the retirement of a sick leader should be arranged, not many people thought it should be done like this.

It seems that Lee knew that Savage's complaint was incurable, but not how long he might live.[13] That much was by this time fairly common knowledge—it had for months been widely rumoured round the country that the Prime Minister had only a few months to live.[14]

This was the most dramatic personal confrontation in New Zealand political history. Lee, a war hero, writer, one of New Zealand's first self-conscious nationalists, feared, hated, and admired, against the sick Prime Minister, beloved by many thousands of people. To understand how strongly most people felt against Lee, it is necessary to recall that large numbers of people almost worshipped Savage. A well-known journalist, O. N. Gillespie, wrote to Nash in December 1938, 'I have never felt such alarm as I did when I accidentally had to pass through the crowd welcoming the Prime Minister at the Railway Station before the election. There was something terrifying to me in the unrestrained emotion of that mob mind, dumbly and sub-consciously due to the fact that they recognised a higher form of a kindred spirit, a personality ruled by heart rather than by mind.'[15]

Lee was still Nash's Under-Secretary, but this was too much. In Fraser's (and Savage's) absence, cabinet resolved that Lee should be asked to resign. Mason and Langstone, as well as Nash and eight others, signed the memorandum to Savage conveying their recommendation. Lee refused to resign and Nash dismissed him. When Fraser heard of cabinet's decision he wrote to Nash that he agreed and said of Lee's article, 'Its cold-blooded cruelty appalled me. It clearly indicates that the author is not a normal person who can be trusted to observe the ordinary decencies of life and friendly association.' When he heard the news, Jim Thorn wrote to Nash that Lee's article was 'cruel and abominable, and was the very reverse of the spirit essential to the development of any brotherly society. His conduct towards yourself was ungenerous from start to finish.'[16]

The trade unionists began to turn on Lee. In Auckland F. G. Young (about whom Lee had, so he said, been writing a 'Labour Novel' during the bitter dispute of 1934-5) moved at an LRC meeting that he be censured for attacking Savage, but the meeting supported Lee. Then the National Executive tried to tie him down to submitting his writings for its approval. This led him into more wild flailing of his verbal fists. He wrote to David Wilson—now in cabinet—that one of his letters sprang from 'niggling autocracy or fascist buffoonery.'[17]

At the Easter party conference in 1940 Lee ran into men as aggressive and ruthless as himself, and politically much shrewder. Fraser and the unionists, led by Roberts and Fintan Patrick Walsh, an ex-Communist, cut him to ribbons. They had prepared the way by placing in the National Executive's report a recommendation—which was adopted when conference accepted the report—greatly strengthening the power of the unions within the party. Previously no delegate to conference could cast more than four votes. Now the 'card-vote' enabled a union's four delegates to cast all the votes to which it was entitled.[18]

Savage's report, scrawled in pencil on a piece of paper or cardboard, said that 'For about two years my life has been a living hell.' He said he had been 'attacked through the public press with all the venom and lying innuendo of the political sewer'. Lee had called him a 'pathological case'. As reports were made that Savage was not expected to live, Wilson said that Lee had stabbed Savage in the back. Fraser said it would have been more decent to shoot him than to spread the idea that he was a physical and mental wreck.

'Big Jim' Roberts was in the chair. The atmosphere was wildly emotional. Speaking from the floor, Lee had little chance to defend himself. He was expelled from the party by 546 to 344. Apparently the strengthening of the card-vote had been an unnecessary precaution.[19] Savage died two days later. His funeral procession by train from Wellington to Auckland was an extraordinary demonstration of public grief. For thirty years or more his photograph was to be found hung in the homes of Labour supporters.

On 4 April Fraser took control of caucus. Dan Sullivan moved to elect him as leader. Nordmeyer nominated McMillan and Barnard nominated Clyde Carr, another dissident, but a very weak candidate. Fraser ruled from the chair that the vote be by show of hands. Nordmeyer's motion for a secret ballot was defeated. Fraser was then elected. He received thirty-three votes, Carr three, and McMillan twelve. At the next meeting Nash was unanimously elected deputy leader. Fraser left it to caucus to nominate and elect a replacement in cabinet for Savage, and McMillan was elected. This sensible concession to caucus feeling at once improved the atmosphere.[20] Fraser gave McMillan a harmless portfolio, Marine.

McMillan was probably disappointed not to get Health. In 1941 he resigned and returned to private medical practice, becoming a considerable political embarrassment to the government. He acted exactly as the BMA leaders had forecast that some doctors would, setting up a panel system with a group of young doctors and acquiring droves of patients, while—allegedly—performing minimal services. In 1942 Moohan wrote to Nash that McMillan 'was about the greatest Social Security beneficiary in the Dominion'. In January 1947 Nash was advised that McMillan had received the very large sum of £13,800 in social security payments in a year.[21]

After Fraser became Prime Minister, Barnard, the Speaker, resigned from the Labour Party. He published a letter to Fraser giving among his reasons for resignation the undemocratic control of caucus, and the political domination of a few powerful 'industrial chiefs'. He said that Nash was stopping the takeover of the Bank of New Zealand, and denounced the continuance of orthodox finance. While asserting that when Great Britain was at war New Zealand was too (which, as a lawyer, he should have known was untrue, or taken to be untrue by the government), he yet complained—as 'a native-born New Zealander'—at the government's servility to Chamberlain.[22] It was not an impressive or a cogent document at the time or to posterity, which might wish the precocious proclamations of native New Zealanders to have revealed a more generous, a larger spirit.

People regarded these events in very different lights. Lee and his supporters thought there was a struggle of radicals and socialists against conservative leaders. But none of the participants were socialists in the sense of wanting to nationalize the resources of production. Lee's definition of socialism was the same as that of William Pember Reeves in about 1890. Lee saw any sort of State enterprise as socialism—pensions, social security, even 'socialist milk', 'socialist telephones', or 'socialist electricity'. Nash and Fraser were socialists too, if socialism were the same thing as State control. The Labour Party had become a welfare party, using State powers to protect the population's standard of living. The leaders and the dissidents were at one on this ground.

The real and substantive difference between leaders and dissidents throughout was credit reform. Whether the latter would have introduced their policies had they won power is debatable. Neither Langstone nor Mason nor McMillan carried enough weight in cabinet to try. Had they done so, New Zealand would have had a wildly inflationary economy. It is impossible to believe that a small country, so dependent on British capital investment, the British market, and overseas trade and one of the least insulated of countries, could have constructed an antipodean autarchy. Certainly the economic writings of the leading dissidents give little reason for confidence that they had the insight and ability to do it.

Much of the trouble arose from powerful individual rivalries. Lee and McMillan rightly felt themselves to be more able than some of the rough diamonds in cabinet. The leading dissidents were New Zealand-born, the leading ministers were not. The rebels were mostly relatively well-educated—two lawyers, a Presbyterian minister, a physician—or well-read, like Lee. Apart from Fraser and Nash, the leading ministers were not well-read. But, what proved more important, none of the dissidents were trade unionists. Langstone had been a shearer, but then he had run a railway refreshment room. The dissidents were a professional non-union group in a party that sprang from the unions and was led by former union activists and by Nash, a former professional political organizer. The ministers had the confidence of the union leaders. Their rivals were cast aside.[23]

Barnard's letter had underlined the facts and their fate. The rebels favoured an unorthodox finance but disliked Labour's close alliance with the industrial and union movement. Where else they hoped to get an equally large electoral support, except in fairyland, was unclear.

Nash did not take the leading part in the disposal of Lee, but he felt strong resentment against him, while rarely showing it.[24] He did not feel merely for himself. Like many Labour politicians, he admired and felt great affection for Savage. He thought he had been the 'Heart, soul and driving force of the Social Security system now in operation, by encouragement and help he enabled his colleagues to overcome unprecedented difficulties'. He was unselfish, unassuming, homely speaking.[25] Still, Nash's financial policies had constantly been attacked both in public and in caucus—not that its proceedings were private, while Lee was there—and he felt it. His dignity amidst difficulties won him much sympathy. In October 1939 some fourteen members of caucus wished to call on him to express their loyalty and support, but decided not to, for fear of giving the impression of forming a clique. Instead they wrote expressing their admiration for the way he had worked under 'enormous pressure' from caucus. One of them said that the 'destructive elements' in the party would have to be dealt with: 'clever but unscrupulous people' were endangering their policy.[26] Probably he valued

Top In the Chancery at Washington. From left: T.R. Aickin, Nash, B.R. Turner, W.N. Pharazyn. *Above* Nash and Peter Fraser with W.J. McKell, Premier of New South Wales, at the Rose Bay air terminal in 1946

WHERE'S WALTER?

THE POTENTATE

Nash at Havana; Nash at home. Two Minhinnick views of 1948

even more a letter from W. J. Lyon, a leading credit-man in caucus and now an officer in the New Zealand army in the Middle East. He had been one of Lee's greatest defenders but was (he wrote to F. Moncur, another MP) disgusted with the 'Psychopathology' article. To Nash he wrote that their goals had been identical, though he still felt that the pace could have been accelerated. 'What a tragedy it was that personal issues were allowed to obscure political ideology and the culminating tragedy, the death of our beloved leader. I realise more than ever how puerile some of our fights in Caucus were, and how ridiculous it was that most of our discussions took place in an atmosphere of distrust and suspicion and the comradeship of 1935 was allowed to be dissipated.'[27]

Lyon wrote that events were approaching a climax; they would soon be 'in the thick of it'. He was killed a few months later. The death of Savage and the fall of Lee occurred during the terrible events of war, which heightened the tension and emotion.

XVI

World War

1939-41

To begin with the attitudes of the Labour leaders towards wars had been very different from those of most New Zealanders. They saw them not as in any sense ennobling, but as imperialist conflicts, fattening the profiteers while oppressing the workers. But—again unlike most New Zealanders— they had keenly studied international affairs if only because, like Harry Holland, they were watching for the first glimmer of the red dawn.

At first Labour had associated the League of Nations with the Treaty of Versailles and capitalist trickery: it was no more than a continuation of the war alliance. The party's 1922 manifesto referred to uniting the world in a federation of peoples, not (like the League) of governments. But by 1925 the manifesto was pro-League. Labour now saw the League as an instrument of arbitration in international affairs. By contrast, the Massey government took little interest in the League, thinking the British Empire and Royal Navy more reliable guarantees. Labour disliked this 'mother complex'. Labour was anti-imperialist, anti-militarist, and internationalist.

Nash was one of the main people in the party, as in the country, encouraging an active interest in the League and in world affairs in general. In 1934, and in 1935 when he was national president, he gave another lead when he said that the party 'is solidly behind the idea of collective security. This can best be achieved through adherence to the Covenant of the League of Nations'. If the League decided to resist aggression, New Zealand might have to 'fight in sorrow for the good of the future'. The occasion for these remarks was the Italian invasion of Abyssinia. Despite criticism from unions about fighting capitalist wars, the party acquiesced in this support for collective security, and the possible use of League of Nations 'sanctions' against aggressors. F. L. W. Wood has written, 'The Labour movement . . . had grasped the nettle of warfare as the ultimate guarantee of collective security.' It was an important point in New Zealand foreign policy.[1]

When he became a wartime minister, Nash was criticized for abandoning his principles, but he was scarcely alone in concluding that Hitler and Mussolini could not be defeated by Christian passive resistance. The fear of a world dominated by militarism and Fascism led him to abandon pacifism.[2]

The Labour government increasingly stood for and strove for economic and political independence. W. K. Hancock wrote, of the Reserve Bank legislation, 'It was New Zealand, traditionally the most dutiful of the Dominions and the one most economically dependent upon Great Britain, who armed herself with the most formidable weapons of monetary self-help.'[3] In foreign affairs it departed further from British policies than the other Dominions. For New Zealand merely to *have* a foreign policy was an exhilarating novelty. At the League meetings in Geneva the New Zealand representative, Bill Jordan, voted for 'collective security', at times in a minority of three or four, with the USSR and China and, on occasion, Bolivia, over the Abyssinian and the Spanish crises. On one occasion Litvinov said that they had between them a majority of the world's population. New Zealand's refusal to condone aggression put her on the opposite side to the rest of the Commonwealth. (She had her moment of self-righteous revenge: after the war New Zealand alone still recognized the government of the Emperor Haile Selassie.)

In 1936 the Secretary-General of the League asked members for suggestions about improving the operations of the League. The British urged the Dominions not to answer, for fear of antagonizing the Germans, but the government decided to reply. Savage—democratic in cabinet, at least— circulated a questionnaire, with ninety questions, among ministers. A copy with Nash's replies is among his papers. His answers included the following:

1. Do you believe that war can be prevented in any other way than by the threat, and if necessary the reality, of war against a declared aggressor?   *Yes*
5. Do you think there can be any security without a fully collective system based on force in the last resort?   *No.*

The first answer was the old Nash and the second was the new. The former pacifist was now in favour of New Zealand going to war to enforce peace. He was against regional pacts, which were likely to lead to mere alliances and to war, but hoped the League could be strengthened. He favoured creating an international peace-keeping force under League control.[4]

New Zealand was one of the few countries which replied. Its memo breathed a fiery idealism. Economic sanctions against aggressors should be immediate; if ineffective they should be followed by automatic combined military action. The League should control an international force. Plebiscites should be held in all countries to see whether the peoples would support these proposals for peace.

Critics of New Zealand's policy thought it naive of a small country to expect to stop aggression by a policy which could involve the armed forces of great countries in major wars. It was also naive of the New Zealand government, in 1936, to place any faith in the League's ability to keep the peace. But the faith of the New Zealand conservatives in the Royal Navy was equally misplaced. Where could a small country turn?

At the 1937 Imperial Conference, Savage pressed New Zealand's views unavailingly. The Conference as a whole leaned heavily towards appeasement. It was asserted in its *Proceedings* that a growth of international trade might prove a step towards political appeasement.[5] Nash, just back from bilateralizing in Berlin, must have smiled at this.

On this occasion New Zealand's defence (as well as foreign and trade) policies were discussed. The security of New Zealand supposedly rested on the Singapore naval base, from which a great British fleet would operate, to protect the Asian and Pacific Dominions and colonies. By the early nineteen-thirties some of the chiefs of the British armed forces had doubts about whether an adequate naval force could be spared from Home waters, or whether Singapore could hold out until a fleet arrived, or whether Britain could face Germany and Japan together. In 1936 Sir William Sinclair-Burgess, major-general commanding the New Zealand military forces, warned the government that if war broke out in the Pacific a British fleet might not be able to come for two or three years, during which a hostile Asian power could consolidate its hold.[6] The government became increasingly sceptical about the increasingly qualified British assurances. Wing Commander Cochrane, a British expert, wrote a report suggesting that an air force would be better for local defence than the two cruisers which New Zealand maintained. If the protection offered by Singapore were dubious, an air force seemed to offer some security against local raids.

Nash had argued this viewpoint strongly before the Chiefs of Staff and MacDonald and Inskip, in March 1937. He said the government would place the defence of New Zealand first, defence of Pacific sea communications second, and of the Commonwealth third in its defence priorities. He thought New Zealand could get better value from twenty-four aircraft than from two cruisers. Sir Maurice Hankey, Secretary of the Committee of Imperial Defence, and Sir Ernle Chatfield were distinctly perturbed and urged that the cruisers could defend the Dominion against raids until the main fleet arrived. The Japanese would not dare send large units south because they would have to meet the main British fleet. Chatfield said that if New Zealand gave up its cruisers it would weaken Commonwealth defence. He presented what had been the Admiralty view since the late nineteenth century, that the defence of the Dominion rested on one thing: the ability of the Royal Navy to defeat the main enemy fleets. Their attitude annoyed Nash, who was still complaining of it two years later, for it invited New Zealand to assume precisely what was doubted, the reliability of the Singapore strategy.[7]

The British authorities had grave doubts about this strategy themselves, but before they distributed copies of their Far Eastern Appreciation to the Dominion leaders, references to the precarious supply situation at Singapore, to the actual time necessary for the navy to relieve the base, and to the precarious position of Hong Kong were deleted. Thus the Dominions were presented with an optimistic picture which the Committee of Imperial Defence did not itself accept. The aim was to encourage them to coordinate their defence planning with Britain, rather than concentrate on local defence.[8]

In June Savage, Nash, and Berendsen attended two more meetings with the Chiefs of Staff. Chatfield again emphasized the role of the main fleet. He explained that, after it arrived, Japan would not be invaded, but would be defeated by economic pressure! Reassured or not, Savage had to agree that New Zealand could do nothing alone, and must 'sink or swim' with the United Kingdom. When asked whether New Zealand would keep its cruisers, Savage said they would get the advice of the Chiefs of Staff before deciding. Nash brought up the government's basic doubt. He said that the latest British estimate was that it would be sixty days before the main fleet could reach Singapore. Was this the maximum estimate or might it be 120 days? And could Singapore hold out even for sixty?[9]

At this time New Zealand's defence policy was, in any case, very undecided. There was no doubt that New Zealand would go to war if Britain did—Forbes, Savage, and Nash had all said so.[10] But the government was opposed to sending an army overseas, as in World War I. So what did Savage's assertion that New Zealand would play its part mean?[11] In July 1939 Nash was widely reported in the British Press as saying that New Zealand was not likely to send an expeditionary force. There was much criticism of him in New Zealand for this statement. He issued a correction: he had said merely that New Zealand had no commitment to send one, but would do what was necessary to defend democracy.[12]

There was still, on the eve of war, opposition within the Labour Party to sending troops abroad. And, there was the persistent doubt about the Royal Navy. In April 1939 the New Zealand government called a New Zealand Defence Conference in Wellington, attended by New Zealand, Australian, and British defence experts, as well as by the leading New Zealand ministers and public servants. Nash took a prominent part and revised the reports of the conference.[13] It was the first attempt to coordinate the Pacific defences of the three countries.[14] New Zealand agreed to strengthen the defences of Fiji and to assist in some other places in the hopefully defensive screen of islands to the north. It was arranged that New Zealand should get some modern aircraft. The British urged that New Zealand's best military contribution would be an expeditionary force, and steps were taken to strengthen the army.

It was agreed that if Singapore fell the Pacific Dominions would be open to invasion, so that their representatives once again wanted to know when a

British fleet would arrive. Although the British authorities already realized that a fleet might *not* arrive, the British Chiefs of Staff had sent a quite misleading paper asserting that if Japan attacked a fleet would be sent whatever the situation in Europe.[15] When Air Marshal Sir Arthur Longmore returned to Britain he told the Chiefs of Staff that it had been embarrassing —the British delegation did not want to encourage doubts about the fleet, yet did not want to discourage New Zealand defence preparations by suggesting that all was well.[16] In the event they were less than frank.

The British now said it might take up to ninety days for a fleet to arrive and twenty more for supply convoys. Bernard Ashwin of Treasury expressed doubts whether Singapore could hold out that long. He noted that the Japanese had experience of coastal landings in China. There might be a 'gap' between the time Singapore could hold out and the fleet arrive. Longmore complained that Berendsen and Nash were firing broadsides at the British. Nash was very pressing and sceptical about how long the fleet would take if Germany and Italy were at war too. Major-General P. J. Mackesy said it might be three months—but fortresses could hold out much longer than expected. Nash asked, 'What do we do then to defend Australia and New Zealand when Singapore is gone and the fleet that comes after is smashed up?' Longmore said, 'I think the answer to that is to take to the Waitomo Caves.' Nash retorted, 'The only place that we can see anything that is glowing.'[17]

One could not call Nash or Fraser or Savage New Zealand nationalists, as Lee was. New Zealand stood between colony and nation; they were leaders entirely appropriate at this stage. They thought much, justifiably, and on the whole wisely, about imperial relations, whether trade or defence or political. But events were pushing the southern Dominion towards national independence. Neither an Australian-born Prime Minister nor his Scottish deputy were likely to kow-tow to the English. If Nash had nostalgic yearnings, his experience in 1939 pushed him strongly towards antipodean and 'Kiwi' rather than Anglo-Saxon attitudes.

When declaring war, Savage said of Britain his famous words, 'Where she goes we go, where she stands we stand'. He did not know for certain that the British had gone, even if it seemed unlikely that they were coming. The overwhelming majority of New Zealanders accepted his sentiment, whether for the love of the motherland or hatred of murderous dictators. By September the government had reversed its attitudes and offered an expeditionary force. Plans were discussed by Fraser with other Common-wealth ministers in London late in the year.[18] He was more abrupt than Nash—and often had to curb his sarcastic or satirical tongue. When he went the rounds of the British ministries he got on famously until he encountered Sir John Simon, the Chancellor, whom the New Zealanders found a slippery and unlikeable man. When discussing the expenses of a New Zealand expeditionary force, Simon said that the Treasury did not intend to finance New Zealand out of its monetary difficulties under cover of a war. In front of a dozen British and a couple of his own officials, Fraser snapped back that 'they were not there as suppliants but as partners.'[19] Fraser recruited Major-General Bernard Freyberg, a famous hero from Gallipoli, to lead the troops. Freyberg took the same view as Fraser, writing later that the New Zealand division was the expeditionary force of a sovereign state, the army of an ally, not part of the British army, but 'a partner in the British Commonwealth of Nations'.[20] In those days, to New Zealanders like Freyberg, and to the thousands of men who rushed to volunteer, pride was not exhausted by patriotism: the words 'British Commonwealth of Nations' had a powerful emotional evocation.

The ministers, ex-pacifists and former opponents of conscription, took a little time to settle down to the realities of war. For instance, they were not very security-minded. When the first echelon of troops sailed for war one minister mentioned the fact in a broadcast and called on his listeners to join in singing 'For those in peril on the sea'! Fraser actually announced the names of the warships convoying them![21] Party bickering, now rendered pettier than usual by great events, continued. A newspaper proclaimed that the nation must fight 'Nashism' at home as well as Nazism abroad.[22] But the great German offensive of May 1940 led to emotional public scenes. There was a growing demand for conscription, for a coalition government, for leadership.

Fraser lacked the inspirational qualities to become a great national war leader in the Churchill mould. But he was determined, dogged, tough, hard-working, and soon rose tremendously to the occasion, even if he did continue to pronounce 'New Zealand', in some northern fashion, as 'New Zil-and', whereas the local fashion was to stress the 'zeal'.

In June the British government cabled that if Japan went to war it was improbable that reinforcements could be sent. Fraser replied that the understanding that a fleet would be sent had formed the basis of all New Zealand's defence undertakings. He requested approval for sending a cabinet minister on a mission to Washington.[23] In July Coates and Adam Hamilton joined with Fraser, Nash, and Fred Jones, the Minister of Defence, to form a War Cabinet. It was to deal with war production and finance and any other matters related to the war. By early 1942 Fraser said that 90 per cent of the country's administration was in its control.[24]

The war continued to go badly. Early in 1941 New Zealand troops went to Greece. The British government had not told the New Zealanders of the full military difficulties of the operation, and, in particular, of the probable lack of air support.[25] In May, when the Commonwealth forces were being evacuated, Fraser went off to the Middle East to see what could be done to extricate New Zealand soldiers from Crete. Nash now became acting Prime Minister until September.

Nash undoubtedly enjoyed this arduous experience. Fraser was a much more dominant Prime Minister than Savage, and in a way, Nash had become *less* prominent as number two than as number three. He had been closer to Savage than Fraser was. Perhaps in wartime all but the number one have to submerge their personalities for the common good. But there was another relevant factor. The government's problems had changed. The great legislation was past; the problems of 1940 and 1941 were not those of the legislator but of the politician, such as relations with pressure groups, and with the Opposition party and with other governments. These problems were, in a concentrated form, the sort of problems at which Fraser excelled. As a creative legislator Nash was his equal; in matters of political tactics no one in New Zealand was his equal. He had the kind of flair, instant reflex, instinct almost, which marks the born politician.

In the absence of his chief, the loyal lieutenant did very well. He did not make any terrible mistakes. He was already, in lesser degree, used to coping with the innumerable diverse problems which crowd in on a prime minister's attention. Fraser and he discussed, by cable, the appointment of a new Chief of the General Staff. Both of them had, as Nash cabled, 'bias towards New Zealander for post'. Edward Puttick was appointed.[26] The Governor-General, Sir Cyril Newall, was reluctant to sign a government recommendation remitting a sentence of flogging on four prisoners in Mt Eden gaol. He wanted the government to announce legislation abolishing flogging. Nash was reluctant to acquiesce in his not accepting advice, but was half inclined to agree to his terms if the government did oppose flogging. Fraser cabled back that cabinet should on no account accept the Governor-General's refusal to act on ministerial advice. However, he too, hesitated. Perhaps they should not press the point. With an election pending, their decision might be misunderstood. On this occasion—probably the last on which a New Zealand Governor-General did not act on ministerial advice—the cabinet gave in. Rex Mason, the Attorney General, announced that flogging would be abolished; the Governor-General then signed.[27]

One problem Nash could not solve was the refusal of the medical profession to accept the proposed medical service. In 1941 Nordmeyer replaced H. T. Armstrong as Minister of Health and began to harry the doctors. They were offered a 15s. capitation fee per patient, plus a mileage allowance, but this was acceptable to few. In desperation Nash and Nordmeyer took up the idea, several times suggested by the profession, of a fee for each treatment a doctor gave to a patient. They met BMA representatives in late August and Nash said 'we will pretty well have to agree to anything to achieve cooperation'. The doctors, however, refused the fee-for-service. The government went ahead and introduced legislation introducing a 5s. fee for each service. The doctors organized protest meetings and published advertisements saying that the people's health was in danger.[28]

In August it was decided to stabilize the prices of thirty-eight commodities, including foods, locally-made clothing and footwear, electric light,
gas, and other fuel. This was the first result of a Stabilization Conference
which had met a year before and agreed that prices, wages, and costs must
all be stabilized. Some sort of action had become necessary. Though New
Zealand was actually selling her exports to Britain 'at prices substantially
stabilized', nothing had been done to control import prices, which rose
rapidly in 1940-1. In August 1940 a 5 per cent wage order by the
Arbitration Court had stimulated further inflation. By September 1941
prices had risen 5 per cent. Wartime 'stabilization' was not yet sufficiently
comprehensive to work.[29]

One of the most difficult problems Nash had to deal with was the
treatment of conscientious objectors. Men who refused military service on
grounds of conscience went before Appeal Boards. The chairmen often
spoke to the 'conchies' as though they were criminals, and only a minority
of appeals, for instance from Quakers, were allowed. Those whose appeals
were declined and who still resisted, were imprisoned. In August 1941 Nash
announced that defaulters' detention camps were to be provided for such
cases. He made no apology. These men had 'come into conflict with the
state' at a time when everyone's rights were suffering. They must pay the
penalty.

At the same time special tribunals were set up to investigate the financial
circumstances of conscientious objectors whose appeals were allowed. They
were not to be permitted to earn more than they would have been paid in
the armed forces. Their income above that level was paid into the social
security fund.[30]

Some pacifists thought Nash hypocritical, but there is no doubt of the
sincerity of his view that civilization and Christianity were alike threatened
by Nazism which had to be resisted by force. The treatment of 'conchies'
was relatively harsh in New Zealand. The Labour government was also
criticized on this ground. But powerful elements of public opinion favoured
a harsher treatment, as became obvious later in the war. The government
was to some extent sheltering the 'conchies' from a warlike democracy.[31]

Most of Nash's reports to the Prime Minister in 1941 related directly to
such political matters, rather than to the economy. This was evidently the
kind of information Fraser required; he wanted to keep his fingers on the
political pulse. When Labour did badly in the municipal elections he
demanded and received an explanation from Nash and the party secretary,
'Mick' Moohan. After reading Nash's long explanation, Fraser cabled back:
'The Municipal results were shocking and no explanation supplied seems
adequate.'[32]

The main political issue at the time was that the triennial general election
was due in 1941. There was much party manoeuvring in case it occurred.
In November 1940 S. G. Holland had supplanted Adam Hamilton as leader

of the Opposition. It would be difficult to detect in him any of the qualities which marked say, J. G. Coates or Peter Fraser, as distinguished national leaders. He was a party politician through and through. But he was resilient and aggressive. The government found him an awkward customer to handle.

Holland declined Fraser's request that he should join the War Cabinet. He considered that Labour was pressing on with 'its full programme for the socialization of New Zealand's industries' under cover of the war, and he would not cooperate unless there were a national non-party government. Otherwise he preferred his freedom of action. Before Fraser went to Egypt, however, he and Holland agreed that active party propaganda should be kept to a minimum.[33]

The next few months were marked by constant political sniping by Holland and his friends, whom Labour people called the 'new gang', as opposed to the 'old gang', led by Coates and Hamilton, who as far as possible maintained a non-party dignity befitting a time of national crisis. Holland claimed that by criticizing the BMA, Nordmeyer had broken the agreement to minimize propaganda, while Dan Sullivan had also broken it over another matter. Nash claimed that their statements were normal ministerial comment. Holland now took it that the arrangement with Fraser was at an end.[34]

The National Party was pressing for a 'national', that is a coalition, government. The Federation of Labour and the Labour Party were almost unanimous in opposing the idea. Nash received many letters from branches and LRC's on this point. It was felt, one branch secretary wrote, that a coalition would be the end of the Labour movement. Caucus unanimously opposed the idea and Nash agreed.[35] In summing up the situation to caucus one of the points Nash made was that if National and Labour formed a wartime coalition, it 'would bring into existence another Opposition led by Lee—That whilst his stocks were at present at a low ebb a National Government would cause them to rise.' It had been suggested publicly that Lee should be included in a wartime government. Nash thought this 'Not worth considering'.

Caucus was nearly unanimous in wanting an election. Indeed, Nash could not see how an election could be avoided if there were to be no coalition. The situation was thus very confused. After a meeting of the War Cabinet on 26 July Nash and Adam Hamilton agreed that a coalition was not possible. Hamilton asked whether the election could somehow be postponed. Nash summarized his feeling in a sentence cabled to Fraser: 'I personally am satisfied that a National Government would send our movement to pieces and yet it appears to be sheer folly to fight an election with the war clouds looming.' He wanted to stop 'the present vicious political propaganda' and thought once again to invite Sid Holland and perhaps Forbes to join the war cabinet.[36]

Fraser had all along taken a different view. At the party conference in

1941 he had flatly refused to accept a commitment not to form a national (coalition) government. Now he cabled back that in his view a national government was advisable both in the country's and Labour's interests. It would unify the nation; the responsibility for difficult and unpopular tasks would be shared. He thought that a national government might be inevitable if Japan entered the war, which he thought was 'likely and imminent'.[37]

When Fraser returned in mid-September he found that there was much disaffection with his leadership and even talk of a 'Nash Party' which wished to make Nash the Prime Minister. The main reason for this unrest was undoubtedly Fraser's opposition to his party over the formation of a wartime non-party government. In contrast, Nash's prestige stood high in the party. In early October a large and enthusiastic gathering of MPs and their friends paid tribute to his work for the party since 1922 and his success as acting Prime Minister. Fraser presented him with a gentleman's tallboy, a razor, and a pair of cuff-links.[38]

Political leaders who travel abroad must often feel uneasy. But in this case there is no reason to suppose that Nash gave any support or encouragement to the critics of Fraser's leadership. He was a loyal deputy. There was however much gossip and speculation about this minor revolt. Carl Berendsen, Head of the Prime Minister's Department, who travelled with Fraser, said that he stamped it out. Colonel W. N. Pharazyn, later the Military Attaché in the Washington legation, who heard about the revolt from the union leader, F. P. Walsh, supposed that the episode may have inclined Nash to go to Washington, since he did not want to undermine his leader. Frank Langstone said that Fraser sent Nash to Washington to get rid of a rival.[39] There is no reason to suppose that any of these opinions is correct. Fraser had a perfectly straightforward reason for choosing Nash as New Zealand's first diplomat in a foreign country, and Nash for accepting.

Fraser found that the Labour movement was too opposed to a coalition to be budged. Holland would not accept anything less than a coalition. However, he did agree that the elections could be postponed for a year, while Fraser promised to keep 'legislation on purely party lines to a minimum'.[40] Fraser was unhappy about this situation. He felt that in such a crisis everyone should put his party second to country. But few politicians were patriots in this sense. At the next Labour conference in 1942, Fraser hinted that circumstances might arise in which he would resign if the country were divided politically in wartime.[41]

The result was that New Zealand continued to be governed by the Labour Party and the Federation of Labour, who had formed a close alliance against 'the brutal aggression of the Nazi dictatorship'.[42] The president of the party was the former union chief, 'Big Jim' Roberts, from County Cork; of the Federation, Angus McLagan, from Midlothian. Fintan Patrick Walsh was a third union chief. Born F. P. Tuohy, in Poverty Bay, he had been involved in IWW affairs in the USA and helped Angus

McLagan to start the New Zealand Communist Party. He changed his name to Walsh and his politics to Labour. McLagan and Walsh were as anti-Communist as only ex-Communists can be. In this attitude they were at one with Fraser and Semple, the ex-'Red Feds'. Fraser ruled in very close consultation with the Federation of Labour. The other powers in the land were Walter Nash and Bernard Ashwin, Secretary to Treasury.

With the service chiefs and, of course, many other important men like Coates, these men forged a powerful war machine, economic and military. In February 1940 the government introduced emergency regulations which gave it great powers of censorship, control of all property, persons, and institutions. It became a 'constitutional autocracy', but one backed by a strong national consensus.

A deputation of Wellington citizens, including G. R. Powles and the historians F. L. Wood and J. C. Beaglehole, called on Fraser and Mason in May 1940 to express their concern at the invasion of popular liberty. Fraser assured them that the powers would not be used arbitrarily, but that they would be used, for instance, against any union or employer who 'tried to hold up the country'.[43] There was, however, little room for dissent in the tight little wartime islands.

One instance of the tightening of censorship on opinion must suffice. Since 1936 Fraser and Nash had taken a keen interest in the plans to celebrate New Zealand's centenary in 1940. They had personally discussed who should be on a National Historical Committee. Nash had listed the names he favoured, including his friend J. B. Condliffe, W. T. G. Airey, a left wing former Christian, and J. C. Beaglehole. It was decided to mark the occasion by publishing two series of books, under the editorship of E. H. McCormick. Dr W. B. Sutch, one of Nash's secretaries, was to write a survey of social services. When he delivered it, it was found to be much too long and very controversial. One official reader for the Press described it as a Marxist history of the working class and bitter in tone. Much of it, such as an account of the rise of Labour, mentioning Fraser and other cabinet ministers as 'Red Feds', seemed barely relevant to the topic. Nash and Fraser read it—indeed Fraser had directed that government approval was needed. It was declined. Sutch then rewrote it in a more popular form which was acceptable to the Under-Secretary, J. W. Heenan, and the editorial advisers. But, after discussion with Fraser—and after two months' delay—Nash directed that it would not be published by the government, on the grounds that it did not fit into the general centennial series. The outcome was not quite what Fraser intended. By courtesy of the Prime Minister's secretary, Sutch sent the first manuscript to England in Fraser's luggage, so as to avoid the New Zealand censor. Penguin Books brought out a large edition. The other manuscript was published in New Zealand.[44]

It was Fraser, not Nash, who pressed the repression of the left. Nash can be associated with few such examples—and, even in this case, Dr Sutch believed that Nash tried to assist him. But Sutch was making himself unpopular for other reasons—notably for delivering a speech criticizing the papacy and very offensive to the Roman Catholics.[45] When Sutch was called up early in 1942 in a military ballot the government did not appeal. Many of those who earned Fraser's displeasure found themselves not in a Siberia but in a military camp.

The illiberal aspects of Fraser's rule were to become more striking in stress of war. It is more fitting to emphasize, early in the war, Nash's and Fraser's encouragement to the arts. For instance, the Centennial Surveys were the most important series of books to be written and published in New Zealand to that time. The government granted annuities to James Cowan and Jessie Mackay, two leading writers.[46] In all sorts of ways, in collaboration with Heenan, they sought to encourage the cultural development of what was still intellectually and artistically a colony.

Nash's main job in 1939-41 was to tune up the war economy. This meant that, as in peacetime, as Minister of Finance he had a say in most important decisions. New Zealand had not been prepared for war. There had been a small measure of rearmament; the territorial army had been enlarged; but the shortage of overseas funds had kept imports for defence purposes to a minimum. There had been negligible planning about the use of manpower before the war. Ironically, the over-importing which produced the exchange crisis proved a godsend. In particular, heavy earth-moving equipment brought in for Bob Semple's public works proved invaluable for defence works.[47] Similarly the introduction of exchange controls and import licensing, not notably skilful in 1938-9, proved useful practice for wartime controls and planning.

It had long been observed, especially by credit reformers, that there was always plenty of money for wars. Once again, the question for Nash was, where is the money coming from? In his budget speeches in 1940 and 1941, in a speech published as a pamphlet in 1940, *Nash replies to the Critics*, in his speech to the Stabilization Conference in 1940, Nash had turned his face sternly against inflationary credit issues. The government's policy for financing the national effort 'on the war front and the "home front",' he said in his 1940 financial statement, 'may be concisely stated as tax to the economic limit for war purposes and borrow for essential productive works and for any balance of war requirements'. In addressing the Stabilization Conference he refurbished his sturdy old favourite phrase and told them that the 'first call' on their resources and energies was now the war.[48]

Tax to the limit: he meant it. It was at this time that he began to earn a reputation as a rapacious taxer. In 1940 he introduced new gift and death duties and a war tax, the national security tax, of 1s. in the £1. The aggregate income, social security, and national security taxes rose to a level that had not been known before. In 1915 a single taxpayer earning £500 paid £6 13s. 4d. tax; now he paid £97 8s. 9d. The man who paid £32 1s. 8d. on £1,000 income in 1915, would now pay £255 5s.[49] Income taxes, which had brought in £4.5 million in 1935-6, yielded £16.5 million in 1941-2. Even so, it scarcely amounted to the 'conscription of wealth' which Labour had long demanded in wartime.

During the war social security expenditure was extended to protect the needy from the effects of the extra taxes. In 1940 the child allowance was extended to the second child, and in 1941 the family benefit was extended to all children in families earning less than £5 per week. The payment was 4s. per child.

In late 1941 the doctors had at last accepted social security. Dr Jamieson wrote to Fraser as soon as he returned from abroad asking for a commission to enquire into health services. Fraser intervened in the battle between the doctors and Nash and Nordmeyer. He suggested a compromise: the patient would pay the doctor and then collect a rebate. The government then went on to raise the payment per service to the high sum of 7s. 6d. and the doctors swallowed their now sugared principles.[50] But they had won the last point, for their services were not 'free' to the patients: they could charge a fee higher than the refund; the patients could be asked to pay more than the state's contribution. Fraser had given in to the demand which Nash resisted in 1938. The doctors had proven themselves the most powerful trade union in the country; tougher even to deal with than the wharfies.

Pension payments were increased in 1941. The cost of social security was now £14.6 million. At this time the government also began to subsidize the prices of bread, sugar, and coal.

In addition to taxes, there were massive internal loans. When Fraser was abroad in 1941, Nash was able to tell him that the second war loan had been oversubscribed. A nominal interest rate was paid. During 1941 the internal government debt rose by £11.8 million to £26 million. But Nash had the great satisfaction of reducing the debt owed in London. An agreement had been reached whereby the British government was to pay for the cost of New Zealand forces abroad, lending the money to the New Zealand government. Nash disliked this arrangement, which would pile up 'dead-weight overseas debt' to become a burden for years. Indeed, he disliked and feared *any* debt in London. In 1941 he was able to report that the borrowings of £5.9 million had been repaid in full.[51] Despite the movement of men and women into the armed forces, manufacturing and farm production rose during 1939-41.[52]

Although stabilization was not yet fully effective, Nash was entitled to some glow of satisfaction at the results of his management of the economy. He deserved his high reputation among Labour supporters.

XVII

Minister to Washington

1942-3

When Fraser suggested in June 1940 that a minister should go to Washington the British government demurred, arguing that it might seem an attempt to influence the forthcoming presidential election. With ironical understatement, Fraser replied that the British government 'do not perhaps completely understand the point of view that is being forced by circumstances upon the Governments and peoples of New Zealand, and it is believed, Australia'. Nevertheless, despite the urgency of arranging for adequate representations in Washington, where the defence of New Zealand must now be decided, Fraser let nearly a year go by without acting.[1] A similar delay had occurred in 1939-40 over the appointment of an Australian minister to Washington, and no doubt for the same reason—the difficulty of finding someone of distinction for the post.[2]

At first it seems that Fraser had in mind a temporary political mission to Washington, but this aim was soon changed to establishing permanent diplomatic relations. From the first Nash's name came to mind as the best man for the job. The country had no experienced diplomats—indeed it had no diplomatic appointments other than the quasi-diplomatic High Commissionership in London, which was always a political appointment. No one else had Nash's experience of dealing with other governments and his knowledge of his own country's policies and problems. Nash's name was raised in cabinet early in 1940. He objected and Fraser said that he could not be spared.[3]

It was announced early in 1941 that the two countries would exchange ministers, but Fraser was still undecided what to do. As a first step towards closer relations with the USA, Gordon Coates and Frank Langstone were sent to Washington in May. Theirs was not a diplomatic mission. Coates was to discuss the supply of munitions. Nash's instructions to Langstone were that he was to negotiate to sell dairy produce and meat and to make such preliminary arrangements as might prove possible to establish a legation.[4]

Langstone was a competent departmental minister, quite capable of discussing trade or buying property, but intellectually he was narrow, personally unpolished, and in both respects unsubtle. Yet Fraser certainly led him to believe that he would—or, at least, might—be appointed Minister to Washington. He admitted in a cable to Nash in 1942 that he had intended to appoint him.[5] Langstone wrote, modestly enough, to Nash that he had been chosen as minister because Fraser could not spare Nash or Dan Sullivan.[6] Instead of appointing someone he could not spare, Fraser had dispatched someone he was glad to see the back of. Others, who could have done it, wanted the job—W. Downie Stewart, for instance, and possibly Coates—but they were not acceptable to Labour, on party political grounds.[7] The result was one of the occasions when Fraser's usually acute political judgement failed him. Possibly part of the explanation was that he made the decision when he had a more important crisis on his mind. He asked Langstone to go to the USA just as he was himself leaving for the Middle East, in mid-1941.

When Coates and Langstone reached Washington R. G. Casey, the Australian Minister, appointed late in 1939, did everything he could to help and advise them.[8] Coates had completed his work by July and went home, but Langstone stayed on. In August Fraser saw him, on his way back to New Zealand from the Middle East and Great Britain. Possibly Fraser learned that Langstone had not made a good impression. A New Zealander who had been working for the Supply Mission in North America later wrote that it was clear in 1941 that Langstone had almost none of the necessary qualifications, and that people had said it would be a tragedy if he were made the minister.[9] Fraser made no move to appoint him, and apparently it was expected that he would go home.[10] However, he remained in Washington, looking for a suitable legation.

As war threatened in the Pacific, Fraser had decided that someone more high-powered was needed in Washington and on 18 November, Nash was appointed. He was, however, to retain his seat in parliament and his cabinet rank. Fraser explained to Langstone that cabinet decided on Nash because of his knowledge of international affairs and because, as a member of the War Cabinet, he was in touch with all aspects of government war policy. (The Australian Minister to Washington, Casey, had been a minister in the Menzies government. Indeed, so important had the Australians considered the post that Menzies had thought of resigning the prime ministership and going himself.)[11] Nash's appointment, Fraser told Langstone, was to be temporary.[12]

Nash's appointment received a good press. The *Taranaki Daily News* described his 'immense capacity for work, the breadth and depth of his intellect, his singleness of purpose and his knowledge of international affairs. . . .' It said he was the 'outstanding personality in the present Cabinet' and also 'the strong man of the Party.'[13]

But before his appointment was announced the Japanese attacked Pearl Harbour on 7 December. They invaded Malaya, Thailand, the Philippines.

Two British warships, the *Prince of Wales* and the *Repulse* (substitutes, not envoys, for the great, fictitious Pacific fleet) which arrived to assist in the defence of Singapore, were sunk on 10 December off the Malayan coast. The way seemed open for a Japanese attack on New Zealand.

The Nashes left on the Trans-Tasman flying-boat *Aotearoa* on 18 January.[14] Their first stop was Fiji, which Nash regarded as the key to the defence of New Zealand. One incident concerning Fiji's defences always stuck in his mind. Shortly before Pearl Harbour some Americans paid an official visit to New Zealand to see what progress was being made with building airfields. One of them was L. J. Sverdrup, a well-known engineer and later a general. It was decided to push ahead with the construction of Nandi airfield, and the Americans were to pay for it. When he was leaving Sverdrup remarked that they had no formal agreement. On the back of one of his cards Sverdrup drew a cross representing the airfield and wrote '£250,000'. He then initialled it, 'L.J.S.'. Nash always said it was a contract. In the mid-nineteen-sixties when General Sverdrup visited New Zealand again, he and Nash drew up a replica. Both copies survive in his papers.[15]

In Suva he inspected the defences, watched Fijian soldiers training for jungle fighting, and attended a service at a Methodist chapel. They then went on to Canton Island, a flight of which he wrote an account twenty-five years later:

Just before we arrived there—perhaps some 50 or 100 miles out—the message came down from the cockpit to Burgess [the pilot] and myself, who were talking in the passenger area, that he was wanted upstairs. So he went upstairs to the cockpit and sent down for me shortly afterwards. He asked me to look through the window, where he pointed out to a warship, which he said he thought was a cruiser. He did not know if it was American, British, or Japanese, and no one would answer. The radio operator, Reid, another New Zealander, was in charge, and they could not get an answer.

We flew round the island because Burgess had said there was no chance of us going on. 'We haven't got enough fuel now to go from here. We might get into all sorts of trouble before we got to Palmyra ; we might even miss it.'

So we flew round the island several times, and it looked a difficult job to get down because no one had any knowledge of the location and the coral atolls were showing up out of the water. At any rate, there came a sharp shout from Reid, 'They're answering ; they're answering ; they're answering.'

So then we were guided down into the water. We got down very comfortably into the lagoon and then we went ashore. We waited for some time, and later in the evening Burgess decided he was not going on, although I wanted to get on. But then some of the Fortresses that were going to relieve MacArthur at Bataan came in—some 20 of them, I think.

In conversation with the man in charge of the 'planes, he said, 'No, there is no chance of you going on tonight, Mr. Nash. It is not good weather and you might miss Palmyra, and then you wouldn't know where you were.'

By the next morning we had found out that it was not a warship ; it was an American destroyer. At any rate, we stayed the night, with a beautiful display of film in the open. We also left a passenger on the island to open a Post Office

to prove that it was a British island and it was occupied. It later became a
condominium island for the Americans and the British.

We left next morning for Palmyra. We came down into the lagoon there at
about half-past-four in the afternoon. We were met by the American officer in
charge of the island, Admiral Rowe. When the launch came alongside the sea-
plane and the door was opened, my wife, as the only lady on board, went on to
the small landing platform, and he said, 'Good God, it's a woman.'

The story was that there had not been a woman on that island for twenty-two
years, and my wife was assigned to Captain Rowe's quarters. I went to his Chief
of Staff's, which were in the next room. We had a very nice night, although the
picture shown was one of the oldest and ugliest that I had seen for many years.

We also went for a walk along the lagoon pathway, a road that was being
constructed by the Seabees for the purpose of connecting the Conference atolls
and making it a road right around the island except to leave open the normal
entrance through the reef.

We left there the next morning for Pearl Harbor.[16]

At Pearl Harbour he met Admiral Nimitz and General Hurley and
inspected the devastation, before flying on to San Francisco. On this
occasion Nash did not relax. He had no sleep that night, nor the next,
flying on to Washington. There they were met by the British Ambassador,
Lord Halifax, the Australian Minister, Richard Casey, Langstone, and other
New Zealanders.

On the 31st he gave his first press conference in Washington, which was
very widely reported. He urged the necessity for a unified war command
for the entire Pacific, possibly under an American naval officer. He
expressed dissatisfaction with the existing arrangement, whereby General
Wavell had been appointed Commander-in-Chief of all Allied forces in
Burma, Malaya, the Philippines, and East Indies, leaving the US Navy to
control the Pacific east of the Philippines, including 'the United States'
approaches to Australasia'—whatever and wherever they may have been.
Fraser had already told Churchill of New Zealand's dissatisfaction.[17] Nash
also expressed a wish that a Pacific War Council should be set up in
Washington. This was another subject which Fraser was discussing, by
cable, with Churchill. New Zealand felt distinctly out in the cold. Its
government had little knowledge of the intentions of the British or
American authorities and no voice in their councils. It had no way of
contributing to discussions and decisions which would determine New
Zealand's fate. It was Nash's task to become a voice for New Zealand.

Fraser had told Churchill that New Zealanders no longer trusted the
opinions of experts—who had frequently and recently asserted that New
Zealand was in no danger of attack.[18] Nash now frankly said that he thought
the Japanese might try to invade New Zealand. A reporter said it was a
long way from Tokyo. Nash said, 'so is Pearl Harbour'.[19] He also said
'Nobody who goes away to fight or help in the war should be worse off
because of going. Nobody ought to be better off for staying behind. Nobody

ought to make any profit out of the war.' The *Boston Globe* remarked, 'If the Minister is correctly interpreting his people the New Zealanders have achieved a great simplicity in dealing with one of the most difficult and explosive of war issues'.[20] The journalist was sceptical—but it was the sort of thing that Nash could sincerely say and sound sincere. He had a perfectly natural openness which enabled him to talk on big issues idealistically without sounding sentimental or canting. It was an admirable quality which went back to his youthful religion and radicalism.

For New Zealand and friendly Pacific countries these were the worst days of the war. The Japanese bombed Rabaul, invaded New Ireland; they bombed Port Moresby, landed in New Britain. Though most of its population were unaware, the invasion of New Zealand seemed not at all unlikely to armed boys on the cliff-tops, to men from World War I, called up again in the National Military Reserve to guard 'vital points', to the government, to the Minister as he presented his credentials to President Roosevelt on 16 February, the day after Singapore fell to the foe.

Fraser had been right to appoint Nash. After working together for twenty years they had an almost instinctive ability to work as a team; each sensed the other's thoughts. They had thought things out together. On almost all issues Nash was not 'representing' his government's policy: it was *his* policy.

Next day he cabled Peter Fraser:

At an interview with the President yesterday I stressed and he understood New Zealand's [problems?], particularly the need for its defence and its value as a base if things went badly and Fiji was not held. He set out reasons for the War Council in London and the Staff Council at Washington. He stated that anything that required action would come to Washington, but that British and Dutch questions would first go to London and, after consideration there, would come to Washington with recommendations for action.

I stressed the need for anti-aircraft defences, with which he agreed. I shall continue to stress to the Chiefs of Staff for their attention our need for all equipment. He urged that our Staff officers should make immediate contact with the United States Chiefs of Staff, which they will do on Wednesday. He maintained he would send for me if questions affecting us required his consideration and also would see me when I wished to represent our case. I asked especially if I could contact personally the United States Chief of Staff, Marshall, to make our case at any time and he answered, 'Yes'.

I hope now to make some contacts with Hopkins, Sumner Welles, the United States Chiefs of Staff and others, and I shall keep you advised.[21]

At this stage it was not at all clear, from day to day, whether Nash was, in fact, going to be in Washington. Although Australia—and now New Zealand—were busily pushing their antipodean barrows in Washington, the United States authorities had very little wish to listen to their cries. The Americans thought that the views and the wishes of the Australians and New Zealanders and of the Dutch, whose government was in London, should be sorted out there and forwarded to Washington by the British. The higher direction of the war would be by a Roosevelt-Churchill tandem; for minor British or other minor allies the British could speak to the Combined (Anglo-American) Chiefs of Staff in Washington. The Anzacs (the term irresistibly reasserts itself at such an hour) were very unhappy. They wanted to see a representative Pacific War Council created in Washington, a 'council of action for the higher direction of the war in the Pacific'. Both countries pressed their views on their great allies.[22]

Churchill and Roosevelt felt that the place for such a council was London, which seemed absurd to the Pacific leaders. Nash cabled Fraser that the proposal was 'disadvantageous politically, strategically, and geographically'. On the first count it would 'lead to the formation of a Commonwealth or sectarian point of view, which will then have to be reconciled from a considerable distance with another sectarian point of view in Washington.' Strategically, it encouraged the idea of a British advance from the Indian Ocean and an American from Hawaii—that is, it would perpetuate a divided strategy. And geographically, London was too far away to enable a proper appreciation of Pacific problems. Nash wanted the British to concentrate on the European and Atlantic wars while Roosevelt, with a War Council in Washington, should direct the Asian and Pacific wars.

They had to accept the creation of a Far Eastern Council in London, but Nash still urged Fraser to induce Churchill to press that Casey, the Dutch minister, and he should have the right to attend meetings of the Combined Chiefs of Staff.[23] However, Fraser had decided that, since London was now more important to New Zealand than Washington, Nash should go there. New Zealand must have 'our best and weightiest representation there'. He was to be a member of the Pacific (Far Eastern) Council and of the British War Cabinet. Fraser asked whether he thought Langstone should become Minister in Washington, or whether Jordan or someone else should go there.

At first Langstone had been helpful to Nash,[24] but now he began a dispute which was to drag on for months. When Nash discussed the situation with him he complained bitterly that Fraser had offered him the post as minister and then changed his mind without consulting him. Nash cabled that Langstone was so angry he doubted whether he would accept an appointment. He favoured sending Langstone to Canberra and Jordan to Washington, if necessary. But again he urged the importance of Washington. 'The great danger in our acceptance of the Churchill-Roosevelt set-up is that it will probably keep us out of all contact with nations other than the United Kingdom, Australia and the Dutch and we will be heard only in the British War Cabinet, and any views we may have on policy may only be voiced in the major councils to the extent that they are approved by the United Kingdom. This will entail consideration as to whether continued pressure at Washington may not be the best policy.'[25]

Nash told Fraser that he was 'flirting' with the idea of going to London
for a few months 'whilst retaining my position as Minister to the United
States'. In this case he would have been in Pooh-Bah's class—Deputy
Prime Minister, Minister of Finance, Minister in Washington, and member
of the Imperial War Cabinet and Far Eastern Council. Fraser refused to
accept this, saying that Nash would have enough to do in London.[26] But
there is this much to be said for Nash's suggestion, that it is hard to think
of anyone else in the Labour front ranks, other than the Prime Minister
himself, who could do the job either in London or in Washington.

In the event the Anglo-American plans collapsed with the fall of
Singapore and Rangoon. Early in March the President decided that there
must after all be a Pacific War Council in Washington, so Nash remained
where he thought he should be. Fraser now asked Nash what he thought
of sending Langstone to London to represent his country on the Imperial
War Cabinet. By now Nash had had enough of Langstone's complaints.
He replied that if 'goodwill, integrity and ability to think' were the only
qualifications he would support Langstone, but it was essential to 'obtain
the goodwill and respect of those from whom you may differ'. After two
month's experience of Langstone he doubted whether he could do this:
'Argument, contrariness and open contradiction with long involved statements . . .' made it impossible for him to get the necessary results.

It is rare to find Nash being so frankly critical. But this was in a
confidential reference, and the appointment was of such enormous importance that anything less than frankness would have been a dereliction.
Writing to other people, Nash was charitable, as usual.[27] At the same time
it is easy to feel sympathy for Langstone, who had stayed on in Washington
partly at his own and partly at Fraser's request. He cabled Fraser, 'My
position unenviable with nothing to do. I resemble a circulating cypher
looking for its index number'.[28] Fraser had messed him about. But he saw
only his personal feelings and ignored Fraser's—and New Zealand's—
difficulties over the first diplomatic appointment.

In April he accepted the first High Commissionership in Ottawa. Later
in the year Fraser passed through North America and Langstone made an
unpleasant scene.[29] Then he resigned. He made press statements both in
Canada and later in New Zealand denouncing Fraser. He seemed to believe
that the only qualifications needed for the country's first diplomat were
that he should be New Zealand-born. People in New Zealand were fairly
generally contemptuous, as Fraser was publicly, of someone not seeing how
insignificant private hurts seemed at a time of national danger. Langstone
returned to New Zealand, full of resentment and spite. He resigned from
cabinet.[30] Fourteen years later he was an unsuccessful Social Credit
candidate for Parliament.

Whenever he was in Washington Nash attended the Pacific War Council throughout its existence, from April 1942 until January 1944. It was always chaired by Roosevelt, and was essentially his own committee. At the first meeting he suggested that no formal minutes be kept, but his naval aide, Captain John McCrea, kept a record for the President. In his absence, Roosevelt's close friend and assistant, Harry Hopkins, occasionally made notes.[31] The members were the British ambassador and the Australian, Canadian, New Zealand, and Dutch ministers. China was represented by her Minister of Foreign Affairs, T. V. Soong, and the Philippines by President Manuel Quezon, who had been evacuated from Corregidor with General MacArthur. Churchill, Evatt, Mackenzie King of Canada, and Peter Fraser attended when they were in Washington, but the Council never achieved the status that the Anzacs had hoped. It never made decisions nor had any direct voice in war strategy. At each meeting Roosevelt would review the war situation. Sometimes he would reminisce, even at length, once for instance about a boyhood trip in Germany. Or he would chat, talk 'off the top of his head', about anything that had caught the attention of his very lively and meandering mind. At one meeting he referred to the need for a world currency, to paying for public works by a credit issue, the need for massive population transfers to unpopulated areas, and the likelihood of widespread miscegenation after the war. (The Australian Minister, Sir Owen Dixon, said to Captain McCrea about the latter point, after the meeting, that in that case 'it would seem to me of little importance who wins the war'.) Nash cabled Fraser that the President's discussion was probably meant to divert them from the bad war situation.[32]

General discussion and questions to the President would follow his review. The representatives could bring up and press their own points of view—though probably this was more often done at private meetings with the President, Hopkins, or the Chiefs of Staff. The general atmosphere, according to Geoffrey Cox, the First Secretary, who attended in Nash's absence, was that of 'a press conference at the highest level'. It was a public relations exercise as much as a meeting of Pacific allies.

Sometimes questions brought up would be referred to the Chiefs of Staff. And no doubt the discussions helped to clarify for the President the various national points of view. But it was possible, as Nash sometimes did, to exaggerate the importance of the War Council. In an article in 1943 he suggested that after individual countries had made their cases 'the reports' went to the Chiefs of Staff, Churchill, and Roosevelt for decision. It is doubtful whether anything as clear-cut as this occurred regularly. In the case in early April 1942, which Nash mentioned in his article, Evatt and he were pressing for more war supplies, so as to stop the Japanese from taking Fiji. Nash wrote, 'It was my job . . . to prove as far as I could —and I think I succeeded—that if the Japanese were wise—this was in March, 1942—they would drive on and seize Fiji.' Evatt and he sought to impress upon the Council the importance of the security of Australia and

New Zealand. Nash had already argued the same point with Hopkins, and given him a list of New Zealand's defence requirements, on 24 March. Not that Hopkins needed convincing. He had already, on 14 March, written to Roosevelt that the defence of Australia, New Zealand, Fiji, and New Caledonia was their first military concern.[33] The Pacific War Council had nothing to do with the decision. Nevertheless, the Council had considerable value as window-dressing: its existence gave New Zealanders the impression that their leaders were participating in decision-making, an opinion which Nash's article—originally an address delivered in Wellington—fostered. The facts were more nearly expressed in a letter he wrote to Fraser in mid-1942 —'The Pacific War Council, by avoiding raising ultra controversial questions, is working fairly well. I personally have reserved questions on our needs for personal discussion with King, Dill, Marshall or the President.'[34]

The American Press sometimes said in 1942 that Nash was 'spokesman' for the War Council, and later in life he used to say so too. What the basis was for this assertion is not clear. Certainly he did sometimes talk to reporters about its meetings, but so did several other members, such as Lord Halifax.[35] There is nothing in Roosevelt's record of the meetings to suggest either that members should not speak to the Press, or that Nash could. *Newsweek* said that newspapermen 'learned to go to him' for news of the meetings. It seems fair to conclude that Geoffrey Cox, John S. Reid, and Carl Berendsen were right in thinking that Nash was a self-appointed spokesman,[36] though not the only one. Certainly Roosevelt did not regard Nash as 'spokesman'. On 17 February 1943 he came to the Council and said (his naval aide, now Rear-Admiral William Brown, wrote) : 'there are several subjects that he would like to discuss with the Council but that he felt he must ask all of the members not to discuss any of the subjects with representatives of the press (he stated smilingly, "looking straight at my friend Walter Nash").'[37]

This smiling criticism possibly related to Nash's press statement after the previous meeting, on 3 February, at which Roosevelt had reported on his meeting with Churchill at Casablanca. Nash had told the Press that the leaders had discussed whether to attack the Nazis in the Mediterranean or somewhere on the Atlantic coast.[38]

The Council did usefully serve to keep the allies in touch with Roosevelt's thinking. He also quite frequently flew kites to test their reaction—for instance he several times suggested that the French should not be permitted to retake Indo-China. Churchill did not agree.

Nash probably learned as much from another series of meetings held fortnightly at the British Embassy of the heads of British Commonwealth missions. He found these 'most informative and helpful'. Besides the various ministers, and a representative of India, these were attended by the British Joint Staff Mission, which included Field Marshall Sir John Dill. Nash wrote to Fraser that the United States staff sought to carry out their own plans in the Pacific without discussion. Often Dill saw plans only after they were completed and then only for information and not comment.[39]

In 1942 Roosevelt invited Smuts, Curtin, and Fraser to visit him. Fraser came in August. This was an opportunity for New Zealand to air its views and grievances at length. One night Roosevelt, Fraser, and Nash talked until 2 a.m.

New Zealand was not at all satisfied with the higher control of the war. The government was critical of the Pacific War Council. It was also unhappy about the fact that the defence of Australia and New Zealand were separated. The former was part of the South-West Pacific Area, under General MacArthur, while New Zealand was in a South Pacific Area under Admiral E. J. King. Both governments strongly opposed this, but Roosevelt had insisted at the Pacific War Council that the defence of Australia was an army and air force matter, while New Zealand was a naval problem.[40] Fraser complained that he only learned of some plans involving Australian and New Zealand forces from the Australians, who had learned of them from the United States army.

Australia and New Zealand—and some American leaders—wanted an early offensive against Japan, as Nash and Fraser urged on the President. But they failed, of course, to alter the fundamental assumption of Roosevelt's and Churchill's strategy, that Germany must be defeated first. Meanwhile, Australia, New Zealand, and India would be defended, China aided, and Japan attacked with whatever weapons could be spared from Europe.[41]

After Fraser's departure Nash continued to press New Zealand's points of view. In October he cabled Fraser that he had urged upon Hopkins that general strategy could at least be discussed at the War Council even if decisions were not made. Hopkins replied that he could always discuss his views with Admiral Ernest King. Roosevelt had some months earlier instructed both King and General George Marshall to discuss their plans with Nash. But, of course, Nash could not trespass too much on their time.[42]

On none of these matters did the Anzacs get what they wanted. But at least their leaders could talk to Roosevelt and the American leaders, could feel that they were not ignored, could feel that they were 'in the picture'. What they failed to get was a direct say in decision-making.

While in Washington the Nashes lived at the legation, which Langstone had purchased for $115,000, at 27 Observatory Circle. Nash arranged to buy the next-door property at number 19 for a chancery. Both were 'modified Georgian' houses, built in the mid-nineteen-twenties. They adjoined the British embassy.[43]

Nash wrote to his successor, Carl Berendsen, that he had come to love the legation in the fourteen months he had lived there, during an appointment of just over two years. He wrote to Senator Claude Pepper that it was one of the happiest periods of his life. He purchased an excellent cellar from a wealthy man. His cook, Margaret Moore, introduced him to 'old fashioneds', which, so he pretended, consisted of fruit juice.[44] His taste for good food and drink expanded with opportunity—not that this had been lacking, for instance, on his missions in the nineteen-thirties. It was generally supposed in New Zealand that Nash was a 'wowser', opposed to such human pleasures. This was so of Fraser but quite untrue of Nash. He loved his food and enjoyed good wine and liquor in moderation.

In some ways, to become a diplomat in Washington was a bigger jump from Selly Oak than being a New Zealand cabinet minister, but if Nash felt any diffidence he certainly did not show it. To start with the Caseys gave the Nashes a good deal of help in finding their feet—not that the USA was quite unfamiliar. Indeed it was Nash's fifth visit. Richard Casey was very definitely Australian top-drawer: a Cambridge graduate, a war hero, who had been attached to the British Foreign Office. He and his wife flew their own plane.[45] He was a very great contrast to Nash, one which points to Nash's rare if not unique quality as a diplomat in war-time Washington. Almost all the English-speaking (and European) diplomats were upper class, or at least professional men. Nash was one of the first of a new breed. He was not an 'élitist'; not a son of the rich, nor a graduate of a great university; nor did he pretend to be. In this respect he stood out. It helps to explain his appeal to the public and to American leaders.

As usual, Nash really enjoyed his new job. Lot was a great success as a diplomat's wife (though one of Nash's staff said he neglected her seven days a week). She took it as the greatest of compliments when someone said that what they liked about the Nashes was that they were natural.[46] People who knew her at that time very frequently were charmed by her unaffected simplicity, her genuineness. There were no pretensions. An American soldier who had met her wrote to her in 1944 that his family would love her—'love you, in fact, because you have the straight convictions and real heart and no frills, that are such rare qualities.'[47] In New Zealand she had led a group of thirty-two women who met in her house once a week to sew clothes for the Patriotic Society. The *Christian Science Monitor* reported that Mrs Nash said one lady made twenty-two pairs of boy's pants in a day, 'So you can see we were not an idle group'.[48]

In the anxious days of early 1942 Nash's task was clear and confined almost entirely to New Zealand's defence, and to making the contacts necessary to ensure that its defence needs were known. He had to keep in touch with the State, War, and Navy Departments and the Combined Chiefs of Staff. Much of his work was concerned with lend-lease and reverse lend-lease. He had signed the letter to Cordell Hull setting out the reciprocal lend-lease agreement between the USA and New Zealand. It is not necessary to follow him through the intricate Washington network of the lend-lease Administration, the War Production Board, the Combined Raw

Materials Board, and so on. A letter from his successor, Carl Berendsen, to
Peter Fraser, about lend-lease goods in 1945 neatly summarized the
problems of life in the administrative maze:

As Mr. Nash will understand, the organization of the United States Government, in its application to matters of supply from this country, as in other cases,
is extremely complicated. It is generally true to say that on any matter there is
no one person among the American officials on the operative level who (a)
knows the facts and (b) has the authority to deal with any subject. Indeed,
there is often no one official who knows which official or officials does know the
facts or is competent to handle the matter, and in very many cases the matter is
dealt with by many separate officials and, indeed, as in these cases, by several
separate agencies of the United States Government. This difficulty, extreme in
itself, is accentuated especially at the present time by the remarkable rapidity of
changes of personnel in practically every agency. The only way really to get a
decision on the two points at issue is to go to the highest level. This is necessarily
a lengthy process as the high level, though it possesses the authority, does not
know the facts. . . .[49]

Later in the year the danger of invasion receded, as Nash told the Empire
Parliamentary Association at a meeting in the House of Commons in
August. He saw the turning point as the Battle of Midway in June. There,
and in the Coral Sea engagement, the Japanese had lost five of their nine
aircraft carriers.[50] They were still, however, capable of invading Papua in
July, but Nash could now turn some of his attention to other tasks, notably
publicity. Geoffrey Cox, a former New Zealand Rhodes Scholar, a success-
ful foreign correspondent in Britain and then soldier, was recruited by
Berendsen and brought over from the Second New Zealand Expeditionary
Force to be First Secretary and, in Nash's prolonged absence in 1943,
Chargé d'Affaires.

Cox regarded himself as a journalist, not a diplomat, and concentrated
on publicity. This happened to be what New Zealand most needed, since
most Americans scarcely knew where it was. In August he wrote to Nash
outlining the aims of their publicity. First it should seek to help the war
effort by maintaining good relations which would ensure a minimum of
difficulty in the supply of United States war materials. Secondly, it was
necessary to keep New Zealand's contribution to the war effort in the minds
of Americans so that New Zealand could eventually speak at the peace
conference with the influence its effort deserved. In general, publicity would
be preparing the way for post-war cultural and trade relations. Good
publicity in the USA would also help to boost morale in New Zealand.
America's other allies were all making a similar effort.[51]

Between 31 January 1942 and 6 March 1943 Nash delivered about
ninety speeches and broadcasts.[52] He travelled very extensively on war
business.

A list of Nash's activities in North America would look like a catalogue.

He gave evidence to a Canadian Special Commission on Reconstruction and Re-establishment. He received honorary doctorates from Tufts College and Temple University. He led a New Zealand delegation, consisting of himself, Jean McKenzie, and Bruce Turner, to an Institute of Pacific Affairs conference at Mont Tremblant, Quebec, in 1942. Mrs Nash went too—the first time she had accompanied him to a conference. An American, Francis Burton Harrison, former Governor-General of the Philippines and now adviser to President M. L. Quezon, recorded his impression of Nash. The theme of the conference was the Atlantic Charter. Churchill had just announced in his Mansion House speech that he had no intention of presiding over the liquidation of the British Empire.

The last plenary session ended on a note of bitter wrangling between the delegates from the British Dominions and those from Great Britain. The ghost of Winston Churchill's Mansion House speech had not been laid. Walter Nash, New Zealand Minister to the United States, and a member of the Pacific War Council made a rousing stump speech taking great patches of skin off the English delegation. It was a thoroughly embittered and masterly address. Various of the English present answered him, maintaining the complete sincerity of their offers, and the good faith of the English Government and especially of the House of Commons on the question of gradual freedom for the component parts of their empire. Mr Arthur Creech Jones, M.P., parliamentary secretary to Hon. Ernest Bevin, Minister of Labour, made an answer of passionate sincerity and deep feeling to Nash's attack.[53]

Nash's speeches made a powerful impact. One of the Second Secretaries, Bruce Turner, wrote many of them, but Nash never stuck to the script. Often he spoke without notes, which impressed many people. *Newsweek* said that his speeches were 'notable for their simplicity, sincerity, and extemporaneous quality'.[54] Geoffrey Cox was struck by the fact that the timbre of Nash's voice conveyed a reassurance. This was probably one of the great secrets of Nash's success in politics.

He spoke often about New Zealand's welfare state, but also about the great issues of war and peace, about what the allies were fighting for, about the better world to come. People had to believe this and wanted to hear it. He came to be referred to very often in the press as a Pacific 'New Dealer'. Cox wrote to him that he represented 'personally and through his country the type of progress which is essential'. His sentiments and opinions on such topics as international aid, peace, social welfare, happily coincided with the very strong streak of idealism in American opinion at that time. He gave speeches called, for instance, 'The End of Imperialism', which were very much in line with liberal American thinking, and would not have been delivered by, for instance, the British Ambassador. Nash very often hit the front pages. Cox also noted that when Nash was away New Zealand got much less press coverage. And Cox was no flatterer: he resisted Nash and refused to write speeches for him.[55]

Cox, Berendsen, Fraser, during his visits to the USA, and, indeed, almost every New Zealander connected with Nash's work in the USA testified to the 'considerable magnitude' of the impression he made. Many Americans said the same thing, both in private and public. Senator Pepper wrote to him that he was 'the most dynamic figure' whom he had met in Washington, and that he thought the Vice-President agreed. And Henry Wallace wrote, in a letter to Harry Laidler, of the League of Industrial Democracy, a testimonial which was read out at a farewell luncheon for Nash in 1944: 'In my opinion Walter Nash is one of the significant figures of the world. He clearly sees the significance of oncoming political trends as they relate to rapid economic and technological changes.' When Berendsen succeeded Nash he wrote to him that literally everyone spoke well of the Nashes—'I am bound to say that I find this a little terrifying. . . .'[56] Thus Nash was a great success at his chief task, representing his country to the Americans and making it known.

Some of Nash's pronouncements pleased the Americans. For instance he publicly agreed with the 'Lick Hitler First' strategy.[57] But he was very outspoken—as Deputy Prime Minister he had less fear of crossing his government than most diplomats. In July 1942 he spoke at an 'On to Victory' War Bond rally in the Lyric Theatre in Baltimore. He quoted one of his favourite poems, James Russell Lowell's 'On the Capture of Fugitive Slaves Near Washington':

> Man is more than Constitutions ; better rot beneath the sod,
> Than be true to Church and State while we are doubly false to God!
>
> We owe allegiance to the State ; but deeper, truer, more,
> To the sympathies that God hath set within our spirit's core ;
> Our country claims our fealty ; we grant it so, but then
> Before Man made us citizens, great Nature made us men.
>
> He's true to God who's true to man ; wherever wrong is done,
> To the humblest and the weakest, 'neath the all-beholding sun,
> That wrong is also done to us ; and they are slaves most base,
> Whose love of right is for themselves, and not for all their race.

It was a huge, star-studded audience. One of the stars was Loretta Young. Nash wrote, many years later, 'I was greeted with tumultuous applause from 500 people, but a terrific silence that could almost have been heard from 9,500 people.' When he had finished Paul Patterson, owner of the *Baltimore Sun*, asked him whether he realized that he was in Baltimore when he chose to speak on race and colour. When he said, 'Yes', Patterson said, 'Then you have got more courage than I have.'[58]

Before he left England in 1909 he had written the last lines of these verses in his sister Emily's autograph album.

Another favourite quotation on the theme of racial equality, which he constantly repeated in speeches, was a remark by Dr J. E. K. Aggrey, an African and negro leader, that one could play a tune using only the white notes or only the black notes but that, for full harmony, one must use both.

In addition to speeches, press interviews, and broadcasts, Nash expressed his views in a book, *New Zealand, A Working Democracy*, published in New York in 1943 and in London and Melbourne in 1944. A journalist called Eric Estorick, who wrote about British Commonwealth history and politics, acted as his agent. The book was put together by Bruce Turner, mainly out of Nash's speeches. Turner wrote the first section, some 12,000 words, 'New Zealand', and probably much of 'New Zealand at War'. He wrote to Nash telling him of the arrangement of these sections. Nash revised the manuscript to some extent. The final section 'Reflections of a New Zealander', gave his own thoughts on the present and future world.

Cox and Reg Aickin helped Turner, for instance in checking proofs in 1943 when Nash was back in New Zealand. But they asked Nash not to thank them by name in the preface. Elsewhere, however, for instance in writing to A. G. B. Fisher, Nash was quite frank about Turner's role as part- or co-author. However, at the time Nash received all the credit. Characteristically, he refused to take any payment. Nor did his co-author get any. The publishers paid $1,500 of which 25 per cent went to Estorick. Nash handed the balance over to the New Zealand Treasury.[59]

It is hard to believe that Nash could have written a satisfactory book. As a speaker he usually had a good sense of audience response—but, speaking or writing, he was very long-winded. He never used one word if he could find six that would do. He rarely used a telling or pithy phrase. His written prose lacked distinctiveness or style. The same could be said of almost all New Zealand politicians.

Much of the book is a compilation describing New Zealand and its government and its war effort. Mr Nash appears in the third person. The final section is more interesting. It explains 'Why We Fight', discusses 'World Organisation', 'Post-war Reconstruction', 'Towards a New Pacific'; and concludes with 'The End of Imperialism'.

Many of his views were the idealistic ones he had expressed for many years. There was a strong element of commonsense—for instance, in discussing the future of the Dutch and French colonies in South-east Asia he expressed fear of a 'Balkanised East Asia'.[60] He could talk—and this section of his book was really that—convincingly on such topics because he had thought about them for years and had some experience. In talking of post-war relief, for instance, he would have thought of the Second Socialist International, where Ramsay MacDonald reported on hunger in Germany. There was a shrewd streak of national self-interest in his idealism about such matters. He spoke of building up reserves of food, to be made available to the starving millions in war-torn countries; he spoke of New Zealand's importance as a food-producing country—and especially of the desirability 'that a large proportion of the foodstuffs shipped to Europe and elsewhere for relief purposes should be milk products, because these are the most nutritive, and can be most easily assimilated by peoples whose stomachs have been weakened by long periods of deprivation'. He said that much trade after the war might be commodity exchange—but he had thought of the idea that the rich states might buy food from New Zealand to give to the poor nations.[61]

One of Nash's constant themes in 1942-3 was the need for the creation of a United Nations Council, a peace council to parallel the great War Councils. He wanted an immediate meeting of the United Nations (that is, at that time, of the Allies against Germany, Italy, and Japan). Roosevelt had spoken in 1941 of the 'four freedoms'. He and Churchill had issued the Atlantic Charter later that year. What was now needed was a meeting of the 'forty-three free nations' to define their aims more precisely and fully, and to translate those aims into terms of specific domestic and international policies. Moreover, initial decisions about the future organization of the world must be made in public and not in secret conclave. He repeatedly urged in speeches that a World Reconstruction and Developmental Council should be set up at once.[62]

Many people were very moved by his talk. In November 1942 Bill Parry, a simple soul, wrote from Wellington, 'Your advocacy Walter, of the International Council to give an interpretation to the Atlantic Charter is an inspiration. . . .' He added that Tim Armstrong, who had just died, had been 'enthused' too. 'Tim said Walter is not going to have our cause fooled this time, he is going to insist upon the world being given to understand what it really means'.[63]

But what did the Atlantic Charter mean? The right to national self-determination, the right of all people to improved labour standards, economic advancement, and social security, for instance, looked differently to British or Americans. Nash pressed his views on this question on Roosevelt, both at private meetings and at the Pacific War Council.[64] At the meeting on 3 February Admiral Brown's notes (which strongly reflected the President's attitudes), recorded:

Mr. Nash of New Zealand then launched upon a rather lengthy plea that another meeting of all United Nations might be called in the near future to make all countries—small, as well as large—feel that they are an important and integral part of the Allied war effort and of the readjustment that follows peace. President Roosevelt and Lord Halifax held that such a discussion at this time might open up discussion of certain phases of post-war adjustment that would be very harmful to united effort. President Quezon appeared to share Mr. Nash's opinion that a conference could be prevented from doing harm by agreeing beforehand to have free discussions behind closed doors and to agree beforehand on what announcement should be made to the world as to the United

Nations' aims and intentions. A rather lengthy discussion followed—pro and con—during which President Roosevelt expressed his belief that the islands of the Pacific must in the future be considered for the good of the entire world rather than for the benefit of particular nations. . . .

Roosevelt felt that such a meeting would be premature and divisive, for instance over the future of colonies. He raised that issue even more forcibly on 17 February. Nash cabled Fraser:

One disturbing statement by President at meeting was a reference to controls of Islands in Pacific particularly referring to Eastern and Western Samoa— inferring that all these islands would be better in one organisation with a High Commissioner. He also stated that whilst Eastern [American] Samoa was completely free of venereal disease—Western [New Zealand] Samoa and Apia in particular was saturated with it Stop Could you let me know the facts.[65]

The future of islands and meetings of the United Nations were both topics Roosevelt had indicated that he wanted kept 'off the record', to prevent rumours, at the meeting at which he rebuked Nash for talking to the press. He now temporarily diverted Nash's attention from the future of the world to explaining, at the next meeting, that there had been no VD in 'British Samoa' a year ago, though there had been some few cases since the arrival of American troops! The President agreed that VD was not a serious problem in the South Pacific, although in Liberia contagion was close to 100 per cent![66]

The discussions were not all so trivial. On 17 February, besides mildly rebuking Nash, Roosevelt had made a positive suggestion, namely that a meeting of the United Nations might be called to discuss world food supplies after the war. Discussion of a single subject 'might prevent the introduction of subjects that would lead to controversy and bad feeling'. Nash and Sir Owen Dixon of Australia went on 'at considerable length' about their countries' control of the marketing of food. The President thought that nations might have to control the sale of some basic commodities in future. Lord Halifax and Leighton McCarthy of Canada were 'luke-warm' about the proposed conference. They thought endless and bitter controversy might arise out of such issues as private enterprise and finance.

Nash suggested, and all agreed, that the conference should meet not in a city but in a rural hotel where members could get to know one another. Once again, Roosevelt asked Nash not to comment publicly on their proposals. He had sought the views of the Russians and other allies, and was awaiting their replies.[67] This discussion was a small part of the political process which led to the first United Nations conference at Hot Springs, Virginia, in May-June 1943, which set up the Food and Agricultural Organization of the United Nations and the conference at Atlantic City in November, at which the United Nations Relief and Rehabilitation Administration was created.

It should not be thought that Nash was not generally on good terms with Roosevelt. Geoffrey Cox said that he was 'extraordinarily skilful at getting in with and keeping in with people of power'.[68] He thought—and so did Peter Fraser—that Roosevelt liked and respected Nash. Both the Roosevelts wrote cordially to Nash after he had left. And when the President died, Harry Hopkins wrote to Nash that he had had 'great confidence' in Nash and Fraser.[69]

XVIII

Wellington, Canberra, Washington, London

1943-4

Nash was still Minister of Finance and Customs, though he had resigned the Marketing portfolio. In early April 1943 he returned to Wellington. It was not certain whether he would return to Washington or not.

During Nash's absence Fraser had succeeded, for a time, in creating a coalition War Administration, consisting of government and Opposition representatives, and bringing Angus McLagan, president of the Federation of Labour, into the government, with a seat in the Legislative Council. The War Administration was to run parallel with the Labour Cabinet. In addition there was an inner War Cabinet.

Most of the party, like Nash, disliked any idea of a coalition. James O'Brien, the Member for Westland, wrote to Nash '. . . Mr. Fraser seems to have most of us hoodooed for, although members of the Cabinet at times express their deep concern about the way things are going, as soon as Fraser cracks the whip they all come to heel. To get this latest idea through Caucus Fraser brought along Jim Roberts, Angus McLagan and others, and finally got an overwhelming majority for the proposals'.[1]

The War Administration lasted only until October. While Fraser was in the USA a miners' strike broke out. The government took strong action against them and some were sentenced to prison. However, on his return Fraser intervened. The state took over the mines for the duration of the war and the men returned to work. The National Party representatives withdrew from the War Administration, on the grounds that the government was not enforcing the law against the strikers. Coates and Hamilton, however, rejoined the War Cabinet as individuals. Mick Moohan, the Labour Party secretary, wrote to Nash that the War Administration had not been welcomed by the Labour movement and 'the bunch of political derelicts' who were given portfolios inspired no confidence. Sid Holland, he added, had 'walked out like a spoilt baby'. Nash wrote that the collapse of the War Administration was probably advantageous to Labour. He thought that Fraser had handled the coal strike very well and had achieved better results than a coercive policy, such as Holland demanded, would have achieved. Fraser himself had argued, against Holland, that gaoling the strikers would simply prevent them from producing coal. Nevertheless, Holland had won a reputation for being tough on strikers—even though he had been no more outspoken against 'wreckers' than Semple and Webb.[2]

Nash wrote to Moohan, 'Fraser stands so far above all others in the Dominion that it would be a tragedy if anything affected his leadership. In spite of his temper and sharp attacks on people, which tend to cause friction, his natural integrity and honesty, his hatred of sham and humbug, his natural intuition of things that are bad, bring him into the class of the big men.'[3] This was an assessment with which many people close to Fraser agreed. By 'intuition of things that are bad' Nash probably meant Fraser's insight into bad, dishonest, or merely 'political' motives, a quality in which Nash was deficient. He was notably charitable for a politician. His distrust of subordinates was of their judgement and accuracy, not of their intentions.

Nash was home for the party conference and for the budget. In 1942 it had been presented by Fraser and enormously increased taxes. Though Nash was able to present this year's budget, economic matters were no longer in his control. Fraser had announced a comprehensive stabilization policy, to control prices, wages, and costs, in December 1942. Stabilization and war finance were the dominant economic themes of the time, and Nash summarized these in his financial statement. So far the war had cost £229 millions—which made his £17 million conversion of 1939 seem a tiny problem.

The budget provided extensive increases in pensions for disabled ex-serviceman, for war and other widows, and in child allowances. Payments to hospitals were also increased. The cost of social security increased to £17 million.[4]

Nash stayed on in New Zealand for the 1943 general election. He spoke to nineteen meetings in three weeks. The credit reformers tried to make a comeback. John A. Lee's breakaway party, Democratic Soldier Labour, advocated a 'new credit system', especially for industrial development. He and Barnard ridiculed Fraser and Nash as financial conservatives. The Reverend C. C. Scrimgeour stood against Fraser in Wellington Central, calling Fraser and Nash the Ramsay MacDonald and Philip Snowden of New Zealand. He, too, pushed credit reform views.[5]

'Scrim' had been an object of suspicion to Labour leaders ever since his friend, Savage, appointed him Controller of Commercial Broadcasting, at a very high salary, in 1937. He did not hesitate to use radio to criticize the government. During the war he was restive about censorship and resisted the censor. Early in 1943 he was temporarily suspended when an uncensored broadcast referred to the arrival of the United States marines.[6] The government also greatly disliked the activities of others associated with radio station 1ZB. One man was inviting listeners to send him money for 'Better

Bonds' which, it was implied, were better than the government war bonds. 'Debt-free' money was being advocated over a government radio station.[7] A programme on Harry Holland, which stressed the 1913 strike, was put off the air on instructions from Fraser's 'Grey Eminence', F. P. Walsh, after discussions with Fraser.[8] As in the case of Sutch's book, Fraser disliked reminders of his radical and prison days. The government was now hunting for reasons to get rid of this insolent priest. A record of a so-called 'orgy' in his office was discovered. Eventually he was sacked.[9]

Labour stood on its record: 'unemployment banished'; 'unrivalled prosperity'; 'Labour's Social Order Gives Freedom from Want'—an Atlantic Charter and up-to-date slogan; the most comprehensive Social Security benefits in the world. Its record, including effective war-time leadership, was enough. Labour's share of the European vote dropped nearly 10 per cent to 47 per cent and the government lost nine seats to National. But it retained a lead, including the four Maori MPs, of 45 to 34. National's share of the vote increased very little—many votes went to John A. Leeites and independents.[10] 'Scrim' won over 2,000 votes and Fraser held only a minority of the votes in his electorate. Thus there were many still willing to listen to the siren cries of credit. Against Nash an independent social creditite came second, with 3,563 votes, beating both the National and Leeite candidates. Nash won 8,823 votes, not as high as in recent elections, but he still had a handsome majority.

In several seats vote-splitting by the John A. Leeites put the Labour MP out. Nevertheless, the rout of those credit reform deviationists was, from the government point of view, the main gain. Lee lost his seat. His party won only four per cent of the vote and won no seats at all. Lee was out. Langstone was merely a nuisance in caucus. McMillan had resigned from cabinet and retired from parliament. The credit reformers were beaten, even though they proved to be capable of fighting another round or two.

While the Nashes were at home their oldest son, Clement Walter, who had been a lawyer and was now in the RNZAF, died of meningitis. Nash had been closer to Walter than to his other sons, and respected him for his independence, but he could not express his feelings. To Jean McKenzie, an assistant in Washington with whom he was very close, he wrote that the shock would take some time to heal.[11] To his brother Albert and his wife a year later he wrote, 'We were rather hard hit when Walter passed on, but the effect of the blow will gradually work away with time, although we are hoping to continue to have many happy memories of him. Lottie has been upset quite a lot, but I hope she also will recover within a reasonable time.'[12]

New Zealand politics were not to reclaim Nash yet. By December 1943, accompanied by his old friend and assistant, John S. Reid, he flew to

Australia, en route to the USA. Their wives followed by sea. On the way his habit, fully developed in the USA, of commenting extempore on world affairs got him into trouble with two Prime Ministers. Reid and he were met in Sydney by Carl Berendsen, who did not get on well with Fraser, and was now the High Commissioner in Australia. They went up to Canberra where Nash held a Press conference on Christmas eve. He suggested that after the war a Pacific Islands federation, under the trusteeship of the USA, the UK, France, Australia, and New Zealand, might be set up. It might prove better than the post-World War I mandates. It would aim at raising the standard of living in the islands. The islands could be used mutually, thus ending any wrangles over air bases. Fraser cabled a rebuke. He had been, 'as you know, particularly anxious that the term confederation should not be used', but even the term 'federation' might give an erroneous impression. He issued a public statement that Nash's views were his own personal suggestions. Neither Nash nor the government, he said, thought of a transfer of sovereignty by Pacific powers to any sort of federation. There was a further protest from the Free French in Tahiti that Nash was envisaging their loss of French citizenship.[13]

Nash had said much the same thing in Wellington in early December when he spoke of an island confederation to give effect to the principles of the Atlantic Charter.[14] Alister McIntosh, now successor to Berendsen as Secretary of External Affairs and presently Head of the Prime Minister's Department, had then written a paper for Nash elaborating the idea of a federation of all the Pacific islands with a regional authority consisting of the Pacific ruling states plus representatives of the island peoples. It might be advisory or have some sovereign powers. The aim was to work out a common economic and social development programme.[15]

Nash was not, of course, the only one to be holding forth on the future of the Pacific. At the Mont Tremblant conference Lord Hailey had fore-shadowed a Pacific Zone Council and much of the discussion had centred round the creation of International Authorities in South-east Asia and the Pacific.[16] This was possibly where Nash got the idea, but not certainly, for discussion of trusteeship was then widespread. At the Pacific War Council, Roosevelt had suggested, and was again to suggest, a united approach to the control of the islands.[17] Evatt had in October 1943 proposed to New Zealand that Australia and New Zealand should take the responsibility for all the British islands. He wished to call a conference of governments interested in the South Pacific.[18]

Many people, including the New Zealand government, were thinking about Pacific futures. But Fraser did not want Nash doing it aloud and in public. He told him that he could discuss his views privately with British and American leaders.

Nash did it again a few days later. In an interview in Sydney on 26 December he referred to post-war immigration policy and said that 'the seeds of another war would most certainly be sown if other nations said they would neither accept the Japanese nor let their goods flow to them'. Though he added that northern Europeans developed best in Australia and New Zealand, this annoyed Curtin. Nash, who had flown up to Noumea to see New Zealand troops, received a message from the Prime Minister that he was 'greatly embarrassed' at being asked to comment on Nash's statement which 'could easily become a matter of difficulty for both Governments'. Nash's statement appeared both to refer to immigration into Australia and to justify Japanese expansion southward.

Nash replied denying that he had suggested any justification for Japanese aggression. He said that one or two Australian ministers had been present at his press interview, which did not touch on subjects to be discussed at the forthcoming conference. He apologized to both Prime Ministers for the embarrassment he had caused them.[19]

On this occasion Nash was criticized in the Press for not speaking for his government, presumably a diplomat's first duty. Diplomats cannot wander lonely and independently in search of golden conceptions of the future. Nash's statements, like many others', sounded all the better for a certain woolliness, a cloudy rhetoric. But the statements of diplomats often require very precise definition at the edges. No ill effects, however, seem to have followed from his indiscretions. Perhaps he benefited from error. Certainly talking indiscreetly was rarely held to be one of his faults thereafter. Rather he cultivated the dubious art, in answering questions, of being obscure to a Delphian degree, not because of too great a brevity, but by interposing garrulous thickets between his meaning and his audience.

Wartime travel was no pleasure. On 2 January Nash flew to Fiji, and then to Tarawa, a scene of recent violent fighting. There was a Japanese air raid not far off while he was there. On 4 January they flew on but had to land at Johnston Island, one 'that was hardly registered either in geography or anywhere else.' The commanding officer introduced Nash as Sir Walter and later begged him not to correct the error, since he had advertised that a Knight of the British Empire was about to land. Thereafter Nash used to tell how he was 'a Knight for a night'. They then flew on to Honolulu. Nash's diary laconically recalls that when he left the plane nearly turned over and had to return. By 7 January he was in San Francisco.

His flight was uneventful in comparison with John S. Reid's. Nash flew on ahead of him from Tarawa, leaving a message that he should guard some secret papers in a satchel. Reid got a lift in an army amphibian, despite cheerful warnings from navy friends that army fliers could not be trusted out of sight of land since they flew by line of sight. They came down in the ocean in a storm and threw all the spare gear they could find overboard. Reid preserved the satchel by sitting on it. Later he wrote that if he had been an experienced diplomat he would have known their likely worth and dumped them without a qualm. Next morning they managed to take off for Canton Island. The general who was a passenger said 'Even if the Japs hold it we have to go in.'[20] Reid presently rejoined his minister in Honolulu.

Nash was a persistent man and unrepentant about his statement on Pacific federation. As soon as he reached the USA he said at a press conference that it was his personal idea that there should be 'an international advisory or consultative council for the Pacific island groups' composed of states with interests in the region. He excluded the Dutch East Indies, the Philippines, Hawaii, and the Japanese mandates from the scheme. There would be some form of international trusteeship: the administering states would report to the supervisory council.[21]

At the Pacific War Council on 12 January Roosevelt meditated on the control of the Pacific Islands. New Zealand's—and Australia's—new assertiveness was becoming a little irritating to the Americans. When Nash said that New Zealand's interests went as far east as the Society and the Tuamotu islands, 'President Roosevelt laughingly suggested that since they were so very ambitious perhaps New Zealand should extend its control to Australia.'[22]

At about this time Anzac relationships with the USA temporarily deteriorated. Australian and New Zealand leaders, notably Evatt, were very disappointed at the failure of the great allied leaders to consult them about post-war planning, especially in making the Cairo declaration that Japan should lose her Pacific islands. They were disturbed at claims by American leaders to sovereignty over Pacific bases after the war.[23]

This was another important issue on which Nash had made his own pronouncements. He had been reported in the American Press as saying that he believed New Zealand would grant air and naval bases to the USA as part of a mutual defence system.[24] This was a very delicate subject indeed.

In January 1944 Fraser went to Australia, on Evatt's invitation, to discuss post-war problems. On Evatt's initiative, the agreement usually called the Canberra pact was drawn up. It affirmed that the doctrine of trusteeship was applicable to all Pacific colonies, and that the aim was ultimate self-government. It proclaimed that the possession of war-time bases afforded no grounds for post-war territorial claims. It called for an international conference to discuss the future of the Pacific. The first doctrine offended some British leaders; the next two points irritated the Americans. The Secretary of State, Cordell Hull, informed Curtin and Fraser that the President and he were disturbed at the proposal to call a conference. It might lead to friction. He thought that the creation of an international security system should precede regional pacts.[25]

Nash does not seem to have felt the sting of American displeasure, except for some Press criticism.[26] He was away in London for two months from the beginning of February. But in April, when Fraser was on his way to a Commonwealth Prime Minister's conference, Hull spoke very strongly to him and Nash, accusing Australia and New Zealand of a dishonesty comparable to the Russians! Roosevelt, however, told Curtin at this time that the whole episode was best forgotten.[27]

From early February 1944 until early April Nash was in London, a member of the War Cabinet for the second time. The first was in 1942, when the war was going badly. Now he was in Britain on the eve of 'D' day. It does not seem from the recorded 'Conclusions' (minutes of decisions) of the meetings of the War Cabinet that Nash contributed any-thing of note to decisions, but, like S. M. Bruce of Australia, he offered his counsel. At least New Zealand was informed in person, as it were, of the great events. They discussed 'unconditional surrender', for instance. Churchill wanted a list made of fifty or a hundred major war criminals, to be executed when caught and without trial.[28]

Though Nash was greatly impressed by Churchill, he thought it was Attlee's 'brain and his quiet reserve that enabled the work to be co-ordinated. . . .' Attlee would seek to sum up towards the end of a meeting, after the others had talked right round a subject.[29]

The British leaders were not all impressed by the Dominion leaders. On one occasion in February Hugh Dalton, President of the Board of Trade (and soon to be Chancellor of the Exchequer), wrote in his diary, after a meeting of the War Cabinet, that there was a row over the question of imperial preference, with Beaverbrook and Brendan Bracken shouting everyone down:

The whole thing develops into the worst pandemonium I have ever seen in the Cabinet. Towards the end, four or five Ministers are often shouting at once, and the P.M., I think, deliberately allows the thing to get out of hand, explaining that he hasn't had time to read the papers, and doesn't pretend to understand it, but thinks it should be thoroughly discussed, and why anyhow should we be hustled, 'just because a few officials from the Dominions are here ; they can be entertained for a few days, and given drinks, and taken round to see the bomb craters.'[30]

Nash's main job in London was to discuss the Dominion's manpower problems. New Zealand had over-extended itself. It was trying to maintain an army division in the Middle East, and then Italy, and another in the Pacific, plus large numbers of men in the navy and air force. By September 1942 there were 153,600 men and 3,400 women in the armed forces. The men were nearly a third of the male labour force.[31] This situation was the result of the government's decision, in 1942 and 1943, to leave the main

division in the Middle East, despite the Japanese attack.[32] Apart from John
A. Lee and Langstone there was little opposition to this decision, which
Fraser and Nash supported. Anglo-American strategy was to beat Germany
first. But the Australians refused to accept Anglo-American advice and
brought their troops home from the Middle East—to fight in New Guinea.

Churchill's and Roosevelt's strategy proved to be sound. But, in retrospect,
it seems extraordinary that, when New Zealand was threatened, the government left the very experienced and efficient New Zealand army in the
Middle East. It is difficult to believe that, had Fraser and Nash been New
Zealanders, they could have accepted this policy.

The result was a demand for manpower which the country could not
sustain if the supply of vital foodstuffs to Britain and the American forces
in the Pacific were to be kept up. Before leaving for Britain Nash discussed
the manpower problem with Roosevelt who said, with a powerful logic, that
in view of its proximity and particular interest, New Zealand troops should
enter Tokyo rather than Berlin.[33] Churchill, however, still thought otherwise. Eventually it was decided to release part of the Pacific (3rd) division
to civilian work, and ultimately to recall it.[34]

New Zealand mobilization for war had now passed its peak. But as a
result of these decisions its army was fighting 12,000 miles away, and making
no impact in New Zealand's own region.

Another of Nash's tasks in London was to see Hugh Dalton about 'price
disparities'. During the war the terms of trade had turned strongly against
New Zealand, which had firmly controlled internal costs. Nash claimed that
New Zealand had lost some £28 million. In other words, Great Britain was
benefiting considerably from New Zealand's successful stabilization policy.
At first the British offered £3 million or £4 million, but in the end they paid
£12 million and £4 million a year for four years. These lump payments
helped Nash to redeem the feared London loans.

Dalton saw Nash a number of times. Once he took him to dine and
wrote, 'I find he is not, as I had feared, teatotal. As usual he talks very
good sense. He has strong "bilateralist" tendencies in trade. He talks much,
and interestingly, about personalities in A. and N.Z., speaking very well
indeed of Curtin [who he?] says, since he became P.M., has grown
immeasurably. . . .'[35]

XIX

Planning for World Peace
and Justice

1943-8

In the years 1943-8 the New Zealand government was engaged in international negotiations on an unprecedented scale. With its scanty resources of qualified people, it had great difficulty in meeting its obligations. In 1946 alone, between February and December, representatives were needed for twenty-one international conferences, including a British Commonwealth Prime Ministers' conference and ILO, UNESCO, and IMF meetings. Essentially all these conferences were concerned with planning the shape of the post-war world. It could not be expected that such a small state as New Zealand could have had an important influence on their conclusions. But it did play a larger role than would have been thought possible before 1935 or is now generally realized. One reason for this was that very few states took part. Most of the independent states of the modern world were then dependent territories. The Germans, Italians, Japanese, and their allies were also absent. Sometimes the USSR stayed away too.

Another circumstance of importance is that very often New Zealand, sometimes in conjunction with Australia, had points of view distinctly different from those of the great allied powers. Fraser and Nash, like Evatt and Chifley, did not hesitate to express them very forcibly. One of Nash's qualities much appreciated by New Zealand officials accompanying him was that he was never apologetic because of New Zealand's smallness and unimportance—nor, indeed, from any other feelings of inferiority or inadequacy. For Fraser and Nash, Berendsen, Ashwin, Campbell, and the others, the great series of conferences at this time were an opportunity to try to apply in post-war planning some of the idealism that had inspired Labour's policy in the League of Nations.

The economic conferences which Nash attended represented the zenith of Labour's aspirations—to do for mankind what social security, full employment, guaranteed prices and other measures had, they believed, done for New Zealand.

Nash's colleagues like Tim Armstrong or Bill Parry were by no means the only people who took seriously his musings, dreams about the world to come. As an occasional preacher, a Student Christian Movement or Institute of International Affairs lecturer, he had in a sense spent his life discussing such things. The British broadcaster and former Minister of Health, Walter Elliot, said in a broadcast to Australia and New Zealand in 1942, while talking about the world to be after the war:

. . . . Much of this I had the good fortune to discuss with your Walter Nash, of New Zealand, in a room overlooking the London River while the slow northern twilight went on and on—8.30—9.30—10.30—and even then, light in the sky. Organisations—ideals—a world standard of living—lease-lend in war and peace —the butter market in years to come, and all that that implied—*and* our rival vital statistics. Some of it he had said in New Zealand; some of it in Pennsylvania; here he was in London; and I had no manner of doubt, seeing and hearing him and thinking of all like him, that we should again find a compass course to sail, and start upon new enterprises as engrossing as any of old.[1]

Of course, Nash enjoyed this kind of idealistic talk. It happened, too, that the idea of *planning* the future world, whether in connection with food resources or rates of exchange, long attractive to him, was in the 1940s very widely influential. Moreover, whether or not his personal contribution was significant on any particular occasion, the great conferences and meetings of the 1940s gave Nash that sense of involvement in great events which he craved.

Nash was taken much more seriously at these conferences than people in New Zealand realized, then or since. This was not only because of the few states participating; it was also because of the impact he made person- ally. For instance, in 1944 the Director-General of UNRRA, Governor Herbert H. Lehmann, wanted Nash to become Senior Deputy Director- General. He declined. When it was suggested to him that Lehmann might soon retire, Nash wrote to Lehmann that it was hard for him to decide to decline, because his mind was set on improving relations between the nations. But decline he did.[2]

In April-May 1944, following his visit to London, Nash represented New Zealand at the twenty-sixth conference of the International Labour Organization, at Philadelphia. On an American nomination he was elected president. The ILO had been almost ignored by New Zealand governments, before 1935. They sent no representatives to its conferences before 1930, and ratified none of its conventions. But it had long interested Nash and the Labour Party. Its effort to improve labour conditions was one of the things which led the Party to become pro-League (the other was the Chanak crisis of 1922, which suggested that the League could have a role as an international arbitrator).[3] As early as 1926 Nash was collecting information about New Zealand conditions for its director.[4]

Representatives of governments, workers, and employers from forty-one countries attended. When *Izvestia* criticized the ILO, Nash called on the Soviet Union to rejoin.[5] In his opening speech, he said that whenever he met servicemen they asked him, 'What is going to happen when this is over, Mr. Nash?' They expected the ILO to give an answer. Its aim, he said, was to free people from want and to give them a full life—words which could be empty rhetoric, but were strongly felt by the speaker.

Various committees laboured to draw up a vast series of recommendations and resolutions on many subjects such as social security, disabled workers, employment of women, and also the Philadelphia Charter, a restatement of the aims of the ILO. Some statements in the declaration sound very like Nash, not because he wrote them, but because they were very much the sort of things he believed in and might have said: 'Labour is not a commodity'; 'Poverty anywhere constitutes a danger to prosperity everywhere'. The ILO aimed at full employment everywhere; at the 'extension of social security measures to provide a basic income to all in need of such protection and comprehensive medical care'.

Nash's final speech was very impressive. His rhetoric was not Churchillian, yet he could communicate to many people a simple dogged will to better things. He produced many of his habitual themes, none of them out of place.

He spoke of racial equality and of social security. The objective approved by the conference had reminded him, he said, of an earlier conference in Geneva in 1920. He spoke of 'the first charge'. It was a 'simple, ordinary, Christian duty', to care for the sick; the aged because we enjoy the fruits of their labour; the young because they are our future. And he spoke of the men fighting all over the world, of the need to abolish war and to rehabilitate the servicemen. A previous speaker had discussed the disabled. Nash referred to men who had lost limbs, but now led useful lives with the aid of mechanical ones. He thought of the man who had said during the depression that no one wanted him, and he said that what the disabled wanted was not pensions but 'the joy of being wanted.'

He spoke of 'freedom', a word, he said, used so loosely in recent years that it had lost its force. Yet it was a word much needed. It implied its own conditions. 'There can be no freedom where there is hunger. There can be no freedom where there is ill health. Only very rarely is there a St. Francis of Assisi who can experience freedom fully in poverty and hunger.' He affirmed that poverty could be abolished.

I don't want to get rid of poverty just to ensure that prosperity is maintained; I want to get rid of poverty because it is bad, it is wrong, it is immoral, it is unethical, it is un-Christian, it is unfair, and it is unjust, and it is everything that is bad. I mean involuntary poverty—where a man is told that his hands are not wanted, and that his wife and his youngsters will be deprived of the necessary things for health.[6]

The American Secretary of Labor, Frances Perkins, and Jan Masaryk,

the Czech foreign minister, praised Nash's kindly and efficient chairman-
ship.[7] A. D. McIntosh wrote to Nash that it had been intended (presumably
by the Americans) that he should act as chairman of the UN interim
Commission on Food and Agriculture,[8] but he was absent in New Zealand.
At the conference at Hot Springs, Virginia, in mid-1943, when this first UN
agency was set up, New Zealand was represented by R. M. Campbell, now
Official Secretary to the High Commissioner's Office in London, George
Duncan of the Marketing Department, and E. J. Fawcett, the Director-
General of Agriculture. Geoffrey Cox went with Campbell, A. G. B. Fisher,
and B. R. Turner to Atlantic City to attend the first meeting of UNRRA
later in the year.[9] Thereafter Fraser and Nash took over the chief roles at
such conferences.

Throughout most of July 1944 Nash attended the United Nations
Monetary and Financial Conference at Bretton Woods, in New Hampshire,
at which the International Monetary Fund, and the International Bank for
Reconstruction and Development were created. The latter was set up to
provide capital for building up war-torn or under-developed economies. Of
greater interest to New Zealand was the IMF.

In 1888 the great economist, Alfred Marshall, had suggested that 'the
time would come at which it would be thought as unreasonable for any
country to regulate its own currency without reference to other countries
as it would be to have signalling codes at sea which took no account of
the signalling codes of other countries.'[10]

During the depression competitive devaluations, prohibitive tariffs,
exchange controls, and other unilateral actions had contributed to causing
a great drop in world trade. The purpose of the Bretton Woods meeting
was to prevent a recurrence of this situation, insofar as monetary causes
were relevant. It was assumed that the world's problems should be solved
through international cooperation, not national individualism. It was
assumed that exchange rates were an international concern.

Bretton Woods arose from articles four and five of the Atlantic Charter,
which looked forward to equal access for all peoples, on equal terms, to
trade and raw materials. To this end the USA and Great Britain declared
in 1942 in their Mutual Aid Agreement that they would seek to expand
production, employment, trade, and consumption, to eliminate all forms of
discriminatory treatment in international commerce, and to reduce tariff
and other trade barriers.[11]

As far as the world's financial structure was concerned, what seemed
needed was some organization to increase international currency reserves,
stabilize exchange rates, facilitate international lending, and encourage both
debtors and creditors to correct large or chronic deficits in their balances
of payments. It was also intended that multi-lateral (not bi-lateral) international payments should be encouraged, and exchange restrictions which
hampered world trade should be eliminated.[12]

Although New Zealand had an obvious interest in the regulated expansion of world trade, international monetary stability, and above all in cooperative measures to cope with balance of payments deficits, the Bretton Woods meeting also held a potential threat. Fraser wrote to Nash in January 1944 that 'there exists a grave danger for New Zealand' in the preliminary talks between London and Washington on post-war policy. He feared that Great Britain might accept the idea of export subsidies, which the USA might want to keep to help its farmers, while being 'inclined to surrender on questions of quantitative restriction of imports, bulk purchase, state trading and imperial preference'. He thought 'it would be a poor reward for our country's immense war effort to be threatened in any way with industrial disaster at the hands of our friends.'[13]

The threat was real, for import licensing and exchange controls, such as New Zealand's, were two of the measures restrictive of trade which the Americans, led by Cordell Hull, and the British wished to eliminate.

The Americans and British had to make concessions to the Russians during the preliminary discussions in London. Nash cabled Fraser from there in March that the trend of thought favoured either private trading or state trading with government monopolies.[14] It was not clear whether there would be room for New Zealand's mixed trading system.

Before the conference began the Australian and New Zealand governments conferred about their policies during discussions on international economic collaboration. They agreed that the main over-all aim was full employment. This objective was a legacy of the depression which was, at least in New Zealand, to dominate Labour thought for many years. The two countries wanted to induce others to pursue domestic policies aimed at the same target. They wanted international economic cooperation after the war. But—Fraser cabled to Nash—they wanted the right to retain government control of imports and exports where necessary in the national interests.[15]

The Bretton Woods conference of forty-four states met to discuss the draft Agreement drawn up during the preliminary discussions. Nash led the New Zealand delegates. He was accompanied by B. C. Ashwin, Secretary to the Treasury, E. C. Fussell of the Reserve Bank, Bruce Turner, and A. G. B. Fisher. The latter had been brought over from Chatham House in London as an 'expert', to the FAO conference. Cox and Campbell had him attached to the New Zealand delegation to the UNRRA conference. When Nash was in London he found that Fisher and Campbell did an excellent job during the preliminary IMF discussions. He now had Fisher appointed a temporary Counsellor to the New Zealand legation.[16] Fisher's understanding of international finance was outstanding. Turner was to become the senior UN financial official. With their economists' knowledge of trade and finance and Nash's politician's knowledge and experience, it was a good team.

Apart from the main Commissions, the one on the IMF chaired by Harry Dexter White, Assistant to the Secretary of the Treasury, and the one on the International Bank chaired by Lord Keynes, there were three committees. Nash was elected Chairman of the Committee on Nominations (to the various commissions and committees). During the conference he was also elected a member of a committee which fixed 'quota' allocations.[17]

Each member of the Fund was allotted a 'quota', which determined its subscription and drawing rights. Both in Committee and in full Commission Nash pressed for a higher quota for New Zealand. He did not get his way, but thought nevertheless, since the establishment of the Fund was of such broad international importance, that New Zealand should join.[18] The Russian request for a much higher quota was approved, and Nash was impressed with what he took to be the USSR's whole-hearted support for the Fund. Nash spoke on various other matters. For instance, he strongly but unsuccessfully protested against the requirement that members of the Fund pay a small service charge on borrowings. He thought this would discourage the use of the Fund.[19] But his main concern was that the Agreement provided that members would not impose restrictions on the making of payments and transfers for current international transactions except during a transition period after joining, or temporarily against currencies which the IMF had declared 'scarce'.

He cabled the Acting Prime Minister and Minister of External Affairs (Dan Sullivan, while Fraser was abroad too, from April to July).

While the intention of this provision is not to interfere with a member's system of exchange control so long as the member is not blocking payments which it owes (i.e. for current imports) I felt that it was unsatisfactory in its present form because it is liable to lead to misunderstanding on the part of the public. I endeavoured to have embodied in the clause a specific statement that reference to restrictions was in no way directed at the control of exchange in its entirety to enable commitments for approved imports and other approved transactions to be met promptly and fully. But the most I could get was an assurance from the Chairmen of the Commission (concurred in by members of the Commission) that there was nothing in the clause as it stands which in any way conflicts with exchange control. Under the present draft we can maintain our import licensing and exchange control procedure subject only to our ensuring that all exchange required for current transactions is made available.

According to the notes he made at this time, he had asked the chairman, Harry D. White, whether exchange controls were permissible, provided that exchange was used to pay for all current transactions. White replied that this was his understanding, and he asked the meeting if there was any dissent. There was none.[20]

Within New Zealand there was much suspicion and hostility to the IMF. Nash was warned not in any way to intimate publicly that if he signed the final Act he was committed to recommending it to his government; nor was

New Zealand committed to adopting it. Sullivan and Fraser both stated that there would be no commitments until the government and parliament had considered the matter.[21]

Nash felt strongly that New Zealand should join the Fund. Before he left he wrote to Harry D. White, 'it can easily be the greatest step in World History with possibilities of removing one of the major causes of war—if not the major cause.'[22] He was not blind to the possible menace to his beloved import and exchange controls. There would be some restrictions on New Zealand. For instance, a member of the IMF could not permit exchange rates to fluctuate greatly without permission. But any international system of payments would involve submitting to rules. As usual, Nash placed international benefits to the fore. But, like A. G. B. Fisher, he was also quite aware of the great help the Fund might offer in coping with balance of payments problems like that in 1939.[23]

Nash had by now been succeeded as Minister to Washington by Carl Berendsen. His colleagues wanted him back in time for the 1944 budget. This gave him a very tight schedule. However, Admiral Ernest J. King arranged for a plane to fly Mrs Nash and himself back home. They left New York by plane on 20 July and San Francisco on 22 July. They landed at Honolulu, Canton Island and Fiji, where Nash received 'budget material' flown up from New Zealand. The flight across the Pacific to Auckland took 33 hours 3 minutes.[24] By 26 July he was in Wellington for the opening of parliament.

While Fraser and Nash were away the credit-men had been playing up in caucus. On Langstone's motion a caucus committee had considered nationalizing the Bank of New Zealand. It resolved unanimously that this should be done though so frightened was caucus of Fraser that it approved the committee's views only as a recommendation to the Prime Minister.[25]

Although Nash had opposed this step in war-time and had said that the banks were doing a good job, this time both he and the Prime Minister had to submit to the majority. They remained entirely—and justifiably—sceptical. Since the government already appointed a majority of the bank's directors and controlled its actions in various ways through the Reserve Bank, and since the other banks were to be left in private ownership, it was not clear what benefits would flow to the public from nationalization.

However, Fraser and Nash could console themselves with the thought that it might be possible to unite the party over an issue which had long divided it. At the 1943 party conference Nash had strongly resisted the demand for nationalization and had been supported by the majority. Now, at the 1944 conference, he seconded H. E. Combs's motion to create a state trading bank. His arguments were luke-warm but he said that, although it would not bring all the advantages people hoped for, it was in the best interests of the country that the proposal should receive unanimous support if possible. He added that conference could not compel the government to act. Still, the applause for him and Combs and Langstone was tumultuous.

Langstone was lyrical: 'Archimedes said "Give me a long enough lever and I will lift the world." ' Turning to Nash he said, 'Here's the lever, Mr. Nash. It will make it possible for the sunshine of economic prosperity and progress to shine in even the darkest places.'[26] There was great applause.

The national president, James Roberts, said that the atmosphere at conference was like a revivalist meeting. An MP wrote to Nash that the decision had 'solidified the movement'.[27] Many unionists agreed with Langstone over this issue. Young of the Hotel Workers' union helped to organize support at the conference.[28] It was one of the last flurries of the Labour Party credit reformers. In 1953 Social Credit supporters—including Langstone—were to transfer their support to their own party. But in 1944 people with such views were still powerful in the Labour Party, in caucus and in cabinet. Consequently the financial policies of Nash—and Fraser— were often neither supported nor understood. On the other hand, the views of the credit reformers were confused and often impenetrable. Langstone was in 1945 going about saying that all credit for national undertakings should be free of interest at its source; its issue should be compatible with a stable price level. The banks were causing inflation—which would be stopped by free credit. He believed that, once there was a state trading bank, the others would not be allowed to create credit but only to lend their deposits. W. E. Parry, the Minister of Internal Affairs, thought that socialism could be achieved if the Reserve Bank and the Bank of New Zealand purchased all local production and then regulated the volume of money needed to purchase it, so as to stabilize prices.[29] These were not the views of a lunatic fringe but part of the central weave of Labour Party— and New Zealand—political thought.

Labour's opponents cried 'socialism' and organized protest meetings. Newspapers ran headings such as 'MONEY REVOLUTION: FINANCIAL PERIL AHEAD'.[30] There was some fear, which seemed reasonable, that there might be political bias or interference in the bank's lending policies.[31] It had long been obvious that, if the government took over one bank, its fearful depositors might move their accounts. Some farmers' organizations now tried to organize a boycott of the Bank of New Zealand.[32] Nash had to issue a statement assuring customers of the bank that they would have the same rights and immunities as before nationalization, that the bank's records would be secret and that its business would be conducted according to 'sound banking practice'.[33] Nash felt that, having been forced to nationalize it, he had then been forced to save it.[34]

Initially the bank lost a few hundred accounts—not as many as was feared. In the long run the nationalization had no significant effects except on the bank's shareholders, who were bought out. The public soon forgot that it was a state bank.

The credit reformers had a further field day with the IMF. In October 1944 caucus resolved that the government should ratify the Bretton Woods agreements.[35] But there was no hurry—the closing date for adherence to the agreement was the end of 1945. Fraser was abroad again for many weeks in mid-1945 at San Francisco. In any case, the government was busily watching the policy of others. In the USA there was much opposition led by Senator Taft.[36] In Australia there was heated debate too. More important in the New Zealand government's eyes, Britain had not joined. As part of the sterling area, New Zealand could not act alone. On 6 December 1945 the government informed caucus that it had decided to ratify Bretton Woods.[37] Next day, Parliament adjourned. Not until mid-December did the British Parliament approve ratification. It was then too late to recall the New Zealand Parliament.

In 1946 both Nash and Fraser were in London and Europe for important conferences. As a newspaper observed, neither party was eager to grasp the IMF nettle in an election year.[38] The government was becoming very reluctant indeed. The Social Creditites and other assorted credit reformers were to a man turning against the Fund. The government had no wish to turn them against Labour. Labour ministers and MPs were receiving very many letters and branch resolutions against ratification. The Fund was 'a diabolical plan to wreck our Empire'. A Social Credit letter said that 'A Return to Gold will Bring Depression'—it was endlessly and incorrectly asserted that joining the Fund meant a return to the gold standard.[39] The leader of the Opposition, S. G. Holland, and F. W. Doidge, Member for Tauranga, were actively denouncing the Fund, on the ground that to join was to hand control of credit to an international organization, and that it meant the end of imperial preference.[40] Both parties were divided in opinion. The public support for the Fund was moderate and well-informed;[41] the opposition was powerful, immoderate, and wildly emotional. So the government did nothing.

In early 1947 Australia decided to join, though Chifley wrote to Nash that he had had a 'difficult time with it here'. One of his ministers had said publicly that 'the sovereignty of the nation' was in jeopardy; the IMF would 'pervert and paganise our Christian ideals'.[42] Hugh Dalton was urging Nash that New Zealand should join too. He wanted to get enough Commonwealth votes to secure an extra Commonwealth director of the Fund.[43]

At some very prolonged government caucus meetings through July the issue was decided. Nash and Ormond Wilson moved approval for ratification. Langstone, Combs, Connolly, Anderton, Baxter, and others fought hard against them. Nash took notes of the various arguments. Langstone said that the USA would take control and had already forced Britain to join. Combs was opposed and asked whether New Zealand could keep import controls. Connolly reported, 'Large Body who are fearful of

International Financiers'. Baxter sounded 'Prejudiced against U.S.A.'
'Suggests we should not surrender to U.S.A.' Nash said that they could not
convert or reform the world 'by keeping out of the Conferences'. He urged
that they did not stay out of the United Nations because they disliked the
veto. Fraser sat on the fence. In the end the discussion was suspended with
no agreement reached.[44]

Nash's own view was that even the Labour dissidents and the National
Party making political capital out of the issue would not have stopped the
government from ratification if only Britain had not postponed a decision
until the last moment in 1945. What had been politically possible in
December 1945 was impossible now.[45] It was a severe defeat for him at the
hands of the caucus currency reformers. It seems clear that Fraser and he
had become so engrossed in world politics that they had temporarily lost
touch with their party.

In these war-time and post-war negotiations Fraser made a stronger
impression than Nash. He was tougher, more down-to-earth, more incisive.
In 1945 he led the New Zealand delegation to the San Francisco conference,
where the United Nations was created. He chaired the international trusteeship committee, and made a considerable impression with his firmness and
skill. The Australian and New Zealand opposition to giving great powers
in the Security Council a veto is well-known.[46] Fraser also attended the first
meeting of the General Assembly in January 1946. Nash, however, went in
his place to the meeting of Commonwealth Prime Ministers in London in
April and May. Having been in London in January Fraser must have
thought it was Nash's turn.

Whenever Nash was in London in the 1940s he had trouble with Bill
Jordan, the High Commissioner, who would scarcely agree to meet or speak
to him. Jordan was an object of much suspicion in the party, because of
his conservative views. Probably he resented Nash arriving and putting him
in the shade so frequently and lengthily.[47] On this occasion he refused to
attend the conference as an observer. Nash went up to him at a reception
for Ben Chifley, shook hands and said 'I hoped I would see a lot more of
him and his reply was "please yourself" '. He refused to cooperate in any
way unless Nash called at his office and apologized in the presence of two
senior officials. Nash wrote to Fraser that he did not know what for.
However, Nash got him an invitation from Attlee, but he was unappeased.
The situation was 'really most unpleasant', Nash wrote to Fraser, and made
him 'feel rather uncomfortable'.[48]

Nash made what was by now, at Commonwealth conferences, the ritual
New Zealand imperialist gesture. He said that a Commonwealth parliament,
such as had been suggested after the first world war, was not wanted, but he
thought there should be more regular and frequent meetings to formulate,
as far as possible, a Commonwealth policy. The *Daily Express* said that

Nash wanted an 'Empire Cabinet' of about twenty men to discuss defence and trade and make recommendations to governments. The *Daily Mail* called it a 'super-cabinet'.[49] This sort of talk was meaningless even before World War I: it was already clear then that the Dominions wanted co-operation not unity. By 1946 it was positively anachronistic. At the conference Field Marshal Smuts and Mackenzie King repudiated all notion of common defence or foreign policies when Bevin and the British Chiefs of Staff suggested them. Nor would they consider any Commonwealth machinery for these purposes. Mackenzie King, indeed, preferred written communications between governments to conferences and said he was reluctant to express views at conferences because he could not consult his colleagues.

The Australians and New Zealanders felt that they were not adequately consulted by the British. The others did not want too much consultation. Nash wrote to Fraser, 'some Dominions felt that, if it were true that if they expressed interest and gave advice to the United Kingdom Government on a matter of foreign policy they would have to accept a share of any resulting commitment, then they would prefer not to express interest or offer advice'.

The Chiefs of Staff wanted to defend certain areas of crucial importance to the Commonwealth, in the event of war. One was the Middle East. Nash wrote:

A test case came up during the Conference over the withdrawal from Egypt. The Suez Canal has traditionally been considered a key point in Commonwealth communications, especially for India, Australia, New Zealand, and South Africa. Mr. Chifley, Dr. Evatt and myself agreed that the British Government's policy towards Egypt was sound, in that there was no practicable alternative. But the important point is that policy towards Egypt was not regarded as one of joint Commonwealth concern, and all except myself were prepared to hold that Egypt and the Canal were primarily United Kingdom responsibilities. If this is so, I question whether there is any area towards which the members of the Commonwealth would accept the position that there must be a joint policy, and we are therefore in the situation that each member of the Commonwealth will take a primary responsibility in its own region, but will not go further.[50]

Attlee assured the House of Commons that the Dominions had been 'fully consulted' about the withdrawal from Egypt. He told the visiting Prime Ministers that he had believed they had 'acquiesced'. Evatt and Smuts denied this and Attlee had to apologize to the House for misleading it. Nash told Fraser that he had 'acquiesced, though I did not share in the responsibility for it'. In the Press he said that he had been fully informed and had agreed.[51] Thus Nash—and Fraser[52]—wanted more consultation. Nash cabled Fraser that there was no major question of foreign policy that was the exclusive responsibility of Britain, though Britain might sometimes have the last word. If New Zealand shared responsibility on any issue, then her voice must be heard and taken note of. He seemed to think that this applied to almost all issues of foreign policy.[53]

The other leaders were not always consistent. For instance Mackenzie King on occasion spoke of the need for consultation.[54] Nevertheless, the New Zealand government, led by an Englishman and a Scot, was markedly more Commonwealth-minded than the other Commonwealth governments. There was certainly no invariable and necessary connection between British birth and British imperial patriotism. And in Nash's case it might have been expected that his unhappy experiences in 1939 would have outweighed love of country. But his reaction was different. He always tried to look charitably upon the actions of those who opposed him. The behaviour of the upper class rulers of 1939 did not altogether dismay him; he bore no resentment; the sins of Oliver Stanley were not visited on Churchill or Attlee. It should be added that New Zealand was moving in the same direction as the others, but more slowly. In 1947 New Zealand adopted the Statute of Westminster which made it in all legal respects a fully independent state. In 1946 the government began discreetly to drop using the expression 'Dominion of New Zealand', the word Dominion being scarcely appropriate to the new post-war Commonwealth.

Perhaps the most important issue for New Zealand to arise at the conference was that of American bases in the Pacific. The Americans were speaking with two voices during and after the war. The sweet American voice said 'trusteeship for colonies'; the tough one said, 'bases'. In early 1946 the Americans were demanding joint bases in New Caledonia, Fiji, Western Samoa, and other islands, some of them Australian, New Zealand, or British. They also wanted exclusive rights in Canton and Christmas Islands and Funafuti. When the Secretary of State, J. F. Byrnes, talked to Commonwealth leaders in January 1946, Peter Fraser told him that some of the islands to which the USA laid claim, in the Northern Cooks, were actually part of New Zealand territory. He asked him, no doubt sarcastically, whether their claims were based on occupation or discovery. Byrnes said that the time for action was now, while the American loan to the United Kingdom was going through Congress. Fraser spoke equally frankly. He said, 'so far as the disputed islands were concerned it was a question of "nothing doing" '.[55]

In April Byrnes was demanding that Tarawa should be ceded by Great Britain. He again told Attlee, in Paris, that this gift would expedite the approval of the American loan then being negotiated.[56] Australia and New Zealand were aiming to negotiate the grant of joint bases to the USA as part of a regional South Pacific defence arrangement. This received some newspaper publicity and Byrnes registered (Nash told Fraser) strong disapproval. He said there was no one against whom the USA need prepare a defence—which made the others wonder why the USA wanted the bases.[57] The Australians were firm that the Americans would get no bases in their island territories without some regional arrangement but, in the last resort, the New Zealanders were willing to give the Americans a base in Western Samoa without this condition, so anxious were they to involve the USA in the defence of the South Pacific.[58] In the end the USA dropped its claims to bases.

Nash represented New Zealand at the Victory Parade. He played a little snooker and billiards for relaxation. He and Lot dined at Buckingham Palace with the King and Queen, Queen Mary, Princess Elizabeth, and other members of the royal family, Smuts, Mackenzie King, and the Attlees. Lot sat next to the King.

Nash attended a big meeting of European socialists which Hugh Dalton chaired. The Germans were not invited. They discussed whether to set up a new socialist international, and decided that the British Labour Party should set up an information bureau in London. Dalton wrote in his diary, 'Nash came and was one of the successes of the Conference. His speech about what they had done in New Zealand and of their general outlook on the world was refreshingly different from all the old European misery.'[59]

In 1947 to early April 1948 Nash seemed to be abroad most of the time. In late January he was in Canberra at a meeting which set up the South Pacific Commission. There was much debate over whether its headquarters should be in Australia or Fiji, and whether New Zealand's financial contribution could be increased so that Australia's influence should not be predominant.[60] But most of Nash's work was at the great trade and tariff conferences at Geneva, Havana, New York, London, and elsewhere.

The General Agreement on Tariffs and Trade (GATT) and the proposed International Trade Organisation (ITO) arose from the same idealistic impulse as the IMF. Once again, it was hoped that international cooperation would prevent any return to the intolerable autarchic policies of between the wars. How to translate the ideal of economic cooperation into commercial practice, and in what form, was the problem. Often, as some Americans fought for a return to the trading system which they imagined had existed before the depression—the capitalist system of the gold standard and market forces—while others, like the New Zealanders, fought to keep quantitative restrictions, international brotherhood seemed far away. Yet most, probably all, of the governments were willing to make concessions to achieve a better climate for world trade than that of dog-eat-dog. The USA, for instance, was willing to make substantial tariff reductions.

Nash took part in some of the preliminary discussions. In June 1946, there were talks with British and other Commonwealth officials on commercial policy. There, as on every possible later occasion, he tried to impress his listeners with New Zealand's determination not to give up import and exchange controls, even though the government favoured the American proposals for an ITO as a whole. He said that during the war New Zealand had built up purchasing power of £250 million beyond available supplies. If there were no import licences, he feared a run on New Zealand's overseas funds. At the same time, there was no guarantee that the goods imported would be essential commodities. In addition, New Zealand wanted to protect new industries. He argued, there and elsewhere, that New Zealand's controls did not diminish world trade, for licences could be issued for all the foreign exchange available for imports. The British and Americans, however, thought quantitative restriction of imports quite unacceptable except during some temporary difficulties.[61]

The first session of the Preparatory Committee of the United Nations Conference on Trade and Employment met in London in late 1946. The New Zealand delegation was led by Mr J. P. D. Johnsen, Assistant Comptroller of Customs. Nash led the team during British Commonwealth talks in March-April 1947 and then to the Second Session of the Preparatory Committee in Geneva in April and May. On his way to England and Europe he visited Washington. He spoke to Dean Acheson, the Under-Secretary of State, and had a talk with Harry Hawkins, a leader of the United States delegation to the London session, and Winthrop Brown, a leader at Geneva. The latter said the basis of New Zealand's policy was industrial development. Nash said that this was relevant, but that the main reason for it was the balance of payments. Hawkins said this was a temporary difficulty; Nash replied that it was likely to be 'a temporary permanent difficulty, like the permanent casuals at the Railway Workshops', as he reported to Fraser. He warned him that there must be no emphasis in New Zealand statements on import selection for development purposes[62] —dirty economics, in orthodox American and British eyes.

While he was in the United States Nash addressed the Economic and Employment Commission of the Economic and Social Council of the UN. The British had moved in favour of international action to maintain 'high and stable levels of world employment'. Nash said this did not go far enough—full employment was what was needed. At the end of his speech there was much applause from delegates and spectators.[63] At all these meetings full employment was widely discussed. There was much fear of countries 'exporting unemployment'. Governments were increasingly reluctant to meet balance of payments difficulties by domestic deflationary measures causing unemployment. This was one of Nash's favourite topics. Moreover he was not one of the numerous economic Vicars of Bray he encountered, new converts from the doctrine of laissez-faire. He was used to the topic. Full employment was now the chief aim of the economic policies of most governments. In the case of Great Britain the Board of Trade officials seemed only now to have noticed the change of government —to Labour, in 1945.

The negotiations at Geneva had two parts. First there were the GATT tariff bargaining, whereby, through bilateral concessions (later extended generally through the operation of most-favoured-nation provisions), levels of tariffs were reduced. British Commonwealth ('imperial') preferences were, however, excluded from the ban on preferences. At Geneva New Zealand negotiated 267 tariff concessions. Nash estimated that the government would lose about £1 million in revenues.[64] The person chiefly responsible for this aspect of negotiations was Johnsen, who—as Nash generously acknowledged—remained a key figure in the delegation throughout this group of conferences because of his expert knowledge.[65]

The text of the General Agreement on Tariffs and Trade was intended to be an interim measure, to be superseded by the Charter for a grand International Trade Organisation, which was to be a specialized agency of the United Nations, and was to administer the 'rules of the game' in world trade. In the meantime some trade rules were included in GATT to protect the tariff concessions from being nullified by other sorts of restrictive measures. Nash played a main role for New Zealand in discussions over the Charter.

From New Zealand's point of view the draft Charter of the ITO which was discussed at Geneva was exceedingly defective. It was based on what Nash called a 'free market philosophy', with friendly gestures towards Russia (which did not take part in the negotiations) in that it also provided for complete state monopolies. There was no room for New Zealand's policies, which were in-between.

This—largely American—blue-print for a world economic order was remarkably one-sided. It banned all quotas and import licences except during a transitional post-war period—but in certain circumstances permitted import restrictions on agricultural products and fish![66] American agriculture could be so protected but not New Zealand industries. The draft heavily favoured the developed countries and, in Nash's view, was likely to keep underdeveloped countries backward. There were other complaints. There were restrictions on quantitative restrictions but not on tariffs or subsidies. Bismarck had once said that free trade was the economic policy of the strong. Nash said in a speech in Geneva that tariffs and subsidies were the policies of the rich. A poor country could not afford a tariff high enough to protect its industries because its population could not afford to pay the resulting high prices. He had circulated a New Zealand amendment to Article 33, giving scope for a New Zealand-type system, a mixed (trading) economy. There was very loud applause, upon which the chairman remarked.[67]

To trace all New Zealand's detailed amendments to various articles of the ITO Charter would lose the man in the maze of his committees—enjoyable as he found them, and at home as he was in adding a sub-paragraph to a paragraph of an article of a draft agreement.

The New Zealand delegation decided that the best tactics would be to press for an amendment of one article, basic from New Zealand's point of view. Article 33 provided that a country with complete state monopoly of

import trade should negotiate with other states to promote its foreign trade
in accordance with the purposes of the Charter. The New Zealand amendment provided that states which maintained 'an effective system of complete
control' of foreign trade by methods other than a complete state monopoly,
should receive the recognition accorded to eastern Europe. Such states were
to use all their overseas receipts for debt repayments and imports.[68]

Only eighteen states were represented at Geneva. On this and other
related amendments Nash received support from the Chileans and Czechs
—Jan Masaryk being not yet defenestrated in Prague. Australia, New
Zealand, Cuba, and Chile pressed hard for more protection for the under-
developed countries. A Cuban delegate later said that his country was 'one
of the other bad boys' who dared to raise their voice against their elder
brothers.[69]

Nash had to leave in late April. Dan Sullivan, the deputy Prime Minister
in his absence, died, and Fraser wanted him back for the party conference
in June.[70] The chairman of the Geneva conference, Max Suetens of Belgium,
said, justly, that Nash had 'taken a most important part in our discussion'.[71]

Leicester Webb, a journalist and political scientist who had become
Director of Stabilization, replaced Nash on the delegation. The Americans
now opened up with some heavy traditional artillery. They moved an
amendment directly attacking the New Zealand amendment. One American
delegate said that the New Zealand amendment would destroy the structure
of the Charter and—horror of free trade horrors—make it possible to
protect all domestic industries.

Clair Wilcox said that the New Zealand amendment was 'a sanctification
of autarchy, an incitement to economic warfare.' Leicester Webb said in
conference that Wilcox had 'descended upon us in wrath rather like an
angel of the Lord'.[72]

Webb spoke more briefly and boldly than Nash, but without the
conciliatory gestures desirable in view of other New Zealand objectives,
not immediately at stake. Nash, however, was clear enough when speaking
to Webb or Johnsen. One American amendment implied more or less free
entry for investors. Nash cabled from Wellington to the delegation:

There can be no question of admitting equality of investment opportunity
and certainly no question of concessions to foreign capital which will be
permitted to exploit New Zealand resources only in circumstances and under
conditions conforming faithfully to our economic and social policies.

The whole of the proposed American amendment is a threat to the economic
and political sovereignty of countries which might be penetrated by the capital
of creditor nations. Moreover read in the light of Charter's insistence on M.F.N.
[Most Favoured Nation: that is, that any tariff advantage given to one state
must be given to all members] . . . and proscription of quantitative regulation
it has the appearance of serving the expansionist aims of economic imperialisms.

New Zealand could not in any circumstances subscribe to an article of such
substance.[73]

It was so rare for Nash not to call a spade a digging implement that it can only be assumed that it was drafted by a knowledgeable, leftist, and patriotic public servant.

Nash cabled to the British and Australian governments that it was becoming very doubtful whether New Zealand would be able to subscribe to the draft charter. He sought their help with Article 33 at Geneva. The British replied that they saw grave dangers in the New Zealand amendment, which opened the door to a widespread use of quantitative restrictions. Britain had to expand her exports, and relied on the renunciation of quantitative restrictions to achieve this.[74]

The New Zealand and Australian delegates had made some impact at Geneva. A Chilean delegate said that every time there was tension the problem of underdeveloped countries was at the centre of it.[75] New Zealand was in the unusual position of being an 'advanced' country, with a high standard of living, yet 'underdeveloped'. It was genuinely on both sides. In the end the main New Zealand amendment was reduced to a footnote to an article—but an important footnote for New Zealand. It said that where countries faced a high demand for imports as a result of their full employment programmes then quantitative regulations were acceptable.[76]

It was during Nash's return to New Zealand, in July 1947, that, as already discussed, the Labour caucus declined to swallow the IMF and accept domination by anonymous, sinister American financiers. GATT was also coming under fire. Nash went to his next United Nations Conference, on Trade and Employment, at Havana, without confidence that the fruit of their labours would be acceptable.

In his report on the Havana conference, which met from 21 December 1947 to 24 March 1948, with his usual love of statistics, Nash recorded that the 500 representatives of fifty-three countries had some 800 meetings, involving 3,000 working hours. He was a hard leader. The New Zealand delegation met each morning at 8.45 a.m. to 10.15 a.m., before attending their various committee and other meetings in the National Capitolum, from 10.30 to 1 p.m. They had no siesta, but met again as a delegation at 3 p.m. The conference resumed from 4 p.m. to 7 or 8 p.m. Where possible Nash got the delegation together again in the evening. They worked every day except Christmas day and New Year's day.[77]

Nash was elected a vice-president and chairman of the sub-committee on state trading. He attended all meetings of the general committee, meetings of heads of delegations, and plenary sessions, besides sub-committees.

In a speech to a plenary meeting Nash warned of the danger of having preconceived and fixed opinions. 'Opinions of all kinds and shades, which are often honestly presented as ethical axioms, are too frequently based on national economic self-interest.' They would have to be prepared to modify their views in the interests of international cooperation.[78]

Nash certainly showed no sign of a willingness to consider that he might be wrong. But he did accept that the final Charter for world trade must be a compromise, entirely suiting no one. He strove to ensure that that compromise included as much of what New Zealand wanted as possible. Once he told a member of the delegation that New Zealand had as much right to have its views fully considered as any great power.[79]

The main difficulties, again, were concerned with the problems of the underdeveloped countries. Nash's concern with these was greatly stimulated by the appalling juxtaposition of luxury and degradation which he saw in Havana, and they were a repetitive theme in his speeches. Basically the New Zealand delegates urged, as at Geneva, that quantitative restrictions might better provide for a regulated expansion of the trade of such countries and for their economic development than any other mechanism.

Naturally all sorts of difficulties arose, for instance about the relationship between the ITO and the IMF. A committee discussed European economic union. British delegates privately expressed their fear that the United Kingdom might ultimately be forced to join. Perhaps for the first time Fraser and Nash had to ponder some of the consequent problems—what would happen, for instance, to the Commonwealth preferential tariffs?[80]

Nash often spoke on small technical points as well as on the big issues, showing a considerable grasp of detail and ability as a committee man. He did not at that time lose sight of the wood for the trees, as he sometimes seemed to do in later years. New Zealand submitted numerous amendments to the Charter.

On this occasion a number of underdeveloped countries supported New Zealand's initiative over quantitative restrictions. Even so, there were many prolonged verbal struggles. On one occasion, when Nash had praised some opinions expressed by a Czech and an American speaker, the American delegate said, 'I might also say, with respect to Mr. Nash coupling Dr. Augenthaler with me, that the United States is not a satellite of Czecho-slovakia.'[81]

As a result of the conferences at Geneva and Havana the original American and free trade draft was very substantially modified. The New Zealand footnote about quantitative restrictions was retained, attached to Article XXI on 'Restrictions to Safeguard the Balance of Payments', which New Zealand had had a hand in drafting at Geneva.[82] The assertion in Article 20 that quantitative restrictions were to be eliminated was heavily qualified. There were now numerous exceptions.[83]

After an absence of over four months Nash walked 'jauntily' down the steps from a Pan-American Clipper at Auckland. He carried a panama hat with a dark red ribbon under his arm, but he wore his almost invariable 'ministerial' homburg.[84]

He was pleased with Article XXI. He said (with a smile), 'This was called the New Zealand clause, and some delegates were sore about it, at first, but later considered it satisfactory.'[85]

In his spoken report to cabinet he said that the Charter was the best compromise that could be achieved. Had Article XXI been further amended in an antipodean direction, the USA, the UK, and Canada would not have joined.[86]

Nash had been criticized in the Press for his 'mystery trip', for being away for months—or more—putting the world right.[87] There were some amusing Minhinnick cartoons asking, 'Where's Walter?'.

Havana and GATT were under heavy credit reform and National Party fire. F. W. Doidge, Member for Tauranga (and an extreme British imperialist), was announcing that GATT was treason and insinuating that it meant the end of imperial preferences. S. G. Holland announced that the National Party would oppose GATT since it was a side entrance to Bretton Woods.[88]

It is not certain that New Zealand would have joined. But the ITO, the first attempt to draw up a code for international trade, was assassinated elsewhere. The USSR had not come to the conferences. The ITO had been mainly an American idea, and Nash had given Cordell Hull and the Americans full credit for pushing it up to the draft stage. But the Charter was now severely criticized by American business groups, for instance because of concessions to exchange controls. They said it accepted most of the practices of economic nationalism. Some groups pictured the ITO as a super-state capable of directing United States policy. Late in 1950 President Truman announced that the proposed Charter would not be resubmitted to Congress.[89] So GATT, which had been intended to form an interim outline of a world trade order, was all that remained—an agreement without any supra-national organization.

XX

The Minister at Work

1936-49

During all his years as a minister in Wellington and Washington Nash enjoyed life's greatest blessing, good health. In 1940, Dr Hardwick-Smith gave him a thorough check-up. His heart, lungs, and blood were in excellent shape. His gall-bladder was not functioning perfectly because (his doctor wrote) he was spending sixteen hours a day sitting down. He wrote to Nash that he thought 'you are really a very healthy man', but that he would benefit from exercise.[1]

Nash took no notice of this. In the United States he was plump, not quite portly. But his face did not fatten. His jaw and features looked most determined. He took virtually no exercise—that part, at least, of his early rules of life had been discarded.

He enjoyed mental as well as physical health, each no doubt supporting the other. Mrs Geoffrey Cox noticed in Washington that he was never downcast, never depressed—or at least not for long. He put failures aside. In 1942 he wrote to Dr Hardwick-Smith in Lower Hutt that Lot longed to return to New Zealand. Certainly, he thought, the 'simplicity in the New Zealand life with all its shortcomings brings elements of joy far above the normal. For myself I live for the future by using the present and although tiredness may sometimes press I can generally overcome it by changing from one interesting problem to another'.[2]

Despite several qualities which suggest the opposite, he had great self-confidence, which had sustained him through failures and long waiting for success. He did not need much sleep, but when he went to bed he slept. He did not often worry or take worries home: another blessing.

In Kidderminster some fairy godmother had granted him bountiful energy, endless zest for new tasks. During two weeks in 1944 his schedule provided for him to spend Tuesday in Tennessee, returning to New York next day to attend the dinner of the United States Veterans to present a trophy from the New Zealand disabled soldiers. That night it was back to Washington until the following Monday. Then he was to go to Ottawa for discussions on mutual aid during Tuesday and Wednesday. He cabled

Fraser, offering to meet him in Montreal next day. On the Friday Nash had to leave for the monetary conference in Bretton Woods.[3]

For Nash such a level of activity was normal. He had a marvellous ability to relax while travelling and to arrive looking refreshed. Gladstone once said that he craved 'the continuous work which ought to fill the life of a Christian without intermission'.[4] Nash could have said the same. His addiction to work was connected with many facets of his life and character. Earlier in his life it would have meant, in part, keeping out of temptation. His drive to power and desire to keep it were strong whips. Increasingly, habit might have been the main source. But perhaps most important was a sense of hours filled by important duties—a sense of significance.

In Washington Nash was an immense success. Most of his closest associates felt that he was then at his peak, or more generally, in the years 1936-49: not in fame, not in power, but in efficient capacity. He had become fully himself so that, whatever he did or said, those who knew him best, whether fondly or critically would nod to themselves or wink to one another, as if to say, 'There is Walter being Walter'.

Some of Nash's most striking characteristics need to be looked at collectively, as fitting together, rather than chronologically, successively and repetitively.

Walter Nash's staff saw much more of him in most weeks than his family did. With some of them, like Dick Campbell, he had long been on friendly personal terms. But what struck his associates most was his suspicion of subordinates, and of public servants in general. It is probably not unusual in Labour Parties, especially long out of office, to feel that top public servants are identified with the conservatives. A generation later Norman Kirk certainly felt something of the sort. In Nash's case this attitude seemed to run deeper. Partly it was associated with a reluctance to share power, even with subordinates. But probably it went back to his unfortunate business experiences in his first years in New Zealand. He had learnt not to trust other people.

His suspicion was sometimes revealed in forms which invited caricature. For instance he never trusted anyone else's arithmetic and always checked the addition of any column of figures put before him. The detection of an error delighted him. Sir Carl Berendsen used to say that wily departmental heads, wishing to divert the Minister's attention from more important things, would include a satisfactory numerical mistake in papers put before him.[5]

Like any other leader, of course, he had to have advice. In addition to his departmental and official advisers, he also had a 'think-tank' of fairly left-wing advisers, including Sutch, Campbell, Jack Lewin, and (only a little left of centre) A. G. B. Fisher.[6] He surrounded himself with very able people. He appreciated their merits. But no one could accuse him of accepting their advice, nor anyone else's, uncritically. Moreover, Nash had few, if any, intimates who were in politics, after he became a minister. (His closest friends were neighbours.) Consequently no one knew all his thoughts; no one had especially strong influence on him.

When Hugh Dalton was in Wellington in 1938 he saw a good deal of the Labour ministers. He found some of them working in parliament on a Sunday (Nash went to work almost every Sunday) and thought they were working too hard. He wrote: 'Nash devolves nothing; carries everything in his own head; is a tremendous Christian. Someone said "these Ministers are a simple, straightforward, transparent lot. All quite unsophisticated except Nash, & he makes up for that with his Christianity". Nash said to me "I have to watch everything!" '[7]

That one brief remark comes close to how Nash saw his own role—he felt he had to watch all his colleagues. Some of them he did need to watch. He dominated Parry, Jones, and Roberts, for example—men who needed to be told what to do.

His distrust of the judgements of others—or, to put it another way, his refusal to share decision-making with subordinates—led him to insist on seeing the evidence on which their recommendations were based, the regulation by which they were authorized. Not merely would they be asked, at whatever hour of the night or weekend, to bring in the relevant file, but Nash began to accumulate in his office the largest collection of files ever to grace a New Zealand ministerial office. Everyone who ever worked with Nash was astonished at the many hundreds of files which covered two or more tables, and any other available horizontal surface above the floor, criss-crossed, and stacked two feet high.

He could not bear to be parted from them. When he went to England in 1936 he insisted on showing Reg Aickin and Bill Sutch how to pack piles of paper into the cabin trunks. His office in Washington was filled up like that in Wellington. He actually took some 800 lbs of files with him to Washington in wartime.[8] At Christmas, 1943, he arrived in Canberra to stay with the new High Commissioner, Carl Berendsen, loaded with files, which he proceeded, as usual, to lay out carefully on window-ledges, the mantelpiece and elsewhere. He worked on them on Christmas Day. A minister in the Labour government of the nineteen-seventies recalls travelling about New Zealand with Nash and watching him do this in hotel rooms. He said that 'Walter appeared to absorb their contents by osmosis'. He would continually sort them, turn them, open them, play with them. Many people testify that he had a quite extraordinary knowledge of what was in them. Mr T. H. McCombs, Nash's Under-Secretary, 1945-7, and then Minister of Education, thought that Nash seemed to read them and let his subconscious eventually reach a conclusion. He recalls that on one occasion a man had sold some American bulldozers in dubious circumstances after the war. He denied that there was any dishonesty and the public servants could find no regulation broken. Nash had not considered the matter for months but when he received their report he said 'Yes, there is something wrong. It's in here'. And he picked up a thick file and at once pounced on one paper in the middle, which indicated an irregularity.[9]

The reasons for or explanations of his hoarding must have been various. One was certainly that it gave him power. As Minister of Finance he could demand to see—and keep—files on almost anything: defence, public works, education. Files and decisions accumulated in his office, to the frustration and fury of other ministers. But without doubt the main reason was simply an extreme caution about trusting anyone else. It is hard to believe, but nevertheless true, that for a time after he became a minister he insisted on opening every envelope addressed to him.[10] Another aspect of this same syndrome was that he took files home—and kept them—including many files that he should not have kept, since they were clearly departmental. Some such files now in his papers, like a report on suspected foreign security risks during the First World War, are difficult to explain in relation to his interests, numerous as those were. Among his papers is a file on the Thames Harbour Board. What significance it had for him is now obscure, but there is in his papers a letter from Sir Joseph Heenan mentioning how indebted he once was to Nash in the nineteen-twenties, when he was a law draughtsman, for helping him to draught a bill on that subject. So he must have known the topic very well.

Occasionally Nash lost all his current stack of files. For instance, Sir Arnold Nordmeyer recalls, when Nash went to Havana he became acting minister. Treasury and other departments wanted their files back, and he returned the lot. When Nash returned he nearly cried—'What have you done? Where are my files?'[11]

Nash had, since he reached New Zealand, and certainly by about 1914, begun to keep every scrap of paper which, however remotely, was concerned with him. Great men like Churchill or Roosevelt often keep, or have people who are keepers of, their papers. But Nash began to collect them when no one could think him important. Why? Suspicion of being done down by partners? A sense of destiny? Perhaps both. But he did so with a thoroughness unique in New Zealand and extraordinary, or odd, anywhere. He kept in-letters and drafts of out-letters and copies of out-letters; diaries; notes saying that Mr Jones was waiting outside at 11.30 a.m. All the notes and memos which accumulated in his drawers were periodically bundled up. When Peter Fraser—and other ministers—died he kept the contents of their drawers too. When he went to the Second Socialist International he kept his Cook's itinerary, passport, tickets, hotel bills, agenda, conference papers, notes taken down at the conference, his draft and published reports on it, and Lot's refusal to go. It could be that he was the greatest lover of paper, and not merely documents related to himself, in history.

That these observations about his papyromania are not at all exaggerated is attested by two letters to Nash from Reg Aickin, one of his secretaries, written after Nash left for Washington in 1942 and before Aickin joined him there. Nash and his staff had occupied ten rooms in Wellington. Aickin had the wearisome job of clearing them out. The files had been stored in and spread out in all these rooms. One of the secretaries kept a card index of references to individuals and topics mentioned in the files. On 30 January Aickin wrote, 'The mass of files is far greater than I had ever imagined. Miss Galt in her filing system alone has reached over 10,000, and we are only in the early hundreds on that. All the rest of the material is now practically under control, and the files that have been retained will be stored in Smithson's room.' On 17 February he wrote again, 'we have retained for your future use a considerable volume of personal, political and policy matter' plus personal correspondence and general economic data. All this had been parcelled and labelled and a proportion of somewhat confidential material had been stored in Nash's study and garage.[12] By this time his study was full of papers. When he went to the USA and the house was let, the study was locked up. The overflow of papers had already spread into his—eventually famous—garage.

There was an obsessional quality about many of Nash's activities. It could be thought that he collected almost everything. He kept innumerable pieces of string and heaps of used stamps in boxes. He collected people. He remembered and valued every old friend and large numbers of more-or-less casual acquaintances. By 1945 he had a very large number of correspondents—pen friends—including generals, Mrs Roosevelt, lords, ladies, children, old friends from Kidderminster days like 'Hitch', Beveridge, Freyberg, Julian Amery, Hobday, W. P. Morrell, Attlee, 'Kitty' Boylin, Miss Bradburn . . . almost everyone, it seems, whom he had met. There are letters from these friends and acquaintances and many others in a single one of the files in Nash's papers.[13]

The Minister had a flaw strange in one who loved power so much. He distrusted his own instinctive judgement. Since he would not rely on the judgements of others, the result was inevitable—delays. When he did make decisions they were usually right—common-sensical, politically sound, morally acceptable, successful. But he had to keep and master every file to ensure that his decision was, in fact, right. Sir Terence McCombs, like the late Dr Sutch, recalls that to alter his sense of priorities was almost impossible. He refused to be rushed. If anyone marked a file 'Urgent' he would move it to the bottom of the pile. If a public servant sneaked in at night to move a file to the top, as many recall, he would notice and reverse the order. Consequently he became famous for his procrastination in making decisions. He loved power, in short, but was not eager to exercise it quickly. Bob Semple was one of the few people, other than Fraser, who could deal with this. If Nash held up *his* decisions he would rush in and swear at him. Nash hated bad language. One can imagine the scene. Most of Semple's Australian adjectives and expletives began with 'b'. Nash would give in.[14]

The lives of lesser ministers and public servants were not easy. While Nash was slow with decisions, Fraser was terribly dilatory about signing correspondence. A. D. McIntosh wrote to Nash in 1943 that, during his absence in the USA, the staff had almost given up the attempt to get Fraser's signature. He liked dealing with business orally; he found writing painful. His writing was clumsy and he spattered ink liberally about. He was like Nash, however, in being unwilling to delegate. To get a signature meant waiting in the queue for hours.[15]

Two further points should be made about Nash's reluctance to make speedy decisions. There was often an element of shrewdness in his indecision. Like any other administrator, he knew that some problems, if left alone, would solve themselves, or go away.

Nash worked hard by conviction, preference, and habit, but given his attitudes to decision-making, he had to work long hours, for he was sorting his papers as a researcher would, rather than a decider. His daily schedule was so gruelling that few people could have stood it.

He always woke, like Peter Fraser, to hear the 6 a.m. radio news. (Critics said that he could not bear to be told anything he did not know.) There followed a breakfast which, with slight variations, was daily consumed for over thirty years. As he travelled, cooks in Russian or Indonesian hotels would be instructed to provide it. A glass of hot water was religiously followed by freshly squeezed orange juice and an egg nog, with the yolks of one or more eggs beaten up with a little cold and then hot milk. Strong men might shudder at the thought of such a dawn potion.

By 8 or 9 a.m. he would be in his office. Like most MPs, at least while in Wellington, he ate his main meal at midday, soup, fish, roast meat and vegetables, pudding or fruit, followed by biscuits and blue vein cheese. In the evening he ate only a few sandwiches. He remained at his desk, when not at a meeting, until midnight or later. He then went home. Sometimes he would have another of his own concoctions before going to sleep: a tablespoon of honey and the juice of a lemon in hot water. Many years later he wrote, 'I find this type of food tends to maintain good health'.[16] He then slept soundly for about four hours a night.

Mrs Nash entered less and less into this scheme of things. During the nineteen-forties she developed a very painful arthritis, which restricted her activities. As before, she devoted herself to looking after Nash, but she saw little of him at home.

Although Nash worked hard, his work was not disciplined, organized. It was thorough, meticulous, but it was not efficient in terms of output in relation to hours. His considerable intelligence was undisciplined. In other words, his work, excessive as his load was, need not have taken up nearly all his waking hours—such, at least, was the opinion of many who worked with him.

In almost every aspect of Nash's work there was this exceptional, excessive attention to detail. One result (though this was much more noticeable later in his life) was that sometimes he seemed not to distinguish big from small issues. Mr Harold Innes recalls that on one occasion during the war, New Zealand was negotiating a revised price for butter sold to Britain. The difference between the British offer and the New Zealand demand amounted to several million pounds. Nash failed to arrive for a 9 a.m. conference on this subject and after a time Innes rang Mrs Nash. She apologized: he had been up until 4 a.m. trying to balance his personal accounts. A donation of £2 2s. to the Petone Bowling Club had been overlooked.[17]

When he was to be away from the Washington legation he would try to lay down every point of procedure to be followed in his absence: two chairs and bookshelves were to be bought for Mr Turner's room; Mr and Mrs E. Buckton (a secretary) were to live in the residence, but were to cook their own food in the absence of the housekeeper.[18] Nothing was so small as to be beneath his notice. In 1949 he sent a hamper of food—sheeps' tongues, corned beef, dripping, lard—from New Zealand to England. It cost 15s. 5d. He asked the Price Control Division of the Department of Industries and Commerce to check up on the price, and was assured by the director himself that it did not contravene price fixation regulations.[19]

Nash's assistants, colleagues, servants often, then and since, discussed in mixed tones his various habits of life and work, but none as much as his almost complete absence of consideration for their comfort and feelings. He was merciless in keeping people at work until midnight, night after night, whether there was anything to do or not; at calling them back to the office at odd hours; at keeping people waiting. He would tell people to call, and then keep them waiting for hours, not because he had someone else there at a meeting, but because he had decided to do, or continue doing, something else—drafting a letter, studying a file, pondering a problem. He was oblivious to the waste of time and the frustration this produced. On this aspect of his behaviour his subordinates were of but one opinion. Reg Aickin and Nash liked one another. But Aickin said to Sir Bernard Ashwin that Nash's heart could bleed only for suffering humanity at large, never for the staff working for him.[20] There was some truth in this. Many reformers have shared this combination of far-seeing and short-sightedness.

He used—and, often enough, wasted—his subordinates' time and energies ruthlessly, yet most of the able men, if not all, who served under him, agreed that he did not give them enough to do, did not make the most of them, did not encourage them to their fullest, because he could not delegate. And many of his assistants, like Campbell, Turner, Cox, Fisher, and Sutch, were extremely able men, as their earlier or later careers reveal. This shortcoming was a respect in which Nash was inefficient.

Numerous stories show the great lengths to which Nash's thoughtlessness could go, but two very well attested examples will suffice. During the war one of Nash's assistants was on leave from the army. He was recalled, and Nash asked him to come back to the office on his last night to clear up one or two matters before returning to the Middle East. It was Nash's chauffeur's night off, so Nash asked his assistant to pick him up at 11 p.m., at the home of one of those hostesses who, during the war, competed in filling their drawing rooms with celebrities. The assistant—a senior one— wanted to leave his job cleanly done, free of loose ends, and at the agreed time turned up at the house. After waiting half an hour, lined up with the chauffeurs of the other guests, he inquired at the door for Nash. The maid told him the guests were listening to a musical quartet and could not be disturbed. It was well after midnight, and then only after the assistant had demanded that two messages be taken in to Nash, that the Minister emerged. They drove back to the office, where it soon became apparent that there was nothing significant which needed doing. It simply did not occur to Nash that this was his assistant's last night with his wife before returning to the war.[21]

Carl Berendsen succeeded Nash as Minister to Washington. When he arrived Nash asked him to come to meet him at Bretton Woods. Peter Fraser, who was in Washington, said 'Don't go', but he and his wife did go. Bruce Turner, who was with Nash, forgot to warn security of their arrival and they were taken to the guardhouse. Berendsen, who was an aggressive man, was very angry, and thought it was an attempt to humiliate him. Nash's diary records that Berendsen arrived at 2 p.m.; Nash had a cocktail party at Morganthau's at 6 p.m. and another with the British representatives at 6.30, followed by a Norwegian dinner at 7.30. Nash kept Berendsen waiting until next morning before seeing him. When Berendsen told Fraser he said, 'I told you so'.[22]

It was characteristic of Nash that he was more thoughtful for his chauffeur than for a senior assistant. When he left the USA he wrote out by hand a reference for Margaret Moore, his cook.[23] When he met New Zealand servicemen in the USA or elsewhere he would take their names and write to their parents that they were well. Two 'broke and unknown' New Zealanders turned up in Washington late one night in 1944 asking for assistance. Nash asked if they could pay a taxi and invited them to call. When they arrived he left a conference to greet them, and gave them $10 to tide them over, put a secretary at their disposal, invited them to a welcome party for Fraser next day and wrote to their parents.[24] That was on the eve of Bretton Woods. He treated the ordinary person better than important people.

Nash believed that he and his close associates were engaged in great deeds, of importance to the world. He did not spare himself. It never occurred to him to spare others. Undoubtedly he wanted to be and came to see himself as a great man. Sometimes his helpers felt that his ego was insatiable; it consumed everyone else. But sometimes posterity may feel that they were indeed engaged in great deeds, of welfare or war, in comparison with which the leisure or comfort of public servants was of small account. Many of his contemporaries thought so.

Public servants and others who knew the Labour leaders inevitably compared Nash with Fraser. Fraser could be a bully, and some preferred Nash. But the senior officials almost invariably considered Fraser the bigger man, more fitted to be Prime Minister. Cox, McIntosh, and many others thought that Fraser had a touch of greatness then lacking in Nash. It was often held that Fraser was more of a statesman. Certainly he was a more dominant, aggressive, and decisive leader. But he was also more of a wily politician. In even the least important appointments—for instance a board administering some Maori scholarships—he thought from a party point of view, preferring a Labour man to the National supporter recommended by Sir Apirana Ngata.[25] Nash was much less of a party politician.

Fraser, too, was a puritan, in the sense that most pleasures were suspect and replaced by work. Most people are laymen, secular in relation to the religion of power, of re-forming the world. Yet obviously it would be a mistake to label Nash a puritan if that were thought to exclude an enjoyment of life. At sixty he had an immense appetite for life, food, power, achievements, praise. Like Fraser, he was uninterested in wealth. When Dalton was in Wellington in 1938 he thought that the salary pool had cut ministers' salaries far too low. He wrote, 'But Savage & Nash have a very simple attitude to money. Savage is a bachelor, neither smokes nor drinks, lodges with old friends. Nash seems to have no interest in money at all. . . .'[26]

XXI

The Collapse of Labour

1946-9

In May 1947 Peter Fraser cabled Nash in Geneva that the party was awaiting his return to discuss various economic problems: 'Regret to inform you that the industrial situation on the waterfront is very serious and from the present trend of events and particularly because of the attitude of Barnes Hill and the majority of the executive it appears inevitable that the Government will be compelled to take drastic action. I will be very glad to welcome you back and to have your assistance in this difficult situation.'[1]

In late January 1948 Fraser cabled Nash that he wanted him back from Havana as soon as possible because of a 'developing situation of industrial unrest centred round the question of prices and wages'.[2]

Not only were one or the other or both of the leaders often abroad but Fraser, who had driven himself mercilessly, was on several occasions ill—in December 1947, for instance, with pneumonia.

The erosion of support for an elected government and its eventual fall may be analysed or described in various ways. Biographically it amounts to leaders losing their grip on the political and economic situation and on the electorate. Absences and illness were certainly significant elements in the decline of New Zealand's first Labour government. So, too, was the creation of a vigorous National Opposition. It was increasingly confident and aggressive. The days of Downie Stewart, Forbes, Coates, or even Adam Hamilton seemed gentlemanly in comparison with the vulgarity and rough tactics of National led by S. G. Holland.

In 1946 Nash's enemies began spreading afresh the rumour that he had been a bankrupt. This non-event came to be so widely believed among National supporters (though probably not by the National leaders) that it was still being repeated after his death. His old tailor friend from New Plymouth, George Pearce, begged him to deny it in one of his broadcast speeches (Labour had introduced the practice of broadcasting parliamentary debates), but Nash thought it not worth the trouble.

The campaign was so rough that various people wrote to Nash lamenting the personal attacks.[3] Like any good politician, Nash could bear this sort of thing with equanimity; like most other people, he felt more upset about the wounds inflicted by his friends. On this occasion his party was to cast him out of his seat, his stronghold for nearly twenty years.

In 1946 there was an electoral boundary revision. Part of Nash's electorate became the new Petone electorate; part went into a new Hutt electorate which included areas previously in Wellington Suburbs. A high proportion of Nash's majorities had been won in what was now Petone. Nash informed the Labour Representation Committee that he would prefer to stand as the candidate there. The chairman told the National Executive that he was the only person nominated for selection for Petone. The president and vice-president of the party, James Roberts and Arnold Nordmeyer, called on Nash to discuss the question. He again made it clear that he would prefer Petone. When asked if he would accept the decision of the National Executive, he agreed on condition that he was consulted before a decision was made. Shortly afterwards he learnt from the Labour newspaper, the *Southern Cross*, that he had been selected for Hutt. He wrote protesting to Roberts that he would do his best to win the new electorate, 'but I cannot understand why I have been turned out of the Electorate which I fought for many years to win for the Party and where I believe I hold the respect and support of a large majority of the electors.' The secretary of the Petone branch wrote to the party's secretary, Mick Moohan, protesting, but conceding, 'Of course the National Executive think that only Mr Nash can win Hutt, anyone can win Petone.' The secretary estimated that in the new Hutt electorate there had been a National majority in 1943 but Nash, clearly very worried, made a more thorough analysis. It suggested that Labour had had a majority of 226 within the boundaries of the new electorate. Since then 1,537 state rental houses—hopefully the homes of grateful Labour voters—had been built in the electorate.[4]

Though its decision was hard the Executive's reasoning was sound. But it was difficult not to think, as many people did, that the source of the decision was its beneficiary, the party's secretary, who received the Petone nomination—a safe seat on a plate. That friendly man from Garrison, Ireland, Mick Moohan, was one of the few Labour people of whom Nash would be frankly critical in speaking to his friends. He was a sly fellow, oozing bonhomie, with an instinct for low politics.

After eleven years of Labour rule, six of them in war conditions, various groups of people, not obviously National, were becoming restive, disenchanted.

The dairy farmers, some of whom Labour had won in 1935 and 1938, while hoping for more, were hostile. They had been brooding since 1938 on Nash's refusal to accept the dairy price recommended by the advisory committee of that year, and unhappy accepting the government's maintenance of the 1938 price throughout the war, with only one small increase in 1942-3.[5] Their leaders were demanding that the industry should actively participate in and share with the government in the control of the industry and in marketing negotiations.[6] The government accepted these demands in the 1946 manifesto. Not quite counting on rural enthusiasm, however, the government also abolished the undemocratic 'country quota', which added a fictitious extra 28 per cent to the population in rural areas.

There were many other dissident groups, large or small. One of the latter were the conscientious objectors and their friends, not of great electoral account, but who weighed on Nash's conscience. In mid-1945, while Fraser was at the San Francisco conference and Nash was acting Prime Minister, the government decided to allow those in detention to appeal for release on parole. There was persistent, almost hysterical protest from the Returned Servicemen's Association and others, who demanded that the 'conchies' should remain in detention and should lose their civil rights for ten years after the war. Nash flatly refused to accept this and stoutly defended the government's policy in the House. When Fraser returned he gave an RSA deputation a deserved tongue-lashing. He said they had lost all credibility since they supported the attitude of soldiers who refused to return to the war after leave in New Zealand.[7] Once again the government was tempering the democratic wind to the shorn lamb. But it gained no credit from the 'conchies'—and their sympathizers denounced the government for oppression.

There was, both in the trade union movement and in the Labour Party, widespread fear of a slump such as had followed World War I, a fear which was expressed, for instance, by both Walsh and Nash. For this reason, among others, the government continued its stabilization policy after the war.[8] This increased the restiveness of many sections of the community including dairy farmers and unions, who wanted more money. In particular there were continual disputes on the wharves, which greatly tried the patience of public and government. The public was also growing weary of the many 'shortages', accepted in good part during the war.[9] It was in this connection, in February 1946, that Nash made one of his most famous utterances. He said, if you are short of a cigarette or a pipe 'have an acid drop. The major part of smoking is having something to do with your mouth'. This observation, the fruit of his own experience (for he used to smoke, and to sell acid drops) caused much hilarity.[10] It was also wrongly interpreted—by smokers—as an example of wowserism. For some time thereafter he appeared in Minhinnick's cartoons with a bag of acid drops.

True to the form of most democratic electorates, collectively the public wanted both less controls and more. The New Zealand Expeditionary Force Association, led by Kenneth H. Melvin, wanted a credit authority set up to stabilize prices and control credit. While opposing inflation, they also wanted cheaper loans for local bodies willing to build houses.[11] The farmers were also complaining about inflation. Nash told them that there was nothing he feared more than rampant inflation.[12] He thought criticism of the government on this score was unfair, for it had been very successful in controlling wartime inflation. The increase in prices was only 14 per cent. Nash boasted at Geneva that no country had a better record.[13]

It was fashionable in leftist and credit reform circles after the war to talk of the government as extreme right wing. But it had made some moves, not all willingly, to refurbish its image in radical or credit reform eyes. The 1946 election manifesto promised the nationalization of the coal mines—which some owners in any case wanted. In 1945 the child allowance had been increased to 10s. a week. At that time this was a significant addition to the income of families. Another such measure was the nationalization of the Bank of New Zealand which pleased socialists and credit reformers.

For the 1946 election Labour came out with an extensive Ten Year Plan for national and regional development. It constantly stressed the danger of unemployment under National. But mainly it stood on its record. One pamphlet, *Labour Guarantees the Future*, had a heading, 'We've never been better off thanks to Labour'. It promised freedom from fear—of unemployment, old age, poverty. . . .

Nash's own publicity, such as a leaflet, *The Hutt Electorate*, placed the main emphasis on these fears. The voters were told that the choice was between 'the jungle economics of unrestricted competition advocated by the Nationalists with its inevitable accompaniment of booms, slumps, insecurity and poverty' and prosperity with Labour. 'Only under Labour's economic and social philosophy is there any security against future unemployment.' Nash wrote one pamphlet himself, *A Personal Message from the Rt. Hon. Walter Nash*, relating his services to his electorate and to the country.[14]

His main opponent was J. E. F. Vogel, a grandson of Julius Vogel. His publicity, like his party's, constantly praised National's supposedly free enterprise as opposed to Labour's supposedly ultimate socialism.[15] The Hutt electors took little notice of this appeal. Nash won the new electorate handsomely. He received 8,025 votes, Vogel 5,438. The other two independent candidates won only a couple of hundred between them. The Labour Party, however, received a set-back. It won the same number of European seats as National—thirty-eight. It continued in office by virtue of winning the four Maori electorates. Thereafter in Minhinnick's cartoons there was often a small Maori—Labour's 'mandate'.

After the election caucus formally re-elected the cabinet, with the exception of the Prime Minister. Fraser nominated ten names. Others nominated five more, including Langstone and E. L. Cullen, the Member for Hastings. Nash and C. F. ('Jerry') Skinner, an ex-serviceman who was Minister of Rehabilitation and Lands, received the most votes, forty each, Dan Sullivan and Nordmeyer thirty-nine. Langstone received only nine. To Fraser's surprise and embarrassment, Cullen beat Rex Mason, the Attorney-General and Minister of Justice. Mason continued to administer his portfolios and was re-elected a few months later when Mabel Howard was also elected to cabinet, the country's first woman minister.[16]

The Labour Party had become an alternative conservative party, acting to protect, to conserve the gains made since 1935. In the leadership Fraser and Semple (who wrote a pamphlet in 1948, *Why I Fight Communism* and received a Communist reply, *Semple Iscariot* by 'The Gadfly') were most identified with the shift to the right. They were fully supported by the ex-Communists, McLagan and Walsh. To emphasize this change in Labour's stance is not, however, to agree with the left wingers of 1949, who believed that Labour was defeated *because* it was conservative. The evidence is overwhelming that a left wing Labour Party would have fared worse at the hands of a greedy, capitalistic electorate.

The thoughtful leftists regarded Nash as not quite beyond the pink pale, possibly redeemable. In January 1946 Mr J. P. Lewin, one of his former assistants, sent Nash a paper on the reasons for the decline of Labour. Like many leftists of the time he attributed it to the decline of the union movement, resulting from compulsory unionism, introduced by the Labour government, as well as to the propaganda initiative of the National Party. More socialist propaganda was needed, and more democracy in the party. Ormond Wilson, now back in parliament, read and commented upon this a year later. He thought that the only remedy for the government's weakness was its demise: 'my basic point of discussion would not be how to avert defeat, but how to prepare for defeat.'[17]

Nash was a member of the New Zealand Fabian Society, 1947-9, and its first president. One of its leading members and a former Communist, Mr George Fraser, wrote a pamphlet, *The Martial Plan*, which was published while he was working in the Information Section of the Prime Minister's Department. Peter Fraser suspected that he had given confidential information to the Fabians. This was investigated by R. M. Campbell, Nash's old friend and Labour supporter, now Chairman of the Public Service Commission. He found no evidence that George Fraser had leaked information, and agreed to remove him from the Prime Minister's office solely because Peter Fraser found his presence an embarrassment. Campbell staunchly defended George Fraser's right to express his opinions.[18] Nash wrote to Fraser that his pamphlet contained errors and was not up to the standards of the British Fabian Society.

Nash could be thought more radical than Peter Fraser on several grounds. For instance he strongly believed in state control. Fraser was politically more flexible or opportunist: some said more effective, others more dishonest. A good example of the difference between the two men is afforded by the government's revision of guaranteed price procedures in 1947. The 1946 manifesto had promised that a joint government-dairy industry tribunal, with an independent chairman, should fix the guaranteed price. Similarly, government and dairying men would form a marketing organization to sell the produce. The government would appoint its chairman.

Early in March 1947, when Nash was in the USA, on his way to Geneva, Fraser cabled that Ashwin, Leicester Webb, and Walsh had been discussing marketing with dairy industry representatives. This group had suggested that a single organization should both fix the price and control marketing. It was to consist of three government and three industry nominees, with a mutually acceptable chairman. While the guaranteed price was to be determined according to the 1936 Act, it was agreed by both parties that any continuous disparity between internal prices to producers and external market realizations would be detrimental both to the dairy industry and to the Dominion.[19]

Nash felt that his own baby was being thrown out with the bathwater. He cabled back in what was for him agitated language: the proposal was opposed to party policy; it would mean 'abolition of foundation principle of guaranteed price'; 'Proposal regarding price fixing appears to be simply an equalisation scheme' as opposed to 'guaranteed price principle', which 'covers cost with reasonable return for farmers labour and capital'. Moreover, 'To give commission control of marketing would tend towards producer control which could be just as anti-social and, in some cases more so than private monopoly.' In a later cable, Nash explained that in the manifesto the *government* was to appoint the chairman of the proposed Marketing Authority.

This was heady stuff coming from Nash, usually so bland. Fraser sent soothing words, assuring his deputy that while government to government agreements covered bulk sales the government would have effective control of marketing. Nash remained dissatisfied, though regretting his disagreement with Fraser, Sullivan, E. L. Cullen, the Minister of Agriculture and Marketing, Leicester Webb, and Walsh.

That line-up—listed by both Fraser and Nash in cables—neatly illustrates Nash's position in New Zealand politics. He was denounced as a conservative by the funny money men, yet he was well to the left of this powerful establishment quintet. Because he was very loyal to his colleagues, and charitable in speech about people he disliked, this was an aspect of Nash which was not always understood.

By 1 April Fraser had determined to get Nash's consent. He cabled that the matter was one of 'extreme urgency as position here is becoming critically difficult'. Nash had to leave the decision to Fraser and cabinet. He was never convinced that it was right.[20]

Nash firmly believed that the guaranteed price could be based on costs plus enough to give dairy farmers a decent living by local standards. It was not merely a levelling mechanism. This was not perverse. In every year, in the years 1936 to 1960, the farmers' working costs were taken into account in fixing the price.[21] Those were almost all booming years. But the government's agreement with the industry made better economic sense, for it was true that local pay-outs could not persistently exceed overseas receipts without causing serious problems.

Fraser was fed up with annual wrangling with cow cockies; glad to hand the problem of prices to a tribunal.[22] The outcome might fittingly be described, in the words of the 1949 Labour Manifesto, as 'a fruitful partnership between the Government and the Industry in the marketing of dairy products'. It might be thought a characteristic feature of New Zealand society—arrived at, in this case, from conflict between and within both parties. Fraser is the one who bows to the democratic winds; Nash is the doctrinaire—sticking to his own doctrines.

Labour won power talking of 'insulating' the economy; a major reason why it lost office was that what happened in New Zealand was so inextricably involved with what was happening in Britain, the Commonwealth, and the world. Economically, politically, strategically, New Zealand could not be 'insulated'. It was this fact that drew Nash and Fraser abroad so often —Fraser was away at a Commonwealth Prime Ministers' Conference, then in Paris, Germany, and North America, from October 1948 to late January 1949. In April he was back in London for another Commonwealth Conference.[23] In July Nash was in London for a Commonwealth Finance Ministers' Conference. They were at this time less intimately in touch with the voters than stay-at-home politicians. The problems which affected New Zealand and influenced governmental policies were global, and were not always understood by voters.

The government felt itself obliged to do everything possible to assist Britain, even if such assistance appeared at first sight to be against New Zealand's interests. Fraser and Nash were British in origin, but there is no reason to attribute their policy in this respect to their birthplaces. No doubt most people's sense of identity is shaped by the associations formed during the process of growing up and being educated. But a British loyalty could be fostered in more countries than one. When S. G. Holland, a New Zealander, became Prime Minister his fervour for royalty and empire or Commonwealth left Nash's in the rear. In this case, however, economic facts spoke louder than national sentiments. New Zealand was utterly dependent on the British market; therefore the reconstruction of the British economy after the war *was* a major, almost the major, New Zealand interest. And beyond nationalism and economic facts there was another loyalty. Fraser and Nash—Chifley and Churchill and other wartime leaders—were Commonwealth men; they *thought* internationally. They knew one another well; they saw the many-sidedness yet interlinked unity of many Commonwealth and world problems.

Aid to 'the old country' took many forms. New Zealand and Australia donated £10 million sterling each as gifts towards British recovery. This was about 10 per cent of New Zealand's overseas funds. Much more important, New Zealand's principal trade policy was a form of aid to Britain. For many years New Zealand sold its dairy produce to Britain at well below ruling world prices. This was the case even though Britain was paying New Zealand 'lump sums' to compensate for the fact that the terms of trade had moved against New Zealand, because she had successfully held local inflation firmly in check.[24]

While he was in London in 1946 Nash renegotiated the bulk sales agreement with Great Britain. New Zealand continued voluntarily to sell her produce at below world rates. In 1947, for instance, the British were paying 242s. per cwt. f.o.b. for Danish butter and only 175s. for New Zealand (before the war the advantage of Danish butter had been only 15s. or 16s.).[25] It could reasonably be argued that the world afforded no comparable market for New Zealand dairy produce—but New Zealand did not try to develop other markets. The agreement with Britain allowed for $2\frac{1}{2}$ per cent of New Zealand production to go to other markets, but this provision was not used. Australian butter, by contrast, was being sent to Asian markets.[26]

During and after the war, as a result of import shortages, New Zealand built up massive reserves of sterling. The banks' overseas assets increased from £7 million in early 1939 to £114 million in February 1947.[27] This was the highest level in New Zealand history. Nash had learnt one thing very clearly in 1939—he never wished to find himself at the mercy of the British moneylenders again. Much of the 'lump sum payments', and other overseas assets were, as has been noted, used to redeem London debts. The overseas debt was reduced during the war by £45 million.[28] Nash could reasonably feel that New Zealand's economic strength had never been greater—and this at the end of a major war.

When in 1948 Nash revalued the New Zealand £ (which had been devalued in 1933 to NZ £125 = sterling £100) to parity with sterling, he explained this to the public in terms of help for Britain. Labour had never liked the devaluation, intended to help farmers with higher export receipts. It seems likely that Nash and his colleagues had an emotional commitment to parity—a deep feeling, as B. C. Ashwin said, that a 'pound is a pound is a pound'.[29]

Nash's principal advisers opposed revaluation. Ashwin wrote that New Zealand would lose £20 million annually in export earnings and also lose the protection afforded to New Zealand industry by the existing exchange rate. The Department of Industries and Commerce and E. C. Fussell of the Reserve Bank were also opposed. The Australian leader, Ben Chifley, wrote that he was now more cautious about appreciation than he had been a year ago.[30]

How Nash revalued always stuck in his mind as one of the exciting events of his life.[31] Only Peter Fraser knew what he intended. Nash called

Ashwin and Fussell to his room on the afternoon before he read the budget. They discussed both a revaluation to NZ£110 = sterling £100 and parity. At 6.30 p.m. there was a cabinet meeting which agreed to Nash's preference for parity. Just before 7.30 p.m. Nash told Ashwin and Fussell the decision. He then wrote out a short note which he read, in a dramatic statement, after he completed the budget. Everyone seemed to be quite taken by surprise. Nash was delighted that no one had made a penny out of speculation.

At a time of rising import prices and high overseas reserves the reaction to the change was fairly favourable and the short-term effects were beneficial.[32] Nash explained his decision by saying, and writing in *Fair Exchange*, a pamphlet put out by the Labour Party,[33] that because New Zealand's stabilization policies had controlled inflation better than in most countries, the terms of trade were unfavourable. He posed the alternatives —either to demand higher prices from Britain or to revalue. He defended the latter choice. It would reduce the cost of imports. The benefits of lower prices would spread through the community.

After the war Britain suffered from a severe US dollar shortage. Even when Britain achieved an overall balance of payments, there was a dollar shortage. The sterling countries pooled their dollars, but still there were not enough. In 1947 Attlee asked Fraser if New Zealand could help in various ways. These included not importing more than current export earnings— thus keeping up the sterling balances; reducing petrol consumption; not ordering supplies from dollar sources even if they were available earlier than those from the sterling area; and, as before, restricting dollar expenditure in general.[34] New Zealand agreed.

Another government policy was to continue food rationing in New Zealand so as to maximize exports to Britain. All these policies meant the continuation of controls and shortages. The public was growing weary of them—and of stabilization. These had been accepted in wartime; but voluntary peacetime restrictions were another matter. E. C. Fussell wrote to Nash in 1948 that importers believed that import limitation was 'more to suit the New Zealand Government's wishes than to help Britain'.[35] Such attitudes were very common. Nash was winning support abroad but not at home. In July 1949, after he had attended a meeting of Commonwealth Finance Ministers, at which Britain's dollar crisis (which soon led to the devaluation of sterling) was discussed, Stafford Cripps wrote thanking Nash for 'all your helpfulness during our meetings and for that ready friendship which you always radiate'.[36]

Resentment against restrictions and controls and shortages was grist for the National Party's propaganda mill. It was easy to say that this was state control, socialism. Nash's and the government's liking for central control made the accusation credible. The resentment was a major determinant of the 1949 election.

Another respect in which the outside world dominated the situation in

New Zealand was defence. Fraser had become a cold war warrior before the hot war ended; psychologically he was ready for an anti-communist crusade.

At Commonwealth Prime Ministers' conferences in 1948 and 1949 Fraser heard much from the lips of the Foreign Secretary, Ernest Bevin, and from senior army officers, about the Russian threat, by all means short of war, to established governments.[37] After his return in 1949 Fraser came out in favour of peacetime conscription.

Though there was a public movement favouring conscription, there was powerful opposition in many trade unions, trades councils, and Labour Party branches to this reversal of Labour's traditional policy.[38] John A. Lee and 'Jock' Barnes, the Auckland watersiders' leader, spoke against conscription. Failing to get Labour Party conference approval, Fraser sought refuge in a national referendum. He then stumped the country as though there were a general election. Public money was spent to get a 'yes' vote. Eventually 533,000 voted in favour, 152,000 against, but 40 per cent did not vote. Conscription was for Labour a self-inflicted wound. No government action did as much harm to the party organization. Branch membership dropped.[39] Old Labour stalwarts, workers at the 'grass roots' in the electorates, were sick at heart at this betrayal of a party article of faith. For the 1949 election the Labour branches were in disarray.

There was a further aspect of the 1949 election atmosphere which needs to be stressed because of its immediate and prospective influence on the fortunes of Labour and its leaders. After the war there were endless union-management disputes in several industries, notably on the wharves. Possibly these were in part a bursting-out of hostilities bottled up during the war. There were more immediate causes of tension. Stabilization was unable in peacetime to resist inflationary pressures from rising import costs and rising wages. Consumer prices rose some 4.5 per cent annually in 1946-9. It also seems that the wage-earner's share of the national cake was declining.[40]

Whatever the causes of industrial disorder, the rest of the community—including many, and probably most trade unionists in the more peaceful industries—was in no mood to put up with it. Many people blamed the disorder on Communists. And there were Communists among the leaders of some unions, including the waterside workers' and carpenters'. At that time Communists were very antagonistic to the government. Clearly it was not serving the interests of Russian foreign policy—which seemed to be their chief interest. The best-known leaders of the watersiders, Harold ('Jock') Barnes and Toby Hill, were not Communists. They were able, aggressive, persistent, and they were very hostile to the government, against which Barnes had a personal grudge: Labour had declined to reinstate him in the public service from which he had been dismissed during the depression.[41]

Work on the wharves became chaotic after the war. There were delays due to 'spelling' and 'go-slows'. There were repeated breaches of agreements newly made.[42] The militant unions were hostile to the arbitration court, although some of them, including the carpenters' union, were registered under the Industrial Conciliation and Arbitration Act. The watersiders, in 1946, secured their own Waterfront Industry Commission, on which they were represented. But, when their representatives did not get their way, the union leaders treated it as just another authority. In their hostility to arbitration these unionists were carrying on the tradition of the 'Red Feds' of 1913 and of the Alliance of Labour in the nineteen-twenties.

Barnes and Hill led their followers into non-stop battles with the government, the Commission, and the Federation of Labour, which supported arbitration. Over some industrial disputes about working conditions or pay it is easy to defend the leaders. Collectively, however, their actions showed a great misjudgement about what the government or public would stand. There was something paranoiac about the scope of their ambitions. It might be necessary in future, Hill announced in 1946, for the watersiders to decide to which countries New Zealand's exports should be sent.[43] Barnes's manner of speaking to cabinet ministers was extremely arrogant, and belligerent.[44]

Nash sometimes received deputations of wharfies or shipowners, either with other ministers or in the absence of Fraser and McLagan. He could speak toughly himself—for instance, to some shipowners in 1949.[45] But he was not as used to dealing with unionists as Fraser or McLagan and he was not quite happy in the openly antagonistic atmosphere of some of these talks. He wished to be conciliatory when no one else seemed willing. His approach must sometimes have astonished his audience on such occasions. When deputations of waterfront employers and workers, including Barnes and Hill, met McLagan and Nash in November 1948, they appeared to have agreed on a compromise reconstitution of the Commission. McLagan had mentioned 'opportunity' which reminded Nash of 'some delightful old lines' he had learnt some sixty years before. He concluded the meeting by quoting them!

> Master of Men, Destinies alive,
> Fame, love, and fortune on my footsteps wait,
> Cities and fields I walk, I penetrate
> Deserts and seas remote, and passing by
> I knock unbidden once at every gate.
> If sleeping wake,
> If feasting rise before I turn away,
> It is the hour of fate ;
> And ere you doubt or hesitate
> Seek me in vain and uselessly implore,
> I answer not, and I return no more.

'That is opportunity', he explained.[46]

The government was capable of taking strong action against a union. In

1949 the Auckland carpenters began a go-slow. They were supported by the wharfies. The government deregistered the carpenters' union and, although there was opposition from some MPs and party branches, registered a new union set up by moderates.[47] Despite Fraser's feeling, in 1947, that 'drastic action' might be needed against the watersiders, the government hesitated to act quite as strongly against the wharfies, because it might split the Labour movement from top to bottom. Wharf disputes continued through 1949 and the union restricted overtime work. The government abolished the Waterfront Industry Commission and a new judicial body, the Waterfront Industry Authority, and suspended the wharfies' 'guaranteed wage'. By August the government had forced the union to resume normal working hours. It was a set-back for the militants. But the government had not done enough to evade the accusation by the National Party and the Press that it was weak in dealing with wharfies.[48]

Nash was closely involved in another arduous union dispute. The Public Service had fallen behind private employees in salaries and wages. The Public Service Association was fighting a vigorous campaign to catch up with the 'private sector'. Its leader was Mr J. P. Lewin, a brash, determined, aggressive left winger, an able man and 'difficult to intimidate or subdue', another outspoken leftist public servant, Dr W. B. Sutch, has written.[49] Their demands for increases in 1948 would have cost some £2 million, Nash estimated.[50] F. P. Walsh, who was a member of the Stabilization Commission, warned Fraser (who was abroad) that if the public servants' maximum demand were accepted an Arbitration Court award would follow giving increases to all salary and wage earners, at a cost of some £45 million. He also cautioned Fraser that if the Public Service Association won it would increase 'Lewin's prestige as the outstanding leader on behalf of wage and salaried workers of this Dominion'.[51]

Lewin had been one of Nash's advisers, and with him in Geneva, but, like other ministers, Nash was finding his aggressive tactics and blunt manner of speaking offensive. At one meeting he told ministers that if their demands were refused they would make war on the government, and that the object of war was the destruction of the enemy. Nash and Semple both thought he was insulting.[52]

The public servants were very agitated and threatened to hold a stop-work meeting. R. M. Campbell, Chairman of the Public Service Commission, warned the service that anyone attending a stop-work meeting was liable to be dismissed. A Communist, Mr Cecil Holmes, in the National Film Studios, then called a stop-work meeting and wrote an impudent letter to Lewin on how to address it, beginning with the advice to 'Butter the buggers up a bit. . . .' Lewin apparently contemplated attending, for he wrote draft resolutions for the occasion.[53] However, better counsels prevailed, the meeting was cancelled, and Lewin returned Holmes's letter. Shortly afterwards another civil servant (not a policeman) took a satchel from Holmes's car. It contained the letter, Lewin's notes and Holmes's Communist Party card. These were handed to the police, who showed them to Nash. Walsh also saw them—and saw the possibility of demonstrating that the public service agitation was Communist-inspired. Certainly it was widely believed that 'toughy', as Walsh was called by his enemies (he had changed his surname from Tuohy) was behind it.[54] It seems certain that Walsh and probably some of the ministers pressed Nash to make a public statement. He was uneasy, since he knew Lewin quite well. Moreover, Lewin's mother was dying. He delayed action for two weeks until after the funeral. Then, after getting legal advice, he issued a public statement about Communist efforts to use industrial disputes for their own disruptive purposes, and published Holmes's letter and Lewin's notes. Walsh wrote to Fraser that 'Lewin and his clique' had been exposed and that Holmes and Lewin should be suspended.[55]

Holmes was sacked and the Public Service Commission recommended that Lewin be dismissed but this was overruled by Fraser and he was reprimanded.[56] Holmes went to court and won. The Supreme Court held that he should have had a hearing before he was dismissed. Campbell then wanted to reinstate him but the government went to the Court of Appeal which held, by a majority, that Holmes was not a probationer and hence could not be dismissed summarily.[57]

The famous 'satchel snatch' was one of the few occasions when Nash— then acting Prime Minister and acting Minister in charge of Police—had a central role in such an illiberal act. His public statement, publicizing the Communists' disruptive techniques, was a 'smear' of Lewin. Holmes certainly had acted aggressively, but the stop-work meeting had been stopped by Lewin and others, so he had merely sought to hold one. The National Party had a great day in parliament. Holland moved a motion of no confidence. He talked of a police state, a breach of the United Nations Charter on Human Rights, and an invasion of personal liberty—the publication of stolen private papers. Nash—and Fraser—swore that when the police brought the papers to Nash they did not disclose their source, so that he did not know they were stolen, which caused some National laughter.[58]

Nash had been pushed by Walsh and others into a kind of action which he found distasteful. It was perhaps the only political action of which he admitted, later in life, to being ashamed.[59] He always, thereafter, spoke to his closest friends of Walsh with something close to loathing. Probably Walsh, like Fraser, could bully him; dominate him by sheer physical presence. He once said that Walsh was the toughest man he ever met in his life. He acknowledged his ability while disapproving of his 'methods'.[60] By that mild remark he meant that Walsh was unscrupulous, ruthless; he would bend people to his will by any means to hand, including threats. In a letter to James Thorn, written in 1947 and before the satchel episode, he had praised Walsh, though rather as one might praise a dog of uncertain temper: 'We are all sorry that Jack Walsh was beaten for the Vice-Presidency of the Federation of Labour. He is easily the best man we have had in the industrial movement for years. His method of approach is often not as good as it might be, but he is sound, he is loyal, and in the long run if people treat him decently he is as good as they make them. He has certainly been the greatest single assistance from the industrial movement since we became the Government, and there is no man in whose judgment with regard to industrial matters and economic matters we have more faith.'[61] After 1948 he revised his judgement of Walsh: he ceased to trust him at all.

In the 1949 election a bouncy Sid Holland led a confident National Party. 'LABOUR is the SHORTAGE Government' they proclaimed; it was socialist, indeed they said Communist; it was inflationary. National would 'make the £ go further'. It would defend personal freedom and private enterprise. It accepted social security. It would deal with militant unions. They said it was 'Time for a Change'. Nash was denounced in the Press as 'a Socialist managing the country's national accounts to a Socialist pattern'; his budgets were written 'from a Socialist angle'.[62] His party was denounced by National for believing in and fostering class antagonism. National stood for all classes.[63] Labour spoke of the danger of depression; of Labour's great record.[64] Labour was now the establishment. National had the enthusiasm, the new image. After fourteen years, Labour was swept aside. National won eight Labour seats, and a majority of forty-six to thirty-four in the new House. Nash himself won easily enough, beating his National opponent by 8,153 to 5,880.

Ben Roberts wrote that not even Fraser had done more for the Party. Ormond Wilson wrote that he 'need no longer worry about what Peter says and thinks' and could come into the Fabian movement. Nash wrote a few months later to another Fabian, George Fraser, that in view of the recent history of the Society he could scarcely become an active member—which he greatly regretted, since research was of urgent importance to the Labour movement. This had been his opinion when he first became the party secretary. Geoffrey Cox wrote praising him for giving a chance to young men like himself, and for selecting and trusting General Freyberg. At midnight on 4 December Freyberg, now the Governor-General, wrote, 'How very much I have valued your help and friendship. The last ten years have not been easy ones. More difficult years lie ahead. But no matter what happens I know our friendship will survive.' Lady Freyberg also wrote from time to time to Mrs Nash. A couple of years later, when he was leaving this country, Freyberg wrote that it was a sad and distressing experience, but they would never forget 'so many acts of kindness' from the Nashes.[65] Such letters must have helped Nash to bear the loss of office with equanimity.

It was scarcely possible, however, in any way to disguise that the voters had decisively rejected Nash's New Zealand. They had not, to be sure, repudiated his total vision of what government and society should be, for Labour's social welfare was regarded by most people as the main pillar of utopia. But they had rejected what Nash regarded as its twin and equal—centralized controls. Nash, more than any other individual, had been responsible for erecting, between 1935 and 1942, the endless series of exchange, import, marketing, price, land sales, rent, and other controls. Fraser had been more flexible in his attitude to private competitive enterprise. More than any other minister, Nash had represented welfare and controls; the controlled welfare state.

According to a newspaper, Fraser took three or four brown paper bags to his new office, while Nash took three lorry loads home.[66] A controversy then followed between Fraser and Holland, who accused the Labour ministers of removing reports on the satchel snatch, the Murupara pulp and paper plans, and secret military papers. Fraser won this round. He retorted that when the Coalition lost office in 1935 they had destroyed all the external affairs papers. The ministers' offices had been denuded of documents. Moreover, he said, outgoing ministers were as capable of deciding which documents were state papers as incoming ministers.[67] The files in the Nash papers from this period suggest that in his view any document he had signed or sighted was his own.

XXII

The Wharf Strike

1951

The historian, J. C. Beaglehole, wrote of the first National Government, 'The naive, the almost childish brutality with which the Chiefs of the National Party fell upon power may seem quite surprising, until one remembers how famished for power they were. . . .' Labour, he wrote, had an exhausted leader, Peter Fraser, who had lost control where his control had once been greatest, over industrial labour.

The new Prime Minister was a very different man indeed. Fraser and Nash had been outstanding leaders in world affairs. Of Holland, Beaglehole wrote, 'The spectacle of the Prime Minister as an exponent of policy in international and Commonwealth affairs was something from which one wished to remove one's eyes hurriedly. . . .'[1]

Fraser and Nash, who had little schooling, were widely read and cared very much for books, the arts, research. Holland, who had been to high school, gave the impression that he felt he had had enough learning. He was notorious for a cheerful vulgarity.[2]

The sensitive or superior might shudder or sneer, but Holland was ebullient, domineering, belligerent. He had some able men in his cabinet, including two future Prime Ministers, K. J. Holyoake and J. R. Marshall. Holland was not as impressive as Fraser or Nash, but his ministers (who included seven lawyers) were probably on average more competent departmental administrators than the Labour men.

Perhaps sensing that Fraser was a spent force, National concentrated its initial political barrage on Nash. Fraser said that it was a 'planned and concerted attack'.[3] Certainly the president of the National Party, W. J. Sim, Holland, and several ministers seemed to take turns in criticizing him. The substance of their criticism was ironical, yet showed that New Zealand politics had not changed. He was accused of creating Reserve Bank credit!

Holland claimed that Labour had borrowed £89 million from the Reserve Bank in 1949 and that New Zealand had been living beyond its income. He claimed to have discovered that Nash concealed a deficit of £25 million. Nash had been adopting inflationary policies—'socialist finance'. It is doubtful whether Nash appreciated the irony of this accusation. He fired back repeated salvoes of figures. Millions of £s flew through the parliamentary air.[4] This pointless dispute went on for years.

National removed the controls over land sales in May 1950. It reduced government subsidies on a wide range of foods and on the carriage of fertilizer. The price of essential foods necessarily rose.[5] It seemed that the government would dismantle Labour's state-regulated economy and that the workers would suffer. At a protest meeting in Auckland, Nash said that he did not think that 'the homes throughout the country have ever been so startled as when the Prime Minister put over his statements regarding subsidies'. He said that 6 May was 'Black Friday'.[6] This sort of alarmist talk was to be characteristic of Labour—and Nash's—speeches for years. The party was increasingly out of touch with the public mood. The country was beginning to enjoy an unparalleled period of prosperity heralded by the Korean war wool boom.

In December Fraser died, worn out by arduous years.[7] After his initial stroke, Nash visited him in hospital every day, and was with him shortly before he died of a heart attack. He was two years older than Nash, who had known him since 1911 or 1912. In 1922 Fraser was one of the men with whom he had discussed becoming the party secretary. Fraser was much the ablest man Nash had known in the New Zealand Labour movement, and one of the country's few great Prime Ministers. He lacked Seddon's or Savage's or, in time, Nash's rapport with the voters. But none of them had greater political gifts or excelled him in their political achievements. Nash and he had worked together for a long time and Nash felt a real affection as well as great respect for his gifts.

When Nash thought of Fraser he had to admit that he could be sarcastic, his temper could flare up. He could be a hard man to work for. Once he told Nash to remember that he was not Prime Minister.[8] When Nash spoke of him after his death, he stressed his insight into people—he 'Saw through people'—and his political intuition, both in domestic and international affairs, which was, Nash thought, remarkable. He praised Fraser's loyalty to colleagues. When others had tried to undermine Harry Holland, Fraser had circumvented them; no one could have been more loyal and helpful to Savage. Yet, Nash added, at his first caucus as leader, Fraser had created a sense of unity and loyalty previously lacking. Unlike himself (Nash implied) Fraser acted on 'immediate urges'; generally he was right.[9]

In January 1951, at the age of sixty-eight, Nash was unanimously elected leader of the party by caucus. There had been newspaper speculation that C. F. (Jerry) Skinner might beat him, but it was idle gossip. Friends like Dick Campbell wrote that the choice was inevitable. Skinner nominated Nash and McLagan seconded the nomination. There were no others nominated. Skinner then beat two others for the deputy leadership.[10] This may have been one of the rare occasions when Nash felt a little awed by the tasks ahead. He wrote to Ormond Wilson,[11] and said at the party conference in 1951, that it was not possible fully to replace Peter Fraser. He would do his best. Other old party friends, like Tom Brindle or Lee Martin, were dead, or ill and inactive, like Semple, or retiring from parliament. Skinner and McLagan were relative newcomers to the leadership. The parliamentary team was changing. Nash persisted. He had immediately to face one of his greatest ordeals, the 1951 wharf strike.

The tactics of Barnes and Hill, in fighting for better pay and conditions for 'wharfies', seemed to be non-stop aggression, apparently on the principle, 'if it moves—hit it'. There was violent friction between Barnes and F. P. Walsh of the Federation of Labour, two very strong men indeed. In April 1950 the Waterside Workers' Union, and some others, walked out of the FOL and started their own Trade Union Congress. By so doing they isolated themselves from the general union movement and sat out on a limb, waiting to be cut off. But of this they seemed entirely unaware. Shortly afterwards there were more of the stoppages on the wharves which so infuriated most of the population. The government threatened to declare a state of emergency and it seemed that there would be a showdown, but Peter Fraser intervened. A meeting of the wharf and FOL leaders with Fraser, Nash, Semple, and McLagan opened the way to a settlement,[12] the making of which could not have pleased the government. A state of emergency was declared, but the government did not use its powers. The next time there was a dispute it was ready to act. In January 1951 an Arbitration Court general wage increase of 15 per cent displeased the 'wharfies'. 'Those who have made the wages decision are like the Bourbons —they have not heard the sound of marching feet', their secretary, Hill, declared ominously.[13] There were further disputes on the wharves about what increase the watersiders, who were not covered by the court order, would receive. The unionists turned down the employers' offer and refused to work overtime. The employers placed the men on a two-day penalty. The men said it was a lock-out; the employers said it was a strike. The union refused to accept arbitration. The government was now able to make a stand on the principle of defending industrial law and order. Once again a state of emergency was proclaimed and some very severe emergency regulations were gazetted. It was illegal to go on strike, to publish anything likely to encourage strikers, to give money to strikers or food to their wives and children. At the end of February the Waterside Workers' Union was deregistered, that is, struck off the list of unions registered under the Industrial Conciliation and Arbitration Act. The 'wharfies' now had no union and no leaders officially recognized.

It was a time of violent emotion, like 1913. The wharf leaders were generally believed to be Communists, acting as agents of the Cominform. These were the days of the Korean War, of the Australian bill to ban the Communist Party, of Senator McCarthy. The Prime Minister said that the country was 'actually at war'; he said that there was a 'very determined effort . . . to overthrow orderly government by force'. Another minister said, 'whether we like to admit it or not, the fact remains that we are at war, and on this occasion we have more traitors within our gates than ever before in our history'. The Minister of Labour, William Sullivan, said that it was not an industrial dispute but 'part of the cold war, engineered by Communists to advance their cause and the cause of Russia'.[14]

The wharf dispute created a situation very threatening to the Labour Party. The union movement was split, though the Trade Union Congress represented only a minority. There was danger for the party in entering into the dispute; yet it was almost impossible to stay out of it.

Nash was very much on his own. He distrusted Walsh. McLagan, the former Minister of Labour, was ill. His experience in union affairs was much needed. At first the Labour caucus lay as low as it could. But in late March Nash decided to make a statement on the crisis. It was the first of a number of steps which placed him and his party in very grave difficulties. Partly, at least, this seems to have been due to his own suspicion of Walsh.

In February he had been invited to speak to a public meeting in Hamilton on the subject of subsidies and wages. It was called by the Waikato Trades Council, a section of the FOL, specifically to create more interest in the work of the Federation. The national secretary of the FOL, K. McL. Baxter, was to speak too. Nash signed 2,000 personal invitations. He agreed to speak on 'Inflation—Subsidies and Wage Rates' and Baxter on the work of the FOL.

Nash had a considerable capacity to see things as he believed they should be. He chose to regard the meeting as one arranged to demonstrate the need for cooperation between unions and party within the Labour movement. Consequently what followed greatly offended him. When he arrived at the meeting he was told that Baxter would speak first and answer questions before he spoke. This Nash quite reasonably objected to. It was agreed that Baxter should speak first, but that questions should follow both speeches. When he reached the Embassy Theatre an inspector of police told him that he was not to refer to the emergency regulations governing the waterfront dispute. Nash very firmly refused to accept this direction. The chairman then announced that Baxter would speak and answer questions first. Nash whispered that he might decline to speak and Baxter agreed that questions should come at the end.

This episode, occurring so early in his leadership, made such a strong impression on him that he wrote by hand a lengthy account:

all the evidence tended to show that the purpose of Waikato Trades Council was to use Leader of Parliamentary Labour Party to attract a crowd to hear Mr Baxter boost the Federation of Labour.
   Doubts as to the purpose and bona-fides of F. of L. were raised in conversation with Mr Walsh prior to my leaving for Hamilton—when he said that

Mr Baxter would be speaking at the meeting on the F. of L. and the waterfront dispute. Mr W's purpose might have been to associate me with the attack on the W.W.U. [Waterside Workers' Union.]

There is more emotion in these remarks than seems justified, for the original invitation had specifically said that the aim was to boost the FOL and the meeting was to be distinctly an industrial and not a Labour Party one.[15]

The emotion was an index of the tension between Nash and Walsh and within the FOL and caucus. This is not surprising, for almost everyone was emotional and many were hysterical at that time. It also shows that from the beginning of his leadership Nash was anxious to demonstrate, not least to himself, that the party was not dictated to by the FOL, nor he by its bullying leader. When interviewed in 1966 about Walsh, Nash said that Walsh 'influenced Government decisions by his ability and knowledge—especially by his ability to present his case'. He tried, as usual, to be fair. He went on, 'I liked him more than he liked me. He thought that I was too soft'. (Which was perfectly true.) 'But I was not going to be dictated to by anyone. I told him that he could put his case to me whenever he liked but that the final decision as far as Government policy went was mine'.[16]

Nash felt, then, that the FOL was trying to line him up. This was no doubt true in general, but not obvious on the particular occasion. Probably he was rattled by the police inspector. But, in addition, he seems to have felt intensely suspicious of Walsh. After all, no matter what Walsh said, Nash had been *asked* to a meeting to boost the FOL. The tension between them was not a good sign for the Labour movement.

In his Hamilton speech Nash said that the 'wharfies' had already agreed to six of the government's seven demands. He called for a compulsory conference to discuss the remaining point, that the union should be an open one. The 'wharfies' must accept the decision of an independent chairman—they would have to accept arbitration if they hoped to have any future in New Zealand. He criticized some of the emergency regulations, especially the right given to officials to open private correspondence, restrictions on freedom of speech and the regulation making it an offence to give food to a watersider's family. He acknowledged, however, that a Labour government would have used emergency powers to see that the population was clothed and fed.

This statement, which now sounds innocently liberal, got him into trouble. He was universally denounced in the Press. Sid Holland attacked him for fence-sitting and for suggesting a conference with law-breakers.[17]

He now made himself unpopular with the FOL by inviting Barnes and Hill to his office for discussions and suggesting that he would invite them to attend caucus with FOL representatives. The FOL promptly declined an invitation and the 'wharfies' were not invited to caucus. However, this proposal was reported in the papers. Nash had to assure Arthur Osborne that he was not 'flirting with Barnes'—as the public supposed.[18] Nash justified seeing them—these public enemies, as they were almost universally felt to be—on the grounds that he had not yet heard their full case.[19]

In 1913 Nash had thought of writing to the Prime Minister about how to settle the strike of that time. Now he wrote to Holland asking why the government did not call a conference to settle the dispute. He also protested at the infringement of civil liberties, and asked that parliament be called together.[20] Nash repeated this request several times, but Holland did not do it. Parliament would have given the Labour Opposition an opportunity to air its views which it did not have during the crisis. The Press was hostile, hysterical, and extremely unfair in its presentation of Labour or union opinion.

Nash and other former Labour ministers had several conferences with the 'wharfies' and had succeeded in encouraging them to make notable concessions to the government's demands. The government refused to treat with Barnes and Hill because they wanted their union to be reregistered. The government would not accept any national union.[21] Moreover, the government was too shrewd to accept proposals brought about by Nash's intervention, and give him credit for any settlement.

As the 'wharfies' and their allies, seamen and miners, found themselves being thrashed by a determined government there was some violence, such as attacks on strike-breakers. ('I done me bun and called him "scabby" ', one deregistered unionist explained in court.) An attempt was made to blow up a railway bridge near a Huntly coal mine. The government now spoke of putting the country on a 'war footing' and thousands of men were enlisted in a Civil Emergency Organization.[22]

The City Council in Auckland refused to permit Nash to hold a public meeting in the Town Hall. The police refused to let another Labour MP hold a meeting with his constituents unless he avoided reference to the strike or the emergency regulations. These episodes, like the police attempt to prevent Nash from speaking about the emergency regulations in Hamilton, suggested that New Zealand was becoming a police state. They made Nash very angry—he related them in a letter to Ben Chifley, in which he described the split between the FOL and the party.[23] On 13 May he spoke to a large audience—he thought 10,000—in the Auckland Domain. He had told Chifley that the party had sought settlement of the dispute 'without supporting the waterside workers or opposing the Federation of Labour, which is opposed to the waterside workers'. He told the Domain audience, 'We are not for the waterside workers, and we are not against them. . . .' They had been wrong in refusing arbitration in the beginning; now the government was wrong in not agreeing to arbitration.[24]

The words were to dog him for most of the rest of his life. He had long had a reputation for being evasive. A cartoonist in the Hutt had in 1946

portrayed Nash being asked if he favoured democracy and replying 'No
Yes No Yes No Yes. . . .'[25] From now on he was constantly ridiculed in
the Press and in parliament as the embodiment of equivocation or fence-
sitting. To many people his attitude towards the 'wharfies', at a time felt to
be a national emergency, was almost treason.

After Nash gave up no one tried to negotiate for a compromise solution.
By early June the strike was over after 151 days. The once powerful
Waterside Workers' Union was split up into twenty-six port unions. The
miners and seamen were beaten too. Militant unionism was crushed. The
union movement was split between the FOL and the defeated militants. The
Labour caucus was split between the extreme anti-Communists, like Semple
and McLagan, and the moderates, like Nash and Nordmeyer. There was a
coolness between the FOL and the Labour Party, and within the Labour
Party.

Nash's first months as leader had been among the most difficult in his
political life. That he felt himself under intense pressure is obvious. He
wrote by hand a very large quantity of personal memos and notes, daily
chronicles of events, like the one on the Hamilton meeting. He only wrote
such records of events where he felt the events to be of great significance—
like his talk with Roosevelt in 1939. Another reaction to the situation which
indicates the importance he attached to it, also shows how deeply he
believed in the power of prayer. The staff of his parish church, St James's,
had an early morning service daily. Lay attendance was rare. Every day
during the strike Nash joined them at 7 a.m. to pray for industrial peace.[26]
He felt very deeply the proscription on giving food or money to strikers'
families. Probably he thought it would be a very bad thing if the Leader of
the Opposition broke—or were caught breaking—the law. So he asked a
local minister to make grants on his behalf to families in distress and repaid
him when the strike was over.[27]

Although the Press denounced and ridiculed him, Nash behaved with
considerable dignity throughout the crisis. He tried to be fair-minded in
evaluating the 'wharfies'' case and the facts of the situation. He told his
audiences that there was no Communist conspiracy behind the dispute,
although doubtless the Communists would use the dispute for their own
ends. He tried to be similarly objective about the 'cold war'. In 1954 he
wrote to a woman in Sydney that he did not think the Russians wanted war
but victory through peaceful penetration.[28]

His effort to be fair, when almost everyone was dominated by emotion,
was what led to the strongest criticism. He never defended the actions of
the watersiders; nor did he denounce them. There is not much doubt that
the reason was the one he gave to an interviewer years later: 'I had spent
my life getting better conditions for the workers and I would not attack
them and lose them their gains. I opposed them but I would not attack
them'.[29]

Nash was leaning over backwards to be fair for, as he wrote to Chifley, the 'wharfies' 'did not always play the game' with the Labour government.[30] Fraser would have said something more pungent.

There is not much doubt that the situation would have worked out somewhat differently had Fraser lived. He had a considerable rapport with Walsh. Nash said that Walsh had 'a sort of reverence' for Fraser[31]—he wept openly at the hospital when Fraser died. The FOL was anti-Barnes; so were the Labour leaders. So there was no intrinsic reason why there should not have been a closer cooperation between FOL and party during the crisis. It seems clear that the personal distrust between Nash and Walsh was a significant source of friction at that time.

The government's stunning victory in the wharf crisis helped it to entrench itself in office. Parliament had scarcely assembled when Holland asked for a dissolution. It was the only 'surprise' election within memory. Obviously Holland meant to ride into stronger and longer political power on the wave of support he had had against the militant unions.

The 1951 election was possibly the roughest Nash ever experienced. A National MP said at a meeting in New Plymouth that Nash's actions had once bankrupted his partner in business. A doctor told the meeting that Nash had 'sold promissory notes in Wellington as a result of which his partner became bankrupt'. Nash took legal advice and was advised that an action for slander would probably fail. The National MP had admitted that Nash had not himself been a bankrupt, but there were so many rumours that his old friend George Pearce published a notice in the local newspaper that he would pay £200 to the local war memorial fund if anyone could prove that Nash had ever been a bankrupt or caused a partner to be bankrupted.[32]

A National pamphlet proclaimed that the issue was 'The People versus The Wreckers'. A sub-heading read 'Bash-gang tactics! Mob-violence! Thuggery!' The government spoke in equally rugged terms: 'we have defended the people against the basher gangs which are the necessary accompaniment of a Communist state', Holland said in a broadcast. Mr K. J. Holyoake said that voters had to decide whether or not they wanted Barnes, Hill, and others restored to their positions. Nash's opponent, J. W. Andrews, who had opposed him in 1938, said that Nash had visited Russia, returned home to praise its planning, and helped to plant Communism in New Zealand.[33]

Labour's chances were not raised by the former strikers. Barnes came out in support of Labour, which was not a life-giving kiss. 'Pat' Potter, who was chairman of the Trade Union Congress, was even less helpful when he said that once Labour were elected 'we can line Mr Nash up'.[34] Nash and his friends thought that two factors, his refusal to denounce the 'wharfies', and the violent anti-Communist campaign by National, decided the election. The Press, as right-wing and capitalist as any in a Communist's dream, equated Labour with Communist. When Ben Roberts, the former Labour Minister of Agriculture, wrote to Nash about the election results, Nash began to write a reply. 'The Communist bogey proved terrifying to thousands, yet it was (in the light of circumstances in New Zealand [where only a tiny minority voted Communist]) so childish that I could not persuade myself that it would terrify grown up men & women'[35]—he stopped at that point, and did not complete the letter, but wrote another four months later.

Possibly Labour's defeat was not entirely due to National aggression. Some of the Labour pamphlets stressed the danger of a depression—which was not very real to most people during the great Korean war wool boom. Labour voters stayed home in droves. There was a very low turn-out. National won another four seats, tightening its grip. Nash was indomitable: alone among Labour MPs he gained an increased majority. He was one of the few remaining Labour leaders who was still a national figure, not to be brushed aside by abuse, however repetitive.

In May 1951 a British newspaper had reported that New Zealand was in the grip of a Communist-inspired reign of terror.[36] Its season of hysteria was not yet over. After the election the government introduced two repressive pieces of legislation. One, to deal with spying, was the Official Secrets Act, which passed without debate except that Nash asked for an assurance that anyone accused could have a jury trial.[37] The other legislation was the Police Offences Amendment Bill, which dealt with sedition and subversion. This time the government had gone too far. There was very widespread protest in the Press, from churchmen and others. The sight of a government which spoke so much about the rule of law and of extending individual freedom—as Holland did during the 1951 election—curtailing individual liberties was hard to stomach. Some of the most illiberal features of the Bill were dropped, but as passed it was bad enough. Like the emergency regulations, the new legislation placed a heavy burden of proof on the accused. In addition summary trial without a jury was introduced.

The government alleged that the strike had been secretly fomented by Communists. The aim, it appeared, was to limit New Zealand's war effort, an assertion for which the evidence appeared to be some anonymous waterside workers' strike pamphlets.[38] The election, the ministers said, had given them a mandate to deal with the Communists. In introducing the Bill the Attorney-General, T. C. Webb, stressed the need to guard the right of the individual to 'legitimate' freedom of speech. Nash attacked strongly. He recalled his conviction in 1921, and described it in detail. This involved him running a gauntlet of National interjections. Holland asked if it were wise to bring the subject up. Nash said the same thing could happen under this legislation. It involved a censorship of literature, of opinion. He quoted the journal *Round Table* that democracy must fight anti-democratic ideologies like Communism with democratic weapons.[39]

In January 1952 Lot and he sailed for Britain in the *Athenic*. At last he had time to reply to his old friend Ben Roberts. Their letters were an excursion into the past, where they found reassurance, and from which they drew strength. Roberts, born in Liverpool, Anglican turned Primitive Methodist lay preacher, a farmer in New Zealand who had joined the United Labour Party in 1913, had much in common with Nash, notably a way of moralizing about politics common among former English socialists of their generation. They spoke of their ideals almost in terms of piety; their dialectic was far from materialistic. To them it was the capitalists— the National Party—who were materialists.

Roberts wrote that Holland's policy was 'an appeal to the lowest traits of fear hatred & cupidity'. National had encouraged speculators. 'Gambling in racing etc. is bad enough; but Gambling in land, houses, homes, food & clothing is stark & unmitigated tragedy!'

In material things Labour should match National—'but the emphasis should be on the deep things of the Spirit'. 'Human Brotherhood & Socialism & the Christian Ethic in the hearts of our people, must become the main spring of our actions.' Many of these passages were much to Nash's taste and he underlined them. There was much more too: democracy encouraged man's 'evolution to higher & nobler things' but, alas, the people had chosen bondage, elected 'to go back to the flesh pots of Egypt. . . . I suppose a generation have grown up that knows not Joseph!!'

Nash replied that the letter had been an inspiration to read in September and was as inspiring in January. He thought that Labour had been losing some of 'the spirit of the founders of the Socialist movement', but that the election had strengthened their movement. 'If the result brings more willingness to serve it will have been a blessing in disguise'—to serve, 'instead of what we can give and get of material things.' Two years of National rule had been marked by a tendency to 'pay more for ownership and cleverness—than for making and serving'. The objective of the Labour and Socialist Movement must be that 'only those who serve (being able) are entitled to the good things of Life'. 'Service must be the title—not ownership'.[40] This was the Nash who had read Ruskin in Selly Oak; who had corresponded with Robert Ahearn.

In 1946 Nash had been appointed a member of the Privy Council. Now he was present, as a Privy Councillor, at the accession of the Queen. He signed the proclamation and two days later attended the Accession Council when Queen Elizabeth subscribed an oath to maintain the true Protestant religion.[41] They were back in New Zealand by April 1952, Nash looking tanned and fit.[42] He told a Lower Hutt audience he had never felt better to carry on the fight.[43]

XXIII

Leader of the Opposition

1951-7

Nash bore his loss of office from 1949 onwards with equanimity. Now he had lost the regular use of an official car he travelled to and from Wellington by bus and train. The sight of this familiar, stocky, neatly-dressed figure, complete with homburg, at first surprised and impressed his fellow commuters. One night when he was coming home on the last train, a cheerful drunk called out, 'What are you doing here Walter?' 'I'm a worker too, you know', he replied in his quiet voice.[1]

He showed no evidence of welcoming the extra leisure available; the first leisure, indeed, for fourteen years. Henry Taylor, who worked in the Colonial Office, observed in 'The Statesman out of Office', a chapter of a satirical book, that the 'craving for office with which statesmen are so often reproached is, perhaps, in the more active of them, quite as much a craving for business as for emolument or power; and their unseasonable love of business grows out of their forfeiture of the love of leisure'.[2]

Nash's former assistant, the irrepressible Dick Campbell, somewhat astringent about Nash in his later years, but who had had unrivalled opportunities of studying him from the nineteen-twenties onwards, used to urge that Nash was to be found summed up in Taylor's book.

Nash contrived to be, or seem, as busy as ever. Much of his work, of course, for several months of the year, was the day-to-day business of the House. A larger proportion of his time could be devoted to his own electorate. He spent hours and hours talking to his constituents—one might almost say his parishioners. He came to regard them as his own people. He tried every little thing he knew to get them a state house, a mortgage from State Advances, an additional pension. In talking to the needy, the helpless, he felt and communicated a deep concern that was instantly and unmistakably recognized.

As Henry Taylor remarked, a statesman's loss of office is often 'attended with but little loss of political importance. . . . he will continue to cover a space in the public mind proportioned to the reputation which he has acquired'. Yet rarely is the change acceptable: 'and the reason would appear to be, that most statesmen do not find themselves enabled to bring home to their own minds a satisfactory sense of their importance merely by the contemplation of that in which it really consists, unaided by impressions upon the senses. A number of very little things, which go to make up the *bustle* of greatness, are necessary to keep up in them a strong and lively assurance that they are great.' It was 'the granting of audiences, the receiving of deputations, the summonses to levees and councils', Taylor wrote, which created 'a pictorial presentiment' of their greatness.[3]

There is little doubt that this bustle of business was very important to Nash. Perhaps that was one reason why he never declined an invitation to any gathering if he could help it. As he grew older his attendance at cocktail parties became sedulous. One of his secretaries at this time, Mr Bruce Brown, once speculated that Nash somehow drew life, energy, from the approbation of crowds.[4]

It is difficult in New Zealand to make much of an impression on the public as Leader of the Opposition. The Prime Minister inevitably inspires a certain awe. But there is no comparable popular feeling about his chief opponent. Indeed the Opposition, in general, seems often to be carping; opposing for the sake of opposing; sometimes almost unpatriotic.

Sir Alister McIntosh, formerly head of the Prime Minister's and the External Affairs departments, once remarked[5] how opposition reduces the most formidable ministers to impotence. When they are separated from their well-informed secretaries of Treasury, of External Affairs or whatever, their statements seem ill-informed, shallow, off the point. Their words sound hollow—for their words no longer make decisions, decide fates.

It is sometimes said that in New Zealand a good Leader of the Opposition should not be too gentlemanly, but rather, abrasive and rough. If so, Nash was not outstanding in the role. He opposed, as well as he could, but often generously, acknowledging merit in his opponents or in their works.

The Labour MPs formed a very weak Opposition—like National after its two defeats in 1935 and 1938. Norman Kirk, while he was himself Leader of the Opposition, said that the Labour Party had received such a battering during 1951 that only Nash's doggedness enabled it to recover.[6] There were only thirty Labour members in a House of eighty, and some of them were very tired warriors, like Semple; there was little new blood. In debate they lacked depth. Nash, Nordmeyer, McLagan, C. F. Skinner, W. W. Freer, and P. G. Connolly were among the stronger men. Only the first three were well known to the public.

Labour's main attack was over financial policy and economic questions generally. Here there were issues, but not very striking ones. The National government settled down to a moderate, middle-of-the-road course which made nonsense of Labour jeremiads. Labour complained constantly that National had wrecked import selection, wrecked state housing, wrecked the economy.[7] But it was not very convincing because the country was enjoying the great post-war prosperity which was to continue, with minor interruptions, for two decades.

The politics of prosperity, at least in New Zealand, are unexciting. There was little for the Opposition to get its teeth into. Nash persistently taunted Holland with issuing more Reserve Bank credit, in 1952-3, than Labour had in its last year of office, after criticizing Labour for such borrowing.[8] This kind of discussion, in New Zealand, seems more entrancing to politicians, radio (later TV) commentators, and political scientists than to anyone else. They have an agreement to pretend that politics matter more than most people think.

National began by removing most import controls. Nash was shocked to find that overseas funds were being spent on unnecessary luxuries. He made much of the fact that, in 1952, he bought a 2 lb tin of Danish ham for 29s. 3d. (when 4 lb tins of New Zealand ham could be purchased for 28s.).[9] But balance of payments difficulties, resulting from over-importing, forced the government to reintroduce controls. It came up with a scheme of 'exchange allocation', a form of disguised import licensing which rationed overseas exchange instead of goods.[10] To the community the effect was much the same. Needless to say, Nash now denounced the government's improvidence with overseas funds. But it did not run into difficulties comparable to those of 1939. Labour's constant criticism of the government's import policy[11] made little impact on prosperous voters.

At the beginning of 1954 a minority of Labour MPs were so dissatisfied with Nash's leadership that they tried to get rid of him. They thought he was too old and too identified with the restrictive controls which had been rejected by voters in 1949. The *Dominion*, reporting these feelings, added 'the fact remains that he is at 71 still a public figure, with an international background'.[12]

The men behind the abortive coup were the remnants of the credit reformers, or Leeites, in the caucus of the 1930s: Mason (who detested Nash), Bill Anderton, and Nordmeyer who, while probably never a creditite, had been numbered in the ranks of the dissidents as an ambitious young 'stirrer'.

As far as Nash knew, it began in May 1953. He wrote a memo by hand:

7-5-53

4 P M

Mason called—and said that a number of members had complained to him about the Leadership of the Party that he had consulted others—and was of opinion that a majority of the Party desired another Leader. I stated that he had approached the members to ensure what he had always desired—my resignation. He said that was incorrect—he had a great respect for myself personally but that the Party would do better under some other Leader.

I pointed out how mean it was to approach me on the eve of my departure for Britain—which gave me the alternative of cancelling the Coronation engagement to meet the Party members or leaving the matter three months to over hang my thoughts during that period.

Why did he not raise the question during the Session whilst he was canvassing the members—when he could have reached a decision at once.

He said he did not consider that I should give up the position now but on my return.

After a lengthy conversation I advised him that I would deal with his representations in my own way.

On the closing day of the Session April 30th Osborne and McLagan advised me that Mason had approached [W. A.] Hudson [MP for Mornington]—asking his opinion regarding displacing W.N. from the Leadership.

McL. said it was unthinable [*sic*] at the present time.

Soon after Nash left for the Coronation, Mason began to suggest that many members of caucus thought that he should retire. On his return there was a letter from Mason awaiting him at the Auckland airport '. . . to say that you may confidently disregard anything I said in our last discussion in your room before you left. There will be no question raised by anyone of departing from ordinary routine or of anticipating it.'[13] This was a reference to caucus rules, drawn up in 1939, that the leader would be elected at 'a meeting to be called in the year of the General Election prior to the opening of the last Session of Parliament'.

At a caucus on 9 February 1954 Angus McLagan referred to the questioning of Nash's leadership in the Press and moved a vote of confidence in him. Mason moved as an amendment that they should fix a date for the selection of the party leader. This was carried as a substantive motion, which was a slap in the face for Nash, but caucus immediately applied a soothing lotion by supporting McLagan's vote of confidence unanimously.

A wrangle now developed over the date of the meeting. Nash's supporters believed that the party at large would back his leadership, so they wanted the meeting to be held after the annual party conference. Jock Mathison, a Christchurch MP and a Scot like McLagan, now moved that the election of the leader should take place after the conference. But John Stewart, an Auckland MP, successfully moved for an April election.

The national executive of the party now entered the fray and came out strongly for Nash, deploring the 'treachery' of some caucus member who had leaked their proceedings to the Press. The executive protested that caucus had broken its own rules about the timing of the election of the leader. This did not seem to be the case, but the executive maintained that the leader had to be elected at 'the' (not 'a') meeting prior to the last session of parliament preceding an election. A long row went on over this point. Nordmeyer was at once Nash's prospective challenger and president of the party. In caucus he moved resolutions denouncing the interference of the executive, which he chaired.[14]

On the executive there were the unpaid 'area representatives', many of them unionists, as well as other unionists like Roberts. The party and the unions both weighed in on Nash's side, heavily and decisively. Branches all over the country passed resolutions supporting him. So did the Federation of Labour, the coolness of 1951 now forgotten.[15] The rebels in short, had sadly misjudged the situation. It seems that they never numbered more than six (Mathison's estimate in July 1953) to nine (according to Nash's later count): Mason, Nordmeyer, P. G. Connolly, Anderton, Hackett, Freer, plus Stewart, Macfarlane, and Kearins. Apparently Mick Moohan had flirted with the anti-Nash minority for a time, but he was now firmly in the winners' camp.[16] At caucus on 23 June he moved that Nash should be leader. Warren Freer, an Auckland MP, nominated Nordmeyer. Nash won and 'Jerry' Skinner, the only nomination, was elected deputy leader.[17]

Labour came out in the 1954 election with a fist-full of promises. The child allowance would be raised to 15s. a week. The government would make available 3 per cent loans for housing. Effective steps were promised to make the state the sole authority for the issue of credit and currency. This was an attempt to keep creditites in the Labour fold, for the Social Credit Political League was now putting up its own candidates. In July Nash had forced the pace by announcing that if elected, Labour would introduce PAYE income taxation. The government then said that PAYE was bound to come.[18] Labour announced during the election that the first £100 of taxation due in 1956 on income earned in the previous year would be cancelled (so that no one would be paying two years' tax at once).

Labour tried to make it a 'cost-of-living' election. Nash always stressed that whereas National had promised in 1949 to 'make the £ go further', it now cost 28s. to buy what a £ would buy in 1949.[19] But, at least to start with, the contest between the main parties aroused little interest. Both Nash and Holland commented on this.[20] By contrast, Social Credit meetings had a revivalist atmosphere.[21]

The lack of fervour reflected the fact that Labour and National had politically drawn closer together so that a failure to tell one from the other was excusable. There were differences between them over policy and in the kinds of voters who supported them. But there was nothing comparable to the ideological gap between the parties in the nineteen-twenties or even the nineteen-thirties. This was obvious to almost everyone except, it seemed, the politicians. They continued to assert that Labour would oppress private enterprise or that National would oppress the unions.

For Nash, at least, things improved towards the end of his campaign. He began to find large and enthusiastic audiences. He spoke to a Labour rally of 10,000 in Auckland. The crowd became impatient with listening to F. P. Walsh speaking on wages and the cost of living and called out, 'Sit down!' and 'We want Walter!'[22] This must have been a soothing shout in the leader's ears.

In the Auckland Town Hall he was greeted by a storm of cheering, whistling, and stamping feet. Elderly men and women pushed into the aisle to shake hands and to pat him on the shoulder.[23] Nash was beginning to arouse a little of the emotional admiration, almost reverence, which people had felt towards Savage, scarcely ever towards Fraser. The touching of the leader is, in New Zealand, one of its main manifestations.

Nash's stamina was astounding. The newspapers commented on the great energy he had put into the campaign; on how fit he was and vigorous his voice. The *Dominion* said that he had rallied the wilted Labour forces of 1951.[24]

The biggest surprise of the election was that the new party, Social Credit, won 11 per cent of the vote. Many people had protested against the main parties by voting for the newcomer. But it won no seats. Labour won more votes than National. Over 55 per cent of the electorate had voted against the government, and for either Labour or Social Credit. But though Labour won five more seats, it took only 35 electorates to National's 45. In the Hutt the vote for National dropped by nearly 2,000 and Nash's majority rose by over 1,000.

One subject on which Nash often spoke in parliament, not always very impressively, was foreign affairs. At first there was substantially a consensus in the House. Labour agreed with the government in supporting the Korean war effort and in wanting a Pacific pact. When the ANZUS Treaty was signed, Nash lamented the absence of Britain. Labour differed from National by 1953 in supporting the recognition of Communist China and its admission to the United Nations.[25]

Being an onlooker of events must have irritated him most in foreign affairs, for it was in this area that increasingly he had come to see himself as authoritative; it was here that the government was weakest. Sometimes —even without receiving the advice of Berendsen or Alister McIntosh— Nash made some useful comments. In 1954 he said of Indo-China, 'Outside nations, no matter how powerfully they assist the French to subdue the Vietnam or the Vietminh people, cannot succeed. . . . The only solution lies in the people of Indo-China governing themselves with their own powers, their own forces, and in their own way.' He believed that the nations of Indo-China could govern themselves without extending the threat of Communism. Nash was by no means alone in holding such views, but few people expressed them in New Zealand, and those few were often so obsessively pro-Russian that their motives were suspect. Nash stressed the need for economic aid: peaceful cooperation was the only sound defence for the future. New Zealand must be careful not to become identified with certain forces looked on by some South-east Asian nations as enemies. On the SEATO treaty, which arose from the situation in Vietnam, his comments were less apt. He called it an extension of the ANZUS pact, and an improvement because Britain, as well as some Asian states, was a member. He thought its terms progressive and constructive.[26]

On some of the great issues of international politics, Nash's caution—growing, if anything, with age—infuriated radical supporters. During the Suez crisis, for instance, he was much more moderate than Evatt or Gaitskell. As early as August, S. G. Holland had said that 'where Britain stands, we stand'[27]—at a time when it was becoming increasingly likely that the British were going to stand along the canal. In September Nash issued a careful statement that military force should not be used until the dispute had been considered by the United Nations and the International Court of Justice.[28] When the French and British attacked Egypt the New Zealand government was the first in the Commonwealth to offer support. All Nash would say was that no information so far available warranted a change in Labour's policy of referring to the UN all disputes likely to lead to armed conflict. Holland and Nash were praised in the conservative *Dominion* for their dignity and restraint and reserve.[29] On 5 November Gaitskell denounced his country's 'act of aggression' while Nash sat on his fence. Then on 7 November, he issued a statement approved by caucus. It denounced aggression by any country, while recognizing that the UN had been unable to enforce its decisions. It appreciated Britain's magnificent contribution to world peace, while regretting its aggression in Egypt.[30]

Much if not all of the text was in Nash's words—on this occasion notably mealy-mouthed, or milk-and-watery. Nash wrote to Evatt that, while agreeing that the denunciations by Gaitskell and Evatt had been factually accurate, his own statement had been based on the hope that better results might be achieved by avoiding continued condemnation of Britain.[31] There was some speculation in the Press that Nash might be having some opposition in caucus. P. N. Holloway, the MP for Heretaunga, wanted a stronger denunciation of the British government. Nash, Skinner, Mason, and others were thought to be pro-British.[32] P. G. Connolly had been saying how good it was to hear the British lion roar when petty dictators tried to twist its tail.[33] It does seem that Nash was extremely pro-Britain, if not pro-Anthony Eden. There was much muttering in some party branches that his statements were not as unequivocal as Gaitskell's. His 'neither-for-nor-against' statement pleased no one.[34] However, the crisis passed quickly and no great or permanent harm was done.

It was sometimes said in the newspapers that Labour was becoming a more effective Opposition after 1954. Nash's leadership was thought to be more positive.[35] After several years of office, the National government was being forced on to the defensive over various issues. There was the 'Parker case' in 1956 about equal pay for women in the public service. And Labour's economic offensive had more to sustain it: the cost of living was said to have gone up by 41.8 per cent between 1949 and 1955; taxation had increased from £72 to £111 per head.[36]

During the 1956 session the confidence of the Opposition rose notably, particularly because of the introduction of PAYE income tax. In his 1957 budget, which was widely held to be an election-winning one, the Minister of Finance, Jack Watts, promised that when PAYE was introduced, in April 1958, there would be certain tax concessions. First, the tax on income earned in the year 1957-8, and due to be paid in February 1959, would be written off. Secondly, on taxes due to be paid in February 1958, on income earned 1956-7, there would be a 25 per cent rebate up to £75. Thirdly, people earning income other than salaries and wages would pay no social security tax on income earned in 1957-8.[37]

This bid was a distinct advance on Labour's offer, during the 1954 election, of a flat rebate of £100 on income tax due in the year when PAYE was to start. Nash did not, in his reply to Watts, suggest that Labour had a new bid in reserve, but it is clear that this was the case. He attacked the government for remitting the social security tax on income earned by the self-employed. The reason given for this concession was not easy to explain to voters. People receiving salaries and wages had had this tax subtracted from their salaries, hence they paid on current income. But the self-employed paid it in instalments on past income. Once PAYE was introduced, the self-employed would become liable for provisional social security tax, under PAYE, as well as for the tax already owing. National held it was unfair for them to be taxed twice in one year, and offered to extinguish the tax owing. But Labour pointed out that the self-employed were to be excused a tax which other people had already paid. In Labour eyes the government was offering a concession to the wealthy, for the self-employed were professional people and businessmen, shopkeepers and farmers. They were also likely to be National voters. Nash and his followers launched a non-stop attack on this proposal.

In addition, in his budget speech, Nash criticized the government for remitting all income tax due to be paid on income earned in 1957-8. Seven people, he said, earned a total of £378,000, on which they paid £92,000 tax. Why should the rich benefit to this extent?[38] He had said the same thing in a speech in Lyttelton in March.[39]

It is clear what Nash thought. He thought the remission of a whole year's tax, on rich and poor alike, was iniquitous. It is also fairly clear that the Labour caucus had decided on a complete remission—a policy he had criticized in Lyttelton. He had been overruled by caucus.[40]

Nordmeyer followed Nash in the debate and said something very different. He said that he could not see that remitting a year's tax was much of a concession: the state would get much the same sum into its coffers. He agreed that a year's tax could be remitted and promised a £100 rebate on the taxes due in February 1958. The National leaders pounced on the discrepancy between Nash's attitude and Nordmeyer's but soon lost the point in a confused debate.[41] Nash began to sing the same tune as caucus. He quoted Sir Bernard Ashwin, who had said that the year's revenue was merely the *basis* of a tax assessment. He did not much care which year's income was taxed as long as the taxes came in.[42]

It was characteristic of Nash that he thought it was *immoral* to hand back their taxes to the rich. This was a *class* way of looking at things, and one which made him more left wing than most of his colleagues since the nineteen-twenties. Fraser, Semple, had moved right. New Zealanders rarely thought, felt, with such emotional immediacy, in class terms. It was an aspect of Nash's make-up which had often caused people to misjudge, underestimate him—to think, for example, that John A. Lee was more radical. In this case his attitude had a unique irony. His colleagues had pushed him, against his judgement and principles, into one of the most shrewd and decisive moves in his political life. This was apparent, however, rather in retrospect.

The differences between Labour and National policy were complex to explain in terms of taxation practice, but simple in their practical effect on voters and taxpayers. Both parties offered the remission of one year's tax. In addition, National offered up to £75 and Labour up to £100 on the previous year's income tax. National at first offered to the self-employed the remission of one year's social security tax. (This was built into the tax tables and, if abolished by Labour, would provide most of the money to pay for Labour's higher income tax remission.)

It is useful to set out what the financial and cynical facts were, because at the time the discussion, among politicians and commentators, grew so complex that the points seemed theological.[43] It was not, however, the remission of sins that was in dispute unless, in a prosperous democracy, poverty is a sin.

What had Labour promised in 1954? Was Labour's £100 off on top of the National tax tables which included a 25 per cent rebate? Was Labour —as National MPs said—offering a monstrous and wicked bribe? Despite all the debate, in fact it was a political auction. As early as March 1957 the well-informed political correspondent of the *Dominion* had written that the issue in the next election would be who would offer the largest rebate —'The swinging voters, who make and break Governments, will have their votes up for auction. . . .'[44]

The debate in parliament grew very tense as the Labour men sensed that they had the government on the defensive. In October the government retreated a little and announced that social security tax for the current year on incomes other than salaries and wages would be payable only when a taxpayer died or left the country. Nash's secretary, Mr Bruce Brown, commented:

Some Opposition members were at first a little crestfallen at the supposed loss of a nice point for the hustings, but brightened when they reflected on the possibilities for ridicule contained in the 'pay it when you're dead' provision. The amendment also assisted Labour's case in its explicit recognition that this tax was owing and should be collected, a point which early Government arguments had tended to deny.

One may doubt whether the amendment mollified any indignant wage and salary earners—and it may have annoyed many self-employed—but the point involved here was the effect of the whole question on morale. It placed the Government very unexpectedly on the defensive, confusing and dividing their number, while Labour began to see the Budget less as an election winner than as a millstone about the Government's neck.[45]

From time to time during 1957 the Labour Party announced other policies very attractive to different groups of people. For instance it proposed to abolish compulsory military training.[46] Nash frequently expressed his party's opposition to nuclear tests. His party supported the British Labour Party in urging the postponement of further British bomb tests in the Pacific.[47] Nash also took a lead in advocating progressive increases in women's pay until equal pay for equal work was achieved.[48] This was incorporated in Labour's policy for the 1957 election.

Another prominent 'plank' in the platform was 3 per cent loans for housing and a scheme whereby the family benefit (which Labour promised to raise to 15s. per child a week) could be drawn in advance as a lump sum, up to £1,000 per family, to repay a mortgage or pay a deposit on a house. Pensions were to be increased. Free schoolbooks would be provided by the state. There was much emphasis on industrialization and on import selection. One proposal was aimed, presumably, at wooing the Social Credit voters of 1954. Labour's manifesto explained that a part of trading bank profit was interest on credit. The net profits from the creation of credit by trading banks would be taken by the state. Surprisingly, this radical proposal attracted little National criticism.[49]

Labour's election manifesto took up twenty-two foolscap pages; National's took seventy-three. National, too, sought to offer something for everyone. It, too, offered increased pensions, more generous housing loans. It offered a grant of £25 to each child commencing secondary school to assist the purchase of books and uniforms. The National government had abolished the upper house of parliament, the Legislative Council, but was having further thoughts. It now proposed to re-examine the role of a second chamber.

Holland's health had been failing and he retired, very reluctantly, at the end of the 1957 session. Although this was announced in August, his continued presence prevented his successor, Keith Holyoake, from establishing himself as a leader until late October, when he at last formed his own ministry. Holyoake had spent years in Holland's shadow. He was a reserved man, who lacked Holland's rapport with audiences, and had not achieved any clear popular image. Nash, by contrast, was one of the best-known people in the country.

Mr Bruce Brown, Nash's private secretary, who travelled with him during the campaign, published an account of it in 1958:

Mr. Nash opened Labour's campaign with his broadcast address from Auckland on the evening of November 5. That date caused some incidental concern because it was feared that the distraction of Guy Fawkes night might heavily reduce the vital radio audience. In the event the crowd in Auckland Town Hall proved very substantial, and, apart from some continual explosions in the near distance all seemed well. The broadcast was regarded as being as important as the rest of the campaign put together. Labour officials and supporters in Auckland and throughout the country agreed that Mr. Nash was in fine form and thought his speech much the best of the opening broadcasts. Many were exultant and believed that the election was won then and there, while all thought the party's prospects had been greatly enhanced.

In this Auckland speech Nash tried to reply to the constant question—how would Labour pay for its promises?—which was the principal National weapon of attack. 'Plenty of money is available to finance the schemes', he said. 'A short while after we become the Government they (the National Party) will be surprised to see how much money we find.'[50]

Mr Brown's account goes on:

In all he addressed twenty-three major meetings and several other lunch-hour and workplace gatherings. The greatest day undoubtedly was in Auckland on Wednesday in the last week. Arriving an hour late because his aircraft had been delayed by head winds (he had flown from Christchurch and had been travelling for something around five hours when he reached Auckland) Mr. Nash was rushed by car to the Auckland waterside. The lunch-hour was now over, but the men unanimously agreed to forfeit an hour's pay to stay and hear Labour's leader, and he was accorded a tremendous reception from two thousand cargo workers. After a factory meeting in the late afternoon Mr. Nash addressed three evening meetings, in the key seats of Roskill, Eden and Tamaki. He began in Roskill where an astonishing meeting of approaching twelve hundred people upset the schedule's timing. Mr. Nash spoke ten minutes over time, and it seemed to take nearly as long to get him through the throng to his waiting car. . . . Altogether Mr. Nash addressed nearly five thousand people that day.

The whole tour, however, from the opening broadcast to the final Wellington meeting (where a packed Town Hall belied some anxiety on the part of the organisers) was counted a great success and a triumph of ability and stamina for Mr. Nash. At its conclusion his own view was that he would have had to go back to the 1938 election to find equal enthusiasm and cordiality in the reception given him.

During the North Island section of Mr. Nash's tour reports were published, emanating from Mr. Holyoake's experiences in the South, that there seemed very little interest in the election in the South Island. A comparison may not be valid since Mr. Nash visited the South Island in the second half of the campaign when interest may have been awakened, but the contention did not seem to be true. As the attendance figures confirm, interest was high in Dunedin and Christchurch, and Timaru, Blenheim and Nelson produced crowds equal to their North Island counterparts. Nor was there a marked difference between North and South Island audiences in liveliness, as had been prophesied. Rather the distinction would appear to be between the Auckland region and the rest of New Zealand. Auckland and Hamilton provided the most volatile crowds.

A remark which there brought forth a storm of applause might elsewhere earn only an appreciative clap. One would hesitate to say whether this reflects any real difference in local temperament or whether it was merely a temporary variation in political interest related to local organisation and other factors, but it is commonly assumed to be a difference in temperament. . . .

Several points concerning audience reaction may be of interest. Firstly, P.A.Y.E. and the £100 rebate did not generally gain any excessive enthusiasm in applause, except perhaps at the opening meeting in Auckland. (It was emphasised in advertising more in Auckland than elsewhere.) Generally, the best received item of policy appeared to be the Family Benefit Home Ownership Scheme, followed by the Housing policy and the Social Security benefit increases. One might assume from their presence that audiences were more interested in politics than the average, yet they often displayed a great lack of knowledge, especially, but not only, about P.A.Y.E. At virtually every meeting Mr. Nash discussed the question of social security charge for self-employed people compared to wage and salary earners, and described in chronological order what the Government had proposed, why the Opposition had opposed it, and the amendment the Government had ultimately introduced making the charge due on the death of the individual taxpayer concerned. The issues and the amendment had actually been discussed night after night in parliamentary broadcasts several weeks prior to the campaign. The Press had featured the introduction of the amendment with large headlines. Yet whenever Mr. Nash got to the 'pay it when you're dead' piece every audience roared with laughter, giving every indication that this was the first they had heard of it.

The dramatic skill of ridicule may have exaggerated this impression, but much ignorance undoubtedly existed. It was indicated in the questions often asked and in the degree of confusion that existed over Labour's rebate proposal. Interpretations of this apparently bloomed between the extremes of those who imagined that if they owed £10 in tax, Labour would write it off and present them with a cheque for £90 as well ; and those who supposed it was merely an extra exemption, so that if their income had been £1,000, exemptions £500 and taxable balance £500, their exemptions would now increase to £600 and they would be required to pay tax only on £400.

During the campaign National became impressed with the popularity of Labour's £100 and announced that the 25 per cent rebate would be granted for three consecutive years. Efforts to suggest that this had been an implied part of policy previously were unconvincing.[51] It was a new bid.

'Mick' Moohan, the Labour Party's president, was under no illusions that the election was an auction. He was responsible for an advertisement which boldly asked: 'DO YOU WANT £100 OR NOT?'

The text beneath the slogan explained: 'If your [tax] assessment is £40, you will pay £30 if you vote in National but you will pay nothing if you vote in Labour. . . . If your assessment is, for instance, £100, you will pay £75 if you vote in National but you will pay nothing if you vote in Labour. . . .'

'CAN YOU AFFORD £20, OR £50, OR £100 to vote Holyoake and his bunglers back for another seven years of squandering, credit squeezing, tax grabbing. . . .'[52]

This was rather too strong for Nash to stomach. He found it distasteful and embarrassing.[53] The slogan could be taken to mean—and National claimed that it was taken to mean—that everyone would receive a £100 rebate, whether or not he or she actually paid £100 in taxes; in other words, most people would receive a cash rebate. Moohan also signed an 'Open Letter to Electors' which said that most people could tear up their tax demand notices[54]—which had been sent out during the campaign.[55] The 'Letter' could be thought to imply that the £100 rebate was on top of National's 25 per cent already incorporated in the tax tables.

That £100, constantly repeated in Labour speeches and denounced in National's through the year, made a powerful impact. It sounded sweet, especially to middle income voters who actually paid that much tax.

At the end of the campaign Nash grew enthusiastic and less cautious. In his final broadcast to the nation before the election his tongue ran ahead of him. He stressed Labour's tax proposals at length. He promised that a Labour government would not alter the existing tax schedules, which incorporated National's 25 per cent rebate—in other words, that Labour would not increase taxes. He went on to say that 'Given normal circumstances, all the finance necessary to run the country will be available next year without any alteration in the rates of tax . . .' and he concluded by reiterating, 'We'll find all the money without increasing the taxation. . . .'[56]

Time would have surprises in store for a politician who made so many promises. But, for the moment, he fought his campaign with gusto. Reporters noted that his energy belied his age; that wherever he went he never 'failed to impress with his personality'.[57] When the votes were counted on 30 November, Nash was to be Prime Minister.

Labour won just over 48 per cent of the vote, giving it a lead of 4 per cent over National. The Social Credit vote had dropped 4 per cent. Six seats had changed to Labour, five of them 'in city suburbs of middling or mixed social composition'. The sixth was the small town, Nelson.[58] Labour had won, but only just. The party had a majority of two—forty-one to thirty-nine; once a Speaker was appointed, a majority of one. A majority of one was music in Labour ears.

It was a remarkable feat. At the age of seventy-five, forty-five years after he became involved in New Zealand politics, thirty-five years after he became party secretary; after the turmoil and defeat of 1951; he was Prime Minister. Labour's victory was widely attributed to his leadership. No one in the party now stood anywhere near him in stature in public esteem. A political scientist wrote at the time, 'Almost without exception, the papers considered Labour's victory to be a personal triumph for Mr Nash'.[59] J. C. Beaglehole wrote that the country was 'genuinely glad to see him at last unequivocally Prime Minister, and not deputy- or acting-Prime Minister. . . . There is no doubt that Mr Nash, also, was genuinely glad to see himself at the top of the tree'.[60]

The minutes of committees rarely tell a lively or satisfactory tale, but the minutes of the Labour caucus on 5 December 1957 are an exception. They read:

THANKS TO LEADER

On the motion of Hon. C. F. Skinner, Caucus expressed its thanks and appreciation for the leadership of the Rt. Hon. Walter Nash during the Election campaign, endorsing the view that to it the victory was largely due. The motion was carried with acclamation, with musical honours, and with cheers, and with a haka from Maori members.

XXIV

Into Power Again

1957-8

Cabinet was elected at the first meeting of caucus after the election. The method was the 'exhaustive ballot'. Nash was already elected as leader. Every other minister had to receive the support of a majority of members. Three of the Maoris did not wish to stand, leaving E. T. Tirikatene as the sole Maori candidate. One of the six new members announced, to the displeasure of some of the others, that they would not stand. They included Norman Kirk, Bob Tizard, and Arthur Faulkner. Forty-one members voted for fifteen ministers. Thirteen were elected on the first ballot. Tirikatene topped the poll with thirty-nine votes. Skinner, Nordmeyer, Mason, and Hackett were next with thirty-seven votes. Hugh Watt and Philip Holloway, relatively new members (with four and three years in the House) were among the next group. Then Ray Boord and Anderton were elected to join them.[1]

The Prime Minister now allocated the portfolios. He made himself Minister of Maori Affairs and of External Affairs, as well as Prime Minister. Jerry Skinner became deputy Prime Minister and Minister of Lands. Although twice a minister—first of all in Fraser's government, during and after the war—he made little impression on national public opinion, remaining always very much in Nash's shadow. He was regarded by his cabinet colleagues as 'an honest Kiwi bloke', a straightforward, reliable chap with much political commonsense but no pretensions to specialized abilities. Arnold Nordmeyer, who became Minister of Finance, was more of a public figure and more able. H. G. R. Mason returned as Attorney-General and Minister of Health. E. T. Tirikatene was made Minister of Forests. Mabel Howard became Minister of Social Security—she wrote thanking Nash for her election: 'I believe you had something to do with it'.[2] She had briefly been a minister under Fraser.

Six of the ministers had been immigrants from Great Britain and Ireland.[3] Seven, including Nash, had held office under Fraser. But Nash gave important portfolios to some relatively new men. Philip Holloway took over Industries and Commerce. Hugh Watt was given Works. Ray Boord, first elected in 1954, was called in to see Nash, who said, 'Customs, Broadcasting, and Publicity'. Boord said thank you and left but, after reflection, returned. He said to Nash that he could understand his selection for the last two port-folios, for he had been the party's press and publicity officer, but not Customs. 'What do I do?' he asked. Nash threw back his head and laughed and said, 'make rules and stick to them'. Mr Boord later believed that Nash knew he would have to reintroduce import licensing and wanted a minister who would not bend the rules.[4] (Other ministers complained later that he would not bend them even when the allocation of an import licence might have been politically invaluable.)

They did not look likely to set anything on fire. Though Nash and Nordmeyer had once been thought very left wing, none of them had that reputation now. They had lost the wild money-men of 1935, so that the ex-credit reformers and ex-socialists in their ranks looked pallid in comparison with their predecessors. They did not *intend* to set anything alight—they had no great schemes like those of 1935. Labour had become an alternative administration, differing from National in support and in emphasis. In the cabinet photographs they looked a *respectable* lot. The historian J. C. Beaglehole remarked that Nash, 'at the age of 76, looked the only young man among them. The impression of eternal youth—or rather eternal splendid maturity—was illusory. . . .'[5]

The responsibilities, as opposed to the joys of power, descended upon Nash with unwelcome speed. Reality asserted itself over euphoria in the nightmare guise that Nash knew so well: another balance of payments crisis.

There had been balance of payments problems in each election year since 1946. That meant that the government had permitted an importing spree in election years—or, in other words, that the public demanded more goodies than exports would pay for while politicians were unwilling to act the stern guardian of the public purse just before elections.[6] 1957 was no exception. A day or two after the election, the economist J. B. Condliffe, an old friend, who was acting as economic consultant to the Reserve Bank, came to Nash with a sorry tale. The Bank had been recommending credit restrictions since August. While the Governor of the Bank, E. C. Fussell, was ill and his deputy, Gilbert Wilson, not very active, Condliffe and the economic staff discovered in early October that the worst balance of payments crisis since 1938 was threatening. Condliffe was forbidden to tell Nash. The Minister of Finance, Jack Watts, was told of the situation, by Wilson, it seems, in October. Fussell wrote to him on 6 November, that urgent action was needed. The government declined to act so near to and during an election campaign.[7]

Only now, after the election but before Labour took office on 12 December, did Condliffe publicly refer to the crisis in a talk to Rotary.[8] The threatening situation had not, however, gone quite unnoticed. In mid-

November F. P. Walsh, President of the Federation of Labour, accused the Prime Minister of studiously avoiding any reference to the country's economic crisis, the over-spending of overseas funds. Holyoake replied that ruin was not just round the corner but that the national finances would require careful handling. The Press commented on the very low overseas reserves, when figures were published later in the month. But at least one newspaper, and also a cabinet minister, Tom Shand, used the signs of a crisis as a stick to beat Labour with. Shand said that there was a clear warning against expensive election promises. The *Evening Post* warned that 'Labour's reckless bid for office' should not be accepted at the expense of 'financial stability'.[9] Labour said very little because an admission of crisis would make its promises look hollow.

The episode was eloquent testimony to the ostrich-like propensities of a prosperous democracy in an election year. The government could more or less conceal, the Opposition and public ignore, approaching unpleasant economic sand-storms. Meanwhile the situation deteriorated.

On the day Labour took office, E. L. Greensmith sent a Treasury report to Arnold Nordmeyer.[10] Export prices had fallen sharply while import payments were running at some £4 million a month above the 1956 level. To ministers who had been so very *promising* his advice was bitterly unpalatable. To restore equilibrium, private imports must be reduced by £30 million. (The estimated total for 1957, before reduction, was £260 million.) This was a task painful, and difficult, though not impossible, without unemployment resulting from shortages of imported raw materials for industries. As a consequence, it would be essential to reduce purchasing power to the same extent: extra taxation and a reduction in government expenditure were essential.

How could the government fulfil its promises while decreasing expenditure and increasing taxes? At a meeting of the Cabinet Committee on Economic Policy on 20 December, chaired by Nordmeyer and attended by Skinner, Holloway, and Boord, as well as Greensmith, Fussell, Sutch, and others, the question was asked in Nash's absence. Nordmeyer said that New Zealand must live within its income so that overseas borrowing should not be thought of at present. The Committee agreed that comprehensive import controls would be the most effective way of dealing with the problem. (Nash must have been present in spirit, with the shades of 1938-9, at this point):

Subsidiary matters were discussed as follows:
(a) it was obvious that import control of itself would not restrain excessive internal demand and that a simultaneous and strongly disinflationary policy was required to reduce the level of demands for imports from the prospected £260 million level to the suggested level of up to £220 million [but hopefully only £200 million].

Many relevant problems were discussed: what to do about imports 'on the water', for instance; and the need to revise the Ottawa Agreement with Great Britain.[11]

Treasury and the Reserve Bank were in agreement. Unless 'forceful and resolute action' were taken quickly, wrote Fussell on 16 December, the situation was more likely to get out of hand than at any time since 1938. Geof Datson, a former private secretary and now in Industries and Commerce, wrote that he thought the public was prepared for 'strong measures'.[12] The advice to the government was loud, clear, and almost unanimous.

On Christmas eve Nash spoke publicly of the crisis, and again in a national radio broadcast on New Year's day. As recently as November he had sounded like Santa Claus: now he had to begin to sound like Scrooge.

In his broadcast he spoke of the blame. In September the deficit in trade figures had been £4 million. The October trade figures, published on 15 November, had shown a deficit of £14.2 million—cause for concern, for government action, not yet for alarm. But by November the deficit was £20 million and by late December £30 million—from £4 million to £30 million in three months—the 'most rapid slide in the history of New Zealand trade and an indictment of the previous government which had allowed New Zealand's overseas reserves to fall from £83 million on 2 October to £45½ million on 25 December'. Putting it even more bluntly, after eight years of very high export prices, the overseas funds would only pay for six weeks' imports.

As Nash spoke he was, in effect, reviewing much of his own life as a Minister of Finance, and the country's history, as he surveyed the alternatives. The first was to borrow abroad—shades of 1939 again. £50 or £60 million (not a mere £17 million now) could not, given the state of the London market, be raised unless at very high interest. He was not going to go through that again.

Rapid deflation, reducing purchasing power sufficiently, and causing unemployment, was not acceptable. Nor would devaluation do the job—devaluation to such an extent that it would deter importing would mean a 25 per cent or 30 per cent rise in the cost of living: inflation instead of an exchange crisis.

Exchange controls, on the lines of National controls in 1952, were a fourth theoretical possibility, but were blunt and clumsy. The remaining possibility, which Labour would adopt, was 'exchange allocation and import selection'.

This kind of thinking aloud, in an attempt to make the public see how an unpalatable decision is reached, has been used successfully by more recent New Zealand political leaders to create a public sense of *participating* in the decision. In his broadcast Nash did it very well. Perhaps the public were swimming, or drinking, and not listening.

At this stage some of the principal newspapers agreed with Nash's criticism of the previous government's inaction.[14] His indignation did not appear to be tempered by any recollection of turning a blind eye himself to the flight of capital and over-importing before the 1938 election. Jack Watts defended himself by making the suggestion—to be repeated endlessly by Nationalists—that Labour's pre-election hint of renewed import controls led to panic importing. This counter-attack, however, seems to have had little weight. Many of the extra imports had been ordered months before the election.[15]

Import controls were reimposed from the beginning of 1958. Extremely detailed import licensing schedules were periodically worked out, specifying how much barley, chaff, flour, rennet, saccharine could be imported. The level was decided at the Cabinet Committee on Economic Policy. Holloway, Boord, Nordmeyer, sometimes Nash or Skinner, with some of the powerful public servants, Henry Lang of Treasury, W. B. Sutch or M. J. Moriarty from Industries and Commerce, J. V. T. Baker of Statistics, would be present.[16] One of them gives a satirical account of proceedings.

The Prime Minister would, for instance, say that no extra tinned salmon was needed. Someone would say, 'But many women use salmon with their Sunday salads.'

'So they do. X extra tons. Now prunes. Many working class families eat prunes. Y extra tons'.

So the engines of state worked away at midnight preserving a small economy.

Import restrictions could not have much effect for several months. In the meantime other steps were necessary. Nordmeyer sold £5 million of New Zealand's London assets.[17] Nash flew to Australia one weekend to meet Menzies. He secured a short-term credit from the Commonwealth Bank of £7.5 million. A £20 million loan was raised in London at the high interest rate of 6 per cent, and $12.3 million USA were borrowed from American bankers. The government borrowed £45 million within a year. This went very much against the grain as far as Nash and Nordmeyer were concerned.

Parliament was called for a short session in January to pass amending legislation to provide for the £100 rebate. The debate was bitter from the start. Labour accused National of concealing from the country the level of the overseas funds, and of not acting to preserve them. National said that importers had stocked up for fear that Labour would be elected and reintroduce import controls. K. J. Holyoake said that Labour's £100 was a dangerous gamble to win the election. Now £19 million was being left in circulation (to pay for the tax rebate), National wanted to know where Labour would recoup that amount of revenue.[18]

The government also made money available at 3 per cent for housing for families on incomes up to £1,000. Both of these actions were inflationary. The tax rebate left some £19 or more million extra in circulation, while building increased the demand for imports. In an effort to reduce inflationary pressures, Nordmeyer asked the trading banks to reduce overdrafts, but this had had little effect by mid-1958.[19]

As the budget was being finalized, in mid-1958, there was no sign of economic hope. Butter prices overseas had fallen so low that they met only 62 per cent of the guaranteed price being paid in New Zealand. Cheese prices had fallen below the guaranteed price and wool prices had fallen heavily too. Declining prices had made the usual election spree worse. Moreover, because of the price falls and the great volume of pre-election importing, overseas funds were not building up as usual from exports.

In March the Secretary to Treasury, E. L. Greensmith, wrote to Nordmeyer that the situation was even worse than in December. Twice in twenty years, he said, New Zealand had been rescued from rather similar problems by inflation abroad caused by wars—in 1939 and 1951. Such help could not be counted on again. 'The measures adopted ought to be adequate and rigorous rather than lenient or chance-taking.'[20]

In the face of this near-unanimous advice to take draconic measures, 'Nordy' prepared his budget. The advice was very much in line with his own stern, straightforward inclination; probably this was less true of Nash, though his 1939 experiences had strengthened his dislike of borrowing or taking economic risks, which left him few options. The other ministers most fully involved in the plans were those on the Economic Policy committee. Several ministers used later to claim that they learned of the budget only just before it was delivered,[21] but in fact the strategy of the budget had been discussed in cabinet for hours, for the benefit of those who could understand and wished to know.[22] What was true was that they learnt the final details only at the last moment.

On 26 June Nordmeyer outlined the details to cabinet just before 7 p.m. As they left the room, Bill Fox said to Mick Moohan and Fred Hackett that the budget had 'shot' the next election. Moohan said it had 'shot' the next three.[23] From 7.10 to 7.25 Nordmeyer outlined the main provisions to caucus and answered questions. As the Labour team entered the House the Leader of the Opposition, K. J. Holyoake, noticed their glum faces and knew some shocks were ahead.[24]

In 1930 J. G. Coates had called Ward's budget 'the Black Budget'[25]— but that was long forgotten. This time the label stuck. Nordmeyer's budget was remembered as 'the black budget' for many years. It can be argued that it was good for 'the country'. For the government it was a suicidal mistake. It was the biggest blunder in Nash's political career. Although he was not immediately and directly responsible, he was the leader and did not say 'No'.

The government's objectives were to restore economic stability and maintain full employment, Nordmeyer said. It did not accept the view that full employment involved inflation. Nevertheless the country was facing an inflationary situation (the Consumers' Price Index had risen 2.1 per cent in a year—an increase then thought unacceptable). Overseas reserves had fallen 60 per cent to the lowest post-war level; reduced export prices suggested a drop of £50 million in export receipts for 1958. This would require a reduction of £82 million in imports to avoid a deficit—double what had been proposed by the Cabinet Committee on Economic Policy in December. Such was the atmosphere of alarm!

The budget implemented some of Labour's promises. Age benefits and some other pensions were raised. Ever since 1938 Labour had wanted to make the age benefit free of a means test at sixty-five. Nordmeyer announced that by stages the means test would be abolished and the universal superannuation raised until it equalled the old age benefit. The family benefit was increased very substantially, from 10s. to 15s. per child per week. But these improvements which might otherwise have made a big impression were soon lost sight of in the general gloom.

Income tax was raised very substantially indeed, especially on unmarried people and childless couples, whose personal exemptions were reduced. Duties on beer, spirits, tobacco, and cars were doubled. The tax on petrol was nearly doubled. Gift and estate duties were raised sharply.[26]

It was an economist's budget; a Treasury budget; but it was not what the voters had been led to expect from Labour's fair promises. Keith Holyoake, Leader of the Opposition, repeatedly attacked Nash for his election-eve broadcast promise not to alter the tax tables. By increasing taxation he had broken his promise. At first Nash did not believe that he had used the words Holyoake quoted, but after hearing the tape replayed he frankly admitted that he had made a mistake.[27] National had dented his reputation a little.

To Holyoake's talk of a £19 million bribe Nash replied that it was nonsense. After all, National had been willing to forego up to £75 in rebate, plus £18.25 million in social security tax on the self-employed.[28]

Neither Nash nor Nordmeyer nor any other Labour man managed to satisfy the public in general that their measures were reasonable and necessary; nor to fix the guilt squarely on the shoulders of the previous National ministers. They took a pride in courageously doing their duty. They did not succeed in convincing the public that their deeds were not supererogatory. Moreover, the budget on 'Black Thursday' contrasted so startlingly with their big promises in November. The people had admittedly been over-indulging in imports, but they did not like the medicine now administered.

The Press and the economists said that stern measures were needed. An economist, Alan Danks, praised the budget as justifiably tough—just what the professor ordered. Dr W. B. Sutch, a member of the Cabinet Economic Committee who advised it, praised the budget as 'the best example of monetary management New Zealand has ever seen.'[29]

The budget did help to restore economic equilibrium. But whatever view is taken of it as an example of managing the economy, it was popularly regarded as a political disaster; indeed it entered the realms of political folk-lore as archetypal in this respect. To say that it was disastrous is not a mere opinion.

The 1951 strike, polarizing 'class' feeling, had led to a resurgence of Labour Party branch activity. There was a steady growth in the number of branches up to 1957. The 1958 budget led to a precipitous decline. In Auckland nearly a third of the branches closed down, and membership fell proportionately within two years. Within the branches that remained there was much criticism of the budget, which was said to have hit low-income groups.[30]

Greensmith had warned Nordmeyer against taking any chances—and neither he nor Nash were gambling men. But a gamble would have worked. Economic conditions—wool prices for instance—rapidly improved. Holyoake said, when import controls were introduced in January, that there was no need for such severity.[31] After a year or two he seemed a better prophet than Nordmeyer. Moreover, he had had experience. The 1954 election spree had shown a run-down in reserves of £39 million.[32]

Why did Nash and cabinet make this error of political judgement? A number of reasons suggest themselves. One, which was noticed by many people at the time, was that neither Nash nor Nordmeyer *paid* taxes on cars, petrol, cigarettes, beer, or spirits.[33] It was a 'wowsers'' budget (in New Zealand a 'wowser' is someone puritanical, refusing alcohol and suspected of opposing pleasures). In this respect it was also a budget out-of-date, for the prohibition and temperance movements belonged to the past.

Mr Nordmeyer was a Presbyterian minister. His own attitude was revealed by an anecdote from the next election. In the final Labour election speech, broadcast throughout the country, he put down an interjector with the jocular remark, 'Looking at our friend, I should say that he would be very interested in the price of beer.'[34] Nash used to smoke a good deal in his youth, and was not a teetotaller, but he was, in a general way, puritanical in his attitudes.

Hitting the working man's fags, beer—and petrol—was related to Nash's lack of rapport with the union chiefs. Neither Nash nor Nordmeyer had been unionists. They did not consult—indeed they would have thought it quite improper to consult—the Federation of Labour. Yet F. P. Walsh, if asked in general terms his views on the situation, would not have suggested beer and cigarette taxes. He used to sneer that it was 'the Reverend Mr. Nordmeyer's budget'. Now he came out and said that the budget was an attack on the workers' standard of living.[35] Nor was his voice a solitary one. F. G. Young, of the Hotel Workers' Union, a rival of Walsh's in reputation for ruthlessness, wrote an almost abusive letter to Nash in January 1958 and, when he did not reply at once, sent a copy to each Labour MP. It then appeared in the Press. He denounced Nash for the large cut in imports of spirits. 'Walter, you won't get away with it, so you had better start doing a little back peddling'. He was censured by his executive and had to apologize, but the harm was done.[36] Later he wrote to A. J. McDonald, the Party secretary, that his union was very dissatisfied with the government for not fully controlling credit; for giving benefits to the workers with one hand and taking them back with the other; for attacking the workers' living standards with duties on liquor and tobacco.[37] The government had moved away from its firm base in the trade union movement.

A psychological factor was important in the government's decision. Nash had been told in London in 1939 that he had introduced import restrictions too late. His enemies were not slow to remind him of what he could never, in any case, forget, the parallel with 1938-9.[38] This time, fighting the battles of 1939 in 1958, he reacted quickly; over-reacted.

The basic fact was that the ministers accepted advice. It is easy for bankers and financiers and public servants to recommend stern measures; it is not always wise for politicians to accept what they are told. Nordmeyer, Boord, Holloway, and Nash did not reveal political creativity. They did not think of new ways to achieve the same results; they did not tell their advisers: 'Go back to your desks and think of something new.'

For various reasons Nash necessarily left the details to Nordmeyer. In April he was abroad in South-east Asia. He was not, in any case, a regular attender at the Economic Policy Committee. Dr Sutch, who was, wrote that Nordmeyer and Holloway came to have a big influence on economic policy.[39] But Nash did not say 'no'. Almost certainly that was because in substance he agreed with the provisions of the budget.

It could be said, then, that he did not rise supremely to his first and major test as Prime Minister, in the sense of superbly mastering and surmounting great difficulties and odds. Like Nordmeyer, he deserves our respect for political honesty and courage, for a willingness to take unpopular steps in the public interest. But *did* courage necessarily mean accepting the advice of bankers and economists? In any case, successful politicians need other qualities besides courage—flair and luck.

It seems that higher taxes on the rich would have hurt fewer people and fewer Labour voters. But Labour had a majority of only one (plus the Speaker); a majority not hard to lose. Perhaps no measures would have been adequate for the problem without undermining that small margin of support. Moreover, it has been argued that, if purchasing power had to be siphoned off quickly, 'it had to come from where it was, in the pockets of lower-income spenders as well as in thick wallets'.[40] From these points of view it could be said that National's election spree left Labour a bill it could not afford to meet. But, of course, unpalatable payments had not been part of Labour's promises.

Short-term borrowing and extra duties on luxuries were meant to be temporary devices until the overall policies took hold. The government's economic strategy involved three lines of attack. First there was stringent import licensing. Second, and in general a long-term measure, was industrial development. Third was the search for new export markets.

For New Zealand a key—sometimes the key—to prosperity had throughout the century been markets; and 'markets' had meant 'the Empire'. When the Ottawa Agreement was negotiated in 1932, the British market had been at the centre of New Zealand's economic thinking. So it had been when Nash tried to negotiate a revision of Ottawa, involving bilateral bulk exports of New Zealand produce, in 1936-7. But during the war, and during the years of post-war shortages, markets had given less anxiety. In the nineteen-fifties, however, it again became apparent that Coates had been right when he wrote in 1933 that the British market was not bottomless.

At Ottawa New Zealand had granted tariff preferences of 20 per cent *ad valorem* on a large number of British exports. Britain had granted duty free entry for most New Zealand exports and had placed quotas on meats. But the quotas were now of little value because of the great expansion of British production. Some of the tariff preferences granted by the British had been defined against weight. For instance New Zealand butter received a preference of 15s. per cwt., but this had become of little value because of great price rises. It had once been equivalent to 15 per cent but now represented only 5 per cent. The preferences New Zealand granted were related to money values and had retained their value to British exporters. Thus the balance of advantage of Ottawa had swung heavily against New Zealand.

Imperial preferences reduced the competitive power of some New Zealand industries because dear British imports were a significant part of their cost structure, potentially cheap competitive imports—trucks, machinery—being kept out by tariffs. They also hindered the development of other industries which were exposed to British competition. Thus both industrialization and the quest for new markets required a revision of Ottawa. More important, however, was the fact that the British market was simply not big enough. (There was now no possibility of introducing Nash's old bulk-goods-swap agreement.) Moreover, to win new markets, New Zealand might need to enter into bilateral bulk exchange agreements, which would involve quantitative restrictions—to men of GATT or of the ill-fated ITO agreement, those dread letters—QRs.[41]

In 1957 K. J. Holyoake led an unsuccessful mission to London. He asked for revised quotas on foreign meats and was promptly declined. QRs were not acceptable at National's suggestion any more than at Labour's. Holyoake then sought to revise the Ottawa tariff preferences. The British dug their heels in, however, and nothing was achieved on this issue.[42]

In 1958 the Labour government returned to the fray with a greater sense of urgency. In January Harold Macmillan visited New Zealand. George

Mallaby, the British High Commissioner, has left an account of this visit
in his memoirs: Macmillan arrived tired and ill to face Nash and dinner
in the Grand Hotel in Auckland:

Mr. Nash, the New Zealand Prime Minister, sat next to him and for once it
seemed to me that old man's tact and charm deserted him. He did not seem to
sense Mr. Macmillan's fatigue and quite contrary to my hopes and expectations
he missed the deep significance of the occasion—the arrival for the first time in
history of a British Prime Minister in New Zealand. Some quiet and elevated
observations would have met the case, but instead of this Mr. Nash became the
party politician, trying to provoke, with old outmoded sneers, the elegant leader
of the British Conservative Party. Mr. Macmillan was clearly put out and had
genuine difficulty, I thought, in concealing his irritation. When at last the
uncomfortable meal ended I had a hasty word with Norman Brook and Alister
McIntosh, Mr. Nash's chief adviser, and suggested that the serious political talk
which was then to take place between the two Prime Ministers should be
postponed. They thought we had better stick to the arrangement and they were
right. For as the discussion proceeded and Brook and McIntosh and I grew
more and more weary and less and less able to concentrate, the two Prime
Ministers, after the manner of politicians, grew more and more animated as the
clock approached midnight. Mr. Nash had quite laid aside his petty spiteful
weapons and listened with thoughtful interest to Mr. Macmillan's account of
his experiences in India. The atmosphere changed completely and wisdom, wit
and friendliness, which both men possessed in good measure, soon prevailed.
It was very late before they were willing to part.
Thereafter all went well. . . .

Later there were two days of political talks in Wellington:

These were a success—more successful, Mr. Nash later confessed to me, than
he had expected. Some of his more extreme colleagues viewed with distaste the
visit of this embodiment of Edwardian Toryism. They found it hard to rise
above the party line, but they were soon disarmed by the strange charm of the
man, his own statesmanlike approach to all problems and the vague look of
uncomprehending idiocy if anyone tried to score a party point. . . .[43]

The two men got on well. However dissimilar they may have appeared
they had much in common. They were not only Englishmen but ones with
a curiously old-fashioned air: they seemed to belong to the nineteenth
century. They were both Empire-men; they both thought that traditional
imperial, now Commonwealth ties, were important.
Macmillan wrote in his memoirs:

Nash himself was an old-fashioned radical, rather than a socialist. His hero
was Gladstone, not Marx. Somewhat 'vain and talkative, but sound and loyal.
I have found him very easy to get on with.' He was passionately fond of
political history and had read widely.
I formed with Nash a close friendship which continued until his death. He
represented a fine tradition of English radicalism of the last century based upon
sincere idealism and genuine piety. In the pursuit of what he thought right he

was both persistent and fearless. Although he was deeply interested in foreign policy, and much of our talk was occupied by a survey of the world situation, the main items for serious discussion were naturally economic. . . .

On 23 January I attended a meeting of the New Zealand Cabinet which lasted nearly two hours. Apart from the immediate economic difficulties, on which I assured them that British exporters would understand the need for temporary import controls, Ministers seemed chiefly interested in the questions of defence. In particular, they expressed anxiety about developments in Indonesia and the future of Malaya. Fortunately for me the Prime Minister conducted the whole affair off his own bat and filled up the greater part of the time with his own exposition. In the evening I had another private conversation with him which lasted until the early hours of the morning. All this was both useful and informative, if somewhat repetitive. Nash was fond of talking, and when he found another Prime Minister ready to listen to the arguments which he thought it right to expound, he enjoyed to the full 'the rare felicity of uniting, in the same pursuit, his duty and his inclination'.[44]

Gladstone and Marx were alike wide of the mark. Macmillan would have done better had he thought of two friends of his grandfather, Charles Kingsley and F. D. Maurice.

Nash told Mallaby that he found it easier to deal with a Conservative than with a Labour government in Britain[45]—he was forgetting Oliver Stanley.

Among other subjects Nash brought up the question of revising Ottawa. They agreed to seek some agreement as soon as possible, and before a Commonwealth economic conference which was to meet in Montreal in September.[46] Nash also raised one of New Zealand's recurrent problems, dairy marketing. Prices had fallen drastically, largely because a number of countries were 'dumping' subsidized butter. Macmillan was sympathetic and himself suggested that New Zealand should invoke the new British anti-dumping laws.[47]

A strong team of officials, led by J. P. D. Johnsen, now of the New Zealand Board of Trade, who had been at Geneva and Havana with Nash, set off for London in April to discuss revising Ottawa. Jerry Skinner, the deputy Prime Minister, went to London to discuss the butter problem. Both he and the officials ran into customary difficult negotiations. The British declined to impose countervailing or anti-dumping duties, but threatened to do so if offending countries did not voluntarily limit supplies.

The delegation of officials found that the British were agreeable to reduced tariff preferences, but demanded a tough concession in return, that the New Zealand government should state, in the revised trade agreement, that it would not apply quantitative restrictions to protect local industry against British trade. New Zealand already had made such an undertaking, in general, under GATT which however, permitted quantitative restrictions for balance of payments purposes, and these could be manipulated so as to give some protection to local industry. The British also wanted New Zealand to agree that import restrictions would not be used so as to alter

Britain's share of New Zealand's imports. This principle, of non-discrimination, was also embodied in GATT.[48]

The British wanted GATT-plus. This was humiliating and unacceptable to New Zealand. It involved publicly stating that it would keep its international commitments. Moreover the British demand would completely prevent New Zealand from negotiating bilateral agreements in order to win new markets.[49] The Earl of Home, Secretary of State for Commonwealth Relations, wrote that since Britain had gone a substantial way towards meeting New Zealand's wishes over butter, they looked to New Zealand to accept reasonable terms for a revision of Ottawa. In New Zealand eyes, of course, these were unconnected matters.[50]

Skinner saw David Eccles, President of the Board of Trade, and told him that unless New Zealand secured an agreement at least as favourable as that recently made with the Australians it would mean the end of the Ottawa Agreement as far as New Zealand was concerned. This tactic had been authorized by cabinet after Johnsen had learnt in Canberra that the Commonwealth government had authorized the same threat to denounce Ottawa.[51] In 1939 it had been the British who had threatened to do this. Now they were not convinced that the loyal Kiwis' bluff could not be called, but Eccles did offer, in a later message to Skinner, that New Zealand's assurances about quantitative restrictions could be covered by a separate confidential minute.[52]

Skinner came home in June but the public servants continued their negotiations, frustrated by varied British delaying tactics, for four months. In June Nash wrote, but did not send, a letter to Macmillan threatening to terminate Ottawa. In July he sent him a message to this effect through the High Commissioner. He expressed appreciation for help from the new Chancellor, Derick Heathcoat Amory, with the recent loan, and said that he was sure that the British action over butter dumping was a result of Macmillan's 'sympathetic understanding'. But he said that, in existing world trading conditions, the British demand about quantitative restrictions would make the initial development of new markets difficult if not impossible. They would have to consider terminating the agreement.[53]

Macmillan replied that he was very much concerned that Nash should contemplate such a step just before the Commonwealth countries assembled at Montreal to discuss ways of increasing Commonwealth trade, and asked him to meet at Montreal. 'It may be that meeting round a table we could find a formula to which we could both subscribe in public and which would meet our respective needs.' This message was laced with some of what used to be called 'the spirit of the Commonwealth'. And he concluded, 'these matters are so tremendously important to both our countries'.[54]

This and other messages from Macmillan, direct or through Mallaby, led Nash to reply for cabinet that it was their wish to make the Montreal Conference a success that had led them to seek an early solution to the problem. He explained New Zealand's problems and said that the British demands for assurances, on tariffs as well as QRs, questioned the mutual good faith which had always been assured. After the Montreal conference New Zealand must give notice of termination. He, too, felt sure that, could they meet, they could find an acceptable formula. But he could not go to Montreal, nor was Macmillan going.[55]

Mallaby had been throughout involved in the negotiations. He was, he wrote, 'in trouble, quite serious trouble, with Mr. Nash. He had made up his mind to take a step which from the point of view of the Commonwealth as a whole I thought rash and dangerous.' He and a senior New Zealand External Affairs officer put their heads together and suggested a compromise face-saving formula, based on a confidential minute which New Zealand had offered in June.[56] A carefully drafted document called 'Heads of Agreement' was prepared. This was not an agreement itself, but a statement of agreed principles.

New Zealand's preferential margins on British imports were to be reduced very substantially or even abolished. The Ottawa formula, that tariff protection would be afforded only to industries 'reasonably assured of sound opportunities of success', was retained. The two governments agreed 'in the operation of their import licensing systems' to ensure that their actions did not 'conflict with their obligations under GATT to operate their controls in a non-discriminatory way'. The two governments accepted that 'in certain conditions New Zealand might resort to a limited measure of bilateral trading'. New Zealand promised that this would aim not at diverting existing trade from Great Britain but at seeking new trade.[57]

It seems clear that no agreement would have been reached without the personal intervention of Macmillan and without some rapport between him and Nash. They were a good deal franker in their personal messages than the officials were in their negotiations. This was the kind of politics that Nash loved, negotiations with governments; and the subject in which he felt most at home, imperial trade. New Zealand was a very small country, but not without some weight in the discussions for it was Great Britain's fifth biggest customer. Hence the negotiations were not as unequal as they might seem.

The Heads of Agreement document was accepted by both governments in early September. Almost simultaneously a trade agreement with Japan was announced which gave New Zealand exports better access to the Japanese market in return for import licences for Japanese exports which did not threaten New Zealand industries.[58]

Sir George Mallaby observed, in connection with these negotiations to revise Ottawa, how Nash differed from Keith Holyoake in one respect. Both were loyal to Great Britain, but the latter's devotion was 'less tender, less compassionate', for he was New Zealand-born:

Mr. Holyoake, like all long-settled and well-established New Zealanders, could quickly take offence at what seemed to him—and sometimes rightly so—patronising affronts from cocksure Englishmen. Most New Zealanders are a little prickly and it is easy to see why. Mr. Nash's attitude to this sort of thing was totally different. If he felt that the British Government or some visiting Englishman had behaved with superior arrogance he would be grieved and unhappy—not affronted—upset, as any man is by the ill-behaviour of his own family. Disputes between the two countries, which, of course, arose from time to time, were a personal worry and distress to him, but when he had taken his position he fought as an equal and made no cringing concession whatever to superior power. And when the quarrel was all over the affection was deeper than ever.

New Zealanders themselves may have been subconsciously aware of this difference of approach. They never quite knew where they had Mr. Nash. Was he one of them or was he still, if you scratched below the surface, just another Pommy? Certainly he never exchanged his Worcestershire accent for the very individual New Zealand version of our language.[59]

It is true that Nash never sounded like a New Zealander: when he said words like 'put' the 'u' had a Kidderminster sound. His sentences had a 'Kiddy', not a Kiwi cadence. And some people thought that he had always remained a 'Pom' at heart. If so, it must be added that he stoutly defended New Zealand's interests on very many occasions. Moreover, to many New Zealand ears, Holyoake sounded more English than Nash, so elocution did not then much influence the fate of politicians.

During the negotiations in London Nash was not the spearhead of New Zealand diplomacy, as in 1936-7 and 1939, but the general commander, 12,000 miles in the rear. For this period, at least, domestic politics took up most of his attention, during an arduous parliamentary session. One unpleasant task was to reduce the guaranteed price to dairy farmers. Dairy produce prices had fallen 45 per cent since 1955 (in comparison with 47 per cent from 1929 to 1934). An Act passed by National in 1956 prevented a reduction of the pay-out to dairy farmers of more than 5 per cent in any one year. The government had to suspend this clause and impose a cut of over 10 per cent.[60] This led to strong attacks on the government from National and from farmers, not so much for the reduction as for reducing the income of one section of the community alone.[61] The Minister of Agriculture, C. F. Skinner, bore the brunt of the negotiations with the industry, but Nash keenly followed the run of play. When Skinner wrote to him arguing that the pay-out should not be reduced below 32d. per pound, for instance, Nash did his own calculations.[62] The measure increased the government's reputation for taking away, not giving, as promised.

The government carried out some more of its promises. Compulsory military training was abolished, despite strenuous opposition from the National Party, the Returned Servicemen's Association, a revived Defence League, and the Chief of the General Staff, General C. E. Weir, who wanted the government to make a public statement of his personal views. Nash said that a public servant's advice to the government was confidential and he did not have the right to publish criticisms of government policy.[63] It seems that the government's tiny majority incited every form of opposition, on the theory that it had no 'mandate' for radical reform.

Other government measures may be listed. For instance families were enabled to 'capitalize' the family benefit payments for children in a lump sum to pay a deposit on a house, pay off a mortgage and the like. This step, plus 3 per cent housing loans, greatly extended the possibilities of the not-so-wealthy acquiring a home.

It was a very arduous year and a wearing parliamentary session. The party whips rallied the Labour ranks so successfully that they won every one of the 104 divisions, with their majority of forty to thirty-nine. Even 'Dobby' Paikea, Member for Northern Maori, notoriously ill and absent from sessions throughout the fifties, was on deck. When twitted by a 'Nat' for his miraculous recovery of health he replied that now forty Members were praying for him.

National fought very hard, and the atmosphere in the House was often ill-tempered, even bitter. Both Nash and Keith Holyoake thought it had been a particularly difficult session. Nash had forced the House to sit very frequently after midnight, for very long hours without precedent for twenty-five years. When the House adjourned Holyoake said he was sure everyone wanted a few days' rest.[64] Nash was overseas, on his second extended trip that year.

XXV

'Summitry'

1958-60

The most notable feature of Walter Nash's prime ministership was his frequent absences from the country. A National Party journal, *Freedom*, had said in 1951 that when he was a minister he 'was never at home except when he was abroad'.[1] While he was Prime Minister his travels inspired many cartoons (hinting, for instance, that he would visit the moon next) and a great deal of criticism. It was said that his absences caused administrative log-jams because he kept so many decisions in his own hands. He took little, if any, notice of such comment and jokingly boasted that he had a flying log of two million miles at the public expense.[2]

As with Harold Macmillan in England, it rapidly became clear to Nash's colleagues that his great passion now was international affairs. This was (and is) unusual among Prime Ministers in New Zealand, where foreign policy has almost never been an election issue. Only Fraser and, more recently, Norman Kirk, have given external affairs anything like the emphasis that Nash did.

There is no doubt that Nash had increasingly, over twenty years, come to see himself as an international figure: not an Eisenhower or a Nehru, but still a statesman. It was in this scene that the inner-Nash acted out his chosen role. Long and arduous travels, far from exhausting him (at the age of seventy-six or so), stimulated fresh reserves of energy. Travel, conferences, meetings with the great, fed his vanity. But his self-image was not mere illusion. He did achieve a measure of international recognition. His fervent idealism came across very strongly, for instance, on British television to watchers in the Midlands and north of England, as it had in the USA in wartime. People repeatedly said—'Here is a *sincere* politician.' His slightly parsonical voice carried conviction. Moreover the great were willing to hear, if not to heed him. Indeed, Nash was perfectly capable of *making* them listen, for he had grown increasingly insistent and loquacious, and although he was willing to listen and learn, it rarely, if ever, occurred to him that he was wrong or that those he was speaking to were better informed. Given his study of international affairs over some thirty years and his experience, his self-confidence was justified. Certainly he was not always right, but he had no need to apologize.

The comment of George Mallaby, the British High Commissioner, on Nash is sufficiently guarded and generous:

He was known to a number of Commonwealth and European politicians and he had a profound interest in international problems. Alone among New Zealand politicians of that time he had some pretensions to being a world figure. Although by no calculation could New Zealand have been regarded as a great or important Power, Mr. Nash spoke with authority and other world statesmen were ready to listen; his views were well informed and liberal and, although occasionally he seemed to be lost in visionary speculations, he arrived in the end at a practical, hard-headed and courageous attitude. Nearly all New Zealanders, whatever their party, were proud to have Mr. Nash representing them overseas.[3]

For Nash, by 1958, the great moral issues were not poverty and social security at home but world affairs, peace and war. He meant to make whatever contribution he could to guiding the world to wiser and more moral courses.

The greatest issue in international affairs in the late nineteen-fifties was undoubtedly disarmament. The Russian sputnik in October 1957 symbolized for the world Russian power, and made the conflict between Russia and the USA more ominous. The world lived in fear of a nuclear confrontation—which seemed very near during the Cuban crisis of 1962. In many countries groups of people cried out for an end to nuclear testing, which might prove a step towards disarmament. But by what system of inspection and control could such an agreement be supervised?

These were the years of crisis in Lebanon, and over the Chinese off-shore islands. Vietnam was quieter, after the defeat of the French and the Geneva Conference in 1954. But there was fighting in Laos. Should the SEATO allies—including New Zealand—intervene? SEATO, a product of the Vietnam crisis, was tested for the first time in those years. Finally, in New Zealand itself, the international issue arousing the greatest emotion was, for the first time, the argument about playing rugby with the South Africans.

In a statement on foreign affairs in January 1958, Nash described the 'vicious circle of mistrust' confining the great powers. 'Cannot the smaller nations—some of whose representatives have much experience and skill—do something to break this deadlock; to bring about a new approach towards peace through disarmament'?[4]

In 1958 Nash's main effort in external affairs was to revise the Ottawa agreement. Otherwise it might be seen as a year of preparation for his more spectacular initiatives in 1959-60. Even so, his travels would have frightened most old men. In five weeks, in February-March 1958, he travelled 24,000 miles through South-east and South Asia, where he visited most of the capital cities and met and talked with the political leaders including Bandaranaike of Ceylon, Nehru, Abdul Rahman, and the leaders of Pakistan, Thailand, Burma, Singapore, the Philippines, and Australia.

His main purpose was to attend some international conferences. In a sense he was voting with his feet. In the past New Zealand had not taken much notice of the Economic Commission for Asia and the Far East, a United Nations commission. Nash showed the importance he had always attached to the economic problems of Asia by going himself to the ECAFE conference in Kuala Lumpur. He found that its members had much in common with New Zealand—which was in an anomalous position in the world, being at once 'under-developed' and rich. Nearly all the representatives told how their countries were suffering from the fall in world prices for exports of primary products. High on the list of ECAFE discussions was another old New Zealand problem: the relative importance of industrialization and agricultural development. Nash donated some $100,000 USA towards the cost of investigating the potential for irrigation, hydro-electric works, and other purposes of the lower Mekong river.[5]

In March he attended a meeting of the SEATO Council in Manila where he met and talked with John Foster Dulles. While acknowledging Dulles's tendencies to 'brinkmanship', Nash defended him later as a man of good intentions.[6] There was much talk in the final communique of the Communist menace in Asia. Nash's sweep through the region was an attempt to evaluate for himself the nature and reality of that threat. He visited New Zealand troops in Malaya who were preparing to take part in operations against the Communist terrorists; and visited refugees from Communism in Hong Kong. At the SEATO conference he stressed that to raise living standards was the best method of resisting Communism. And, on his return to New Zealand he broadcast two radio talks in which he stressed, not the threat of Communism, but the horrors of Asian poverty. In 1959 he said the same thing to a SEATO conference in Wellington. The greatest threats to security were not political philosophies but poverty and hunger.[7] During the cold war such views were positively red.

While in Asia he visited New Zealand Colombo Plan projects. This aspect of foreign relations was very close to his heart. In October 1958 he went off on another trip to attend a meeting of the Colombo Plan Consultative Committee in Seattle and part of a session of the United Nations. He spoke to the Third (Social, Humanitarian and Cultural) Committee of the UN on 6 October, a platitudinous speech with many references to 'basic human rights' and 'ultimate human values'.[8]

Sometimes on these trips his age showed, but he was not easily put down on such occasions. In New Zealand there was talk of a cable to carry electric power over Cook Strait. After the Colombo conference Nash went to Vancouver and was taken for a flight over the underwater power transmission cable. This was followed by an excellent lunch and a fifty-five minute film on the cable. The host was the Prime Minister of British Columbia, W. A. C. Bennett, and there were other local notables. Nash fell asleep and snored. His secretary, seated too far away to rouse him, sat 'slipping two discs for my country', he says.[9] When the film ended Nash was asked what he thought of it. He replied, 'Hm, well, I've seen it in the air and now I've seen it on the ground. Thank you very much.'

In February 1959 Nash visited one more Asian country, Japan, where he met the emperor and held trade and political talks with ministers and businessmen.[10] It was thought by many people that Nash's journeys were not strictly necessary,[11] and amounted to not much more than receptions and tourism. But there was much more to it. Nash was a very strong and effective spokesman for his government's—which were substantially his own—policies. Indeed it may be doubted whether New Zealand has had a more outspoken representative in international affairs.

In 1959 there was a crisis in Laos which could possibly have led to a major war, like the later war in Vietnam, or even to a great power confrontation. In late 1958 and early 1959 there were accusations from the Royal Laotian Government of North Vietnamese intrusions, and counter claims of American military bases in Laos, contrary to the Geneva agreements. There was frontier fighting between government forces and the insurgent Pathet Lao. In September 1959 the government asked the UN for military aid to stop North Vietnamese aggression.[12]

Laos had been designated, under the protection of SEATO, as a 'protocol' state, so there was immediate talk of intervention, which Nash strongly deprecated. In statements in early September he tried to cool such talk in New Zealand by saying that the situation in Laos was unclear. In particular, it was not at all certain that there was outside aggression rather than Laotian rebellion. It was, however, appropriate for its government to seek UN assistance. The situation was a dangerous one which might involve New Zealand.[13]

In October Nash attended a meeting of the ANZUS Council in Washington, where he was extremely outspoken against American views. He asked how long the Laotian government would have lasted without American aid, and questioned whether it was right to interfere in local politics. One of the Americans, J. Graham Parsons, an assistant Secretary of State, said that Laos naturally looked to the USA for aid, since the USA paid much of its budget. Nash asked if this were a breach of the Geneva agreement, and the American said the USA was not a signatory.

There was a warmer exchange with the Secretary of State, Christian Herter. Nash said that the USA was trying to maintain the type of government the USA wanted, not what the Laotians wanted.

Mr Herter: 'No! We have not selected those who run for office, who form the government.'

Mr [Robert] Murphy [an Under Secretary of State]: 'Mr Prime Minister, you are suggesting that we are trying to impose a government on the Laotians.'

Mr Nash: 'No, trying to maintain an existing government.'

Nash asked whether the West had the right to interfere in the internal politics of a country like Laos, and asked why American aid to the government was right, yet Vietminh aid to the Pathet Lao was wrong.

The other point which he stressed very strongly was that there must be clear evidence of external aggression, not merely internal insurgency, before SEATO intervention could take place. He was most emphatic that the planning for armed intervention should not run ahead of agreement by the governments. He clearly felt that the planners in the armed forces were taking political agreement for granted. After the meeting of the SEATO Council in Wellington in 1959 there had been public reference to SEATO planning. He said that the allies would be charged with planning an intervention, not to save Laos, but to influence the internal political situation. He went on in this strain at length. New Zealand would live up to its SEATO obligations, he said, to the extent that the Vietminh or the Chinese had intervened.[14] He did not get any support. Casey, of Australia, sided with the Americans. But Nash certainly startled New Zealand's allies.

Nash went to see President Eisenhower. They talked at length about de Gaulle, East Berlin, Formosa, disarmament. Eisenhower asked him about New Zealand's attitude to Laos. Nash expressed his concern that 'military planning in SEATO in respect of Laos was going ahead at a pace faster than the development of agreement at the highest political levels'. He wanted to make sure that the plans were not implemented before there was political agreement.[15] A few days later he saw Dag Hammarskjöld, Secretary-General of the UN, who agreed with him that there was no evidence whatsoever of aggression. The Vietminh had sent in supplies—so had the Americans—and the whole affair had been on a very small scale. A UN sub-committee had just reported back from Laos to that effect. The Secretary-General expressed 'particular appreciation of New Zealand's attitude in SEATO and our opposition to military action. It would be a very grave situation indeed if SEATO were brought directly into the problem.'[16]

Nash's papers do not reveal what he, or other New Zealand representatives, said at SEATO meetings, but their policy is clear enough. Nash certainly played a part in preventing any precipitate SEATO action. In years to come, during the Vietnam war, he always considered that his resistance to American pressure had been one of his most important deeds. At the end of 1960 and in 1961 the situation in Laos was again disturbed. Harold Macmillan found the Americans 'anxious to intervene overtly as well as covertly'. He set himself to prevent great power intervention or SEATO intervention. The Australian government and the New Zealand (National) government now supported the Americans; Eisenhower seemed at one point 'strangely hysterical'. Macmillan gave himself some credit for preventing intervention and cooling the situation.[17] Nash deserves some credit for playing a similar role in 1959. His opposition and that of

Macmillan later were responsible for a joint USA-Thai declaration in March 1962 that intervention under SEATO did not require unanimous agreement by the allies. There was an individual as well as a collective responsibility to act.

While he was in the USA Nash spoke to the First Committee of the UN on disarmament, commenting on the British and Russian plans announced by Selwyn Lloyd and Krushchev. He spoke to the Trusteeship Committee on the progress of Western Samoa towards independence and to the Second Committee on the development of under-developed countries. He also spent a few days at the Antarctic Conference, which had not yet concluded, though it was clear that it would not produce all that he had hoped when President Eisenhower had invited New Zealand to attend a year earlier.

Nash had discussed the Antarctic with Harold Macmillan in early 1958. He then wrote to Menzies, pressing New Zealand's view that it would soon be impossible to maintain 'exclusive jurisdiction' there. The aims should be some 'international regime' and demilitarization. There was the disadvantage that Australia and New Zealand would have to surrender their 'monopoly rights' to raw materials, but internationalization was more important. Menzies said that he agreed with much that Nash said, but he did not think there was any need for the 'transfer to international regime of any substantial range of attributes of our sovereignty'.[18]

The British substantially agreed with Nash and had, late in 1957, proposed some Authority with a measure of control over the continent. The Americans had suggested an international regime ten years earlier. But now, the French, Chileans, and Argentinians, like the Australians, would not relinquish their national rights. New Zealand alone proclaimed publicly its willingness to surrender sovereignty and pressed at the Antarctic Conference for a 'completely international regime'. This policy was certainly mainly due to Nash himself. He was very disappointed with the attitude of these countries, and because the eventual Antarctic Treaty did not provide a role for the United Nations, which would have shown that the treaty was not simply an assertion by a few countries of a right to dispose of the Antarctic. Both the British and Australians tried to reassure him that all was not lost.[19] The treaty did provide for non-militarization and forbid nuclear tests on the continent. It was not internationalized, but existing national claims were frozen: no nation was to make new or enlarged territorial claims while the treaty was in force. This was a self-denying ordinance by the twelve signatory states, which included the USA, the USSR, Japan, and the two South American states.

Harold Macmillan was devoted to the idea that, where normal diplomacy had failed, 'summit' meetings of the world's leading politicians might produce at least some small steps towards ending the 'Cold War', disarmament, and peace. For this strategy he invented the term 'summitry'.[20] Early in 1959 he visited Russia; Krushchev visited the USA. In late 1959 these leaders were busy planning a grand summit meeting. Macmillan wrote in his memoirs, 'At this point my friend and colleague, Walter Nash, the much respected Prime Minister of New Zealand, made a suggestion which, however well meant, was rather disturbing.' Nash wrote to Macmillan (and to Menzies) suggesting that a meeting of Prime Ministers, a Commonwealth summit, should precede the great power leaders' meeting.

He urged that President Eisenhower's hand for his Camp David discussions with Krushchev had been strengthened by his prior consultation with Macmillan, de Gaulle, and Adenauer. Similarly, Macmillan's might be strengthened by consulting the Commonwealth leaders. The 'fabric of the Commonwealth' would be strengthened by such a consultation. Macmillan replied that, while he had been 'greatly fortified' by Nash's support, it was impossible to arrange a Commonwealth meeting in time. He suggested that Nash might visit him in November.[21]

In early November Nash left the UN and flew to England for a five-day visit. He saw Macmillan and Hugh Gaitskell. On Saturday he drove up to Birmingham, where he saw his sister Emily and a sister-in-law. He saw Blackpool play West Bromwich Albion—watching association football was his favourite relaxation. On Sunday he went to Chequers. He went for a walk with R. A. Butler, and sat between him and Selwyn Lloyd at dinner, where they discussed Cyprus. 'All Ministers present agreed with me,' Nash wrote, 'on the undesirability of having someone like Makarios and Grivas turning up at Prime Ministers' meetings'. Most of the evening was spent discussing 'summitry'. Macmillan said that he and Nash had an 'Anglo-Saxon' approach to problems. He had, he said, no difficulty in coming to an understanding with Nash, but he did with Adenauer, de Gaulle, or Eisenhower. Nash outlined his apprehensions about SEATO planning over Laos 'at the urgent insistence of the Americans'. Nash thought that 'the talks were delightfully informal and discursive'.[22] Next day he left for Indonesia.

Nash seems to have been relatively insensitive to his surroundings. He was prose, not poetry. This was one of the rare occasions when he commented on them. He said in a radio statement when he reached New Zealand that the 'English countryside was dressed in its autumn colours but it was soon apparent from fog thickening that winter was at hand. It was an extraordinary contrast to be driving through the lanes and roads of England between Chequers and London one morning, and through the paddy fields of Indonesia two days later.'[23]

During his state visit to Indonesia Nash talked to Sukarno about his discussions in the USA and Great Britain. He attended the Colombo Plan conference at Jogjakarta. The Colombo Plan was one of his main interests in foreign policy—aid and economic development being equally to his taste, and it was the third such conference he had attended, the first as Leader of the Opposition in 1956. In speaking to the gathering he was able to apply New Zealand's experience to the problems of under-developed countries. He spoke of their 'critical dependence' on world commodity prices. They had just 'been through it' in New Zealand, he said. In seeking to grapple with poverty, hunger, ignorance, and disease, the instability of commodity prices, which could wreck development plans, was one of the greatest problems. When asked at a Press conference how to solve it, he spoke vaguely of commodity agreements such as the Wheat Pool.[24]

1960 saw even greater efforts in diplomacy than 1958 and 1959. It is likely that Nash felt his two overseas journeys in 1960 marked the peak of his life, not perhaps in results, but in satisfaction, and for achievement of a sort. Many facets of Nash's personality were deeply engaged in the international contacts of these years, culminating in 1960. Many Nashes met: the man of prayer, the man of peace; the student of foreign affairs who helped to start the New Zealand Institute of International Affairs; the vain Nash who liked meeting the great and (like most people) thought better of himself for having done so; the Commonwealth man, the world traveller.

This time he was away for nine weeks, from 5 April to 7 June. His main object was to attend Commonwealth Prime Ministers' and SEATO conferences, but he managed to fit in Singapore (Mr Lee Kuan Yew), Karachi (President Ayub), Kuala Lumpur (Tun Abdul Razak), and many European capitals besides.

First he went to France where he talked with the premier, Mr Debré, and with General de Gaulle. With the latter a twenty minute appointment extended to forty-five as they discussed East-West relations.[25] Then he was off to Moscow, for the first time since 1937, to military guards of honour, to visits to Leningrad, Kiev, and Moscow. He had talks with A. I. Mikoyan, A. A. Gromyko, A. N. Kosygin, and other leaders, who were all very friendly. At a state luncheon in the Kremlin Mikoyan referred to New Zealand's membership of a 'military aggressive bloc' and added jocularly, 'but I cannot see you being a member of such a bloc. You are such a nice man.'[26]

Accompanied by his grandson, Hal, and Mr A. D. McIntosh, Nash went down to visit Nikita Krushchev, who was resting at his villa, near Gagra on the Black Sea. They met on the afternoon of 20 April when they talked for three hours about disarmament and Germany. Krushchev expressed bitter disappointment with the lack of progress at the talks on disarmament taking place at Geneva. At the UN in 1959 Krushchev had proposed a reduction in conventional arms before a reduction in nuclear weapons. The Russians had now reversed this priority. Krushchev said that the USSR had already reduced her armed forces below the level proposed by the West. He demanded rapid disarmament: a system of controls and inspection could be worked out later. He brushed aside the West's demand for a system of controls first. Nash tried to convince him that the West's leaders wanted disarmament too:

Mr Nash: . . . There will be four persons at the Summit. I have met two out of the four leaders, and they both agree that you want disarmament. It would not be worth their trying to deceive me on the point. I am sure that the French and British leaders were sincere. I do know inside the British mind, and although I cannot be as sure in the case of France, I believe de Gaulle wants it. It will help me in my discussion in London to know your point of view.

Mr Krushchev: It is very gratifying for me to hear about Macmillan's and de Gaulle's attitude but their plenipotentiaries at Geneva are speaking in a contrary sense.

Mr Nash: It is what the leaders say that matters.

Mr Krushchev: But Jules Moch and [W.D.] Ormsby-Gore and the other representatives speak differently—and Moch is a brother of yours [i.e. a socialist].

Mr Nash: Yes, but Ormsby-Gore is not a Socialist. [He was the British Minister of State for Foreign Affairs.]

Mr Krushchev: Is that better or worse?

Mr Nash: You have mentioned the prime essential in this matter. It is important to avoid statements imputing ill-will to others. If you believe that people are lying or deceiving, where can we possibly get? We can get trust. Three of the partners want disarmament I know and there is only one left. Why can't we find a way?

Mr Krushchev: I said nothing that would give grounds for thinking I disbelieved de Gaulle or Macmillan, and I believe Eisenhower also wants disarmament.

Mr Nash: All right. All four of you want it. Power is with the four leaders. I believe there is more faith today in the highest places than ever before.

Mr Krushchev: I fully agree, but I cannot go against facts. The representatives in Geneva speak differently. Disarmament won't move ahead of its own accord.

Mr Nash: If the four leaders want it—and I believe that you want it—then we can have disarmament.

Mr Krushchev: I want to believe that that is so but the negotiations in Geneva make me apprehensive. The representatives do not come to light with any solution. . . .

When Nash said presently, of the British, 'They have abolished compulsory military training.' Krushchev was scornful: 'Oh, we are not worried about United Kingdom armaments. If war broke out Britain would be destroyed and armaments can give the United Kingdom nothing but expense.'

Nash found him quite unwilling even to consider any disarmament plans but the Russian. On the question of Germany he was even more uncompromising and truculent. The Russians were threatening to make a separate peace with East Germany, which would end allied rights in West Berlin. He told Nash Russia intended to go ahead alone and bitterly denounced the western powers for intervention in Russia after the October revolution:

Mr Krushchev: If we had trusted the Western Powers more then, we would have been made fools of. Now we do trust people but nevertheless we check up on them. You tell Churchill that the next time you see him.

Mr Nash: I do not think there is much point in our spending too much time on the lessons of the past. I know there have been bad things in the past and the Soviet Union also has a record of bad actions.

Mr Krushchev: What bad actions in the Soviet record—can you name them —can you name one.

Mr Nash: I could ask whether you remembered signing a Treaty with Germany to attack us. . . .

'Mr Nash terminated the discussion on this point by stating that he had never wished anything but good to the Soviet people. He had come to the U.S.S.R. to help Krushchev to make history and not to rake over old quarrels. . . .'

Nash changed the subject and asked about twelve Russians who wanted to join their relatives in New Zealand. Krushchev produced one of his innumerable proverbs: 'I don't mind mothers joining their families. I am reminded of the Russian saying that when the mother-in-law falls out of the cart the horse can draw it more easily.'

Krushchev apparently found Nash an intriguing visitor—a 'labourite socialist', as he called him, whose memories of international socialism went back to the meeting of the Second International at Geneva in 1920. He invited him to his villa for dinner. Nash, his grandson, and some of his staff spent hours talking with Krushchev and his wife and son over dinner. Nash enjoyed it immensely. Mr Hal Nash thought the conversation was like a good-humoured, verbal boxing match. Nash said that Hal was a solicitor. Krushchev said his son was an engineer, at a military engineering academy. Nash said, 'You're a militarist'. Later Nash mentioned that his grandfather had gone to Russia 'and had rather a rough time'.

Krushchev asked, 'How was that?'
Nash: 'He fought in the Crimean War.'
Krushchev: 'You mean he came here to attack us?'
Nash: 'When he got back home he died of wounds.'

Now it was Krushchev's turn to accuse Nash of being a militarist. Then they talked on about disarmament. Nash told him about New Zealand's social security system. It seems to have been an evening they both enjoyed. Krushchev said, 'I boast better than you do!'[27]

On Moscow television and in Press interviews Nash spoke of the remarkable progress he had observed since his previous visit in 1937. Some of his remarks, or alleged remarks, got him into hot water at home. He was attacked by the Opposition, allegedly for saying that he hoped Krushchev would be 'victorious'. He said that, if he *did* say this, he was referring to disarmament. He was also accused of supporting the Russian proposals for disarmament and not the American. And he was reported in

the Press as saying that he had never enjoyed an experience as much as
dining with Krushchev, which was taken to reflect on the hospitality of
western leaders. One writer later sneered that Nash's 'mercifully brief entry
into global politics' was marked by 'diplomatic gaucherie'.[28] Nash, however,
saw himself as helping to make history. He said, in Kiev, 'I am proud also
that I am playing a part, although only a modest one, in the great task of
building a better peaceful way of life by means of bringing about the
realization of the proposals [for disarmament] put forward by your
leaders. . . .'[29] He certainly did not mind, in this great enterprise, if he
embarrassed the British and Americans a little by praising Krushchev's
disarmament plans.

In early May Nash returned from Europe, where he had visited Italy
and been received by the Pope, to London for his third Commonwealth
conference—the others having been in 1937 and 1946. This time there was
Macmillan, Nehru, Diefenbaker, Menzies, Tunku Abdul Rahman, Nkrumah,
Sir Roy Welensky, Eric Louw representing South Africa, Mohammad Ayub
Khan from Pakistan. There was much dining and royalizing as well as
pontificating. Nash's diary (in his own handwriting) records on 3 May a
luncheon at 10 Downing Street, dinner at Windsor Castle (evening dress
and decorations); on 4 May a dinner at No. 10 and a reception at
Buckingham Palace; on 5 May an audience with the Queen.

At the conference, while feeling not at all inferior, he was overshadowed
by Nehru and Macmillan, who did much of the talking on world affairs
and peace. Nehru had recently met Chou En-lai as well as Russian leaders.
Still, Nash told them of his talks with Krushchev. He was convinced from
his talk with the Russian leader that he did not want war, but he would be
willing to take risks, for instance over West Berlin.[30] While they were
discussing the summit conference, to meet in Paris in mid-May, an
American U-2 spy plane was shot down over Russia and its pilot taken.
The summit looked less hopeful now.

Other dark shadows were on the horizon. Nash spoke of New Zealand's
great anxieties if Great Britain drew closer to the EEC. Subsidized EEC
agricultural exports flooding the British market posed a great threat. (On
this trip he visited the six capitals of the EEC countries and discussed their
emerging common agricultural policy.)

The main issue was apartheid in South Africa, with the Tunku leading
the attack. The Union government was to hold a referendum on the question
of South Africa becoming a republic. One issue was whether it could then
stay in the Commonwealth. But there were already republican members, so
that question should have had a foregone answer. The real issue was the
attitudes of Commonwealth governments to apartheid. The Sharpeville
shootings and Macmillan's famous 'winds of change' speech in Capetown
earlier in the year had intensified world criticism of South African racial

policies. Macmillan found some of the discussions difficult to control. He wrote, 'If we *do nothing* the Commonwealth will seem to have no faith and no purpose. If we *do too much* South Africa will secede and this may mean the beginning of a general break-up.'[31]

Macmillan fought hard to get the others to agree that South Africa could remain a member of 'our company'. Menzies stoutly supported him. Nash was less helpful. He said that he intensely disliked some South African policies, but he came down on the same side: it would be better for the Commonwealth and for South Africa if that country continued a member.[32] Macmillan wrote, 'Nash is a nice, good-natured, well-intentioned old-fashioned Liberal—a bore, but a sincere and Christian gentleman.'[33] In the end they agreed that if South Africa decided to become a republic its government should then ask the consent of the other governments to remain in the Commonwealth.

Nash now paid visits to Germany, where he talked with Adenauer and Willy Brandt, and other European capitals. Macmillan went off to his summit meeting in Paris. Eisenhower publicly acknowledged that he had known and approved of the spy flights. The Russian attitude hardened. Krushchev came to Paris blustering, angry, and feeling betrayed, demanded an apology from Eisenhower, and went home. The world's hopes of a thaw in the cold war were dashed for a time.

By 1 June Nash was talking to Eisenhower in the White House. He praised the president's moderate behaviour in the face of Krushchev's abuse. They talked generally about the world situation; Eisenhower still thought that there would be a détente. Nash brought up the question of the recognition of the government in Peking and the admission of China to the UN. He advocated a status of neutrality for Formosa, with a great power guarantee. Eisenhower said that on this question United States policy was very strong. The seating of Communist China in the UN might even lead the United States to withdraw.[34]

Nash had returned to the USA for a SEATO conference. He discussed the Laotian (and world) situation with Hammarskjöld again. They still agreed that there was no aggression in Laos. There had been rigged elections, which Nash called 'selections', that did not please them. The Secretary-General still felt that a military approach would solve nothing.[35] Richard Nixon, the vice-president, opened the conference. On the second day Christian Herter asked Nash to open the discussion. Fresh from visits to the four members of the abortive summit conference, he spoke confidently and at some length.

Some of his free-wheeling remarks at these two sessions, referring to weaknesses on the non-Communist side, such as undemocratic behaviour, gave offence to the Thai and Pakistan leaders, whose governments had a military and authoritarian character. But over two points Nash had moderated his attitude, possibly because the Laotian situation was for the moment less threatening. He argued repetitively for the recognition of Communist China. No disarmament agreement was worthwhile without China's participation. But he no longer proposed that New Zealand should do it unilaterally. Macmillan had told him that though the British had recognized China it had not done them much good.[36] But what had led him to change his mind was the Chinese activities in Tibet and along its borders. The other argument, strongly advanced by the Philippines representative and by Menzies as well as by Nash's security advisers in New Zealand, was that the recognition of China would be regarded as a Communist victory, which would disturb the confidence or shatter the morale of the millions of Chinese living in South-east Asia. This view may have influenced him too.

On this subject Nash stood alone in a cold war sea. But he also spoke about military planning. He now agreed that this was essential, but still stoutly insisted that it should stop short of involving any automatic political commitment. This was a complex matter. For instance, military planning for a certain contingency might involve actions, such as arranging for oil supplies, which could indicate an intention and encourage extremists. Complete secrecy was essential. On this point his views were strongly backed up by Selwyn Lloyd, who remarked that any military plan involved assumptions and, in this case, these had been made by the military and not approved by the political authorities. Nevertheless, political decisions could not be made in time of crisis unless the military plans were ready.

At these meetings, and at a later meeting of Nash with the Secretary of State, Herter expressed some pleasure that Nash was agreeable to military planning taking place and that the New Zealand government did not propose to recognize Communist China at once. Nash mentioned that while he had advocated recognition the New Zealand representative at the UN had voted for a continuance of the moratorium. He would have to handle that in his own way on his return to New Zealand.

Nash said that if ever Herter felt he was 'doing something which Mr. Herter regarded as hurtful or harmful to U.S. and associated interests, he would be glad to have him say so. This would not mean that he would take action if he were requested to do so by the United States, but he would be very willing to listen to the facts and judge for himself. Mr. Herter said that he had no such comment to make, and agreed that any action by Mr. Nash was a matter entirely for his own judgement and not a matter for any pressure from U.S. . . .'[37]

All this was not enough for the apparently inexhaustible premier, now in overdrive. He returned to New Zealand by way of Malaya, where he opened the agricultural college at the University of Malaya donated by New Zealand.

Nor was this too much. With an election due in a month, in October, like a large proportion of the world's leaders, he shot off to the USA again to a session of the United Nations. He was fully committed to a far larger enterprise than an election. Harold Macmillan had sent a message suggesting that it might be useful if a few Commonwealth heads of government were there. Nash replied that he had not thought of going, because of the election, but would now reconsider. He wrote warmly (and often said the same in public) praising Macmillan's efforts for peace. Perhaps in New York Macmillan could test whether there was any chance of starting the movement for peace again: 'now is the time to restate the Western democracies' case and to make the most strenuous appeal in favour of the ideals and objectives of the free world while leading representatives of the United Nations are attending the Assembly.'[38]

A very large number of the world's leaders attended this session of the UN. After disputes about the role of the UN in the Congo, Krushchev was proposing to replace the Secretary-General with a troika—a three-man commission representing different groups in the UN and thus reflecting the power situation. He denounced Hammarskjöld heatedly and demanded his resignation. Hammarskjöld replied that he worked for all countries, not just the great powers. Krushchev's behaviour at the UN astonished and dismayed his audience. He bellowed out interjections, hammered the desk so hard with his wrist that he broke his watch (Nash wrote) and then hammered it with his shoe.[39] Nash hated this 'stupid violence'. He now made one of his most powerful speeches, which was broadcast direct to New Zealand. The *New York Times* said that he made the strongest defence of the Secretary-General.[40] He pointed out that the great powers at the San Francisco conference had proposed something similar, a system of great power deputies, controlling the senior UN jobs. New Zealand and other states had successfully opposed the proposal. He now argued strenuously for a neutral and strong UN executive.

When he began to speak Macmillan, Nehru, Menzies were absent; there was a sense of anti-climax; but as he spoke they drifted in; so did Hammarskjöld. He quoted from a chapter, 'The End of Imperialism', from his book, *New Zealand*. His voice rang out passionately as he restated, in the world's greatest assembly, the belief which he had held for sixty years or more, that there are no inherently superior persons or races. There was applause from the 300 or so people there. When he finished Macmillan and Menzies congratulated him; Nehru went straight out. He had been making his own criticisms of the Secretary-Generalship and suggestions for reform. He and Nash had quarrelled over this. Nash's speech had a very good press at home: it was said that he had truly spoken for his country. Once again Nash hobnobbed with the Commonwealth leaders, talked to Krushchev and to Herter. Nash obviously felt that perhaps he had been a little too outspoken for a leader of a small ally. He asked Herter, ' "Is there anything you want to tell me that I don't know—not anything that I ought to do!" Mr Herter laughed and said he had never wished or attempted to tell Mr Nash what he ought to do'![41]

This speech marked the end of one of the most active periods of New Zealand diplomacy, rivalled previously only by Peter Fraser's efforts during World War II. It would have been extraordinary if the spokesman for so small a people as the New Zealanders had achieved a significant influence in these great international affairs. And of course Nash did not. Not even Macmillan had succeeded in exerting much influence on USA-USSR hostility. That Nash had achieved a status, arising from his wide knowledge and experience and personality, where he could talk with the world's leaders, on equal personal terms, was in itself a considerable achievement. No other New Zealand Prime Minister, except Fraser, has been able to make such informed personal comment on world affairs. Nash played a significant role in interesting the generally apathetic public in these matters.

On the whole he received little credit in New Zealand for his efforts and much criticism for his absences. On balance, his attempt to help bring about world peace was politically disadvantageous. Moreover, his critics, especially radical critics, took more account of his failures. The government had not fulfilled its promise to recognize China, which lost it credit with the small left wing. Nor did it, as many supporters expected, refuse to help the British with their bomb tests. Nash discussed with Macmillan Labour's wish for a cessation of tests, and wrote to him about it early in 1958. In fulfilment of an earlier agreement, New Zealand had sent a frigate to Christmas Island to help with weather reporting during a British thermonuclear bomb test, in April 1958. For this the government was criticized and Nash was anxious that the British tests should cease. He told Macmillan that the American reluctance to accept a test-ban might be due in part to British and French attitudes. Macmillan urged the desirability of dealing with tests not in isolation, but as part of a general and genuine disarmament. Nash accepted this point of view and in turn pressed it on the local Movement for Nuclear Disarmament. However, in mid-1958, the USA, the UK, and the USSR halted their nuclear testing programmes while disarmament discussions went ahead. There were no further nuclear tests while Nash was Prime Minister. While being criticized for aiding the British test in 1958, Nash neither gained nor deserved credit for the (temporary) halt in testing.[42]

More important, as a public issue, was that of rugby and race. Here many people felt very strongly that Nash had fallen flat on his face on his chosen political ground, the field of morality. They felt that he had not recognized a moral issue when he saw one, or had run away from it.

In 1948 there had been some protests against sending a rugby team without Maoris to play in South Africa. Peter Fraser had kept aloof. But racism was becoming a major issue in world politics. In 1959, when the Rugby Football Union proposed to send another all-white All Black team to play the Springboks there was one of the biggest protest movements in New Zealand history. A huge petition, one of the biggest ever, of 153,000 signatures, called for the abandonment of the tour. It was claimed that a

majority of the voters agreed with CABTA, the Citizens All Black Tour
Association, which led the protest.[43] Certainly public opinion was closely
divided. The National Council of Churches, some (but not all) Maori
leaders and organizations, some Labour Party branches and important
unions, weighed in against the tour. In their view, the exclusion of Maoris
from a national team was a gross act of racial discrimination.

Nash had long been an outspoken critic of apartheid. He had said
publicly that it was a bigger threat to peace than nuclear bombs.[44] In 1958,
after he became Prime Minister, New Zealand voted against apartheid for
the first time at the UN. Now, almost without exception, his official advisers,
including secretaries and top public servants, urged him at least to denounce
the Rugby Union's decision, if he would not (as he said) interfere in it.
The decision to exclude Maoris was being widely reported and condemned
in other countries. Only the recently constituted New Zealand Security
Service, an impeccably right wing source of advice, thought differently.
They advised that but for the Communists the controversy would not have
become so heated—a secret insult to the intelligence and conscience of half
the adult population.[45]

It could be expected that Nash would side with the protesters, but he did
not. Both cabinet and caucus (except for Tirikatene, who made his own
public statement) agreed with Nash and Skinner that the correct policy was
not to intervene in the controversy.[46] Neither political party wished to touch
this hot issue. But Nash eventually went a long way towards supporting the
Rugby Union.

Nash frequently said the chairman of the Rugby Union, a company
director, Mr C. S. Hogg, was a real friend of the Maoris and acting in their
highest interests in excluding them. Hogg was an acquaintance and Nash
kept in close touch with him, reading, for example, a letter to Hogg from
the South African rugby leader, Dr Danie Craven, saying that it would be
better if the Maoris did not come.[47]

In a speech in April 1960 Nash defended the decision of the Rugby Union.
Its leaders were men of integrity; 'it would be an act of the greatest folly
and cruelty to the Maori race to allow their representatives to visit a country
where colour is considered to be a mark of inferiority'. He refused to
interfere in the decision of a sports body.[48] Elsewhere he argued that to
ostracize apartheid would merely accentuate bitterness in South Africa.[49]

It may be—and this is a matter of opinion—that Nash made the right
political decision in not interfering with the Rugby Union's decision. But it
is clear that, although he had personally denounced racism for most of his
life, he did not realize how racism in sport had become an escalating issue
in the world. When the rugby team returned he told Hogg that next time
South Africa must accept Maoris or clearly state in the invitation that it
was restricted to Europeans only, 'so that there will be no repetition of the
unpleasantness over this tour.'[50]

In general, from 1958 to 1960, Nash's mind had been preoccupied with world affairs for much of the time. In the case of the All Black issue, he, and the parliamentary Labour Party, had not given priority to the anticipated adverse effects on New Zealand's international standing of allowing the tour to proceed without Maoris. What domestic political effect that had is debatable. But Labour supporters outnumbered National among the protesters.[51] Many of them must have been disheartened. For them, the image of a Labour government fighting on the side of international morality, which the Prime Minister's tours had repolished, must have seemed tarnished.

XXVI

Prime Minister

1958-60

Many journalists and others tried to write portraits of Nash. One of the most successful brief attempts was by J. C. Beaglehole. He wrote in 1961 that it was necessary, in order to avoid exasperation,

to appreciate Mr Nash philosophically, as a connoisseur is said to appreciate a fine, though imperfect, wine. The tremendous energy, so often spent in running away from reality; the moral fervour and the grand statement, so often carrying an escape clause as appendix; the unwillingness to face the paper that is the daily fuel of administration together with that extraordinary devotion to the detail that is its least important aspect; the refusal to make decisions, or the decisions made so late that they seem extorted and not intended; the general benevolence, and the insistence on the last word and the personal signature; the quite honest hesitations and the ability to envelop a plain question in a cloud of irrelevance and misunderstanding in which there is no possibility at all of an answer: all these characteristics, added to a great deal more, made up a certain quality that had to be respected, even while it could not be entirely approved.[1]

In these comments Beaglehole caught a number of Nash's characteristics very well, although the remark about facing paper was mistaken. He also said that Nash 'is not a simple man'. This might be debated at length. For there were the complexities, the endless qualifying clauses (often with no main clause), the shifts and stratagems, the guile, the use of the blind eye —there was, in short, much of the personal stock-in-trade of the professional politician. Yet the most striking thing about Nash was what underlay these: a great simplicity, of character and beliefs, which lent a unity to the many actions in his long life.

In his memoirs Sir George Mallaby, the British High Commissioner in New Zealand while Nash was Prime Minister, has written a sympathetic portrait which has already been quoted:

For my part I was immediately taken with this man. He had style and quality and immense courage and tenacity. Squat and foursquare he stumped boldly through life, indefatigable, talkative to the point of tedium, but always saved by a touch of humour or a visitation of grace. He was close on eighty when he became Prime Minister, but age meant nothing to him. He was determined to make the most of his great office. He loved the power and influence it brought him and he loved still more the wider personal contacts, the visiting politicians, the politicians overseas—he was an unwearied and inveterate traveller—and his own countrymen, of every party and profession, up and down New Zealand. He missed nothing. The annual dinner of the local rugby team was to him as interesting and exciting as a state banquet for the Queen Mother, and he gave himself equally and tirelessly to both, talking on, reminiscing, holding the floor, while men of half his age prayed in silence for their beds.[2]

Nash had become a machine in almost perpetual motion:

I was bold enough—bold through his confidence and affection—to tell him that he must relax and relent in some directions, that the Bata Shoe Company could survive without his welcome intrusion into their annual dinner, that the social evenings with various societies and clubs in the Lower Hutt would not resent his absence, the great man of New Zealand. He could have spared himself all this, but he would not. It was his strength and his weakness. More and more New Zealanders became aware of the stocky figure with white hair, firm and amiable expression and shabby clothes, who exuded good nature and Christian companionship, who spoke to them, at length, but with obvious friendliness and good humour. Was this King Dick Seddon come to life again? On the other hand, his in-tray became very full. His colleagues and his official advisers waited not very hopefully for his decisions.

The most famous story, at the time, about his too restless energies referred to an occasion when he turned up at the Bata Company's annual ball supposing himself to be at the Poneke Football Club Ball. The company's executives, flattered by his presence, asked him to speak and he regaled the bemused guests with his views on rugby football. Next day the Poneke Club officials expressed surprise since they had not invited him to speak or even to attend their ball. Presumably someone on his staff had blundered. In the House the Opposition asked questions about penalties for gate-crashing private functions, and various cartoonists were inspired to visual witticisms.[3]

Every weekend, at certain times of the year, he must have been poised perilously on the brink of a similar error. He insisted on opening as many clubs as possible, several a day. His friend Mary Mackenzie would drive him from one to the next.

Nash's fault of making himself 'absurdly accessible to every Tom, Dick, and Harry, so that Cabinet Ministers, High Commissioners, Ambassadors, and high officials often had to wait in a queue' was not his own, but that of New Zealand democracy. It was a hereditary burden he loved.

He never declined an invitation to any function if he could possibly attend. So he could be found speaking at the Pets Parade in Newtown Park on 4 October 1959, or presenting the prizes at the National Apple Pie Baking Contest on 31 July, and similar occasions every week. No Russian or Chinese Communist, no American populist politician, has surpassed him in this democratic respect.

He continued to work the extremely long hours that had become habitual, which was very hard on his secretaries. The presence of the most senior public servants would be demanded at all hours of the night. If the Director-General of Education, for instance, recommended a certain decision, Nash would insist that he go personally to find and bring the relevant file. Almost all of his assistants now tell stories illustrating his ruthless use of his subordinates and his self-centredness. When import licensing was to be imposed he rang Mr G. H. Datson of Industries and Commerce, asking him to come in to work during a weekend. Mr Datson said that he was in bed with bad influenza. The Prime Minister said, 'That's all right. I don't think I'll catch it'—and insisted that he come.

Nash used to boast that he needed only four or five hours sleep, but as he grew older he used to cat-nap frequently. Sometimes, if he went to a cocktail party, he would lie down briefly in his office before resuming work. This did not endear him to the officials who had to wait while their master slept. Nevertheless, he arose as fresh as a keen adolescent.

Nash did almost everything with gusto. This included eating his four or five course midday meal. 'It is substantial', he wrote to a correspondent, 'and I usually enjoy it very much'. He also enjoyed both wine and spirits, whenever they were offered to him. He never drank excessively and never drank in bars, which perhaps contributed to his widespread reputation for declining all alcohol. He did nothing to contradict it and in small ways encouraged it in the sense of allowing people to believe it. At parties he would try to get one large glass of some innocuous-looking drink, such as gin and orange, and make it last for an hour or two. At one function, where people were drinking lager, Nash had a large glass full of whisky and water. A very little water. He had a good 'head' for liquor.

Although his intimates and associates were aware that Nash often 'nodded off', he rarely seemed tired out, as most people would have been at his age. Once, during the Hamilton by-election in 1959, Arthur Faulkner, a back-bench Labour MP, was at a meeting when Nash seemed to lose the thread of his argument, to become quite confused and, indeed, to be mispronouncing his words. Mr Faulkner put it down to complete exhaustion. He told Nash he needed a rest. The Prime Minister asked whether it had occurred to him that 'if I put the load down I may not be strong enough to lift it again'.[4]

No one who knew Nash seems to have believed that his long hours of work were really necessary. Had he planned his time differently, delegated more, relied on others more, he could have worked a shorter day. The long hours were essential, not for the work, but for him. Hard, long hours of work were central to his self-regard.

Nash was often criticized, by other politicians and officials, for neglecting his wife. Lot had been suffering severely from arthritis since about 1946, and had had a severe operation. She had, in any case, never much liked official travel, official functions. Now she was left behind. By the mid-nineteen-fifties (Nash wrote to a correspondent), they rarely went out together or entertained guests at home. Nash's critics felt that he stayed at work or went to functions when he could have been with her. He and his wife were, however, as devoted as ever. He was her life, and his life was work.

In 1956 they had celebrated their golden wedding. Hundreds of people were invited to the several receptions, which included parliamentary and Labour Party functions. They received heaps of letters, cards, and telegrams. The Press was generous. Nash's feelings were, as usual, self-centred. He wrote to their old friend in Wanganui, Eva Beard, 'I think the greatest happiness that has come to Lottie in the past month or so is contained within the statement that she made—"Well, they have said it of you before you passed away—I always wondered whether they would have done, and now they have". There is some satisfaction in reading of what you have accomplished throughout the years'.[5]

There was near-unanimous agreement among those who worked with Nash that, though he bore a huge load of work, he did not cope with it very well. Those who knew him best thought him past his best—even if he still dwarfed most of his cabinet colleagues. There were endless, notorious delays in getting decisions. The files—hundreds of them, as in the period 1935-49—were stacked in his office. His critics and assistants called the great pile Walter's 'compost heap'. He now had rationalizations for their presence. He told Philip Holloway that he kept them because if there were a nigger in the woodpile, he would pop his head out if he waited long enough. For instance, if someone was 'up to something' he would get nervous at the delay, and want to revise his submission, report, application, or tender.[6]

He often regarded decisions as things to be deferred to defuse explosive situations. The basic reasons for his collection of paper and slow decisions had not, however, changed. The files were comforting, essential to him; he was a careful man, as a result, perhaps, of unhappy business experiences of trusting others; he wanted to get his decisions right. He was less of a 'gut politician' than Peter Fraser or Sid Holland; he trusted facts rather than instinct. It is debatable, but arguable, that most great politicians have followed their noses more often than logic or what Nash used to call 'research'. But it must be added that Nash still had an extraordinary memory—for facts, an invaluable quality for an administrator, and for people, a marvellous quality for a politician. Very many people testify that when they met Nash for the second time he would say—Oh, I met you at such-and-such a place in Washington in 1944; or on an aircraft in 1938; or, even more flatteringly, at your mother's when you were eight. Thus his obvious vanity was balanced by striking evidence of an interest in people. Nash was a cautious man about whom people usually used cautious praise.

'Summitry' *Above* With
Nehru and Diefenbaker
Left With Krushchev

Right Walter and Lotty

Above Left Nash went to the Antarctic in January 1964; *Below* He did not go to the Antarctic in 1959 (the turnkeys are Nordmeyer and Skinner)

"HANG ON—DID WE LOCK THE WINDOW?"

But he did have some qualities which cannot fairly be described without superlatives.

Nash's surviving ministerial colleagues, interviewed in the early nineteen-seventies, were unanimous that he did not interfere in the administration of their portfolios. But he did, of course, have a say, often the main say, in any important economic, financial, or political decision. Sometimes he took over quite minor decisions too. The files would have to go to his room. There, very often, they would stay. He held up decisions endlessly, to the fury of colleagues, public servants, and the public.

He was not domineering. Bill Fox, the Minister of Housing and Marine, said very shrewdly that Peter Fraser was a disciplinarian, but Nash wanted people to think well of him.[7] He was always courteous and kindly.

In cabinet he did not take votes. He waited, sometimes putting up with interminable, repetitive speeches, until there was a consensus. If necessary he dozed until there was a consensus. But they agreed.[8] He had a cunning obvious from his long, successful political career, yet belied by his mild demeanour.

Another aspect of Walter Nash's regime deserves emphasis. When he became Prime Minister he had to deal with the recently established New Zealand Security Service, under Brigadier H. E. Gilbert. Previously the police had been responsible for preventing subversion and espionage. Nash absolutely loathed the methods used by security men and greatly distrusted their judgement about who was, in fact, a 'security' risk. They appeared to regard only Communists and radicals as potentially disloyal.

In 1960 a Public Service Association deputation complained to Nash about having to fill in forms for security clearances. He replied that security clearance procedures were 'repugnant' to him, too, but he could not have a Communist working in his own office, and it was necessary to investigate any organization likely to 'disintegrate in any way the State or the Government'. He admitted that fifty years ago any socialist, including himself, would have been suspect (though he refrained from mentioning that he had himself been under surveillance). He said that he found the whole subject difficult; they were 'talking to him about something that he had got strange views on but he could not afford to be the head of the state and take risks'.[9]

In practice, though this was not of course publicly known, Nash did on occasions back his own judgement and overrule security police advice. One of these must be regarded as a crucial episode in his life, in any discussion of his soundness of judgement. It concerned the late Dr W. B. Sutch, one of the most controversial and equivocal figures in New Zealand political life, even before his arrest in 1974, when he was unsuccessfully prosecuted for a breach of the Official Secrets Act following clandestine meetings with a Russian agent. Sutch repeatedly aroused the suspicions or hostility of his masters—for instance, he was on the advisory committee of the journal *Tomorrow* which published Lee's attack on Savage.[10] In 1937 he was suspected by British security of leaking Commonwealth defence information to a Communist newspaper. When he was a member of the New Zealand delegation to the UN in the late nineteen-forties there were FBI reports that he had contacts with Communists. After he became Prime Minister, Nash was informed by the Security Service that the National government had blocked Sutch's promotion to the head of the Department of Industries and Commerce because the Americans said that they would regard New Zealand's security as suspect.[11] (The United States communicated secret information to its ANZUS and SEATO ally.) Nash, however, appointed Sutch to be permanent head of the department. He did not discuss with the minister, Holloway, the objections of the Security Service, nor raise the matter at cabinet.[12] Nash knew Sutch very well, and had long experience of his ability, intelligence, and deviousness. It was a courageous decision. Whether it was wise may never be known.

In the anti-Communist atmosphere of Chamberlain's Great Britain or the United States during the 'cold war' any pink radical might seem a red threat. Many people—in New Zealand too—were secretly condemned often without their knowledge, on slender or suspect evidence, perhaps mere tittle-tattle collected by anonymous agents.[13] On the other hand, in Sutch's case, cool and uninvolved enquirers may wonder whether there was not some fire below so much smoke. Nash was quite aware of both these points of view and decided to trust his old adviser. Leading National Party MPs did not conceal that they regarded Sutch as a Communist.[14]

One other example of Nash overruling the security service may be given. A European who had in his youth been associated with Marxists wished to become a naturalized New Zealander. He had lived in New Zealand for many years and had a New Zealand wife and children. The security police would not give him a clearance because, they said, he had not accepted New Zealand ideals. Nash minuted in 1960 that he should be allowed to naturalize. The file lay on his desk without action, however, until the election. A backbench Labour MP, Mr R. J. Tizard, took the file to the Minister of Internal Affairs, W. T. Anderton, who was the only Minister in Wellington during much of the election period, because he was not standing, and he signed the necessary approval.

Dr Sutch played a major part in New Zealand politics during the Nash government. His role was not that of a socialist but of a New Zealand nationalist—one of the most conspicuous, indeed, up to that time. His field was that of economic nationalism.

In the Labour government's policy from 1958 onwards, import licensing, the search for new markets, and industrialization went hand in hand. New industries were to provide import-substitutes. But much more important in the long run, they were to help New Zealand to outgrow its colonial economy. To its most ardent advocates, industrialization was almost a religion. The encouragement of industries had been one of Labour's policies since 1931. The inauguration of new industries by guaranteeing them a large share of the local market had been in the forefront of Nash's thoughts as long ago as 1936-7. The Minister, Philip Holloway, was also a well-informed enthusiast. Nevertheless, the driving force behind this greater emphasis on industries was Dr Sutch.

In 1960 Dr Sutch organized an Industrial Development Conference. The gospel according to Sutch was there preached: 'Manufacturing in depth'. Nash told the conference that New Zealand had been living beyond its means for years. But the solution was not to permit the rise and fall of overseas assets to dictate the rise and fall of New Zealand's standard of living as happened before World War II, when banks cut credit if overseas assets fell. It was necessary to cure the fundamental ill—to make the country less dependent on overseas conditions—to industrialize and to encourage exports. The address 'Building the Future', was written by Sutch and slightly revised by Nash while in Brussels in May 1960.[15] In a new way, it was a return to Labour's cry in 1935, for economic 'insulation'.

Mr P. N. Holloway, the Minister of Industries and Commerce, announced that an industrial development fund had been created for the purchase of capital equipment, a mere £1 million to start with. The government and the Department pursued their goal with great zeal. Secret agreements were signed with overseas companies for the establishment of several major industrial projects. New Zealand was to have its own steel rolling mill, glassworks, gin distillery, oil refinery, an aluminium industry, and a cotton mill.

The last two items produced great political problems. In January 1960 Hugh Watt signed an agreement with Consolidated Zinc Proprietary to set up one of the biggest industries in New Zealand. An aluminium smelter was to be built—in Southland, Nash announced later—to make aluminium out of alumina shipped from Queensland. The government was to sell very cheap power made from a huge hydro-electric project at Lakes Manapouri and Te Anau. Later, many features of this agreement, including the price of electricity used, were much criticized.[16] A senior, able and influential public servant, Mr J. P. Lewin, assistant secretary of Industries and Commerce (who had crossed swords with Nash over the famous satchel-snatch, and won), warned the government at the time that it was giving too much away.[17] Over a decade later this agreement was to produce the biggest protest petition ever. But complaints arose at once over raising the level of the lakes to make electricity. A few hundred people and groups wrote to Nash or Watt protesting against the damage to the scenery which would follow from raising the lake levels.

Although they treated their critics cautiously it would not—indeed could not—have occurred to them that environment would so soon become one of the hottest political issues. When the New Zealand Scenery Preservation

Society sent a deputation to Nash and Watt the latter told them that the so-called Manapouri beaches were not beaches at all but marks left by the rise and fall of the lake! Within a few years such words would have been fighting talk. The agreement signed merely said that the lake was not to be raised so high as to endanger the township of Te Anau. The government was later to inform the company what the maximum levels would be. The agreement provided no protection for the scenery except that the township itself could not be flooded.[18] Nash contented himself with getting assurances from the company that the lake level would not be raised in the early stages. The vice-chairman of Consolidated Zinc wrote to him that the engineering works would be constructed so as to enhance the scenic effects. Watt quoted this assurance in the debate and it was also included in a schedule to the agreement with the company as though it was useful to know that the company was 'conscious of the scenic attractions', as the vice-chairman wrote; as though, indeed, the company was about to add to the beauty of those superb lakes some concrete improvements.[19]

On the day of the debate Nash wrote a note saying that the Opposition wanted both the industry and the scenery. 'What happens when you cannot have both?'[20] He did not live to know the answer. But he did see the end of the other and then greater dispute over New Zealand's cotton industry.

In 1946 a man had called on Nash wanting to set up a £800,000 plant to manufacture cotton piece-goods.[21] Nothing came of this. By the nineteen-fifties the British were losing their market in New Zealand for cotton exports to Japanese and other Asian rivals. The British firm of Smith and Nephew Ltd approached the Department of Industries and Commerce with a proposal to set up a small industry in New Zealand. British textiles made locally and protected against imports might be able to hold the market. The project grew. In early 1960 it was proposed that Smith and Nephew should combine with Joanna Mills of South Carolina to establish a cotton mill in New Zealand.

While discussions were proceeding between the companies and the Department, Nash was to speak at the commencement of construction of the Nelson railway which would join Nelson to the main South Island lines. This proposal had helped Labour to win Nelson. Nash wanted to tell the faithful of their further good fortune—they were to have the cotton mill. The boards of the companies had not yet approved the project. Neither they nor the Department nor the Minister wanted the project announced. But Nash *liked* giving away presents. At the railway ceremony he said that Nelson was to have a £4 million cotton spinning, weaving, and processing mill. Initially it would produce meat wraps, denim, drills, sheetings and the like. Nash said that the railway would facilitate the transport of products of the new textile industry.[22]

Nash had acted without his usual caution. His announcement enabled National critics to say that the whole project was designed to justify the railway, whereas in fact the companies had selected Nelson for commercial reasons. Moreover discussions with the companies were far from complete. Within a month the Joanna Mills' board turned down the project. Smith and Nephew now felt unable to go ahead and pulled out too. Nash was left with a promised mill and an election on his hands. When he was in England at the Prime Ministers' conference in May he called on the directors of Smith and Nephew and asked them to submit a new proposal. This they did and an agreement was signed in New Zealand after talks between the company and the Department which lasted only a few days.[23]

Until 1964 the company was guaranteed 80 per cent of the New Zealand market for its products other than meat wraps, for which it was guaranteed $33\frac{1}{3}$ per cent. And after that date, if the company was observing its undertaking, it was promised 'a reasonable assurance of a New Zealand market' indefinitely.[24]

There was a public outcry. Most newspapers opposed the scheme. It was denounced by the Federated Farmers, the Chambers of Commerce, the Textile and Garment Manufacturers' Federation, the Softgoods Federation. F. P. Walsh, a wealthy dairy farmer as well as president of the Federation of Labour, said it was 'the best racket ever'. He was widely considered an expert on rackets. The Plunket Society feared that napkins would be dearer.

The cotton project was criticized on many grounds. For instance, it hindered the expansion of trade with Asia. To many conservatives and economists the whole concept of a state-guaranteed monopoly was anathema. But probably more important was a feeling that there was something ludicrous about starting a *cotton* industry, based on imported cotton, in New Zealand. There was probably widespread support for the views of J. B. Condliffe, an old friend of Nash and now a professor in the USA, who was visiting New Zealand in 1957. He thought that New Zealand's industrialization should be based on naturally strong industries which could compete on export markets—for instance pulp and paper. Dr Sutch's more expansive views received more publicity but, almost certainly, less support.

This is not to suggest that all the arguments were on one side. After all, England became a great producer of cotton cloths without growing cotton. And Smith and Nephew intended to export from New Zealand to Australia cloths at the time exported from Britain. Thus it was intended to develop an export business. But that aim was not greatly stressed at the time.

It turned out, on closer examination, that the cotton mill agreement had been very carelessly drawn up. For instance, the company promised to try to produce its goods at prices not exceeding those of imports. A dispute later arose about whether this price included duty and at what date it was to be fixed. Nash said that the date for fixing the price was when manufacturing commenced; the company claimed that it was the date of the agreement. Since the price of cotton textiles was falling, as Asian imports supplanted

British, this was of major importance.[25]

The Labour government certainly injected an element of urgency into industrial development. Some 240 new or expanded industrial projects were initiated in the three years 1958-60. Yet the results are doubtful. A study of industrialization by an economist, Professor C. A. Blyth, suggests that industrial development has paralleled population growth, the growth of a local market; has not been much affected by government action or inaction; nor by war nor slumps.[26]

It is also doubtful whether the doctrine of 'manufacturing in depth' had much electoral attraction.[27] It may have appealed more to the few manufacturers rather than the many trade unionists. Despite the government and Sutchian rhetoric, it was a *long-term* plan. Indeed New Zealand experience suggests that industries require a very long time to take root. The first sample of New Zealand steel was made in the mid-nineteenth century. A steel industry based on ironsands was talked of and attempted late in the nineteenth century. It was investigated under the National government in the nineteen-fifties and while Nash was Prime Minister. By the nineteen-seventies it was in operation.[28] A party hoisting the flag of industrialization was not waiting for pie-in-the-sky; but it was certainly pinning its hopes on the sweet by-and-by.

Walter Nash's government neither promised in 1957 nor brought in great reforms equivalent to social security or guaranteed prices. Nevertheless, it did pass important measures in addition to its industrial legislation. For example it introduced equal pay for equal work regardless of sex, in the public service. That principle had been part of the policy of the Independent Political Labour League in 1905, and from time to time since. It had become a big public issue in the mid-nineteen-fifties when an Equal Pay Council was formed. In parliament Nash and the other Labour members pressed for the introduction of equal pay in the public service. The principle was included in Labour's election policy in 1957. The Public Service Association fought hard for equality of opportunity for both sexes and was strongly opposed by the Public Service Commission which advanced various arguments against reform, including the view that men's wages included a 'social' element for their families' upkeep. It also objected to paying women more than the 'market rate' for female labour. And it was argued that equal pay would be inflationary.

Nash rejected these views but was unwilling to take positive action during the economic crisis of 1958. He adopted delaying tactics which angered the equal pay advocates. There were several tough discussions during deputations from the Council for Equal Pay and Opportunity to Nash. The Council wanted New Zealand to ratify a 1958 ILO convention opposing discrimination in employment on the basis of sex, race, or politics. Nash told them that New Zealand could not adopt it immediately because there was discrimination which could not at once be ended.[29] In the vote at the ILO conference the New Zealand government delegate abstained.

Nash introduced the Government Service Equal Pay Bill at the end of the 1960 session. He recalled how fifty years ago (in Modern Tailors) he had found women doing for £2 what men received £4 10s. a week for. (At that time, the union had been demanding equal pay.) He affirmed his belief that men were not superior—indeed, he thought the expression 'the better half' was more correct. Equal pay was to be introduced in the public service, in three stages, by 1964.[30]

In the final term of the 1960 session Nordmeyer introduced a short Reserve Bank of New Zealand Amendment Bill affirming that it was the sovereign right of the Crown to control currency and credit.[31] This measure was less of a genuine reform than a ritualistic propitiatory gesture to Labour's credit reform past and credit reform supporters.

In 1960 the government repealed the potentially oppressive clauses of the Police Offences Act which National had passed after the 1951 wharf strike. Some of the debate grew very bitter. J. K. McAlpine, a former National Minister, brought up Nash's conviction for bringing seditious literature into New Zealand. He also misquoted a statement Nash had made in 1951 and said that Nash had been to a conference in Geneva called 'The Second Communist International'. Nash was angry at this apparently intentional error and explained that the Second International was completely anti-Communist.[32]

These two connected episodes, the conferences and the prosecution, had followed Nash throughout his political career. At almost every election leaflets had been distributed in his electorate giving the details. Judging from his huge majorities they failed to convince the voters that he was a dangerous 'red', and did him no harm.

A political scientist has commented that to the Labour leaders the 1958 budget was 'a matter of morality'. To reverse the policies of that year before the imbalances of the economy had been corrected would be to cast doubt on the government's original assessment of the problem.[33] But the terms of trade had begun to improve almost from the time of that budget. It seems, in the light of after-knowledge, that the government had over-reacted in 1958—had guessed wrong. But the economic improvement did not seem to Mr Nordmeyer to justify much generosity in his 1959 budget. He did, however, reduce income tax, by two stages, to about the 1957 level. By early 1960 retail turnover was at a record level; the country was enjoying near-boom conditions. The Minister of Customs, Ray Boord, eased up on import controls. In the 1960 budget Nordmeyer gave some hand-outs to the voters, but he was not open-handed. Pensions and benefits were raised; so were state employees' salaries; duties on petrol and cigarettes and sales tax on motor vehicles were somewhat reduced. Taxes on beer, petrol, and cigarettes were reduced again at the end of the year, just before the election.

It would seem in retrospect that Labour had a very good story to tell. They could claim that the country had weathered a severe economic storm, under their prudent management. Taxes had now been reduced to a pre-1958 level, while substantial improvements had been made in social security benefits. In foreign affairs, in industrialization, the government had much to be proud of. They had a good story, but they failed to tell it and make it heard. For that failure several reasons may be suggested. One is that the piecemeal reduction in taxes and duties, 'the sheer complexity of the four changes in tax tables over three years', confused the electors and concealed the real position from them.[34]

Nash's frequent absences had hindered and were hindering decisions. Some policy decisions had to be postponed well into October when he went off to the UN with the result that some policies were still being worked out during the election. This delayed the preparation of attractive pamphlets.[35] His absences had also necessitated the neglect of some aspects of his administration. He had failed to make any mark, for instance, as Minister of Maori Affairs. There was a great deal of criticism of him in this role, and much dissatisfaction among Maoris. The Maori Policy Committee of the Labour Party pressed on him that Maoris should be Secretary and Minister for Maori Affairs. Nash minuted: 'Tirikatene represents them'.[36] But he kept E. T. Tirikatene as Minister of Forests and merely 'Associate to Minister of Maori Affairs'.

Tirikatene was an engaging man, but full of tricks. It was not always clear to his colleagues what his motives or aims were in any particular matter. Nash was nervous about what he might do. He may also have had reservations about his ability. He probably also felt that a Maori appointed as Minister of Maori Affairs might favour his own tribe, of which Ngata had been accused, in a well-remembered scandal. In any case, following Fraser's example, Nash believed that the best way to keep Maori loyalty was to lend the mana of the Prime Minister to the portfolio.

Nash asked one of the Public Service Commissioners, Mr J. K. Hunn, to act as Secretary for Maori Affairs and 'get an accounting of Maori assets and see what we can do with them'. Mr Hunn believed that the Prime Minister had in mind the fragmentation of Maori land titles, but he chose to interpret 'assets' to mean human as well as physical assets. The result was the famous and contentious 'Hunn report' on the problems and future of the Maoris, which he completed in August 1960. Nash made a single remark to him about it—he would not have time to study it until after the election. The outcome was that it was disinterred early in 1961 and became the basis of National's policy, to the fury of Labour. Similarly a caucus committee on Maori affairs was set up but never met. Nash opted out of chairing the monthly meetings of the Board of Maori Affairs, but left the duty not to his Associate Minister but to the Acting Secretary.[37]

Nash often spoke on Maori marae, almost invariably repeating that there were no inferior or superior races. But, in a real situation of inter-racial contact, this endlessly repeated principle led to no spontaneous empathy, identification. He had contacts with and contributed to many sides of New Zealand life, but he did little in Maori affairs. Peter Fraser had felt a personal commitment to the Maoris and had been a most successful minister. Somehow Maori culture failed to excite Nash's imagination. But some failure at a personal level did not mean that Nash's profession of faith in equality was insincere.

Within the party at large it was felt that the parliamentary Labour Party was out of touch with its traditional supporters.[38] This view was shared by some of the MPs, who blamed Nash's leadership. At a caucus meeting on 16 December 1959 there was some very frank discussion. Nash made some notes on the views of two backbenchers:

'*Tizard* . . . Feeling against Government. . . . Party has drifted away from Workers. W.N. main [person] responsible. . . .'

'*Deas* Lost confidence of Workers. . . . Mr Nash more interested in things overseas than in N.Z.'[39]

Within the Labour Party, from the branches up to cabinet, there was a general malaise. Philip Holloway wrote to Nash early in 1960 to say that he would not be standing again for personal reasons. He remarked that he thought the party organization was pathetically weak and that the future of the party and of the government was 'not bright until there is a re-assessment of our policy and objectives, and also a re-vitalizing of our organisation'. He lamented the fact that party meetings no longer had 'the atmosphere almost of a crusade'.[40] In June Nash was re-elected leader by caucus; they would not drop him in an election year; but there was widespread dissatisfaction with his leadership.

The 1960 election was the subject of a very thorough study by three political scientists.[41] They concluded that in most respects National Party preparations for the election, organization, and publicity were much better. The differences between the parties lay more in organization than in policy. The difference between them, measured from left to right, was slight. In comparison with the vigorous Labour Party of 1935-8 or National in 1949-51, both parties looked tired.

Labour's main policy was industrialization. This was what Nash most stressed. And he constantly repeated one theme: 'You've never been so well-off in New Zealand as you are today. You wouldn't have been so well-off if we had not taken the measures we did in 1958'.[42] One of the Labour pamphlets had a message from the Prime Minister: 'everyone is better off. When these plans are implemented, everyone will be better off still'. 'Labour's policy ensures that everyone, everywhere, will again be better off', the pamphlet was entitled. It was close to Harold Macmillan's winning slogan in 1959, 'You've never had it so good'.

At his early meetings it was remarked—a rare occurrence—that Nash appeared tired, but by the third week of the campaign he seemed to have recovered, and to be his old self. 'Forgive me for using some millions, but it wouldn't be me if I didn't use some millions',[43] he joked at one meeting.

'The parties busied themselves with the history of a bungle. They differed only as to what the bungle was, 1957-8 crisis, or 1958 Budget.'[44] Keith Holyoake tried to argue that overseas funds had not fallen as much as Nash said in 1957, and that Labour had produced a panic budget. Moreover, the over-importing was due to a fear of import controls if Labour should win. Walter Nash continued to stress that National had produced the worst economic crisis since the depression and that Labour had saved the ship. Just before and during the election there was another severe drop in overseas funds, but neither leader said much about it.[45]

The shadow of the 'black budget' dominated the election. There was a drop in the vote for the government of 5.87 per cent. Labour won 43 per cent of the votes; National won 48 per cent. Labour lost seven seats. National now had forty-six seats to Labour's thirty-four. Labour's biggest gain was in Nelson, where the vote rose by 2.76 per cent. Apparently the cotton mill had pleased some people.

What was most significant about the voting was that while Labour's vote fell by 5.87 per cent, National's rose by only 1.64 per cent. Former Labour voters had not voted National or Social Credit: they had stayed home in droves and not gone to the polling booths.[46]

Nash had achieved his life's ambition, but he had not managed to hold on to it. He took defeat philosophically. Mallaby wrote expressing his sympathy and Nash replied that the result was not unexpected. The younger voters had never known anything but prosperity, he wrote, and might have resented the level of taxation. He also thought—as did F. P. Walsh—that the Roman Catholics had turned against Labour. Some leading Catholics urged their co-religionists to throw Labour out because it did not give full support to state aid for private schools. (It seems doubtful whether this was a significant factor.)[47] As for himself, he added, 'No, there was some disappointment; there was nothing great'.[48]

XXVII

The Grand Old Man

1960-8

Walter Nash was an MP to the end of his life, but power had gone. The long reign of Sir Keith Holyoake had begun and Nash did not live to see it end. The National government rapidly altered or reversed some of Labour's policies. In 1961 there was mounting public criticism of the Nelson cotton mill. Within the National Party caucus some backbenchers, including Mr R. D. Muldoon, an assertive and loquacious new MP, attacked the decision of cabinet to honour Labour's agreement.

Eventually, when the factory buildings were nearly complete, the government cancelled the contract and paid £1.4 million compensation. In this rough game Labour's opposition was weak, ineffectual, indeed almost irrelevant. Nash found himself in a position, very different from those he had adopted a generation earlier, of defending overseas borrowing for development: 'we cannot develop this country as it should be developed in this decade or generation out of our own savings or out of our own capital in general. Overseas investment is imperative. . . .' The attack on the cotton mill would, he claimed, deter overseas investors.[1]

During the major parliamentary battle of 1961 Nash was in a position much less comfortable, though assumed with apparent ease. The government decided that New Zealand should become a member of the International Monetary Fund and the World Bank. This stirred up all sorts of slumbering prejudices.

Nash's personal feelings were still favourable to the IMF. In 1958 his old friend A. G. B. Fisher, now a high IMF official, had written saying that now only the Soviet Bloc, Portugal, Switzerland, Liberia, and New Zealand remained non-members. He thought New Zealand's opposition arose from fear of sinister American financial powers. Nash wrote back agreeing that the opposition was emotional. He thought the time would come when the advantages would be seen to outweigh the disadvantages.[2] But the Labour caucus voted against joining and Nash found himself leading the serried ranks of anti-American leftists, anti-American funny-money men, Social Creditites and economic troglodytes in general. He received large numbers of letters opposing the IMF and supporting his opposition. Fifty-eight thousand people signed petitions to parliament, organized by the Labour Party, opposing joining.[3] Many people regarded joining the IMF as an abrogation of sovereignty and submission to 'alien control'.[4] (The 'gnomes of Zurich' had apparently been replaced by Martians or Venusians.) Nash denounced the government for not submitting the issue to the people during the election and demanded that a referendum should be held. In the House he explained his position by saying that the Opposition were unanimous in opposing every clause of the Bill. They agreed with the principles originally set out as the objectives of the IMF, but disagreed ('some of us differ more than others') with the later interpretation and effect of the Fund. He said that the directors of the Fund considered that 'full employment' might involve some unemployment. Labour wanted *no* unemployment at all. He stressed this point repeatedly; arguing his case with a great fund of knowledge and by experience not matched by anyone in the House.[5] To the accusation of inconsistency, he had a ready answer. He said that when he —and the government—wanted to ratify Bretton Woods in 1945-6 the Opposition 'destroyed the possibility' when S. G. Holland announced that every National MP would vote against it.[6] This was a simplification of the events of that time which even he did not believe.

In his speech on the IMF on 15 August Nash was on his top form. The Speaker, R. M. Algie, found him hard to stop or to control.[7] This debate was very heated and prolonged. The Opposition fought hard. On 11 August they argued until just on 5 a.m. The government members constantly praised Nash for his role at Bretton Woods. On 11 August W. A. Sheat, the Member for Egmont, moved a facetious amendment that a list of the delegates at Bretton Woods conference and a copy of Nash's letter of commendation to Harry Dexter White approving of the Fund, and a copy of Nash's statement after the conference should be added as a schedule to the Bill. There was a great deal of shouting, banging (of desks and a tin) and disorder in the House. Tom Shand and possibly Keith Holyoake, it was claimed later, had helped to draft the amendment. Nash was very hurt and indignantly defended his honour: he had believed every word he wrote to White. 'I believe I act up to my integrity always', he said. 'I may have made mistakes and I know I have many faults but I have always tried to do what I thought was right'. The Labour men voted for the amendment and the National men, including Sheat, against. The episode was very generally interpreted in the Press not as a malicious joke that misfired but as an unwarranted personal attack. Nash's changing public image was revealed by press statements that he should not be subject to such indignities. He received many letters of sympathy.[8]

Nash was mellowing in ripe old age—indeed his left wing critics thought that this softening had been going on for a quarter of a century. In foreign policy debates he sounded above the heat of battle and was praised, for instance by J. R. Marshall, the Deputy Prime Minister, for his statesmanlike remarks, placing country before party politics[9]—not the kind of acclaim that would be welcomed by the rising politician. The National government supported United States policies in South-east Asia, much less critically and more supinely that Labour had. In 1962 there was a crisis in Thailand. Communists were infiltrating in the northeast from Laos. The Americans, determined not to be thwarted by allies again, published the joint Thanat-Rusk communique in March that intervention under SEATO could be unilateral. The New Zealand government, however, joined the USA, the UK, and Australia in sending aid. A Special Air Service Squadron was sent from New Zealand. It was soon withdrawn. Nash made no protest and confined himself to a statement of New Zealand's position, that it was committed to preventing aggression from outside Thailand. The Laotian conflict, he said, should be left to the international commission of Poland, India, and Canada to solve. When the secretary of the Westland LRC wrote saying that parliament should have been called before troops were sent, and linking the government's policy with a visit by Dean Rusk, Nash replied that he doubted the connection and pointed out that the Thais had asked for assistance.[10] It should be added that Nash was not alone in accepting government policy. In the country at large there was very little protest. Nash likewise supported the government decision in 1963 to send a small non-combatant advisory force to Vietnam, while adding that he knew of no real evidence of 'aggression from outside'.[11] He sounded milder. But if his opponents thought that the sweeter, more soothing Nash was to become permanent, they were to be surprised.

On 15 December 1961 Mrs Nash died, after many years of suffering. Few people could be more generally liked and loved. Her warm, homely, selfless life, her good humour and good cheer, were acknowledged by all who met her. So too was her role as the devoted wife and mother, supporting her husband through all troubles. The press obituaries were appropriately generous.[12] Possibly her death helps to explain Nash's relatively weak opposition to the government, for instance, over Thailand in 1962.

Lord Sanderson, a British shipping and business magnate, who had become very friendly with Nash since they met at the end of the war, wrote that he was shocked to hear of Lot's death and offered a sea voyage for Nash. In May, Hugh Gaitskell wrote that he would like Nash, Arthur Calwell, and other Labour leaders to come to London for discussions on Britain's entry into the EEC and for a socialist conference.[13] Then Holyoake asked Nash to come to London during the forthcoming Commonwealth Prime Ministers' Conference, when the EEC would be discussed, so that New Zealand would be as united as possible.

Nash flew to London and spent September there. On 6 and 7 September Labour leaders representing eight countries, including some colonies, met in Gaitskell's rooms. They discussed the EEC's agricultural policies. The British Labour Party was now very sceptical about the EEC and Gaitskell had called his own Commonwealth conference to underline its difference with the government. It published a communiqué, from the conference not the British Labour Party, 'that great damage would be done to many Commonwealth countries if Britain joined'. According to George Brown, Nash's influence on Gaitskell had been considerable and had made things more difficult for those Labour men who favoured entry.[14]

On the afternoon of 7 September and next day Nash attended a meeting of the Socialist International in Transport House. There were the representatives of the European members of the International—Danes, Finns, Austrians, and representatives of Commonwealth Labour and socialist parties, including Lee Kuan Yew. The Commonwealth representatives were told why European socialists supported the EEC. It was a very far cry from the Second Socialist International in Geneva. Then they wanted to reform the world: now they issued a statement about safeguarding the Commonwealth countries' economies when Britain entered the EEC.[15]

Before Nash went to England a joint meeting of the New Zealand Labour Party and Federation of Labour executives had decided that, on evidence then available, the UK should stay with the Commonwealth, so Nash's views had been forthright, and very close to those of the government. While in England, Nash had three talks with Macmillan, their discussions, the latter wrote, 'ranging from butter to utopia'. He had been briefed by the government before these talks. On his return Holyoake thanked him, in the House, for his cooperation.[16] On this issue it was reasonable for the parties to agree in substance; but at the same time it helped to build up for Nash a public image of being above the party fray.

Nash took the opportunity in England of seeing Dick Campbell, the Freybergs, the Mallabys, Churchill, Nehru, Heath; he had audiences with the Queen and the Queen Mother.[17] Much more important, he saw his sister Emily, a devoted admirer and correspondent ever since 1909. It was decided that she should migrate to New Zealand and live with and look after him. Lord Sanderson arranged a half-price fare in the *Gothic*. When the ship reached Wellington, Nash met it by launch, climbing up a suspended ladder to meet her! 'Knowing Walter, I wasn't a bit surprised to see him', smiled Miss Nash, 'Not even at 6 a.m.', so a journalist reported.[18]

Emily Nash, who was born in 1893 and died in 1975, was a delightful person, with an extremely pleasant voice and presence. She looked after her brother with a devotion comparable with his wife's. Anyone who met her felt at once that their family must have had a remarkable mother and upbringing. Emily perfectly sustained the impression he made himself, of down-to-earth, very respectable, slightly puritanical soundness and reliability.

After the 1960 election, there was serious talk in the party, for the first time since 1954, of changing the leader. The President of the party, Dr A. M. Finlay, a lawyer and formerly an MP, was highly critical of the lack of drive in the party. He felt that Labour should take the offensive over industrialization, not sit about and answer criticisms as National made them.

In October 1961 he gave notice of motion to the national executive that the Parliamentary Labour Party should be asked to consider the leadership.[19]

In February 1962 Nash addressed the national executive and Dr Finlay withdrew his notice of motion.[20] Nash simply repeated what he had said at a dinner put on by the national executive, caucus, and the Hutt Labour Representation Committee for his eightieth birthday on 12 February—that it was his intention to resign before the end of the year, unless caucus specifically requested otherwise. Thus his successor would have a year before the next election.[21]

Such had been Nash's intention in late 1961, and known to Jerry Skinner, Nordmeyer, and Fred Hackett, but various circumstances, as usual, provided reasons for delay. Lot's death led him to think of hanging on longer. Then Skinner died in April 1962, which complicated the situation. Many MPs, and party members did not think that the party could win the next election under Nordmeyer, now Nash's obvious successor, but handicapped by the 'black budget' on his back.

Nash wrote and discussed his thoughts with Ray Boord, who had been beaten in the 1960 election. He agreed with Boord that if he kept on as leader, as some of his supporters urged, it would be 'Anti-Nordy'. But since so many people thought Nordmeyer could not yet lead Labour to victory, Nash wondered if he would be willing to postpone his ambition to lead until 1964 or 1965, if a majority of caucus preferred Nash. Of the other possible leaders Boord thought that Watt and Norman Kirk might need to wait a few years. Boord inclined to favour Fred Hackett, a party hack, though well-liked, who had been a trade union official and a cabinet minister in the years 1946 to 1949 as well as in 1957-60.

Nash admitted to Boord that his hearing and memory had deteriorated. But he still partly inclined to hang on. He wrote, thinking aloud on paper: 'Can Walter Nash win in 1963 if majority of P.L.P. want him. Can A.H.N. win the election in 1963 if a majority of the P.L.P. want him. If he can then that should be the decision.'[22]

He added, 'Can Fred Hackett win in 1963 if the P.L.P. select him', but crossed this out. Thus he dithered, but tried to be fair.

In June caucus elected a deputy leader. Hugh Watt was eliminated on the first ballot and then Hackett beat Nordmeyer on the second. Some of Hackett's support may have been a sympathy vote, for he was known to be ill—he died early in 1963—but there was also an active anti-Nordmeyer group, including Moohan and Fox. They constantly expressed the view that Nordmeyer could never be a leader and, when occasion arose, reminded their colleagues that Nordmeyer used to be a John A. Leeite. This group was strongly trade unionist.[23] (It was three years later to line up in favour of Norman Kirk against Nordmeyer.)

After the election of Hackett, Nash told caucus that he would resign at the end of the year unless caucus requested otherwise. But Dr Finlay

continued to be extremely dissatisfied with the condition of the party. In
June he complained to Nash that the Policy Committee, of which they were
both members, and which met in Nash's office, did almost nothing except
to defer discussions.[24]

In December, when Nash had still made no move to resign that year,
Dr Finlay addressed a statement to the members of caucus, including Nash.
He wrote:

I am convinced I would be failing in my duty to the members of the Party
as President if I did not express the deeply held conviction that the time has
come for a change in the leadership of the Parliamentary Party. I say this with
sorrow as I would be the first of all of us to acknowledge the tremendous and
self-sacrificing services made to the Party by the Right Hon. Walter Nash, and
to acknowledge that those actions have built for him a monument that will be
treasured forever in our hearts. I am, however, saddened by the thought that
continuation in this present office is likely to tarnish that monument, and for
his sake and the sake of the Party I am deeply concerned about this possibility.

This statement must necessarily be construed as an attack, and it would be
unseemly and undignified if an attack made, as it were at second-hand, were
pressed too far. I content myself, therefore, with confessing to the feeling I have
had for some months, which becomes stronger day by day, that there is at
present a vacuum in the leadership of the Party. A Policy Committee was set
up at the last Conference and it has held a number of meetings in the interven-
ing period. In my view it has achieved precisely nothing, and I have publicly
expressed sympathy with the view of those members of National Executive who
have at least hinted that they would prefer to withdraw from it rather than
waste further time. As a member of that committee I must accept some of the
responsibility for this, but I believe the chief responsibility rests with its
chairman, the leader of the Party. After two years of deliberation, and within
one year of the next election, what passes for policy is nothing but a restatement
of principles we have already adhered to in the past. No attempt has been made
to grapple with the very evident problems that are facing us, and in my opinion
we are, as a Party, totally unfitted to govern at the present time; in fact, if we
did become the government I feel it would be a fraud on the people, and the
melancholy prospect is that I can see, under the present regime, no likelihood
of a change in this.

I must say frankly and bluntly that I see no prospect of the Party securing
the confidence of the electors under the leadership of Mr Nash, and if by some
chance this were to occur I see less prospect of virile and effective government
thereafter. The challenge that faces us, whatever its form may be, demands
administration of this kind, and if we are to be honest with the electors we
must offer them not only a promise but the likelihood of its being carried out.

If we are to be honest, too, we must admit that the record of our last
administration is not a distinguished or a reassuring one. The non-publication
of the Hunn Report, the hesitancy and indecision about licensing legislation,
the manner in which certain new industries were set up are all regrettable, and,
unhappily, typical. The spirited way in which rank-and-file members of caucus
have supported and defended decisions of which, I understand, they were not
aware and which many of them had they been informed, would have challenged,
speaks volumes for their integrity and responsibility.

As a member of the National Executive and not of caucus I can offer no

At a wine festival

Right With Sir Bernard Fergusson,
after Nash was invested with the
GCMG in 1965

Below The last call at Parliament,
May 1968

suggestion as to a likely successor, and have no intention of doing so. I am satisfied, however, that *any* change would be better than no change, and in saying this I sincerely believe I express the view of the Party membership as a whole. With no change we will continue to drift, temporise, and compromise. A change, whatever be its character, would at least provide new blood, and I hope new drive, and new appreciation of the reality of the problems that face us in 1963. . . .[25]

The letter itself and the manner of its presentation caused a great deal of criticism of Dr Finlay. Instead of attending caucus and presenting it him-self, he went off to Auckland, apparently to appear in court, and left it to Mr J. Collins, a trade union member of the executive, to read to caucus on 6 December.

Nash told caucus that he would resign at a caucus meeting in February and would not be a candidate for re-election. Hackett then said that he would not stand either. Collins then read Finlay's letter. After much discussion caucus resolved unanimously 'that the letter be not received, and that Dr. Finlay be requested to attend a later caucus'. At the next caucus, on 26 February 1963, A. H. Nordmeyer was the only nomination for leader. Nash congratulated him and promised his loyal support.[26]

Nash was one of the few important New Zealand leaders who lived a long time after losing power. He became—and was often called in the press—the 'elder Statesman', 'grand old man' of New Zealand politics; a 'father figure'. His status, his *mana*, was probably greater after 1960 than ever before. Carpenters would call out to him, from their jobs, 'Hullo Walter'. A very wide range of people, whether Labour or not, felt an affectionate regard.[27] In his last years he achieved a little of Micky Savage's prestige. At meetings people still tried to touch him.

Honours were given in good measure. In 1963 Victoria University of Wellington awarded him an honorary Doctorate of Laws to add to British and American degrees. He had been a Privy Councillor since 1946 and been made a Companion of Honour in 1959. In 1965 he was created Knight Grand Cross of St Michael and St George (an order which, incidentally, Sir George Grey had denounced as created to keep colonials out of the great orders of knighthood).

He received over 1,000 congratulatory letters (and one against). Of the many felicitous messages perhaps the best was from J. C. Beaglehole who said he would not congratulate Nash but St George, on acquiring a great dragon-slayer. Nash told one friend that it took him two years to decide whether he could accept a knighthood in conformity with the principles of the Labour Party. He discussed it first with Nordmeyer and the executive. In the end he loved being Sir Walter. He twice, however, declined sugges-tions that he accept a life peerage in the House of Lords.[28]

One of Nash's secretaries said of him when he was Prime Minister that he should have been Governor-General. There was much insight in this remark; he did now have an air of being non-partisan. A lady wrote to him in 1963 suggesting that he should be the next Governor. He replied that he had no notion of doing so.[29]

Nash got on extremely well with the Governors-General, especially Sir Bernard Fergusson and Sir Bernard Freyberg, with whom he was very friendly. He liked them and respected their position. When he died Fergusson wrote a tribute in *The Times* which referred to Nash's 'passionate loyalty to the Royal Family'.[30] Certainly he loved meeting royalty, and never had a republican, a 'disloyal' thought, in his life.

More generally Nash derived much of his sense of significance, his self-importance, from knowing the great, especially those engaged in great causes. In Nash's sitting room he had a collection of mementos, treasured things given to him—a Kidderminster carpet, a silver Indian water carrier presented by Nehru, a wooden carving from Sukarno. On the wall was his picture gallery, photographs of those he most admired, some of them autographed and with a personal message, for instance, 'For Walter Nash from his old friend Franklin D. Roosevelt'. The photographs included General Freyberg, Harry Hopkins, and Albert Schweitzer. There was a photograph of the Attlees, of Nash with Hugh Gaitskell. There was one of the Queen and the Duke with the New Zealand members of the Privy Council in 1954—Nash, S. G. Holland, K. J. Holyoake, and W. J. Jordan. There was a photograph of the Prime Ministers and other leaders at the 1946 Commonwealth conference.

In 1921 Nash replied to a letter from his brother Will: 'The greatest danger for any one who aspires to help alter things is that he should fall a victim to the idea of his own importance and this danger is accentuated by praise from his friends so DONT RUB IT IN TOO MUCH.'[31] Nash did not always keep this advice in mind. His closest associates were almost unanimous that vanity was his greatest weakness. His worst enemies, like F. P. Walsh, used to say that he thought he was Jesus Christ. And he did once write to a man, who had congratulated him on his birthday, thanking him for his good wishes on 'my attaining the seventy-fourth anniversary of my nativity'.[32]

In the mid-nineteen-sixties he once said that J. C. Beaglehole was New Zealand's greatest historian; that Beaglehole had written in 1930 or so, 'watch Nash, the coming man'. In fact Beaglehole had written in his *New Zealand, A Short History*, in 1936, that Nash (now the Minister of Finance) was 'the party's most persuasive intellectual force'. Dr Beaglehole had no recollection of writing elsewhere about Nash at that time.[33] Nash gave him a CMG.

Nash was sensitive to petty slights. In 1959, while he was Prime Minister, a Victoria University capping magazine showed Nash speaking frenetically, his long upper lip growing longer, and then dashing to the men's toilet. The caption was a childish 'lavatory' joke. He rang the Chancellor and told him that it was 'completely undesirable and harmful'.[34] No more than in his youth could one imagine him telling a dirty joke.

Some people were very critical of Nash's personality. After his death a Wellington journalist wrote that he had been 'imperious, demanding and vain'.[35] But this Nash, the selfish Nash, was known only to his family, assistants, and colleagues.

Many of Nash's habits came to have the repetitive, compulsive qualities of rituals. One of these was the famous Nash Christmas cards. Every year, starting in the nineteen-thirties or nineteen-forties, Mr and Mrs Nash sent out large numbers of personally designed Christmas cards. In his later life he devoted much thought and time to these. Usually there was a photograph of New Zealand scenery. Always there were one or more inspiring messages which he had chosen, and which grew more numerous and longer as he grew older. Quotations from hymns, Rupert Brooke, Tennyson, Kipling, James Russell Lowell, Einstein, Harry Holland and many others were called on.

In his last years Nash began to write some of the texts himself, in the form of comments on the pictures. One year, alongside a picture of Mt Sefton, he wrote:

THE MOUNTAIN
Grim Rocks—never changing, never yielding . . .
The Snow comes for a season . . .
Then the tumbling Streams—
To awaken the Land . . . and bring Power
For Town and Farm . . . for Work and Light . . .
The lure of the Mountain . . . Snow and Birch . . .
Ever inspiring the Climber, and the Thinker
To Achievement.
Man has climbed the highest Mountain—
Can he not attain the serene summit of Peace?

On another card, featuring the Matukituki Valley, he wrote:

The Peace of the Valley
With its flowing streams
And fertile land
Under protective
Snow-clad Mountains
Greets the young Climbers,
Encouraging them
In the effort
To reach Higher Points
Where the Vision
Of a developing world
Brings nearer
The potential day

> When Truth and Equity,
> Justice and Mercy
> Shall govern
> The mutual dealings
> Of men and of nations.
>   W.N.

In case anyone paid inadequate attention, on several of these cards Nash put on the cover: 'Reading of full text would be appreciated—W.N.'; or, 'The reward of courtesy is realised when you study the illustration and read the text in full. W.N.' Lot would have had the sense to stop this.

Once Nash put his favourite photograph of himself talking to the Governor-General, Sir Bernard Fergusson, after the investiture, inside his Christmas card. It won a prize for the photographer for the best news picture of 1965.

Nash never did things by halves. He sent out many hundreds of these cards annually. In 1957, for instance, he ordered 1,600 to be printed. By the nineteen-sixties he was ordering 3,000. In 1962 he posted 1,991 cards. They went to constituents, acquaintances, friends . . . and to the royal family. According to a journalist the Queen Mother told a visitor that she had kept the card picturing the two knights 'because it contained such a happy photo'.[36]

Various views were held of Nash's Christmas cards. Some people treasured and collected them, moved by his thoughtfulness in remembering them, or by the messages. Others thought them sentimental. F. P. Walsh was moved to exclaim, 'If you have any doubts about him being Christ, have a look at the Christmas card he is sending out. . . .'[37]

Nash's 'verses' (as they were called in a press report) were apparently his only venture into literature. He did not regard them lightly. When he was writing one Christmas card Mary Mackenzie gathered up his notes and drafts when he had finished, to put them in the rubbish basket. He remonstrated: people might want to know by what stages he had reached the final version! With such additions, his collection of papers grew at a rapid pace.

In his old age Nash thought about religion more than he had for years. He had not ceased to go to church regularly, usually at St James's, in the Lower Hutt. One of his secretaries in the nineteen-fifties, Mr Bruce Brown, recalls that Nash's first action when they were to spend a night or so in a new town was to ring the local Anglican Church to learn the time of the first communion, which he would attend if at all possible. He told Mr Brown that it always made him 'feel better'.

The activist side of Christianity still strongly appealed. He wrote characteristic little notes to himself:

> 'A Christian does not merely record history—he makes it.'
> 'Don't be satisfied with reading the lesson—carry it out.'

And most memorably and fittingly:

> God give me work
> Till my life shall end
> And life
> Till my work is done.[38]

In the talks, lay sermons, which he sometimes gave in church he always stressed universal Christian love: love must not be exclusive but must extend to all men, to the universe.[39] In a letter to Mr Robert Ahearn, son of his old friend, he wrote of love:

Love—without making any special effort to define it—is the feeling for the other people, their benefit, their advantage, and their constructive integrity, and preferring their benefits which they can obtain to any benefit which may come to ourselves. When this is achieved, the benefit that comes to the person putting out the love is invaluable and indescribable; but it does not come if they are expecting it. It is part of the results of the work that they do.[40]

Nash's pastor in his old age was Archdeacon W. A. Scott, Minister of St James's Church, Lower Hutt. He says that Nash went to church twice every Sunday. He was there at 8 a.m. the morning after he was elected Prime Minister, in 1957. He was always the last to leave, after a word with the minister, expressing appreciation of the sermon, for instance.

All of Nash's helpers noticed that he could not resist revising any draft manuscript placed before him, a characteristic which was almost without limits. Jim O'Brien, the Minister of Transport, once said to him, 'Walter, you'd alter the Lord's prayer'. And he did, indeed, once revise holy scripture. In church he always read the lesson, if requested. On one occasion, when reading 1 Corinthians 13, each time the word 'charity' appeared he wrote in, and read, 'love' (as in the 1885 Revised Authorized Version). Mr Scott says that Nash was the only man he knew who would revise the bible.[41]

Like many people, Archdeacon Scott believes that Nash was a licensed lay reader. It is very unlikely that he was, for he would not subscribe to all of the Thirty Nine Articles. In reciting the Apostles' Creed he would leave out the word 'only' in front of 'Son'. Probably the idea that he was a lay reader was another of the Nash legends, one which he did not discourage.

In his old age Nash continued to read a great deal. He always enjoyed short stories. Asked to name the three books by Commonwealth authors he most enjoyed reading in 1965-6 he placed first Frank Sargeson's collected stories.[42] But one book above all others impressed him at this time, Teilhard de Chardin's *The Phenomenon of Man*. He thought it the most important book of the last decade,[43] and talked about it endlessly.

Père Teilhard's talk of a universal love uniting mankind, of future spiritual progress towards some collective 'super-life', indeed his great, optimistic, cloudy, cosmic vision appealed to Nash enormously. Above all, it took him back to earlier argumentative, thoughtful days. He wrote to Robert Ahearn that if a change is continuous, as he (and de Chardin) believed, 'then God changes with time and space'. The idea of a 'developing absolute' he knew long before he read de Chardin.

My interest in the subject of 'developing absolute' is linked up with the Vicar of Brooklyn, [R. H. Hobday] Wellington, in 1910, a very great Greek scholar. In conversation with him at that time—that is, fifty years ago—he said that I had been talking about a 'developing absolute' and I then told him that it seemed nonsense to be talking about such a subject. How could anything 'absolute' develop and how could anything 'developing' be absolute? I had a different opinion on the subject after reading D'Chardin's book.[44]

He read a number of Père Teilhard's books with great enthusiasm. On one of his Christmas cards he told 2,000 or so friends and acquaintances that de Chardin's ideas had been anticipated in the sixth century BC by Lao Tzu, who wrote of universal love, as also by Jesus Christ. Nash wrote, the 'Blending of Science and Universal Love is the nearest method yet propounded for solving the nuclear destruction problem,—the feeding of the hungry—and the building of a saner world.'

In his old age Nash's life marched on much as before. He continued to sacrifice his family to his mission in life. He stayed out late at night, quite unnecessarily, and knew it. The impulse to put in an appearance was irresistible. One night, after attending some other function, he dropped in very late at a Christmas party given by various voluntary aid organizations for blind people in Wellington. He said, 'my sister will say I'm being naughty'.[45] No one (except Lot) could have looked after him with more selfless, loving devotion than Emily. Each night, when the House was in session, when he came home there would be an affectionate note, saying there were lambs' tongue or some other sandwiches in the refrigerator, and expressing a doubtless vain hope that he would not be too late: 'Good night God Bless you Love Emily X'.[46] His family in England had always believed in his destiny and Emily still did. If Walter Nash did not always live up to his own ideals of loving, uncomplaining service to others, he certainly inspired his wife and sister to do so.

He was very fond of his grandchildren. Yet they were somewhat objective about his qualities. One of them, as a young man, worked in a printing works. When Nash visited Napier he would sometimes visit the works. The manager would ask his grandson if he would like to see his grandfather. It was never the case, he felt, that 'grandie' (as Nash was called by the grandchildren) was asking to see him. He felt that his grandfather never came to see *them*; but visited them when business called him to Napier. His daughter-in-law, Mrs Lorna Nash, wife of his oldest son Walter, who died during the war, felt that his immediate family never stood up to him. When her youngest son was married, on 11 May 1968 (and shortly before Nash's death), some people he knew were killed in a bus accident, and he decided to go and see their relatives. He insisted that she pack his bag, amidst all the celebrations and excitement. She said to him, 'I hope you know what you're asking.' (It would not have occurred to him, since he was doing what he thought his duty, that he was asking too much.) But Mrs Nash also remarks that when people needed help, Walter would give their problem his whole attention until they had it. If he was needed, he would put himself out for you.[47] Such conflicting aspects show that it would be completely wrong to say that he was so self-centred that he lacked human sympathy for individuals. Like many people, he strongly related to some people some of the time, but not to all or all the time. Perhaps it is a point that cannot be made too strongly—that we know so much about him. Few of us could be so closely scrutinized without showing some contradictions, paradoxes, weaknesses, compulsions, in our conduct of our lives.

He still worked endlessly away. On one of the few occasions when his biographer met him, he called at his room in Parliament Building, to sit outside and wait, like so many thousands. At last Sir Walter, in a kindly way, showed out a very old man. He presently said: 'I'm sorry you had to wait, but I had to talk to him. There's nothing else that anyone can do. He has been evicted and had his belongings put in storage because he did not pay any rent. His wife died and he was in hospital for so long. He does not understand this. But I talk to him.' It was clear from the old man's face that he did feel helped.

In these simple, feeling ways, Sir Walter was still the unpaid social worker, alias democratic representative, of 1930. His files of the 1960s show the same Nash helping pensioners to get pensions, young couples to get mortgages, people with their troubles.[48]

He still travelled abroad. In 1963 he went to a Commonwealth Parliamentary Conference at Kuala Lumpur, enjoying the dinners and trips as much as anyone. In January 1964—to everyone's astonishment—he was off to the Antarctic. He flew to McMurdo Sound in a US Navy Super Constellation and to the South Pole in a ski-equipped Hercules.[49] The newspapers said that he was the oldest man to have reached the South Pole. In 1966 Emily and he sailed in a cargo ship, the *Durango*, to England for a three months trip. A newspaper said that it was his first holiday in the UK since 1909. On board the *Ceramic*, coming home in May, he wrote to Robert Ahearn:

We have had a interesting change from normal duties in New Zealand. With visits to *Eire* for lunch with President de Valera and other Ministers & Diplomats—also to the Island of Mull off the west coast of Scotland—and to Cardiff Wales to see the Welsh Team defeat the team from France and win the International Rugby Championship.

We have had a very full experience with visits to between 40/50 Towns and Cities—and about 50 official and personal Engagements in the Midlands— London—Yorkshire and Lancashire. A very enjoyable and interesting change.[50]

He still fought elections, not only in the Hutt but round the country. In November 1966 he went up to Auckland to speak in the Milford School to help Dr Michael Bassett, the Labour candidate. One hundred and seventy people crowded into the room to hear him. It was not obvious that his speech did help. He kept talking about his loan negotiations in London in 1939—tossing millions of pounds in the air as usual. Critics felt that such backward-looking speeches gave the Labour Party an out-dated image. But the audience had come to hear Sir Walter, and gave him a warm reception.[51]

On this occasion Nash's support was wilting. His majority was cut from 3,648 in 1963 to 1,949, the smallest he had had since 1929. National won the election and the Social Credit vote rose. On this occasion, too, Nash seems to have overestimated his strength. One of his veins (he wrote to Dr Bassett) 'clotted a little'. He had to spend three weeks in hospital and wrote to A. G. B. Fisher in London that the doctors said he had 'been trying to do too much with an aging body. No one knows that it is aging; I do not think it is except in years. I feel as well as I ever did.' He explained Social Credit's increased vote to Fisher by saying that people did not want Labour because of its anti-Vietnam war policy, which was an asset to National, and did not want National because of its economic policy, so they voted Social Credit.[52]

Elections were not his only battlegrounds. In 1965 Nash took a prominent part in the early phase of the great protest movement against sending New Zealand troops to fight in Vietnam.

In mid-1965 the Holyoake government was considering the despatch of troops to assist the South Vietnamese and Americans, on the invitation of the current South Vietnamese leader. This led to one of the strongest and most prolonged public protests in New Zealand history. Several great 'teach-ins' were held, at which speakers presented facts and arguments on both sides.

At the first of these, in July 1965 at the Victoria University, there was a very large audience of about 1,000, by no means all of them students. The lectures went on all day and until late at night, on a Sunday. The atmosphere was very excited, almost revivalist, though most speakers were fairly heard. The presence of Tom Shand and other National MPs, as well as Sir Walter, added a sense that the occasion was as momentous as the audience was unprecedented.

On this occasion Sir Walter's speech, though enthusiastically received, was below his best and he made some errors in referring to the provisions of the SEATO treaty, which, so government speakers claimed, would justify sending troops. It was noticeable that Mr Shand and his colleague, Mr

D. S. Thomson, did not press Sir Walter but asked a later speaker, who happened to have the text of SEATO in his pocket, questions relevant to Sir Walter's address.

A man wrote to Nash shortly afterwards saying that he had enjoyed the 'spate of wonderful oratory from the "intelligenzia" of the University'. Nash replied that he had enjoyed it all and that there were some very good speeches. He thought the best were the two last, by Professor W. H. Oliver and Professor Keith Buchanan, 'so confirming the experience of the very early Christians that the last wine at the wedding was best of all'.[53]

Two months later Sir Walter was to speak to an all-day-and-late-night 'teach-in' session at Auckland University. As the time drew near for him to speak, he could not be found. Anxious organizers hunted about and discovered him alone in another room (at the age of eighty-three) swotting up the text of the SEATO treaty.

He rose, when Sir Leslie Munro, a National MP, concluded, to launch into a survey of the text of SEATO, with its American 'understanding' (that 'aggression' meant 'Communist aggression'), protocols and all. He reviewed the Korean war; explained and justified his stand over Laos when he was Prime Minister. The statements now made about Vietnam had then been made about Laos, and wrongly. He was long-winded, exceeding by far the allotted time. But he was passionate, and the passion was transferred to the audience. He denounced the American bombing of North Vietnam:

All that I am concerned about is to stop this horrifying killing that is going on all over the place, and stop the napalm and phosphorous bombs. It is a horrifying thing when you come to think about it. Look, when once phosphorous has got you, it has got you. You can't get rid of it. It sticks to you. I want to see an end to all the atrocities. If you could tell me the way, I would be an advocate for stopping all Vietcong atrocities too. But don't add to Vietcong atrocities by doing something worse. The Vietcong have got no napalm. Thank you ladies and gentlemen. I would like to end by quoting a poem:
> 'O veiled and secret Power
> Whose paths we seek in vain
> Be with us in our hour
> Of overthrow and pain
> That we: by which sure token
> We know thy ways are true
> In spite of being broken
> May rise and build anew.'

This was one of Nash's favourite quotations, used on a Christmas card and often elsewhere. The effect in the context of reference to the beaten-down North Vietnamese was stunning.

There was a tumultuous standing ovation, even more emotional than at the Wellington 'teach-in'. Such scenes are rare in New Zealand. Nash had seldom, if ever, aroused such fervent admiration.

It was a courageous, a fitting, last campaign. He received large numbers of letters of support afterwards. Among them was a letter from a man, possibly a farmer, in Feilding. After the first 'teach-in', he wrote that he had often criticized Nash, 'but must record unreserved admiration for you in the stand you have taken on Vietnam—a stand that many men would have avoided in the twilight of a long and distinguished service to your country, and one so recently honoured'.[54]

During the early anti-Vietnam protest, Nash joined in the first great debate on foreign policy in New Zealand history. Few people knew that he had been one of the founders of the Institute of International Affairs and the Institute of Pacific Affairs a generation earlier. These bodies had helped to educate some of the university speakers at the 'teach-ins' in problems of foreign affairs. Nash had helped to make a meaningful debate possible, and had lived to take part in it. There was no shilly-shallying when he spoke. One of his old friends, Mr Ormond Wilson, said that he had never heard Walter *so clear* about an issue. His outspokenness did a great deal to restore Nash's reputation with the left wing; for the first time for a generation. His public image was again one very acceptable to dissenters.

Early in 1966 H. N. Blundell, the managing director of the *Evening Post*, asked Nash to write six articles on his career for the far from princely fee of £35 each. This offer arose from a radio programme, 'Reflections of an Elder Statesman', in which he had been interviewed at length by Pam Carson, and which had been very well received. He wrote two articles at sea while travelling to England. One was about Montagu Norman's generosity in 1939 and the other about meeting Roosevelt. He never wrote the others, but he began to think of writing his autobiography. He asked Blundell if he thought he had the capacity and was advised to cooperate with a journalist.[55]

It is very difficult to believe that he could, in fact, have written an autobiography. Although he was a natural orator, with a fine flow of words, his prose was at best clumsy. However, he now spoke of sorting out his papers, but kept procrastinating. Sir Bernard Fergusson said that Nash 'seemed as though he were as convinced as everybody else that he would live almost for ever and would have unlimited time for the task'.[56] However, he did write voluminous notes on the main events of his life, headed 'Reminder Notes' and 'Highlights'. Almost all of them can be interpreted, for instance:

> 1921 'a first charge'
>
> Roosevelt How do you get on with your wife
>
> Cambridge-Doctorate of Law . . . Rutherford's
> Mortar Board Cap & Gown

Maddex—U.K. Actuary
>   you cannot do it
We are going to *do* it
M but you cannot you will bring chaos and
>   ruin to NZ
We are going to pass a *Bill*

Sutch Nazi flags Moscow Visit[57]

Carefully studied these notes show what people and episodes and deeds stuck in his mind as of great significance, as he reviewed his life. It is noticeable that they mostly refer to the years 1935-45.

Nash went to the Labour Party Conference in May 1968 and spoke twice. 'Toby' Hill, the former waterside union secretary, called for further revision of the Police Offences Act and the Public Safety Conservation Act of 1932 which, he said, had been used by the police to prohibit Nash from speaking on one occasion during the wharf strike, though for reasons of political expediency Sidney Holland had intervened and allowed him to speak. It sounded as though Hill was going to repeat an inaccurate statement made by a journalist, Leslie Hobbs, in a recent book, *The Thirty Year Wonders*, about Nash's Hamilton meeting, that 'Nash gave in, did what the policeman said and the meeting was cancelled'.[58] Nash shouted out, while Hill was speaking, that he had not been prevented from speaking. He then took over the microphone and made a very emotional speech denying that he had run away, as Hobbs had implied. He tried, at length, to explain his 'neither for nor against' statement on the strike. Next day he spoke again, on Malaysia. This was his last speech.[59]

In mid-May Sir Walter was taken to the Hutt Hospital for 'observation and rest'. A few days later he had a heart attack. He died peacefully on 4 June. His son Jim and his sister Emily were with him. He was given a state funeral, the first since Peter Fraser died. His estate was valued at $85,000 for duty purposes. He left $38,000 in bequests to his family, the use of his house to his sister in her lifetime, and the residue of his estate to CORSO. His garage full of papers he left to the National Archives.

During the anti-Vietnam war agitation Nash had said that New Zealand should provide a hospital instead of artillery. He began to consider how it might be possible to help the Vietnamese war orphans. This was a very characteristic concern: he always aimed to give some practical assistance to those in need; he preferred to act positively and not merely to *oppose*. In July 1967 he made a public proposal to establish a children's village in Vietnam, and set about trying to raise funds for this purpose. It became doubtful whether this was the best way to help the orphans, but after his death the Prime Minister and the Leader of the Opposition announced that the project would be continued as a tribute to Nash. A children's ward was erected at the Qui Nhon provincial hospital in Vietnam.[60] Nash would have liked that memorial.

References

ABBREVIATIONS USED IN REFERENCES

AJHR *Appendices to the Journals of the House of Representatives.*

N Nash Papers The numbers of bundles and files are prefixed by the letter N: e.g. N1170. Some of these bundles are not yet open to general inspection.

In references to letters etc. Sir Walter Nash is referred to as 'WN' and his wife as 'Lot'.

PD *New Zealand Parliamentary Debates.*

'Reflections of an Elder Statesman' Typed notes for a radio interview with Miss Pam Carson of Wellington, in the possession of Mr J. A. D. Nash of Lower Hutt. Miss Carson has a tape.

I: THE OLD COUNTRY, 1882-1909

1. Will Nash/WN, [c. 20 May 1922], N2175.
2. Various addresses have been gleaned from street directories: *Littlebury's Directory of Worcester and District*, 1879, *Kelly's Directory of Birmingham, Staffordshire, Warwickshire, and Worcestershire*, 1892. The street numbers have been changed from time to time, but most of the houses above and near the 'Reindeer Inn' still stood in 1973.
3. John T. Bunce, *Josiah Mason: A Biography*, Birmingham, 1882, p. 1; see also Asa Briggs, *History of Birmingham*, Oxford, 1952, II, 108-9.
4. *Littlebury's Directory*, 1879; WN birth certificate, Somerset House, London; WN wedding certificate, St Mary's Church, Selly Oak.
5. Will Nash/WN, [c. 20 May 1922], N2175.
6. Public Library, Kidderminster.
7. John R. Burton, *A History of Kidderminster*, London, 1890, pp. 171-82.
8. *Kidderminster Shuttle*, 20 May 1960.
9. Ibid., 6 March 1937.
10. Nash often referred to her in letters and interviews etc. See *Kidderminster Shuttle*, 20 May 1960; also WN/G. Parry, 29 March 1963, N2423. Some of her letters are in N1599, N2140, N2259. For information about the school see Burton, p. 144; *Kelly's Directory*, 1892. The St John's (Street) School was a storeroom in 1973.
11. Ernest Nash/WN, 27 Feb. 1927.
12. WN/G. Parry, 29 March 1963, N2423; *Birmingham Post*, 5 June 1968; *Kidderminster Shuttle*, 3 April 1937; *Dominion*, 2 April 1937.
13. K. Middlemas and J. Barnes, *Baldwin. A Biography*, London, 1969, pp. 40-41.
14. *Kidderminster Shuttle*, 3 April 1937, 20 May 1960; correspondence with Thursfield in N1229; WN/Janet White, 7 June 1961, N1626.

15. *Evening Post,* 23 Aug. 1969, M. Kelly article.
16. 'From Mill-boy to Office Manager. "How to Succeed" ', N2130.
17. 11 Dec. 1913, N308.
18. Will Nash/WN, [c. 20 May 1922], N2175.
19. *Kidderminster Shuttle,* 1 March 1937. Speech when he received the Freedom of the City of Kidderminster.
20. His name does not appear in the register in the Church of St Mary and All Saints. See below, pp. 16-17.
21. Mrs A. Nash/WN and Lot, 13 Oct. 1910, N2130; Will Nash/WN, 10 Feb. 1931 and [Christmas] 1934, N2191; Emily Nash/author, 2 Oct. 1972.
22. B. Jacobs, *The Story of British Carpets,* 2nd ed., London, 1972, p. 107.
23. Such was the impression of Miss Emily Nash.
24. Briggs, p. 158; A. G. Gardiner, *Life of George Cadbury,* London, 1923. On bicycles, see, G. C. Allen, *The Industrial Development of Birmingham and the Black Country 1860-1927,* London, 1929, pp. 294-5. See also, A. Mansbridge, *An Adventure in Working Class Education,* London, 1920, p. 7.
25. The essay is in N2130. There was a magazine put out by the Bournville Works Youths' Club, *The Camaraderie,* in 1901.
26. *Birmingham Mail,* 18 Feb. 1937; 'Reflections of an Elder Statesman', notes for a radio interview in the possession of Mr J. A. D. Nash.
27. Allen, pp. 337-9.
28. Correspondence in N1404, N1706, N2142, N2172, N2558.
29. P.O. testimonial for Mrs Nash, N2172; marriage certificate; notes on WN by Miss Emily Nash in the possession of Mr J. A. D. Nash.
30. *Kelly's Directory of Birmingham,* 1905-9; papers in N2172.
31. Thomas Halward Trust, papers in N1321, N2258.
32. N2172.
33. N2535.
34. Testimonial, 14 March 1905; WN/Cadbury, [March 1909], N2172; WN/H. J. Sabin, n. d., N2130; Ratepayers' Association programme, N1320.
35. *Birmingham Mail,* 2 Jan. 1919; also reports in Sept.-Oct. 1911 during the Council elections. Mr R. A. Wright, of Birmingham, kindly supplied some details.
36. 'Reflections of an Elder Statesman'.
37. 25 Dec. [1934], N2191.
38. In blue notebook, N2557; WN/A. Wedgwood Benn, 3 April 1962, N1674.
39. E. M. Winslow, *The Pattern of Imperialism,* New York, 1948, p. 96; J. A. Hobson, *John Ruskin: Social Reformer,* London, 1898, pp. 121-2.
40. There is a useful, brief summary of George's doctrines and influence in P. d'A. Jones's excellent book, *The Christian Socialist Revival 1877-1914,* Princeton, 1968. It is the best 'background' book for a study of Nash's opinions. There are references to his reading in letters from Hitchinson and Boylin. He listed early readings in several draft notes for his radio talk, 'Reflections of an Elder Statesman'.
41. See, e.g., G. H. Sabine, *A History of Political Theory* 3rd ed., London, 1948, pp. 607-15.
42. Letters from Boylin, N2130 and N2160; from Hitchinson, in N2140; notes for a talk on commercial morality, blue notebook, N2557.
43. Boylin/WN, [1908], N2130; Will Nash/WN, 25 Dec. [1934], N2191.
44. W. K. Hancock's term, *Survey of British Commonwealth Affairs,* London, 1940, II, Part I, pp. 92-93; F. Daniel/WN, 24 April 1910, N308.
45. Papers in N2172; J. Boylin/WN, [1908], N2130; F. B. Darling/WN, 10 Oct. 19[12], N308; WN speech, *Kidderminster Shuttle,* 3 April 1937.

46. A. E. Brooker/WN, [1910], N308; Mrs A. Nash/WN, 2 Dec. 1909, N2130.
47. [1909], N2172.
48. Will Nash/WN, 11 Feb. 1909, N2172; Albert Nash/Lot, 19 July 1936, N2139; other papers in N2172; 'Reflections of an Elder Statesman'; WN/S. Clarke, 18 Jan. 1946, N1188.
49. N2175.
50. WN/Mrs A. Nash, 7 April 1909, in possession of Mr J. A. D. Nash; Will/WN, [1921], N2175; papers in N2130, N2172.

II: THE NEW CHUM, 1909-12

1. WN/Mrs A. Nash, 20 May 1909, in possession of Mr J. A. D. Nash.
2. W. A. Smith/'Hutchie', 31 March 1909; N308; Dr W. J. Garbutt/Laing, 28 March 1909, N2172.
3. Mrs A. Nash/WN and Lot, 6 Oct. 1910, N2130.
4. Nell/Lot and WN, 10 Dec. 1909, 13 Jan., 30 June 1910, N2130; rent book; N2168; personal ledger, N3020.
5. WN statement, [1909], N1693. For valuable advice on the affairs of the company, including explaining some of its records, I am much indebted to Professor R. C. J. Stone.
6. Arch/WN, 8 June 1910; Mrs A. Nash/WN and Lot, 21 Aug. 1910; Nell/Lot and WN, 3 Sept. [1910], N2130; 'Hitch'/WN, 12 Oct. 1912, N308.
7. Records of St Matthew's Church; WN/Mrs E. Hobday, 10 Jan. 1967, N1706.
8. Sixtieth Anniversary booklet, St Matthew's Church; papers in N308.
9. Letters in N2130.
10. Ibid.
11. Mrs Judy Brooker, who helped me by examining church (and Christian Socialist) records, could not find him listed as a lay reader in Diocesan Synod records anywhere. See below, p. 361.
12. 2 May 1913, N1316; other CEMS papers in N308.
13. WN/Holdsworth, 10 July 1916, N2130; WN/P. Powell, 20 Sept. 1932, N2188.
14. Papers in N1317.
15. See, for instance, L. N. Tolstoy, My Religion, New York, 1922; pp. 79, 102; H. Troyat, Tolstoy, London, 1968, p. 397.
16. The Kingdom of God is within you, New York, 1922, p. 324.
17. First draft, 13 April 1917, in N2188; second in N2167.
18. The Kingdom of God . . .; What is Religion, New York, 1922, pp. 337-8.
19. 17 Nov. 1911, N1316.
20. P. d'A. Jones, pp. 167ff., 214.
21. Society for Promoting Christian Knowledge, Pan-Anglican Congress, Official Report, Vol. II, London, 1908.
22. 2 May 1913, N1316.
23. WN notebook, 1913, N2552.
24. WN/Frankland, 1913, N1316.
25. See, e.g., J. Ruskin, Unto This Last, London, [1907], with introduction by J. A. Hobson; J. A. Hobson, John Ruskin: Social Reformer, London, 1898; D. Leon, Ruskin The Great Victorian, London, 1949.
26. Will Nash/WN and Lot, 20 May 1913.
27. P. H. Hickey, "Red" Fed. Memoirs, [Wellington, 1925], p. 30. The best account of early Labour history is B. S. Gustafson, 'The Advent of the New Zealand Labour Party 1900-1919', unpub. M.A. thesis, University of New Zealand (Auckland), 1961.

28. Hobday/WN, 6 April 1914, N1577; WN/Lot, 14 April 1914, N2153; H. E. Holland/WN, 23 March 1914, N308.
29. Thorn/WN, 1 Dec. 1914, N308; Nell Hinton/Lot and WN, 1 Feb. 1912; WN notes for radio interview, in possession of Mr J. A. D. Nash.
30. 29 Aug. 1912, N1577.
31. Gustafson, Chapter 9.
32. W. Nash, *Social Progress in New Zealand*, Labour Party, London, [1944-5] copy in N1209; *N.Z. Labour Party Journal*, 2, 2, April 1966; B. Brown, *The Rise of New Zealand Labour*, Wellington, 1962, p. 37; B. Brown to author, 12 Feb. 1973.
33. WN/Brown, 25 July 1962, N1098.
34. WN/Frankland, [1913], N1316. The reference to politics probably relates to the 1913 strike.
35. N2183, N1317; cf. H. Troyat, *Tolstoy*, p. 51.
36. These include the 'Memorandum of Association', correspondence, some financial statements, and other papers in N308. Further papers are in N1693, N2168, N306, N1561, and N2153. Notice of the company's registration was published in *The Mercantile Gazette of New Zealand*, 7 July 1909; the new debenture was published in the same journal on 16 March 1910. The creditors' petition to bankrupt Edgar Jones is listed in the Supreme Court Bankruptcy Register, Wellington Registry, No. 942, 1 Aug. 1912 and withdrawn on 16 Aug. 1912.
37. 3 Dec. 1911, N230.
38. F. B. Darling/WN, 10 Oct. 19[12], N308.
39. *Kidderminster Shuttle*, 3 April 1937.
40. 6 Aug. 1912, N2153.
41. Correspondence in N2153.
42. 19 Nov. 1914, N1577.
43. WN/H. Jones, n.d., [c. 1916], N308.
44. WN/Lot, 11 Feb. 1915, N2153.

III: THE TRAVELLING MAN, 1912-16

1. WN/Lot, 24 Jan. 1916, N2153.
2. 4 March 1914, N1561.
3. Draft letter, c. 1914, N308.
4. WN/Lot, 15 June 1915, N2153.
5. WN's submission to arbitrator, N2260; also letters to Lot at this time.
6. 19 Feb. 1918, 11 March 1920, N2269.
7. n.d., N308.
8. W. F. Howlett/WN, 28 Nov. 1913, N1316. On Frankland see papers in N1316, N1317, N1577, including WN/George Shann, n.d., N1316.
9. Leaflets on Oneida in N1317. See J. McK. Whitworth, *God's Blueprints: A Sociological Study of Three Utopian Sects*, London, 1975, pp. 121ff., on the sexual practices of this community.
10. WN/Mrs E. Aimley, 25 Sept. 1962, N2247.
11. J. B. Condliffe, *The Beginnings of the W.E.A.*, Wellington, 1968, pp. 14-19; letter to author, 13 Nov. 1972; WN speech notes, 8 Aug. 1959, N187; Hobday/WN, 6 Oct. 1914, N1577; Gustafson, p. 233.
12. 27 Sept. 1913, N1316.
13. P. J. O'Farrell, *Harry Holland. Militant Socialist*, Canberra, 1964, pp. 13, 34-37; P. J. O'Farrell, 'History of the New South Wales Labor Movement 1890-1910', *Journal of Religious History*, II, Dec. 1962.
14. 'Reflections of an Elder Statesman'.

15. Gustafson, p. 232; Hobday/Frankland, 22 Sept. 1913, N1317.
16. There is a useful account of these events in Hickey, *"Red" Fed. Memoirs.*
17. See below, note 36.
18. *Maoriland Worker*, 8, 15, 22, 29 Oct. 1913, 28 Jan., 4 Feb., 11 Feb. 1914. The correspondence and many entries are preserved in Nash's papers.
19. 5, 12 Nov. 1913.
20. 9 Jan. 1936, N2142.
21. Hobday/WN, 31 Oct. 1913, N1577; 26 Aug. 1916, N2167.
22. 18 Nov. 1913, 13 Jan. 1914, N1577.
23. Hobday/Frankland, 24 Nov. [1913]; Hobday/Nash, [1914], N1577.
24. B. Crompton-Smith/WN, 9 Feb. 1916, N308.
25. 8 Nov. 1913, N1577.
26. O'Farrell, pp. 58ff.
27. 'Reflections of an Elder Statesman'.
28. 21 Nov. 1913, N1577.
29. WN/Howlett, 6 Dec. 1913, N1316.
30. 8 Nov. 1913, N1577.
31. 10 to 15 Nov. 1913, correspondence and editorials.
32. WN/Frankland, 8 Nov. 1913, N1577; WN/Hickey, 13 Nov. 1913, N1316.
33. WN/Lot, 23 July 1914, N2153.
34. 13 April 1916, 4 Sept. 1912, N1577.
35. Gustafson, pp. 132ff.
36. Holland/WN, 10 March 1914, N1316; 23 March 1914, N308.
37. 19 March 1914, N1577.
38. E.g. Will Nash/WN, [1933], N2191.
39. Hobday/WN, 4 June 1914, N1577.
40. Drafts in N2552 and 31 May [1914], N1316.
41. Hobday/WN, 4 June 1914, N1577, and letters in N308; Boylin/WN, 6 Oct. 1908, N2130.
42. *New Zealand Year Book*, 1916, pp. 199-20.
43. Hobday/WN, 14 Dec. [1915], 14 Feb. 1915, 11 Aug. 1915, N1577; 3 Aug. 1916, N2167; Hobday's speech, 13 Dec. 1915, N1316; *Dominion*, 30 Nov., 4 Dec. 1915.
44. Notes for a talk, N1317.
45. *Dominion*, 27 Feb., 10, 11, 13, 15, 22 March 1915; WN drafts of letter in N1317.
46. *The Kingdom of God is Within You.*
47. Mrs A. Nash/WN, [1914-15]; Will/WN and Lot, [1914-15], N308.
48. Cit. Gustafson, p. 187.
49. G. Haupt, *Socialism and the Great War*, Oxford, 1972, pp. 1-2, 219.
50. 'The Vag'/WN, 5 July 1917 (in New Zealand 'The Vag' was Ted Howard); Hobday/WN, 21 Dec. 1916, N2167.
51. *Taranaki Daily News*, 12 Dec. 1916.
52. O'Farrell, chapter 4.
53. WN speech, N2104.
54. 28 June 1916, N2167.
55. 9 Aug. 1915, N2153.
56. Letters in N2153, N1317.
57. WN submission to arbitrator, N2260; WN note on Ahearn/WN, 30 March 1916, N2260.
58. 26 Jan. 1916, N2153.
59. WN/Miller and Ahearn, 13 July 1916, N2130.

IV: PROFIT-SHARING AND POLITICS IN NEW PLYMOUTH, 1916-20

1. Draft of scheme, N308. A large quantity of papers about Modern Tailors Ltd is filed in N308, N2153, N2175, N2260, N2167, N1577, N246, and N2236. The National Archives hold the company's minute book, which substantiates Nash's own account of events (see Chapter V) in N2260.
2. See R. B. Martin, *The Dust of Combat. A Life of Charles Kingsley*, London, 1969.
3. Besley/WN, 14 June 1916 and other letters, N2260.
4. 5 July 1916, N2167; n.d. [1916], N1577.
5. 25, 27 June 1916, N2153; WN submissions to arbitrator, N2260.
6. WN submissions; Besley/WN, 5 June 1916, N2260; Minute Book of Modern Tailors Ltd.
7. Interview with Mr Charles Reed, 6 July 1970. He worked for Besley both before and after World War I.
8. N1343, N2260, correspondence and clippings. Advertisements in *Taranaki Daily News*, 2 Aug., 18 Nov. 1919.
9. *Daily News*, 9 April 1919.
10. Holland/WN, 5 Nov. 1918, N2147.
11. Minute Book, National Archives; draft in N2260.
12. Interview with Mrs Olive Clarke, Auckland, 1972.
13. — Nov., 16 Nov. 1916, N2167.
14. Mary Dowling/WN, 30 Aug. 1937, N1099.
15. Notices 13 June 1918, N2147; 22 June 1918, N246.
16. Interview with Miss Hirst, Mahina Bay, 19 Jan. 1973.
17. *Taranaki Daily News*, 15 Nov. to 19 Dec. 1919; interview with Mr H. D. Mullon, New Plymouth, Jan. 1973; F. T. Bellringer/Nash, 16 June 1959, N369.
18. WN/Frankland, [1913], N1316.
19. F. Rogers, 'The Single Tax Movement in New Zealand', unpub. MA thesis, University of New Zealand (Auckland), 1949, p. 112; *Taranaki Daily News*, 25 April 1919, P. J. O'Regan speech.
20. *Taranaki Herald*, 22, 28 April 1919; *Taranaki Daily News*, 20 March 1919; WN notes, N246.
21. For early references see *Taranaki Daily News*, 27, 30 Jan., 3 March 1919.
22. *Taranaki Daily News*, 21 March, 10, 25, 26 April, 1 May 1919; *Taranaki Herald*, 22, 25 April 1919.
23. Interview with Mr H. D. Mullon, New Plymouth, Jan. 1973. He saw a file in the local Post Office on this surveillance.
24. 5 Nov. 1918, N2147.
25. 9 July 1919.
26. O'Farrell, pp. 77ff.; J. Thorn, *Peter Fraser*, London 1952, p. 52.
27. Letters from Holland, Glover, Fraser, and Nash in N2147.
28. N358.
29. 24, 29 April, 1 May 1919.
30. WN/S. W. Fitzherbert, draft letter, N246.
31. Ibid., WN/*Taranaki Daily News*, 4 Dec. 1919, N1343; *Taranaki Herald*, 16 April 1919.
32. U.L.P. *Constitution and Platform*, 1912, 'Municipal Platform'.
33. *Taranaki Herald*, 28 April 1919.
34. *Taranaki Daily News* (clipping), 16 June 1919; WN draft letter, 17 June 1919, N1343.
35. Speech notes, N1577.

36. N246.
37. WN/N. Krushchev, [April 1964], N2558; WN/B. T. Ford, MP (UK), 28 April 1966, N1706; WN notes for speech, [1963], N2263.
38. I am indebted to Mrs Judy Brooker for assistance on this point. See Society for Promoting Christian Knowledge, *Pan-Anglican Congress, Official Report*, Vol. II, Section A, *The Church and Human Society*, Preface, p. iv, and 'Religion and Wages' by A. J. Carlyle (a Christian Social Union paper), p. 34. The phrase also appears in *Christianity and Industrial Problems Being the Report of the Archbishop's Fifth Committee of Enquiry*, London, 1919, Part 1, para 110; and in the *Report of the Lambeth Conference*, 1920, pp. 70-71; and was probably common in Anglican publications and speeches.
39. June 1913, N1317.
40. Hobday/WN, 13 March 1914, N1577.
41. 30 April 1919; *Taranaki Herald*, 16 April 1919.
42. *Taranaki Herald*, 1 May 1919.
43. [May 1919], N2147.
44. Draft WN minutes of Labour Party meeting, N246.
45. Ibid; Parry/WN, 16 June 1919; WN/Holland, 5 June 1919, N2147; *Taranaki Daily News*, 4, 10 March 1919.
46. 4 Oct. 1919, N2147, and correspondence with Fitzherbert, Read, Savage, and Schwieters, in N2147 and N246.
47. Brown, p. 63; *Maoriland Worker*, 9, 30 July, 13 Aug. 1919.
48. *Maoriland Worker*, 6 Aug. 1919, cit. Gustafson, p. 211.
49. 16 Aug. 1919, N2147.
50. WN/Holland, 5 June 1919, N2147.
51. Mrs A. Nash/WN and Lot, 1916, N308; 18 Nov. 1909, N2130.
52. WN/Mrs A. Nash, 11 Jan. 1914, in possession Mr J. A. D. Nash; Emily Nash/WN, 11 Dec. 1913, Emily Nash/WN and Lot, 23 Feb. 1914, N308; Records of Lodge Hill Cemetery, Birmingham. He died on 10 Dec. 1913. The grave is unmarked.
53. WN/A. Hinton, 29 April 1952, N2535. There is a photograph of a very decrepit, poor, and sad old man in this file, probably the father.
54. *Kidderminster Shuttle*, 1 March 1937.
55. 10 Sept. 1917, N2260.
56. Averill/WN, 26 Nov. [1919]; WN/Averill, 27 Nov. 1919, N1230.

V: THE SECOND SOCIALIST INTERNATIONAL—TRAVELS
AND TROUBLES, 1920-1

1. For correspondence on their travels see N377; WN article, 'European Impressions', *Maoriland Worker*, 12 Jan. 1921.
2. Diary, 22 Aug. 1920, N377.
3. On agencies, see N255, N1552, N2175.
4. WN/Ahearn, 28 Aug. 1919, N2147; Savage/WN, 20 Jan. 1921, N2151.
5. Typed statement for *Dominion*, 17 Jan. 1936, N1232.
6. 25 Feb. 1920, N2179.
7. Savage/Chairman, 21 Jan. 1920, Savage/WN, 17 July 1920, N2269; Brindle/WN, 20 Sept. 1920, N2175.
8. Diary, 11 July 1920, and typescript report, N377.
9. WN/Editor, 24 Aug. 1920, N2160; *Maoriland Worker*, 25 Aug., 1 Sept., 15 Sept., 27 Oct. 1920; Brown, pp. 110-11.
10. WN/Lot, July 1920, N2118.

11. Diary, N377.
12. F. Brockway, *Socialism over Sixty Years. The Life of Jowett of Bradford,* London, 1946, p. 176. For another discussion of the conference see G. D. H. Cole, *A History of Socialist Thought,* London, 1958, IV, Part 1, 323ff.
13. Brockway, p. 177.
14. Ibid., p. 179. Nash's notes (in N1343), written at the time, include some additions and variations including control of commodity prices and the provision of capital for socialized industries.
15. WN's reports, MS and typed, in N377; *Maoriland Worker,* 6 Oct., 13 Oct., 1 Dec. 1920. Cf. Brockway, p. 179. The account given here is based on the typed version.
16. 10 Jan. 1921, N377.
17. N377.
18. *Evening Post,* 2 March 1921; *N.Z. Times,* 1 March 1921, *Dominion,* 1 March 1921; *Taranaki News* clipping in N2260. Nash later found that Bukharin's pamphlet was in the parliamentary library. See Nash's accounts, PD, 1951, 296, 1221ff; 1960, 323, 1783.
19. 10 Feb. 1921, N2173.
20. Correspondence in N2173.
21. 3 March 1921, N2175.
22. Chapman, Skerrett, Tripp and Blair/WN, 20 Jan. 1921; WN/Ahearn, 30 Jan. 1920; N2260.
23. Ahearn/WN, 10 May, 14 June, 16 July, 1920; WN's submissions to arbitrator, N2260, Besley's attitude is also referred to in P. B. Cooke (Solicitor)/WN, 9 March 1921.
24. This is what Nash wrote in his draft submissions to the arbitrator (N2260), but if the stated income of over £100 per month was correct he must have earned that amount only very recently. Cf. above, p. 44, on his income. See also WN/Stanton, Johnstone & Spence, 17 April 1921, N2260.
25. Cooke/WN, 9 March 1921; Roy & Nicholson/WN, 26 Jan. 1921, N2260.
26. These paragraphs are based on extensive correspondence in N2175, N2120 and N2145.
27. Award issued 13 Jan. 1922; draft Agreement to go to arbitration, (1921), N2260; WN/Ahearn, 31 Jan. 1922, N2175.
28. WN/W. Kraig, 11 Nov. 1921, N2151; correspondence and cards in N255, N2145, N2175.
29. 11 July 1921, N2173.
30. Holland/WN, 10 Feb. 1921, N2173.
31. 29 July 1921, N2175.
32. 26 Aug. 1921, N2175.
33. 24 Feb. 1921, N2175.
34. 20 Aug. 1921, N2175.
35. WN/P. Fraser (now an MP), 3 Nov., 9 Dec. 1921, N2151.
36. Correspondence with Commissioner of Taxes, N2151; Commission Account, N1553.
37. WN/Lot, 13 Jan. 1923, N2145.

VI: SECRETARY OF THE LABOUR PARTY, 1922-32

1. See correspondence with T. Brindle and F. R. Cooke in N2118, N2151, N2173, N2175; with D. Wilson and G. T. Scott in N2188.
2. McCulloch resigned from the court in 1922 after a dispute with the judge.

WN/C. W. Nash, 13 March 1936, N2198; WN/Fraser, 9 March, Fraser/WN, 18 March 1922, N2188; Lot/WN, July 1922, N2175.

3. WN/W. Ensom, 20 Aug. 1922, N2151.
4. *Maoriland Worker,* 9 Aug. 1922; *National Record* (Hocken Library), Nov. 1922.
5. *N.Z. Worker,* 14 May 1924; Conference Report, Labour Party Head Office. The estimate of his salary is based on total salary expenditure of Head Office, recorded in Labour Party Executive Minutes in Head Office.
6. WN/Lot, 20 May 1923, N2145.
7. *Maoriland Worker,* 25 April 1923.
8. Wilson/WN, 15 Sept. 1922, N2151; *Evening Post,* 23 Aug. 1969, M. Kelly article.
9. 23 May 1923 and other issues in April and May. Cf. Fraser's Report to the 1923 conference on the National Office. Nash gave some credit for originating the bureau to Fraser, *Maoriland Worker,* 9 Jan. 1924.
10. *Maoriland Worker,* 1 Aug. 1923, 9, 16 Jan., 20 Feb. 1924.
11. Ibid., 19 Dec. 1923. On the Labour Party's role in directing the journal see file in NZLP Head Office; also *N.Z. Worker,* 26 Sept. 1928.
12 WN/J. Meech, 11 Oct. 1923, N2151.
13. E. Spurr/WN, 7 Aug. 1922, N2151. On membership, see B. Brown, pp. 36, 76. E. Olssen, 'John Alexander Lee; The Stormy Petrel', unpub. MA thesis, Otago University, 1965, p. 22, gives somewhat different figures.
14. R. M. Chapman, *The Political Scene, 1919-1931,* Auckland, 1969, p. 40.
15. WN/Lot, 11 Jan. 1923, N2145; WN correspondence with Fraser and others on railway strike, 1924, N1540. See also R. C. J. Stone, 'A History of Trade Unionism in New Zealand, 1913-37', unpub. MA thesis, University of New Zealand (Auckland), 1948.
16. There are a mass of papers on this firm in several files in the Nash Papers.
17. 'Reflections of an Elder Statesman'. For another version, see WN/Mr and Mrs Rush-Munro, 9 July 1965, N197.
18. WN/W. Bullock, 18 Jan. 1924, N2151; Fraser/WN, 9 May 1924, N1540; *N.Z. Worker,* 30 July, 1 Oct. 1924.
19. 1934 Conference Report; list of stock in N156.
20. A remark made to the author.
21. WN/D. Grant, 27 Nov. 1928, N2173; WN/J. D. Salmond, 26 Nov. 1925, N1230.
22. N1233.
23. 8 Oct. 1941, N2273.
24. *N.Z. Worker,* 20 April 1927, 23 April, 7 May 1930.
25. Ibid., 12 March 1924.
26. Brown, pp. 76-77.
27. Langstone/WN, 9 Dec. 1926, N2098.
28. WN/Lot, 26 Dec. 1922, N2145.
29. E.g. on board ship going to Canada in 1933—wine bill in N75.
30. Holland/J. Cocking, 29 Dec. 1921, in P. J. O'Farrell notes (see bibliography).
31. Mrs Holland/J. Cocking, 28 May 1922; T. Batho ('The Vag'), 'Random Ramblings', in P. J. O'Farrell notes.
32. Holland/Nash, 30 Jan. 1924, 15 Nov. 1929, N2416; Holland/WN, 7 April 1930, P. J. O'Farrell notes; NZLP Conference Report, 1927.
33. Cards in N2416, N2151.
34. Chapman, p. 17.
35. Ibid., p. 16.
36. *Fors Clavigera,* New York, n.d. (Ruskin's Complete Works), Letter LXXXIX.
37. Brown, pp. 63-7 and 79ff. There is much material from the land policy com-

mittees in the Nash papers.

38. E.g. letter to *Evening Post,* 18 Dec. 1922, N2098; article in *N.Z. Worker,* 9 April 1924.

39. N2141.

40. Brown, p. 80.

41. Lee/WN, 1 Feb. 1923, N2141 and, in full, in P. J. O'Farrell notes.

42. Langstone letter in N2141.

43. Brown, p. 67.

44. Cit. O'Farrell, *Harry Holland,* p. 145.

45. B. Whyte/WN, [1925], N2188. There are other letters from her in N1481 and N2139. Mr J. A. Lee once said in conversation with the author that Bertha Whyte was Nash's mistress, and he later wrote (in *Political Notebooks,* Welling-ton, 1973, pp. 39-40) that Nash was 'doing a line' with her. Her letters, of which a number, spread over many years, survive in the Nash papers, suggest a family acquaintanceship and a slight friendship. and that she was a strong Labour sup-porter. More important, a lady living in Wellington in 1974, who lived with Bertha Whyte for many years, says that she was in fact the friend of another Labour MP, Ted Howard, and certainly not of Nash. It is very difficult for Nash's closest friends to believe that he ever had an affair.

46. 29 Oct. 1925.

47. Speeches in *N.Z. Worker,* 12 Nov., 10 Dec. 1924, 14 Oct. 1925; *Dominion,* 7 Oct., 2 Nov. 1925.

48. E. Spurr/WN, 29 Jan. 1923, P. J. O'Farrell notes.

49. Wellington, 1925.

50. 21 Oct. 1925.

51. Chapman, pp. 16, 32.

52. 7 Dec. 1926, in 1927 Land Sub-committee file, N2098.

53. Brown, pp. 87-95; N2098. Nash wrote the report.

54. O'Farrell, pp. 100-2, 138; Holland/WN, 2 Sept. 1926, N2098.

55. Parry/WN, 18 Oct. 1923; WN/Parry, 2 Feb. 1927, P. J. O'Farrell notes.

56. Chapman, pp. 49-50. There is an interesting letter from Lee to his wife, 18 Oct. 1935, Lee 541/5, quoting Forbes's views on the loan.

57. *Evening Post,* 25 Oct. 1928; *Hutt News,* 8 Nov. 1928.

58. 7 Nov. 1928.

59. *Hutt News,* 8 Nov. 1928.

60. Ibid., 22 Nov. 1928.

61. 18 Nov. 1928, letter in possession of Mr J. A. D. Nash.

62. Chapman, pp. 54-57.

63. *N.Z. Worker,* 6 April, 4 May 1927; 17, 24 April, 8 May 1929. Harbour Board papers in N1182, N1291.

64. *N.Z. Worker,* 20 Nov. 1929.

65. 10 Dec. 1929, N2188.

66. 27 Nov. 1929.

67. Ibid., also 1 Jan. 1930.

68. *Evening Post,* 29 Nov. 1929.

69. *N.Z. Worker,* 18 Dec. 1929; *Evening Post,* 10 Dec. 1929, P. Fraser letter.

70. 12 Dec. 1929.

71. *Evening Post,* 28 Nov., 3, 5, 6 Dec. 1929.

72. Ibid., 6, 15 Dec. 1929.

73. Ibid., 6 Dec. 1929.

74. R. H. E. Slacke/WN, 16 June 1956, N2188.

75. 23 Dec. 1929.

76. 29 Dec. 1929, N1230
77. 18 Nov. 1930, N2188.
78. 14 Nov. 1929, N2160.

VII: INTERNATIONAL RELATIONS, ELECTORAL AFFAIRS, AND
PRIVATE LIFE, 1922-32

1. Airey/WN, 23 May 1929, N2132.
2. WN/J. S. Reid, 28 Dec. 1944, N2259.
3. 1 Aug. 1927, N30.
4. 12 Dec. 1927, 1 May 1929, N1556.
5. WN/Campbell letters, N2148; PD, 1943, 262, 544.
6. *Maoriland Worker,* 10 Jan. 1923.
7. Correspondence with Hobday in N2123, and other letters in N2151.
8. A. S. J. Reid, 'Church and State in New Zealand, 1930-1935', unpub. MA
   thesis, University of New Zealand (Victoria), 1961, pp. 12, 87-88.
9. 'Recollections of Sir Walter Nash', typescript kindly sent to the author by Dr
   Salmond; 'Some Recollections of Walter Nash', typescript kindly sent by Dr
   A. C. Watson; Rev. J. Gilman Dunn/WN, 12 Feb. 1962, N368; WN/Fraser,
   9 May 1923, N1540.
10. *Standard,* 16 Oct. 1941; Lee/Mrs Lee, 5 Sept. [1925], Lee MSS 541/1.
11. *N.Z. Worker,* 19 Oct. 1927; for papers on the founding of the IPR and the
    NZIIA, see N20.
12. N78; *N.Z. Worker,* 29 Feb. 1928.
13. Correspondence in N20.
14. See N18, N3018, for its papers; Sir John Ilott/WN, 13 June, WN/Ilott, 28
    June 1960, N1628.
15. *N.Z. Worker,* 9, 16 Nov. 1927; WN letters to Lot, N2145.
16. W. Nash, 'A New Zealand Outlook on Pacific Affairs', in J. B. Condliffe (ed.),
    Problems of the Pacific, Chicago, 1928, (the proceedings of the conference), p. 40.
17. *N.Z. Worker,* 16 Nov. 1927.
18. *Dunedin Evening Star,* 8 Oct. 1927.
19. Condliffe (ed.), *Problems of the Pacific,* p. 39.
20. PD, 1927, 214, pp. 259-66.
21. *Dunedin Evening Star,* 8 Oct. 1927.
22. H. Northey, 'Singapore: New Zealand's Great Illusion', unpub. MA thesis,
    University of Auckland, 1971, p. 165.
23. A. P. Ngata . . . Nash and others, *New Zealand Affairs,* Christchurch, 1929,
    pp. 158, 176.
24. Bloodworth/WN, 8 July 1929 and other letters, N1556.
25. 10 May 1933, N1480.
26. O'Farrell, p. 203.
27. Fisher/WN, 26 May 1933, N2416; Fisher/WN, 5 June 1933, N75.
28. N97, Conference papers.
29. Mogi/WN and WN draft reply [1933], N75; WN/J. Thorn, 2 April 1934, N1543;
    WN note, National Executive papers, N2077.
30. Notes for 'Memoirs'. The following remarks about the Nash family are based
    on interviews with Mr and Mrs L. Nash, and Mrs Lorna Nash, 24 Jan. 1972,
    and with the late Hon. T. and Mrs Bloodworth, on 6 July 1970. Many letters
    from the Nash boys to their father are in his papers.
31. Notebook, N2325.
32. WN/C. W. Nash, 15 Sept. 1933, N75.

33. 28 Jan. 1931, N1321.
34. Papers in N1279, N1540, about the Golding family. There are many other similar examples in Nash's papers. E.g. in a file of correspondence with a friend, Mrs Olga Williams, N1446.
35. Papers in N2191; Mrs M. Kirk to author, 14 June 1970.
36. Chapman, pp. 33-34.
37. Reid/WN, 6 Dec. 1935, N1480.
38. Papers in N1071.
39. Papers in N1039; PD, 1932, 232, 152-3.
40. PD, 1934, 239, 692-3; 240, 284; papers in N76, N1242, and N2196.
41. 10 Nov. 1930 and later minutes, N1029; *N.Z. Worker,* 12 March 1930.
42. *N.Z. Worker,* 12 March 1930.
43. Bell/WN, 5 Jan. 1931; letter from fourteen men, 28 Dec. 1931, N1025.
44. J. Parker (editor)/J. Anderson, 7 Oct. 1932, N1024.
45. This and the following cases are samples from the papers in N1024, N1230, N1477, N1480.
46. Mrs L. Benson/WN, 9 Jan. 1958, N2149; WN/Mrs E. Prestidge, 14 Dec. 1931, N1480.
47. 'Reflections of an Elder Statesman'.
48. List in N1543; for 1931 see N2098 (twenty-seven clubs).
49. Interview with Mrs L. Nash and Mrs M. Nash, 24 Jan. 1972.
50. Interview, 9 Dec. 1972.

VIII: THE WAY OUT OF THE LABYRINTH, 1930-1

1. PD, 1930, 224. 44ff; cf. Brown, pp. 62, 132-3.
2. 2 July 1930.
3. 28 June 1930.
4. PD, 1931, 227, 140.
5. 11 Sept. 1932, N2188.
6. E.g. PD, 1930, 225, 44-45; *The Sun* (Christchurch), 9 Aug. 1932, speech on international settlement of war debts.
7. PD, 1930, 226, 647.
8. 2 March 1935, Lee MSS, 541/5.
9. Lee/Mrs Lee, 2 Aug. 1934, Lee MSS, 541/4.
10. *Wanganui Chronicle,* 18 May 1938.
11. J. B. Condliffe, *The Welfare State in New Zealand,* London, 1959, p. 16, gives indices for 'barter terms of trade'.
12. Ibid., pp. 14-15, 17; J. P. Belshaw, 'The Crisis In New Zealand, 1930-34', unpub. MA thesis, University of New Zealand (Auckland), 1934, pp. 18, 19, 25.
13. J. Macrae and K. Sinclair, 'Unemployment in New Zealand during the Depression of the late 1920s and early 1930s', *Australian Economic History Review,* XV, I, 1975.
14. G. R. Hawke, 'Towards a Re-Appraisal of the "Long Depression" in New Zealand 1879-1895', unpub. paper presented to Department of Economics Seminar, University of Auckland, July 1975, p. 25.
15. Hawke, 'The Government and the Depression of the 1930s in New Zealand' *Australian Economic History Review,* XIII, I, p. 86; Condliffe, p. 51.
16. Condliffe, pp. 38-9.
17. PD, 1931, 227, 251.
18. 25 Aug. 1930, N1556.
19. Conference Report, 1930; Brown, pp. 138ff.; O'Farrell, pp. 197-9.
20. *N.Z. Worker,* 3 Dec. 1930.

21. Letter to *Evening Post*, 8 June 1932, N1220.
22. *N.Z. Worker*, 21 May 1930.
23. 10, 12 Dec. 1930, P. J. O'Farrell notes.
24. PD, 1931, 227; Holland to Cocking, 7 May 1931, P. J. O'Farrell notes.
25. *N.Z. Worker*, 15 Oct. 1930, deputation (including Nash) to Forbes.
26. PD, 1931, 229, 707 (Holland).
27. Ibid., pp. 709-11.
28. Ibid., 1932, 233, 59ff.
29. O'Farrell, p. 187.
30. Brown, pp. 137-8.
31. O'Farrell, pp. 181-2; Brown, pp. 135-8.
32. Pp. 2-5, 21; cf. G. R. Hawke, *Between Governments and Banks. A History of the Reserve Bank of New Zealand*, Wellington, 1973, pp. 9-10, 14-5.
33. See, e.g., S. A. and M. Ensom/WN, 15 March 1922, and his reply, 17 March 1922; A. E. Mander/WN, 21 March 1922, N1230.
34. For a socialist criticism of Douglas, see John Strachey's pamphlet, *Social Credit. An Economic Analysis*, London, 1936; for a New Zealand criticism, see A. J. Danks, *What Everyone Should Know About Social Credit*, Christchurch, 1955.
35. O'Farrell, p. 184; PD, 1931, 228, 22-23; 229, 183ff.
36. O'Farrell, p. 187; see below, p. 106 re 1933 policy.
37. Brown, p. 65.
38. Suggestion to the land committee, 1924, N2141.
39. *N.Z. Worker*, 15 Oct. 1924; 24 Nov. 1926 (this article, 'Supplied' by Nash, was clearly written by him. It contains his favourite ideas and phrases); WN/Parry, 2 Feb. 1927, P. J. O'Farrell notes, General Secretary's correspondence.
40. On the whole question of the origins of guaranteed prices, see R. J. M. Hill, 'The Quest for Control. The New Zealand Dairy Industry and the Guaranteed Price, 1921-36', unpub. MA thesis, University of Auckland, 1974, which I supervised. Although I had read some of the main sources in the Nash Papers before Mr Hill, I rely on his work, and on discussions with him, for much of the interpretation and detail offered in this section of the book.
41. PD, 1923, 202, 353-6, 468, 480; 1926, 210, 26-29, 54-56; Hill, pp. 108ff.
42. Letter to a farmer, 14 June 1927, N2141; WN/Hinton, 10 Nov. 1930, N2140. Cf. article, possibly by Nash, on Land Settlement, *N.Z. Worker*, 24 Nov. 1926. Cf. A. P. Ngata and others, *New Zealand Affairs*, pp. 161, 166.
43. PD, 1930, 224, 334; cf. Savage, 163, 879ff.; 225, 113ff. See below, Chapter XII, pp. 133-5.
44. Mr Mason did not (in 1973) recall helping to write the manifesto. He remembered that he was in North Auckland helping candidates, including Captain Rushworth, the president of the Country Party, who had strong Social Credit views. Mason helped to write his election propaganda. Labour did not put up a candidate against him.
45. Brown, p. 150. A report drawn up by Parry, Nash, Semple, Clyde Carr, Barnard, and Roberts stressing that credit should be available through existing financial agencies (19 March 1932) was submitted, after the election, to the 1932 Conference. PD, 1932, 232, 198ff.
46. This episode has been ignored by historians except in two unpublished theses. Only R. Clifton, 'Douglas Social Credit and the Labour Party, 1930-35', unpub. MA thesis, University of New Zealand (Victoria), 1961, pp. 178-80, emphasized it. It had been referred to earlier by E. P. Malone, 'The Rural Voter—voting trends in the Waikato, 1922-35', unpub. MA thesis, University of New Zealand (Auckland), 1958, p. 164.

47. *Dominion, The Press*, 5 Nov., 17 Nov. 1931.
48. *Dominion, Auckland Star*, 17 Nov. 1931; *The Press*, 18, 23, 24 Nov. 1931.
49. *Dominion*, 21, 25, 26, 27, 30 Nov., 1 Dec. 1931; *Hutt News*, 1 Dec. 1931.
50. *Hutt News*, 25 Nov., 1 Dec. 1931.
51. PD, 1932, 231, 180ff., 246ff.
52. 9 Dec. 1931; WN/Semple, 4 Dec. 1931, N1229.
53. Letters in N2145, N2151, N2191.
54. Dowse/WN, 15 Jan. 1932, N2188.
55. Letter from Mr John A. Lee to the author, 14 Nov. 1972. Wright referred to some of these positions, PD, 1932, 233, 917-18.
56. PD, 1932, 233, 420; 1933, 235, 911; 237, 224; 1935, 242, 514-15.
57. PD, 1935, 242, 58.

IX: THE POLITICS OF DEPRESSION, 1932-4

1. PD, 1932, 232, 178-81, 206.
2. Lee/Mrs Lee, 18 Oct. 1932; 30 [—] 1932, 2 Dec. 1932, Lee MSS, 541/2.
3. See K. Sinclair and W. F. Mandle, *Open Account. A History of the Bank of New South Wales in New Zealand, 1861-1961*, Wellington, 1961, Chapter XI.
4. I am not quite convinced by the argument of G. R. Hawke, *Between Government and Banks*, pp. 36-37. Currency 'personality', like tariff 'personality', was an aspiration of Dominion nationalism.
5. Hawke, *Between Governments and Banks*, Chapter 3. See also, G. R. Hawke, 'The Government and the Depression of the 1930s', loc. cit. Hawke's is much the best account of the facts of these events. Cf. review of his *Between Governments and Banks* by W. B. Sutch, *New Zealand Listener*. 16 Feb. 1974, and Hawke's letter, 18 May 1974.
6. Hawke, 'The Government and the Depression', *loc. cit.*, p. 85; C. A. Blyth, 'The Industrialisation of New Zealand', *New Zealand Economic Papers*, 8, 1974, p. 18.
7. PD, 1934, 238, 733-8; Blyth, loc. cit.
8. WN/McMillan correspondence and notes of meeting in 1933 in N2133; M. C. Pugh, 'The New Zealand Legion and Conservative Protest in the Great Depression', unpub. MA thesis, University of Auckland, 1969.
9. S. A. and M. Ensom/WN, 15 March; WN/Ensom, 17 March 1922; A. E. Mander/WN, 21 March 1922, N1230.
10. O'Farrell, pp. 177-8, 192; Lee/Mrs Lee, 6 Sept., 6 Oct., 19 Oct. 1932, Lee MSS, 541/2.
11. 10 May 1927, N1556.
12. PD, 1932, 234, p. 782; 233, 917.
13. 31 Jan. 1933, Lee MSS, 541/3; Savage/WN, 20 Feb. 1931, P. J. O'Farrell Notes.
14. WN/McCombs, 30 June 1933, N1230; Lee/ Mrs Lee, 6 March 1933, Lee MSS 541/2.
15. PD, 1933, 236, 90ff. On this point the remark by P. J. O'Farrell, p. 203, that to Holland a loan was a capitalist levy on the people, is unconvincing. He had advocated a large loan during the 1931 election.
16. Lee/Mrs Lee, 6 March (3 letters), 7 March 1933, Lee MSS 541/2. Lee told his wife that the voting was 13 to 6 but actually names 21 MPs.
17. WN/McCombs, 30 June 1933, N1230; PD, 1933, 235, 1073ff., 1102-03.
18. PD, 1932, 232, 149-50.
19. PD, 1931, 229, 464; 1930, 225, 368 (Nash); 1931, 229, 711 (Holland); cf. Nash's evidence to Monetary Commission, AJHR, 1934, B-3, p. 334.

20. AJHR, loc. cit., p. 336; PD, 1934, 239, 697.

21. In 1957 Langstone became a Social Credit candidate for parliament, but even in 1934 he was closer to Douglas than the others.

22. A. H. Tocker, 'The Monetary Standards of New Zealand and Australia', *Economic Journal*, XXXIV, Dec. 1924.

23. Hawke, *Between Governments and Banks*, pp. 15-17.

24. PD, 1932, 233, 57-8; 1933, 236, 418; H. G. R. Mason, *Common Sense of the Money Question*, Wellington [1934].

25. WN/D. Wilson, 18 April 1934, N2077.

26. *The First Step in the March from Bankruptcy to Prosperity. Labour's Plan!* Mr Mason wrote to the author (26 June 1973) that Langstone was 'a mere sentimentalist, with no more idea of finance than a child'. Sir Bernard Ashwin (interview, 1971) said he never succeeded in explaining the most elementary financial points to him.

27. Copies in envelopes addressed to MPs in N2104.

28. PD, 1933, 235, 84.

29. Copies in N2098.

30. *A Letter which every New Zealander should read*, Auckland, 1938.

31. Clifton, pp. 68ff.

32. 11 July 1933, P. J. O'Farrell Notes.

33. Wilson/Lee, 13 June 1933, P. J. O'Farrell Notes.

34. R. S. Mackay/Thorn, 28 April 1933, N2098.

35. Barnard/Thorn, 18 Aug. 1932, 15 Jan. 1934; Thorn/Barnard, 19 Jan. 1934, P. J. O'Farrell Notes.

36. WN/Mrs K. M. Tannahill, 3 Nov. 1934, N485.

37. Clifton, p. 189.

38. Minutes, 15 Sept. 1932, P. J. O'Farrell Notes.

39. Clifton, e.g. pp. 194-5.

40. Brown, pp. 170-2. The socialist 'Objective' was not formally dropped until 1951.

41. Drafts in N1540, N2098; other papers in N1275.

42. Letters in N1540.

43. Clifton, pp. 211ff.

44. O'Farrell, pp. 206-9.

45. 15 Oct. [1933], N75.

46. Wilson/WN, 15 Oct. 1933, N75.

47. 13 Oct. 1933, Lee MSS 541/2. Lee headed this letter, 'A note for reference ten years hence'. It is still of interest after thirty-three years.

X: 'THIS IS THE YEAR', 1935-6

1. Lee/F. Young, [c. March 1935], N1186; this episode is extensively documented, with letters from Lee, Mason, Savage, etc., in N1186, N2077; National Executive minutes, N2077; letters in Lee MSS, 541/5; *Truth*, 24 April, 1 May 1935.

2. Brown, p. 176.

3. D. Wilson/WN, 21 Aug. 1933; N75; 1934 Conference Report.

4. C. G. Rollo, 'The Election of 1935 in New Zealand', unpub. MA thesis, University of New Zealand (Canterbury), 1950, pp. 13ff.

5. WN/C. B. Whitmore, 12 Sept. 1935, N1481.

6. E.g., PD, 1933, 237, 215-16, Adam Hamilton.

7. S. Wigglesworth, 'The Depression and the Election of 1935', unpub. MA thesis, University of New Zealand (Auckland), 1954, p. 47.

8. Ibid., p. 140; PD, 1935, 242, 4, 517-8.

9. Rollo, pp. 146ff. For Nationalist and Democrat election manifestos see *Dominion*, 2 Oct., 29 Oct. 1935.
10. Handwritten draft in N1275; draft notes and WN/Savage, [3 Nov. 1935], N304; WN/Thorn, 11 Nov. 1935, N2104.
11. Many of his speeches etc. expound these views. E.g. *N.Z. Worker*, 12 June 1929, 19 Feb. 1930; *Dominion*, 7 Nov. 1935; *Poverty Bay Herald*, 25 Oct. 1930; *Star* (Wairoa), 30 Oct. 1935.
12. *Winnipeg Free Press*, 2 Nov. 1936; PD, 1937, 248, 1107.
13. W. Nash, *New Zealand A Working Democracy*, New York, 1943, p. 265.
14. *N.Z. Worker*, 11 March 1925.
15. 8 Aug. 1935, N1477.
16. 12 May 1933, N2416.
17. PD, 1936, 244, 686.
18. 8 Dec. 1935, N1444. On the history of this pamphlet see Hill, pp. 288ff.
19. 19 Aug. 1935, N316, a file which also contains proofs of *Guaranteed Prices Why and How*.
20. PD, 1935, 242, 59, (Semple); Hill, pp. 137 (Fraser); 187, 352 (Nash); Williams/WN, 16 Oct. 1935, N1481.
21. E.g. P. Neilson/WN, 26 Sept. 1935, N1479; WN/J. E. Keenan, 27 Sept. 1935, N2077.
22. Sections on pp. 9 and 12 of proof copy, N316, deleted. See Hill, pp. 242-3. Nash certainly thought that a deficit would be repayable. See his speech in Whangarei, *N.Z. Herald*, 5 Nov. 1935.
23. Central Executive minutes, 9 Dec. 1935, N2077.
24. R. S. Milne, *Political Parties in New Zealand*, Oxford, 1966, p. 76; Parry, Langstone, Nash letters in N2077 about C. A. Barrell; Clifton, pp. 231ff.
25. WN report 19 Aug. 1935, N1479; also papers in N2104.
26. N2104.
27. Wilson/WN, 24 Oct. 1935, N1481.
28. Central Executive minutes, 24 Oct., 9 Dec. 1935, N2077; sample pamphlets and other papers in N2104; *Evening Post*, 21 Nov. 1935; poster in N2104.
29. D. Wilson report, 23 May 1938, N2088; 1936 conference report; A. Spurr/WN, 20 Dec. 1935, N1268.
30. Wigglesworth, pp. 144-5; Rollo, pp. 74-8; Clifton, Chapter VI.
31. *Dominion*, 23, 24 Nov. 1935; Lee/Mrs Lee, 3 Dec. 1935, Lee MSS, 541/5.
32. L. Edwards, *Scrim*, Auckland, 1971, pp. 81-3; PD, 1936, 244, 347.
33. Clifton, pp. 235, 254; for samples see *N.Z. Herald*, 1, 6, 22 Nov. 1935, *Evening Post*, 21 Nov. 1935.
34. *Socialism in New Zealand*, London, 1938, p. 43.
35. E.g. *Evening Post*, 12 Nov. 1935. Most of his speeches stressed guaranteed prices.
36. *Dominion*, 15 Aug. 1935; PD, 1935, 241, 49; Clifton, p. 259.
37. 11 July 1935, N2188.
38. Ibid.; Rollo, p. 102.
39 L. Lipson, *The Politics of Equality*, Chicago, 1948, p. 231.
40. Wigglesworth, Appendix 5.
41. Closey/WN, 20 Dec., WN/Closey, 31 Dec. 1935, N1477.
42. Hill, pp. 262ff.; Clifton, pp. 307ff.
43. Lee MSS, 541/6.
44. Interview with Mr Ormond Wilson; WN/R. M. Campbell, 18 Dec. 1935, N2148.
45. Lists in N2269.
46. Lee/Mrs Lee, 3 Dec. 1935, (the third of four notes of that date), Lee MSS, 541/6; Fraser/Lee, 3 June 1937 (a copy sent to the author by Mr Lee); WN/B.

Brown, 15 Oct. 1962, N1098; Brown, p. 190. Nash seems to have included Lee's name in a list when he was drawing up his own cabinet proposals, N2269. The comments on newspaper opinion are based on a search of the two main newspapers in each of the four cities, 29 Nov. to 6 Dec. 1935, carried out by Mrs Jane Thomson.

47. Lee/Mrs Lee, 3 Dec. 1935 (two notes), loc. cit.; Minutes of the Caucus of the Parliamentary Labour Party, in the Nash Papers. These were read by kind permission of the late Mr Norman Kirk, then Leader of the Opposition.
48. 22 May 1935, N1478.
49. Lee/Mrs Lee, 13 Dec. 1935, loc. cit.
50. 14 Jan. 1936, loc. cit.
51. A recollection of Mr Ormond Wilson.
52. R. Chapman and K. Sinclair (eds.), *Studies of a Small Democracy*, Auckland, 1963, pp. 172-3 (F. Rogers's article).
53. R. J. Stanton/WN, 22 Dec.; Heenan/WN, 5 Dec.; Thorn/WN, 4 Dec. 1935, N2134.
54. Lee/WN, 26 Dec., WN/Lee, 31 Dec. 1935, N1479. In *Simple on a Soap Box*, Auckland, 1963, p. 38, Mr Lee says that he wrote to Savage about Nash being a quartermaster general.
55. Lee/WN, 24 Dec. 1935, N1479.
56. Labour Party Conference Report, 1935; *Truth*, 1 May 1935; WN cabinet-making (etc.) notes, N2269; Minutes of the Parliamentary Labour Party, 20-21 Feb. 1936.
57. Mason/J. B. Sleeman, 19 May 1953, filed in Vol. 3 of Minutes of the Parliamentary Labour Party.
58. Fraser/WN, 2 April; Wilson et. al./WN, 3 June 1936, N2537.

XI: MINISTER OF FINANCE, 1936

1. Lee/Mrs Lee, 12, 20 Feb., 18 March 1936, Lee MSS 541/6; 3 April 1936, Lee MSS 541/7.
2. 7 Dec. 1935.
3. WN/C. Carr, 4 Feb. 1932, P. J. O'Farrell notes.
4. Ashwin/WN, 13, 16 Dec. 1935, N1231; Campbell/WN, 7 Dec. 1935; Crick/Campbell, 1 Dec. 1935; WN/Campbell, 29 Jan. 1936, N2148; Hill, pp. 328-30.
5. Lee/Mrs Lee, 20 Feb. 1936, Lee MSS 541/6.
6. PD, 1935, 244, 140ff.; Hawke, *Between Governments and Banks*, pp. 52ff., 61ff.
7. A. Hempton/WN, 18 March 1936, N76; PD, 1936, 244, 147-8.
8. Lee/Mrs Lee, 6 April 1936, Lee MSS, 541/7.
9. Silverstone/WN, 26 Sept. 1936, N2143; Ashwin/WN, 27 April 1937, N1589; Lee, *Simple*, pp. 85-86; Hawke, pp. 63-67, 83. It does seem, from Silverstone's and Lee's comments, and from what Nash said later in the House, that (contrary to Hawke's view, p. 68), the fixing of interest rates was an initial cause of friction between Nash and Lefeaux.
10. *Evening Post*, 12 Nov. 1935; Labour's Election Manifesto, 1935.
11. See J. A. Hobson's introduction to *Unto This Last*, London, [1907].
12. These are discussed at length by Hill, Chapters V to VIII, to which this brief comment is heavily indebted.
13. D. Barnes/WN, 18 Sept.; WN/Barnes, 24 Sept. 1935, N1477.
14. Hill, p. 245; Fisher/WN, 5 Aug. 1935, N316.
15. Lee/Mrs Lee, 23 Jan., 13, 14, 19 Feb. 1936, Lee MSS, 541/6; *Simple*, pp. 62ff.; cf. a criticism of Lee's assertions, Hill, p. 323, footnote. The government in fact

paid more than it promised. See Hill, p. 303, on the Savage, Nash, Lee Martin meetings.

16. Hill, pp. 379-81.
17. Ibid., pp. 324-7.
18. PD, 1936, 244, 675ff.; the quotation from Fisher is from his letter to Nash, 5 Aug. 1935, N316.
19. PD, 1936, 244, 684ff. (Coates), 856 (Hamilton).
20. Ibid., 876ff.; cf. Coates, 686, 690.
21. Hill, pp. 322-3; 'Summary of Developments—Guaranteed Price. . . .', 5 Aug. 1959, paper in N2403.
22. Hill, pp. 284-5, 383.
23. PD, 1936, 245, 443ff.
24. PD, 1936, 246, 261ff., 336ff.
25. 15 May 1937.
26. Lee/Mrs Lee, 4 Aug. 1936, Lee MSS, 541/8.
27. Report of the Special Departmental Committee, N1014; E. A. Hanson, 'The Social Security Story', unpub. MA thesis, University of Auckland, 1975, pp. 57-58, 66-67; K. Sinclair, 'The Lee-Sutch Syndrome', *New Zealand Journal of History*, 8, 2 Oct. 1974.
28 Minutes of the Parliamentary Labour Party; Lee, *Simple*, p. 86.

XII: LONDON AND OTHER CAPITALS, 1936-7

1. Notes on deputation, 15 Sept. 1936; WN/P. Fraser, 19 Oct. 1936, N1599.
2. PD, 1933, 237, 246-7; Hill, pp. 152ff.; IPR Conference document CS 74, in N364 and N67.
3. PD, 1935, 242, 511.
4. But see PD, 1933, 237, 246.
5. 'Preliminary notes of Address' on 15 Oct. 1934, W. Downie Stewart MSS, Hocken Library.
6. H. W. Arndt, *Economic Lessons of the 1930s*, Oxford, 1944, *passim*.
7. W. B. Sutch, *Recent Economic Changes in New Zealand*, New Zealand, 1936, p. 21. This book and Arndt's give excellent accounts of the imperial and international economic problems of the time. The best commentary on the Ottawa agreements, their origins and outcome, is still W. K. Hancock's *Survey of British Commonwealth Affairs*, II, Part I.
8. See Sutch, *Recent Economic Changes, passim*, for a review of these events.
9. Hancock, p. 279.
10. Ibid., p. 226.
11. Sutch, *Recent Economic Changes*, p. 56.
12. Arndt, pp. 88, 112ff.; J. A. Richardson, *British Economic Foreign Policy*, London, 1936, pp. 101ff.
13. *World Trade and its Future*, London, 1936, p. 94.
14. Memo 22 Oct. 1936, BT 11/607, PRO London. Nash's discussions in London in 1936-7 and 1939 are documented in great detail in Dominions Office, Board of Trade, Treasury, and Ministry of Agriculture and Fisheries series. Only a fraction of this material is referred to in this book.
15. For reference to information from Lefeaux, see Lord Hartington/Malcolm MacDonald, n.d.; E. Harding memo, 21 Nov. 1936, BT 11/637; Board of Trade Brief for British ministers for meeting with Nash on 16 Dec. 1936, BT 11/631.
16. Notes sent by the Dominions Office to the Board of Trade, 22 May 1937, BT 11/637.

17. Boulter/E. R. Eddison, 24 Dec. 1936, BT 11/637.

18. Minutes and correspondence in BT 11/626.

19. BT 11/637. Professor P. S. O'Connor found this suggestion and wondered what was on the menu.

20. E.g. MacDonald/WN, 28 April 1958, N1413.

21. MacDonald notes, DO 35/274.

22. BT 11/631, notes of meeting on 19 Nov. 1936.

23. *Survey,* II, 1, 198.

24. K. Sinclair, 'The Lee-Sutch Syndrome', loc. cit., pp. 101-2.

25. Governor-General/Secretary of State, 2 Dec.; Secretary of State/Governor-General, 3 Dec.; Governor-General/Secretary of State, 5 Dec. 1936 and other cables filed in N2537.

26. WN/Savage, 7 Dec.; Governor-General/Secretary of State, 10 Dec. 1936 (with message for the King).

27. Middlemas and Barnes, *Baldwin A Biography,* pp. 1000-03. The 'minister' referred to, p. 1003, footnote, was Nash. Nash signed the Proclamation of George VI on 12 Dec. 1936. (Information and relevant documents kindly provided by the Privy Council Office, Whitehall.) See also, *Dominion,* 5 Jan., *Evening Post,* 11 Jan. 1937, N66.

28. 'Basis suggested for a new Trade Agreement', Brief prepared for President of Board of Trade, 8 Nov. 1936, BT 11/637.

29. For the arguments used, see Board of Trade Brief and notes on meeting of 16 Dec., BT 11/631; note furnished to Nash on 19 Dec. of observations made by Euan Wallace, DO 35/764; notes of meeting of 23 Dec., DO 35/763.

30. Machtig/MacDonald, 22 Dec., DO 35/763; notes of meeting, 23 Dec., DO 35/763; minutes by S. D. Waley and S. P. Woods, T 161/772. (The latter were found by Professor P. S. O'Connor.) MacDonald/WN, 19 Feb. 1937, DO 35/763.

31. Arndt, pp. 68-69.

32. DO 35/763, meeting on 9 Feb. 1937; DO 35/116, meeting on 8 March and WN's draft agreement presented then; for British draft proposals see DO 35/763/0116/5.

33. Meeting on 2 July 1937, DO 35/763; meeting on 15 Feb. 1937, BT 11/631. On exchange controls etc. see Nash's remarks at meeting on 8 March 1937, DO 35/116, and WN/Savage, 7 Dec. 1936, N66, re meeting with Norman.

34. 'Memorandum by the Official Committee on the Negotiations with New Zealand', 7 April 1937, BT 11/631.

35. Meeting on 16 Dec. 1936, BT 11/631.

36. Meetings of 15 March, 24 March, DO 35/763.

37. Meeting of British Ministers on 7 April, DO 35/763; also meetings of 22 March, BT 11/631, and 25 March, DO 35/763.

38. Memo by the Minister of Agriculture, 7 April, DO 35/763.

39. 'Memo by the Official Committee . . .', 7 April 1937, BT 11/631; draft of letter to Nash re mutton and lamb, Feb. 1937, and revised draft, 6 April 1937, DO 35/763/116/45.

40. H. Clay, *Lord Norman,* London, 1957, p. 414.

41. Documents on Nash's European tour are in N66, N72, N134, N152, N209, N303, N1083, N1311, N1599, N2062. The late Dr R. M. Campbell recalled (in conversation) the visit to Litvinov, and the Nazi flag episode. I also heard Dr Sutch's and Mr J. P. D. Johnsen's version of the latter episode. When Nash was very old he wrote in some biographical notes: 'Sutch. Nazi flags. Moscow visit'.

42. *Dominion,* 29 April 1937.

43. Mrs Fraser/Mrs Nash, 20 Feb. 1937, N2143.

44. WN/Savage, 11 Jan., 1 Feb. 1937, N2197; 15 March 1937, N1599; Hobday/Mrs Nash, 29 April 1937, N2143.
45. N2143.
46. Mrs Fraser/Mrs Nash, 20 Feb., 30 March, 13 May 1937, N2143.
47. Sutch, *The Quest for Security in New Zealand 1840 to 1966,* Wellington, 1966, p. 211.
48. Wilson/WN, 5 April 1937, N2143. Revised draft of speech and final version in N2292. Other papers on the conference are in N45 and N2537.
49. Text in N2537.
50. Dalton Diaries, 18, 22 June 1937 (London School of Economics). Jordan told Dalton that it was quite untrue, as had been reported in the *New Statesman,* that Eden had blue-pencilled his speech at the recent League of Nations meeting. 'He said that this story was an insult to N.Z. and an insult to him. He always spoke from notes and not from manuscript. What had actually happened was that Eden came across and showed him the manuscript speech which Eden himself intended to deliver. He made some comments on certain passages and Eden then marked these with a blue pencil, and, when he spoke, modified. Jordan was furiously angry with the *New Statesman,* but said that he thought it below the dignity of the High Commissioner for New Zealand to write to the Press and contradict such stories.' Cf. the version by W. B. Sutch, *Quest for Security,* p. 205. Sutch was in Geneva with Jordan, but what Dalton records seems more likely to be correct.
51. *Evening Post,* 25 Aug. 1937. On the conference in general see R. Tamchina, 'In Search of Common Causes: The Imperial Conference of 1937', *Journal of Imperial and Commonwealth History,* I, 1, 1972.
52. See below, XXVI, footnote 11.
53. Meeting on 9 June 1937, DO 35/763.
54. Paper on 'U.K.-N.Z. Trade Negotiations', NZ 11/36, June 1936; meeting on 2 July 1937, DO 35/763; C. W. D. [ixon] minute, 31 May 1937, DO 35/763/0116/43.
55. Memo of 7 April 1937, DO 35/763.
56. Stanley/Morrison, 2 Sept. 1937; Secretary of State cable, 25 Nov. 1937, DO 35/763; see also BT 11/950.
57. *Quest for Security,* p. 210.
58. Interview with Mr Harold Innes, 29 March 1973; on Nash's interest in interlocking directorates, see PD 1931, 227, 414.
59. Lord Davies/WN, 23 June 1937, and WN's reply, N2143.
60. *Evening Post,* 30 Aug. 1969, M. Kelly article.
61. Papers in N134.
62. Draft 'memoirs', in possession Mr J. A. D. Nash.
63. *Star,* 26 Feb. 1937; *Daily Express,* 9 Nov. 1936; *Tobacco,* 2 Dec. 1936.
64. WN/Mrs A. Day, 6 March 1937, N1599; J. P. Balmforth letter in *St John's Parish Magazine* (Kidderminster), April 1937.
65. Press release, 23 July 1937, N38; *Dominion,* 19 July 1937.
66. N2258.
67. 18 May 1937, N2089.
68. N2143.
69. 19 Aug. 1937.
70. WN/Savage, 30 June 1937, N134; *Standard,* 8 July 1937; WN Press statement for *The Exporter,* Aug. 1937, N38.
71. *Dominion,* 5 July 1937.
72. PD 1937, 248, 424.
73. Sutch, *Quest for Security,* p. 211.

XIII: TRIUMPHS AND TROUBLES, 1937-8

1. Savage/Mrs P. M. K. Knights, 24 March 1938, N1460.
2. Wilson/WN, 5 April 1937, N2143.
3. 20 Feb., 30 March, 13 May 1937, N2143.
4. Mrs Fraser/Mrs Nash, 13 May 1937, N2143; *Dominion* and *Evening Post,* 29 April 1937; PD, 1937, 249, 144ff.; Edwards, *Scrim,* p. 93.
5. 23 June 1937, N2537.
6. See, e.g., *N.Z. News,* 27 April 1937; *Financial News,* 18 May 1937; *Dominion,* 14, 20 April, 11 May 1937; *Evening Post,* 17 Aug. 1937; R. M. (?) Sunley/Rodda, 7 July 1936, N2198.
7. PD, 1937, 248, 738-9.
8. Ashwin/WN, 27 April 1937, N1589.
9. PD, 1937, 248, 417ff.; 672ff.
19. *N.Z. Worker,* 6 Oct. 1926.
11. PD, 1937, 249, 738-9.
12. Fletcher/Lee, 13 Jan. 1937, Treasury 25/139, National Archives.
13. Fletcher/WN, 20 Feb. 1937, Treasury 25/139; Fletcher/WN, 9 Dec. 1938, in Nash file, 'Confidential and other important historical papers', in possession of Mr J. A. D. Nash. The original government offer to purchase Fletcher's firm was made in June 1936 or earlier. See R. T. Metge, 'The House that Jack Built. The Origins of Labour State Housing 1935-8 . . .', unpub. MA thesis, University of Auckland, 1972, p. 24; and *passim* on this subject in general. Other letters between Fletcher and Nash are in N217, N1232, N1478, N1563.
14. Fletcher/Lee, 13 Jan. 1937; Fletcher/WN, 20 Feb. 1937, Treasury 25/139.
15. Ashwin/WN, 29 Nov. 1940, N1232; N. Robinson, *James Fletcher: Builder,* London, 1970, pp. 117-9.
16. Lee/WN, 1 Dec. 1936, N217; WN/Fletcher, 19 Oct. 1936, N217; 1 March 1940, 10 Jan. 1941, N1232.
17. Metge, p. 25.
18. In an interview with the author. The housing report is in N2196.
19. Minutes of Parliamentary Labour Party, 17 June 1937. By 24 Aug. 1937, he was proposing extensive inflationary measures, Lee/Nordmeyer, N2197. See below, p. 159.
20. 6 March 1937, N1084; 4 Nov. 1936, WN/Lee, 12 Dec. 1936, N217.
21. Robinson, p. 116; PD, 1937, 248, 420.
22. *Dominion,* 8 Dec. 1972.
23. Metge, pp. 44-45, Lee/WN, 20 May 1937, N1084.
24. Ashwin/Fraser, 19 March 1937, N1084.
25. Metge, p. 46; Savage/Mrs K. Simmons, 2 Nov. 1937, WN/J. O'Brien, 19 Jan. 1938, N217.
26. N2139.
27. Lee/WN, 1 Dec. 1936, N217; 16 April 1937, N1084; Lee/Savage, 18 March 1938, N217; see E. Olssen, 'John A. Lee, The Amalgamated Society of Carpenters and Joiners and "Worker Control" of the Building Industry', *Political Science,* 27, 1-2, July-Dec. 1975. Lee does not seem to me to have been as favourably disposed to worker control as Olssen suggests.
28. Metge, pp. 24-25, 61-63.
29. Lee/WN, 28 Sept. 1937, N217.
30. 14 March 1940, Lee MSS 441/9.
31. PD, 1933, 235, 160; 236, 188.
32. Ibid., 1939, 255, 229.

33. 13 May [1936], Lee MSS 541/8.
34. 26 March 1936, Lee MSS, 541/6; 11 June 1936, Lee MSS, 541/8.
35. Minutes of Parliamentary Labour Party, 17 Feb., 14 Sept. 1937.
36. Ibid., 8 Sept., 23, 24, 30 Nov. 1937; Lee/Nordmeyer, 24 Aug. 1937, N2197; Lee/Savage, 8 Feb. 1938, N2318.
37. *Labour Has a Plan*, p. 3.
38. 27 April 1937, N1589.
39. Minutes of Parliamentary Labour Party, 30 Nov. 1937.
40. Hanson, pp. 59-67. The following pages on the social security legislation are based in substance on Miss Hanson's excellent detailed study of the subject.
41. Ibid., pp. 69ff.; *Third Report,* 18 March 1937, is filed with the other three reports, N1014.
42. See J. B. Lovell-Smith, *The New Zealand Doctor and The Welfare State,* Auckland, 1966, pp. 37-54. This is a useful account largely from the point of view of the BMA.
43. See, e.g., D. Robb, *Medicine and Health in New Zealand,* Christchurch, 1940; *Health Services or Doctors and Hospitals,* Wellington, [1942]; *Medical Odyssey,* Auckland, 1967. Dr D. G. McMillan's pamphlet, *A National Health Service. New Zealand of Tomorrow,* Wellington, [1935], also deserves its perpetuity, as a source of Social Security—the ideas of a young, radical, rural GP.
44. Hanson, pp. 79ff.
45. Ibid., p. 87.
46. 13 April 1938, N256.
47. For their arguments, see Hanson, pp. 79ff. and *passim;* Lovell-Smith, *passim.*
48. Hanson, p. 85; Lovell-Smith, p. 99.
49. Hanson, p. 96; Robb, *Health Services,* pp. 8-9; *Medical Odyssey,* Chapter 3; statements by Jamieson at conference with Nash and Fraser, 21 Dec. 1937, Minutes, N1007, pp. 3, 6, 7.
50. Hanson, pp. 97-98; Jamieson statement, Minutes of 21 Dec. 1937, p. 13; Dr Jamieson to National Health and Superannuation Committee, Le I/1938/10, Vol. 3, National Archives.
51. Lovell-Smith, p. 71. Other doctors called social security a 'revolution': T. D. M. Stout, Evidence Submitted to National Health and Superannuation Committee.
52. Lovell-Smith, pp. 68-69; Minutes of meeting on 21 Dec. 1937, N1007.
53. Lovell-Smith, pp. 74-75; Hanson, pp. 99-100; Minutes of meeting, N1007.
54. *I Fight For New Zealand,* p. 22.
55. Copies of the two schemes submitted to caucus are in the Lee MSS, 441/22; see also Hanson, pp. 100ff.; 178ff.
56. J. S. Reid/WN, 5 Nov. 1936, N1311; Hanson, pp. 62-63; WN/Fraser, 19 Jan. 1937, N271.
57. Hanson, pp. 102-3.
58. Ibid., p. 102.
59. 15 March 1937, N1311.
60. Handwritten note by WN [early 1938] and notes from caucus meeting 10-11 Feb. 1938, found by Miss E. A. Hanson in N1006.
61. Lee, *I Fight,* p. 22; *Simple,* pp. 99-103.
62. Lee minute, Lee MSS, 441/22.
63. Minutes of Parliamentary Labour Party, 10, 11 Feb. 1938.
64. Lee, *I Fight,* p. 23; Hanson, pp. 112-14.
65. BMA Evidence Submitted to National Health and Superannuation Committee. For Jamieson's later version see Lovell-Smith, pp. 78-80.
66. Reid/WN, 9 Feb. 1937, N1311; Third Report of Interdepartmental Committee,

18 March 1937, pp. 12-13.
67. Hanson, pp. 136, 146.
68. PD, 1938, 252, 321ff.
69. 28 June 1946, N1544.
70. WN notes for memoirs, in possession Mr J. A. D. Nash.
71. PD, 1938, 252, 416-23.
72. WN/B. Brown, draft letter, 1962, N1098; Hanson, pp. 143-4.
73. Milne, *Political Parties in New Zealand,* p. 54.
74. N2098; *Standard,* 19 May 1938.
75. Hamilton speeches, 12 Oct. 1938, N1231; PD, 1938, 251, 124ff., 673; election pamphlet, N2098; *Dominion,* 30 Sept., 4 Oct. 1938.
76. Report to 1938 Conference; election manifesto—copies in N2083, N2087, N2436.
77. D. Wilson memo, 23 May 1938, N2088.
78. Wilson/WN, 18 May 1938, N2538; [K. ?] Lee Martin/WN, 13 June 1938, N2139; Hill, p. 394. See file of press clippings, N1681.
79. *Dominion,* 17 Feb. 1938; Clark/WN, 29 June 1938, N2139.
80. Hill, p. 392.
81. Press statement, 16 Sept. 1938, N1308; W. E. Hale/WN, 20 Nov. 1946, N420.
82. W. E. Hale/WN, 20 Nov. 1946, N420.
83. Lipson, pp. 205, 232; Milne, p. 55; Brown, p. 185.
84. PD, 1938, 251, 639.

XIV: THE EXCHANGE CRISIS, 1938-9

1. H. Belshaw, 'Import and Exchange Control in New Zealand', *Economic Record,* Dec. 1939; WN speech to importers' conference, 25 Jan. 1939, N2308; WN/W. H. Ridge, 7 May 1940, N2056.
2. See Chapter IX above, p. 104.
3. Hawke, *Between Governments and Banks,* p. 105; WN press statement, N2088; PD, 1938, 251, 640.
4. [Littlejohn] National Bank/WN, 20, 25 Oct. 1938, N2259; letters on the rumours in N1462, N1464, N1456, N1467, N1569.
5. H. Belshaw, 'Import and Exchange Control', loc. cit.; cf. Hawke, pp. 110-11.
6. [Littlejohn] National Bank/WN, 20, 25 Oct. 1938, N2259.
7. Hawke, p. 106.
8. WN speech to importers' conference, 25 Jan. 1939, N2308.
9. See the discussion in Hawke, p. 103.
10. Minutes of Parliamentary Labour Party, 10 Dec. 1937.
11. E.g. W. B. Sutch memo, 8 June 1938, N348.
12. Comptroller of Customs memo, 19 Oct. 1937, N2308.
13. Hawke, pp. 103-8.
14. N2269.
15. *Simple,* p. 124.
16. 23 Jan. 1939, N349; Sutch/WN, 6 Dec. 1938, N348; Milne, p. 52.
17. Letters dated 25 Nov., 17 Dec. 1938, N2308.
18. Minutes of Parliamentary Labour Party, 26 May, 3 June 1936.
19. Ibid., 3, 4 Nov. 1938; cf. Lee's account in *Simple,* pp. 125-8.
20. Minutes of Parliamentary Labour Party, 9, 10, 11 Feb. 1939.
21. 6 Nov. 1938, N2537.
22. Auckland, [1939]; *Simple,* pp. 139ff.; Olssen, pp. 210ff.
23. Minutes of Parliamentary Labour Party, 5 Oct., 10 Dec. 1937; K. Sinclair, 'Fruit Fly, Fireblight and Powdery Scab: Australia-New Zealand Trade Relations, 1919-1939', *Journal of Imperial and Commonwealth History,* I, 1, Oct. 1972,

pp. 43-44.
24. N2305.
25. Meeting on 29 June 1939, BT 11/1112.
26. WN Notes, 16 April 1939, N2305; Governor-General/Secretary of State, 21 Jan. 1939; Secretary of State/Governor-General, 22 April 1939, N2305; Meeting at Board of Trade, 15 May 1939, DO35/764 (Sir Eric Machtig).
27. Press clippings—e.g. *Reynolds News,* 28 May 1939—in N86.
28. R. M. Sunley (NZ Finance Officer)/WN, 15 Jan. 1939, N348.
29. Machtig minute, 25 Feb. 1939; Waley/C. W. Dixon, 3 April 1939, DO35/548 A; draft cable, T160/876.
30. MacDonald/Jordan, 9 Dec. 1938, DO35/764; Secretary of State/Governor-General, 2 Dec. 1938, N2305.
31. Secretary of State/Governor-General, 15 March 1939, N2305; meeting at Board of Trade, 15 May 1939, DO35/764 (Sir Eric Machtig).
32. Meeting at Board of Trade, DO35/764 and many other minutes and statements in records in the PRO.
33. J. A. P. Edgcumbe, 'Whither New Zealand'; Boulter/Edgcumbe, 5 Jan. 1939; Kershaw notes, 19 Dec. 1938; DO35/764.
34. Meeting of British Ministers, 5 June 1939, BT 11/1112. He had just seen Nash.
35. Minute, 28 June 1939, DO35/765.
36. Shannon/E. Harding, 1 March 1939, T160/876.
37. Meeting of officials, 15 May 1939, DO35/764; meeting of ministers, 5 June 1939, BT11/1112.
38. N2305; draft cables to Batterbee, T160/876.
39. W. A. Brooker, 'Exchange Control in New Zealand 1936-1945', unpub. PhD thesis, University of New Zealand (Otago), 1949, *passim.* WN statement to British Ministers, meeting on 7 June 1939, BT11/1112.
40. *N.Z. Herald,* 23 May 1939; papers in N2308.
41. Savage/WN, 29 May 1939; WN/Savage, 9 June 1939; Ashwin/WN, 14 June 1939, N342; *Dominion,* 25, 27 May 1939; *Evening Post,* 8 June 1939.
42. *Dominion,* 1 June 1939. Meeting of Nash with British Ministers, 5 July 1939, DO35/765; New Zealand version of minutes of the meeting in N2310. Nash's 1939 negotiations are documented in detail in BT, DO, and T files in the PRO. The cables between WN and Savage are in N342, and other papers in N346, N347, and N2310.
43. Inskip's report to meeting of British Ministers, 5 June 1939, BT11/1112.
44. WN/Savage, 2 June 1939, N342.
45. BT11/1112.
46. Note by Phillips, 9 June 1939, DO35/765.
47. WN/Savage, 9 June 1939, N342.
48. Interview with Kershaw at Bank of England, 5 June 1939, N347; WN/Savage, 19 June 1939, N342.
49. CAB 23/100 (cabinet minutes, PRO).
50. E.g. *Manchester Daily Express,* 22 June 1939.
51. 24 May 1939, DO35/765.
52. BT brief, 24 May 1939, ibid.; P. F. Bennett/O. Stanley, 7 June 1939, ibid.
53. WN/Savage, 24 June 1939, N342; T. minute, 22 June 1939, T160/876.
54. WN/Savage 24 June 1939, N342; T. memo to Waley, 23 June 1939, T160/876.
55. BT11/1112; WN/Savage, 1 July 1939, N342.
56. New Zealand minutes of meeting at 4 p.m. 29 June 1939, N2310; British minutes, DO35/765; the meeting with the group of ministers was at 3 p.m. Also WN/Savage, 1 July 1939, N342.

57. WN/Savage, 5 July 1939, N342.
58. 6 July, 7 July 1939, N342. WN spoke on proposed cuts at the meeting on 7 June with British Ministers, BT11/1112.
59. Minutes, N347; WN/Savage, 8 July 1939, N342; 'A Maturing Loan', draft article in possession of Mr J. A. D. Nash.
60. N349.
61. 10 July 1939, N342. Many of the events of these days are related in a detailed letter, E. Machtig/H. Batterbee, 25 July 1939, DO35/765.
62. Minutes in N2310.
63. Machtig letter, cited note 61.
64. Meetings on 5 and 7 July 1939, DO35/765; NZ minutes of 5 July, N2310.
65. Machtig/Batterbee, 25 July 1939, DO35/765; transcript of telephone conversation between Savage and Nash, 11 July 1939, N346; Savage/WN (cables), 10, 11 July 1939, N342; drafts of statement in N346 and N2310.
66. *Trade Discussions between United Kingdom Ministers and the Honourable Walter Nash . . ., July 1939*, HMSO, Cmd. 6059 (British Parliamentary Paper).
67. Transcript in N347.
68. *Tribune*, 4 Aug.; *Weekly Review*, 3 Aug. 1939, and other clippings in N86, N347.
69. WN/Savage, 14 July 1939, N342.
70. *Lord Norman*, London, 1957, pp. 413-4.
71. WN/Savage, 27 July 1939, N346.
72. Jordan/WN, 16 Aug. 1939, N2310.
73. 22 July 1939.
74. WN/Inskip, 17 July 1939, N342; WN notes for 'Memoirs' in possession Mr J. A. D. Nash.
75. WN/Norman, 24 March 1945; Norman/WN, 5 June 1945, N2259.
76. WN/Mrs Nash, 2 Aug. 1939, N349.
77. 'Sir Walter's Story How Banker Montagu Norman Came to New Zealand's Aid', *Evening Post*, 5 June 1968; and drafts of this article with Nash's notes for 'Memoirs'.
78. Hodson/WN, 4 Aug.; WN/Hodson, 18 Aug. 1939, N349.
79. 9 July 1939, N342.
80. *The Sky is a Limpet*, Auckland, 1939.
81. A. Boyle, *Montagu Norman*, London, 1967, pp. 300ff.
82. Book in N2537; WN notes of interview, N2545; typescript (several versions) 'A Meeting in the United States' (section of projected newspaper article by Nash in the possession of Mr J. A. D. Nash). Dr John Stagg has suggested that the President was apparently referring to the Nootka Sound crisis of 1790, when Adams recommended that the British should be refused permission to march across United States territory to attack the Spanish on the Mississippi. If so, the analogy with the Japanese crossing ocean was tenuous. See C. F. Adams (ed.), *The Works of John Adams*, Boston, 1850-56, VIII, 497-500, J. Adams/President Washington, 29 Aug. 1790.
83. WN Report, 1940, cited J. V. T. Baker, *The New Zealand People at War. War Economy*, Wellington 1965, pp. 42-43.

XV: PARTY STRIFE, 1939-40

1. Fraser/WN, 4 Aug. 1939, N349.
2. *I Fight For New Zealand*, p. 29; cf. Barnard's statements in *The Speech of a New Zealander*, Wellington, 1940.

3. Barnard, *Speech;* Wood, pp. 104ff.; Lee/Barnard, 15 Dec. 1939; Lee/WN, 15 Dec. 1939, Lee MSS 441/34.
4. PD, 1939, 255, 130-9, 194-5, 226-31.
5. Summary of statements made by McMillan at Dunedin West branches, 7 March 1940, sent by Bill Clarke (Seaman's Union) to Nash or Fraser, 14 March 1940, N2318; Barnard, *Speech;* Barnard/Fraser, 7 April 1940, N.Z. Labour Party MS, 270/31, Alexander Turnbull Library, Wellington; J. A. Lee, *Debt Finance for War and Peace versus Democracy,* Auckland, 1940.
6. Minutes of Parliamentary Labour Party, 8, 9, 10 Sept. 1939; Olssen, pp. 222-3; Lee, *I Fight,* p. 29. Caucus had not resolved, as Lee said in *Simple,* p. 155, 'to vote for a soldier or ex-soldier if it wanted to', though if cabinet were enlarged, an ex-serviceman could have been elected/selected. On Lee's further attack in *Tomorrow* see Olssen, pp. 220-1.
7. Hawke, pp. 39-40, 63ff.; Lefeaux/WN, 11 Oct. 1939, and other letters, 1939-40, N1590.
8. N244.
9. *Letter,* p. 11.
10. Minutes of Parliamentary Labour Party, 3, 5 Oct. 1939.
11. Lee/Barnard, 20 Dec. 1939; Lee's typewritten account of the meeting, Lee MSS 441/34; *Simple,* pp. 155ff. His account in *Simple* is inaccurate in one respect: The minutes of the Parliamentary Labour Party, 4 Nov. 1939, show that Nordmeyer nominated McMillan against Wilson, not to be an Under-Secretary.
12. 6 Dec. 1939. See Olssen, p. 227ff.
13. *Simple,* cf. statements on pp. 156, 158, 175-6; Olssen, pp. 229ff.
14. E.g. J. M. Murray/WN, 29 March 1938; 18 Nov. 1939, N2139.
15. 20 Dec. 1938, N2269.
16. WN and cabinet/Savage, 8 Dec.; WN/Lee, 18 Dec.; Lee/WN, 19 Dec.; Fraser/WN, 12 Jan. 1940, in file, 'J. A. Lee and W. E. Barnard', in possession of Mr J. A. D. Nash; Thorn/WN, 22 Dec. 1939, N2537.
17. 14 March 1940, Lee MSS 441/34. The best account of these events is in Olssen, pp. 232ff.
18. Brown, pp. 210-11.
19. R. J. Northey, 'The Annual Conferences of the New Zealand Labour Party', unpub. MA thesis, University of Auckland, 1973, p. 338. There is a photocopy of Savage's message in the Lee Papers.
20. Minutes of Parliamentary Labour Party, 4 April, 24 May 1940; J. Lyon/F. Moncur, 2 Jan. 1941, N2307; P. Neilson/WN, 8 Aug. 1940, N2537.
21. WN/Fraser, 15 Jan. 1947, N2304; Moohan/WN, 11 May 1942, N2258; *Evening Post,* 14 Sept. 1943. Dr W. Newlands said three doctors were earning £10,000 each. See also, Lovell-Smith, pp. 155-6. For Jamieson's prophecy, see Notes of Conference, 21 Dec. 1937, N1007.
22. Barnard/Fraser, 7 April 1940, NZ Labour Party MS 270/31.
23. For an analysis of the conflict see K. Sinclair, 'The Lee-Sutch Syndrome', loc. cit.
24. Cf. WN/B. Brown, 15 Oct. 1962, N1098.
25. WN speech, 11 Oct. 1959, N2244; W. Nash, *New Zealand. A Working Democracy,* New York, 1943, Preface, p. viii. Nash wrote this himself—draft in N287.
26. J. Robertson, B. Roberts, J. Thorn, and others, including credit reformers like C. A. Barrell, to WN, N2537.
27. Lyon/Moncur, 2 Jan. 1941, N2304; Lyon/WN, 25 Nov. 1940, N2139.

XVI: WORLD WAR 1939-41

1. *The New Zealand People at War: Political and External Affairs,* Wellington 1958, pp. 38-39; *N.Z. Worker,* 25 Sept. 1935, WN; PD, 1934, 239, 8-9.
2. PD, 1941, 260, 326.
3. *Survey,* II, 1, 197.
4. Copy in N2545. On this episode see K. Peters, 'New Zealand's Attitudes to the Reform of the League of Nations', *New Zealand Journal of History,* 6, 1, April 1972.
5. N. Mansergh, *Survey of British Commonwealth Affairs. Problems of External Policy 1931-1939,* London, 1952, pp. 88-89.
6. W. D. McIntyre, 'New Zealand and the Singapore Base on the Eve of the Pacific War'. Institute of Commonwealth Studies seminar paper, RHC/73/6, cited with the author's permission.
7. Committee of Imperial Defence, COS Sub-Committee, meeting 16 March 1937, CAB 53/7, Public Record Office, London.
8. Tamchina, pp. 93-94.
9. Committee of Imperial Defence, COS Sub-Committee, meetings of 1 June, 7 June, CAB 53/7.
10. Mansergh, pp. 192, 201; Tamchina, p. 86 and n. 38.
11. Mansergh, pp. 199-200.
12. WN/Savage, 5 July 1939, N347; files of clippings in N86, N347.
13. Drafts in N2243.
14. Wood, pp. 76ff.; B. K. Gordon, *New Zealand Becomes a Pacific Power,* Chicago, 1960, p. 96.
15. McIntyre, loc. cit.; see Berendsen's remarks at New Zealand Defence Conference, 14 April 1939.
16. COS Sub-Committee meeting, 25 May 1939, CAB 53/11.
17. Proceedings of Defence Conference, N2243.
18. Wood, pp. 99-100.
19. Information from the late Dr R. M. Campbell, who was present.
20. Wood, pp. 100-3.
21. Jordan/Fraser, 13 Feb. 1940, N2304; James Shelley evidence, N2251.
22. Wood, p. 122, and Chapters 10-11 in general.
23. Ibid., pp. 194-5.
24. Ibid., pp. 141-2; correspondence in N2071, N286.
25. Ibid., pp. 182-9.
26. WN/Fraser, 7 July, 15 July 1941, N2294.
27. WN/Fraser, 5 Aug., 12 Aug.; Fraser/WN, 12 Aug. 1941, N2294.
28. *The Press,* 10 May 1941; *Auckland Star,* 23 Sept. 1941; WN/Fraser, 5 Sept. 1941, N2294; Lovell-Smith, pp. 124-41; file of clippings in N1300.
29. WN/Fraser, 5 Sept. 1941, N2294; Baker, pp. 278ff.; R. M. Campbell memo, 14 July 1941, N2148.
30. WN/Fraser, 5 Aug. 1941, N2294; PD, 1941, 260, 325ff.
31. Wood, pp. 145ff.; see below, p. 267.
32. WN/Fraser, 1 July; Fraser/WN, 3 June, 28 July 1941, N2294.
33. Wood, pp. 166-9.
34. WN/Fraser, 1 July 1941, Holland/Nash correspondence, May-June 1941, N2294.
35. Correspondence in N1268, N2056, N2294; J. Williams/WN, 27 June 1941, N1268. Langstone press statement, *Evening Post,* 12 Jan. 1943.
36. WN/Fraser, 1 July, 26 July, 5 Aug. 1941, N2294.
37. Fraser/WN, 28 July 1941, N2294.

38. *Evening Post*, 8 Oct.; *Standard,* 16 Oct. 1941.
39. Interview with Colonel Pharazyn, 18 Jan. 1971, and with Sir Carl Berendsen, 8 Jan. 1971; Langstone press statements, N345.
40. Wood, pp. 170-1; Fraser/Holland correspondence in N2071.
41. *Dominion,* 16 April 1942.
42. 'Joint Statement on War Policy' by the National Council of the NZFOL, and the National Executive of the NZLP, 1939, 'Statement on the International Situation' by the National Council of the NZFOL, 1939.
43. 17 May 1940, N1162. For general comment, see Wood, pp. 124-5, 142-3, and *passim.*
44. W. B. Sutch, *The Quest for Security; Poverty and Progress in New Zealand,* Wellington, 1941. W. B. Sutch/K. Sinclair, 13 March 1973; WN/Fraser, 15 Sept. 1936, N1453; J. W. Heenan/WN, 19 Sept. 1940, N2544; documents in Internal Affairs 62/12; 62/110/5, National Archives.
45. T. B. Gusscott/WN, 1 June, WN/Gusscott, 19 June 1938, N2139; T. O'Shea (the Archbishop of Wellington)/P. Fraser, 25 June 1940, N2318; Reg Aickin/WN, 30 Jan. 1942, N1609.
46. N1448, file of 1936.
47. Baker, pp. 27ff.
48. PD, 1940, 257, 302ff.; 1941, 259, 353ff.; *Nash Replies to the Critics,* published by the N.Z. Labour Party, 1940.
49. *Nash Replies,* p. 29.
50. Lovell-Smith, pp. 139ff.
51. PD, 1940, 257, 303; 1941, 259, 361-4.
52. Baker, p. 441.

XVII: MINISTER TO WASHINGTON, 1942-43

1. Wood, pp. 194-6.
2. A. Watt, *The Evolution of Australian Foreign Policy 1938-65,* Cambridge, 1967, pp. 29-30.
3. Langstone/WN, 21 Feb. 1942, N345.
4. WN/Langstone, 13 May 1941, N2249.
5. 17 Feb. 1942, N345.
6. Letter cited note 3.
7. Stewart/Fraser, 10 Jan. 1940, N2304; Stewart/WN, 6 Jan. 1942, N2259; J. L. Kember, 'The Establishment of the New Zealand Legation at Washington, 1940-1944', unpub. research essay, Victoria University, 1971, p. 17, on Coates. Mr Kember's useful essay sorts out many details of his subject. Some of his sources were not used by me, but I had read the relevant Nash papers before he had.
8. Coates/WN, 6 June 1941, N130; Casey/Langstone, 6 June 1941; Casey/Coates, 2 June 1941, N2543.
9. E. H. Scott/Fraser, 10 March 1943, N2180.
10. Kember, pp. 20-21.
11. M. R. Megaw, 'Undiplomatic Channels: Australian Representation in the United States, 1918-1939', *Historical Studies,* 15, 60, 1973, p. 629.
12. Fraser/Langstone, 27 Nov., 1 Dec. 1941, N2545.
13. 2 Jan. 1942.
14. WN diary, N2539; typescript 'Memoirs', in possession of Mr J. A. D. Nash.
15. Filed in N2325, N2539; E. A. Gibson (formerly RNZAF) to author, 1971. Nash did not, as he later supposed, initial it himself.
16. Typescript 'Memoirs'; 1942 diary, N2539.

17. *Documents Relating to New Zealand's Participation in the Second World War 1939-45*, War History Branch, Wellington, 1963, Vol. III, pp. 113ff.
18. Ibid., pp. 122-8, Fraser's important message to the British government, 12 Jan. 1942.
19. *Chicago Daily Tribune*, 1 Feb. 1942, and other clippings in N1728; summary of press interview in N141.
20. [1 Feb. 1942], press clipping in N1728; press interview, N141.
21. *Documents*, p. 155.
22. Paul Hasluck, *The Government and the People 1942-1945*, Canberra, 1970, pp. 47-48.
23. WN/Fraser, 6 Feb., 18 Feb. 1942, *Documents*, pp. 149-50, 156.
24. WN/Fraser, 3 Feb. 1942, cit. Kember, p. 31.
25. WN/Fraser, 11, 12 Feb. 1942, N345; Langstone/WN, 21 Feb. 1942, N345, which recounts his grievances.
26. WN/Fraser, 14 Feb., Fraser/WN, 17 Feb. 1942, N345.
27. Fraser/WN, 27 March, WN/Fraser, 30 March 1942, N345. Cf. WN/H. Combs, 11 Feb. 1943, N2413.
28. [March] 1942, N345.
29. Langstone/WN, 24 Sept. 1942, N345; Kember, p. 52; minutes of Parliamentary Labour Party, 14 Oct. 1942.
30. Fraser press statement, N345; A. McIntosh/WN, 11 Feb. 1943, N345; WN/M. Moohan (draft), N17; M. Moohan/WN, 22 Dec. 1942, N2258; E. H. Scott/Fraser, 10 March 1943, N2180; C. W. Nash/WN, 16 Oct. 1942, N2413; Langstone press statements, N345.
31. The minutes of the Council, which are in the Roosevelt Papers, Hyde Park, were kindly sent to me by Professor W. R. Louis. It is still widely believed that there are no minutes. E.g. Hasluck, p. 228.
32. Minutes, 28 Oct. 1942; WN/Fraser, draft cable, 28 Oct. 1942, N17.
33. W. Nash, 'Administrative Organisations in Washington', *Journal of Public Administration*, 6, 1, Sept. 1943, pp. 75-76; minutes of Pacific War Council, 3 April 1942; R. E. Sherwood, *Roosevelt and Hopkins. An Intimate History*, New York, 1950, p. 518; WN/Hopkins, 24 March 1942, N345.
34. 4 May 1942, N2545.
35. E.g. *New York Times*, 1 April, 28 Aug., 10 Dec. 1942; 18 March 1943; *Washington Post*, 9 July 1942. See clippings in N1728.
36. *Newsweek*, 29 March 1943; interviews.
37. Minutes.
38. *Baltimore Sun*, 5 Feb. 1943, clipping in N1728.
39. WN/Fraser, 4 May 1942, N2545; WN/Fraser, 30 Oct. 1942, N17.
40. Minutes, 10 April 1942.
41. Fraser/WN, 5 Aug. 1942; H. L. Ismay/WN, 6 Aug. 1942, N1328; draft Fraser cable, 27 Aug. 1942, summarising points to be discussed with Roosevelt, N135; WN notes, 27 Aug. 1942, N135, for War Council meeting of that day, which Fraser attended too. List of Fraser's engagements and topics to be discussed with Nash, N2223.
42. WN/Fraser, 9 Oct. 1942, N17; WN/Fraser, 4 May 1942, N2545.
43. Fraser/Langstone, 11 Oct. 1941, N2545; papers in N1728.
44. Interviews with Sir Carl Berendsen, Sir Geoffrey Cox; WN/Berendsen, 28 Dec. 1944; WN/Pepper, 22 Sept. 1944, N2259.
45. Watt, pp. 31-33.
46. *Evening Post*, 30 Aug. 1969, article by Margaret Kelly.
47. Miles/Mrs Nash, 21 Feb. 1944, N16.

48 5 June 1942.
49. PD, 1943, 263, 430ff. (WN); WN/W. J. Green, 23 June 1942, N130; Berendsen/ Fraser, 31 July 1945, N223.
50. WN address, 5 Aug. 1942, 'Relations of the United Nations in Defence of the Pacific', Empire Parliamentary Association, (Confidential), London 1942, N2316. On the Japanese losses, see Hasluck, p. 167.
51 Cox/WN, 22 Aug. 1942, N1298.
52. List in N142.
53. M. P. Onorato (ed.), *Origins of the Philippine Republic. Extracts from the Diaries and Records of Francis Burton Harrison,* Cornell University, South East Asia Programme Data Paper, 1974; Institute of Pacific Relations, *War and Peace in the Pacific,* N.Y., 1943; papers in N2160, N2316.
54. 29 March 1943.
55. Cox/WN, 1 May, 2 Aug. 1943, and other letters in N143; interview with Sir Geoffrey Cox, 1974.
56. Wallace/Laidler, 7 April 1944; Pepper/WN, 14 Aug. 1944, N2259; Paul Patterson (*Baltimore Sun*)/J. W. Heenan, 5 April 1944, N2273; Berendsen/WN, 10 Aug. 1944, N2259.
57. *Newsweek,* 29 March 1943; *Wisconsin State Journal,* 23 Nov. 1942; *Washington Post,* 2 Feb. 1943.
58. Nash's unfinished 'Memoirs' in possession of Mr J. A. D. Nash; list of speeches, etc., N142.
59. Interview with Sir Geoffrey Cox, 1974; with Mr B. R. Turner, March 1975; WN/Fisher, 27 Dec. 1966, N1706; correspondence between Nash and Estorick, Turner, Cox and J. C. Beaglehole in N2176.
60. *New Zealand,* p. 285.
61. Ibid., pp. 248-9.
62. See text of speeches in N141, N142, e.g. speech to Foreign Policy Association, Philadelphia, 16 Jan. 1943; Chapter 10 of Nash's *New Zealand;* press clippings, N1728, e.g. *Washington Post,* 16 Feb. 1943.
63. 10 Nov. 1942, N2535.
64. WN/Fraser, draft cable, [Feb. 1943?], N17; minutes, 3 Feb. 1943.
65. Draft cable, 17 Feb. 1943, N17.
66. Minutes, 17 March 1943.
67. WN 'Memoirs', typed version.
68. Interview with Sir Geoffrey Cox, 4 Feb. 1974.
69. D. Wilson/WN, 30 Sept. 1942, citing Fraser, N2413; Roosevelt/WN, 16 Dec. 1944; Hopkins/WN, 2 May 1945, N2545. N2259 contains letters from the Roosevelts and many famous Americans and other leaders. See also, J. P. Lash, *Eleanor: The Years Alone,* New York, 1972, p. 19.

XVIII: WELLINGTON, CANBERRA, WASHINGTON, LONDON, 1943-4

1. 28 May 1942; WN/O'Brien 21 July 1942, N345; minutes of Parliamentary Labour Party, 11 May 1942.
2. Moohan/WN, 11 May, 29 Sept. 1942, WN/Moohan, 9 Nov. 1942, N2258; Wood, pp. 232-9.
3. 24 June 1942, N2258.
4. PD, 1943, 262, 552ff.
5. *Evening Post,* 1 Sept. 1943 (Lee's party programme); *Dominion,* 30 Aug., 6 Sept. 1943 (Scrimgeour).
6. D. Wilson/Scrimgeour, 15 April 1942; J. T. Paul/Wilson, 1 March 1943, and other papers in N2029.

7. Papers on Brian Dunningham's 'Crusade for Social Justice', etc., N2090, N2029; Thorn/WN, 13 Nov. 1939, N2537.

8. Minute in N2029.

9. The account of these events in Edwards, *Scrim.*, is substantially the Rev. C. C. Scrimgeour's. The Nash files are less sympathetic. He was a great trial to the government in wartime, and it might be thought that he was treated lightly, being allowed to serve in the Air Force. Dictatorships had shorter ways with dissenters.

10. On the election in general, see J. R. S. Daniels, 'The General Election of 1943', unpub. MA thesis, Victoria University, 1961.

11. WN/J. McKenzie, 14 Oct. 1943, N429.

12. WN/Albert and Becky, 4 Nov. 1944, N351.

13. *Evening Post*, 27 Dec. 1943; Fraser/WN, 27 Dec. 1943, N130; *Dominion*, 28 Dec. 1943.

14. *Dominion*, 8 Dec. 1943.

15. 'Notes for Hon. W. Nash on Pacific Federation', 18 Dec. 1943, N1326.

16. Institute of Pacific Relations, *War and Peace in the Pacific*, New York, 1943, pp. 13, 56, 78, 82, 117ff. This is cited by R. M. D. Munro, 'New Zealand's Role in the Establishment of the South Pacific Commission', unpub. MA thesis, Victoria University, 1970. Nash did not, however, as Munro asserts (p. 24) refer to colonial territories in his final statement.

17. Minutes of Pacific War Council, 3, 17 Feb. 1943, 12 Jan. 1944.

18. R. Kay (ed.), *The Australian-New Zealand Agreement 1944*, Wellington, 1972, pp. 47-48.

19. WN/Fraser, 24 Dec., 31 Dec. 1943; WN/Curtin, 31 Dec. 1943, N130.

20. WN diary, 1943, N2539; WN/H. H. Dobie, 1 July 1959, N369; MS memoirs Episode 1, in possession of Mr J. S. Reid.

21. B. Lasker, 'The Pacific Front: Planning for Oceania', *Far Eastern Survey*, XIII, 2, 1944, p. 13.

22. Minutes. The Council had not met for three months and did not meet again. Also WN/Fraser, 12 Jan. 1944, N1326.

23. M. P. Lissington, *New Zealand and the United States 1840-1944*, Wellington, 1972, pp. 77ff.

24. *Baltimore Sun*, 25 Feb. 1943; WN/Kingsbury Smith (International News Service), 24 Feb. 1943, N135.

25. N1326; Kay, pp. 159-62.

26. Carroll Binder *(Chicago Daily News)*/WN, 1 Feb. 1944, N1326.

27. Lissington, pp. 93-95; Wilson Brown memo, 25 April 1944 (re Curtin's talks with Roosevelt), Roosevelt Papers, copy kindly provided by Professor W. Roger Louis.

28. Conclusions of War Cabinet, CAB 65/41, Public Record Office, London, 13 March 1944. Nash was present 28 February to 3 April, but had reached London by 8 February.

29. WN/Lord Moyle, 24 Jan. 1968, N2481.

30. Dalton Diaries, 30, 23 Feb. 1944.

31. Baker, p. 82.

32. Wood, pp. 249-61.

33. WN/Fraser, 15 Jan. 1944, N133.

34. [Fraser]/WN, 31 March 1944, N133; Wood, Chapter 20. Some of the WN/Fraser cables are in N114.

35. Dalton Diaries, 30, 21 Feb. 1944; papers in N1327; Baker, pp. 382-4.

XIX: PLANNING FOR WORLD PEACE AND JUSTICE, 1943-8

1. W. Elliot, *Long Distance,* London, 1943, p. 84.
2. WN/Lehmann, 6 Aug. 1944, and papers in N2259.
3. G. F. Matthews, 'The New Zealand Labour Party's Attitudes to the League of Nations 1918-1935', unpub. MA research essay, University of Auckland, 1975.
4. *N.Z. Worker,* 16 June 1926, 18 June 1930.
5. *New York Herald Tribune,* 29 April 1944. Conference papers in N2241, N2251, N2259, N2562.
6. Text in AJHR, 1944, A-7, pp. 21-24.
7. Papers in N2259.
8. 13 Oct. 1943, N130.
9. Reports in AJHR, 1943, A-1; 1944, A-3A.
10. A. G. B. Fisher, 'The Political Framework of an International Institution' [the IMF], *The Manchester School,* May 1962, p. 125.
11. Cited Department of External Affairs, *International Monetary Fund,* Wellington, 1944.
12. Articles of Agreement of the IMF, AJHR, 1944, A-8, p. 19. The Reserve Bank of New Zealand published a useful summary, *Bretton Woods, G.A.T.T., and Related Topics,* Wellington, 1953.
13. 12 Jan. 1944, N1098.
14. 14 March 1944, N90.
15. Fraser/WN, 17 Feb. 1944, N1327.
16. Draft WN cables, N2160.
17. WN/Sullivan, 2 July, 17 July 1944, No. 1015, N1098.
18. WN/Sullivan, 18, 19 July 1944, N1098.
19. *Dominion,* 27 July 1944; WN/Minister External Affairs, 12, 17, 18 July 1944, N1098.
20. WN/Sullivan, 18 July 1944, No. 1017, N1098; WN pencil notes, N1581.
21. Sullivan/WN, 19 July 1944, No. 189; Chifley/Sullivan, 18 July 1944, N1098.
22. 20 July 1944 (draft), N1581.
23. Fisher/WN, 14 Aug. 1944, N1098.
24. WN/King, 31 July 1944, N2535; WN diary, N2539.
25. Minutes of the Parliamentary Labour Party, 2 May, 14 June, 5 Nov. 1944; Sullivan/Fraser, 3 July 1944, N2545.
26. *Standard,* 16 Nov. 1944; cited C. G. F. Simkin, 'The Nationalisation of the Bank of New Zealand', *Economic Record,* 1946, Vol. 22.
27. P. Neilson/WN, 15 Feb. 1945, N2410.
28. WN/B. Brown, 15 Oct. 1962, N1098.
29. Langstone/WN, 16 Jan. 1947, N2247; Langstone statements, *Auckland Star,* 19 June 1945, *Dominion,* 26 May 1945; Parry/Fraser, 31 Jan. 1949, N2004.
30. *Dominion,* 9 Nov. 1945.
31. Ibid., 26 May 1945.
32. General Manager Bank of New Zealand/WN, 16 Nov. 1945, and other letters in N1088; *Dominion,* 16 May 1945, 31 Jan. 1946.
33. *Waikato Independent,* 9 April 1945.
34. WN/B. Brown, 15 Oct. 1962, N1098; P. L. Porter, (General Manager Bank of New Zealand)/WN, 18 Jan. 1946, N1088.
35. Minutes of Parliamentary Labour Party 14-16 Oct. 1944.
36. Berendsen/Fraser, 18 July 1945, and other reports in N2403.
37. Minutes of Parliamentary Labour Party, 6 Dec. 1945.
38. *Nelson Evening Mail,* 4 Dec. 1946.

39. Mrs A. P. Mullins/Fraser, 28 Sept. 1946, and other letters in N2276 and N2160.
40. *Nelson Evening Mail,* 4 Dec. 1946, and papers in N1318, N2334. On Holland's views see also PD, 1946, 274, 335-6.
41. E.g. C. G. F. Simkin and H. R. Rodwell, *An Open Letter to the Members of the General Assembly on the Bretton Woods Agreements,* Auckland, 1946.
42. L. F. Crisp, *Ben Chifley,* London, 1961, p. 205, footnote; Chifley/WN, 7 Aug. 1947, N151.
43. Dalton/WN, 30 April, 23 May 1947, N151; E. C. Fussell/WN, 14 April 1946, N2277.
44. Minutes of Parliamentary Labour Party, July 1947; typed caucus minute, N2083; Nash's notes, notebook, N151.
45. WN/A. G. B. Fisher, 8 Jan. 1951, N2112; WN notes for newspaper article with 'memoirs' in possession Mr J. A. D. Nash; PD, 1961, 326, 988.
46. For a kindly portrait of Fraser at San Francisco see Hasluck, pp. 504-5; see also Sir Alister McIntosh, 'Working with Peter Fraser in Wartime', *New Zealand Journal of History,* X, 1, 1976.
47. WN/B. Martin, 3 Nov. 1922, N2151; Jordan/WN, 9 April 1930, P. J. O'Farrell papers; Jordan/Fraser, 16 Dec. 1948, N2304.
48. Fraser/WN, 2 May, WN/Fraser, 2 May 1946, N2278; WN/Fraser, 10 May 1946 (2 letters), WN/Jordan, 2 May 1946 (2 letters), N2259.
49. *Daily Express, Daily Mail,* 24 April 1946.
50. WN report on the conference to Fraser, 22 July 1946, N2288; WN/Fraser, 22 May 1946, N2278.
51. WN/Fraser, 9, 10 May 1946, N2278.
52. Fraser/WN, 11 May 1946, N2278; 1 June 1946, N65.
53. WN/Fraser, 9 May 1946, N2278.
54. WN/Fraser, 22, 23 May 1946, N2278.
55. *Meetings of Prime Ministers April-May 1946. Full Record of Minutes of Meetings and Memoranda,* (minutes of meeting on 22 Jan. 1946), Colonial Office, London; paper in N2288.
56. WN/Fraser, 3 May 1946, N2288.
57. WN/Fraser, 24 April, 5 May, 7 May 1946, N2278 and N2288; press clippings, N21; WN address, *The South Pacific and World Affairs,* printed for private circulation by the Empire Parliamentary Association, London, 1946.
58 WN/Fraser, 26 April 1946, N2278; and draft USA-NZ agreement re Upolu, 1946, N2288; WN/Fraser, 22 July 1946, N2288.
59. Dalton diaries, 34, 20 May 1946; *Daily Telegraph,* 20 May 1946.
60. WN/Fraser, 31 Jan. 1947; Fraser/WN, 4 Feb. 1947, N233.
61. Minutes of Meetings in London, 5 June, 14 June 1946, e.g. remarks by Sir P. Liesching, N80.
62. WN/Fraser, 10 March 1947, N151.
63. WN/Fraser, 7 March 1947, N1298.
64. *Evening Post,* 23 July 1948.
65. WN/Fraser, 1 May 1947, N113.
66. *Report of the First Session of the Preparatory Committee of the United Nations Conference on Trade and Employment,* London, 1946, p. 29, Article 25.
67. WN speech 20 May 1947 to Preparatory Committee, papers in N2565 and N70.
68. Papers in N70, N80, N137; WN/Fraser draft, c.8 May 1947, N80.
69 Official Record of Conference, 22 May, 24 June, 30 June, 1 July 1947, N2565; papers in N63.
70. Fraser/WN, 9 April, 2 May 1947, N13.
71. Official Record, 20 May 1947, N2565.

72. Ibid., 5 July 1947, N2565; also John W. Evans (USA delegate), 24 June 1947.
73. Cable, 9 June 1947, N13.
74. WN/Cripps, Dalton, Chifley, 19 June 1947, N276 and N13; Secretary of State/ Fraser, 19 July 1947, N111.
75. F. Garcia Oldini, Official Record, 16 July 1947, N2565.
76. Footnote to Article 31; Article 21, on full employment is also relevant. See *United Nations Conference on Trade and Employment,* Department of External Affairs, Publication No. 40, Wellington, 1947, pp. 16-17, 20-21.
77. *United Nations Conference on Trade and Employment,* Department of External Affairs, Publication No. 58, Wellington, 1948; WN/J. Thorn, 31 Dec. 1947, N122; G. H. Datson press statement, N63.
78. 28 Nov. 1947, N63.
79. WN/Johnsen, 19 July 1947, N13.
80. WN/Fraser, 10 Feb., N116; WN/Fraser, 17 March; Fraser/WN, [12], 19 March 1948, N93.
81. In Committee 3, on 3 Jan. 1948, N137.
82. WN speech, 29 Dec. 1947, N237; papers in N137.
83. In Articles 20, 21, 23 and in Annex K, Annex P. For New Zealand's views see explanation in Publication No. 58 of the Department of External Affairs, cited note 77; for text, see *United Nations Conference on Trade and Employment, Final Act and Related Documents,* Havana, 1948.
84. *New Zealand Herald,* 2 April 1948.
85. Ibid., 3 April 1948.
86. Outline notes, N108; another version in N2379.
87. *Truth,* 18 Feb. 1948.
88. *Dominion,* 22 May (Doidge); *Evening Post,* 25 May (Nash); *Evening Post,* 6, 7 April, 25 June (S. G. Holland); *New Zealand Herald,* 8 Sept. 1948 (Empire Industries Association).
89. W. Diebold, *The End of the I.T.O.,* Princeton, 1952.

XX: THE MINISTER AT WORK, 1936-49

1. Hardwick-Smith/WN, 1 May 1940, N2543.
2. 2 Nov. 1942, N17.
3. Draft cable, N2160.
4. Cit. D. Hamer, 'Understanding Mr Gladstone', *New Zealand Journal of History,* 6, 2, 1972, p. 125.
5. Interview, 8 Jan. 1971.
6. Interview with Mr Lewin, 22 May 1972.
7. Dalton diaries, 55, 27 Feb. 1938.
8. Interview with Sir Carl Berendsen, 8 Jan. 1971; *Evening Post,* 30 Aug. 1969, p. 42.
9. Interview with Sir Terence McCombs in London, 1974.
10. Interview with Berendsen; W. P. Reeves article in *Dominion,* 17 June 1968; and other informants.
11. Interview with Sir Arnold Nordmeyer, 26 May 1970.
12. Aickin/WN, 30 Jan., 17 Feb. 1942, N1609.
13. N2259.
14. *Evening Post,* 30 Aug. 1969, p. 42.
15. McIntosh/WN, 22 Dec. 1943, N130; McIntosh to author, 4 Dec. 1974.
16. Leah Newick, article on Nash, *New Zealand Women's Weekly,* 8 Feb. 1965; *Newsweek,* 19 March 1943. Nash described his meals in letters, WN/Mrs M. M. Dennehy, 15 March 1968, N2375; WN/J. P. Hearne, 4 May 1961, N644.

17. Interview, 29 March 1973.
18. WN/G. Cox, 17 March 1943 (two letters), N2535.
19. Papers in N2250 re hamper sent 3 Aug. 1949.
20. Interview, 18 Jan. 1971; Aickin/WN, 21 Aug.; WN/Aickin, 28 Dec. 1944, N2259.
21. Interview with a well-known New Zealander who wishes to be anonymous.
22. Interviews with Sir Carl Berendsen and Mr Turner; WN diary 1944, N2539.
23. 30 June 1944, N2259.
24. Mervyn Robinson/WN, 15 June 1965, N197.
25. Fraser/Minister of Education, re Ngarimu Scholarships, N2067.
26. Dalton diaries, 55, 26 Feb. 1938.

XXI: THE COLLAPSE OF LABOUR, 1946-9

1. 19 May 1947, N13.
2. 29 Jan. 1948, N2450.
3. Pearce/WN, 2 Sept., WN/Pearce, 6 Sept. 1946, N2273; correspondence in N2146. A National Party Research Office paper, 'The Labour Party's Leader', 9 Feb. 1953, specifically stated that he had not been a bankrupt. Earlier papers on Nash do not mention this topic. Mr Martin Nestor arranged for me to read the Nash file.
4. WN/[Roberts], [1946], (draft), N2093; Secretary Petone Branch/M. Moohan, 16 Aug. 1946, N2273. The Executive was petitioned to reverse its decision (N2093). Nash's analysis is also in N2093.
5. M. J. Moriarty, 'The Marketing of Dairy Produce', N.Z. Journal of Public Administration, 10, 2, March 1948, pp. 17-18; C. P. Agar statements during N.Z. Dairy Board deputation to Fraser and Ben Roberts, 28 June 1946, N1166.
6. E.g. A. Linton, a member of the Dairy Board, Taranaki Herald, 1 Oct. 1945.
7. WN/S. J. Harrison (General Secretary RSA), 7 June 1945, and other papers in N1253, N384, N1. Nash remarks to RSA deputation, 7 March 1945; Fraser remarks to deputation, 26 July 1945. On the furlough men, see Wood, pp. 266-71.
8. R. McLennan, 'The Last Years of the First Labour Government, 1945-1949', unpub. MA thesis, University of Auckland, 1963, Introduction and pp. 92ff.
9. E.g. Truth, 21 Aug. 1946.
10. N.Z. Herald, 8, 9 Feb. 1946.
11. Secretary 2nd N.Z.E.F. Association/WN, 16 Oct. 1946, N2558; Melvin/WN, 14 Nov. 1946, N2093; Melvin/WN, 17 May 1949, N1110; Melvin speech, 21 May 1947, N1074.
12. Deputation to D. Sullivan and Nash 30 May 1945, N1093.
13. Baker, p. 340; Minutes of Preparatory Committee, E/PC/T/EC/PV. 2.5, 20 May 1947, N2565.
14. N2093.
15. Dominion, 1 Aug. 1946.
16. Minutes of Parliamentary Labour Party 17 Dec. 1946, 26 Feb., 13-16 May 1947; list of caucus votes in N2304.
17. Lewin memo, 13 Jan. 1946; Wilson/WN, 14 Jan. 1947, N2251.
18. Campbell/P. Fraser, 5, 18 Aug. 1948, N2304; Campbell/WN, 2 Aug. 1948, N1209; WN/G. Fraser, 28 June 1948, N1209; P. Fraser/Lewin, 17 Oct., Lewin/ P. Fraser, 8 Nov. 1949, N2318.
19. 8 March 1947; WN/Fraser, 10, 17 March. These and the series of cables referred to are filed in N1554 and in N363.
20. E.g. WN/J. H. Furniss, 8 June 1967, N2430.

21. 'Summary of Developments—Guaranteed Price for Dairy Industry', 5 Aug. 1959, N2403, lists farm costs 1936-60; F. P. Walsh/WN, 20 Sept. 1949, N363, describes how the price was fixed in 1949.
22. See his remarks to Dairy Board deputation, 4 Sept. 1946, N1166.
23. Thorn, pp. 262-8.
24. Baker, 378-84; see above, Chapter XVIII, p. 236.
25. Ashwin/WN, 11 July 1947, N1311.
26. 'Review of New Zealand Contracts', Ministry of Food summary of discussions with Nash, 4 June 1946, N1313.
27. Baker, p. 389; W. Nash, *Fair Exchange,* Wellington, 1948, p. 13.
28. Baker, pp. 266, 390.
29. Hawke, *Between Governments and Banks,* p. 123.
30. Ibid., pp. 122-3; Ashwin/WN, 30 May, 9 Dec. 1947, N1120, and other papers in N1120, N2072; Chifley/WN, 30 Aug. 1948, and A. D. McIntosh memo on discussion with Chifley, N2545.
31. Typescript draft article on parity, in possession Mr J. A. D. Nash.
32. Hawke, *Between Governments and Banks,* p. 123.
33. Wellington, 1948; broadcast speech, 22 Aug. 1948, text filed in N1120.
34. Attlee/Fraser, 13 Aug. 1947, N131.
35. 24 March 1948, N293.
36. 18 July 1949, N2545.
37. E.g. Minutes of 1948 conference, N482; Fraser talked to Field Marshal Slim in 1949. See minutes of 2nd NZEF deputation to Nordmeyer, 29 July 1949, N2072.
38. Papers in N10, N1295.
39. M. E. R. Bassett, *Confrontation '51. The 1951 Waterfront Dispute,* Wellington, 1972, pp. 32, 217-8, 219-20.
40. McLennan, pp. 183, 189ff.
41. G. Fraser, *Ungrateful People,* Auckland, 1952, pp. 55-57.
42. See A. McLagan/T. Hill, 31 March 1949, N1215; Nash remarks to shipowners' delegation, 30 May 1949, N209. On the wharf situation in general see Bassett.
43. Cited Bassett, pp. 20-21.
44. E.g. during deputation to McLagan, 30 April 1947, N1324.
45. Meeting on 30 May 1949, p. 8, N209.
46. 19 Nov. 1948, N479.
47. WN notes on cabinet meeting, 6 May 1949, WN/C. J. Cadman, 29 April 1949; and other papers in N383.
48. Bassett, pp. 30-33, 217.
49. *Quest for Security,* p. 346.
50. WN/Fraser, draft, [Nov. 1948], N215.
51. Walsh/Fraser, 25 Nov. 1948, Walsh Papers, in possession of the late Dr C. Bollinger, Wellington.
52. Deputation of Lewin and others to Nash, Semple, and other ministers, 23 Nov. 1948, N215; deputation to Fraser, Nash and others, 1 Feb. 1949, N215; draft cable, WN/Fraser, 15 Nov. 1948, N276.
53. These documents were released to the press by Nash on 14 December 1948. Lewin called the letter 'impudent' during a deputation to ministers, 1 Feb. 1949, N215; interview with Mr Lewin, 22 May 1972.
54. Sutch, p. 347. His account seems substantially accurate. *News-Report* (a journal), 30 March 1949, N2304. For other accounts see Nash's statement in parliament, PD, 1949, 287, 2088ff. and Nash's press statement, 14 Dec. 1948. The late R. M. Campbell told the author in an interview in 1973 that when he was first called

to Nash's office to discuss the satchel case, Walsh was there too. The statement of Charles H. Williams, who took the satchel from the car, is in N2322.

55. 21 Dec. 1948, in WN file 'Confidential and other important historical papers' in possession of Mr J. A. D. Nash.
56. R. M. Campbell and G. T. Bolt/Fraser, 7 Feb. 1949, N2322; L. A. Atkinson/J. Turnbull, 5 April 1949, N1075.
57. Papers in N2322, including Campbell notes, 18, 25 May 1949.
58. PD, 1949, 287, 2083ff.
59. He said so in conversation with the late Dr C. Bollinger of Wellington.
60. Text of interview with Mr W. Gibbons, 7 Sept. 1966, N2295.
61. 28 June 1947, N2275.
62. *Auckland Star,* 25 Nov. 1949.
63. National Party pamphlet, N2083.
64. On the election, see McLennan and S. E. Fraser, 'The 1949 General Election', unpub. MA thesis, University of Otago, 1967.
65. Roberts/WN, 6 Dec. 1949; Wilson/WN, 2 Dec. 1949, N1198; WN/G. Fraser, 5 Jan., 17 May 1950, N1209; Cox/WN, 7 Dec. 1949, N2535; Freyberg/WN, 4 Dec. 1949, N2535; 30 Aug. 1952, N2543.
66. *Marlborough Express,* 25 March 1950.
67. Correspondence in N1286.

XXII: THE WHARF STRIKE, 1951

1. *Landfall,* 58, June 1961, pp. 139-41.
2. See G. Mallaby, *From My Level. Unwritten Minutes,* London, 1965, pp. 73-74. Mallaby was the British High Commissioner.
3. *N.Z. Herald,* 12 July 1950.
4. Ibid. 2, 3 Feb. 1950; Holland/WN correspondence, 1950, N2259; papers in N2383 and N2236; PD, 1950, 290, 1907ff.
5. *Evening Post,* 6 May 1950.
6. Text of speech in N1347.
7. Apparently he left no papers except the contents of his drawer and a number of volumes about his wife's death now filed in the Nash Papers.
8. 'Reflections of an Elder Statesman'.
9. PD, 1951, 294, 29-31; WN notes for speeches about Fraser, N287, N1184.
10. Minutes of the Parliamentary Labour Party, 17 Jan. 1951; letters in N2190; *Auckland Star,* 16 Dec. 1950 (speculation about Skinner).
11. WN/Wilson, 6 Jan. 1951, N2112.
12. Bassett, pp. 39-60. Dr Bassett's book provides a thorough discussion of the 1951 dispute and is especially valuable on Nash's role in it. Nash's papers include voluminous documentation of the strike, which Dr Bassett read.
13. Ibid., pp. 67-68.
14. Ibid., pp. 87, 231; *Evening Post,* 2 March; *Dominion* 2 May 1951.
15. R. P. Smith (Waikato Trades Council)/WN, 16 Feb. 1951; WN/Smith, 19 March 1951; and other papers in N2234; WN memo, 'March 29 1951', on the meeting, N2235.
16. Text of interview with Mr W. Gibbons, 7 Sept. 1966, N2295.
17. Bassett, pp. 145-8; *Dominion,* 30 March 1951.
18. Osborne/WN, 10 April; WN/Osborne, 12 April 1951, N2234.
19. *Standard,* 2 May 1951, WN speech to FOL.

20. 4 April 1951, in cyclostyled 'Summary of statements by Parliamentary Labour Party', N2235.
21. Summary of WN speech to FOL conference, 26 April 1951, N2234; *Standard,* 2 May 1951; Bassett, pp. 148ff.
22. J. M. Murray/WN, 2 May 1951, N2234; *Auckland Star,* 1 May 1951.
23. 14 May 1951, N2111; Bassett, pp. 171-4.
24. *Evening Post,* 14 May 1951; Bassett, pp. 174-5.
25. *Hutt News,* 26 Nov. 1946.
26. Rev. D. Edmiston/Mrs Judy Brooker, 23 Jan. 1973. Letter in possession of Mrs Brooker, Wellington.
27. WN/Rev. I. Dixon, 27 July 1951, N2111.
28. WN/Mrs B. Barnett, 16 Feb. 1954, N1434.
29. Text of interview with Mr W. Gibbons, 1966, N2295.
30. 14 May 1951, N2111.
31. Interview cited in note 29.
32. Affidavit sworn by Joyce Lash and Eileen Hoskin, 30 Aug. 1951; WN/A. H. Johnstone, 14 Sept. 1951; A. H. Johnstone's Opinion, 9 Oct. 1951; E. G. Pearce's advertisement and other papers in a file in the possession of Mr J. A. D. Nash.
33. Text of Holland broadcast, 30 Aug.; Holyoake, 28 Aug. 1951, N2091; *Hutt News,* 22 Aug. 1951 (Andrews).
34. Bassett, p. 198.
35. Incomplete draft reply to Roberts's letter, 2 Sept. 1951, N2112; see also WN/ Emily Nash, 1 Oct. 1951, N2082; A. Osborne/WN, 5 Sept.; WN/Osborne, 7 Sept. 1951, N2086; H. Combs/C. W. Boswell [1951], N2470.
36. *The People,* quoted in *Otago Daily Times,* 21 May 1951.
37. PD, 1951, 296, 1359-60.
38. Ibid., 1212, 1230. For a contemporary comment on the Act, see G. S. Orr, 'Some Recent Legislation', *Landfall,* 21, March 1952, pp. 54-60.
39. PD, 1951, 296, 1219ff.
40. Roberts/WN, 2 Sept. 1951; WN/Roberts, 2 Jan. 1952, N2112.
41. Proclamations of 6 and 8 February 1952, kindly provided by the Privy Council Office.
42. *Standard,* 16 April; *Dominion,* 10 April 1952.
43. Speech notes, 21 May 1952, N1183.

XXIII: LEADER OF THE OPPOSITION, 1951-7

1. A story from Mr Barry Mitcalfe, who was on the train.
2. *The Statesman,* Cambridge, 1897, p. 181.
3. Ibid., pp. 183-4.
4. In conversation with author.
5. To the author, 16 May 1972.
6. To the author, in 1969.
7. E.g. Nash's budget speech, *Evening Post,* 13 Aug. 1952.
8. *Standard,* 4 Feb. 1953; *Dominion,* 31 Jan. 1953.
9. *Standard,* 18 June 1952; *N.Z. Herald,* 12 June 1952.
10. Hawke, pp. 115-17.
11. E.g. *Dominion,* 28 June, 3 July 1952.
12. 15 Feb. 1954.
13. WN memo, 7 May 1953; J. Mathison/WN, 24 July 1953; Mason/WN, 16 July 1953, in file 'Party Leadership', in possession of Mr J. A. D. Nash.

14. Minutes of National Executive, 17 Feb. 1954 (N.Z. Labour Party Head Office); Minutes of Parliamentary Labour Party, 9 Feb., 17 March, 27 April 1954.
15. *Dominion*, 13 April 1954. Telegrams and letters of support in file, 'Party Leadership' in possession of Mr J. A. D. Nash.
16. Mathison/WN, 24 July 1953 and Nash's list of Nash and Nordmeyer supporters and doubtfuls in file 'Party Leadership'. Information about Moohan from Sir Arnold Nordmeyer.
17. Minutes of Parliamentary Labour Party, 23 June 1954.
18. *Dominion*, 1 July 1954; *Standard*, 7 July 1954.
19. *Dominion*, 20 Oct. 1954.
20. Ibid., 20 Oct. (Holland); 22 Oct. 1954 (Nash).
21. R. G. Durrant, 'The Elections', *Landfall*, 33, March 1955, pp. 70-76.
22. *Dominion*, 8 Nov., also 12 Nov. 1954 (meeting in Wellington).
23. Ibid., 11 Nov. 1954.
24. Ibid., 15 Nov., 11 Nov. 1954.
25. Ibid., 17 July 1952 (foreign policy debate); 24 Oct. 1952 (ANZUS); 13, 14, Aug. 1953 (ANZUS and China).
26. PD, 1954, 303, 215-6; 304, 2104ff.; *Dominion*, 7 July, 25 Aug., 1 Oct. 1954. Anthony Eden had considered in April 1954 that it was doubtful whether a military solution was possible in Vietnam: *Memoirs. Full Circle*, London, 1960.
27. *Dominion*, 8 Aug. 1956.
28. 17 Sept. 1956; text in N2567.
29. *Dominion*, 2, 3, 5 Nov. 1956.
30. Text in N2069.
31. 8 Nov. 1956, N2069.
32. *Dominion*, 10 Dec. 1956.
33. Ibid., 9 Aug. 1956.
34. Ibid., 10 Dec. 1956.
35. Ibid., 31 Oct. 1955; 1 Oct. 1956, 11 March 1957; *Standard*, 16 Nov. 1955.
36. *Dominion*, 7 April, 27 July 1955.
37. PD, 1957, 312, 1187-90.
38. Ibid., 1241-2.
39. Ibid., 1305. Harry Lake cited a press report of 19 March.
40. Information from Dr Martyn Finlay and Mrs Craig McKenzie; A. Robinson, 'The National Campaign', *Political Science*, 10, 1, March 1958, p. 27.
41. PD, 1957, 312, 1298-9 (Nordmeyer); 1305 (Lake).
42. Ibid., 1957, 314, 2912.
43. If anyone doubts this, see A. Robinson, cited in footnote 40, B. Brown's article 'The Labour Campaign', p. 11, in the same issue of *Political Science*, and the debates on the budget and the Income Tax Assessment Bill, 1957.
44. 18 March 1957.
45. *Political Science*, 10, 1, March 1958, p. 12. I am indebted to Mr Brown for permission to quote extensively from his well-informed article.
46. *Dominion*, 13 April 1957.
47. Ibid., 6, 8 May, 13 June 1957.
48. Ibid., 29 March 1957.
49. B. Brown, loc. cit., pp. 14-15.
50. *Dominion*, 6 Nov. 1957.
51. Robinson, loc. cit., p. 32; PD, 1958, 316, 818 (Holyoake).
52. *Standard*, 27 Nov. 1957.
53. He said so to many friends. See speech notes on this in N211.
54. 29 Nov. 1957; see PD, 1958, 315, 175; partial transcript in National Party

Research Office file. Nash was somewhat concerned about this advice, which was repeated the day after the election. Mr Bruce Brown has pointed out to me that because the National Party's rebate was incorporated in the tax tables it was not necessarily true that anyone whose tax demand was for £100 or less would have nothing to pay when Labour's £100 rebate was enacted, for this calculation had to be made on the basis of the sum due before the National rebate. This point illustrates the unlikelihood that the average voter would appreciate all the issues.

55. *Dominion,* 25 Nov. 1957.
56. Text of broadcast, 29 Nov. 1957, N2437.
57. *Dominion,* 18 Nov. 1957.
58. R. M. Chapman, W. K. Jackson, and A. V. Mitchell, *New Zealand Politics in Action: the 1960 General Election,* London, 1962, p. 30.
59. J. K. Cunningham, 'Editorial Opinion and the 1957 Election', *Landfall,* 46, June 1958, p. 173.
60. *Landfall,* 58, June 1961, p. 143.

XXIV: INTO POWER AGAIN, 1957-8

1. Votes for cabinet, N376.
2. 9 Dec. 1957, N2551.
3. Nash, Hackett, Fox, Moohan, Mathison, Anderton. Three more had been born in Australia, but educated in New Zealand: Watt, Howard, Skinner.
4. Interview with Mr R. Boord, 24 Jan. 1973.
5. *Landfall,* 58, June 1961, p. 143.
6. Chapman, Jackson, Mitchell, pp. 39ff.
7. J. B. Condliffe, 'Autobiography', typescript in Alexander Turnbull Library; Hawke, *Between Governments and Banks,* p. 117; WN speech 24 Jan. 1958, speech notes, N191.
8. *Evening Post,* 9 Dec. 1957.
9. Ibid., 14 Nov. (Walsh); 15 Nov. (Holyoake); 16 Nov. (Shand); 19, 20 Nov. (editorials); 22 Nov. 1957 (overseas reserves).
10. 12 Dec. 1957, N1100; PD, 1958, 315, 61ff.
11. Draft minutes, N1100.
12. Fussell/Nordmeyer, 16 Dec. 1957, N1100; Datson/WN, 18 Dec. 1957, N2551.
13. Text in N1100.
14. Chapman, Jackson, Mitchell, p. 45; press quotations in N191.
15. Chapman, Jackson, Mitchell, pp. 43-45; *Hawera Star,* 2 Jan. 1958 (Watts's statement).
16. Minutes in N242.
17. *Dominion,* 17 Jan. 1958.
18. E.g. PD, 1958, 315, 152 (Holyoake); 11 (Marshall).
19. Chapman, Jackson, Mitchell, pp. 47-88; Hawke, p. 161.
20. 5 March 1958, N1587.
21. Interview with Mr W. A. Fox, 11 Oct. 1972; interview with Mr P. Skoglund, 20 Jan. 1973. Moohan used to dissociate himself from the budget.
22. Interview with Mr P. N. Holloway, 1 March 1973.
23. Interview with Mr Fox.
24. PD, 1958, 316, 342.
25. Ibid., 1931, 229, 88 (Holland).
26. Ibid., 1958, 316, 276ff.

27. Ibid., 351 (Holyoake); 798, 817-18 (Nash); 318, 1831 (Holyoake). See above p. 302

28. PD, 1958, 316, 353.

29. Ibid., 356; *Quest for Security*, p. 426.

30. B. S. Gustafson, 'Continuing Transformation. The structure, composition and functioning of the New Zealand Labour Party in the Auckland region, 1949-70', unpub. PhD thesis, University of Auckland, 1973, I, 86ff., 248ff., 264-5.

31. *Otago Daily Times*, 16 Jan. 1958.

32. Chapman, Jackson, Mitchell, p. 42 and table p. 41.

33. E.g. PD, 1958, 316, 358.

34. Chapman, Jackson, Mitchell, p. 117. (Professor Jackson quotes this sally with approval.)

35. Walsh/J. A. Lee, 12 Oct. 1959, Lee MSS 441/9; Walsh/T. F. Anderson, 13 Dec. 1960, N403.

36. Young/WN, 3 Jan. 1958, N1623; *N.Z. Herald*, 28 Jan. 1958; papers in N2059.

37. 19 March 1959, N1655.

38. PD, 1956, 315, 50 (Watts).

39. *Quest for Security*, p. 426.

40. By R. M. Chapman, in Chapman, Jackson, Mitchell, p. 50.

41. For general comment on the problems, see S. A. McLeod (Secretary N.Z. delegation), 'Trade Discussions . . . . London, 8 April-29 May 1957', N2341; E. L. Greensmith/Chairman, Cabinet Committee on Economic Policy, January 1958, N1623, and other documents in N2341.

42. Holyoake/D. Eccles, 8 May 1957, in S. A. McLeod memo, loc. cit.; AJHR 1957, A-15, 'Trade Discussions. . . .'

43. *From My Level*, pp. 64-67.

44. H. Macmillan, *Riding the Storm 1956-1959*, London, 1971, pp. 398-9.

45. Mallaby, pp. 67-68.

46. Minutes of Cabinet Committee on Economic and Financial Policy (extract), 2 May 1958, N2341.

47. WN press statement, 21 May 1958, N2433.

48. E. L. Greensmith/Chairman Cabinet Committee on Economic and Financial Policy, 19 May 1958, sending a paper on the negotiations. There is very detailed documentation of these negotiations in N2341.

49. E.g., WN/High Commissioner (London) (message for Macmillan), 25 July 1958; WN/Macmillan, 18 Aug. 1958, N2341.

50. Skinner/WN, 14 May 1958; WN/Skinner, 16 May 1958, N1682; Johnsen/WN, 30 May 1958, N2341.

51. Skinner/WN, 4 June 1958, N2341; Deputy High Commissioner (London)/WN, 19 April 1958; External Affairs/Johnsen, 5 May 1958, N2341.

52. 23 June, enclos. Mallaby/WN, 25 June 1958, N2341.

53. 6 June (not sent); 25 July 1958, N2341.

54. 12 Aug. (in reply to a further Nash message of 8 Aug. 1958), N2341.

55. Exchange of letters, 18 Aug. 1958, N2341, N2059.

56. *From My Level*, p. 70; Sir Alister McIntosh wrote to Sir George Mallaby at my request and he explained that he and Mr George Laking had found a solution. Sir Alister McIntosh to the author, 17 March 1973. See also, Mallaby/WN, 14 Aug. 1958, N2341. For New Zealand's offer of 4 June, see Greensmith/Chairman Cabinet Committee on Economic and Financial Policy, 4 Sept. 1958, Annex A, N2341.

57. *New Zealand-United Kingdom Trade Discussions, 1958*, Department of External Affairs Publication No. 195.

58. *Agreement on Commerce between New Zealand and Japan, 1958,* Department of External Affairs Publication No. 194.
59. *From My Level,* pp. 79-80.
60. Chapman, Jackson, Mitchell, pp. 50-51; PLP report to Labour Party Conference, 1959, presented by Nash.
61. PD, 1958, 318, 1991ff., 2188ff.
62. Skinner/WN, 15 Aug. 1958, and WN calculations on carbon copy, N1682.
63. Weir/WN, 14 July 1958; WN speech notes for joint meeting of Defence and External Affairs Committees, attended by Weir, 3 Sept. 1958, N1678.
64. PLP Report to 1959 Labour Party Conference (Nash); PD, 1958, 318, 2240-1 (Holyoake).

XXV: 'SUMMITRY', 1958-60

1. 1 Aug. 1951.
2. *Evening Star,* 10 Nov. 1958.
3. *From My Level,* p. 78. R. G. Casey wrote that Nash was the one man in the government who had any 'broad and balanced grasp' of world affairs. T. B. Millar (ed.), *Australian Foreign Minister. The Diaries of R. G. Casey 1951-60,* London, 1972, pp. 296-7.
4. Press statement, N117.
5. WN radio broadcast, 20 April 1958, N201.
6. WN interview for 'John Foster Dulles Oral History Project', 11 Sept. 1964, N2432; notes of discussion with Eisenhower, 28 Oct. 1959, N2343.
7. 6, 20 April 1958, N201; *External Affairs Review,* Department of External Affairs, April 1959, p. 9.
8. *External Affairs Review,* Nov. 1958. (The same speech writer seemed to write Norman Kirk's speeches on foreign policy, which were peppered with references to the 'human family'.)
9. Interview, August 1970; papers in N2340.
10. Papers in N2445; *External Affairs Review,* Feb. 1959.
11. E.g., *Evening Post,* 26, 27 Jan. 1959.
12. *External Affairs Review,* Dec. 1959, pp. 10-12.
13. Press statements, 4, 7 Sept. 1959, N201; PD, 1959, 320, 1707-8.
14. Notes on ANZUS Council meeting, N2343.
15. Note of discussion, 28 Oct. 1959, N2343.
16. Note of meeting, 2 Nov. 1959, N2343.
17. *Pointing the Way 1959-1961,* London, 1972, pp. 330ff., 344-7.
18. WN/Menzies, 20 Feb. 1958; Menzies/WN, 25 Feb. 1958. Letter book, 'Correspondence on Important Policy Issues during Mr Nash's Term of Office', N2325.
19. See Foreign Office Note, 28 Sept. 1959, further letters from Menzies and other documents in N2325. On the general issue see C. Beeby, *The Antarctic Treaty,* Wellington, 1972.
20. For the term, see WN account of visit to Chequers, 8 Nov. 1959, N2343; for an account of 'summitry' see Anthony Sampson, *Macmillan. A Study in Ambiguity,* London, 1967, chapter IX, and Macmillan's autobiography, IV, *Riding the Storm* and V, *Pointing the Way.*
21. Macmillan, *Pointing the Way,* p. 94; WN/Macmillan, 12 Oct.; Macmillan/WN, 15 Oct.; WN/Macmillan, 16 Oct.; Macmillan/WN, 17 Oct. 1959, N2325.
22. WN account of visit to Chequers, 8 Nov. 1959; also memo of talks with Macmillan on 4 Nov., N2343.
23. *External Affairs Review,* Nov. 1959.

24. Interview, 13 Nov. 1959; notes for speech to conference and other papers in N2340.
25. Nash kept an account of this tour in N2325. Read in conjunction with his letter book, 'Correspondence on Important Policy Issues During Mr Nash's Term of Office' (N2325), it gives a good account of his views, discussions, and negotiations at this time.
26. *Dominion,* 26 April 1960.
27. WN's summary and transcript of conversation, N2325; WN/Eisenhower, 30 April 1960, N2328; interview with Mr Hal Nash, 23 Jan. 1972; WN/Walter Lippmann, 2 May 1961, N1649; account of conversation about WN's grandfather in press clipping, 27 April 1960, in N2209; Leah Newick, article on WN, *New Zealand Women's Weekly,* 8 Feb. 1965.
28. *Dominion,* 26, 27 April 1960 (remarks on Khrushchev being 'victorious'); PD, 1960, 322, 591ff, (Holyoake); T. R. Reese, *Australia, New Zealand and the United States,* Oxford, 1969, pp. 205-6. Dr Reese, an Englishman, at once criticizes Menzies for seeming a flunkey of the Americans and Nash for being too independent over disarmament policy.
29. Notes on visit to Russia, N2325.
30. 'Meeting of Commonwealth Prime Ministers May 1960. Minutes of Meetings and Memoranda', N373; 'Prime Minister's Tour, 5 April-7 June 1960', 6, p. 9, N2325.
31. *Pointing the Way,* p. 172.
32. 'Meeting of Commonwealth Prime Ministers . . . .' 6, p. 28, N373.
33. *Pointing the Way,* p. 174.
34. 'Prime Minister's Tour, 5 April-7 June 1960', 'Note of Discussion between the Prime Minister and President Eisenhower', June 1960, N2325.
35. Ibid., 27 May 1960.
36. *Riding the Storm,* p. 542.
37. Items 16-18 in N2325.
38. Macmillan/WN, 15 Sept.; WN/High Commissioner, 20 Sept. 1960, and other communications, N2325.
39. 'Reflections of an Elder Statesman'.
40. 5 Oct. 1960. Text of speech is in *External Affairs Review,* Oct. 1960.
41. *Dominion,* 11 Oct. 1960, report by Mr J. A. Kelleher; WN discussion with Herter, 3 Oct. 1960, N2304.
42. WN/Macmillan, 16 April; Macmillan/WN, 5 June 1958; WN/Burton, 12 Aug. 1960; Campaign for Nuclear Disarmament deputation to Nash, 4 Aug. 1960, N2325; N. Roberts, *New Zealand and Nuclear Testing in the Pacific,* Wellington, 1972.
43. *'No Maoris No Tour',* CABTA, 1960 (a pamphlet), p. 11. For surveys of this issue see K. G. M. Graham, 'New Zealand on Apartheid', unpub. research essay, Political Science Department, Victoria University, 1971, and R. Thompson, *Retreat from Apartheid: New Zealand's Sporting Contacts with South Africa,* Wellington, 1975.
44. *Dominion,* 23 Feb. 1955, and other papers in N1437.
45. For advice from External Affairs, Security, and elsewhere, see documents in N1172 and N1324.
46. WN/Skinner, 5 Nov. 1959, N1172.
47. WN/Sir John Maud, U.K. High Commissioner in South Africa, 6 April 1960 *(not sent),* N1224; WN/Rev. J. D. Grocott, 17 March 1960, N2011; Craven/Hogg, 23 Nov. 1958, copy in N1224; Hogg/P. A. Barnes (WN's Secretary), 8 April 1960, N1224.

48. WN speech, 5 April 1960, *External Affairs Review,* April 1960, pp. 20-23.
49. WN/Rev. J. D. Grocott, 17 March 1960, N2011.
50. 14 Sept. 1960, N1224.
51. Chapman, Jackson, Mitchell, p. 72.

XXVI: PRIME MINISTER, 1958-60

1. *Landfall,* 58, June 1961, pp. 143-4.
2. *From My Level,* pp. 80-82.
3. *Evening Post,* 15, 18 Sept.; *Auckland Star, New Zealand Herald,* 16 Sept. 1958.
4. Interview, 10 May 1973.
5. 20 July 1956, N2188. This bundle has a mass of material about the celebration.
6. Interview, 1 March 1973.
7. Interview, 11 Oct. 1972.
8. Interviews with Mr Watt and Mr Boord.
9. Notes of deputation, 26 July 1960, N1656.
10. Norma Campbell/WN, [1939], N349.
11. There are reports in the Nash Papers on Sutch. There is nothing to prove or disprove the suspicions of MI5, the FBI, or the SIS.
12. Mr Holloway denied in evidence during Sutch's trial that he knew he was suspect; also P. N. Holloway/author, 17 Feb. 1976.
13. The late Dr R. M. Campbell, the former Chairman of the Public Service Commission, felt very angry about such cases and wrote an article in the *New Zealand Listener* (23 Feb. 1974) about the subject: he discussed the names of the people concerned and the evidence with me on several occasions.
14. PD, 1960, 322, 522 (D. J. Eyre).
15. Sutch/WN, 5 May; WN/Sutch, 19 May 1960, N1130.
16. E.g. N. L. Macbeth, 'The Cotton Mill—and After', Canterbury Chamber of Commerce, *Economic Bulletin,* No. 447, March 1962.
17. Memo 12 Jan. 1960, N2286.
18. Notes of deputation 27 Sept. 1960, N2286; on the agreement see papers in N2286. See also PD, 1960, 324, pp. 2130ff. (Hugh Watt).
19. PD, 1960, 324, p. 2186.
20. 7 Sept. 1960, N2288.
21. WN/Jim Nash, 6 July 1946, N2402.
22. *Nelson Evening Mail,* 1 March 1960. For a detailed study see A. Mitchell *Politics and People in New Zealand,* Christchurch, 1969, 'A case study: The Nelson cotton mill', and D. J. Mitchell, 'Nelson Cotton Mill', unpub. MA thesis, Canterbury University, 1967. This account is based on their work.
23. A. Mitchell, pp. 75-76; D. J. Mitchell, pp. 44-47; PD, 1962, 331, 1613-4 (Nash).
24. P. N. Holloway/G. Whittaker (Deputy Chairman Smith & Nephew), 12 Aug. 1960, N1131.
25. A. Mitchell, pp. 77ff.; D. J. Mitchell, pp. 51ff.
26. C. A. Blyth, 'The Industrialisation of New Zealand', *New Zealand Economic Papers,* 8, 1974.
27. Cf. Chapman, Jackson, Mitchell, p. 55.
28. File on steel industry, N1111.
29. Notes of deputation, 10 June 1959, N1171. On the whole question, see M. A. Kane, 'The History of Equal Pay in New Zealand 1890-1960', unpub. MA thesis, University of Auckland, 1972.
30. PD, 1960, 325, 3222ff.
31. Ibid., pp. 3298ff.
32. Ibid., 323, 1783-7.

33. Chapman, Jackson, Mitchell, p. 62 (R. M. Chapman).
34. Ibid., p. 65.
35. Ibid., p. 83 (A. Mitchell).
36. WN note on P. T. Watene/WN, 14 Jan. 1959; see also Report of Maori Policy Committee, 1958 Conference and 1960 Conference, N1151.
37. These two paragraphs are based on a lively letter from Mr J. K. Hunn to the author, 7 June 1975, and on some remarks by Mr R. J. Tizard, 30 Sept. 1972.
38. Gustafson, 'Continuing Transformation', I, 247ff.
39. N376.
40. 27 April 1960, N1645.
41. Chapman, Jackson, Mitchell.
42. Ibid., p. 98.
43. Ibid., pp. 98, 116.
44. Ibid., p. 90.
45. Ibid., pp. 66-67, 106-7.
46. Ibid., pp. 264ff.
47. Ibid., pp. 103-4, 289-92; Walsh/T. F. Anderson, 13 Dec. 1960, N403.
48. WN/Mallaby, 26 Dec. 1960, N1652.

XXVII: THE GRAND OLD MAN, 1960-8

1. PD, 1961, 329, 3507.
2. Fisher/WN, 19 Nov., WN/Fisher, 21 Nov. 1958, N1401.
3. Letters in N2334, N2338, N2473; on the petitions, Minutes of the Parliamentary Labour Party, 27 July 1961, N2020.
4. E.g. G. O'Brien (Secretary Wellington City Branch of Labour Party)/WN, 15 June 1961, N2338.
5. PD, 1961, 326, 986ff.; 327, 1356ff.
6. Ibid., 326, 988.
7. Ibid., 327, 1356ff.
8. Greymouth Evening Star, 16 Aug.; Press, Christchurch, 14 Aug. 1961, and other press clippings and letters in N2334.
9. E.g. PD, 1961, 326, 478, during a debate on the EEC. Such remarks were not uncommon.
10. E.g. Ibid., 1963, 335, 417ff., J. E. Laing/WN, 19 May; WN/Laing, 25 May 1962, N2451; and file in N91.
11. PD, 1963, 335, 419.
12. Dominion, 18 Dec.; Evening Post, 16 Dec. 1961.
13. Sanderson/WN, 19 Dec. 1961; WN/Sanderson, 25 Sept. 1962, N2247; Lord Sanderson of Ayot, Ships and Sealing Wax, London, 1967, p. 202; Gaitskell/WN, 29 May, 1 Aug. 1962, N2247.
14. The Times, 10 Sept. 1962, cited J. D. B. Miller, Survey of Commonwealth Affairs . . . 1953-1969, London, 1974, pp. 328-9. These remarks are based on Miller and on Nash's notes, Sept. 1962, N328.
15. WN notes, N328; Socialist International Information, XII, 37, 15 Sept. 1962 (cyclostyled news-sheet), N2246.
16. PD, 1962, 332, 2024-9; H. Macmillan, At the End of the Day, London, 1973, p. 130.
17. Papers in N2247.
18. Leah Newick, article, New Zealand Woman's Weekly, 8 Feb. 1965.
19. Minutes of National Executive, 3 Oct. 1961; extract from Finlay letter, 6 Feb. 1962 (which Nash read to caucus), N2020.
20. Minutes of National Executive, 27 Feb. 1962.

21. Finlay/Members of PLP, 3 Dec. 1962, N2558; WN speech notes, N368.
22. Boord/WN, [May 1962], WN/Boord (draft) [May-June 1962], N2465.
23. Minutes of the Parliamentary Labour Party, 7 June 1962, N2020.
24. Finlay/WN, 22 June; Finlay memo to Policy Committee, 16 Aug. 1962, N471.
25. 3 Dec. 1962, N2558.
26 Minutes of the Parliamentary Labour Party, N2020.
27. See, e.g., Leah Newick article, *New Zealand Woman's Weekly,* 8 Feb. 1965.
28. Letters in N197; on the House of Lords, see WN/O. Wilson, 1 Sept. 1965, N476; A. G. B. Fisher/author, 19 May 1971.
29. M. A. Brereton/WN, 12 Aug., WN/M. A. Brereton, 16 Aug. 1963, N2339. The secretary was Mr B. M. Brown.
30. Cit. *Evening Post,* 13 June 1968.
31. 19 March 1921, N2175.
32. WN/J. M. Caughey, 17 Feb. 1956, N2406.
33. He said it to his biographer, who discussed it with Dr Beaglehole. See Beaglehole, pp. 122-3.
34. *Cappicade,* 1959; WN handwritten note, 8 May 1959, N504.
35. W. P. Reeves, article on Nash, *Dominion,* 17 June 1968.
36. Margaret Kelly article on Nash, *Evening Post,* 6 Sept. 1969. Numbers of copies and details of orders etc. of Nash's Christmas cards are in N321.
37. Walsh/T. F. Anderson, 13 Dec. 1960, N403.
38. N1695, on Prime Minister's notepaper.
39. E.g. talk in St. James's Church, Riccarton, 22 March 1953, N1174.
40. 30 April 1963, in the possession of Mr Ahearn, Martinborough.
41. Interview with Archdeacon Scott, December 1972; interview with Sir Terence McCombs, 1974.
42. WN notes, 17 Aug. 1966, N2480.
43. WN/Mrs C. Saggers, 10 Sept. 1963, N2348.
44. 14 June 1967.
45. Interview with Mr and Mrs A. E. Campbell, 18 May 1972.
46. N2555.
47. Interviews 23, 24 Jan. 1972.
48. E.g. N2412.
49. *Evening Post,* 23, 25, 27, 30 Jan. 1964.
50. 25 May 1966.
51. His biographer was in the audience.
52. WN/Bassett, 8 Dec. 1966, N2262; WN/Fisher, 27 Dec. 1966, N1706.
53. T. R. Livesey/WN, 27 July; WN/Livesey, 27 July 1965, N2456. For Press reports see any New Zealand newspaper, 19 July 1965. The *third* to last speaker was Sir Walter's biographer, who had SEATO in his pocket. He was the second of two speakers following Sir Walter at Auckland.
54. J. Crawley/WN, 20 July 1965, N2456. For Nash's speech see M. Bassett and R. Nola (eds), *New Zealand and South-East Asia,* Auckland, 1965 (texts of lectures).
55. Blundell/WN, 10 March 1966, and other letters in file with Nash's notes for memoirs in possession of Mr J. A. D. Nash.
56. *Evening Post,* 13 June 1968.
57. In possession of Mr J. A. D. Nash.
58. Christchurch, 1967, pp. 65-66.
59. *Evening Post,* 8 May 1968. The author was in the audience.
60. *A Final Report. The Sir Walter Nash Vietnam Appeal,* Trentham, [1971], (a pamphlet).

Bibliography

This bibliography is in certain sections highly selective. In particular the lists of pamphlets, newspapers, and official publications include only items of especial significance. In the Nash Papers and elsewhere I read or glanced at hundreds of political pamphlets, many of which had only a minor bearing on Sir Walter's biography. These latter have been ignored here. So have the numerous newspapers referred to, often in the voluminous clippings in the Nash papers. The newspapers listed were consulted extensively. Large numbers of official publications—reports on conferences, treaties, etc.—were consulted on points of fact but are not included in this bibliography.

The main source of information was Sir Walter's papers, which have been described in the preface and referred to in the text. Many of the other sources consulted are duplicated in those papers—for instance Labour Party Executive and conference papers and quantities of Labour Party correspondence. The scope of the papers is that of Nash's life. Most of the activities in which he was involved are documented, though with varying degrees of completeness.

PRIMARY

1. UNPUBLISHED

A. Official Papers

BOARD OF TRADE RECORDS, Public Record Office, London.
CABINET MINUTES, Public Record Office, London.
DOMINIONS OFFICE RECORDS, Public Record Office, London.
EVIDENCE SUBMITTED TO NATIONAL HEALTH AND SUPERANNUATION COMMITTEE, Le I/1938/10, National Archives, Wellington.
INTERNAL AFFAIRS RECORDS, National Archives, Wellington.
MINUTES OF PACIFIC WAR COUNCIL, Roosevelt Papers, Hyde Park, New York.
TREASURY RECORDS, National Archives, Wellington.
TREASURY RECORDS, Public Record Office, London.
WAR CABINET RECORDS, Public Record Office, London.

B. Private Papers

CONDLIFFE, J. B. 'Autobiography', typescript in Alexander Turnbull Library.
HUGH DALTON DIARIES, British Library of Political and Economic Science, London School of Economics.
MINUTES OF NATIONAL EXECUTIVE OF THE NEW ZEALAND LABOUR PARTY, Head Office, Wellington.
MINUTES OF PARLIAMENTARY LABOUR PARTY, 1935-60. These caucus minutes are in the Nash Papers but deposited with the Public Trustee, Wellington. The only known earlier minutes, 1920-8, plus some notes for minutes, 1931, are in the Alexander Turnbull Library, Wellington. NZLP MSS 270/11.

NEW ZEALAND LABOUR PARTY CONFERENCE REPORTS, Head Office, Wellington.
JOHN A. LEE PAPERS, Auckland Public Library.
MINUTE BOOK OF MODERN TAILORS LTD, National Archives.
NATIONAL PARTY RESEARCH OFFICE FILE ON SIR WALTER NASH, Wellington.
PAPERS OF SIR WALTER NASH, National Archives, Wellington.
PAPERS OF SIR WALTER NASH in the possession of Mr J. A. D. Nash (a few files and Nash's autobiographical notes and 'Reflections of an Elder Statesman', notes for a radio interview with Miss Pam Carson of Wellington, who has a tape, and draft articles for the *Evening Post*).
P. J. O'FARRELL NOTES ON NEW ZEALAND LABOUR PARTY CORRESPONDENCE. Many files of Labour Party Head Office correspondence, etc., including the National Secretaries' correspondence, have been destroyed since he read them. His voluminous notes are the only surviving record of these letters. Professor O'Farrell generously sent me a copy of his notes. This is now, with his permission, deposited in the Alexander Turnbull Library.
PAPERS OF WILLIAM DOWNIE STEWART, Hocken Library, Dunedin.
F. P. WALSH PAPERS, in possession of the late Dr C. Bollinger.
CHARLES MORGAN WILLIAMS PAPERS, in the possession of Mr Ormond Wilson, Wellington.

2. PUBLISHED

A. Official Papers

Appendices to the Journals of the House of Representatives.
Documents Relating to New Zealand's Participation in the Second World War 1939-45, War History Branch, Department of Internal Affairs, 3 vols, Wellington, 1949-63.
External Affairs Review.
General Agreement on Tariffs and Trade, Department of External Affairs Publication No. 43, Wellington, 1947.
Protocols and Declaration to the General Agreement on Tariffs and Trade, Department of External Affairs Publication No. 59, Wellington, 1948.
International Monetary Fund, Department of External Affairs, Wellington, 1944.
International Monetary Fund and World Bank. Implications of New Zealand Membership, Presented by Hon. H. R. Lake, Wellington, 1961 (AJHR, 1961, A-12, but issued as a booklet).
Meetings of Prime Ministers April-May 1946. Full Record of Minutes of Meetings and Memoranda, Colonial Office, London.
Meeting of Commonwealth Prime Ministers May 1960. Minutes of Meetings and Memoranda (filed in Nash Papers, N373).
The Mercantile Gazette of New Zealand.
New Zealand Parliamentary Debates.
Trade Discussion between the United Kingdom Ministers and Honourable Walter Nash . . . July 1939, HMSO, Cmd. 6059 (British Parliamentary Paper).
Report of the First Session of the Preparatory Committee of United Nations Conference on Trade and Employment, London, 1946.
United Nations Conference on Trade and Employment, Department of External Affairs Publication No. 40, Wellington, 1947.
United Nations Conference on Trade and Employment . . . Held at Havana . . ., Department of External Affairs Publication No. 58, Wellington, 1948.
United Nations Conference on Trade and Employment, Final Act and Related Documents, Havana, 1948.

The United Nations Monetary and Financial Conference Held at Bretton Woods . . .,
    Department of External Affairs Publication No. 22, Wellington, 1946.

B   *Newspapers*

Auckland Star
Dominion
Evening Post
Kidderminster Shuttle
Maoriland Worker
New Zealand Herald
New Zealand Worker
Standard
Taranaki Daily News
Taranaki Herald

C. *Books*

CASEY, LORD, *Personal Experience 1939-1946,* London, 1962.
CONDLIFFE, J. B. (ed.), *Problems of the Pacific,* Chicago, 1928.
FAIRBURN, A. R. D., *The Sky is a Limpet,* Auckland, 1939.
HICKEY, P. H., *"Red" Fed. Memoirs,* [Wellington], 1925.
INSTITUTE OF PACIFIC RELATIONS, *War and Peace in the Pacific,* New York, 1943.
Kelly's Directory of Birmingham, Staffordshire, Warwickshire, and Worcestershire,
    London, 1892.
Kelly's Directory of Birmingham, London, 1905-9.
LEE, JOHN A., *Political Notebooks,* Wellington, 1973.
LEE, JOHN A., *Simple on a Soap-Box,* Auckland, 1963.
Littlebury's Directory of Worcester and District, London, 1879.
MACMILLAN, H., *Riding the Storm 1956-1959,* London, 1971.
MACMILLAN, H., *Pointing the Way 1959-1961,* London, 1972.
MALLABY, GEORGE, *From My Level. Unwritten Minutes,* London, 1965.
MILLAR, T. B. (ed.), *Australian Foreign Minister. The Diaries of R. G. Casey 1951-60,*
    London, 1972.
NASH, W., *New Zealand. A Working Democracy,* New York, 1943.
NGATA, A. P. . . . NASH, W. and others, *New Zealand Affairs,* Christchurch, 1929.
ONORATO, M. P. (ed.), *Origins of the Philippine Republic. Extracts from the Diaries
    and Records of Francis Burton Harrison,* Cornell University, Southeast Asia
    Program Data Paper, 1974.
ROBB, SIR DOUGLAS, *Medical Odyssey,* Auckland, 1967.
ROBB, D., *Medicine and Health in New Zealand,* Christchurch, 1940.
RUSKIN, J., *Fors Clavigera,* New York, n.d.
RUSKIN, J., *Unto This Last,* London, [1907].
SOCIETY FOR PROMOTING CHRISTIAN KNOWLEDGE, *Pan-Anglican Congress. Official
    Report,* Vol. II, London, 1908.
TAYLOR, HENRY, *The Statesman,* Cambridge, 1897.
TOLSTOY, L. N., *The Kingdom of God is within you,* New York, 1922.
TOLSTOY, L. N., *My Religion,* New York, 1922.
TOLSTOY, L. N., *What is Religion,* New York, 1922.

D. *Pamphlets*

BARNARD, W. E., *The Speech of a New Zealander,* Wellington, 1940.
CITIZENS ALL BLACK TOUR ASSOCIATION, *'No Maoris No Tour',* [Wellington], 1960.

Christianity and Industrial Problems Being the Report of the Archbishop's Fifth Committee of Enquiry, London, 1919.

COATES, J. G., *A Butter Quota or a Free Market?*, Wellington, 1933.

DANKS, A. J., *What Everyone Should Know About Social Credit*, Christchurch, 1955.

'THE GADFLY', *Semple Iscariot*, Auckland, [1948].

HOLLAND, H. E., 'BALLOT BOX', AND ROSS, R. S.,*The Tragic Story of the Waihi Strike*, Wellington, 1913.

HOLLAND, H. E., *The Way Out of the Labyrinth*, Wellington, 1932.

Joint Statement on War Policy by the National Council of the New Zealand Federation of Labour and the National Executive of the New Zealand Labour Party, [Wellington], [1939].

LANGSTONE, F., *The First Step in the March from Bankruptcy to Prosperity. Labour's Plan!*, Ohakune, [1934].

LEE, JOHN A., *Debt Finance for War and Peace versus Democracy*, Auckland, [1940].

LEE, JOHN A., *I Fight for New Zealand*, Auckland, [1940].

LEE, JOHN A., *Labour Has a Plan*, Wellington, 1934.

[LEE, JOHN A.], *A Letter which every New Zealander should read*, Auckland, [1938].

LEE, JOHN A., *Money Power for the People. Labour's Way Out*, Wellington, 1937.

McMILLAN, D. G., *A National Health Service. New Zealand of Tomorrow*, Wellington, [1935].

MASON, H. G. R., *Common Sense of the Money Question*, Wellington, [1934].

NASH, W., *Fair Exchange*, Wellington, 1948.

NASH, W., *Financial Power in New Zealand. The Case for a State Bank*, Wellington, [1925].

NASH, W., *Guaranteed Prices—Why and How*, Wellington, 1935.

NASH, W., *Guaranteed Prices—A Successful Reality*, Wellington, 1938.

NASH, W., *Labour Rule in New Zealand*, London, 1936.

NASH, W., *Nash Replies to the Critics*, Wellington, 1940.

NASH, W., *Social Progress in New Zealand*, London, [1944-5].

Report of the Lambeth Conference, 1920.

RESERVE BANK OF NEW ZEALAND, *Bretton Woods, G.A.T.T., and Related Topics*, Wellington, 1953.

ROBB, D., *Health Services or Doctors and Hospitals*, Wellington, [1942].

ROBERTS, J., *The Conquest of Depression*, Wellington, [1934].

SAVAGE, M. J., *The Case for Labour*, Auckland, [1935].

SEMPLE, R., *Why I Fight Communism*, Wellington, 1948.

SIMKIN, C. G. F., AND RODWELL, H. R., *An Open Letter to the Members of the General Assembly on the Bretton Woods Agreements*, Auckland, 1946.

Statement on the International Situation, by the National Council of the New Zealand Federation of Labour, [1939].

STRACHEY, JOHN, *Social Credit. An Economic Analysis*, London, 1936.

WILSON, DAVID, *History in the Making*, Wellington, 1937.

E. Articles and Addresses

LEE, JOHN A., 'Psycho-Pathology in Politics', *Tomorrow*, 6, 3, 6 Dec. 1939.

NASH, W., 'Administrative Organisations in Washington', *Journal of Public Administration*, 6, 1, Sept. 1943.

NASH, W., *New Zealand's Experience with Land-value Taxation*, New York, 1943 (an address, 23 Jan. 1943).

NASH, W., 'A New Zealand Outlook on Pacific Affairs', in J. B. Condliffe (ed.), *Problems of the Pacific*, Chicago, 1928.

NASH, W., *Relations of the United Nations in Defence of the Pacific*, Empire
   Parliamentary Association, (Confidential) (an address, 5 Aug. 1942).
NASH, W., *Social Security in New Zealand*, Toronto, 1944 (an address, 24 May 1944).
NASH, W., *The South Pacific and World Affairs*, Empire Parliamentary Association,
   London, 1946 (for private circulation) (an address, 15 May 1946).

3. INTERVIEWS. One of the important sources of information was interviews
with many of Sir Walter Nash's family, friends, colleagues and acquaintances.
The tapes have been deposited in the National Archives.

SECONDARY

A. Books

ALLEN, G. C., *The Industrial Development of Birmingham and the Black Country*,
   London, 1929.
ARNDT, H. W., *Economic Lessons of the 1930s*, Oxford, 1944.
BAKER, J. V. T., *The New Zealand People at War. War Economy*, Wellington, 1965.
BASSETT, MICHAEL, *Confrontation '51 the 1951 Waterfront Dispute*, Wellington, 1972.
BASSETT, M., AND NOLA, R. (eds.), *New Zealand and South-East Asia*, Auckland,
   1965.
BEAGLEHOLE, J. C., *New Zealand. A Short History*, London, 1936.
BEEBY, C., *The Antarctic Treaty*, Wellington, 1972.
BOYLE, ANDREW, *Montagu Norman*, London, 1967.
BRIGGS, ASA, *History of Birmingham*, Oxford, Vol. 2, 1952.
BROCKWAY, F., *Socialism over Sixty Years. The Life of Jowett of Bradford*, London,
   1946.
BROWN, BRUCE, *The Rise of New Zealand Labour*, Wellington, 1962.
BUNCE, JOHN T., *Josiah Mason: A Biography*, Birmingham, 1882.
BURTON, JOHN R., *A History of Kidderminster*, London, 1890.
CHAPMAN, R. M., *The Political Scene, 1919-1931*, Auckland, 1969.
CHAPMAN, R. M., JACKSON, W. K., AND MITCHELL, A. V., *New Zealand Politics in
   Action: The 1960 General Election*, London, 1962.
CHAPMAN, R., AND SINCLAIR, K., (eds.), *Studies of a Small Democracy*, Auckland,
   1963.
COLE, G. D. H., *A History of Socialist Thought*, London, 1958.
COLEMAN, M. D., *The New Zealand Labour Party 1916-1966. A Bibliography*,
   Wellington, 1972.
CONDLIFFE, J. B., *The Beginnings of the W.E.A.*, Wellington, 1968.
CONDLIFFE, J. B., *The Welfare State in New Zealand*, London, 1959.
CLAY, SIR HENRY, *Lord Norman*, London, 1957.
CRISP, L. F., *Ben Chifley*, London, 1961.
DIEBOLD, W., *The End of the I.T.O.*, Princeton, 1952.
EDWARDS, L., *Scrim*, Auckland, 1971.
ELLIOT, W., *Long Distance*, London, 1943.
FRASER, G., *Ungrateful People*, Auckland, 1952.
GARDINER, A. G., *Life of George Cadbury*, London, 1923.
GORDON, B. K., *New Zealand Becomes a Pacific Power*, Chicago, 1960.
HANCOCK, W. K., *Survey of British Commonwealth Affairs*, Oxford, Vol. 2, Part 1,
   1940.
HASLUCK, PAUL, *The Government and the People 1942-1945*, Canberra, 1970.
HAUPT, G., *Socialism and the Great War*, Oxford, 1972.
HAWKE, G. R., *Between Governments and Banks: A History of the Reserve Bank
   of New Zealand*, Wellington, 1973.

HOBSON, J. A., *John Ruskin. Social Reformer,* London, 1898.

JACOBS, B., *The Story of British Carpets,* 2nd ed., London, 1972.

JONES, P. D'A., *The Christian Socialist Revival 1877-1914,* Princeton, 1968.

KAY, R. (ed.), *The Australian-New Zealand Agreement 1944,* Wellington, 1972.

LASH, J. P., *Eleanor: The Years Alone,* New York, 1972.

LEE, J. A., *Socialism in New Zealand,* London, 1938.

LEON, D., *Ruskin The Great Victorian,* London, 1949.

LIPSON, LESLIE, *The Politics of Equality,* Chicago, 1948.

LISSINGTON, M. P., *New Zealand and the United States 1840-1944,* Wellington, 1972.

LOVELL-SMITH, J. B., *The New Zealand Doctor and the Welfare State,* Auckland, 1966.

MACKENZIE, CRAIG, *Walter Nash Pioneer and Prophet,* Palmerston North, 1975.

MANSBRIDGE, A., *An Adventure in Working Class Eduction,* London, 1920.

MANSERGH, N., *Survey of British Commonwealth Affairs. Problems of External Policy 1931-1939,* London, 1952.

MARTIN, R. B., *The Dust of Combat. A Life of Charles Kingsley,* London, 1969.

MIDDLEMAS K., AND BARNES, J., *Baldwin—A Biography,* London, 1969.

MILLER, J. D. B., *Survey of Commonwealth Affairs . . . 1953-1969,* London, 1974.

MILNE, R. S., *Political Parties in New Zealand,* Oxford, 1966.

MITCHELL, A., *Politics and People in New Zealand,* Christchurch, 1969.

O'FARRELL, P. J., *Harry Holland. Militant Socialist,* Canberra, 1964.

PAUL, J. T., *Humanism in Politics,* Wellington, 1946.

REESE, T. R., *Australia, New Zealand and the United States,* Oxford, 1969.

RICHARDSON, J. A., *British Economic Foreign Policy,* London, 1936.

ROBERTS, N., *New Zealand and Nuclear Testing in the Pacific,* Wellington, 1972.

ROBINSON, N., *James Fletcher: Builder,* London, 1970.

ROTH, H., *Trade Unions in New Zealand. Past and Present,* Wellington, 1973.

SABINE, G. H., *A History of Political Theory,* 3rd ed., London, 1948.

SALTER, A., *World Trade and its Future,* London, 1936.

SHERWOOD, R. E., *Roosevelt and Hopkins. An Intimate Biography,* New York, 1950.

SINCLAIR, K., AND MANDLE, W. F., *Open Account. A History of the Bank of New South Wales in New Zealand, 1861-1961,* Wellington, 1961.

SUTCH, W. B., *Poverty and Progress in New Zealand,* Wellington, 1941.

SUTCH, W. B., *Quest for Security in New Zealand,* Harmondsworth, 1941.

SUTCH, W. B., *Recent Economic Changes in New Zealand,* New Zealand, 1936.

THOMPSON, R., *Retreat from Apartheid: New Zealand's Sporting Contacts with South Africa,* Wellington, 1975.

THORN, J., *Peter Fraser,* London, 1952.

TROYAT, H., *Tolstoy,* London, 1968.

WATT, A., *The Evolution of Australian Foreign Policy 1938-65,* Cambridge, 1966.

WINSLOW, E. M., *The Pattern of Imperialism,* New York, 1948.

WOOD, F. L. W., *The New Zealand People at War: Political and External Affairs,* Wellington, 1958.

B. Articles

BEAGLEHOLE, J. C., 'New Zealand since the War', *Landfall,* 58, June 1961.

BELSHAW, H., 'Import and Exchange Control in New Zealand', *Economic Record,* Vol. 15, 1939.

BLYTH, C. A., 'The Industrialisation of New Zealand', *New Zealand Economic Papers,* 8, 1974.

BROWN, B., 'The Labour Campaign', *Political Science,* 10, 1, March 1958.

CUNNINGHAM, J. K., 'Editorial Opinion and the 1957 Election', *Landfall*, 46, June 1958.

DURRANT, R. G., 'The Elections', *Landfall*, 33, March 1955.

FISHER, A. G. B.. 'The Political Framework of an International Institution', *The Manchester School*, May 1962.

TOCKER, A. H., 'The Monetary Standards of New Zealand and Australia', *Economic Journal*, 34, December 1924.

HAMER, D., 'Understanding Mr Gladstone', *New Zealand Journal of History*, 6, 2, October 1972.

HAWKE, G. R., 'The Government and the Depression of the 1930s', *Australian Economic History Review*, 13, 1, March 1973.

MACBETH, N. L., 'The Cotton Mll—and After', *Canterbury Chamber of Commerce, Economic Bulletin*, No. 447, March 1962.

McINTOSH, ALISTER, 'Working with Peter Fraser in Wartime: Personal Reminiscences', *New Zealand Journal of History*, 10, 1, April 1976.

MACRAE, J., AND SINCLAIR, K., 'Unemployment in New Zealand during the Depression of the late 1920s and early 1930s', *Australian Economic History Review*, 15, 1, 1975.

MEGAW, M. R., ' . . . Australian Representation in the United States, 1918-1939', *Historical Studies*, 15, 60, 1973.

MORIARTY, M. J., 'The Marketing of Dairy Produce', *New Zealand Journal of Public Administration*, 10, 2, March 1948.

O'FARRELL, P. J., 'History of the New South Wales Labour Movement . . .', *Journal of Religious History*, II, Dec. 1962.

OLSSEN, E., 'John A. Lee, the Amalgamated Society of Carpenters and Joiners and "Worker Control" of the Building Industry', *Political Science*, 27, 1-2, July-Dec. 1975.

ORR, GORDON S., 'Some Recent Legislation', *Landfall*, 21, March 1952.

PETERS, K., 'New Zealand's Attitudes to the Reform of the League of Nations', *New Zealand Journal of History*, 6, 1, April 1972.

ROBINSON, A., 'The National Campaign', *Political Science*, 10, 1, March 1958.

SIMKIN, C. G. F., 'The Nationalisation of the Bank of New Zealand', *Economic Record*, 22, 1946.

SINCLAIR, K., 'Fruit Fly, Fireblight and Powdery Scab: Australia-New Zealand Trade Relations, 1919-39', *Journal of Imperial and Commonwealth History*, 1, 1, October 1972.

SINCLAIR, K., 'The Lee-Sutch Syndrome', *The New Zealand Journal of History*, 8, 2, October 1974.

TAMCHINA, R., 'In Search of Common Causes: The Imperial Conference of 1937', *Journal of Imperial and Commonwealth History*, 1, 1, 1972.

C. *Unpublished Theses and Research Essays*

BELSHAW, J. P., 'The Crisis in New Zealand, 1930-34', unpub. MA thesis, University of New Zealand (Auckland), 1934.

BROOKER, W. A., 'Exchange Control in New Zealand 1936-1945', unpub. PhD thesis, University of New Zealand (Otago), 1949.

CLIFTON, R., 'Douglas Credit and the Labour Party 1930-1935', unpub. MA thesis, University of New Zealand (Victoria), 1961.

DANIELS, J. R. S., 'The General Election of 1943', unpub. MA thesis, University of New Zealand (Victoria), 1961.

FRASER, S. E., 'The 1949 General Election', unpub. MA thesis, University of Otago, 1967.

GRAHAM, K. G. M., 'New Zealand on Apartheid', unpub. research essay, Victoria University, 1971.

GUSTAFSON, B. S., 'The Advent of the New Zealand Labour Party 1900-1919', unpub. MA thesis, University of New Zealand (Auckland), 1961.

GUSTAFSON, B. S., 'Continuing Transformation. The structure, composition and functioning of the New Zealand Labour Party in the Auckland region, 1949-70', PhD thesis, University of Auckland, 1973.

HANSON, E. A., 'The Social Security Story. A Study of the Origins of the 1938 Social Security Act', unpub. MA thesis, University of Auckland, 1975.

HILL, R. J. M., 'The Quest for Control. The New Zealand Dairy Industry and the Guaranteed Price, 1921-36', unpubl. MA thesis, University of Auckland, 1974.

KANE, M. A., 'The History of Equal Pay in New Zealand 1890-1960', unpub. MA thesis, University of Auckland, 1972.

KEMBER, J. L., 'The Establishment of the New Zealand Legation at Washington, 1940-44', unpub. research essay, Victoria University, 1971.

McINTYRE, W. D., 'New Zealand and the Singapore Base on the Eve of the Pacific War', Institute of Commonwealth Studies (London) seminar paper, RHC.73/6.

McLENNAN, R., 'The Last Years of the First Labour Government, 1945-1949', unpub. MA thesis, University of Auckland, 1963.

MALONE, E. P., 'The Rural Voter—voting trends in the Waikato, 1922-35', unpub. MA thesis, University of New Zealand (Auckland), 1958.

MATTHEWS, G. F., 'The New Zealand Labour Party's Attitudes to the League of Nations 1918-1935', unpub. MA research essay, University of Auckland, 1975.

METGE, R. T., 'The House that Jack Built. The Origins of Labour State Housing 1935-8', unpub. MA thesis, University of Auckland, 1972.

MITCHELL, D. J., 'Nelson Cotton Mill', unpub. MA thesis, Canterbury University, 1967.

MUNRO, R. M. D., 'New Zealand's Role in the Establishment of the South Pacific Commission', unpub. MA thesis, Victoria University, 1970.

NORTHEY, H., 'Singapore: New Zealand's Great Illusion', unpub. MA thesis, University of Auckland, 1971.

NORTHEY, R. J., 'The Annual Conferences of the New Zealand Labour Party', unpub. MA thesis, University of Auckland, 1973.

OLSSEN, ERIK, 'John Alexander Lee; the Stormy Petrel', unpub. MA thesis, University of Otago, 1965.

PUGH, M. C., 'The New Zealand Legion and Conservative Protest in the Great Depression', unpub. MA thesis, University of Auckland, 1969.

REID, A. S. J., 'Church and State in New Zealand, 1930-1935', unpub. MA thesis, University of New Zealand (Victoria), 1961.

ROGERS, F., 'The Single Tax Movement in New Zealand', unpub. MA thesis, University of New Zealand (Auckland), 1949.

ROLLO, C. G., 'The Election of 1935 in New Zealand', unpub. MA thesis, University of New Zealand (Canterbury), 1950.

STONE, R. C. J., 'A History of Trade Unionism in New Zealand, 1913-37', unpub. MA thesis, University of New Zealand (Auckland), 1948.

WIGGLESWORTH, S., 'The Depression and the Election of 1935', unpub. MA thesis, University of New Zealand (Auckland), 195[4].

Index